INFORMATION SYSTEMS

Video training courses are available on the subjects of these books in the
James Martin ADVANCED TECHNOLOGY LIBRARY of over 300 tapes and disks,
from Applied Learning, 1751 West Diehl Road, Naperville, IL 60540 (tel: 312-369-3000).

Database	Telecommunications	Networks and Data Communications	Society
AN END USER'S GUIDE TO DATABASE	TELECOMMUNICATIONS AND THE COMPUTER (third edition)	PRINCIPLES OF DATA COMMUNICATION	THE COMPUTERIZED SOCIETY
PRINCIPLES OF DATABASE MANAGEMENT (second edition)	COMMUNICATIONS SATELLITE SYSTEMS	TELEPROCESSING NETWORK ORGANIZATION	TELEMATIC SOCIETY: A CHALLENGE FOR TOMORROW
COMPUTER DATABASE ORGANIZATION (third edition)	**Distributed Processing**	SYSTEMS ANALYSIS FOR DATA TRANSMISSION	TECHNOLOGY'S CRUCIBLE
MANAGING THE DATABASE ENVIRONMENT (second edition)	COMPUTER NETWORKS AND DISTRIBUTED PROCESSING	DATA COMMUNICATION TECHNOLOGY	VIEWDATA AND THE INFORMATION SOCIETY
DATABASE ANALYSIS AND DESIGN	DESIGN AND STRATEGY FOR DISTRIBUTED DATA PROCESSING	DATA COMMUNICATION DESIGN TECHNIQUES	**SAA: Systems Application Architecture**
VSAM: ACCESS METHOD SERVICES AND PROGRAMMING TECHNIQUES	**Office Automation**	SNA: IBM's NETWORKING SOLUTION	SAA: COMMON USER ACCESS
DB2: CONCEPTS, DESIGN, AND PROGRAMMING	IBM OFFICE SYSTEMS: ARCHITECTURES AND IMPLEMENTATIONS	LOCAL AREA NETWORKS: ARCHITECTURES AND IMPLEMENTATIONS	SAA: COMMON COMMUNICATIONS SUPPORT: DISTRIBUTED APPLICATIONS
IDMS/R: CONCEPTS, DESIGN, AND PROGRAMMING		OFFICE AUTOMATION STANDARDS	SAA: COMMON COMMUNICATIONS SUPPORT: NETWORK INFRASTRUCTURE
Security		DATA COMMUNICATION STANDARDS	SAA: COMMON PROGRAMMING INTERFACE
SECURITY, ACCURACY, AND PRIVACY IN COMPUTER SYSTEMS		COMPUTER NETWORKS AND DISTRIBUTED PROCESSING: SOFTWARE, TECHNIQUES, AND ARCHITECTURE	

STRUCTURED TECHNIQUES
The Basis for CASE

A ——————— BOOK

THE JAMES MARTIN BOOKS

- Application Development Without Programmers
- Communications Satellite Systems
- Computer Data-Base Organization, Second Edition
- Computer Networks and Distributed Processing: Software, Techniques, and Architecture
- Design and Strategy of Distributed Data Processing
- Design of Man-Computer Dialogues
- Design of Real-Time Computer Systems
- An End User's Guide to Data Base
- Fourth-Generation Languages, Volume I: Principles
- Future Developments in Telecommunications, Second Edition
- Information Engineering
- An Information Systems Manifesto
- Introduction to Teleprocessing
- Managing the Data-Base Environment
- Principles of Data-Base Management
- Programming Real-Time Computer Systems
- Recommended Diagramming Standards for Analysts and Programmers
- Security, Accuracy, and Privacy in Computer Systems
- Strategic Data-Planning Methodologies
- Systems Analysis for Data Transmission
- System Design from Provably Correct Constructs
- Technology's Crucible
- Telecommunications and the Computer, Second Edition
- Telematic Society: A Challenge for Tomorrow
- Teleprocessing Network Organization
- Viewdata and the Information Society

with Carma McClure

- Action Diagrams: Clearly Structured Program Design
- Diagramming Techniques for Analysts and Programmers
- Software Maintenance: The Problem and Its Solutions
- Structured Techniques: The Basis for CASE, Revised Edition

with The ARBEN Group, Inc.

- A Breakthrough in Making Computers Friendly: The Macintosh Computer
- Data Communication Technology
- Fourth-Generation Languages, Volume II: Representative Fourth-Generation Languages
- Fourth-Generation Languages, Volume III: 4GLs from IBM
- Principles of Data Communication
- SNA: IBM's Networking Solution
- VSAM: Access Method Services and Programming Techniques

with Adrian Norman

- The Computerized Society

Revised Edition

STRUCTURED TECHNIQUES:
The Basis for CASE

JAMES MARTIN
CARMA McCLURE

PRENTICE HALL, Englewood Cliffs, New Jersey 07632

Library of Congress Cataloging-in-Publication Data

Martin, James, (date)
  Structured techniques.

  Previously published as: Structured techniques for
computing.
  Includes index.
  1. Electronic data processing—Structured techniques.
2. Computer software—Development. I. McClure,
Carma L. II. Martin, James. Structured
techniques for computing. III. Title.
QA76.9.S84M37 1988   005.1'13   87-7174
ISBN 0-13-854936-2

Editorial/production supervision: *Kathryn Gollin Marshak*
Jacket design: *Bruce Kenselaar*
Jacket photograph courtesy of *KnowledgeWare*
Manufacturing buyer: *Richard Washburn*

Previously published under the title:
Structured Techniques for Computing

Printed in the United States of America

10 9 8 7 6

ISBN 0-13-854936-2 025

PRENTICE-HALL INTERNATIONAL (UK) LIMITED, *London*
PRENTICE-HALL OF AUSTRALIA PTY. LIMITED, *Sydney*
PRENTICE-HALL CANADA INC., *Toronto*
PRENTICE-HALL HISPANOAMERICANA, S.A., *Mexico*
PRENTICE-HALL OF INDIA PRIVATE LIMITED, *New Delhi*
PRENTICE-HALL OF JAPAN, INC., *Tokyo*
SIMON & SCHUSTER ASIA PTE. LTD., *Singapore*
EDITORA PRENTICE-HALL DO BRASIL, LTDA., *Rio de Janeiro*

CASE

COMPUTER-AIDED SYSTEMS ENGINEERING

```
1 Help    2 Insert 3 MrkBeg 4 MrkEnd 5 Cut    6 Paste 7 Find   8 Draw   9 Cntrct 10 Expand

[0.46] subscrip.▲   line=13   column=1   buffer lines=0      Insert
 * Subscription system
   ┌ Do while there are subscription transactions
   │ ┌ Get valid transaction
   │ │
   │ │   Read  │ transaction │
   │ │
   │ │ ┌ Validate transaction
   │ │ │   Check general format
   │ │ ├ If error
   │ │ │   o──────────────o
   │ │ │   │ Process error │
   │ │ │   o──────────────o
   │ │ │
   │ │ ├ If transaction type is new
   │ │ │   Check name and address
   │ │ │   Check for numeric ZIP
   │ │ │   Check for valid terms
   │ │ │   Check for payment
   │ │ ┌ If  errors
   │ │ │      Set invalid indicator
   │ │ ├ Else
```

A sample action diagram, showing code structure, created with Action Diagrammer from KnowledgeWare.

CASE: The change from plastic templates and pencils to planning and design with structured techniques at a workbench screen where the design-automation tools drive a code generator.

IPSE (Integrated Programming Support Environment): Sometimes, especially in Europe, the term *IPSE* is used, rather than *CASE*. IPSE tools sometimes emphasize verbal specifications and programming more than design automation.

CASE or IPSE tools should support the entire development life cycle.

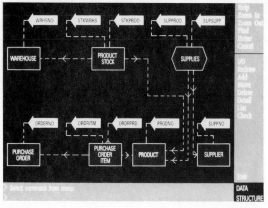

Data Structure Diagram from Information Enginnering Facility™. Copyright © 1986 Texas Instruments.

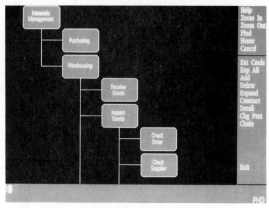

Process Hierarchy Diagram from Information Engineering Facility™. Copyright © 1986 Texas Instruments.

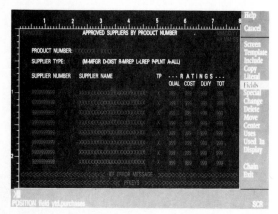

Clustered Natural Business Systems Matrix from Information Engineering Facility™. Copyright © 1986 Texas Instruments.

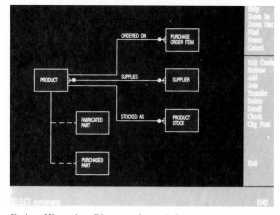

Entity Hierarchy Diagram from Information Engineering Facility™. Copyright © 1986 Texas Instruments.

Screen Designer Diagram from Information Engineering Facility™. Copyright © 1986 Texas Instruments.

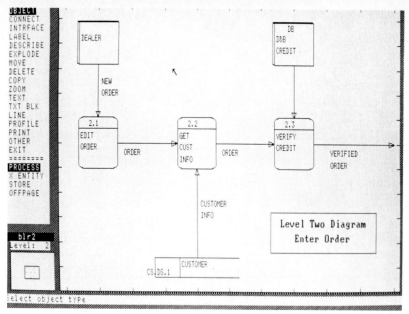

A Data Flow Diagram created using Excelerator. Copyright © 1987 Index Technology Corporation.

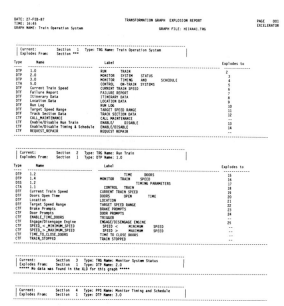

A report from Excelerator/RTS that automatically analyzes, for a set of graphs, the status and relationships between levels of a design. Copyright © 1987 Index Technology Corporation.

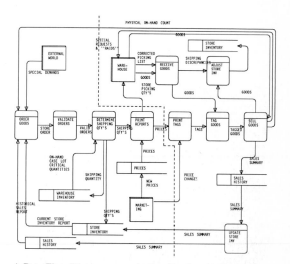

A Data Flow Diagram created using Excelerator. Copyright © 1987 Index Technology Corporation.

TO
CORINTHIA,
NATALIE,
AND
ROSE

CONTENTS

Table of Boxes   *xxiii*
Preface   *xxv*

PART **I**   PHILOSOPHY

1   **Why Structured Techniques and CASE?**   *3*

Objectives 3; Evolution 8; Mathematical Rigor 11;
CASE: Computer-Aided Systems Engineering 12;
Important Characteristics 13; Loyalty to Old Techniques 13

2   **Philosophies of Structured Techniques**   *15*

Introduction 15; Basic Principles 15;
Basic Principles of Software Engineering 20;
The Data-Base Environment 23;
Automation of Analysis, Design, and Coding 24;
Graphics 26; Provably Correct Constructs 26;
Management of Complexity 27; Changing Computer Languages 28;
End-User Involvement 28; User-Friendly Structured Techniques 30;
The Design Process 30

PART II PROGRAMMING METHODOLOGIES

3 Structured Programming 37

The Shift to Software 37; Introduction of Structured Programming 38;
GO TO–less Programming 38; Objectives 39; Definitions 39

4 Structured Programs 45

Properties of a Structured Program 45; Limited Control Constructs 45;
Nested IF 48; Case Statement 49; Escape 50;
Highest-Level Control Constructs 50; Standardized Module Format 51;
Hierarchical Organization 51; Program Control Structure 52;
Program Paths 53; Documentation 54; Indentation 59;
Structured Coding Standards 59

5 Modular Programming and Control of Complexity 67

Divide and Conquer 67; Program Modules 67; Black Box Model 68;
Modularization Schemes 68; Module Size 70; Complexity Metrics 70;
Module Relationships 75; Program Shape 80

6 Programming by Stepwise Refinement 83

Changing Programming from Craft to Science 83;
Stepwise Refinement 83; Levels of Abstraction 84;
An Example of the Refinement Process 85

7 Top-Down, Bottom-Up, and Structured Programming 91

Structured Programming Methodologies 91; Top-Down Programming 91;
Bottom-Up Versus Top-Down Programming 95;
Bottom-Up Programming 96; Choosing a Development Approach 98;
Combinations 99

8　Commentary on Structured Programming Methodologies *103*

The Problem of Programming in the Large 103;
Program Complexity 103; The Absence of Rigor 104;
Recommendation 105

PART **III** DIAGRAMMING TECHNIQUES

9　Diagrams and Clear Thinking *109*

Introduction 109; Changing Methods 110;
Categories of Structured Diagrams 111; End-User Involvement 111;
Program Documentation Tools 117; Utility of Documentation 118;
Computer-Aided Diagramming 120; Functions of Structured Diagrams 120

10　Forms of Structured Diagrams *123*

Introduction 123; Forms of Tree Structure 123; Inhibition of Change 125;
Left-to-Right Trees 126; Sequence of Operations 131;
Mesh-Structured Diagrams 131; COW Charts 133; Nested Charts 134;
Data-Model Charts 138; Root Nodes 141; Find the Trees 142;
Computer Magic 145; Symbols with Obvious Meaning 145; Summary 148

11　Data Flow Diagrams *149*

Introduction 149; Defining Data Flow 149; Components of a DFD 149;
Leveling a DFD 152; Process Specification and Data Dictionary 154;
Gane and Sarson Notation 155; Use of Computer Graphics 158;
Commentary 163; Data Layering 164

12　Three Species of Functional Decomposition *165*

Introduction 165;
Levels of Thoroughness in Functional Decomposition 165;
Species I Functional Decomposition: Corporate Model 166;
Species II Functional Decomposition 170;
Species III Functional Decomposition 176; Commentary 177

13   Structure Charts   *181*

Hierarchical Diagram 181; Components of a Structure Chart 181;
Control Relationships 183; Common Modules 183; Library Modules 184;
Data Transfer 184; Sequence, Selection, and Iteration 186;
Transaction Center 188; Computer Graphics 188

14   HIPO Diagrams   *191*

Introduction 191; Diagram Components 192;
Analysis and Design Tools 194; Commentary 194

15   Warnier-Orr Diagrams   *197*

Introduction 197; Representation of Data 197;
Representation of Program Structure 199;
Critique of Warnier-Orr Diagrams 201

16   Michael Jackson Diagrams   *207*

Introduction 207; Tree-Structure Diagrams 207;
Data-Structure Diagrams 209; Program-Structure Diagrams 211;
System Network Diagram 212; From Data to Programs 213;
Critique of Jackson Diagrams 214

17   Flowcharts   *219*

Overview Versus Detailed Structure 219; Flowcharts 220;
Flowchart Symbols 222; Critique of Flowcharts 222

18   Structured English and Pseudocode   *227*

Introduction 227; Why Should English Be Structured? 227;
Ambiguities 228; Structured English 229; Four Basic Structure Types 230;
Keywords from Fourth-Generation Languages 232;
Rules for Structured English 233; Pseudocode 234;
Jackson's Structure Text 234; Critique of Structured English 237

19   Nassi-Shneiderman Charts   *239*

Introduction 239; Control Constructs 240;
Critique of the Nassi-Schneiderman Chart 243

20   Action Diagrams   *245*

Overview Versus Detailed Logic Diagramming 245; Brackets 246;
Ultimate Decomposition 247; Conditions 248; Loops 250;
Sets of Data 250; Subprocedures 251;
Subprocedures Not Yet Designed 251; Common Procedures 251;
Terminations 252; Fourth-Generation Languages 252;
Decomposition to Program Code 253; Titles Versus Code Structure 254;
Concurrency 256; Input and Output Data 258; Advantages 261

21   Decision Trees and Decision Tables   *275*

A Broadly Used Diagramming Technique 275; Decision Tree 275;
Decision Table 276; Decision Tree or Table? 279;
Using Decision Trees and Decision Tables 279; Commentary 279

22   Data Analysis Diagrams   *281*

Introduction 281; Bubble Charts 281;
Associations Between Data Items 282;
One-to-One and One-to-Many Associations 283; Types and Instances 284;
Reverse Associations 284; Keys and Attributes 286;
Data-Item Groups 287; Records 287; Concatenated Keys 288;
Derived Data 290; Optional Data Items 293

23   Entity-Relationship Diagrams   *297*

Introduction 297; Entities 297; Entity Diagrams 298;
Concatenated Entity Type 299; Labels and Sentences 302;
Subject and Predicate 304; Basic Constructs 307;
Semantic Independence 307; Inverted-L Diagrams 308;
Entity Subtypes 310;
Multiple Subtype Groupings 311; Subtype Hierarchies 312;
Computer Representation of the Diagram 314; Notation Styles 315

24   Data Navigation Diagrams   *325*

Introduction 325; Divide and Conquer 325;
Separating Data from Procedures 326; Data Navigation Diagrams 327;
Procedure Design 331; Physical Design 333; Complexity 334;
Standard Procedure 335

25   Compound Data Accesses *339*

Introduction 339; Relational Joins 340; Automatic Navigation 343;
Simple Versus Compound Data-Base Accesses 343;
Intermixing Simple and Compound Actions 344; Three-Way Joins 347;
Semantic Disintegrity 348; Navigation Paths 350;
Fourth-Generation Languages 351

26   HOS Charts *355*

Introduction 355; HOS 355; Binary Trees 355; Functions 357;
From Requirements Statements to Detailed Design 361;
Three Primitive Control Structures 361;
Control Maps 364; Generation of Code 364;
Four Types of Leaf Nodes 364;
Static and Dynamic Testing of Programs 367; Embellishments 367;
Other Control Structures 368; Simplification 370;
User Functions Employed in a Defined Structure 370;
Extending the Power of HOS 370; Discussion 372

27   A Consumer's Guide to Diagramming Techniques *377*

Introduction 377; Criteria for Choice 378; Data and Processes 382;
Data Flow Diagrams 382; The Essential Trilogy 383;
Comprehensive Capabilities 383; Ultimate Decomposition 384;
Drawing Speed 384; Integrity Checking 386; Code Generation 387;
User Friendliness 387; Computer Graphics 388;
Summary of Properties 388; Our Choice of Techniques 394;
Challenge 395

PART IV   ANALYSIS AND DESIGN

28   Structured Analysis and Design Techniques *399*

Software Analysis and Design 399; The Desire to Skip Analysis 399;
Changing Requirements 399; System Specification 400;
Poor Specification and Expensive Errors 400; Importance of Analysis 401;
A Building Analogy 401; Importance of Design 402;
A Systematic Design Approach 403; Types of Software Design 403;
Structured Design Methodologies 405

29 Structured Analysis 407

A Critical Step 407; A Structured Discipline 407;
System Specification 408; Data-Flow Diagram 410; Data Dictionary 410;
Process Specification 411; Steps of Structured Analysis 412;
Critique of Structured Analysis 414; When to Use Structured Analysis 415

30 Top-Down Design 417

Informal Design Strategy 417; Design Process 417;
Decision Making 418; Principles of Top-Down Design 419;
Documentation for Top-Down Design 419; Top-Down Design of Data 419;
When to Use Top-Down Design 420

31 Structured Design 423

Systematic Design Approach 423;
Structured Design: Step 1: Draw Data-Flow Diagram 424;
Step 2: Draw Structure Chart 424; Step 3: Evaluate the Design 431;
Step 4: Prepare the Design for Implementation 435

32 An Evaluation of Structured Design 441

Structured Design of the Credit Verification System 441;
Applying Transform Analysis 441;
Evaluating the Quality of the Design 443;
Critique of Structured Design 446;
Critique of Transform and Transaction Analysis 447;
Comparison with Top-Down Design 451;
Critique of Coupling and Cohesion 452; Lack of Data Design 453

33 Jackson Design Methodology 455

Jackson Design Versus Structured Design 455;
Data-Driven Program Design 455; Example: Employee Skills System 457;
Designing Simple Programs 462; Designing Complex Programs 464;
Structure Clash 465; Program Inversion 466

34 An Evaluation of Jackson Design Methodology 469

Constructive Design Method 469; Designing the Subscription System 469;
Limitations of the Jackson Design Methodology 475;
Designing the Credit Verification System 478; Summary 484

35 **Warnier-Orr Design Methodology** *489*

Background 489; Set Theory 489; Top-Down Approach 490;
Data-Driven Approach 491; Design of the Employee Skills System 491

36 **An Evaluation of the Warnier-Orr Design**
Methodology *503*

Input-Process-Output Model 503;
Objective of the Warnier-Orr Design Methodology 504;
Benefits of the Warnier-Orr Diagram 504;
Problems with the Warnier-Orr Diagram 506;
Bracketed Pseudocode 507; Major Criticisms 507;
Design of the Subscription System 507;
Problems with Multiple Output Structures 508;
Incompatible Hierarchies 511; Inadequate Input Design Guidelines 511;
Overemphasis on Output 511; Recommendations 513

PART V **MORE AUTOMATED TECHNIQUES**

37 **A Higher Level of Automation** *517*

Introduction 517; Problems with Specifications 517;
Specification Languages 518; Computer-Aided Specification Design 519;
Two Types of Languages 519; Computable Specifications 520;
Automation of Design 521; Integration of Definition Levels 523;
A Common Communication Vehicle 523;
Integrated Top-Down and Bottom-Up Design 524;
Mathematically Rigorous Languages 525; User Friendliness 525;
Properties Needed 525; Spectrum of Specification Languages 526

38 **HOS Methodology** *533*

Introduction 533; USE.IT 533; JOIN, INCLUDE, and OR 535;
Generation of Code 535; Four Types of Leaf Nodes 537;
Co-control Structures 538; Local Variables 545; N-way Branches 546;
Interactive Graphics Editor 546; Simulation 551;
External Modules of Code 554; Generation of Documentation 555

39 The Impact of Design Automation 557

The Revolution 557; Effect on Programming 557;
Effect on Specifications 558; What Does "Provably Correct" Mean? 559;
Syntax and Semantics 559; Internal and External Semantics 560;
Standards 561; Verification and Testing 561;
Building Higher Levels of Trust 562; Improvements in Productivity 562;
Cost Savings 563; Effect of Program Size 564; Error Statistics 565;
Human System Components 567;
Use of Other Front-End Methodologies 567;
Incorporation of Nonprocedural Languages 569; Software Factories 569;

40 Data-Base Planning 575

Introduction 575; Separate Developments with Incompatible Data 576;
Stable Foundation 578; Stable Data Bases 580;
Logical Design of Data Bases 581;
The Failure of Data Administration 582

41 Third Normal Form 585

Normalization of Data 585; First Normal Form 587;
Functional Dependency 590; Full Functional Dependency 591;
Second Normal Form 592; Candidate Keys 594; Third Normal Form 595;
Storage and Performance 596; Semantic Disintegrity 598;
Clear Thinking About Data 598; A Suggested Exercise 602;
An Example of Normalization 602

42 Automated Data Modeling 605

Introduction 605; The Synthesis Process 606; Bubble Charts 607;
Synthesizing User Views 607; Illustration of the Synthesis Process 607;
Levels of Primary Keys 610; Canonical Data Structures 612;
Canonical Synthesis 613; Elimination of Redundancies 614;
Candidate Keys 616; Transitive Dependencies 617;
Concatenated Keys 618; Intersection Data 619;
Many-to-Many Associations 620; Mapping Between Primary Keys 620;
Intersecting Attributes 620; Isolated Attributes 623; Record Sequence 623;
Automating the Procedure 623; Data Designer 624;
Conversion to HOS Notation 629

43   Computer-Aided Design   *631*

Introduction 631; Computerized Help in Design 632;
Developing a Data-Base Application 633; Automatic Conversion 640;
Four Stages 643; Logical and Physical Navigation Diagrams 645;
Physical Design 649; Objectives of the Design Dialogue 649;
Variations 650

44   Information Engineering   *651*

Introduction 651; What Is Information Engineering? 652;
Building Blocks of Information Engineering 654;
Computerization of Information Engineering 661;
Essential Need for User Participation 661; A House on the Sand 663;
Two Images 663

PART VI   VERIFICATION AND TESTING

45   Software Verification, Validation, and Testing   *667*

The Case of the $18.5-Million Hyphen 667;
The Case of the Infinite Loop 667;
Demonstrating Software Correctness 667;
Verification and Validation Techniques 671

46   Testing   *675*

The Testing Process 675; Testing Heuristics 675;
Four-Phase Testing Procedure 678; Unit Testing 679;
Integration Testing 681; System Testing 684; Acceptance Testing 685;
Test Data 685

47   Debugging   *689*

The Case of the Missing Period 689; The Difficulty of Debugging 689;
Debugging Methods 690; Program Debugging Tools 691;
Locating Program Errors 693; Predicting Error-Proneness 699

48   Automated Test Tools *701*

Test Tools 701; General Research's RXVP 701;
Software Renovation Technology's RE-LEARN 706;
Software Environments 714; Bell Labs' UNIX 715

49   An Evaluation of Verification Techniques *717*

Introduction 717; Limitations of Testing 717;
Problems with Test Tools 718; Lack of Theory 718;
Testing Fourth-Generation-Language Programs 719;
Improvement Through Formality 723;
Formal Proof-of-Correctness Techniques 724

PART VII   TOWARD AN ENGINEERING DISCIPLINE

50   Where Do Structured Techniques Go from Here? *731*

Patterns of Evolution 731;
Phases of Growth of Management Science 732;
Phases of Growth of Structured Techniques 734; Shock 736;
Inadequacy 738; The Automation of Automation 739;
Rigorous Specification 740; Meat Machines 740;
Theoretical Principles 741; Future Growth of Automated Methods 742

51   The Move Toward True Engineering *745*

Introduction 745; Software Misengineering 745;
Characteristics of Engineering 746; Power Tools 749;
Information Engineering 752; Resistance to New Methods 753

52   Epilogue: The Future *757*

The Revolution: Its Causes and Outcome 757;
A Way to Think About Systems 760;
The Changing Computer Industry 760

Index *763*

TABLE OF BOXES

Box 1.1 Objectives of structured techniques *5*
Box 2.1 Basic principles of the structured philosophy *16*
Box 2.2 Principles of software engineering *22*
Box 2.3 Principles of information engineering *25*
Box 2.4 Principles of computer-aided systems design *29*
Box 2.5 Principles of end-user involvement *32*
Box 3.1 Objectives of structured programming *40*
Box 3.2 Definition of structured programming *42*
Box 4.1 Properties of a structured program *46*
Box 4.2 Rules for program control flow in a structured program *53*
Box 4.3 Overview documentation items *55*
Box 4.4 Module comment-block items *56*
Box 4.5 Structured programming standards *58*
Box 5.1 Properties of a module *69*
Box 5.2 Advantages of modular programming *70*
Box 5.3 Decoupling guidelines *78*
Box 5.4 Guidelines for determining the level of module cohesion *81*
Box 6.1 Airline Reservations program *86*
Box 7.1 Basic principles of top-down programming *95*
Box 9.1 Categorization of the diagramming techniques described in the following chapters *112*
Box 10.1 Properties of a good system diagramming technique *148*
Box 13.1 Control rules for a structure chart *183*
Box 15.1 Basic constructs of the Warnier-Orr diagram *202*
Box 18.1 Rules for writing structured English *232*
Box 20.1 Summary of notation used in action diagrams *269*
Box 22.1 Notation used on bubble charts for data analysis *294*
Box 23.1 Basic constructs used for describing data *308*
Box 23.2 Notation used on entity-relationship diagrams *320*
Box 27.1 Summary of the capabilities of diagramming techniques *378*
Box 27.2 Other properties of diagramming techniques *389*
Box 29.1 Structured analysis process *413*
Box 31.1 Guidelines for determining the level of module cohesion *434*
Box 31.2 Packaging guidelines *438*

Box 33.1   Jackson program design procedure *456*
Box 34.1   Properties of a simple program *481*
Box 35.1   Steps in the Warnier-Orr design procedure *490*
Box 37.1   Desirable properties of a specification *526*
Box 37.2   Desirable properties of a specification tool *528*
Box 39.1   Traditional development versus HOS-like methodology *572*
Box 40.1   Reasons for failure of corporate data administration *582*
Box 40.2   Essentials for the overall control of data in an enterprise *583*
Box 41.1   Conversion to third normal form *586*
Box 41.2   Vocabulary used in discussing data *588*
Box 42.1   Avoidance of hidden transitive dependencies in the representation of user
           views of data *618*
Box 42.2   Reorganizing intersecting attributes *622*
Box 45.1   Verification techniques used at each software development stage *668*
Box 45.2   Categories of verification and validation techniques *672*
Box 46.1   Where verification and validation techniques are primarily used in testing *676*
Box 46.2   Steps in unit testing *680*
Box 46.3   Guidelines for integration testing *684*
Box 46.4   Guidelines for system testing *685*
Box 46.5   Guidelines for test data *686*
Box 47.1   Debugging tools and aids *692*
Box 47.2   Error report *694*
Box 47.3   Error correction data *695*
Box 47.4   Error categories *696*
Box 47.5   Debugging guidelines *698*
Box 48.1   Types of test tools *702*
Box 48.2   Automated test tools *704*
Box 48.3   Test-support functions provided by RXVP *706*
Box 49.1   Test tools that support functional testing *720*
Box 49.2   Guidelines for verifying procedural code *723*
Box 51.1   Ways in which computers can help in the automation of systems analysis,
           design, and programming *750*
Box 51.2   Software engineering curriculum *753*
Box 51.3   Information engineering curriculum *754*

PREFACE

The structured revolution has substantially changed systems analysis, design, and programming. Any DP installation that is not using structured techniques throughout, today, is badly managed.

The revolution in structured techniques paved the way for a more fundamental change in the job of the system designer and implementor: *CASE* (Computer-Aided Systems Engineering). CASE technology provides the implementor with a workbench (usually a personal computer) with graphics for the planning and design of systems. The workbench collects enough information about the design to drive a code generator. The code generator and central repository of the design may reside on a mainframe.

The term *IPSE* (Integrated Programming Support Environment) is common in Europe, rather than CASE. IPSE is sometimes more concerned with verbal specifications and programming; CASE is sometimes more concerned with design automation and code generation.

There are many different structured techniques, and their advocates tend to make conflicting claims. In attending courses on the techniques we found no course that represented the whole body of knowledge that structured techniques that we think an analyst, designer, programmer, or DP manager ought to have today. This book addresses that body of knowledge, attempting to describe the techniques tutorially and put them into perspective.

Of the many techniques, some are minor variants on others. We have selected the techniques that are in most common use or represent an advancement of system development methodology.

STRUCTURE OF THIS BOOK

Much of this book is a tutorial on traditional structured techniques. Some of the chapters describe new, more automated techniques. The book emphasizes the philosophies of structured methodologies. Techniques that at first sight appear to be different often share a common philosophy. We have separated the tutorial descriptions of the techniques from the comparisons and critiques of the techniques.

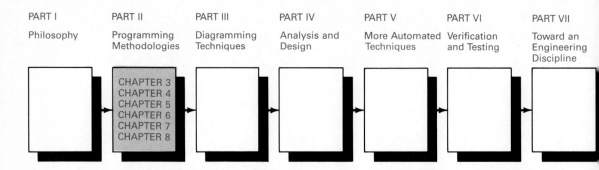

Software engineering and information engineering (which are built on the structured philosophy) encompass management methods and controls as well as analysis, design, and programming techniques. This book limits itself to the analysis, design, and programming techniques and does not discuss management issues.

Part II of the book is concerned with programming methodologies. If you are concerned mainly with analysis and design, you might skip this section at first reading. Somewhat related, Part VI is concerned with testing and verification. This is mainly about programming but includes some considerations important for analysts and designers.

For the analyst and designer, the meat of the book is in Parts III, IV, and V.

A vital aspect of using structured techniques is to employ the best types of diagrams. A diagram is worth a thousand words (and much more with some of the specifications we examined!). Diagramming techniques are so important that a major segment of the book has been devoted to them. The section on diagramming techniques is followed by the section on design and analysis methodologies.

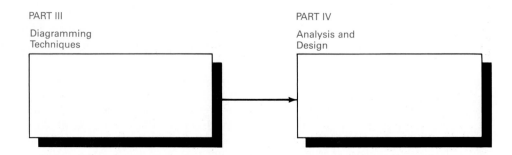

There are logical connections between these two sections. The diagramming technique for a particular structured approach is discussed in Part III, and detailed use of the methodology is discussed in Part IV. For example:

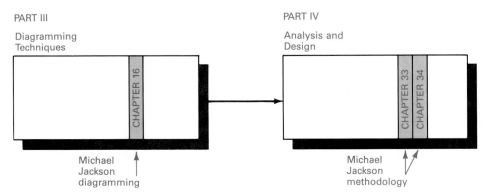

PART III

Diagramming
Techniques

CHAPTER 16

Michael
Jackson
diagramming

PART IV

Analysis and
Design

CHAPTER 33   CHAPTER 34

Michael
Jackson
methodology

You can obtain a quick overview of the techniques by reading through the diagramming section.

The *philosophy* of structured techniques permeates the entire book, but we have attempted to distill it into the first and last sections.

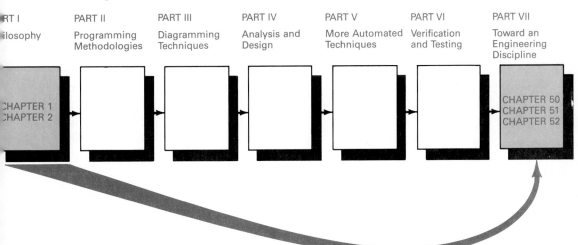

PART I
Philosophy

PART II
Programming
Methodologies

PART III
Diagramming
Techniques

PART IV
Analysis and
Design

PART V
More Automated
Techniques

PART VI
Verification
and Testing

PART VII
Toward an
Engineering
Discipline

CHAPTER 1
CHAPTER 2

CHAPTER 50
CHAPTER 51
CHAPTER 52

The structured revolution is not yet complete. Better structured techniques are evolving, dramatically different from those of the 1970s. We describe some of this change, but it is an ongoing story with surprises yet to come. The most important trend is the move to techniques that are the basis for CASE. The analyst of the future will design systems at a screen in such a way that code can be generated from his design. This needs more rigorous design techniques than those commonly used by systems analysts in the past. When a computer is used as part of the design process, much more intricate and precise techniques are possible which would be too tedious or difficult to do manually. The challenge today is to harness the computer as powerfully as possible in the entire process of developing systems.

James Martin
Carma McClure

PART **I** PHILOSOPHY

1 WHY STRUCTURED TECHNIQUES AND CASE?

OBJECTIVES   In the early days of systems analysis and programming, there were few rules other than those of the programming language itself. Pioneers headed into an uncharted territory and made up their own methods. As in the early days of the Wild West, their methods were often inefficient and caused many problems. The barrooms of the Wild West were full of talk about gunfights and robberies; the cocktail parties of 1960s and 1970s were full of tales about computer errors.

To the dismay of the gunslingers, the Wild West was changed by the spread of machinery, the car, highways, and big money. Computers became powerful and widespread, and vast industries depended on them. The demands for programs greatly overtook the capabilities of programmers and analysts. Programs had to be created faster and at lower cost. Program quality became vital. It was fun at cocktail parties to hear of receiving overdue notices for $0.00, but it was no joke to think of software bugs in a cruise missile carrying a hydrogen bomb finding its way by incredibly complex computing.

Analysis and programming had to change from amateur, ad hoc methods to disciplined, well-thought-out methods. Structured techniques represent a search for discipline in analysis and programming. They have done much to improve the quality of programs and the predictability of the analysis and programming process. Structured techniques are not static but are steadily evolving into better forms. We are likely to see major changes in techniques in the years ahead that will lead to more automated and hence much faster application development.

The need for better techniques is illustrated in some of the quotations from computer authorities:

> We build systems like the Wright brothers built airplanes—build the whole thing, push it off a cliff, let it crash, and start over again.
>
> *Professor R. M. Graham [1]*

You software guys are too much like the weavers in the story about the Emperor and his new clothes. When I go out and check on a software development the answers I get sound like "We're fantastically busy weaving this magic cloth. Just wait awhile and it'll look terrific." But there's nothing I can see or touch, no numbers I can relate to, no way to pick up signals that things aren't really all that great. And there are too many people I know who have come out at the end wearing a bunch of expensive rags or nothing at all.

U.S. Air Force decision maker [2]

There is a widening gap between ambitions and achievements in software engineering. This gap appears in several dimensions: between promises to users and performance by software; between what seems to be ultimately possible and what is achievable now; and between estimates of software costs and expenditures. This gap is arising at a time when the consequences of software failures in all its aspects are becoming increasingly serious.

Dr. E. E. David and A. G. Fraser [3]

If builders built buildings the same way that programmers wrote programs, the first woodpecker would destroy civilization.

Dr. Gerald Weinberg [4]

The attempt to build a discipline of software engineering on such shoddy foundations must surely be doomed, like trying to base chemical engineering on the phlogiston theory, or astronomy on the assumption of a flat earth.

C. A. R. Hoare, Professor of Computing, Oxford [5]

The primary objectives of structured techniques are as follows:

- Achieve high-quality programs of predictable behavior
- Achieve programs that are easily modifiable (maintainable)
- Simplify programs and the program development process
- Achieve more predictability and control in the development process
- Speed up system development
- Lower the cost of system development

To achieve these primary objectives, a number of secondary objectives can be stated. These are listed in Box 1.1.

BOX 1.1   Objectives of structured techniques

Primary Objectives

- Achieve high-quality programs of predictable behavior
- Create programs that are easily modifiable (maintainable)
- Simplify programs and the program development process
- Achieve more predictability and control in the development process
- Speed up system development
- Lower the cost of system development

Secondary (More Technical) Objectives Desirable in Order to Meet the Primary Objectives

- Decompose complex problems and constructs into successively simpler ones. Complex functions are decomposed into lower-level functions, these are decomposed into simpler functions, and so on. This should break the design into a hierarchy of modules with precisely defined interfaces between them.

- Achieve simplicity of design. Good design usually has elegant simplicity with clean interfaces between simple modules; bad design has complex, convoluted patterns of interaction.

- Control complexity. In computing we are going to build systems of ever-increasing complexity. This is true not only of programs but also of chip design, mainframe design, networks, and other areas. It is vital to divide complex designs in an orderly fashion so that the humans can handle the complexity without errors. Control of complexity is achieved by minimizing the number of interactions among separate modules and standardizing the control structure.

- Achieve clear thinking about systems and programs.

- Use diagramming techniques that are as clear as possible. Good diagrams are a great help in understanding complex problems. We believe that they are so important that we have devoted the whole of Part III of this book to diagramming techniques.

- Improve the readability of diagrams and code. One person needs to be able to understand another's design and code. Maintainers need to be able to modify the code. Clarity and readability are essential for this. Improved program readability is achieved through standardization of program style.

(Continued)

BOX 1.1 *(Continued)*

- Improve communication with end users. Many systems have failed or operated poorly because they do not meet the users' requirements well. The techniques used should enable end users to sketch their requirements and enable them to check the designs thoroughly before implementation.

- Achieve unity of architecture. Good design achieves clear, unified architecture. Similar design principles and constructs apply to the entire system. Messy design has separate fragments of different design concepts.

- Employ consistent, teachable methods. The analysis, design, and programming techniques need to be easily teachable. The techniques must be suitable for easily packaged training courses and must apply to all types of programs in an installation. A standard set of control structures should be used.

- Employ a standard set of control structures that can be converted into code with minimum effort. Fourth-generation languages facilitate the representation of such control structures with much less work than third-generation languages [6].

- Achieve precise communication among people in a development team. One of the biggest sources of problems is mismatches in the work of different developers and programmers. The technique should minimize the need for complex interaction among team members and accomplish this interaction through formal representations, preferably computerized.

- Minimize the number of developers on a team, achieving one-person teams where possible. This minimizes human interaction problems. One-person teams can often be achieved by using fourth-generation languages, automated design tools, code generators, and computerized data models.

- Use techniques that work well for large systems as well as small ones. Large systems require much more control of interactions between modules.

- Minimize errors. Designers and programmers make fewer errors if the tools they use are well designed. Where possible, techniques employing a workstation should catch errors as soon as they are made, giving the designer or programmer immediate feedback.

- Catch errors as early as possible. Errors are much less expensive if they are caught at the specification stage rather than during design, in the design stage rather than during coding, or in the coding and debugging stage rather than during maintenance.

BOX 1.1 *(Continued)*

- Achieve provably correct design where possible. **This requires more advanced forms of structured techniques as well as computerized verification, preferably on-line at a screen.**

- Achieve rigorous interfaces between separately developed modules. **Most errors in very large projects are in program-program interfaces. Rigorous control of software interfaces requires more advanced structured techniques.**

- Achieve ever more powerful building blocks and libraries. **As more complex software modules are created, the power of the designer increases. It is necessary to achieve library control and interface control to permit the correct use of more powerful building blocks.**

- Achieve sound data administration. **Data administration is concerned with the correct structuring of data and the uniformity of data definition and design throughout an enterprise. Done well, this speeds up analysis and design and permits the building of information resources.**

- Achieve sound data analysis. **Data analysis clarifies the structure of data and leads to stable data structures, resulting in lower maintenance costs. In the view of data-base authorities, good data analysis should always be done before programs are designed.**

- Provide an analyst's and programmer's workbench with which to maximize help from the computers in achieving objectives. **Interactive computerized tools are needed for many aspects of structured analysis and design. They speed up the work, facilitate modifications, and help to enforce rigorous controls.**

- Achieve the maximum automation of system design with techniques that make possible the automatic generation of code. **Structured techniques are steadily evolving into forms that permit automated checking, modification, and code generation. This automation of the design and programming process allows much higher quality code to be generated quickly.**

In the first decade of structured techniques, some of the objectives in Box 1.1 were not commonly stated. For example:

- *Improve communication with end users.* Recent emphasis on end-user involvement in computing has led to an emphasis on user languages, prototyping, and information center management [7].

- *Minimize the number of developers on a team achieving one-person teams where possible.* Computerized data models and fourth-generation languages enable one person to accomplish what might have required five to ten people [6]. One-person teams are much easier to manage and often lead to greater creativity.

- *Achieve provably correct design where possible.* This objective was clearly stated in computer science departments but omitted completely in the mass commercial courses on structured techniques. For 20 years of applying mathematical proofs to programs, this remained a capability beyond the reach of practical analysts. Recently, new automated approaches have enabled ordinary analysts to create programs that are guaranteed to be free from internal design or coding bugs (see Chapters 26, 38, and 39).

- *Achieve sound data administration* and *achieve sound data analysis.* Data administration and data analysis were missing from the early structured methodologies but are now recognized as vitally important (see Chapters 22, 23, 40, 41, and 42).

- *Provide an analyst's and programmer's workbench with which to maximize help from the computers in achieving objectives.* There has been much discussion of a "programmer's workbench." What is needed is an "analyst's workbench" giving analysts a kit of computerized tools for building systems and generating executable code.

- *Achieve the maximum automation of system design with techniques that make possible the automatic generation of code.* Code generators barely existed in the 1970s, but now there is a proliferation of them. They have a major effect on speed of development, reduction of bugs, and ease of maintenance.

EVOLUTION

Structured techniques evolved from a coding methodology (structured programming) to techniques including analysis, design, and testing methodologies as well as project management concepts and documentation tools. Structured techniques were intended to be a step toward changing software building from a manual craft to an engineering-like discipline. In a sense, they are more an attitude than a particular methodology.

They assumed a more fundamental importance with the advent of CASE (computer-aided systems engineering) tools. They were essential to achieving automated aids to system design, computerized verification of the design, and automated generation of code from the design.

Structured techniques were introduced to the academic community in the late 1960s. They became well known in industry in the early 1970s after the work of F. Terry Baker and Harlan Mills in IBM, particularly their work on the New York *Times* project [8]. Since that time they have gained immense popularity and have had a profound impact on the art of programming.

By the late 1970s, structured techniques had evolved into a set of technologies encompassing the whole software life cycle. They addressed both technical and management issues. They ranged from programming language constructs to problem-solving procedures. Figure 1.1 lists some of the better-known techniques and the time sequence of their evolution.

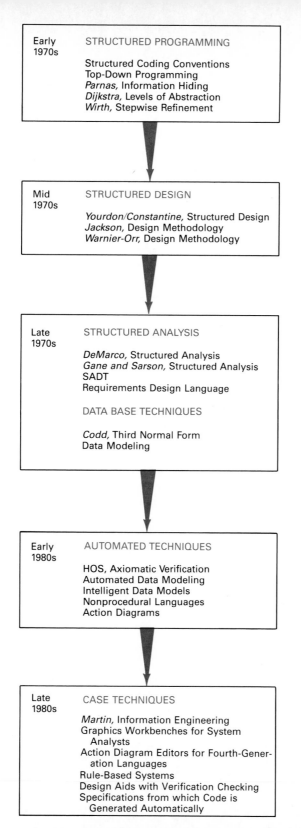

Early 1970s

STRUCTURED PROGRAMMING

Structured Coding Conventions
Top-Down Programming
Parnas, Information Hiding
Dijkstra, Levels of Abstraction
Wirth, Stepwise Refinement

Mid 1970s

STRUCTURED DESIGN

Yourdon/Constantine, Structured Design
Jackson, Design Methodology
Warnier-Orr, Design Methodology

Late 1970s

STRUCTURED ANALYSIS

DeMarco, Structured Analysis
Gane and Sarson, Structured Analysis
SADT
Requirements Design Language

DATA BASE TECHNIQUES

Codd, Third Normal Form
Data Modeling

Early 1980s

AUTOMATED TECHNIQUES

HOS, Axiomatic Verification
Automated Data Modeling
Intelligent Data Models
Nonprocedural Languages
Action Diagrams

Late 1980s

CASE TECHNIQUES

Martin, Information Engineering
Graphics Workbenches for System
    Analysts
Action Diagram Editors for Fourth-Gener-
    ation Languages
Rule-Based Systems
Design Aids with Verification Checking
Specifications from which Code is
    Generated Automatically

9

Figure 1.1 The evolution of structured techniques into CASE technology.

Structured Programming

Early structured techniques focused on the program itself. They addressed questions on the form of the program. What should a program look like? What is the relationship between its static form and its dynamic run-time structure? How can program code be made more understandable? How can complexity be controlled as programs grow in size?

Standardization of form was the key. The notion of standardization was applied to program control constructs and program modules.

Structured Design

By the mid-1970s the structured philosophy spread to the design phase. The notion of standardization was applied to the problem-solving process as a way of introducing organization and discipline into program design. Whereas the earlier structured techniques concentrated on a detailed instruction-level view of the program, structured design focused on a higher-level view of the program, using the program module as the basic building block. The relationship between the problem and its program solution was studied. The concept of modularization was refined by standardizing the structure of a program module, restricting the interfaces between modules, and defining program quality metrics.

Structured Analysis

When it became apparent that many software problems arose from poor definition of requirements, attention turned to the analysis phase. Structured techniques for systems analysis and requirements specification were developed in the late 1970s. The use of data flow diagrams spread rapidly. Data-base techniques were developed.

Many different structured techniques had been introduced. Structured techniques became a composite of methodologies, strategies, and tools offering a systematic approach for developing software. Although they differed in their function, where they were used in the software life cycle, and by whom they were used, all structured techniques shared a common philosophy.

Information Engineering

Information engineering (Chapter 44) applied structured techniques not to one system but to an entire enterprise. Its goal is to create a structured framework into which separately designed systems fit. The framework consists of structured data models and models of the enterprise and its processes.

Automated Techniques

By the early 1980s low productivity in programming had reached crisis proportions. Computers and particularly microcomputers were spreading furiously and dropping in cost. Many end users had become computer-literate and were clamoring for more applications. DP, using the methodologies of the top three blocks in Fig. 1.1, was simply not building applications fast enough and was bogging down in worse and worse maintenance problems. The search for productivity led to new languages [6], report generators, application generators, data-base tools, software for decision support, tools for end users, and various ways of creating specifications from which code could be generated automatically.

By the early 1980s the urgent need was for higher levels of automation in system development. It was realized that if computers were employed as a design workbench, *much* more powerful design techniques could be used. The power and usefulness of structured techniques could be raised by an order of magnitude and more by the appropriate use of computers.

Computers were employed for creating, editing, expanding, and changing structured diagrams. They were used for maintaining dictionaries, directories, and encyclopedias to aid the designer and programmer. They were used to automate data modeling and extract subsets of data models for individual developers. They were used to check and cross-check the designs being created. Elaborate and sometimes mathematically based verification techniques came into use. Above all, software was used, where possible, to avoid the slow and error-prone process of coding in conventional languages, and to automate the generation of code.

The term *encyclopedia* came into use to mean a computerized repository containing the design of systems in such a way that the computer could check the consistency and completeness of the design.

MATHEMATICAL RIGOR

A problem with traditional programming languages is that they permit programmers to create constructs that cannot be validated. Dijkstra shocked the programming world in the late 1960s by stating that GO TO statements and flowcharts should be eliminated because they encouraged unruly, nonverifiable structures. Today GO TO–less programming and avoidance of flowcharts are accepted as normal among programmers who are appropriately trained. Nobody, however, dared to suggest that COBOL or PL/I or PASCAL or ADA should be avoided on the grounds that they encourage nonverifiable structures. Indeed, von Neumann constructs, which have been the basis of computing since it all began, encourage problems.

Great leaps forward in science occur when scientists dare to challenge the most cherished beliefs. Copernicus dared to think that the earth was not the center of the universe. Einstein dared to challenge Newtonian physics. Today we must dare to challenge von Neumann. We must challenge the concept of programming. All applications of computers can be created without conventional programming, including the most complex ones. Indeed, it is with the most complex applications that we most need to avoid conventional programming. Programmers will be replaced, screaming and kicking, by analysts, and sometimes end users, who create designs and generate programs with computerized tools. CASE tools will permit a diversity of constructs to be used in design from which code can be generated automatically.

The structured techniques which are now regarded as traditional (Constantine, Yourdon, De Marco, Jackson, Warnier-Orr) made a substantial improvement to the process of programming and design but do not yield to automatic verification of design or generation of executable, bug-free code. By further refining or changing the constructs they use, we can achieve a higher-level of automation, higher-quality results, better management of complexity, and faster system development.

To achieve truly rigorous verification of design, all constructs used must be based on mathematical axioms such that the overall design can be mathematically verified. The constructs of the first wave of structured techniques eliminated GO TOs but did not use constructs based on mathematical axioms. Hamilton and Zeldin demonstrated how to build systems that employ *only* axiomatically based constructs [8]. With their extension of structured design, a computer can rigorously check the entire design, eliminating inconsistencies and misuse of the constructs, and can automatically generate code. Different CASE tools use different computerized techniques for verifying the consistency of a design and, as far as possible, eliminating design errors.

CASE: COMPUTER-AIDED SYSTEMS ENGINEERING

By the early 1970s the term *computer-aided design* (CAD) was common for design engineers. Many CAD software packages were sold. Amazingly, ten years later the terms *computer-aided systems analysis* (CASA) and *computer-aided programming* (CAP) were still not common. Systems analysts and programmers, who had done so much to automate everybody else's job, were remarkably reluctant to have their own job automated. They sat at their desks with pencils creating designs full of errors, inconsistencies, and omissions that a computerized tool could have detected.

Structured techniques are an excellent basis for CASA and CAP. Today the two terms have been combined into the term *computer-aided systems engineering (CASE)*. However, the power of the computer is such that it invites drastic improvements in the techniques themselves. Rigorous methods that would be far too tedious to use by hand can be made easy and fast to use with computers.

New structured techniques designed around the notion that the analyst and designer will employ a computer with computerized graphics are coming into existence. They can do comprehensive verification of the constructs that are built.

It might be thought that structured techniques are not needed in a world of automatic code generators or that application development without programmers implies application development without structured techniques, but the opposite is the case. The basic problem of computing is the mastering of complexity.

That is really what structured techniques are all about. They enable us to break complex problems into small problems, to extract order from confusion. They enable us to think clearly about complex situations. The world of computing is destined to tackle worse and worse complexity—complexity far beyond what we can imagine. Computerized design tools, with an encyclopedia storing different parts of the design and ensuring their consistency, enable us to build systems of ever greater complexity and to modify (maintain) those systems as needed. We will need all the help we can find in tackling complexity.

Structured techniques are an aid to clear thinking. As such, they are an essential part of any basic course on computing. As end users become more involved with system design and fourth-generation languages, they should be taught structured techniques from the start. The constructs of these techniques should feed the new languages, as we shall illustrate.

IMPORTANT CHARACTERISTICS   Several characteristics are required in structured techniques that were not present or emphasized in the early methods. The following are among the most important characteristics of new techniques:

- *The technique is designed to be user-friendly* so that end users can be fully involved in thinking about computerized procedures and discussing and validating the designs of analysts.

- *The technique is designed for direct use with fourth-generation languages or code generators* so that slow hand coding in third-generation languages (COBOL, PL/I, FORTRAN, etc.) is largely avoided.

- *The technique is designed to be as rigorous as possible.* The word *rigor* was used in the advertising for every structured method, but most of these methods had no mathematical rigor. The techniques for achieving rigor need to be applicable to large systems, not just to textbook problems.

- *The technique should be data-base oriented for commercial DP.* Many early methods were inadequate in a data-base environment.

- *The technique should be designed for operation with automated design tools.* Design with CASE tools is much faster, more thorough, and more easily changeable than manual design.

- *Different and far more powerful methods are practicable with automated tools than with manual design.* Structured techniques need to be changed to take full advantage of the power of the computer. In the long run, this idea and the need to achieve provably correct design will completely change the nature of programming and the design of systems.

LOYALTY TO OLD TECHNIQUES   It is clear that structured techniques are still evolving. In fact, they are probably still in an early stage of their evolution. When the design process is automated, it is clearly possible to have methods that are *much* better than the traditional ones. Traditional structured techniques are failing to solve the increasingly urgent problems of DP.

However, there tends to be a fierce, emotional loyalty among the practitioners and advocates of each technique. Some of the old and rather inadequate techniques are vigorously and irrationally defended against any suggestion of alternate methods.

There have been several revolutions in microchip design methodology. Some of the designers who were skilled with one technique failed to adapt to the next technique; some adapted well; some became managers. New graduates learned the new technique without preconceived notions about the old, and because the field was expanding so fast, they came to occupy the majority of design positions. Programming is comparable in complexity to chip design, but the pressures to change to new techniques are not nearly as great. In chip design there was often no option. Efficient DP organizations *will* change, and analysts and programmers everywhere ought to recognize that better methods are necessary.

REFERENCES

1. R. M. Graham, panel discussion in *Software Engineering,* ed. P. Naur and B. Randall. Brussels: NATO Scientific Affairs Division, 1969.

2. B. W. Boehm, "Software and Its Impact: A Quantitative Assessment," *Datamation,* May 1973.

3. E. E. David and A. G. Fraser, panel discussion in *Software Engineering,* ed. P. Naur and B. Randall. Brussels: NATO Scientific Affairs Division, 1969.

4. Personal communication.

5. C. A. R. Hoare, *The Engineering of Software: A Startling Contradiction,* Computer Bulletin, British Computer Society, December 1975.

6. J. Martin, *Fourth-Generation Languages,* Englewood Cliffs, NJ: Prentice-Hall, Inc., 1985.

7. J. Martin, *Application Development Without Programmers.* Englewood Cliffs, NJ: Prentice-Hall, Inc., 1982.

8. M. Hamilton and S. Zeldin, "Higher Order Software: A Methodology for Defining Software," *IEEE Trans. on Software Engineering,* SE-2, no. 1, 9–32, 1976.

2 PHILOSOPHIES OF STRUCTURED TECHNIQUES

INTRODUCTION   The structured philosophy began in the world of programming. As indicated in Fig. 1.1, it steadily extended into the design, analysis, and information-planning areas.

The original philosophies applied to programming will remain important as the techniques for creating systems change. They are principles relevant to managing *complexity,* whether in software, chip design, or complex system design. They relate to the introduction of standardization and discipline to both the *process* of design and the final *form* of the design. They seek to improve the management of system development, the process of system development, and the resulting system through the introduction of well-defined procedures, tools, techniques, project controls, and communication mechanisms. They structure the development life cycle into a sequence of step-by-step procedures. They use standardization, review, and documentation to provide order and visibility to the process of system development.

BASIC PRINCIPLES   The basic structured philosophy formalized good programming practices. It applies to many aspects of system development other than programming. Some of its practices existed long ago but were not formalized, standardized, or taught until the structured revolution.

The original structured philosophy is a composite of the following problem-solving strategies:

- Principle of abstraction
- Principle of formality

BOX 2.1   Basic principles of the structured philosophy

Principle of Abstraction

To solve a problem, separate the aspects that are tied to a particular reality in order to represent the problem in a simplified, general form.

Principle of Formality

Follow a rigorous, methodical approach to solve a problem.

Divide-and-Conquer Concept

Solve a difficult problem by dividing the problem into a set of smaller, independent problems that are easier to understand and to solve.

Hierarchical Ordering Concept

Organize the components of a solution into a tree-like hierarchical structure. Then the solution can be understood and constructed level by level, each new level adding more detail.

- Divide-and-conquer concept
- Hierarchical ordering concept

Box 2.1 summarizes this structured philosophy.

Principle of Abstraction

Without the principle of abstraction, the structured revolution in programming might never have happened. *Abstraction* is the conception or view of something separate from its realities. It is a simplification of facts describing what is being done without explaining how it is being done. Abstraction allows us to imagine a desired problem solution without immediately being restricted by the peripheral and irrelevant details surrounding reality. Some of our most creative and best solutions are derived in this way.

Abstraction is the best tool we have found for dealing with complexity that involves many interrelated pieces. It is a way of cutting out a simple, clear view of what can be done from a tightly interwoven mass of details.

Using the principle of abstraction, we can view a program in levels or layers. The topmost level shows us the most abstract, simplified view, while the bottommost level shows the atomic details of reality. We can move down a level at a time, gradually seeing more and more detailed program components, or we can move up a level at a time until the entire program solution can be expressed in one powerful, high-level instruction. (See Chapter 6.)

Each level of abstraction is composed of a group of functions that are deemed logically related. Functions belonging to the same level and to different levels are allowed to communicate in restricted ways. There are two communication rules [1]:

1. Lower levels are not aware of and therefore do not access higher levels. But higher levels can invoke lower levels to perform tasks.

2. Each level has its own data, which belong exclusively to functions at that level and cannot be accessed by functions at another level. Data are explicitly passed from one level to another. (Each level may access a common, formally structured data base.)

The principle of abstraction is found in many structured techniques. For example, it is the basis of top-down and bottom-up programming. (See Chapter 7.)

Principle of Formality

The second fundamental principle of the structured philosophy is the principle of formality. The word *formality* suggests a rigorous, methodical approach. This is precisely what it implies in the structured philosophy. The principle of formality is the basis for moving programming from an ad hoc, intuitive art closer to an engineering-like discipline. Without formality, there would be no basis for instituting software project controls and product quality controls. Furthermore, there would be no basis for proving programs correct. Formality enables us to study programs (algorithms) as mathematical objects. Finally, and perhaps most important, formality enables us to communicate ideas and instructions unambiguously in a computable form. In other words, it enables us to automate them.

Introducing formality into programming means that program development is guided by systematic, step-by-step procedures, that the results to be produced by each procedure can be rigorously defined, and that an evaluation step is included to determine whether a procedure has been executed correctly and whether the result produced is correct. It does *not* mean that programming is reduced to a rote procedure in which neither problem-solving skills nor creativity is needed.

Introducing formality into any process, technical or otherwise, is often resisted on the grounds that it stifles creativity. However, the structured philosophy uses formality to nurture creativity through discipline and rigor. Formality is a positive and powerful way of blending the craft and engineering aspects of programming to clarify communication and to focus creativity.

The software life cycle is one example of applying the principle of for-

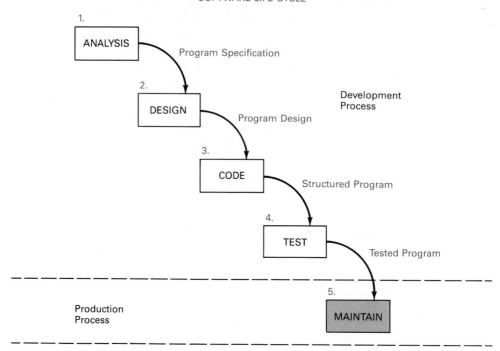

Figure 2.1 The software life cycle is a multistep process consisting of five basic sequential phases: analysis, design, code, test, and maintain.

mality to programming. The software life cycle defines the programming process as a sequence of phases, as shown in Fig. 2.1. For each life-cycle phase, detailed step-by-step procedures have been defined. For example, there are a variety of structured design methodologies, each with its own procedures (e.g., Yourdon Structured Design Methodology, Jackson Design Methodology, Warnier-Orr Methodology). Figure 2.2 shows the four basic design steps in the Yourdon Structured Design Methodology.

Proofs of correctness are another example of applying formality. Dijkstra, Wirth, and Hoare were responsible for much of the early work done in defining the constructive approach to program correctness.

Divide-and-Conquer Concept

Divide and conquer is the concept of solving difficult problems by dividing a problem into a set of smaller, independent problems that are easier to understand and solve (see Fig. 2.3). It is a powerful and essential tool for dealing with complexity. It allows the software developer to work confidently on one piece of a larger system without worrying about the enormous number of details cov-

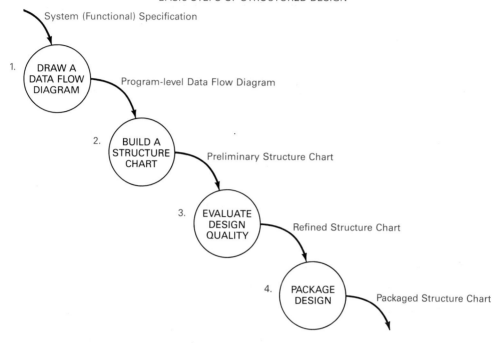

Figure 2.2   The program design process as defined by Yourdon and Constantine consists of four basic sequential steps.

ering the entire system. Divide and conquer has been used since the days of Julius Caesar.

When applied to a software system, the divide-and-conquer concept means partitioning a program into independent pieces that are manageably small and separately testable. Each piece can be developed by one individual. The program is called *modular*. When applied to the software development process, it means partitioning the process into steps that are manageably small. *Stepwise refinement* (or *functional decomposition*) is an example of such a step-by-step programming method. (See Chapter 6.)

Hierarchical Ordering Concept

The concept of *hierarchical ordering* is closely related to that of divide and conquer. In addition to finding that it is easier to understand a program if it is divided into pieces, the arrangement of the pieces is equally important to understandability. Always organizing program modules into a tree-like hierarchical structure enhances understandability. The program can be understood and built level by level where each new level adds more detail.

DIVIDE AND CONQUER

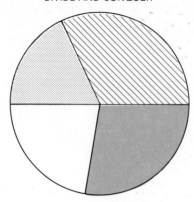

Figure 2.3 Divide and conquer is the strategy of solving difficult problems by dividing a problem into a set of smaller problems that are easier to understand and solve. It is used to simplify the program (modularization) and the programming process (stepwise refinement).

The concept of hierarchical ordering is used in many natural systems as well as in business organizations (see Fig. 2.4). Hierarchical organization make it possible to handle control, delegation, and communication problems that can arise in complex systems involving many parts. In the same way, hierarchical organization can help solve complexity problems in large programs and systems. In addition, it makes more thorough coverage possible in program testing.

Like divide and conquer, hierarchical ordering is the foundation for many structured techniques such as top-down programming, chief programmer team, and structured design methodologies. Although it is theoretically possible to use them separately, combining the divide-and-conquer and hierarchical ordering concepts was instrumental in advancing programming beyond the less powerful modular programming method. Without hierarchical ordering, structured programming would be little more than modular programming.

One of the essential differences between structured and unstructured programs is that structured programs are ordered hierarchically whereas unstructured programs are ordered only sequentially. A hierarchical structure allows us to remove upper layers and still have usable lower-level layers, which can become the building blocks for a variation of the system or the base of a new system. This can be a powerful mechanism for creating programs that are easy to change.

BASIC PRINCIPLES OF SOFTWARE ENGINEERING

In many ways it has become difficult to distinguish between software engineering and structured techniques. *Software engineering* is the study of the principles and their application to the development and

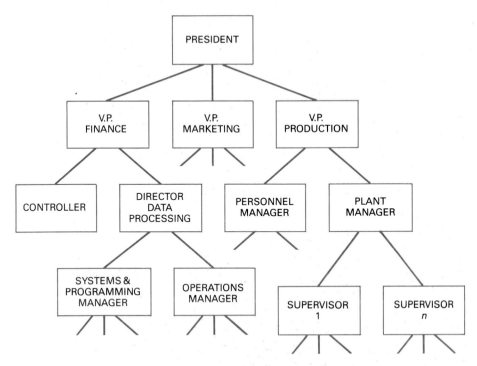

Figure 2.4   A hierarchical organizational structure for a company can make it possible to handle the complexities arising from large business organizations.

maintenance of software systems. Thus software engineering and structured techniques are both collections of software methodologies and tools. They share many of the same goals and basic principles. However, software engineering is a much broader discipline than structured techniques. Software engineering includes the structured methodology and the collection of structured techniques as well as many other software methodologies and tools.

Software engineering is founded on the basic structured principles defined in Box 2.1. In addition, software engineering expands this list to include four more principles (see Box 2.2):

- Principle of hiding
- Principle of localization
- Principle of conceptual integrity
- Principle of completeness

The *principle of hiding* is used to guide the functional decomposition process. To control complexity a system should be modularized, and the interfaces between modules should be kept as simple as possible. The principle of hiding

BOX 2.2   Principles of software engineering

NUCLEUS PRINCIPLES OF
STRUCTURED TECHNIQUES
Principle of Abstraction
Principle of Formality
Divide-and-Conquer Concept
Hierarchical Ordering Concept

OTHER PRINCIPLES OF SOFTWARE ENGINEERING

Principle of Hiding

Hide inessential information. Enable a module to see only the information needed for that module.

Principle of Localization

Place logically related items close together.

Principle of Conceptual Integrity

Follow a consistent design philosophy and architecture.

Principle of Completeness

Check to make certain that nothing is left out.

Principle of Logical Independence

In analysis and design, concentrate on the logical functions to be accomplished independently of the physical implementation.

---

accomplishes this objective by making visible outside a module only the information necessary for interfacing with other modules. Hiding inessential information makes a system easier to understand since each module is aware of and deals with only the information that it requires to perform its function. Hiding also makes a system easier to maintain since it helps minimize the parts of the system affected by a change.

The *principle of localization* is concerned with grouping together logically related items physically. This applies to data and process steps. Arrays, records, subroutines, and procedures are all applications of the principle of localization. The avoidance of GOTOs in well-structured code helps enforce the principle of localization.

The *principle of conceptual integrity* is perhaps the most important principle of software engineering. When combined with the principles of abstraction and hierarchical ordering, the principle of conceptual integrity greatly enhances our ability to master complexity. The principle of conceptual integrity stresses the value of one design plan consistently followed in building every component of a system. The result of following the principle of conceptual integrity is a unified system architecture. This promotes the quality of understandability more than any other factor. Consistently following one style, one design plan, or one system architecture is often more important than which particular one is chosen.

Completeness implies that everything has been included and nothing has been left out. In a complex system that involves many components, it must be presumed that there will be omissions. The *principle of completeness* directs attention to the importance of checking that a system completely meets all the requirements. It involves data and function checks as well as correctness and robustness (i.e., systems ability to recover from errors) checks.

THE DATA-BASE ENVIRONMENT

While the principles of structured programming and process design were emerging, another branch of computing was groping into existence—data bases and information systems. It became clear that a major function of commercial data processing was to get the right data to the right people when they needed it. A vision emerged of all office workers having a workstation on their desk from which they could access data bases. Easy to use, nonprocedural data-base languages grew up. They did not express *how* to process data but rather *what* was to be done to the data. These languages, at least for most of their uses, did not need the techniques that had grown up for structured programming. They did require that the data bases they accessed be well designed and well implemented.

It became clear that the running of a corporation required certain specific data and that these data existed independently of the design of any computer processes that might use them. The data had an inherent structure that was independent of how they were processed. A data-base management system permits many different processes to use the same data and to have different views of the same data.

This led to the principle of *data independence:* Data models representing the inherent logical structure of data should be formally designed, independent of the physical access techniques and distribution of the data. In well-managed data processing installations, such data models become the foundation stones of the data processing. Many different programs used subsets of the same data models. Different programmers and analysts used a common data dictionary. A data administrator who was independent of individual projects was the custodian of the data models and dictionary. It was considered necessary to analyze the data formally before programs were designed. This is a basic, rigorous, and not difficult task for the systems analyst. The data in question may already have been analyzed and are represented in the data administrator's data models.

Strategic planning of data throughout a corporation became desirable. Data require planning, defining, and structuring throughout an enterprise so that they can be exchanged among processes and so that management can obtain the information most valuable in running the enterprise.

Languages, tools, and management techniques quite different from the traditional programming processes are needed to enable managers and users throughout an enterprise to obtain the information.

This set of ideas and the methodologies for implementing it became known as *information engineering*. Box 2.3 lists principles of information engineering. These principles converge with the structured principles of Boxes 2.1 and 2.2.

AUTOMATION OF ANALYSIS, DESIGN, AND CODING

Perhaps the biggest change in structured techniques is likely to come from the use of the computer itself. Early structured techniques were all intended for manual design. As long as systems design and programming uses manual methods, it is restricted to methodologies with which a humble human can cope. More powerful methodologies have been suggested, but they have been too tedious to be practical for our error-prone brains. Powerful methodologies need automation.

The human brain makes endless mistakes when it has to handle a mass of detail. It makes mistakes in programming; it makes mistakes in data modeling; the inputs and outputs do not correlate in layered data flow diagrams; specifications are full of errors, ambiguities, omissions, and inconsistencies. Structured techniques will be designed in the future so that a computer can check them all. It can check that inputs and outputs correlate, it can detect omissions and inconsistencies, it can automate data modeling, and it can automatically generate program code. Software exists today to do these things. It needs to be better integrated, better human-factored, and taught to systems analysts everywhere.

Programming is one of the most labor-intensive and error-prone of human activities. Increasingly in the future it will be avoided by using program generators. Generators are used today for generating report programs, graphics programs, screen dialogues, data-base accesses, and in many cases generating complete applications. It is desirable for most applications that specification languages should replace programming languages. Specification languages state

BOX 2.3 Principles of information engineering

Principle of Rigorous Data Analysis

Data have an inherent structure. Data analysis, which formally identifies this structure, should be done *before* process logic is designed.

Principle of Data Independence

Data models representing the inherent logical structure of data should be formally designed independently of how the data are used and independently of the physical structure and distribution of the data.

Principle of Strategic Data Planning

Data require planning, defining, and structuring throughout an enterprise so that data can be exchanged among processes and so that management can obtain the information most valuable in running the enterprise.

Principle of End-User Access

End users should be given tools for accessing data bases that they can use themselves, without programming.

Principle of Enterprise-Wide Modeling

Data models and process models are constructed across an enterprise (or major division of an enterprise) so that separately developed systems fit into this framework, and hence work together.

what is to be accomplished rather than *how* it is to be programmed in detail. The specifications created should be precise enough that program code can be generated from them. A diversity of specification tools are on the market today. Many generate relatively simple systems, such as report processing and database updating. Some generate complex systems and permit thorough cross-checking of the design. With one specification tool, a complex and efficient compiler was generated without programmers [1].

A principle of design automation then should be that programming is avoided wherever possible. This does not invalidate the principles in Boxes 2.1 and 2.2. On the contrary, as we design increasingly complex systems, those principles become more important. They apply to the design and specification process rather than to program coding.

GRAPHICS   Computer-aided design requires good graphics. The
                         analyst and end user should employ diagrams of sys-
tems that are as meaningful and as easy to understand as possible. These diagrams will often be sketched on blackboards and pieces of paper but should be
designed so that they can be created, edited, manipulated, and added to on a
computer screen. As we will see later, some diagramming techniques are more
appropriate for this than others. The graphics design should be capable of being
decomposed into successively more detail until code can be generated from it.

The computer graphics should be designed so that all manner of checks
can be applied to the design. The designer should be given immediate feedback
when he makes errors. Inconsistencies, omissions, and errors should be highlighted on the screen, and the designer should be given help to correct them.

PROVABLY   Mathematical proofs of correctness of conventional
CORRECT   programs are extremely sophisticated and tedious.
CONSTRUCTS   There is no hope that the ordinary analyst or pro-
                         grammer could apply them. Where proofs of correct-
ness have been applied, the programs have generally been very small and the
mathematics highly complex. What was claimed to be the largest program mathematically proved correct was a 433-statement ALGOL program to perform er-
ror-bounded arithmetic; the proof required 46 pages of difficult mathematical
reasoning [2].

As Hoare defined it, a correctness proof involves the application of valid
rules of inference to sets of valid axioms [3]. For example, some axioms concern the elementary operations of addition or multiplication relevant to integers
(e.g., $x + y = y + x$, $x \times 0 = 0$), and some rules concern the functions of
assignment and iteration (e.g., X: = F, WHILE B DO S). Assertions made about
initial preconditions and the values of relevant variables at the end of the execution (or some intermediate points) of the program are used to prove the correctness of the program. Notations of mathematical logic are used to express
these assertions based on the axioms. For example, *(P) ⊃ S ⊃ (Q)* means "if
proposition P is true when control is at the beginning of statement S, then proposition Q will be true when control is at the end of statement S" [4].

Proofs of correctness are possible for structured programs because the control structures are limited. For each control structure allowed in a structured
program there is a well-known rule of inference: linear reasoning for concatenation, induction for iteration, and case analysis for selection.

Hamilton and Zeldin showed that verification of correctness can be made
to work in practice and can be easily automated if control structures different
from those of conventional programming are used [5]. They employed three
basic control structures, each based on mathematical axioms. This approach
enabled them to build a methodology which is fully automated and easy to use

and which produces programs for which the internal logic is provably correct. This is described in Chapters 26, 38, and 39.

The reason Hamilton and Zeldin's methodology is usable by ordinary systems analysts is that it is fully computerized. The analyst creates diagrams on a computer screen and decomposes these into sufficient detail that code can be generated, and the computer checks every step of this process. The analyst can be entirely unaware of the mathematics underlying the checking. If an attempt were made to use the method by hand, it would be *extremely* tedious, and the analyst would normally make many errors.

CASE tools, then, make possible the use of methods that would be much too tedious and error-prone when done by hand. The computer can check relentlessly everything that is done, aiding the user at each step and allowing the user to employ powerful libraries of constructs. In the long run the only way we will build systems of the level of complexity now envisioned is to use the computer to assist, with structured techniques much more powerful and thorough than the early ones. These techniques need to be designed for comprehensive checking of the entire design (and this may involve many millions of checks) and the automatic creation of program code.

Once such powerful and thorough techniques are in common use, building blocks of greater and greater complexity will be created. Designers, standing on the shoulders of others, will employ these building blocks to create more interesting building blocks. This is the way the computer industry will progress.

MANAGEMENT OF COMPLEXITY

The challenge of much of today's high technology is the management of complexity. This applies to future software, chip design, weapons systems, worldwide computer networks, robots, and many other areas. As we climb the exponential curves of advancing technology, the need to manage complexity grows at a furious pace.

A microchip designer of the late 1960s had to keep the design in his head. This was like keeping the street map of a small town in his head, and he had no difficulty doing it.

By the mid-1970s he needed to keep in his head the equivalent of the street map of a medium-sized city. A taxi driver does this, occasionally needing to look at his street guide.

By the early 1980s the chip designer had to handle complexity roughly equivalent to the street map of a state. Now he could not cope efficiently without help from computers.

By the end of the 1980s, advanced chip designs were equivalent in complexity to a street map of the entire United States, and the cost of errors in the design were very high. New computerized methods that allow the design to be validated at every step are needed. Cells, like subroutines, from a library were used extensively, and their use needs to be validated. A human could not cope without computer assistance, and the design methods have to change to facilitate computer assistance.

By the late 1990s advanced chip design will be equivalent in complexity to a street map of the whole world.

Programming, if we tap the true potential of the computer, will grow to levels of greater complexity than chip design. The program designer, like the chip designer, needs new design methods that are built to use the power and relentless accuracy of the computer.

CHANGING COMPUTER LANGUAGES

The chip designer had to employ new "languages" as the need to manage complexity grew. The programmer also needs to adopt new languages.

Starting in the late 1970s, a flood of new languages came into existence, referred to as fourth-generation languages [6]. The broad objective of these languages was to obtain quality results much faster than with conventional (third-generation) languages such as COBOL, PL/I, FORTRAN and PASCAL. Some fourth-generation languages were intended to simplify the creation of certain applications so that end users, rather than programmers, could create the results they needed.

New computer languages (or at least a major subset of them) should be designed for the analyst rather than for the programmer. They should allow him to generate screens, reports, dialogues, and data bases, navigate through data bases, and update data with nonprocedural, non-programming-like techniques. They should allow him to translate his structured designs, preferably built on a computer graphics screen, directly into code. We may no longer refer to these as *languages*; we may call them *tools,* CASE tools.

This concept of computer-aided systems design is likely to change both structured techniques and computer languages. It is a principle of design automation that *the language should be tailored to the design techniques*. This is going to cause fundamental changes in languages, especially when we limit the design constructs to those that can be mathematically verified to be correct.

Box 2.4 lists principles that apply to computer-aided systems design. Again, these principles do not negate the ones in Boxes 2.1, 2.2, and 2.3 but build upon them, reaching for higher levels of automation.

END-USER INVOLVEMENT

It is essential in computer system design to involve the end users. Some designers and programmers have a proclivity to work in isolation, creating elegant designs without end-user interference or discussion. This is dangerous. It has resulted in many systems that do not meet user needs. In some cases there have been multimillion-dollar disasters.

BOX 2.4   Principles of computer-aided systems design

Powerful Design Techniques Need Automation

The human brain is very limited in its capability to handle detail, complexity, mathematical rigor, and extensive cross-checking without errors. When the computer is harnessed, designers can pass far beyond the confines of the human brain.

Computer-Aided Design Requires Graphics

All structured analysis and design uses graphics. The diagrams become complex and very time-consuming to change. They need constant refinement. A computerized tool should facilitate building, editing, refining, expanding, and extracting subsets from design diagrams so that complexity is made easy to handle.

The Computerized Tool Should Guide the Designer

CASE tools should incorporate methodologies and guide the designer through steps that reflect good design. The tool should ask the designer for information so that it has a complete set of information from which to generate code.

Programming Should Be Avoided Wherever Possible

Design diagrams should be decomposable into successively more detail until code can be generated automatically from them. Reports, charts, data bases, dialogues, data updating, etc., should be specifiable for automatic code generation.

Constructs That Lead to Axiomatically Provable Design Should Be Employed

It is practical to achieve much greater rigor than the currently popular structured techniques provide. Maximum use should be made of constructs that lead to mathematically rigorous automation of design.

Languages Should Be Tailored to Design Techniques

New (fourth-generation) computer languages are evolving rapidly. These should employ appropriate constructs so that the best techniques for automated design are reflected in the computer language.

A vitally important principle in systems analysis and design is to involve the end users fully. This should be done in a number of ways:

1. Users should be taught how to sketch and discuss the computer procedures that would be useful to them.

2. Users should participate in *joint requirements planning* (JRP) and *joint application design* (JAD) workshops at the start of the development life cycle.

3. Users should be able to read and critique the designs created by DP staff.

4. Users should be given tools with which they can build for themselves certain classes of computer applications [7]. A wide variety of user-friendly tools for different purposes now exists.

5. Users should be fully involved in the data administration process of defining and modeling shared data.

6. User management should be fully involved in the planning process of determining the data most important for managing the enterprise.

7. For all DP systems, prototypes should be built and operated experimentally with users before the major development money is spent.

8. Maximum user creativity with computers should be encouraged.

USER-FRIENDLY STRUCTURED TECHNIQUES

To involve users in analysis, design, and data administration it is desirable to employ structured techniques that are as user-friendly as possible. Good diagramming techniques are essential for this. The users should be taught to think about systems with clear diagrams. They should be encouraged to sketch the procedures they want and to discuss and modify the sketches of the systems analysts.

Diagramming should often be done at two levels. It should begin with user-friendly sketches that the users can draw and argue about. The sketches should be designed so that they can be steadily refined into rigorous designs. Rigorous designs that permit axiomatic verification are not necessarily user-friendly. The transition from user-friendly sketches to rigorous design should be a natural one, not one that involves a fundamentally different representation or language. The transition should be an evolution in which more detail is steadily added, preferably on a computer screen with computerized checking. The diagrams should be decomposable into sufficient detail that executable code can be generated automatically.

THE DESIGN PROCESS

Figure 2.5 represents how structured techniques *ought* to be used. First there is a sketching process with full user involvement. The sketching may start on a blackboard or paper and be transferred to a computer screen. At this stage

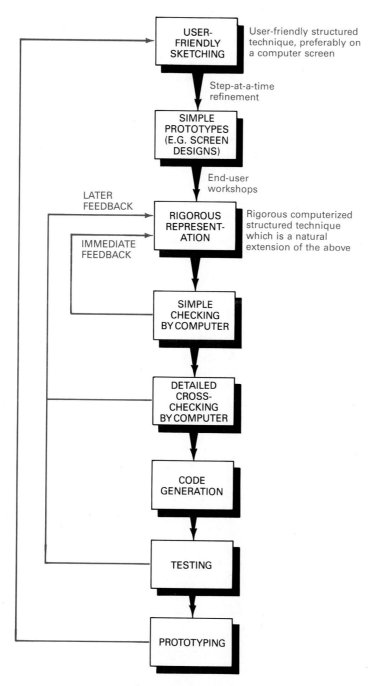

Figure 2.5 The design process with computerized tools and user participation.

there should be as much user interaction as possible. The sketch is then refined, using a computerized tool, to form a rigorous representation designed for axiomatic checking that is as complete and comprehensive as possible. Syntax and simple semantic checking takes place as the design is created. There should be as much *immediate* feedback of error information as possible. Complete cross-

BOX 2.5   Principles of end-user involvement

End Users Should Be Fully Involved in Analysis, Design, and Data Administration

Users should be able to check at every stage what is being planned and built for them. Users should participate thoroughly in design workshops (JAD, joint application design sessions).

Structured Techniques Should Be Designed to Aid User Comprehension and Creativity

Users should be able to sketch procedures that can help them and read, discuss, and modify the analysts' sketches. This requires highly user-friendly structured techniques.

User-Friendly Sketches Should Be Directly Decomposable into Designs That Are Fully Rigorous

Sketches that are easy to understand should be extendable, with a computerized tool, to form a rigorous representation designed for axiomatic checking that is as complete and comprehensive as possible.

Prototypes Should Be Built Wherever Practical

The earliest possible reality testing is needed on all systems.

Information Center Tools Should Be Used Wherever Practical

Tools for end users, including query languages, report generators, spreadsheet manipulation, and user application generators, should be employed to provide maximum flexibility and to create prototypes.

NUCLEUS PRINCIPLES OF STRUCTURED TECHNIQUES
- Principle of Abstraction
- Principle of Formality
- Divide-and-Conquer Concept
- Hierarchical Ordering Concept

OTHER PRINCIPLES OF SOFTWARE ENGINEERING
- Principle of Information Hiding
- Principle of Localization
- Principle of Conceptual Integrity
- Principle of Completeness
- Principle of Logical Independence

PRINCIPLES OF INFORMATION ENGINEERING
- Principle of Rigorous Data Analysis
- Principle of Data Independence
- Principle of Strategic Data Planning
- Principle of End-User Access
- Principle of Enterprise-wide Models

PRINCIPLES OF COMPUTER-AIDED SYSTEMS DESIGN
- Powerful Design Techniques Need Automation
- Computer-Aided Design Requires Graphics
- The Computerized Tool Should Guide the Designer
- Programming Should Be Avoided Wherever Possible
- Constructs That Lead to Axiomatically Provable Design Should Be Employed
- Languages Should Be Tailored to Design Techniques

PRINCIPLES OF END-USER INVOLVEMENT
- End Users Should Be Fully Involved in Analysis, Design, and Data Administration
- Structured Techniques Should Be Designed to Aid User Comprehension and Creativity
- User-Friendly Sketches Should Be Directly Decomposable in Designs That Are Fully Rigorous
- Prototypes Should Be Built Wherever Practical
- Information Center Tools Should Be Used Wherever Practical

Figure 2.6 Principles of structured techniques (a combination of Boxes 2.1 through 2.5).

checking and full semantic checking take place in a later computer run to verify the design. When the designer has corrected all detectable mistakes, executable code is generated and tested. The users are given a prototype, often at first a partial prototype. They work with the prototype and are likely to make many refinements, which are fed through the top steps of Fig. 2.5 until the designer decides to generate another version of the prototype or move on to the final design.

The process we describe here is far from what we find in practice with the most commonly used methodologies at the time of writing. This emphasizes the point we made in Chapter 1: Structured techniques are evolving. Vast improvements are needed over the techniques most commonly taught and practiced.

Box 2.5 lists principles of end-user involvement. Figure 2.6 puts the whole picture together to illustrate the philosophies of structured techniques. Many practitioners and authorities on structured techniques have not progressed beyond the inner two boxes of Fig. 2.6. It is necessary that the whole computer industry evolves to more thorough, more rigorous, and more automated techniques designed for full user involvement.

REFERENCES

1. Higher Order Software, Inc., Cambridge, MA, generating its own software.

2. D. I. Good and R. L. London, "Computer Interval Arithmetic: Definition and Proof of Correct Implementation," *ACM Journal,* October 1970, pp. 603–613. The claim that this was the largest program that has been mathematically proved correct was in B. W. Boehm, "Software and Its Impact: A Quantitative Assessment," reprinted in *Software Design Techniques,* ed. P. Freeman and A. I. Wasserman, Long Beach, CA: IEEE Computer Society, 1980.

3. B. Liskof, "A Design Methodology for Reliable Software Systems," Proceedings, Fall Joint Computer Conference, 1972.

4. C. A. R. Hoare, "An Axiomatic Basis for Computer Programming," *CACM,* 12, no. 10 (October 1969), 576–580.

5. M. Hamilton and S. Zeldin, "Higher Order Software: A Methodology for Defining Software," *IEEE Trans. on Software Engineering* SE-2(1): 9–32, 1976.

6. J. Martin, *Fourth-Generation Languages,* Englewood Cliffs, NJ: Prentice-Hall, Inc., 1985.

7. J. Martin, *Application Development Without Programmers.* Englewood Cliffs, NJ: Prentice-Hall, Inc., 1982.

PART **II**   PROGRAMMING METHODOLOGIES

3 STRUCTURED PROGRAMMING

**THE SHIFT
TO SOFTWARE**
By the late 1960s it became obvious that software systems were complex. They were difficult to design, to write, and to test and virtually impossible to understand and to maintain. The programming task could no longer be viewed as a trivial one. The emphasis shifted from hardware to software. As Wirth explained,

> . . . the true challenge does not consist in pushing computers to their limits by saving bits and microseconds, but in being capable of organizing large and complex programs, and assuring that they specify a process that for all admitted inputs produces the desired results. [1]

There was critical need for improved technologies. This need became so severe that it became referred to as the "software crisis." The serious shortcomings of software technologies were discussed at the 1968 NATO Conference on Software Engineering. For example, Graham stated:

> Today we tend to go on for years, with tremendous investments, to find that the system, which was not well understood to start with, does not work as anticipated. We build systems like the Wright brothers built airplanes— build the whole thing, push it off the cliff, let it crash, and start over again. [2]

Advances in software technologies lagged far behind those in hardware technologies. Installations that bought the latest computers continued to use ad hoc programming methods from the 1950s and early 1960s.

INTRODUCTION
OF STRUCTURED
PROGRAMMING

It was at this point that structured programming was introduced. The 1969 NATO Conference on Software Engineering was one of the first times Dijkstra used the expression "structured programming" [3]. He discussed his concern for the complexity of large programs and the problem of program correctness. He also introduced a new conceptual way of viewing a program as layers or levels of abstractions.

The "THE" Multiprogramming System was developed by Dijkstra using this concept of levels [4]. The system was hierarchically layered to permit exhaustive testing. The utility of levels of abstraction was demonstrated by an a priori proof of the system correctness by which Dijkstra guaranteed the reliability of THE. During testing, only trivial coding errors were found, with a frequency of one error per 500 instructions. The errors were both easy to locate and easy to correct.

We can surmise from the literature that Dijkstra is the founder of structured programming. However, this distinction is not attributed to him because of his 1969 NATO paper on THE; rather it is because of his new famous letter to the editor of the CACM entitled "GO TO Statement Considered Harmful" [5]. Probably more than any other piece of literature, this letter kindled the interest and began the controversy in structured programming. Dijkstra presented several reasons to abolish the GO TO statement from higher-level programming languages. First, it is too primitive a control structure. Programmers do not use the unconditional branch as a control structure. They use it as a building block in the construction of more sophisticated control structures such as DO WHILE structures and case statements. Second, the GO TO statement gives the programmer an opportunity to "make a mess out of" a program. Finally, it obscures the program structure by widening the "gap between the static representation of the program and its dynamic process." In other words, a programmer could not sequentially read a program to determine execution control flow.

GO TO–LESS
PROGRAMMING

Dijkstra was not alone in his dismay over the subtle problems that the GO TO statement can present. Others were also skeptical about its usefulness. Wirth and Hoare published a paper in which they noted that the conditional or case statement showed the execution flow of a program more clearly than the GO TO statement [6]. Also, a theoretical argument that supported the abolishment of the GO TO statement had been presented two years earlier by Bohm and Jacopini [7]. They proved that any program could be written using only simple sequence and iteration as its control constructs. In another version of the proof, the selection structure was also included. Theoretically, then, the GO TO statement is *not* a necessary control construct in structured programming.

Results from programming experiments conducted to study the use of control structures support Dijkstra's position [8]. The more GO TO statements in a program, the more errors the program is likely to have. Higher-level control structures (e.g., DO WHILE and case structures) appear to be easier to comprehend, easier to modify, and less error-prone because they have a higher semantic level and avoid machine-related issues. Also, programmers expressed a preference for using higher-level control structures because they improve program readability and reduce the number of instructions that must be coded.

OBJECTIVES

Unfortunately, in the years following Dijkstra's letter, the GO TO controversy overshadowed the more significant issues of structured programming. Sometimes GO TO–less programming and structured programming are thought to be synonymous concepts. But the objective of structured programming is much more far reaching than the creation of programs without GO TO statements. The objective of structured programming is to solve the software crisis by providing a programming discipline to accomplish the following:

- Improve program reliability
- Improve program readability
- Minimize program complexity
- Simplify program maintenance
- Increase programmer productivity
- Provide a disciplined programming methodology

As the structured programming methodology evolved, it grew closer to the software engineering concept. It became more difficult to differentiate between structured programming and software engineering than between structured programming and GO TO–less programming. For example, structured programming and software engineering share many of the same objectives, making it difficult to decide where the structured programming methodology ends and software engineering begins. Box 3.1 lists the objectives of structured programming.

DEFINITIONS

Rather than one generally accepted definition, there are several schools of thought on what structured programming is.

In the narrowest sense, the concept of structured programming is concerned with only the program form and the coding process. It is a set of conventions that the programmer can follow to produce structured code. The coding rules impose restrictions on the use of control constructs, data structures, mod-

BOX 3.1 Objectives of structured programming

Improve Program Readability

- Make the correspondence between the source program and the execution process as trivial as possible (Dijkstra [5]).
- Encourage locality of control structures and data use (Dijkstra [5]).
- Reduce program complexity by simplifying control paths (Miller and Lindamood [9]).
- Enable programs to be read from beginning to end with no control jumps (Baker [10]).

Improve Program Efficiency

- Make programs efficient with respect to core requirements (Baker [10]).
- Make programs efficient with respect to execution time (Baker [10]).
- Make programs efficient with respect to maintainability:

    Structure the program so that bugs are easy to find and easy to correct (Donaldson [11]).

    Structure the program so that it can be easily modified (Donaldson [11]).

Enhance Program Reliability

- Construct the program so that there is no need to debug it (Wirth [1]).
- Structure the program so that it is amenable to thorough testing (Benson [12], Donaldson [11]).
- Prove the program correct as part of the construction process (Dijkstra [5]).
- Introduce a new level of precision in programming (Mills [13]).

Provide a Discipline for Programming

- Force programmers to think (Benson [12]).
- Systematize the programming process (Mills [14]).
- Enforce system integrity (Brooks [15]).

Reduce the Cost of Programming

- Allow programmers to control larger amounts of code (Wirth [1]).
- Increase programmer productivity (Brown [16]).

ule composition, and documentation. Structured programming in this sense focuses on topics such as:

1. GOTO–less programming (complete or partial banishment of the GOTO statement)
2. Programming with only three control constructs: sequence, selection, and iteration
3. Form of a structured program
4. Applying structured coding conventions in a particular programming language

In a broader sense, structured programming addresses programming methods as well as program form. Structured programming implies following a structured methodology to order program design and implementation. Topics include:

1. Modular programming
2. Stepwise refinement
3. Levels of abstraction
4. Top-down and bottom-up programming

In its broadest sense, the concept of structured programming encompasses the entire programming process. It imposes a discipline on each stage of the creation of a software system and the organization of programmers. Structured programming includes ideas such as:

1. Analytic verification of algorithm correctness to ensure program reliability
2. Systematization of the programming process
3. Relating the programming task to the program design structure and the programming team structure
4. Application of management techniques to the programming process
5. Systematic use of abstraction to control a mass of detail and to produce meaningful documentation

When used in its narrowest sense, structured programming is usually called *structured coding;* when used in its broadest sense, structured programming is viewed as a collection of programming methodologies rather than a single method and is usually called *structured techniques*. It is the second definition that is most generally understood to mean structured programming. *Structured programming* is a methodology that lends structure and discipline to the program form, program design, program coding, and program testing. It is a programming methodology for constructing hierarchically ordered, modular programs using standardized control constructs (see Box 3.2).

BOX 3.2 Definition of structured programming

Structured programming is a methodology that lends structure and discipline to the program form, program design process, program coding, and program testing. It is a programming methodology for constructing hierarchically ordered, modular programs using standardized control constructs.

Structured coding is a method of constructing a program according to a set of rules requiring a strict style format, a standardized control structure, and a restricted set of logic constructs.

Structured techniques are a collection of techniques, methodologies, and tools whose common objective is to build high-quality, low-cost software systems. They include programming methodologies for analysis, design, coding, and testing, project management concepts, and documentation tools.

REFERENCES

1. N. Wirth, "On the Composition of Well-Structured Programs," *Computing Surveys,* 6, no. 4 (December 1974), 247.

2. P. Naur and B. Randell, eds., *Software Engineering 1968*. Brussels: NATO Scientific Affairs Division.

3. E. Dijkstra, "Structured Programming," in *Software Engineering 1969*. Brussels: NATO Scientific Affairs Division.

4. E. Dijkstra, "The Structure of the THE Multiprogramming System," *CACM,* 11, no. 5 (May 1968), 341–346.

5. E. Dijkstra, "GO TO Statement Considered Harmful," *CACM* 11, no. 3 (March 1968), 147–148.

6. N. Wirth and C. A. R. Hoare, "A Contribution to the Development of ALGOL," *CACM,* 9, no. 6 (June 1966), 413.

7. C. Bohm and G. Jacopini, "Flow Diagrams, Turning Machines and Languages with Only Two Formation Rules," *CACM,* 9, no. 5 (May 1966), 366-371.

8. B. Shneiderman, *Software Psychology*. Cambridge, MA: Winthrop, 1980, pp. 66–90.

9. E. Miller and G. Lindamood, "Structured Programming: Top-Down Approach," *Datamation,* 19, no. 12 (December 1973), 55.

10. F. Baker, "Chief Programmer Team Management of Production Programming," *IBM Systems Journal,* 11, no. 1 (January 1972), 58.

11. J. Donaldson, "Structure Programming," *Datamation,* 19, no. 12 (December 1972), 52.

12. J. Benson, *Structured Programming Techniques,* IEEE Symposium on Computer Software Reliability, New York, 1973.

13. H. Mills, *Mathematical Foundations for Structured Programming,* IBM FSD:RSC, 71-5108.

14. H. Mills, "The New Math of Computer Programming," *CACM,* 18, no. 1 (January 1975), 43.

15. F. Brooks, *The Mythical Man-Month.* Reading, MA: Addison-Wesley Publishing Co., 1975.

16. P. Brown, "Programming and Documenting Software Projects," *Computing Surveys,* 6, no. 4 (December 1974), 213.

4 STRUCTURED PROGRAMS

PROPERTIES OF A STRUCTURED PROGRAM

The primary goal of structured programming is to produce a program of high quality at low cost. How effective the structured programming methodologies are in achieving this objective can only be determined if we have a clear understanding of what constitutes a structured program and some practical measures of program structure.

The most prominent characteristics of a structured program are its hierarchical form and restricted set of control constructs. In addition, however, a standardized control structure, documentation requirements, and style conventions are considered equally important properties of a structured program. Box 4.1 summarizes the properties of a structured program.

LIMITED CONTROL CONSTRUCTS

The three basic control constructs identified by Bohm and Jacopini became the basic constructs for building structured programs [1]:

1. Sequence
2. Selection
3. Iteration

When *sequence* is used to control program execution, statements are executed in the same order as they appear in the source code. Figure 4.1 illustrates the sequence construct. The selection, iteration, and branch structures are used to alter program execution flow from its normal sequential statement-by-statement order.

When the *selection* structure is used, a condition is tested, and then de-

BOX 4.1   Properties of a structured program

Property 1

The program is divided into a set of modules arranged in a hierarchy defining their logical and execution-time relationships.

Property 2

The execution flow from module to module is restricted to one simple, easily understood scheme in which control must enter the module at its one entry-point, must leave the module from its one exit point, and must always be passed back to the invoking module.

Property 3

Module construction is standardized according to the traditional modularization rules, and legal control constructs are restricted to sequence, selection, iteration, and the escape.

Property 4

Documentation is required in the source code to define the overall program function and to introduce each module by explaining its function, its data structures, and its relationship to other modules in the program.

pending on whether the test is true or false, one of two alternative sets of instructions is executed. Figure 4.2 illustrates the selection structure.

The *iteration* structure is used to execute a set of instructions an integral number of times—that is, to build a loop. The iteration structure is illustrated in Fig. 4.3. Notice that there are two basic forms for the iteration structure: DO UNTIL and DO WHILE. Either form can be used to create a program loop in a structured program.

Usually the restriction to allow only these three control constructs in a structured program is relaxed to include extensions such as the nested IF, the case statement, and the escape. Allowing these extensions makes the program easier to code and to maintain.

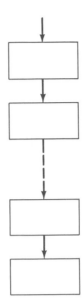

Figure 4.1   When the sequence control construct is used to control program execution, statements are executed one after another in the same order as they appear in the source code.

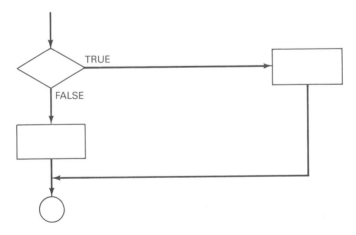

Figure 4.2   When the selection structure (IF-THEN-ELSE structure) is used, a condition is tested. If the condition is true, one set of instructions is executed; if the condition is false, another set of instructions is executed. Then both sets join at a common point to continue execution.

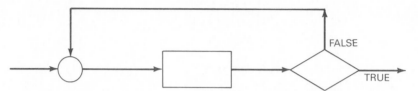

DO UNTIL: A block of instructions is executed. Then a loop termination condition is tested. If the condition is true, the loop is terminated and execution continues with the next sequential instruction. If the condition is false, the instruction block is executed again. Note that the DO UNTIL loop is always executed at least once.

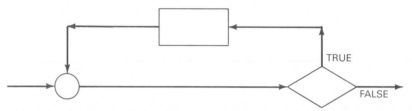

DO WHILE: A termination condition is tested. If the condition is false, the loop is terminated and execution continues with the next sequential instruction. If the condition is true, a block of instructions is executed and the condition is tested again. Note that if the condition is initially false, the loop will *not* be executed at all.

Figure 4.3   The iteration construct is used to execute a set of instructions an integral ($n \geq 0$) number of times. There are two basic forms: DO UNTIL and DO WHILE.

NESTED IF

The selection structure has the following basic format:

```
IF  condition
        statement-1
ELSE
        statement-2
```

where statement-1 is executed when the condition is true and statement-2 is executed when the condition is false. When statement-1 of a selection structure contains a selection structure, it is called a *nested IF*. At each level of nesting, indentation is suggested to make the next level more obvious:

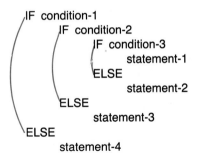

```
IF condition-1
    IF condition-2
        IF condition-3
            statement-1
        ELSE
            statement-2
    ELSE
        statement-3
ELSE
    statement-4
```

In a structured program, at most *three* levels of nesting are allowed. The purpose of this restriction is to control readability. Beyond three levels of nested IFs, it becomes difficult for most programmers to understand the code.

CASE STATEMENT   In the case statement and the *n*-way branch, the selection structure is extended so that a choice is made from more than two alternative sets of code depending on a condition test. In some languages it is implemented using the IF-THEN-ELSE structure or a special case structure. An example of an *n*-way branch coded using the COBOL IF statement and the GO TO–DEPENDING ON statement is shown in Fig. 4.4.

```
IF FORMAT-TYPE = 01
        PERFORM TYPE-1-PROCESSING
ELSE IF FORMAT-TYPE = 02
        PERFORM TYPE-2-PROCESSING
ELSE IF FORMAT-TYPE = 03
        PERFORM TYPE-3-PROCESSING
ELSE
        PERFORM TYPE-ERROR-PROCESSING.
```

(a) Using the COBOL IF statement to implement an *n*-way branch.

```
GO TO TYPE-1-PROCESSING
        TYPE-2-PROCESSING
        TYPE-3-PROCESSING
DEPENDING ON FORMAT-TYPE.
PERFORM TYPE-ERROR-PROCESSING.
```

(b) Using the COBOL GO TO–DEPENDING ON statement to implement an *n*-way branch.

Figure 4.4   The selection construct is extended to allow the case statement or *n*-way branch in a structured program.

ESCAPE   Allowing an escape (branch) to an exit point is a very
                              useful coding technique when certain instructions are
not to be executed due to an error or some other exceptional situation. In many
programming languages, the escape is implemented with the GO TO statement.
Figure 4.5 shows one example.

Using the GO TO statement in a structured program may seem to be a
violation of the fundamental structured philosophy, but here it is not. This is
because the use of the GO TO is restricted to implementing a forward branch
to the exit point of the module in which it appears.

HIGHEST-LEVEL   By limiting the use of the GO TO statement, struc-
CONTROL   tured programming is a form of GO TO–less pro-
CONSTRUCTS   gramming. But structured programming goes beyond
                              GO TO–less programming by standardizing the use
and implementation of *all* program control constructs. The objectives are to
improve program readability and to simplify the program structure.

The structured philosophy advocates the use of the highest-level control
construct available in the programming language. For example, the DO WHILE
(or DO UNTIL) structure rather than the GO TO statement is used to create a
loop in a structured program. Higher-level control constructs decrease program
complexity by reducing the number of instructions coded and by imposing a
single-entry-point/single-exit-point rule.

```
TYPE-1-PROCESS SECTION.
TYPE-1-PROCESS-ENTRY.

        .
        .
        .

    READ DATA-INPUT-FILE
         AT END GO TO TYPE-1-PROCESS-EXIT.
        .
        .
        .

    IF ROW-TYPE = 40
         GO TO TYPE-1-PROCESS-EXIT
    ELSE
         NEXT SENTENCE.
        .
        .
        .

TYPE-1-PROCESS-EXIT.
    EXIT.
```

Figure 4.5   Legal use of the GO TO statement in a structured program allows
a forward branch to the exit point of the module in which the branch appears.

STANDARDIZED MODULE FORMAT

A structured program is a modular program. But in addition to the basic modularization rules, module form is further restricted in a structured program. Strict format rules for constructing a structured module are another means of simplifying the program structure. This allows the programmer to concentrate on the program meaning rather than on the form of the program.

The rules for constructing a structured module are as follows:

- A module has one unique entry point and one unique exit point.

- A module is a self-contained structure.
  It performs one logical task in the program.
  It is bounded by its entry point and its exit point. The exit point must follow the entry point in the code, with no other module entry point or exit point intervening or coinciding.

- Legal control constructs are restricted to sequence, selection (with accepted extensions), iteration, and escape to the module exit point.

HIERARCHICAL ORGANIZATION

The modules in a structured program are hierarchically ordered. Although hierarchical organization is usually considered an inherent part of modular programming, it is possible to organize a modular program in a nonhierarchical manner. For example, a simple modular program containing only a few modules can be organized sequentially. One module is executed after another. When the last module in the sequence has been executed, program execution stops.

Since sequential organization is not an effective means of controlling program complexity as programs grow in size, a structured program is not sequentially ordered. It is always hierarchically ordered in the following manner:

- Level 1 of the hierarchy contains one module. This module, called the *root module,* represents the overall program function at its highest level.

- Level 2 of the hierarchy contains modules that further define the function of the root module.

- In general, each successive level of modules in the hierarchy provides a more detailed functional description of what the program does.

Figure 4.6 shows the hierarchical arrangement for the modules in a Master-file Update program. Level 1 contains the root module, UPDATE MASTER FILE. The function of UPDATE MASTER FILE is defined by three functions, GET VALID TRANSACTION, FETCH MASTER RECORD, and UPDATE MASTER RECORD. The definition of these functions is further explained by the modules at level 3.

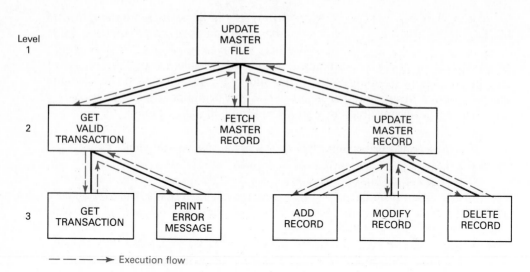

Figure 4.6 Hierarchical organization of modules in the classic Master-File Update program showing the first three levels of program modules.

PROGRAM CONTROL STRUCTURE

An *invocation relationship* exists between two modules, A and B (see Fig. 4.7), in a structured program if module A requires module B in order to perform its function. From the viewpoint of the program control structure, this means that module A invokes module B. When module A invokes module B, program control is passed from module A to module B. The code in module B is then executed. When module B has completed its execution, it passes control back to module A. Program control always enters a module at its entry point and leaves the module from its exit point.

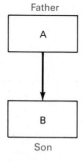

Figure 4.7 An invocation relationship exists between two modules, A and B, if A requires B in order to perform its function. Module A is the *father* of module B, and module B is the *son* of module A. Module B cannot also invoke module A, nor can a module invoke itself.

Module A, the invoking module, is called the *father* of module B, the invoked module; module B is called the *son* of module A. The invocation relationship between two modules in a structured program works only one way; that is, if module A invokes module B, module B cannot also invoke module A directly or indirectly through a son or grandson. Furthermore, a module cannot invoke itself. These relationships are not allowed because they cannot be easily implemented in many programming languages and because they tend to increase program complexity.

The rules for program control flow in a structured program are summarized in Box 4.2.

The smallest structured program consists of only a root module. All other structured programs contain one root module and one or more sons. Except for the root module, all other modules must have at least one father. If a module has multiple fathers, it is called a *common module*. Any module, including the root module, may have zero, one, or multiple sons. A module that has no sons is called a *leaf*. Every branch in the module hierarchy must end with a leaf module.

PROGRAM PATHS   Restricting the organization of modules and the invocation relationship between modules is a very powerful technique for controlling complexity, especially in large programs. By imposing a simple module-invocation system, the total number of possible program paths is reduced. By requiring the flow of program control to return to the invoking module it is easy to trace each program path. By restricting the set

BOX 4.2   Rules for program control flow in a structured program

- There is one and only one root module in a structured program.
- Program execution must begin with the root module.
- A module is executed if and only if it is invoked by its father.
- Only a father can invoke a son. A son cannot invoke its father, nor can a module invoke itself.
- Program control must enter a module at its entry point and must leave at its exit point.
- Control always returns to the invoking module when the invoked module completes execution.

of allowable control constructs, path patterns are reduced. Thus a programmer can use one standard road map to follow the logic through any structured program, regardless of its complexity. Because of the hierarchical organization of modules, the programmer can understand a structured program in degrees, dealing with the next level of detail only when necessary.

DOCUMENTATION Documentation is an integral part of a well-structured program. It addresses three levels of program understanding.

1. Overview
2. Program organization
3. Program instruction

Each successive level provides a more detailed view of the program. All three levels are necessary to the understanding and maintenance of the program.

Overview Documentation

Overview documentation introduces the program to its readers. The need for this first level of program documentation has often been overlooked. Yet it is essential to all levels of program understanding. If one must choose among the three levels of program documentation, overview documentation is the most fundamental and therefore the most essential. Also, it is the easiest to provide and the most stable. Throughout the life of the program, overview documentation is the least likely to require changes. Although the program may be modified frequently to meet changing user requirements, the overall function is likely to remain unchanged.

Overview documentation should be included within the program code in the form of commentary at the beginning of the source code. It should be brief and general. It should also be readable by both nontechnical and technical readers. An example is shown in Figure 4.8. Box 4.3 lists the items normally included in the overview documentation for a structured program.

Program Organization Documentation

Program organization documentation serves as the program table of contents, defining the name, location, and function of each procedural component. Two types of program organization documentation are suggested for a structured program:

1. Graphic documentation representing the program procedural, data, and control structures
2. Program comments introducing each program module and data structure

```
*   VERTICAL-SPACING-DIRECTORY
*
*   THIS ANS COBOL PROGRAM CREATES THE USER CHART
*   FORMAT
*   DIRECTORY BY COMPUTING ALL
*   VALID VERTICAL SPACING COMBINATIONS
*   FOR EACH CHART FORMAT OF THE SMCS
*   SYSTEM. FOR NON-ROTATED CHARTS
*   (FORMATS 1, 2, 4, 9, 10, 12), VERTICAL
*   REFERS TO THE 8½ INCH DIMENSION
*   ON AN 8½ INCH PAGE. FOR ROTATED
*   CHARTS (FORMATS 5, 6, 8, 11) VERTICAL
*   REFERS TO THE 11 INCH DIMENSION.
*   THERE ARE FOUR VERSIONS OF SCALING
*   COMBINATIONS:
*   1) BARS, CHARACTER DATA (FORMATS 1, 5, 6, 8, 9, 11)
*   2) BARS, CHARACTER DATA, GRIDS, LINE
*       GRAPHS (FORMAT 2)
*   3) BARS, CHARACTER DATA, GRIDS (FORMAT 4)
*   4) BARS, CHARACTER DATA, LINE GRAPHS
*       (FORMATS 10, 12)
*
*   CHART FORMAT DATA IS SUPPLIED BY THE
*   SMCS CHART-PIC-INFO FILE
*
*   ADDITIONAL DOCUMENTATION IS AVAILABLE
*   WITH THE SMCS SYSTEM DOCUMENTATION FILE
```

Figure 4.8 Overview documentation for the Vertical Spacing Directory program.

BOX 4.3   Overview documentation items

- An overall function summary defining the basic fundamental components and their relationship to one another

- An overall data-base summary showing the role of data in the total system, including major files, major data structures, and major clusters

- A brief explanation of the underlying design philosophy and the programming style used; the portion of a logical data model used, with logical access maps drawn on it (see Chapters 24 and 25)

- Pointers to historic documentation, including design notes, problem reports, version descriptions, new release notices, and error statistics

- Pointers to more detailed levels of internal program documentation, operating instructions, and user manuals

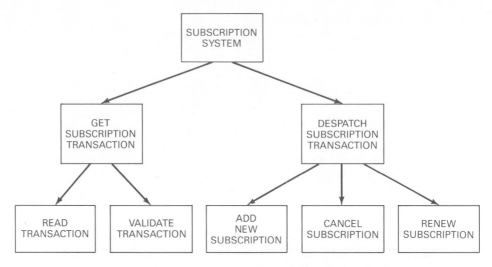

Figure 4.9   A structure chart is used to show the hierarchical arrangement of the modules in a structured program. Each rectangular box represents one module. The name of the module is written inside the box. An arrow joins two modules that have an invocation relationship.

A structure chart (see Chapter 13) is used to show the hierarchical arrangement of program modules. Figure 4.9 shows a structure chart for a subscription system. Each rectangular box represents one module. The name of the module is written inside the box. An arrow joins two modules that have an invocation relationship. The module at the top of the pair is the father, and the module at the bottom of the pair is the son.

BOX 4.4   Module comment-block items

- Module purpose (one or two sentences explaining what the module does)
- Effective date (last revision)
- Limitations, restrictions, and algorithmic idiosyncrasies
- Accuracy requirements
- Inputs/outputs
- Assumptions
- Error recovery types and procedures
- Information explaining the impact of changes on the other portions of the program, especially in the case of common modules

```
*    INITIALIZE-PLOT-SPACE.
*    THIS MODULE COMPUTES THE VERTICAL AND
*    HORIZONTAL PLOT SPACE AVAILABLE AND
*    THE MINIMUM AND MAXIMUM BAR SIZE FOR
*    A PARTICULAR CHART FORMAT. VERTICAL
*    PLOT SPACE IS "DOWN" THE CHART FOR NON-
*    ROTATED CHARTS AND "ACROSS" THE CHART
*    FOR ROTATED CHARTS.
*
*    VARIABLES CHANGED IN THIS MODULE
*         SD-PLOT-SPACE-AVAIL
*         SD-MIN-BAR-HEIGHT
*         SD-MAX-BAR-HEIGHT
*         SD-BAR-COUNT
*         SD-CHAR-COUNT
*         SD-GRID-COUNT
*         SD-LINE-GRAPH-COUNT
*         SD-NO-MORE-SPACE
*
*    DATE OF LAST REVISION: 10/20/80
```

Figure 4.10 Module comment block for the INITIALIZE-PLOT-SPACE module in the Vertical Spacing Directory program.

A comment block precedes each program module in a structured program. Its purpose is to introduce the module to the reader by describing what the module does. How the module works is *not* described. This is best ascertained by actually reading the code. Information included in the module comment block is listed in Box 4.4. An example of a module comment block is shown in Fig. 4.10.

Program Instruction Comments

Instruction-level comments rarely should be used in a structured program. Good documentation does not imply that a source comment is required for each program instruction, each control structure, each decision point, or some such arbitrary rule. For example, a programmer does not have to be told that the line counter is incremented by 1 in the COBOL instruction ADD +1 TO LINE-COUNT; it is obvious from reading the instruction. This sort of documentation is useless. It may even be detrimental to understandability. Weinberg explains that the purpose of a comment is "to prepare the mind of the reader for a proper interpretation of the instruction" [2]. If the instruction is clear as well as correct, the comment is probably not necessary. But if the instruction is incorrect, the comment may lead the reader to believe, mistakenly, that the instruction is correct and in this way make an error more difficult to detect.

BOX 4.5 Structured programming standards

1. The program is divided into independent pieces called modules.

2. A module is a self-contained unit whose code is physically and logically separate from the code of any other module in the program.

3. A module represents one unique logical program function (e.g., FETCH A TRANSACTION).

4. The size of a module should not exceed 100 instructions.

5. A module is bounded by one entry point and one exit point. During execution, program control can enter a module only at its entry point and can leave the module only from its exit point.

6. Modules are related to one another by a hierarchical control structure. Each level in the control structure represents a more detailed functional description of what the program does. It also dictates the transfer of program control from module to module during execution.

7. No loops are allowed in the control structure. This means that a module cannot call itself, nor can it call any module that has called it.

8. Each module should begin with a comment block explaining the function that the module performs, the values passed to the module, the values returned, the modules that call this module, and the modules that this module calls.

9. Comments embedded in the module code should be separated from instructions by one blank line.

10. All comments should be meaningful (i.e., should not repeat information that is obvious from the code).

11. Avoid unnecessary labels; do not use labels as comments.

12. All variable and module names should be meaningful. Module names should suggest the logical function they perform (e.g., EDIT), and variable names should suggest their purpose in the program (e.g., ERRORSW).

13. Names of variables that belong to the same table or that are local (i.e., used only in one module) should begin with the same prefix.

14. The only allowable control constructs are concatenation, selection, repetition, and escape.

15. No more than one instruction is coded on a line. If an instruction requires more than one line, successive lines are indented.

16. IF statements should not be nested more than three levels.

BOX 4.5   *(Continued)*

17. The scope of a GOTO statement (branch instruction) should be limited to the module in which it occurs. This means that the GOTO should not be used to transfer control from one module to another; it is used only to branch to the entry point or the exit point of the module in which it occurs.

18. As a general rule, nonstandard language features should not be used.

19. Obscure (trick) code should be avoided.

Instruction-level comments should be used only in exceptional circumstances, such as explaining an unusual or complex algorithm or highlighting error-prone program segments and potential ambiguities. Instead, meaningful procedure and variable names, standardized control constructs, and a consistent coding style should be emphasized to make a structured program more readable.

INDENTATION

The rules for writing in a conventional language include paragraphing, spacing, and indenting guidelines to improve readability. Similar guidelines for writing structured programs are used to improve program readability. A basic principle of structured programming is that a standardized program form will improve readability. Structured coding rules typically include the following:

1. Do not code more than one statement per line.

2. If a statement requires multiple lines, indent all continuation lines.

3. Indent the true and false portions of the selection structure to identify its scope more clearly.

4. Use an indentation scheme that accentuates the control structures used to direct statement execution order.

STRUCTURED CODING STANDARDS

Many organizations now require that structured programs conform to a set of structured programming standards. A list of structuring rules that are representative of those typically suggested for high-level, procedure-oriented languages such as FORTRAN, COBOL, and PL/I is given in Box 4.5.

```
000100 PROCEDURE DIVISION.
000200 INITIAL-READS.
000300     OPEN INPUT OLD-MASTER TRANS OUTPUT NEW-MASTER.
000400     READ OLD-MASTER READ TRANS.
000401 DATE-CHECK.
000402     MOVE DATE-OM TO DATE-WS IF DATE-WS NOT EQUAL DATE-ET
000403     DISPLAY 'DATES OUT OF SEQUENCE'
000404     GO FINISH-UP.
000405     GO TO FINISH-STATUS.
000406 YEAR-END-CHECK.
000407     IF YEAR-WS = 74 PERFORM YEAR-END-ROUTINE.
000410 FINISH-STATUS.
000420     GO TO INIT.
000430 EDIT.
000440     CALL 'EDIT' USING NEW-MAST-REC-WS.
000450     GO TO LAST-THING.
000453 INIT.
000460     SET SUB TO 1.
000470     GO INITIALIZE-TOTALS.
000650 DETAIL-PREP.
000700     PERFORM PREPARE-DETAIL THRU RESET-READ.
001300 PROCESS-CONT.
001400     ADD 1 TO MASTER-RECS-PROCESSED.
001500     GO TO EDIT.
001600 LAST-THING.
001700     CALL 'PSTMSTR' USING MASTER-REC-WS.
001800     GO TO FINISH-STATUS.
001930 READ-MASTER.
002000     READ OLD-MASTER.
002100     IF END-OF-OLD-MASTER = YES
002200     ALTER FINISH-STATUS TO FINISH-UP.
002210     PERFORM DO-DETAIL-GROUP THRU LOG-TRANSACTION-DETAILS.
002240 DO-TOTALS.
002250     ADD DETAILS-WS TO TOTAL(SUB).
002260     GO TO WHERE-NEXT.
002300 WRITE-MASTER.
002310     WRITE NEW-MASTER.
002311     ADD 1 TO WRITE-MASTER-COUNT.
002312 UPDATE-A-MASTER.
002313     MOVE MASTER-REC TO NEW-MASTER-WS GO RESET-READ.
002314 PREPARE-DETAIL.
002315     MOVE ZEROES TO TABLE-SIZE-WS TRNS-CT-WS RJCT-CT-WS
002316     MOVE 'YES' TO JUST-STARTED-WS
002317     MOVE SPACE TO CURRENT-DESC-WS.
002320 WHERE-NEXT.
002330     GO TO READ-MASTER.
002340 ROUTINE3.
002350     CALL ROUTN31 USING TRANSACTION-REC-ET.
002360     CALL ROUTN32 USING TRANSACTION-REC-ET.
002370     GO TO QR-CODE-CHECK.
002400 FINISH-UP.
002500     DISPLAY 'FINISH-UP'.
002600     CLOSE OLD-MASTER NEW-MASTER TRANS GOBACK.
002601 RESET-READ.
002602     ALTER WHERE-NEXT TO READ-MASTER.
002610 LOG-TRANSACTION-DETAILS.
```

Figure 4.11   Sample of unstructured COBOL code.

```
002620      CALL 'LOGTRNS' USING DETAILS-WS.
002700 DO-DETAIL-GROUP.
002711      READ TRANS AT END GO TO PREPARE-FOR-WRITE.
002720      GO TO SECURITIES RENTALS CASE4 DO-DETAIL-GROUP
002721      PREPARE-FOR-WRITE
002722      DEPENDING TRANS-TYPE.
002723 GROUP3.
002724      GO TO ROUTINE3.
002744 OTHERS.
002745      IF RENTAL-TYPE-ET = 1 GO TO GROUP2.
002746      IF RENTAL-CODE-ET = 4 GO TO GROUP3.
002748      IF RENTAL-CODE-ET LESS 10
002749      GO TO GROUP3.
002750      DISPLAY 'FOUND NON-STANDARD RENTAL TRANSACTION'
002752      GO TO QR-CODE-CHECK.
002753 YEAR-END-ROUTINE.
002754      CALL 'YEAREND' USING DATE-WS.
002755 GROUP2.
002756      GO TO ROUTINE2.
002757 CASE3.
002758      DISPLAY 'TYPE 3 TRANS NOT POSTED'.
002759      GO TO QR-CODE-CHECK.
002770 QR-CODE-CHECK.
002780      GO TO DO-DETAIL-GROUP.
002790 CASE4.
002791      GO GROUP1.
002800 PREPARE-FOR-WRITE.
002900      ALTER WHERE-NEXT TO WRITE-MASTER GO
002901      LOG-TRANSACTION-DETAILS.
002910 INITIALIZE-TOTALS.
002920      IF SUB > 5 GO TO DETAIL-PREP.
002930      MOVE ZEROES TO TOTAL (SUB)
002940      SET SUB UP BY 1
002950      GO TO INITIALIZE-TOTALS.
003020 ROUTINE1.
003021      CALL ROUTN11 USING TRANSACTION-REC-ET.
003028      CALL ROUTN12 USING TRANSACTION-REC-ET.
003029      GO TO QR-CODE-CHECK.
003035 SECURITIES.
003036      IF SECURITY-CLASS-ET = 355 GO TO GROUP1.
003037      IF SECURITY-CLASS-ET = 276  GO TO GROUP2.
003038      IF SECURITY-CLASS-ET GREATER 100
003039      GO TO GROUP3.
003040      DISPLAY 'INVALID SECURITY TRANSACTION'
003041      GO TO QR-CODE-CHECK.
003042 ROUTINE2.
003043      CALL ROUTN21 USING TRANSACTION-REC-ET.
003044      CALL ROUTN22 USING TRANSACTION-REC-ET.
003045      GO TO QR-CODE-CHECK.
003046 GROUP1.
003047      GO TO ROUTINE1.
003048 RENTALS.
003049      IF RENTAL-TYPE-ET = 2 OR LESS 10 AND > 5 GO GROUP1 ELSE
003050      GO OTHERS.
003051
003052
003053
003060
003070
003080
```

Figure 4.11   (Continued)

```
000570                                                        REGIMENT
000580                                                        REGIMENT
000590 A1-MAINLINE.                                           REGIMENT
000600     PERFORM B1-INITIAL-READS.                          REGIMENT
000610     MOVE DATE-OM TO DATE-WS.                           REGIMENT
000620     IF DATE-WS NOT = DATE-ET                           REGIMENT
000630        THEN DISPLAY 'DATES OUT OF SEQUENCE'            REGIMENT
000640             PERFORM B2-FINISH-UP                       REGIMENT
000650        ELSE PERFORM B3-NEEDS-A-NAME-X                  REGIMENT
000660             UNTIL ( FINISH-STATUS-TARGET = FINISH-UP-PARA ) REGIMENT
000670                      OR ( RETURN_STATUS NOT = RESOLVED )  REGIMENT
000680            IF RETURN_STATUS = TRANS-TYPE-OUT-OF-RANGE  REGIMENT
000690               THEN MOVE RESOLVED TO RETURN_STATUS      REGIMENT
000700                    PERFORM B4-VALUE_OUT_OF_RANGE       REGIMENT
000710               ELSE PERFORM B2-FINISH-UP.              REGIMENT
000720     GOBACK.                                            REGIMENT
000730*END-A1-MAINLINE                                        REGIMENT
000740                                                        REGIMENT
000750                                                        REGIMENT
000760 B1-INITIAL-READS.                                      REGIMENT
000770     OPEN   INPUT   OLD-MASTER                          REGIMENT
000780     OPEN   INPUT   TRANS                               REGIMENT
000790     OPEN   OUTPUT  NEW-MASTER   .                      REGIMENT
000800     READ OLD-MASTER                                    REGIMENT
000810     READ TRANS.                                        REGIMENT
000820*END-B1-INITIAL-READS                                   REGIMENT
000830                                                        REGIMENT
000840 B2-FINISH-UP.                                          REGIMENT
000850     DISPLAY 'FINISH-UP'.                               REGIMENT
000860     CLOSE OLD-MASTER.                                  REGIMENT
000870     CLOSE NEW-MASTER.                                  REGIMENT
000880     CLOSE TRANS.                                       REGIMENT
000890*END-B2-FINISH-UP                                       REGIMENT
000900                                                        REGIMENT
000910 B3-NEEDS-A-NAME-X.                                     REGIMENT
000920     SET SUB TO 1.                                      REGIMENT
000930     PERFORM C1-INITIALIZE-TOTALS                       REGIMENT
000940        UNTIL SUB > 5.                                  REGIMENT
000950     PERFORM C2-UPDATE-A-MASTER.                        REGIMENT
000960     IF RETURN_STATUS NOT = RESOLVED                    REGIMENT
000970        THEN NEXT SENTENCE                              REGIMENT
000980        ELSE COMPUTE MASTER-RECS-PARAESSED =            REGIMENT
000990                  MASTER-RECS-PARAESSED + 1             REGIMENT
001000             CALL 'EDIT' USING NEW-MAST-REC-WS          REGIMENT
001010             CALL 'PSTMSTR' USING MASTER-REC-WS.        REGIMENT
001020*END-B3-NEEDS-A-NAME-X                                  REGIMENT
001030                                                        REGIMENT
001040 B4-VALUE_OUT_OF_RANGE.                                 REGIMENT
001050*END-B4-VALUE_OUT_OF_RANGE                              REGIMENT
001060                                                        REGIMENT
001070                                                        REGIMENT
001080 C1-INITIALIZE-TOTALS.                                  REGIMENT
001090     MOVE ZEROES TO TOTAL ( SUB ).                      REGIMENT
001100     SET SUB UP BY 1.                                   REGIMENT
001110*END-C1-INITIALIZE-TOTALS                               REGIMENT
001120                                                        REGIMENT
```

Figure 4.12   The restructured version of the COBOL code shown in Fig.
4.11. It was automatically restructured by the Recoder from Language Technology Inc. [3]. Tools which automatically restructure old programs should be
linked to CASE tools for software engineering so that old, badly structured
code can be *reverse engineered* into tools which facilitate good design.

```
001130 C2-UPDATE-A-MASTER.                                           REGIMENT
001140      PERFORM D1-PREPARE-DETAIL.                               REGIMENT
001150      PERFORM D2-NEEDS-A-NAME-Z                                REGIMENT
001160          UNTIL ( WHERE-NEXT-TARGET = WRITE-MASTER-PARA ) OR ( REGIMENT
001170              RETURN_STATUS NOT = RESOLVED ).                  REGIMENT
001180      IF RETURN_STATUS NOT = RESOLVED                          REGIMENT
001190          THEN NEXT SENTENCE                                   REGIMENT
001200          ELSE PERFORM D3-WRITE-MASTER                         REGIMENT
001210              MOVE MASTER-REC TO NEW-MASTER-WS                 REGIMENT
001220              PERFORM D4 RESET-READ.                           REGIMENT
001230*END-C2-UPDATE-A-MASTER                                        REGIMENT
001240                                                               REGIMENT
001250                                                               REGIMENT
001260 D1-PREPARE-DETAIL.                                            REGIMENT
001270      MOVE ZEROES TO TABLE-SIZE-WS                             REGIMENT
001280      MOVE ZEROES TO TRNS-CT-WS                                REGIMENT
001290      MOVE ZEROES TO RJCT-CT-WS                                REGIMENT
001300      MOVE 'YES' TO JUST-STARTED-WS                            REGIMENT
001310      MOVE SPACE TO CURRENT-DESC-WS.                           REGIMENT
001320*END-D1-PREPARE-DETAIL                                         REGIMENT
001330                                                               REGIMENT
001340 D2-NEEDS-A-NAME-Z.                                            REGIMENT
001350      READ OLD-MASTER.                                         REGIMENT
001360      IF END-OF-OLD-MASTER = YES                               REGIMENT
001370          THEN MOVE FINISH-UP-PARA TO FINISH-STATUS-TARGET.    REGIMENT
001380      PERFORM E1-NEEDS-A-NAME-Q.                               REGIMENT
001390      IF RETURN_STATUS NOT = RESOLVED                          REGIMENT
001400          THEN NEXT SENTENCE                                   REGIMENT
001410          ELSE COMPUTE TOTAL ( SUB ) = TOTAL ( SUB ) + DETAILS-WS. REGIMENT
001420*END-D2-NEEDS-A-NAME-Z                                         REGIMENT
001430                                                               REGIMENT
001440 D3-WRITE-MASTER.                                              REGIMENT
001450      WRITE NEW-MASTER.                                        REGIMENT
001460      COMPUTE WRITE-MASTER-COUNT = WRITE-MASTER-COUNT + 1.     REGIM_NT
001470*END-D3-WRITE-MASTER                                           REGIMENT
001480                                                               REGIMENT
001490 D4-RESET-READ.                                                REGIMENT
001500      MOVE READ-MASTER-PARA TO WHERE-NEXT-TARGET.              REGIMENT
001510*END-D4-RESET-READ                                             REGIMENT
001520                                                               REGIMENT
001530                                                               REGIMENT
001540 E1-NEEDS-A-NAME-Q.                                            REGIMENT
001550      PERFORM F1-NEEDS-A-NAME                                  REGIMENT
001560          UNTIL RETURN_STATUS NOT = RESOLVED.                  REGIMENT
001570      IF RETURN_STATUS = END-OF-TRANS-FILE                     REGIMENT
001580          MOVE RESOLVED TO RETURN_STATUS                       REGIMENT
001590          MOVE WRITE-MASTER-PARA TO WHERE-NEXT-TARGET          REGIMENT
001600          PERFORM F2-LOG-TRANSACTION-DETAILS                   REGIMENT
001610      ELSE IF RETURN_STATUS = EVENT1-DETECTED-IN-F1            REGIMENT
001620          MOVE RESOLVED TO RETURN_STATUS                       REGIMENT
001630          IF TRANS-TYPE = 5                                    REGIMENT
001640              THEN MOVE WRITE-MASTER-PARA TO WHERE-NEXT-TARGET REGIMENT
001650                  PERFORM F2-LOG-TRANSACTION-DETAILS           REGIMENT
001660              ELSE MOVE TRANS-TYPE-OUT-OF-RANGE TO RETURN_STATUS. REGIMENT
001670*END-E1-NEEDS-A-NAME-Q                                         REGIMENT
001680                                                               REGIMENT
001690                                                               REGIMENT
001700 F1-NEEDS-A-NAME.                                              REGIMENT
001710      MOVE FALSE TO AT-END-OCCURED.                            REGIMENT
001720      READ TRANS                                               REGIMENT
001730          AT END                                               REGIMENT
```

Figure 4.12   (Continued)   *(Continued)*

```
001740              MOVE TRUE TO AT-END-OCCURED.                      REGIMENT
001750        IF AT-END-OCCURED = TRUE                                REGIMENT
001760           MOVE END-OF-TRANS-FILE TO RETURN_STATUS              REGIMENT
001770        ELSE IF TRANS-TYPE = 1                                  REGIMENT
001780           IF SECURITY-CLASS-ET = 355                           REGIMENT
001790              CALL ROUTN11 USING TRANSACTION-REC-ET             REGIMENT
001800              CALL ROUTN12 USING TRANSACTION-REC-ET             REGIMENT
001810           ELSE IF SECURITY-CLASS-ET = 276                      REGIMENT
001820              CALL ROUTN21 USING TRANSACTION-REC-ET             REGIMENT
001830              CALL ROUTN22 USING TRANSACTION-REC-ET             REGIMENT
001840           ELSE IF SECURITY-CLASS-ET > 100                      REGIMENT
001850              CALL ROUTN31 USING TRANSACTION-REC-ET             REGIMENT
001860              CALL ROUTN32 USING TRANSACTION-REC-ET             REGIMENT
001870           ELSE DISPLAY 'INVALID SECURITY TRANSACTION'          REGIMENT
001880        ELSE IF TRANS-TYPE = 2                                  REGIMENT
001890           IF ( RENTAL-TYPE-ET = 2 ) OR ( ( RENTAL-TYPE-ET < 10 )  REGIMENT
001900              AND ( RENTAL-TYPE-ET > 5 ) )                      REGIMENT
001910              CALL ROUTN11 USING TRANSACTION-REC-ET             REGIMENT
001920              CALL ROUTN12 USING TRANSACTION-REC-ET             REGIMENT
001930           ELSE IF RENTAL-TYPE-ET = 1                           REGIMENT
001940              CALL ROUTN21 USING TRANSACTION-REC-ET             REGIMENT
001950              CALL ROUTN22 USING TRANSACTION-REC-ET             REGIMENT
001960           ELSE IF RENTAL-CODE-ET = 4                           REGIMENT
001970              CALL ROUTN31 USING TRANSACTION-REC-ET             REGIMENT
001980              CALL ROUTN32 USING TRANSACTION-REC-ET             REGIMENT
001990           ELSE IF RENTAL-CODE-ET < 10                          REGIMENT
002000              CALL ROUTN31 USING TRANSACTION-REC-ET             REGIMENT
002010              CALL ROUTN32 USING TRANSACTION-REC-ET             REGIMENT
002020           ELSE DISPLAY 'FOUND NON-STANDARD RENTAL TRANSACTION' REGIMENT
002030        ELSE IF TRANS-TYPE = 3                                  REGIMENT
002040           CALL ROUTN11 USING TRANSACTION-REC-ET                REGIMENT
002050           CALL ROUTN12 USING TRANSACTION-REC-ET                REGIMENT
002060        ELSE IF TRANS-TYPE = 4                                  REGIMENT
002070           NEXT SENTENCE                                        REGIMENT
002080        ELSE MOVE EVENT1-DETECTED-IN-F1 TO RETURN_STATUS.       REGIMENT
002090*END-F1-NEEDS-A-NAME                                            REGIMENT
002100                                                                REGIMENT
002110 F2-LOG-TRANSACTION-DETAILS.                                    REGIMENT
002120     CALL 'LOGTRNS' USING DETAILS-WS.                           REGIMENT
002130*END-F2-LOG-TRANSACTION-DETAILS                                 REGIMENT
002140                                                                REGIMENT
002150                                                                REGIMENT
```

Figure 4.12   (Continued)

Automated tools that can convert unstructured code to structured code now exist for languages such as FORTRAN and COBOL. Figure 4.11 is a sample of unstructured COBOL code. Figure 4.12 shows how this code has been automatically restructured by a tool called Recoder from Language Technology Inc. [3].

Tools for restructuring programs should be linked to CASE design and coding tools so that poorly designed old programs can be *reverse engineered* into tools which facilitate clean software engineering.

REFERENCES

1. C. Bohm and G. Jacopini, ''Flow Diagrams, Turning Machines and Languages with Only Two Formation Rules,'' *CACM,* 9, no. 5 (May 1966), 366–371.

2. G. Weinberg, *Psychology of Computer Programming.* New York, NY: Von Nostrand Reinhold, 1971, pp. 162–164.

3. Recoder, from Language Technology Inc., Boston, MA.

REFERENCES

5 MODULAR PROGRAMMING AND CONTROL OF COMPLEXITY

DIVIDE AND CONQUER

The beginnings of structured programming can be traced back to modular programming. Much of the structured philosophy is built on the modularization philosophy of divide and conquer. Modular programming uses divide and conquer to solve the program complexity problem. When a program is divided into independent, easy-to-understand pieces, its complexity can be greatly reduced. The structured philosophy uses divide and conquer and extends the modularization philosophy by adding the very important concepts of hierarchical organization and levels of abstraction to govern module relationships.

Modular programming may be defined as organizing a program into small, independent units, called *modules,* whose behavior is governed by a set of rules. Its goals are the following:

1. To decompose a program into independent pieces
2. To divide a complex problem into smaller, simpler problems
3. To verify the correctness of a program module independently of its use as a unit in a larger system

Modularization can be applied at different levels. It can be used to separate a problem into systems, a system into programs, and a program into modules.

PROGRAM MODULES

The program module is the basic building block of a structured program. Each program module represents one problem-related task, such as VALIDATE TRANSACTION DATA or BILL NEW SUBSCRIBER. A module is imple-

```
CHECK-BAR-HEIGHT.                ◄─────── Entry point
  IF BAR-COUNT > 0
    COMPUTE BAR-HEIGHT = Y-SPACE / BAR-COUNT
  ELSE IF Y-SPACE > 0
    MOVE "YES" TO EXTRA-Y-SPACE
    GO TO CHECK-BAR-HEIGHT-EXIT
  ELSE
    MOVE "NO" TO EXTRA-Y-SPACE
    GO TO CHECK-BAR-HEIGHT-EXIT.
  IF BAR-HEIGHT < TO MIN-BAR-HEIGHT
    MOVE 1 TO NO-MORE-SPACE.
CHECK-BAR-HEIGHT-EXIT.
  EXIT.                          ◄─────── Exit point
```

Figure 5.1 The program module is the basic building block of a structured program. A module is implemented as a sequence of programming instructions bounded by an entry point and an exit point.

mented as a sequence of programming instructions bounded by an entry point and an exit point (see Fig. 5.1). The properties of a module are summarized in Box 5.1.

BLACK BOX MODEL

As shown in Fig. 5.2, the standard model of a program module consists of three parts: input, process, and output [1].

Data enter a module as input, are operated on by a process, and leave as output.

A fundamental requirement of the structured approach is the ability to treat this model as a black box. A *black box* is a system in which the inputs, the outputs, and the function performed by the process are known, but the details of how the process is implemented are unknown. A true black box can be used without understanding its contents. There are many examples of commonly used black boxes. Radios, televisions, many household appliances, and automobiles are black boxes to most users.

The black box concept is extremely important because it allows each part of a program to be built and tested independently.

MODULARIZATION SCHEMES

Dividing a program into modules can be a very effective way of controlling complexity. The advantages are listed in Box 5.2. The problem is how to divide the program. For even a simple program, there are countless ways in which to divide it into a set of structured modules. The way chosen can greatly affect program complexity. For example, making modules too large or too small increases program complexity, program costs, and the likelihood of program errors.

BOX 5.1   Properties of a module

- Each module represents one logical, self-contained task.
- Modules are simple.
- Modules are closed.
- Modules are discrete and visible.
- Modules are separately testable.
- Each module is implemented as a single, independent program function.
- Each module has a single entry point and a single exit point.
- Each module exits to a standard return point in the module from which it was executed.
- Modules may be combined into larger modules without the knowledge of the internal construction of the modules.
- Modules have well-defined interfaces. Modules have control connections via their entry points and exit points; modules have data connections via passed parameters and shared data; modules have functional connections via the services they perform for each other.

How a program is divided into modules is called its *modularization scheme*. Defining a good modularization scheme (one that closely reflects the components of the problem to be programmed, minimizes complexity, and can be easily and efficiently implemented) is a major objective of modular programming.

Figure 5.2   The standard model of a program module consists of three parts: input, process, and output. It is treated as a black box where the input, output, and what the process does are known but how the process works is unknown.

BOX 5.2   Advantages of modular programming

- Modular programs are easier to understand because it is possible to study the program one module at a time.
- Program testing is easier.
- Program errors are easier to isolate and correct.
- Machine-dependent functions can be separated for improved portability.
- Program changes can be limited to only a few modules rather than rippling through most of the program code.
- Program efficiency is easier to improve.
- Program modules can be reused as building blocks in other programs.
- Program development time can be shortened because different modules can be assigned to different programmers who can work more or less independently.

MODULE SIZE   Module size guidelines have been developed to help the program designer choose a good modularization scheme. IBM, for example, advises that a module should not exceed 50 lines of program code [2]. The reasoning is that confining a module to one page of source listing (or what will fit on a CRT screen) allows the reader to see and therefore understand all the code at once.

A similar number comes from Weinberg, whose studies show that modules larger than 30 programming instructions are difficult to understand [3].

In general, the size of a module should lie in the range of 10 to 100 instructions. Modules larger than 100 instructions are more expensive to test and to maintain, while modules smaller than 10 instructions can break the program into too many pieces, adversely affecting program efficiency.

Restricting module size to a certain number of lines of code is only a rough rule-of-thumb guideline. When used alone, it is probably too simplistic, since the length of a piece of code is often not an accurate indicator of complexity. The logical tasks performed, the control constructs employed, and the program variables referenced also affect how easily a program can be understood.

COMPLEXITY METRICS   In the 1970s several measures of complexity were developed based on module size. Three examples of program complexity metrics are:

1. Halstead's software science
2. McCabe's cyclomatic number
3. McClure's control variable complexity

These three metrics are easy to calculate and to automate, are generally applicable to any high-level language, and have been successfully used in industry as predictors of programming effort and program reliability. Their common objective is to provide a quantitative measure of program complexity that can guide the design of modular programs.

Software Science

Halstead's theory, called *software science,* is one of the most promising complexity metrics [4]. Numerous studies and experiments from both the university and industrial communities have shown software science metrics to be amazingly accurate. In addition to measuring software complexity and overall quality, Halstead's metrics have been used to measure program reliability, predict program length, and estimate programming effort.

What is most impressive about Halstead's theory is that it is based on a simple count of program operators and operands that can be computed automatically during compilation. Operators include arithmetic operators (e.g., $+$, $-$, $*$, $/$), logical operators (e.g., greater than, equal to), and keywords (e.g., FORTRAN DO, COBOL PERFORM). Operands include constants and variables.

Software science metrics for any program can be derived from four basic counts:

n_1 Number of distinct operators in a program

n_2 Number of distinct operands in a program

N_1 Total number of operators in a program

N_2 Total number of operands in a program

Several simple complexity theories have been developed to relate these counts to program properties such as length and difficulty. For example, the length, N, of a program (module) is computed as

$$N = N_1 + N_2$$

N is a simple measure of program (module) size. The larger the value of N, the more difficult the program is to understand and the more effort required to maintain it. N is preferred over an instruction count because N does not assume that all instructions are equally understandable. In Fig. 5.3, $N = 28$ is the size of the module CHECK-BAR-HEIGHT.

```
CHECK-BAR-HEIGHT.
    IF BAR-COUNT > 0
        COMPUTE BAR-HEIGHT = Y-SPACE / BAR-COUNT
    ELSE IF Y-SPACE > 0
        MOVE "YES" TO EXTRA-Y-SPACE
        GOTO CHECK-BAR-HEIGHT-EXIT
    ELSE
        MOVE "NO" TO EXTRA-Y-SPACE
        GOTO CHECK-BAR-HEIGHT-EXIT.
    IF BAR-HEIGHT < MIN-BAR-HEIGHT
        MOVE 1 TO NO-MORE-SPACE.
CHECK-BAR-HEIGHT-EXIT.
    EXIT.
```

OPERATORS	COUNT	OPERANDS	COUNT
IF	3	BAR-COUNT	2
>	2	0	2
COMPUTE	1	BAR-HEIGHT	2
=	1	Y-SPACE	2
/	1	"YES"	1
MOVE	3	EXTRA-Y-SPACE	2
GO TO	2	"NO"	1
<	1	MIN-BAR-HEIGHT	1
	14	NO-MORE-SPACE	1
			14

$$n_1 = 8 \qquad\qquad N_1 = 14$$
$$n_2 = 9 \qquad\qquad N_2 = 14$$

Figure 5.3　Software science metrics for any program can be derived from four basic counts:

n_1　　Number of distinct operators in the program

n_2　　Number of distinct operands in the program

N_1　　Total number of operators in the program

N_2　　Total number of operands in the program

The values for n_1, n_2, N_1, and N_2 are shown for a section of COBOL program code.

Regardless of the programming language, any program (module) has an integer number of unique operands, n_2. The simplest useful program has one input and one output, or $n_2 = 2$. The next simplest program has a value of $n_2 = 3$, and so on. Therefore, n_2 can be used as another measure of complexity. Experiments have shown that as n_2 increases, programming effort also increases. For example, in an experiment that involved converting *ALGOL* programs to FORTRAN and then expanding the number of outputs by 1, Woodfield observed that a 25 percent increase in n_2 doubled the programming effort [5].

Cyclomatic Number

McCabe proposes a graph-theoretic complexity measure in which program complexity is determined by counting the number of linearly independent paths through a program [6].

    Complexity evaluation is performed at the module level. McCabe uses the cyclomatic number to regulate the size of a module. In a structured program, the cyclomatic number can be calculated by simply counting the number of compares in a module (see Fig. 5.4):

$$\text{Cyclomatic number} = \text{Compares} + 1$$

    To ensure that a program is understandable, the cyclomatic number for each module should not exceed 10. McCabe arrived at 10 as the upper limit for module size after examining several industrial FORTRAN programs. He found that a module whose cyclomatic number is greater than 10 is generally more troublesome and less reliable.

```
CHECK-BAR-HEIGHT.
    IF BAR-COUNT > 0
        COMPUTE BAR-HEIGHT = Y-SPACE / BAR-COUNT
    ELSE IF Y-SPACE > 0
        MOVE "YES" TO EXTRA-Y-SPACE
        GO TO CHECK-BAR-HEIGHT-EXIT
    ELSE
        MOVE "NO" TO EXTRA-Y-SPACE
        GO TO CHECK-BAR-HEIGHT-EXIT
    IF BAR-HEIGHT < MIN-BAR-HEIGHT
        MOVE 1 TO NO-MORE-SPACE.
CHECK-BAR-HEIGHT-EXIT.
    EXIT.
```

COMPARES

BAR-COUNT > 0
Y-SPACE > 0
BAR-HEIGHT < MIN-BAR-HEIGHT
CYCLOMATIC NUMBER = 4

Figure 5.4   McCabe uses the cyclomatic number to regulate the size of a module. It should not exceed 10. In a structured program, the cyclomatic number is calculated by:

$$\text{Cyclomatic number} = \text{compares} + 1$$

Control Variable Complexity

McClure's research indicates that a more accurate complexity metric must examine the variables referenced in the compares as well as the number of compares [7]. She calculates the complexity of a module, C_m, as follows:

$$C_m = C + V$$

where C is the number of compares in the module and V is the number of unique variables referenced in the compares (see Fig. 5.5).

McClure claims that a modularization scheme is good if the complexity of each module is minimized and if it is evenly distributed throughout the program. Avoiding "pockets" of complexity (modules that are much more complex rel-

```
CHECK-BAR-HEIGHT.
    IF BAR-COUNT > 0
        COMPUTE BAR-HEIGHT = Y-SPACE / BAR-COUNT
    ELSE IF Y-SPACE > 0
        MOVE "YES" TO EXTRA-Y-SPACE
        GO TO CHECK-BAR-HEIGHT-EXIT
    ELSE
        MOVE "NO" TO EXTRA-Y-SPACE
        GO TO CHECK-BAR-HEIGHT-EXIT.
    IF BAR-HEIGHT < MIN-BAR-HEIGHT
        MOVE 1 TO NO-MORE-SPACE.
CHECK-BAR-HEIGHT-EXIT.
    EXIT.
```

COMPARES	VARIABLES REFERENCED IN COMPARES
BAR-COUNT > 0	BAR-COUNT
Y-SPACE > 0	Y-SPACE
BAR-HEIGHT < MIN-BAR-HEIGHT	BAR-HEIGHT
	MIN-BAR-HEIGHT
	(Note that constants are not counted)

CHECK-BAR-HEIGHT = 7

Figure 5.5 McClure's research indicates that the variables referenced in the compares is an important factor in measuring complexity. She calculates the complexity of a module, C_m, as follows:

$$C_m = C + V$$

where C is the number of compares in the module and V is the number of unique variables referenced in the compares.

ative to other modules in the program) will increase overall program understandability.

McClure does not suggest a complexity limit, as McCabe does. Instead she suggests computing an average module-complexity value for a program. Each module whose complexity is high or low relative to this average is examined. Since dividing a program into too many modules may be just as detrimental to understandability as dividing it into too few modules, both complexity extremes are examined.

MODULE RELATIONSHIPS

In addition to module size, the relationship between the internal elements of a module and the relationship between program modules can affect program complexity. Parnas explained that "the connections between modules are the assumptions which the modules make about each other" [8]. Modules are connected by the program control structure and by data. Explicit data connections occur when parameters are passed between modules, and implicit data connections occur when modules reference the same data. To control complexity the connections between modules must be controlled and minimized. Parnas suggests the concept of *information hiding,* which states that only necessary data should be known to and accessible by a module. Stevens, Myers, and Constantine suggest *coupling* and *cohesion* as two evaluative measures of module connections [9].

Coupling

In general, the best way to control complexity is to apply the divide-and-conquer concept; that is, divide the program into small, easy-to-understand modules. But unless the modules are also independent and the interaction between them is restricted, complexity will not be controlled. *Coupling* measures the degree of independence between modules.

When there is little interaction between two modules, the modules are described as *loosely coupled;* when there is a great deal of interaction, they are *tightly coupled.* The more tightly coupled its modules are, the more difficult a program is to understand. If two modules are loosely coupled, one module can be understood without examining the other, and one module often can be changed without changing the other. But if two modules are tightly coupled, it may be difficult to understand one without also examining the other or to change one without also changing the other.

Three factors affect the coupling between modules:

1. The number of data items passed between modules (The more data passed, the tighter the coupling.)

2. The amount of control data passed between modules (The more control data passed, the tighter the coupling.)

3. The number of global data elements shared by modules (The more global data elements shared, the tighter the coupling.)

The number of data elements passed between modules refers to the number of arguments or parameters that are passed in a module call. For example, a subroutine call involving 100 parameters is more complex than a subroutine call involving one parameter. A high number of parameters passed in a module call is often an indication that the called module is performing more than one function. Not only the amount of data but also the type of data passed between modules affects complexity.

Control data are data that direct the execution order of program instructions and module calls. End-of-file switches and transaction codes are commonly used as control data. The more control data passed between modules, the greater the complexity.

Shared data are data implicitly referenced by a module rather than explicitly passed as a parameter. Usually shared data are referenced by more than one module. FORTRAN COMMON is an example of shared data when they are referenced by multiple subroutines. Global data is another example. A program that uses a great deal of shared data can be difficult to understand and change because its data are often used in subtle and multiple ways.

Five types of coupling can occur between two modules in a program:

1. Data coupling

2. Stamp coupling

3. Control coupling

4. Common coupling

5. Content coupling

Data coupling is the loosest and the best type of coupling; content coupling is the tightest and the worst type of coupling. Figure 5.6 summarizes each type of coupling. Tight coupling can be the result if a program is arbitrarily divided into modules without regard for the complexity of the data interfaces connecting the modules.

Decoupling

Decoupling is a method of making modules more independent. Decoupling is best performed during program design. Each type of coupling suggests ways to decouple modules. For example, the designer should evaluate the goodness of a modularization scheme by asking questions such as these:

(tight)

CONTENT COUPLING: Two modules are content coupled if one module refers to or changes the internals of another module (e.g., a branch or fall through from one module's code into another module).

COMMON COUPLING: Two modules are common coupled if they share the same global data areas (e.g., FORTRAN COMMON,PL/I EXTERNAL attribute.)

CONTROL COUPLING: Two modules are control coupled if data from one is used to direct the order of instruction execution in the other (e.g., a flag set in one module and tested in a compare in another module).

STAMP COUPLING: Two modules are stamp coupled if they communicate via a composite data item (e.g., record or COBOL group item). The composite data item may contain pieces of data that are not used by a module even though they are passed to it.

DATA COUPLING: Two modules are data coupled if they communicate via a variable or array (table) that is passed directly as a parameter between the two modules. The data is used in problem-related processing not for program control purposes.

(loose)

Figure 5.6   Definition of the five types of coupling.

1. Is each module designed as a black box, or must I look inside to understand the interface?

2. How is each module likely to be changed in the future, and how will these changes affect other parts of the program?

3. Has each module interface been designed to pass as few data as necessary to the module?

4. Is the use of program switches and flags reduced as much as possible by placing decisions that affect the processing steps of a module inside that module?

In addition to asking these questions, the designer should follow the decoupling guidelines listed in Box 5.3.

BOX 5.3   Decoupling guidelines

1. To reduce *data coupling* minimize the number of data couples by:
   Passing only necessary data to a module.
   Not passing data through one or a series of modules to reach another module. (For example, instead of passing an error message through many levels of the structure chart, process that error message at the point where the error occurs.)

2. To reduce *stamp coupling* do not create composite data items containing many logically unrelated pieces of data. Instead, group together only related data into a composite data structure and pass unrelated stand-alone items individually.

3. To reduce *control coupling* attempt to redesign the modularization scheme to eliminate as many control flags as possible. Watch for program functions that have been split into multiple modules. Try to avoid non-problem-related control flags.

4. To reduce *common coupling* avoid shared data areas by:
   Localizing data access to as few modules as possible.
   Passing data explicitly as parameters between the called and the calling modules.
   Dividing shared data areas into logical subregions.

5. Completely eliminate *content coupling* from the design.

Cohesion

In addition to coupling, Constantine proposed cohesion as another measure of the goodness of a modularization scheme [10]. Whereas coupling measures the interdependences between modules, *cohesion* measures how strongly the elements within a module are related.

Figure 5.7 shows examples of the seven levels of cohesion. Coincidental is the weakest and least desirable level; functional is the strongest and most desirable level. The scale between levels is continuous, not discrete, since we cannot draw a sharp line separating any two levels. Also, the scale is not really linear since cohesion is a qualitative, not a quantitative, measure. Figure 5.8 provides definitions of each level of cohesion.

To apply the cohesion measure practically at design time, it must be possible to determine module cohesiveness by examining the module at a black-box level, rather than having to look at the individual instruction-level elements

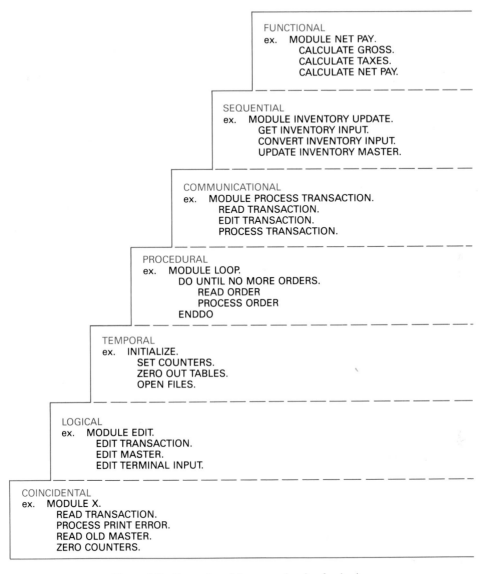

Figure 5.7   Examples of the seven levels of cohesion.

within the module. Yourdon suggests that an effective way of doing this is to describe the module's function in one sentence [10]. If the module is functional, it should be possible to describe its operation fully in a simple imperative sentence. The guidelines in Box 5.4 can be used to distinguish nonfunctional levels of cohesion.

Although coupling and cohesion are normally used to evaluate the good-

Strongest

FUNCTIONAL: Each element in a module is a necessary and essential part of one and only one function.

SEQUENTIAL: The elements of a module are related by performing different parts of a sequence of operations where the output of one operation is the input to the next.

COMMUNICATIONAL: The elements of a module all operate on the same data.

PROCEDURAL: The elements of a module are all part of a procedure — a certain sequence of steps that have to be done in a certain order.

TEMPORAL: The elements of a module are related by time but need not occur in a certain order or operate on the same data.

LOGICAL: The elements of a module are all oriented toward performing a certain class of operations.

COINCIDENTAL: The elements of a module are essentially unrelated by any common function, procedure, data, or anything.

Weakest

Figure 5.8 Definition of the seven levels of cohesion.

ness of a modularization scheme, they are also measures of program modifiability. Both the internal structure of each module and the interrelationships among modules influence the ease with which a program can be changed. A modifiable program is made up of modules that have high cohesion and loose coupling.

PROGRAM SHAPE

Controlling the "shape" of a modular program is another way to choose a good modularization scheme. The number of modules that a module invokes and the number of modules that invoke a module can affect program complexity. Yourdon defines the number of modules invoked by a module as its *fan-out* or *span of control* [11]. As with module size, very high or very low spans are possible indicators of a poor modularization scheme. In general, a module span of control should not exceed 10. This number is closely related to the "magic" number 7, based on psychological studies and in particular the "chunking" theory [12].

The human short-term memory has a limited capacity for retaining "chunks" of information. Well-known experiments show that the capacity of our short-term memory is about 7 ± 2 chunks. It can handle about seven chunks at once. When we go much above this limit, we are much more prone to making errors and becoming frustrated. Reorganizing information into appro-

BOX 5.4   Guidelines for determining the level of module cohesion

- If the only way to describe the module's function is using a compound sentence, its level of cohesion is most likely sequential, communicational, or logical.

- If the description of the module's function contains time-oriented words like *first, next, after,* or *for all,* the module probably has temporal or procedural cohesion.

- If the module's function is described as performing some operation for a class of items (e.g., all types of transaction), the module probably has logical cohesion.

- If the module's function can be described as "initialization," "cleanup," or "housekeeping," the module probably has temporal cohesion.

priate chunks is important for effective use of our short-term memory and for comprehension. We do this subconsciously in performing many of life's tasks. We can help by performing it consciously when doing certain types of program design tasks. For example, designing a module that invokes more than seven other modules may cause the programmer to be more susceptible to making errors.

The number 10 is a reasonable upper limit for handling chunks of program information. It agrees with McCabe's findings that the number of compares in a module should not exceed 10.

Shneiderman also suggests applying the chunking theory to program design [13]. He explains that understanding a program is very much like understanding natural language. The syntax of a natural-language sentence is used to derive its semantic meaning. Though the syntax is remembered only briefly, the semantic structure is retained for a longer time. This is because syntax items are not remembered one at a time but rather are grouped together to form a chunk of information that the human memory retains more easily. Sentences themselves are also grouped together into higher-level semantic structures that can be remembered in one chunk.

Similarly, programmers do not understand programs in a line-by-line manner. They group instructions to form higher-level, more understandable chunks (e.g., a module that calculates the net pay for an employee). This is the primary reason why modularization is such a powerful technique for improving program understandability.

REFERENCES

1. R. Armstrong, *Modular Programming in COBOL*. New York: Wiley, 1973, pp. 62–68.

2. F. Baker, "Chief Programmer Team Management of Production Programming," *IBM Systems Journal*, 11, no. 1, 56–73.

3. G. Weinberg, *The Psychology of Computer Programming*. New York: Van Nostrand Reinhold, 1971, pp. 1–41.

4. A. Fitzsimmons and T. Love, "A Review and Evaluation of Software Science," *ACM Computing Surveys*, 10, no. 1 (March 1978), 3–18.

5. S. Woodfield, "An Experiment on Unit Increase in Problem Complexity," *IEEE Transactions on Software Engineering*, SE-5, no. 2 (March 1979), 76–78.

6. T. McCabe, "A Complexity Measure," *IEEE Transactions on Software Engineering*, SE-2, no. 4 (December 1976), 308–320.

7. C. McClure, *Reducing COBOL Complexity Through Structured Programming*. New York: Van Nostrand Reinhold, 1978, pp. 77–121.

8. D. Parnas, *Information Distribution Aspects of Design Methodology*. Pittsburgh: Technical Report Department of Computer Science, Carnegie-Mellon University, 1971.

9. W. Stevens, G. Myers, and L. Constantine, "Structured Design," *IBM Systems Journal*, 13, no. 2 (1974), 115–139.

10. E. Yourdon and L. Constantine, *Structured Design*. New York: Yourdon, Inc., 1975, pp. 95–126.

11. Ibid., pp. 148–170.

12. G. Miller, "The Magical Number Seven, Plus or Minus Two: Some Limits on Our Capacity for Processing Information," *The Psychological Review*, 1956.

13. B. Shneiderman, *Software Psychology*. Cambridge, MA: Winthrop, 1980, pp. 49–53.

6 PROGRAMMING BY STEPWISE REFINEMENT

CHANGING PROGRAMMING FROM CRAFT TO SCIENCE
Until the structured revolution, programming was to a great extent viewed as a craft whose rules and practice were left to each individual programmer. The work of Wirth, Dijkstra, and others laid the foundations for changing programming from a craft to a structured discipline. They introduced a programming methodology that defines the basic steps to follow in developing structured programs. Wirth called this methodology "programming by stepwise refinement." Dijkstra explained it in terms of "levels of abstraction." The two concepts lie at the heart of the structured programming methodology.

STEPWISE REFINEMENT
Stepwise refinement is the process of developing a program by performing a sequence of refinement steps [1]. The process begins by defining the basic procedural tasks and data needed to solve the programming problem. This initial definition is at a very high, general level. The process stops when all program tasks are expressed in a form that is directly translatable into the programming language(s).

At each refinement step, one or several program tasks are decomposed into more detailed subtasks. The definition of a subtask is often accompanied by a refinement of the definition of the data needed to interface tasks. For this reason, task refinement and data refinement are performed in parallel.

Refinement Characteristics

The characteristics of the refinement process are as follows [2]:

1. The process proceeds in explicit steps.

2. At each step, a set of tasks and data structures is introduced. The program as evolved to that point is defined in terms of this set.

3. The set of tasks and data structures used at a step defines in greater detail the set that was introduced in the previous refinement step.

4. The notation used to define the tasks and data structures is general but becomes more detailed and more like the actual programming language as the refinement process nears completion.

5. The refinement steps are the product of program design decisions involving a further determination of the functional pieces of the program and its data structures.

How well the program design decisions are made determines how well the program is structured into easy-to-understand, easy-to-modify modules. Although there is no single "right" way to make refinement decisions for any programming problem, the following guidelines can help direct the refinement process [1, 3]:

1. Decompose decisions as much as possible in order to separate aspects that initially may appear related but really are not.

2. Defer decisions concerning implementation details as long as possible.

3. Base decisions on criteria such as efficiency, storage economy, clarity, and consistency of structure.

4. Attempt to make the easiest decisions first.

5. Consider alternative decisions at each step.

6. Build the program in minute steps, deciding as little as possible with each step.

We have defined the refinement process as a one-pass procedure, but in practice this is seldom the case. At each refinement step, decisions must be made after considering many alternatives. Because many decisions and many choices must be made when developing even a small program, some oversights and mistakes are likely to occur causing the programmer to back up and redo at least parts of the program. This is considered a normal happening in the refinement process.

LEVELS OF ABSTRACTION

Dijkstra's *levels of abstraction* can be used to describe the refinement process [3]. From Dijkstra's viewpoint, the program is divided into conceptual layers or levels (see Fig. 6.1). The topmost level (level 1 in Fig. 6.1) represents the program in its most abstract (general) form. All successive levels serve to define the components of this level. In the bottommost level (level n in Fig.

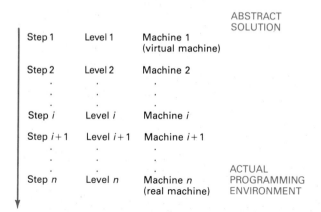

Figure 6.1 Levels of abstraction can be used to define the refinement process. The topmost level represents the program (or machine) in its most abstract form. The bottommost level describes the program (machine) in terms of components available in the actual programming environment. During the refinement steps, the program components are defined in ever greater detail.

6.1), program components can be easily described in terms of the programming language.

Each level is composed of a set of program components deemed logically related and addressable at that point in the program development process. A program component is either a functional component that performs a program subtask, or a data structure. A level is considered logically complete because its components can be combined by means of an algorithm to form a solution to the programming problem.

Alternatively, Dijkstra describes a level as a *machine*. To begin, the program is conceived as a dedicated virtual machine, complete with the necessary data structures, instruction set, and program. When the program is executed on this machine, the desired task is accomplished.

During the refinement process, a real machine is constructed from the virtual machine. At each step a new machine is built. The purpose of the machine is to simulate components from the previous, more abstract machine. As the process continues, the components of each successive machine become less abstract and more like instructions and data structures from the programming language. The process is complete when a machine can be built entirely of components available in the programming languages.

AN EXAMPLE OF THE REFINEMENT PROCESS

Box 6.1 defines a simple programming problem for building an airline reservation system. We can use this problem to illustrate the steps of the refinement

BOX 6.1   Airline Reservations program

The purpose of the Airline Reservations program is to process reservation transactions. There are two basic program tasks:

1. Update the reservations file with new reservations and delete canceled reservations.
2. Print out the updated reservations file after the update step is finished.

(Note that each flight can carry at most two passengers.)

Step 1: The reservations program is divided into two components corresponding to the two basic program tasks.

Machine M_1

```
D₁ (file)
I₁ (update (file), print (file))
A₁:
      update (reservations-file).
      print (reservations-file).
      stop.
```

Step 2: Machine M_1 is defined in terms of machine 2. This is accomplished by refining the instruction set and/or data structure set for M_1. In this example, the decision is to refine the update instruction. The refinement is also accompanied by a refinement of the set D_1 since this is required to explain the new instruction set I_2.

Machine 2

```
D₂   (file, record)
I₂   (read (file), print (file/record), find (record), add
     (record), delete (record))
A₂:
      *update reservations file.
      while not file-end do
            read (transaction-file);
            find (reservations-record);
```

BOX 6.1 *(Continued)*

if reservation-record found
    if add reservation
        add (reservations-record);
    else if delete reservation
        delete (reservations-record);
    else if new reservation to be added
        add (reservations-record);
enddo.
print (reservations-file).
stop.

Step 3: The instructions for adding a new reservation and deleting a reservation from the reservations file are refined.

Machine M_3

D_3 (file, record)
I_3 (read (file), find (record), insert (record), print (record),
     delete (record), modify (record), rewrite (record))

Definition of a transaction record:
    Flight-number
    Date-of-flight
    Name-of-passenger-1
    Name-of-passenger-2
    Transaction-code:

      0-add reservation to file
      1-delete reservation from file

Definition of reservations record:
    Flight-number
    Date-of-flight
    Name-of-passenger-1
    Name-of-passenger-2

A_3:
    while not file-end **do**
        read (transaction-file);
        if update-code = 0

(Continued)

BOX 6.1 *(Continued)*

```
        *add a reservation to the reservations file.
            find (reservations-record) invalid key
                insert (transaction-record);
                print ("New record added", transaction-record)
                invalid-key: = 1;
            *check to see if room on flight for new reservation.
            if invalid-key not = 1
                if passenger-name-1 or passenger-name-2 =
                blanks
                    modify (reservations-record);
                    print ("reservation added", transaction-record);
                else
                    rewrite (reservations-record);
                    print ("no room on flight", transaction-record);
            else
                invalid-key: = 0
    else
        *Delete reservation from reservations-record
            find (reservations-record) invalid-key
                print ("nonexistent record", transaction-record);
                invalid-key: = 1;
        *Delete reservation.
            if invalid-key not = 1
                modify (reservations-record);
                if passenger-name-1 and passenger-name-2
                = blanks
                    delete (reservations-record);
                    print ("record deleted", reservations-record);
                else
                    rewrite (reservations-record);
                    print ("reservation deleted",
                        transaction-record);
            else
                invalid-key: = 0.
enddo.
print (reservations-file).
stop.
```

process. The notation we use is based on Dijkstra's machine notation. The three components of machine M_i are as follows:

1. A data structure set, denoted by D_i
2. An instruction set, denoted by I_i
3. An algorithm, denoted by A_i

The data structure set, D_i, contains the data structures defined thus far by the refinement process. These may be actual data structures from the programming environment, such as files or tables, or abstract data structures to be defined in some later refinement step.

The instruction set, I_i, is composed of instructions from the programming language and/or abstract instructions to be defined in some later refinement step.

The algorithm, A_i, represents the complete program expressed in terms of instructional and data components designed thus far. In the notation used here, instructions in A_i are terminated by a period and subinstructions are terminated by a semicolon. A comment is delimited by an asterisk and a period. An instruction begins with a keyword, and the data it references follow and are enclosed in parentheses.

At step 3 in Box 6.1 all the program components can be easily translated into actual code. Some instructions can be translated one for one directly into a programming language instructions (e.g. IF, STOP). Others will become program procedures (e.g. MODIFY, REWRITE). This represents one possible refinement for the reservations program. Countless others are also possible.

REFERENCES

1. N. Wirth, "Program Development by Stepwise Refinement," *CACM,* 14, no. 4 (April 1971), 221–227.

2. C. McClure, "Top-Down, Bottom-Up, and Structured Programming," *IEEE Transactions on Software Engineering,* SE-1, no. 4 (December 1975), 397–403.

3. O. Dahl, E. Dijkstra, and C. Hoare, *Structured Programming.* New York: Academic Press, 1972, pp. 1–82.

7 TOP-DOWN, BOTTOM-UP, AND STRUCTURED PROGRAMMING

STRUCTURED PROGRAMMING METHODOLOGIES

Programs can be developed from the top down or from the bottom up. Both of these are adaptations of Wirth's programming by stepwise refinement and Dijkstra's programming by levels of abstraction. When a system is built bottom up, the designer creates the components first, makes each component work well, and then fits the components together.

When a designer works top down, he first creates the overall structure, defining but not yet building the components. As the design progresses, he fills in the details by building the lower-level components.

Top-down and bottom-up design are practiced in many fields of engineering other than programming. On complex projects, a combination of top-down and bottom-up design is usually required.

TOP-DOWN PROGRAMMING

Top-down programming is an orderly method of designing, coding, and testing a program in progressive steps. The method is based on programming by stepwise refinement as defined by Wirth [1].

Top-down programming produces a hierarchically structured, modular program. The top-level module in the hierarchy represents the overall function of the program. Lower-level modules represent subfunctions that define the program tasks in greater detail.

In top-down programming, the order of the design, coding, and testing steps is different from traditional program development. In traditional program development, first the entire program is designed, then the program is coded, and finally it is tested. The three steps are performed separately and sequentially. This is called the *phased approach* or the *all-in-one approach*. In contrast, in top-down development the three steps are performed in parallel (see

Fig. 7.1). This is called the *incremental approach* or the *step-by-step approach*. First one module is designed, coded, and tested. Then another module is designed, coded, and tested, and so on, until all modules in the program are finished. As part of the testing step, each newly coded module is integrated and tested with all modules completed to that point. The program grows gradually, one module at a time. Integration is done in steps instead of in big chunks at the end of the project as is done in the phased approach.

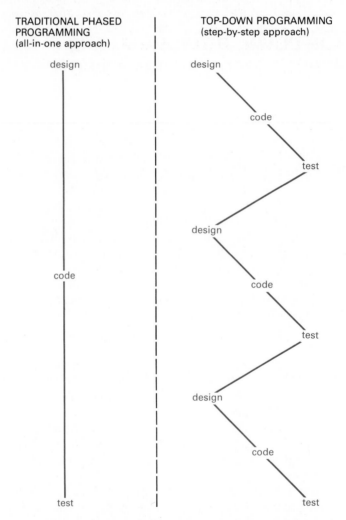

Figure 7.1 In traditional phased program development, the program is designed first, then coded, and finally tested. The three steps are performed sequentially. In top-down programming, the three steps are performed at module level and repeated until all modules are finished.

In practice, the traditional phased approach has not been very successful. It tends to delay the discovery of serious problems and the need for project resources, such as personnel and computer time, until late in the project. The curves shown in Fig. 7.2 illustrate this tendency. Both problems and resource needs seem to build up enormously as the project nears its planned completion point. The situation manifests itself in schedule and budget overruns and in serious integration testing problems. As a result, testing is historically the most poorly executed and most misscheduled development phase. Furthermore, problems are likely to spill over into the maintenance phase, making the program a costly nightmare to maintain.

The top-down approach can avoid many of these problems. It has the advantage of beginning testing earlier in the development process. In this way integration problems can be discovered and corrected earlier and at a lower cost.

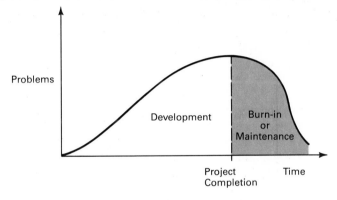

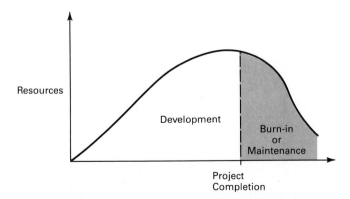

Figure 7.2 In phased program development, serious problems and resource needs often build up enormously as the project nears its planned completion point.

A second advantage is that the need for resources can be more evenly distributed throughout the development process. Finally, a skeleton of the program exists from the early development steps, giving the user a partial version of the program long before the entire program is completed.

Steps of Top-Down Programming

Top-down program development follows the logical structure of the program, beginning with the highest-level module and proceeding to lower-level modules in well-ordered steps. The steps are as follows:

Step 1: Begin with an examination of the problem and then propose a plan of attack, given as the general structure of the program. Express the solution as an outline that identifies the general procedural and data components of the program. At this point the contents of the components are not defined in detail. The outline is obtained by cutting the problem into logical pieces reflecting the functional tasks the program must perform to accomplish its objective (e.g., calculate gross pay, select screen format).

Step 2–n: Expand the program outline into the complete program in steps. The expansion process follows the rules of the refinement process (discussed in Chapter 6). Program components are refined into subcomponents, then the subcomponents are refined, and so on. The process stops when the program is describable as a set of components that can be directly expressed in the pro-

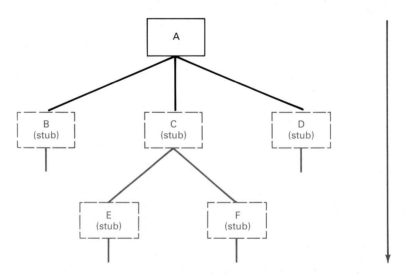

Figure 7.3　The top-down method for designing, coding, and testing follows the logical structure of the program, beginning with the highest-level module and proceeding to lower-level modules in refinement steps. Stubs are used to represent lower-level modules that will be developed later.

gramming language. The degree of detail needed for this description depends on the difficulty of the problem and the judgment of the developers.

As shown in Fig. 7.3, top-down development begins with module A after the general program hierarchical structure has been outlined. Modules B, C, and D are represented as dummy modules called *stubs*. Usually a stub can be coded as an ''empty'' module containing only an entry point and an exit point. When a stub is invoked, it simply returns control to the invoking module. If necessary, it can return a constant value if some output is expected. Stubs stand in as place holders until they are replaced by the actual modules in later refinement steps.

After module A has been designed, coded, and tested, top-down development moves down to modules in level 2. In steps, the stubs for modules B, C, and D are replaced by the actual modules. The process continues in a downward direction until program development is complete.

Box 7.1 lists some basic principles to be followed for successful application of the top-down method.

BOTTOM-UP VERSUS TOP-DOWN PROGRAMMING

Although top-down programming is usually considered the better method for developing a structured program, bottom-up programming is sometimes a viable alternative. Both methods share the same objectives:

- To systematize the programming process
- To provide a framework for problem solving
- To produce a modular program

BOX 7.1   Basic principles of top-down programming

- Design decisions should be made in a way that will separate the problem into parts in which the components of each part are problem-related.
- Implementation details should not be addressed until late in the development process, but alternatives should be explored at each step.
- Data should receive as much attention as functional components because the interfaces between modules must be carefully specified.
- Refinement steps should be simple and explicit.

Both are compatible with the structured programming methodology. However, they approach program development from the opposite direction. The construction technique for program development in top-down programming is *decomposition*. Program functions are decomposed into subfunctions and so on until the whole program can be defined in terms of components from the programming language. As shown in Fig. 7.4, the development direction is from an abstract, high-level solution to the actual programming environment.

In bottom-up programming, the opposite development direction is followed. The program is built by combining simple, atomic components to form more abstract, higher-level components. This construction technique is *concatenation*.

BOTTOM-UP PROGRAMMING

Bottom-up programming develops a program in steps. Just as in top-down programming, the process can be divided into two parts. First an initial solution for the program is proposed. Then the detailed components of the program are developed.

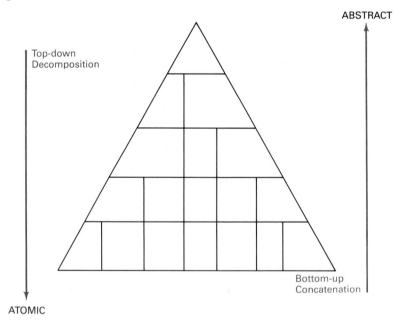

Figure 7.4   Top-down and bottom-up programming approach program development from opposite directions. The top-down program construction technique is *decomposition:* An abstract, high-level view of the program is divided in steps into lower-level subcomponents. The bottom-up program construction technique is *concatenation:* Simple, atomic components are combined in steps to form the program.

Step 1: Begin with an outline of the proposed program. This outline includes the general functional and data components of the program.

Step 2–n: In explicit steps, develop the program by combining low-level components to form higher-level components. This process is called the *concatenation* process. The concatenation process stops when a set of program functions and data structures that are able to solve the programming problem have been constructed from the elements available in the actual programming environment.

As shown in Fig. 7.5, bottom-up program development begins with module E. Following module E, module F is designed, coded, and tested. Then modules E and F are combined and tested. Since module C does not yet exist, its function must be simulated by a test driver. A *test driver* is usually just a skeleton model of the module to be built in a later development step. Development proceeds up the program structure module by module until the entire program has been designed, coded, and tested.

The Concatenation Process

The concatenation process can also be described in terms of levels of abstraction. This is illustrated in Fig. 7.6. Notice that the concatenation process proceeds in the direction opposite the refinement process. Instead of moving downward from a general solution to a low-level component definition, as the refinement process dictates, the concatenation process moves upward from low-level components to a solution.

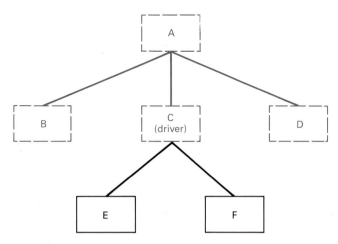

Figure 7.5   The bottom-up method for developing a program moves from the lowest-level modules to the highest-level module in steps. Test drivers are used to represent higher-level modules that will be developed in later steps.

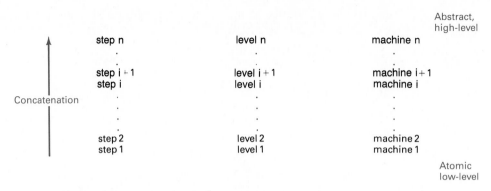

Figure 7.6   The concatenation process moves upward in steps from low-level programming language components to a high-level program solution.

The characteristics of the concatenation process are as follows:

1. The process proceeds in explicit steps.

2. At each step, a machine is built. The components of this machine are constructed from the components of the machine developed during the previous concatenation step.

3. Each step is the result of a decision to combine some components of the previous machine.

In practice, the concatenation process, like the refinement process, is not a one-pass procedure. Errors and oversights can cause part or all of the process to be repeated.

CHOOSING A DEVELOPMENT APPROACH

Top-down and bottom-up programming attempt to order the program development process. The result of either approach is a hierarchically structured, modular program. How well the process works in practice depends on the skills of the developers, the computing and personnel resources available, and the particulars of the programming problem. Both methods can offer only a framework for structuring the development steps. They do not give developers answers to design questions other than the advice that decisions be made as simply and as explicitly as possible.

For particular problems, one approach may be preferred over another. For example, the top-down approach is preferred when the developer "has faith in his ability to estimate the feasibility of constructing a component to match a set of specifications" [2]. It also is preferred when decisions concerning data representations must be delayed. On the other hand, a bottom-up approach allows a large number of programmers to work in parallel on bottom-level modules.

Also, it may be the most practical way to generate test data. Dijkstra's THE operating system was developed primarily bottom up because he considered the program interfaces with the hardware critical to a successful project [3].

However, following a pure top-down or bottom-up approach can cause problems. For example, when following a top-down approach, common functions may not be recognized, or the development process may require too much time, especially for a large program. Following a pure bottom-up approach may result in undefined data and poorly tested module interfaces. The pieces may not fit together.

COMBINATIONS

A combination approach is often more practical than following a strict top-down or bottom-up approach. For example, it may be desirable to implement utility or common modules bottom up since they will be invoked in more than one part of the program. The rest of the program then can be developed top down. This is simpler than creating a stub everywhere in the program where the utility module is invoked.

Many mixtures of top-down and bottom-up programming are possible. For example, Yourdon suggests a strategy in which the input side of the program is developed top down and the output side is developed bottom up [4]. The advantage of this strategy is that testing is performed with live data.

Using this strategy to develop the program shown in Fig. 7.7 would mean the following module development sequence:

1. GET EMPLOYEE TIME CARD
2. VALIDATE TIME CARD
3. COLLECT EMPLOYEE PAY INFO
4. PRODUCE EMPLOYEE PAYROLL
5. COMPUTE NET PAY
6. COMPUTE GROSS PAY
7. PRODUCE PAYCHECK INFORMATION
8. UPDATE PAYROLL REGISTER
9. PRODUCE FEDERAL REPORT
10. PRODUCE STATE REPORT
11. PRINT PAYCHECK

The modules GET EMPLOYEE TIME CARD, VALIDATE TIME CARD, and COLLECT EMPLOYEE PAY INFO would be tested with test drivers. The modules PRODUCE EMPLOYEE PAYROLL, COMPUTE NET PAY, PRODUCE PAYCHECK INFORMATION, and UPDATE PAYROLL REGISTER would be tested with stubs.

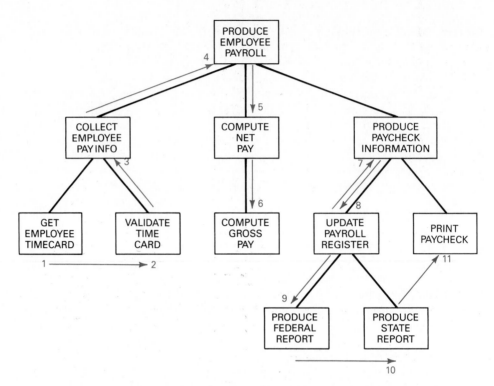

Figure 7.7   Often it is useful to use a combination of the top-down and bottom-up approaches in which part of the program is developed top down and part of the program is developed bottom up. In this example, the modules GET EMPLOYEE TIME CARD, VALIDATE TIME CARD, and COLLECT EMPLOYEE PAY INFO are developed first following a bottom-up strategy. Then the remaining modules are developed following a top-down strategy.

Even in this example, other variations are possible. For example, the module PRODUCE PAYCHECK INFORMATION could be implemented before the module COMPUTE GROSS PAY, or the module PRINT PAYCHECK before the modules PRODUCE FEDERAL REPORT and PRODUCE STATE REPORT.

Every development experience has elements of the top-down and bottom-up methods. At the very least, when developing a program essentially top down, programmers normally must peek below into low-level implementation requirements to guide their high-level decisions. And when following a bottom-up approach, programmers must always keep in mind the general program control structure and the program objective ultimately to be achieved.

REFERENCES

1. N. Wirth, "Program Development by Stepwise Refinement," *CACM*, 14, no. 4 (April 1971), 221–227.

2. B. Randell, "Towards a Methodology of Computing System Design," in Conf. Rec., 1968 NATO Conference on Software Engineering, pp. 204–208.

3. E. Dijkstra, "The Structure of the THE Multi Programming System," *CACM*, 11, no. 5 (May 1968), 341–346.

4. E. Yourdon and L. Constantine, *Structured Design*. Englewood Cliffs, NJ: Prentice-Hall, Inc., 1979, pp. 375–394.

8 COMMENTARY ON STRUCTURED PROGRAMMING METHODOLOGIES

THE PROBLEM OF PROGRAMMING IN THE LARGE

The one programming problem of paramount concern in the 1970s was complexity. This is the problem of programming in the large. It became possible and necessary to develop large, highly interrelated systems of programs. When the same heuristic programming practices used to develop small, stand-alone applications were tried in this new environment, they failed miserably. It soon became obvious that the problem of scaling up was indeed very difficult.

PROGRAM COMPLEXITY

Program complexity is introduced by the difficulty of the programming problem and the size of the program. It is a function of the number of procedural and data components in the program and the number of possible execution paths in the program. Program complexity increases quadratically, not linearly, with program size. This is mainly because of the connections between the components. If n is the number of components, the number of connections between the n components is on the order of n^2. Programming in the large involves a gigantic number of components and possible interconnections.

Once the problem of managing program complexity was recognized, there was no doubt that finding a solution was imperative for the advancement of programming.

According to Dijkstra,

Widespread underestimation of the specific difficulties of size seems one of the major underlying causes of the current software failure . . . . The art of programming is the art of organizing complexity, of mastering multitude and avoiding its master chaos as effectively as possible. [1]

The motivation for the interest in structured programming can be summarized in one word: *complexity*. The objective of structured programming was to introduce order and rigor into the programming process as a way of controlling complexity. As Mills explained, "the essence of structured programming is the presence of rigor and structure in programming" [2].

THE ABSENCE OF RIGOR

Unfortunately, the structured programming methodologies fell short of their objective. They are not rigorous. In fact, they are still very much heuristic methods. *Rigorous* means "exact, precise." But the use of structured methodologies expects intuition, judgment, and common sense of their users. There is no one right way to apply the methods. There is no guarantee of a correct outcome. Structured methodologies are at best rough sketches of rigorous methodologies. They are incomplete, fragmented rules and guidelines that the developers must fill in as best they can. There is much confusion as to exactly what these methodologies entail and how to apply them in practice.

Top-down programming is one example. Top-down programming is a popularized version of Wirth's stepwise refinement method. It represents an important advancement over earlier, ad hoc programming methods because it is an orderly way of attacking large programming problems. However, it is an informal, nonrigorous method. It does not provide complete rules for determining how to subdivide a problem, when to stop the process, or how to control quality. To work in practice, top-down programming must be supplemented with the skills and experience of the developers. For inexperienced developers, top-down programming offers at best a false sense of security. They believe that a correct program will automatically result from evolving it in systematic steps. Of course, this is not the case. A poor program can be produced systematically just as easily as a good one. The same criticisms can be made of bottom-up programming.

Another serious shortcoming is the vagueness of the boundaries between the basic development phases, leaving developers uncertain as to when one phase is finished and when it is appropriate to continue on to the next. For example, there is no clear boundary between analysis and design. The objective of analysis is to state the requirements of the problem to be solved. The objective of design is to formulate a solution meeting the stated requirements. In practice, the development process iterates between analysis and design until the design is judged satisfactory. This iteration is necessary because during the design phase the system requirements become clearer and often change. The design phase is used to refine the requirements. However, many of the structured methodologies work well only if the requirements can be completely defined *before* the design is started. Therefore, developers find themselves in a quandary, disagreeing on what the next step should be and who is responsible for analysis versus design decisions.

Another boundary problem concerns determining when a development phase is finished. None of the structured methodologies answers this question adequately. For example, they explain that the design is finished when each procedural component "has been defined to its logical conclusion" or "can be implemented easily." But what does this really mean? It means that the determination is left to the intuition and experience of the developers.

A similar problem exists for program verification. The structured methodologies do not provide adequate methods for verifying the correctness of a program. Although mathematical methods for formal correctness proofs were developed in the late 1960s, they are not practical techniques in the commercial programming environment. Instead, developers have relied mainly on structured testing methods to demonstrate correctness. Really all they can demonstrate is the presence of errors. The decision on when testing should stop is based on the developers' experience and instinct.

RECOMMENDATION   In short, programming has advanced about as much as possible with the existing structured methodologies and programming languages. Time and experience have proved the structured methodologies to be inadequate tools for solving the complexity problem.

The problem of programming in the large was correctly recognized. It is the problem of managing complexity. The solution was also correctly recognized. It is the structured philosophy—the principles of abstraction and formality and the concepts of divide and conquer and hierarchical ordering. But the implementation of the structured philosophy as embodied in the structured techniques of the 1970s is incomplete. Structured programming, as currently practiced, remains an ad hoc intuitive process. What is needed now is the same as what was needed 20 years ago: a mathematically rigorous *and* automatable programming methodology.

The CASE tools provide aids for creating complex designs and verifying their consistency, independently of programming and programming languages. The tools (or at least the better tools) can then generate code structures or working programs from the design. Programming is thus evolving by means of design tools more than by coding methods.

REFERENCES

1. E. Dijkstra, "Notes on Structured Programming," in *Structured Programming*. New York: Academic Press, 1972.

2. H. Mills, "Software Development," *IEEE Transactions on Software Engineering,* SE-2, no. 4 (December 1976), 265–273.

PART **III** DIAGRAMMING TECHNIQUES

9 DIAGRAMS AND CLEAR THINKING

INTRODUCTION   Good, clear diagrams play an essential part in designing complex systems and developing programs. They are essential to computer-aided design and CASE technology.

Philosophers have often described how what we are capable of thinking depends on the language we use for thinking. When we used only Roman numerals, ordinary people could not multiply or divide. That capability spread when Arabic numbers become widely used. The diagrams we draw of complex processes are a form of language. With computers we may want to create processes more complex than those we would perform manually. Appropriate diagrams help us to visualize and invent those processes.

If only one person is developing a system design or program, the diagrams he uses are an aid to clear thinking. A poor choice of diagramming technique can inhibit his thinking. A good choice can speed up his work and improve the quality of the results.

When several people work on a system or program, the diagrams are an essential communication tool. A formal diagramming technique is needed to enable the developers to interchange ideas and to make their separate components fit together with precision.

Clear diagrams are an essential aid to maintenance. They make it possible for a new team to understand how the programs work and to design changes. A change in one place often affects other parts of the program. Clear diagrams of the program structure enable maintenance programmers to understand the consequential effects of changes they make.

When debugging, clear diagrams are a highly valuable tool for understanding how the programs ought to work and tracking down what might be wrong.

Architects, surveyors, and designers of machine parts have *formal* techniques for diagramming that they *must* follow. Systems analysis and program design have an even greater need for clear diagrams because these activities are more complex and the work of different people must interlock in intricate ways. There tends, however, to be less formality in programming, perhaps because it is a young discipline full of brilliant people who want to make up their own rules.

One of the reasons why building and maintaining software systems is so expensive and error-prone is the difficulty we have in clearly communicating our ideas to one another. Whether we are reading a functional specification, a program design, or a program listing, we often experience great difficulty in understanding precisely what its author is telling us. Whenever we must rely on our own interpretation of the meaning, the chance of a misunderstanding that can lead to program errors is very great.

The larger the team, the greater the need for precision in diagramming. It is difficult or impossible for members of a large team to understand in detail the work of the others. Instead, each team member should be familiar with an overview of the system and see where his component fits into it. He should be able to develop his component with as little ongoing interchange with the rest of the team as possible. He has clear, precisely defined and diagrammed interfaces with the work of the others. When one programmer changes his design, it should not affect the designs of the other programmers, unless this is unavoidable. The interfaces between the work of different programmers need to be unchanging. Achieving this requires high-precision techniques for designing the overall structure of the system.

Structured diagramming techniques offer many advantages. First, they combine graphic and narrative notations to increase understandability. Graphics are especially useful because they tend to be less ambiguous than a narrative description. Also, because they tend to be more concise, graphics can be drawn in much less time than it would take to write a narrative document containing the same amount of information.

Second, structured diagramming techniques support a top-down, structured development approach. They can describe a system or program at varying degrees of detail during each step of the functional decomposition process. They clarify the steps and the results of the functional decomposition process by providing a standardized way of describing procedural logic and data structures.

Structured diagramming techniques help developers deal with the large volume of detail generated during the program development process.

CHANGING METHODS   Diagramming techniques in computing are still evolving. This is necessary because when we examine techniques in common use today, many of them have serious deficiencies. Flowcharts are falling out of use because they do not give a structured view of a program. Some of the early structured diagramming techniques need replacing because they fail to represent some important constructs. We are inventing more rigorous methods for creating better specifications. Vast improvements are needed and are clearly possible in the specification process. These improvements bring new diagramming methods.

One of the problems with computing is that it is so easy to make a mess. Very tidy thinking is needed about the complex logic, or a rat's nest results. Today's structured techniques are an improvement over earlier techniques. However, we can still make a mess with them. Most specifications for complex systems are full of ambiguities, inconsistencies, and omissions. More precise, mathematically based techniques are evolving so that we can use the *computer* to help create specifications without these problems. As better, more automated techniques evolve, they need appropriate diagramming methods.

The best of the CASE impose a discipline on analysts and designers, helping to ensure that complex systems are better engineered and easier to modify.

CATEGORIES OF STRUCTURED DIAGRAMS

Diagrams are used in several areas:

1. Overview model of the enterprise. An overall model of an enterprise and its systems may be drawn. The functions and processes of an enterprise are decomposed hierarchically.

2. Overview systems analysis. The overall flow of data among business events and processes is drawn.

3. System design. The relationships among components of a system are drawn.

4. Program architecture. The overall architecture of a program or set of programs is drawn, showing the separate modules.

5. Program detail. The detailed logic within one program module is drawn.

6. Data models. An overall logical model of the data is drawn. It is important to distinguish here between data-base models and file representation.

7. Data structures. The structures of data bases or files are drawn.

8. Dialog structures. The possible sequences of screens and interactions in a person-computer dialog may be drawn.

Box 9.1 lists the diagramming techniques that are described in the following chapters and shows in which areas they are applicable. Figure 9.1 shows some examples of structured diagrams.

END-USER INVOLVEMENT

Particularly important in computing today is the involvement of end users. We want them to communicate well with systems analysts and to understand the diagrams that are drawn so that they can think about them and be involved in discussions about them.

BOX 9.1 Categorization of the diagramming techniques described in the following chapters

Diagramming Technique	Chapter	Applicability				
		Overview Systems Analysis	Program Architecture	Detailed Program Logic	File Structure	Data-Base Structure
Data-flow diagrams	11	✓				
Functional decomposition	12	✓				
Structure charts	13	✓	✓			
HIPO diagrams	14	✓	✓	✓		
Warnier-Orr diagrams	15	✓	✓	✓	✓	
Michael Jackson diagrams	16		✓		✓	
Flowcharts	17			✓		
Structured English and pseudocode	18			✓		
Nassi-Shneiderman charts	19			✓		
Action diagrams	20, 25	✓	✓	✓	✓	
Decision trees	21	✓		✓		
Decision tables	21			✓		
Data structure diagrams	22					✓
Entity-relationship diagrams	23					✓
Data navigation diagrams	24		✓			✓
HOS charts	26	✓	✓	✓	✓	

Increasingly, some end users are likely to create their own applications with user-friendly fourth-generation languages. Where they do not build the application themselves, we would like them to sketch their needs and work hand in hand with an analyst, perhaps from an information center, who builds the application for them. User-driven computing is a vitally important trend for enabling users to get their problems solved with computers [1].

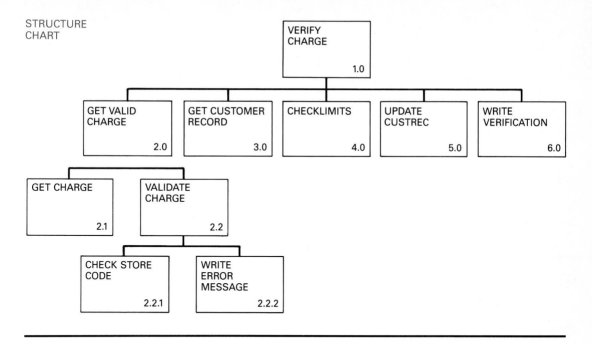

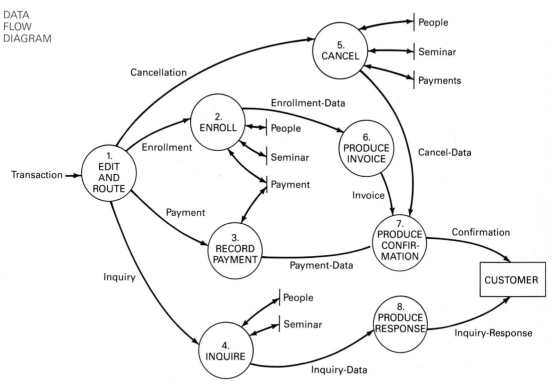

Figure 9.1 Good diagrams form a very important part of external documentation.   *(Continued)*

HIPO
DIAGRAM

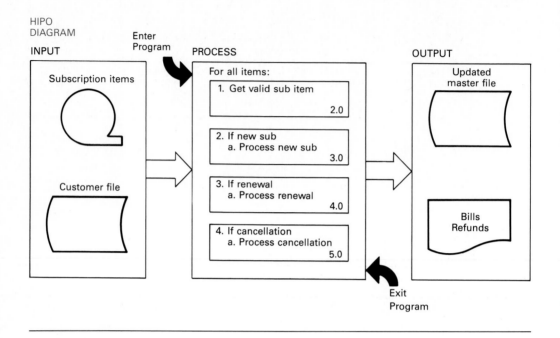

INPUT   Enter Program   PROCESS   OUTPUT

Subscription items

Customer file

For all items:

1. Get valid sub item

   2.0

2. If new sub
   a. Process new sub

   3.0

3. If renewal
   a. Process renewal

   4.0

4. If cancellation
   a. Process cancellation

   5.0

Exit Program

Updated master file

Bills Refunds

WARNIER–ORR
DIAGRAM

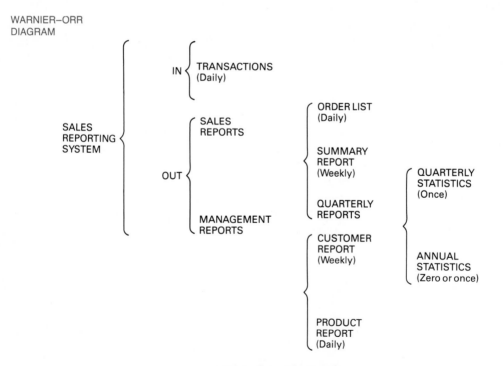

SALES REPORTING SYSTEM

IN { TRANSACTIONS (Daily)

OUT {

SALES REPORTS { ORDER LIST (Daily)

SUMMARY REPORT (Weekly)

QUARTERLY REPORTS { QUARTERLY STATISTICS (Once)

ANNUAL STATISTICS (Zero or once)

MANAGEMENT REPORTS {

CUSTOMER REPORT (Weekly)

PRODUCT REPORT (Daily)

Figure 9.1   (Continued)

MICHAEL
JACKSON
DIAGRAM

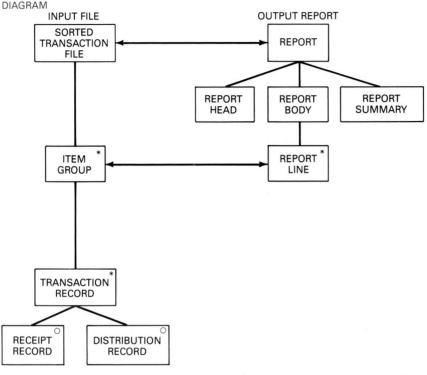

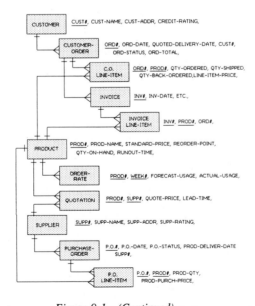

DATA MODEL

Figure 9.1   (Continued)   (Continued)

DATA
NAVIGATION
DIAGRAM

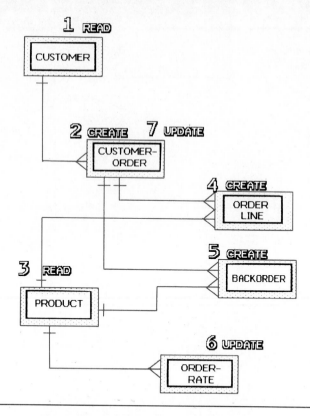

ACTION
DIAGRAM

```
┌─ ENTER BUZZWORD GENERATOR
│
│    CLEAR
│    SHOW "I WILL GENERATE A SCREEN FULL OF 'BUZZ PHRASES' EVERY"
│    "TIME YOU HIT 'ENTER.' WHEN YOU WANT TO STOP, HIT 'ESC.'
│
│    TEXT ADJECTIVE1 (10,16), ADJECTIVE2 (10,16), NOUN (10,16)
│
│    ADJECTIVE1 (1) = "INTEGRATED," "TOTAL," "SYSTEMATIZED," "PARALLEL,"
│       "FUNCTIONAL," "RESPONSIVE," "OPTIONAL," "SYNCHRONIZED,"
│       "COMPATIBLE," BALANCED"
│
│    ADJECTIVE2 (1) = "MANAGEMENT," "ORGANIZATIONAL," "MONITORED,"
│       "RECIPROCAL," "DIGITAL," "LOGISTICAL," "TRANSITIONAL,"
│       "INCREMENTAL," "THIRD GENERATION," "POLICY"
│
│    NOUN(1) = "OPTION," "FLEXIBILITY," "CAPABILITY," "MOBILITY,"
│       "PROGRAMMING," "CONCEPT," "TIME PHASE," "PROJECTION,"
│       "HARDWARE," "CONTINGENCY"
│
│    SEED
│
├─ WHILE KEY NOT = "ESC"
│    COUNT = 1
│
│  ┌─ WHILE COUNT < 23
│  │    A = INT(RND(10) + 1)
│  │    B = INT(RND(10) + 1)
│  │    C = INT(RND(10) + 1)
│  │
│  │    SHOW ADJECTIVE1(A) + " " + ADJECTIVE2(B) + " " + NOUN(C)
│  │
│  │    COUNT = COUNT + 1
│  └─ END
│
│     WAIT
└─ END
│
│    CHAIN "GAMES_MENU"
└─ EXIT
```

Figure 9.1   (Continued)

PSEUDOCODE

```
UPDATE-COMPONENT.
  end-of-reserv = 0.
  PERFORM READ-RESERVATION-COMPONENT.
  PFUNTIL end-of-trans = 1 AND end-of-reserv = 1
    IF end-of-reserv = 1 AND end-of-trans = 0
      PERFORM FINISH-TRANSACTION-COMPONENT
    ENDIF;
    IF end-of-trans = 1 AND end-of-reserv = 0
      PERFORM FINISH-RESERVATION-COMPONENT
    ENDIF;
    *Compare flight-number of Reservations-record
    and Transaction-record for an update match.
    IF end-of-trans = 0 OR end-of-reserv = 0
      IF reservation-flight-number <
        transaction-flight-number
        write(New-reservations-record);
        PERFORM READ-RESERVATION-COMPONENT
      ELSIF reservation-flight-number >
        transaction-flight-number
        print("Reservations record added".
          Transaction-record);
        write(New-reservations-record);
        PERFORM READ-TRANSACTION-COMPONENT
      ELSIF reservation-flight-number =
        transaction-flight-number
        PERFORM UPDATE-RESERVATION-COMPONENT;
        PERFORM READ-RESERVATION-COMPONENT;
        PERFORM READ-TRANSACTION-COMPONENT
      ENDIF
    ENDIF
  ENDPF.
```

Figure 9.1   (Continued)

For these reasons, diagramming techniques should be user-friendly. They should be designed to encourage user understanding, participation, and sketching. Many DP diagramming techniques have been designed for the DP professional only. To be user-friendly, a diagram should be as obvious in meaning as possible. It should avoid symbols and mnemonics that the user may not understand.

PROGRAM DOCUMENTATION TOOLS

Structured diagramming techniques are very important as program documentation tools.

They are used to define the program specifications and to represent the program design. They provide the blueprint for implementing the design into program code. *Structure charts* and *Nassi-Shneiderman charts* are two examples. Together they describe the program organization structure and its internal workings. The programmer translates them into actual programming-language instructions during the coding phase.

Diagrams can give both high-level and detailed descriptions of a program. For example, structure charts can give a high-level overview. They can be used to explain in general terms what major functions the program performs. On the other hand, pseudocode and Nassi-Shneiderman charts can give an instruction-level view of a program. They show where each program variable is initialized, tested, or referenced in the program code.

A high-level and/or detailed view of a program are important, depending on the user's purpose. If he is searching for a bug, detailed documentation may guide him to the exact location of the error. If he wants to determine in which of several programs a certain function is performed, high-level documentation may be the most helpful.

The tool used for high-level design is often different from the tool used for low-level design. For example, HIPO diagrams may be suitable for high-level documentation, but at a low level they become too cluttered and do not show structured coding constructs. Nassi-Shneiderman diagrams show detailed program logic with structuring coding constructs but do not show overall program architecture.

To use different and incompatible techniques for high-level design and low-level design is generally undesirable. It dates back to an era when the program architect was a separate person from the detail coder. Today it is desirable that the high-level design be steadily decomposed into low-level design using the same diagramming technique. This decomposition should often be done by one person, preferably at a computer screen. As fourth-generation languages become more popular, the era of the separate coder will go. We need one diagramming technique that enables a person to sketch an overview of a program and decompose it into detailed logic. *Action diagrams* give this ability. The program design process needs to be linked into the data-base design.

UTILITY OF DOCUMENTATION

Diagramming techniques produce both internal and external program documentation. *Internal documentation* is embedded in the program source code or generated at compile time. Program comments and cross-reference listings are examples of internal documentation.

External documentation is separate from the source code. *HIPO diagrams* and *Warnier-Orr diagrams* are examples of external program documentation.

External program documentation, such as data flow diagrams and pseudocode, is often discarded once the program is developed. It is considered unnecessary and too expensive to keep up-to-date during the remainder of the system life cycle. If a program is well-structured and properly documented internally, external program documentation becomes ignored.

Maintenance programmers mistrust most external documentation because they know that in practice it is seldom updated. Even the external documentation for a newly released system is unlikely to describe a program accurately. The most accurate source of information about a program is the program code and any information generated from the code (e.g., cross-reference listings, automatically generated structure charts, flowcharts). Keeping all the program documentation within or generated from the source code will make it more accessible and more accurate.

We should distinguish between different types of external documentation:

1. High-level structure versus detailed logic

2. Procedural structure versus data structure

High-level documentation will change very little, can be easily updated, and is a valuable source of information about a program throughout its life. *Data flow diagrams, structure charts,* and *action diagrams* are valuable introductions to understanding a complex program.

Two types of high-level documentation are useful: control flow information and data structure information. Although often overlooked, data structure information can be the most useful of the two in aiding overall program understanding because many common data processing application programs have a relatively simple control flow structure but complex data structures. Experiments by Shneiderman support this position. He found that data structure documentation was more helpful to programmers than even more comprehensive control flow information (such as pseudocode) for overall program comprehension, including the procedural aspects [2].

The subject of data administration is particularly important. A data administrator is the custodian of an organization's data dictionary and data structures. He is responsible for maintaining and creating a model of data that will be used on many different projects. This central representation of data is a basic foundation stone of multiple programs. Having separate programs employ views of data extracted from a common data model ensures that data can be exchanged among these programs and that data can be extracted from a common data base for management reporting and decision-support purposes. A clear diagramming technique is needed to represent the data models and views of data that are extracted from it.

The programmer must often navigate through a complex data base. Data navigation diagrams give a diagramming technique for this, linked to the data model and to action diagrams, which represent program structures that use the model.

If the data model is properly designed, the data structures should not usually change in disruptive ways throughout the system life. A canonical data model can be largely independent of individual applications of the data and also of the software or hardware mechanisms that are employed in representing and using the data [3]. The data model and the data dictionary are valuable tools to aid program understanding. Many logical access maps may be associated with the data model.

COMPUTER-AIDED DIAGRAMMING

Architects, engineers, and circuit designers have tools with which they can draw and manipulate diagrams on a computer screen. It is perhaps surprising that so many systems analysts and programmers still draw diagrams by hand. We have CAI, CAD, and CAM (computer-aided instruction, design, and manufacturing, respectively); we need CASA and CAP (computer-aided systems analysis and programming), and their combination: CASE (computer-aided systems engineering).

Interactive diagramming with CASE tools has major advantages. It speeds up the process greatly. It enforces standards. The computer may apply many checks to what is being created. It can automate the documentation process. The designers are less likely to do sloppy work.

Some diagramming techniques are more appropriate for CASE tools than others. Automation of diagramming should lead to automated checking of specifications and automatic generation of program code.

FUNCTIONS OF STRUCTURED DIAGRAMS

Structured diagramming techniques, then, have the following important functions:

- An aid to clear thinking
- Precise communication between members of the development team
- Standard interfaces between modules
- Enforcement of good structuring
- An aid to debugging
- An aid to changing systems (maintenance)
- Fast development (with computer-aided diagramming)
- Enforcing rigor in specifications (when linked to computerized specification tools)
- Linkage to data administration tools
- Enabling end users to review the design
- Encouraging end users to sketch their needs clearly
- Linkage to automatic checking and generation of code

A function that is achieved only on a few systems today ought to be emphasized and may become extremely important. The diagram, drawn on a computer screen, is decomposed into finer detail until executable program code can be generated from it *automatically*. Conventional programming then disappears.

Our objectives are to create specifications that are internally bug-free for exceedingly complex systems, to represent the specifications diagramatically, making them easy to modify, and to generate code from them [4]. The automatic conversion of diagrams to code on existing tools can clearly be improved. It has major advantages in speed of development, quality of code, and ease of maintenance.

REFERENCES

1. J. Martin, *Application Development Without Programmers*. Englewood Cliffs, NJ: Prentice-Hall, Inc., 1982.

2. B. Shneiderman, "Control Flow and Data Structure Documentation: Two Experiments," *CACM,* 25, no. 1 (January 1982), 55–63.

3. J. Martin, *Managing the Data Base Environment*. Englewood Cliffs, NJ: Prentice-Hall, Inc., 1983.

4. J. Martin, *System Design from Provably Correct Constructs*. Englewood Cliffs, NJ: Prentice-Hall, Inc., 1985.

10 FORMS OF STRUCTURED DIAGRAMS

INTRODUCTION The form or style of a diagram has a major effect on its usefulness. Complex charts can be drawn with a variety of techniques.

Humans like to draw artistic charts with curvy arrows sweeping gracefully from one block to another. We position the blocks as our fancy takes us. Such charts may look nice, but they cannot be easily maintained by computer. To enlist the computer's help in drawing and modifying our diagrams, the diagrams have to be reasonably disciplined.

Undisciplined diagramming becomes a mess when the diagrams grow in complexity (Fig. 10.1). Many diagrams that look nice in textbooks grow out of control in the real world when they have hundreds of blocks instead of ten. It is necessary to select forms of diagramming that can handle complexity.

FORMS OF TREE STRUCTURE A construct that appears in many different places in structured design is the hierarchy or tree structure. There are various ways to draw a tree structure. You should be familiar with them and understand that they are equivalent.

A tree structure is used to indicate that an overall facility, such as DOG-MEAT CORPORATION, includes lower-level facilities, such as SALES DIVISION, MANUFACTURING DIVISION, and PLANNING DIVISION. One of these, say, MANUFACTURING DIVISION, includes still lower-level facilities such as PURCHASING, PRODUCTION, and WAREHOUSE. We could draw this inclusion property as in Fig. 10.2.

Figure 10.2 makes it clear what includes what but would be clumsy to draw if there were many levels in the hierarchy. We can make it smaller by drawing it as subdivided rectangles, as in Fig. 10.3. This is neat and indicates clearly what includes what. This type of drawing is used in Nassi-Shneiderman

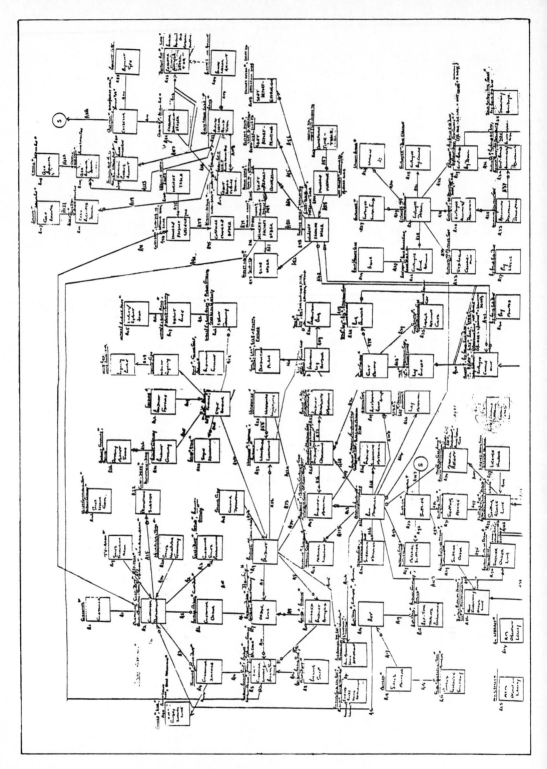

Figure 10.1   Example of a complex hand-drawn diagram.

charts (see Chapter 19). A concern with Fig. 10.3 is that the writing of the lowest level is sideways. A normal printer cannot print sideways letters. It could print letters in a column like in Japan:

P
U
R
C
H
A
S
I
N
G

but this becomes tedious to read in English.

A more usual way to draw a tree structure is like Fig. 10.4. This form of diagram is used by many analysts and programmers. It is the basis of structure charts showing hierarchical structure in programs. It is also used to draw hierarchical data structures.

It looks good in textbooks because there it has a relatively small number of blocks. In real life there can be a large number of blocks at the lower levels, and it will not fit on the width of a page. It might need paper 6 feet wide to draw it, and this is exactly what analysts, programmers, and data administrators do. They know that their work looks more impressive if it occupies a wall rather than resides in a binder. It is still more impressive if they draw it in many colors.

INHIBITION OF CHANGE

The problem with wall charts or hand-drawn works of art is that they are difficult to change. They inhibit change. In the design and analysis process there is usually much change. The more a design can be discussed and modified in its early stages, the more the end result is likely to be satisfactory.

The best way to make a design easy to change is to draw it with a computer, on a screen, with software that makes it simple to modify. Automation of structured analysis, design, and programming using a workstation that draws graphics is generally desirable. We will need a printout of the diagrams created with a computer. With a Calcomp plotter we can produce a 6-foot wall chart, in color, that is sure to impress our colleagues.

Such plotters, however, are not freely available to every analyst and programmer. We would like to obtain a printout from our terminal or personal computer that does not produce 6-foot wall charts unless we are prepared to

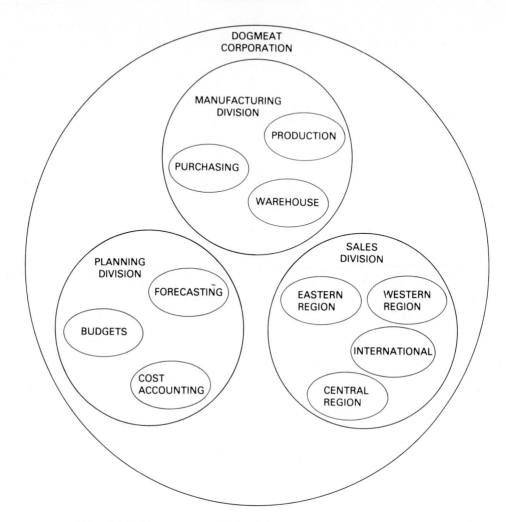

Figure 10.2   Tree structure showing what facilities include other facilities.

stick many pieces of paper together with tape. In any case, wall charts are difficult to send to other people or to take home. They are a real problem to work with on airplanes!

LEFT-TO-RIGHT TREES   We can solve the problem by turning the tree on its side. Figure 10.5 redraws the tree of Fig. 10.4. Now if there are many, many items at level 3, it spreads out vertically rather than horizontally and can be printed with a cheap printer.

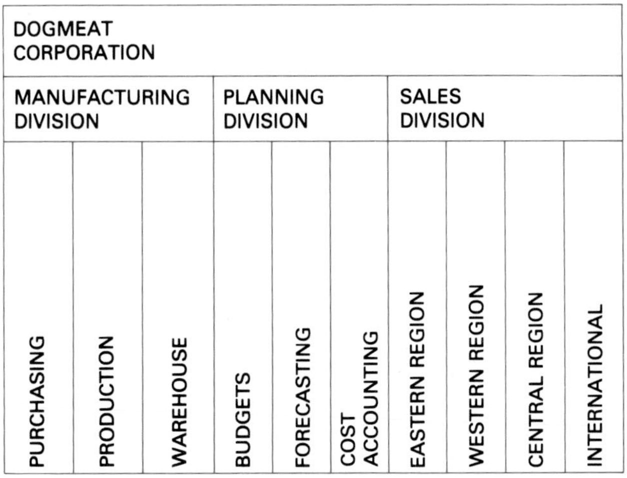

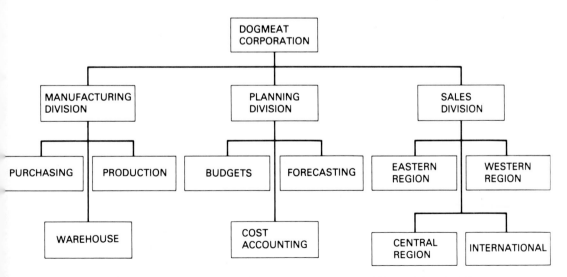

DOGMEAT
CORPORATION
MANUFACTURING
DIVISION
PLANNING
DIVISION
SALES
DIVISION
PURCHASING
PRODUCTION
WAREHOUSE
BUDGETS
FORECASTING
COST
ACCOUNTING
EASTERN REGION
WESTERN REGION
CENTRAL REGION
INTERNATIONAL

Figure 10.3 Box representation of a tree structure.

DOGMEAT
CORPORATION
MANUFACTURING
DIVISION
PLANNING
DIVISION
SALES
DIVISION
PURCHASING
PRODUCTION
BUDGETS
FORECASTING
EASTERN
REGION
WESTERN
REGION
WAREHOUSE
COST
ACCOUNTING
CENTRAL
REGION
INTERNATIONAL

Figure 10.4 A common way of drawing the tree structure of Figs. 10.2 and 10.3.

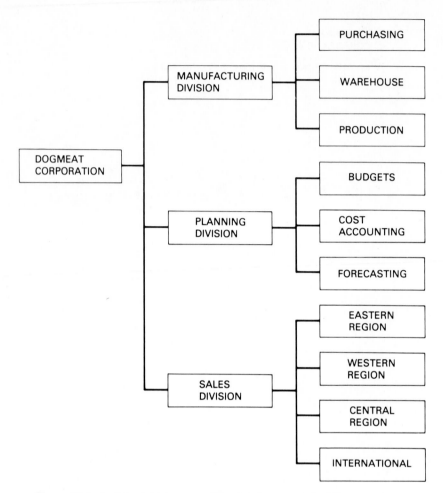

Figure 10.5 Left-to-right trees can be printed on normal-width paper even when they have many items at one level.

Tree structures are used for drawing organization charts of people. Here the tree may not be turned on its side because the person who runs the show wants to see his name at the top of the tree. With program or data structures there are no such ego problems, so left-to-right trees are fine.

Warnier-Orr notation, described in Chapter 15, draws a tree with brackets, as in Fig. 10.6. The left bracket implies that DOGMEAT CORPORATION *includes* MANUFACTURING DIVISION, PLANNING DIVISION, and SALES DIVISION, and so on.

Suppose there are many levels in the tree (we have seen trees with 35

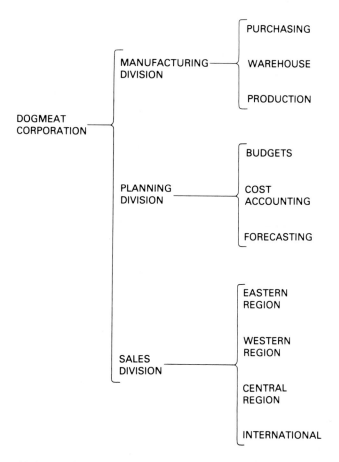

Figure 10.6   Warnier-Orr notation uses brackets to draw a tree structure, as in Fig. 10.5.

levels!). A many-level tree drawn as in Fig. 10.4 or Fig. 10.6 would again spill off the right-hand edge of the page. To solve this we can have a more compact version of a left-to-right tree, as shown in Fig. 10.7.

Incidentally, Fig. 10.7 solves the ego problem. The great leader can again be at the top of the tree.

The analyst has quite a number of lines to draw in Fig. 10.7. We would like him to have a small number of lines to draw so that he can make sketches quickly. Figure 10.8 shows a variant of Fig. 10.7 drawn with square brackets. This makes the hierarchical structure clear with a small number of lines. Each line of text in Fig. 10.8 could occupy much of the page. It could be a paragraph if so desired.

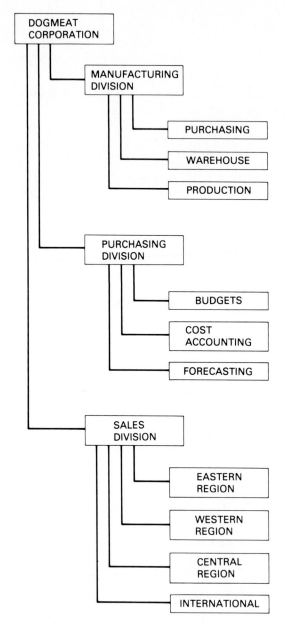

Figure 10.7 A more compact version of Fig. 10.5. With this form, many levels could be included on one page.

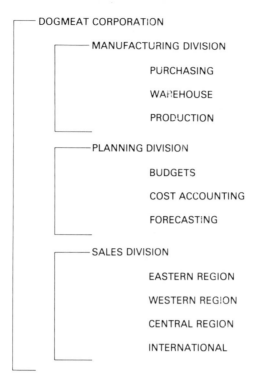

Figure 10.8   Square brackets enable us to draw Fig. 10.7 with a small number of lines.

SEQUENCE OF OPERATIONS

Structure charts (Chapter 13) are drawn like Fig. 10.4. As commonly used they do not show *sequence*.

In much structured design it is necessary to show sequence—of data items, of programs modules, of instructions. If blocks are clustered—more clustered than at the bottom right of Fig. 10.4—their sequence may not be clear unless precise sequencing rules are used. In Figs. 10.5 through 10.8 the sequence is clear. The items are implemented in a top-to-bottom sequence.

Figure 10.8 is much closer than the other diagrams to structured program code. If we remove the lines, it looks like Fig. 10.9.

We must eventually convert our diagrams into code. This conversion should change the format as little as possible to minimize the likelihood of making mistakes and to make checking simple.

MESH-STRUCTURED DIAGRAMS

It is easier to make a mess with mesh-structured diagrams than tree structures. Figure 10.10 shows a mesh structure, often called a network structure.

DOGMEAT CORPORATION

MANUFACTURING DIVISION
PURCHASING
WAREHOUSE
PRODUCTION
PLANNING DIVISION
BUDGETS
COST ACCOUNTING
FORECASTING
SALES DIVISION
EASTERN REGION
WESTERN REGION
CENTRAL REGION
INTERNATIONAL

Figure 10.9 Figure 10.6 drawn without lines and boxes has a structure like program code.

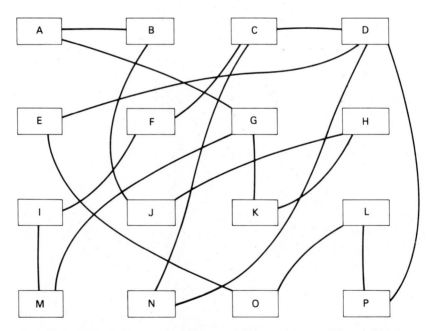

Figure 10.10 Mesh-structure (network-structure) diagram. This would become a mess if it had a large number of nodes.

In a tree structure there is one overall node called the *root,* which we draw at the top in diagrams like Figs. 10.3, 10.4, 10.7, and 10.8 and at the left in diagrams like Figs. 10.5 through 10.8. This node has children, drawn below or to the right of their parent. They, in turn, have children, and so on until the lowest or most detailed node is reached. This terminal node is called a leaf.

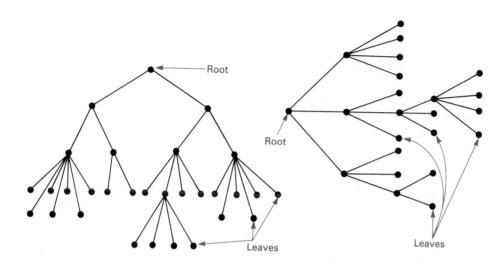

In a mesh structure there is no such neat ordering. A node may have several parents. Anything can point to anything. Chaos rules.

The objective of structured design is to prevent chaos from ruling, to impose neatness on what otherwise might be disorder. GO TO instructions in programs can go to *anywhere,* permitting the programmer to weave a tangled mess. So structured design bans GO TOs and decomposes programs hierarchically.

Program structures, file structures, and document structures can, and should, be decomposed hierarchically. Unfortunately, some types of structures cannot be decomposed hierarchically. A diagram showing how data flows through an organization cannot be beaten into a tree-like shape. A chart showing the relationship between entities in a data model is not tree-like.

Some structured methodologists almost refuse to accept the existence of anything that is not hierarchical. Because data models cannot be drawn with their hierarchical diagrams, they refuse to work with data models and will not look at the theories that regard data models as the foundation stone of modern DP methods.

COW CHARTS   Nevertheless it is necessary to draw mesh-structured diagrams for some important aspects of design.

Figure 10.10 has 16 blocks. Its spaghetti-like structure makes it difficult to work with. Real life is worse, and often such charts have several hundred items. Such a chart may be cut up into pieces, but this does not clarify it unless it is done in a carefully structured way. The spaghetti-like pointers wander among the pages in a way that is confusing and difficult to follow.

Some designers create hand-drawn charts that are too big to redraw quickly, and attempts to modify them create a rapidly worsening mess. The much modified chart is at last redrawn by hand and becomes regarded as a work of art—a triumphant achievement, but don't dare to modify it again!

We have been horrified by some of the charts that data administrators keep. There is no question that these charts inhibit progress in and improvement of the data structure. The data administrators will not dare to let end users propose changes to them. Sometimes these are called COW ("can of worms") charts.

Most COW chart creators are impressed by their rococo masterpieces and pin them up on the wall.

NESTED CHARTS   To ease modification, certain types of charts can be nested. They are divided into modules that fit on normal-sized pages. In a tree structure, any of the blocks or brackets may be expanded in detail on another page. In a data flow diagram, any of the processes may be expanded on another page.

Figure 10.11 shows a data flow diagram. Many data flow diagrams in practice have much larger numbers of processes (drawn as circles in Fig. 10.11) and would require vast charts unless they were broken into nested pieces. Figure 10.12 shows Fig. 10.11 divided into two pieces.

The block labeled PROCESS 17 is expanded in a separate diagram, as shown. Blocks from this diagram, for example PROCESS 17.3, could be shown in further detail on another page. This subdividing of data flow diagrams is called *layering*. The layered structure of data flow diagrams within data flow diagrams within data flow diagrams is itself a hierarchy, like Fig. 10.2, and is often drawn as a tree structure.

Most analysts draw free-form data flow diagrams with curvy lines like Fig. 10.12. Using a computer to draw the diagrams speeds up the process, and the software can perform some checking. Automated checking is very valuable in large projects with many data flow diagrams nested down to many layers. When the diagrams are computerized, they are easy to change, which is important because of the cost and difficulties of maintenance.

Some computerized data flow diagrams need large paper and plotting machines to print them. Like other diagrams, they can be designed to spread out vertically rather than horizontally so that they can be printed by personal com-

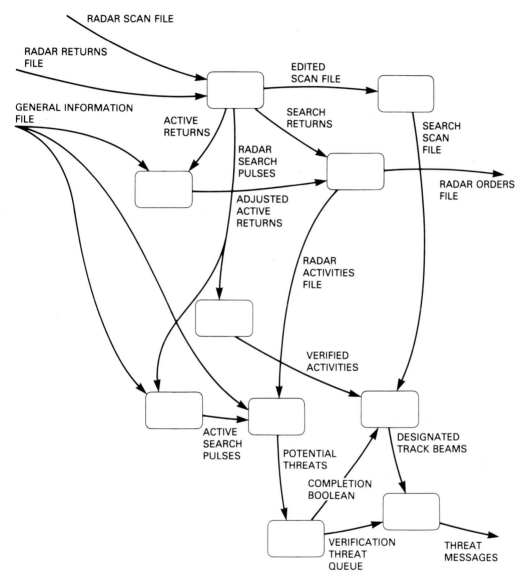

RADAR SCAN FILE

RADAR RETURNS
FILE

GENERAL INFORMATION
FILE

EDITED
SCAN FILE

ACTIVE
RETURNS

SEARCH
RETURNS

SEARCH
SCAN
FILE

RADAR
SEARCH
PULSES

RADAR ORDERS
FILE

ADJUSTED
ACTIVE
RETURNS

RADAR
ACTIVITIES
FILE

VERIFIED
ACTIVITIES

ACTIVE
SEARCH
PULSES

DESIGNATED
TRACK BEAMS

POTENTIAL
THREATS

COMPLETION
BOOLEAN

VERIFICATION
THREAT
QUEUE

THREAT
MESSAGES

Figure 10.11 Data flow diagram (the boxes are computer processes; the arrows are data). It is desirable to divide complex mesh structures into modules of less complexity. This diagram is divided ("layered") in Fig. 10.12.

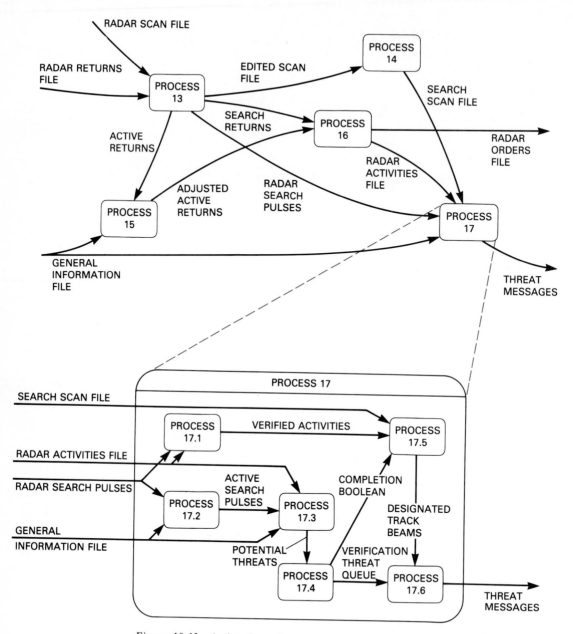

Figure 10.12 A data-flow diagram can be layered, that is, divided into nested modules. The bottom diagram shows details of PROCESS 17 in the upper diagram.

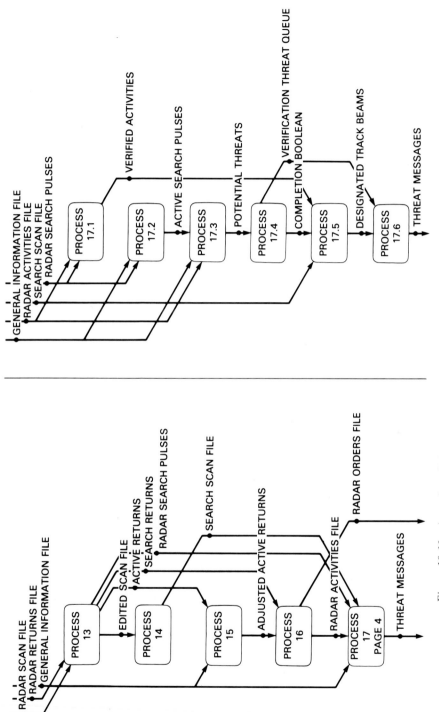

Figure 10.13 A version of Fig. 10.12 drawn vertically so that it can be manipulated and changed by computer.

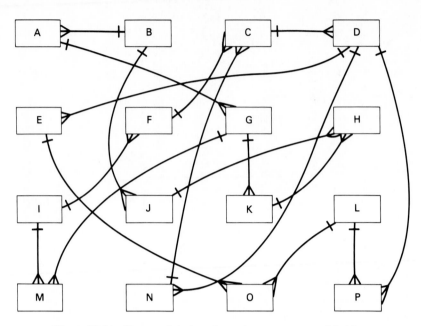

Figure 10.14   Data-model chart drawn in an unstructured fashion.

puters or normal printers and can be put in three-ring binders rather than pinned on the wall.

Figure 10.13 shows a version of Fig. 10.12 designed for computer editing and normal printers.

DATA-MODEL CHARTS

Whereas program structure diagrams and data flow diagrams can be modularized and nested, data models are more difficult to break into pieces. Teaching and insisting on modular design stopped programmers and analysts from papering the walls of their offices with huge charts, but now the data administrator is doing it.

Figure 10.14 shows 16 entities in a data model and the associations among these entities. A line with a bar shows a one-to-one association, for example:

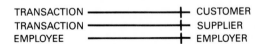

A line with a crow's foot means a one-to-many association, for example:

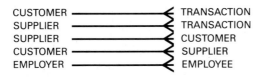

With this notation a hierarchical structure of data is drawn with the crow's feet pointing down or to the right and the one-to-one bars pointing up or to the left. Figure 10.15 shows this structure.

Such tree structures work well for representing a file or a document. One can draw a purchase order or bank statement with a tree structure, as we will see in later chapters when discussing Jackson and Warnier-Orr techniques.

However, it does not work by itself with data bases. The problem is apparent in Fig. 10.15. An order item is for a product. We would therefore like to draw a one-to-one link from ORDER ITEM to PRODUCT. We will do that, but then we no longer have a pure tree structure. Worse, a spare part is a product; it has a product number. We do not really want to regard it as a separate entity. Some PRODUCT records need to point to other PRODUCT records, indicating that the latter PRODUCT is a spare part for the former or that the former contains the latter. We can draw this by labeling two one-to-many links, thus:

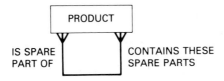

Figure 10.16 redraws the right-hand version of Fig. 10.15 to show these associations. Still more complications are introduced if we include customers in the diagram. You might like to explore this.

The data-base world, then, is full of constructs that cannot be drawn as pure tree structures. In drawing the associations among entity types, network structures like Fig. 10.14 grow up. A medium-sized corporation has many hundreds of entity types and needs to represent them in a data model. The data model cannot be nested simply like a data flow diagram, so how should we draw a king-sized version of Fig. 10.14? How can we make it clear and more structured? An important variant of the same question is, How can we structure it so that it can be drawn and manipulated by a computer?

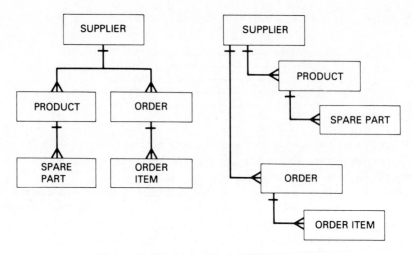

Figure 10.15   Hierarchical structure of data.

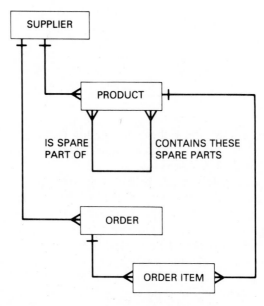

Figure 10.16   Figure 10.15 redrawn with associations between entities that are not hierarchical.

ROOT NODES We can describe certain nodes in a mesh-structured chart as *root nodes*. A tree has one root node. We draw it at the top or at the left. A mesh structure has multiple root nodes. We can pull these also to the top or the left. If we pull them to the top, we will end up with a diagram that spreads out horizontally, which is difficult to print. So let us pull them to the left.

Using our line with a bar and crow's foot notation, the root of a tree structure is the only node with no single-headed arrows leaving it. This can be seen in Fig. 10.15. We can use the same rule for discovering the root nodes of a mesh structure. Figure 10.17 marks the root nodes of Fig. 10.14.

We could remove the root nodes and their links from Fig. 10.17 and the remaining chart could again identify the roots. We will call the original roots *depth 1* nodes, these second-level roots *depth 2* nodes, and so on.

A *depth 2 node* can then be defined as a node that has a one-to-one link pointing to a depth 1 node.

A *depth 3 node* can be defined as a node that has a one-to-one link pointing to a depth 2 node but no one-to-one link pointing to a depth 1 node.

A *depth N node* ($N > 1$) can be defined as a node with a one-to-one link pointing to a depth ($N - 1$) node but no one-to-one link pointing to a lower-depth node.

Figure 10.18 shows the depth numbers of the nodes on the chart in Fig. 10.17.

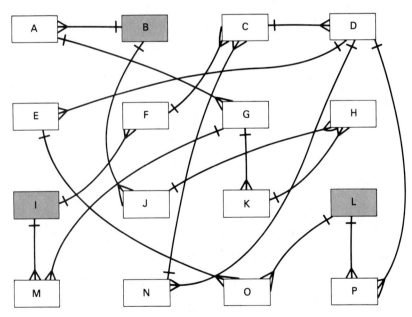

Figure 10.17   The root nodes of this mesh structure are shown in color. They are the nodes that have no one-to-one links to another node.

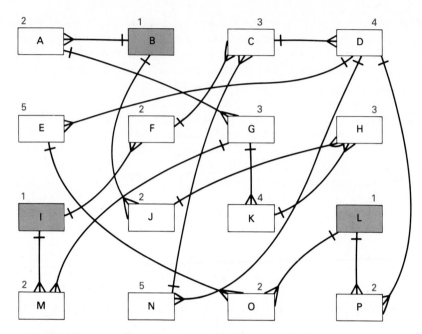

Figure 10.18   The figures indicate the depth of each node and are the basis for restructuring the diagram as shown in Figs. 10.19 and 10.20.

The depth 1 nodes are then plotted on the left-hand side of the chart. The depth 2 nodes are offset by one offset distance. The depth N nodes are offset by $(N - 1)$ offset distances. The depth N node $(N > 1)$ is plotted underneath the depth $(N - 1)$ node to which it points. The nodes under one depth 1 node form a cluster. Arrows that span these clusters are drawn on the left of the chart, away from the clusters, as shown in Fig. 10.19, which redraws Fig. 10.14.

The redrawing of a chart such as Fig. 10.14 begins with the identification of the depth 1 nodes (no one-to-one links leaving them). Then the depth 2 nodes can be marked, next the depth 3 nodes, and so on until all the nodes have been given a depth number. The clusters under each root node are drawn; then the links spanning these clusters are added.

FIND THE TREES   Every mesh structure has little tree structures hidden in it. The process we have just performed might be called "find the trees." In Fig. 10.14 you cannot see the trees for the forest. We can extract the trees, draw them as in Fig. 10.20, and then complete the diagram by drawing the links that span the trees.

In some mesh structures there is a choice of trees that could be extracted. A level 2 node might have two level 1 parents, for example. We make a choice based on which is the most natural grouping or which is the most frequently

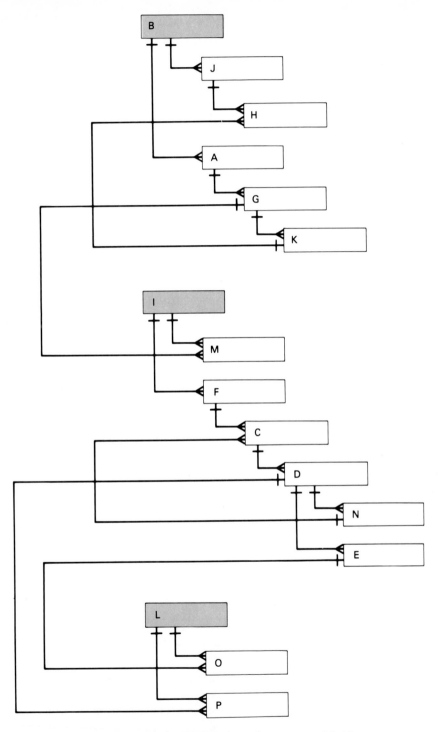

Figure 10.19　Figure 10.18 redrawn in a structured fashion.

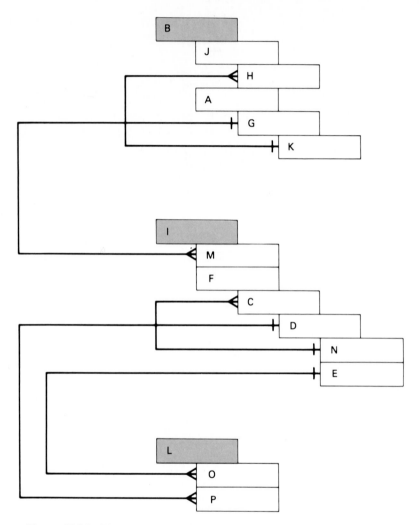

Figure 10.20 Figure 10.19 simplified by drawing its internal hierarchies without one-to-one links.

traversed path. Usually the trees extracted from a mesh structure turn out to be items that belong together naturally. Drawing an entity chart as in Fig. 10.20 clarifies these natural associations.

Figure 10.20, like Figs. 10.8 and 10.13, is a well-structured version of a chart that was messier. It is designed for computerized drawing and modification and for a normal computer printer. Even though Fig. 10.20 looks relatively neat, an entity chart with hundreds of entities becomes complex, with too many lines to be easy to follow. Such a chart should be kept in a computer, and users should not normally see the whole chart. The computer presents them with a portion of the chart when they need it. Computerized extraction of subsets of large charts is extremely helpful.

COMPUTER MAGIC   Once we use a computer, all sorts of magic becomes possible in the manipulation of diagrams.

A good CASE workbench enables us to build big charts, which it checks for consistency with a thoroughness far beyond that of most humans. We can see an overview summary—just the highest layer. We can drop down to detail, descending through several layers. The computer can add color to show items of different meaning. It can highlight whole areas of a chart. It can extend the brackets of Fig. 10.8 into boxes. It can show detailed program logic or code within any box we point to.

Windowing is important in CASE tools. The tool can display a window to ask for details about any block or line on the diagram. The detail window may be text, a form to fill in, or another diagram. We can have windows within windows within windows . . . going to successive levels of detail.

The diagramming technique may be designed so that humans draw relatively few lines when they do it by hand, but once the computer goes to work, it can dress up the diagrams to make them elegant and clear.

Some graphics software enables us to zoom into a diagram like a movie director with a zoom lens. As we move the cursor to an item and zoom in, the diagram changes to show us more detail—and more, and more, until perhaps we reach the coding level. Similarly, we can zoom out to see the overview.

When we change an item on a computerized chart, we may have to change other items to keep the chart consistent. The software should point out all such consequential changes and insist that they be completed. In some cases it can make the consequential changes automatically.

Once computer graphics is employed, the diagramming technique needs to be designed so that the computer can give the maximum help.

SYMBOLS WITH   It is desirable that the symbols and constructs on a
OBVIOUS   diagram have obvious meaning, as far as possible.
MEANING   For example a diagram showing the components
of a process needs to show *selection* and *repetition*.
Some diagramming techniques do not show these. Some show them with symbols that are not obvious in meaning. With Michael Jackson diagramming, the symbol * drawn in the top right-hand corner of a block means repetition, and ○ means selection. In Fig. 10.21, for example, one of the blocks marked ○ is selected. The block PRINT BUZZWORDS, marked *, is repeated several times.

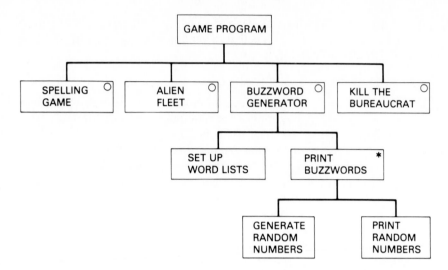

Figure 10.21 The ○ and * in the top right-hand corner of blocks on charts such as this do not have obvious meaning. The form of the diagram should be selected to make the meaning as obvious as possible to relatively uninitiated users.

Unless a key is written on the diagram, it would not be clear to an uninitiated reader what the ○ and * mean. People who once learned to read these charts forget the meaning of the ○ and * and would forget the meaning of other abstract symbols or mnemonics.

A mapmaker has the same problem. He chooses symbols that are as obvious in meaning as possible:

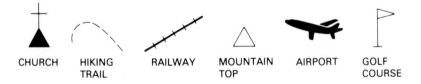

In addition, just to be sure, he puts a key on the diagram explaining the symbols.

A more memorable means of illustrating repetition would be to use a double line or double arrowhead. This is done in music. A double line in a score means repetition:

In structured diagrams, a double line to a block or at the head of a bracket could mean that that block or bracket is repeated:

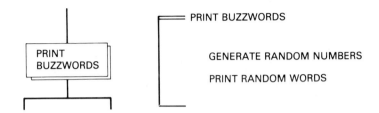

A memorable way of illustrating selection is to use a subdivided bracket:

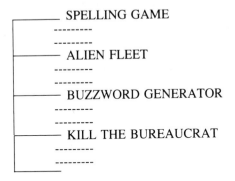

In the bracket just shown, *one* of the four items is performed, whereas in a nonsubdivided bracket, *everything* inside is performed.

> PRINT REPORT HEADER
> PRINT REPORT BODY
> PRINT TOTALS
> PRINT STATISTICS

If a block or bracket is conditional, it is not enough to write a condition symbol or number (0,1) as on Warnier-Orr charts. The bracket should be able to show the nature of the condition:

```
┌─── IF STOCK < 500
│        PERFORM REORDER
└───     UPDATE INVENTORY STATISTICS
```

SUMMARY   Box 10.1 summarizes characteristics that are desirable in diagramming techniques.

BOX 10.1 Properties of a good system diagramming technique

- The diagram can be manipulated easily on a computer graphics screen.

- End users can learn to read, critique, and draw the diagrams quickly.

- Hand-drawn diagrams should be designed for speed of drawing; computer-drawn diagrams can have more lines and elaboration.

- In a diagram, use constructs that are obvious in meaning, and avoid mnemonics and symbols that are not explained in the diagram.

- Diagrams can be printed on normal-sized paper. Wall charts of vast size are to be avoided because they tend to inhibit change and portability.

- Complex diagrams are structured so that they can be subdivided into easy-to-understand modules.

- The overview diagram can be decomposed into detail, this can be shown in greater detail, and so on.

- Windows should be used to collect and display detail. There may be windows within windows within windows . . . . The use of windows for detail can avoid clutter on the diagram.

11 DATA FLOW DIAGRAMS

INTRODUCTION   A data flow diagram shows processes and the flow of data among these processes. At a high level it is used to show business events and the transactions resulting from these events, whether on-paper or computer transactions. At a lower level it is used to show programs or program modules and the flow of data among these routines.

A data flow diagram is used as the first step in one form of structured design. It shows the *overall data flow through a system or program*. It is primarily a systems analysis tool used to draw the basic procedural components and data that pass among them.

DEFINING   Figure 11.1 is an example of a data flow diagram for
DATA FLOW   a procedure for processing customer orders. When an order is placed, the customer record is inspected to determine if the customer exists and whether the customer credit is in good standing. Then, for each product on the order of a valid customer, product availability is checked to determine if the product is available and when it can be supplied. If there is an insufficient quantity on hand, a backorder is created. Finally, an order confirmation is created, and the customer order is completed with order status, total amount due, and delivery information.

The data flow diagram shows how data flow through a logical system, but it does *not* give control or sequence information.

COMPONENTS   A data flow diagram (DFD) is a network representa-
OF A DFD   tion of a system showing the processes and data interfaces between them [1]. The DFD is built from four basic components: the data flow, the process, the data store, and the terminator.

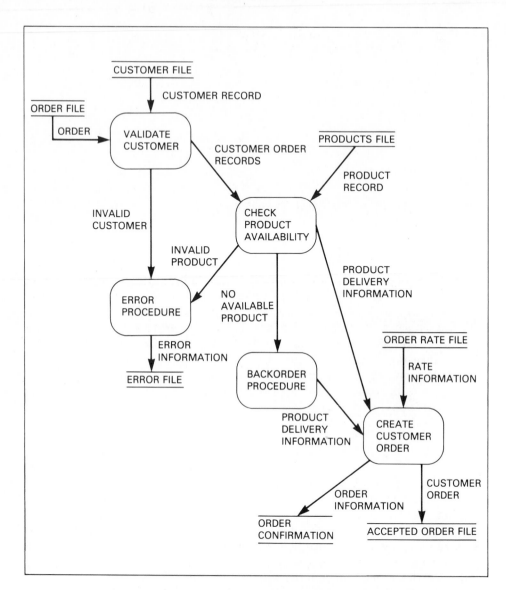

Figure 11.1   Data flow diagram for an order acceptance procedure shows the
data flow and processes performed to handle customer orders.

Data Flow

The *data flow* traces the flow of data through a system of processes. Direction
of data flow is indicated by an arrow. The data are identified by name, with the
name written alongside its corresponding arrow; for example,

PRODUCTS ORDERED

In effect, the data flow shows how the processes are connected.

Process

The *process* is a procedural component in the system. It operates on (or transforms) data. For example, it may perform arithmetic or logic operations on data to produce some result(s). Each process is represented by a circle or round-cornered rectangle on the DFD. The name of the process is written inside the circle. A meaningful name should be used to define the operation performed by the process; for example,

No other information about what the process does is shown in the DFD.

Normally data flow in and out of each process. Often there are multiple data flows in and out of a process; for example,

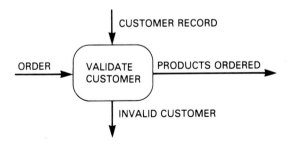

Data Store

A *data store* represents a logical file. It is drawn as a pair of parallel lines (sometimes closed at the left side) on the DFD. The name of the data store is written between the lines; for example,

PRODUCTS FILE   PRODUCTS FILE

Each data store is connected to a process "box" by means of a data flow. The direction of the data-flow arrow shows whether data are being read from the data store into the process or produced by the process and then output to the data store.

In the example shown below, error information is produced by the ERROR PROCEDURE and written out to ERROR FILE:

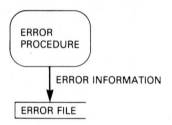

Terminator

A *terminator* shows the origin of data used by the system and the ultimate recipient of data produced by the system. The origin of data is called a *source*, and the recipient of data is called a *sink*. A rectangular box (as shown) or a double square is used to represent a terminator in a DFD:

Terminators actually lie outside the DFD.

LEVELING A DFD

A DFD is a tool for top-down analysis. We can use DFDs to provide both high-level *and* detailed views of a system or program [2]. What takes place within one box on a DFD can be shown in detail on another DFD.

Figure 11.2 shows the top level view of the order acceptance procedure. It shows us that the order acceptance procedure is one of four procedures in the sales distribution system. But this view provides us with no detailed information about the processes and data flow needed to enter an order. If we need more detail, we must look inside the process box to see what subprocesses are contained in the ORDER ACCEPTANCE PROCEDURE. This was the view provided by Fig. 11.1. Figure 11.3 gives an even more expanded view of this procedure by showing the subprocess contained in the VALIDATE CUSTOMER box.

We can continue to expand our view of the system by looking inside each process as far as we like. How detailed should our view be? A general rule of thumb is as follows: Keep expanding process boxes to create more detailed DFDs until the operations performed by each process box can be described in a one-page specification [3].

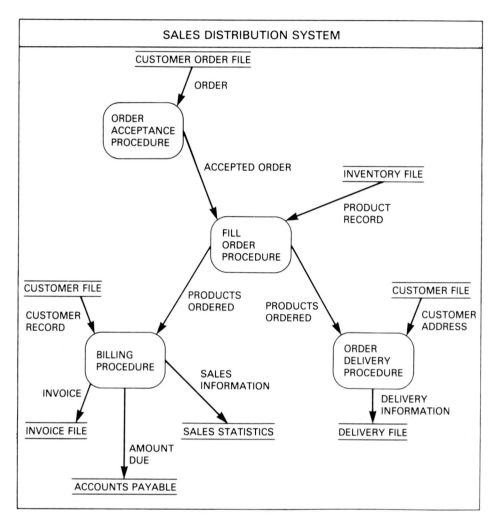

Figure 11.2 A top-level view of the ORDER ACCEPTANCE PROCEDURE shows that it is one of four subprocedures in the sales distribution system.

At each level, the DFD should probably contain fewer than 12 process boxes, preferably only six or seven. Larger DFDs are a sign of trying to show too much detail and are difficult to read.

This process of defining a system in a top-down manner is called *leveling* a DFD.

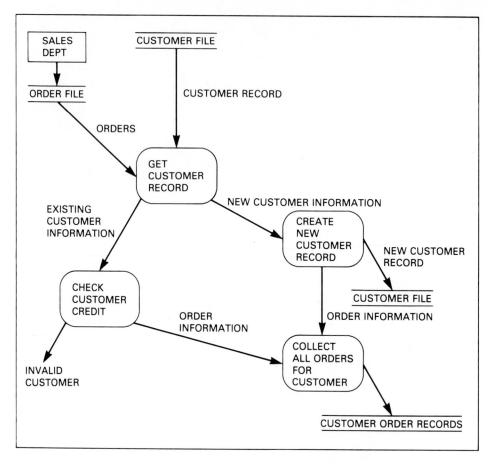

Figure 11.3   An expanded view of the VALIDATE CUSTOMER procedure shows four subprocedures: GET CUSTOMER RECORD, CREATE NEW CUSTOMER RECORD, CHECK CUSTOMER CREDIT, and COLLECT ALL ORDERS FOR CUSTOMER.

PROCESS SPECIFICATION AND DATA DICTIONARY

When a DFD is developed during structured analysis, a process specification and a data dictionary are also developed to give additional system information.

A *process specification* is created for each box in the lowest-level DFD. It defines how data flow in and out of the process and what operations are performed on the data. A process specification is described with other techniques illustrated in subsequent chapters. Figure 11.4 shows a structured-English version of what takes place in the box labeled VALIDATE CUSTOMER in Fig. 11.1.

VALIDATE CUSTOMER

```
FOR EACH ORDER REQUEST:
    FIND MATCHING CUSTOMER RECORD;
    IF CUSTOMER FOUND
        IF CUSTOMER CREDIT IS IN GOOD STANDING
            COLLECT ALL PRODUCT ORDERS FOR THAT CUSTOMER;
            CREATE CUSTOMER_ORDER RECORD
        ELSE (CUSTOMER NOT IN GOOD STANDING)
            WRITE INVALID CUSTOMER ERROR MESSAGE
        ENDIF.
    ELSE (NEW CUSTOMER TO BE ADDED TO FILE)
        CREATE NEW CUSTOMER RECORD;
        COLLECT ALL PRODUCT ORDERS FOR THAT CUSTOMER;
        CREATE CUSTOMER_ORDER RECORD
    ENDIF.
```

Figure 11.4   A process specification shows what happens inside one DFD box (at the lowest level of a leveled DFD). This specification, written in structured English, shows what happens in the VALIDATE CUSTOMER box of Fig. 11.1.

The *data dictionary* contains definitions of all data in the DFD. It can also include physical information about the data, such as data storage devices and data access methods. An example is shown in Fig. 11.5. The term *data dictionary* used in conjunction with defining a DFD is *not* the same as when used in conjunction with data-base management systems.

GANE AND SARSON NOTATION

Gane and Sarson [4] adopted slightly different diagramming conventions for data flow diagrams from those popularized by Yourdon and De Marco. In some ways the Gane and Sarson notation is better. Figure 11.6 summarizes the two.

Gane and Sarson draw a process as a rounded rectangle, (Yourdon and De

CUSTOMER FILE = [customer records]
The brackets [ ] indicate that in this example
CUSTOMER FILE is *iterations* of customer records.

**customer-record = customer-name + customer-address
                    + payment-information + outstanding-orders
                    + cust-type**
The + sign indicates that in this example a customer record is
a composite data item made up of a *sequence* of the data
items listed above.

cust-type = corp | individual
The vertical bar | indicates that cust-type is either a corporation
or an individual.

Figure 11.5   The data dictionary contains definitions of all the data in the DFD.

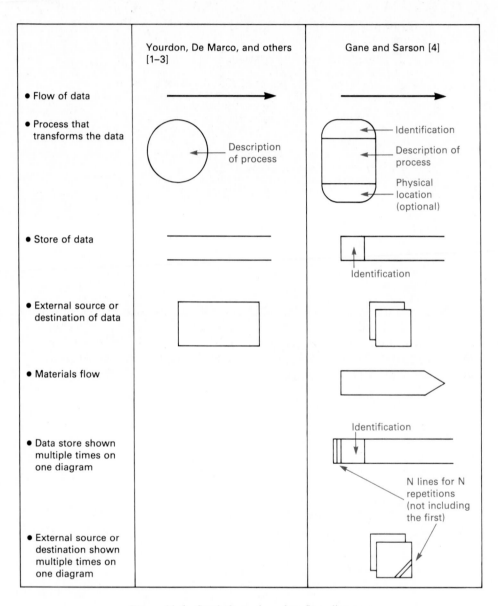

Figure 11.6 Symbols used on data flow diagrams.

Marco draw it as a circle.) In computerized drawing, a machine can more easily link multiple arrows to the block:

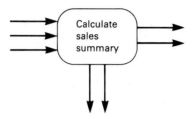

At the top of this block, a block number or other identifier is written:

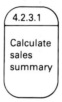

At the bottom the designer may optionally draw the physical location where the process takes place or the name of the computer program that executes the process:

The data store is drawn with a block at the left that may give its number or identification. It may link it to a data model:

| 17.1 | EMPLOYEE FILE |

An external source or destination of data is drawn with a double square:

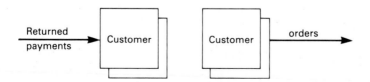

To simplify the mesh of lines on a drawing, a data store or external source or destination may appear several times. If a data store appears twice, a vertical line is drawn at the left side of its block. If an external block appears twice, a diagonal line is drawn in its bottom right corner:

If either of these appear three times, two such lines are drawn:

If they appear N times, $N - 1$ such lines are drawn.

Data flow diagrams are useful for showing the flow of materials as well as of computer data. It is important to indicate what is computer data and what is not. Gane and Sarson use thick arrows for showing the flow of materials:

Sometimes computer data accompany materials. Gane and Sarson draw the two together as shown in Fig. 11.7.

Figure 11.8 shows a typical Gane and Sarson data flow diagram.

USE OF COMPUTER GRAPHICS   Data flow diagrams for complex projects become large, unwieldy, and difficult to maintain. The use of computer graphics solves these problems. When such tools are used, a developer creates his diagrams on a workstation screen, updating the set of charts for the project, which are available to all developers.

Various computerized versions of data flow diagramming exist. We will illustrate STRADIS/DRAW from MCAUTO [5] and EXCELERATOR from InTech [6]. This software provides graphics for the Gane and Sarson method-

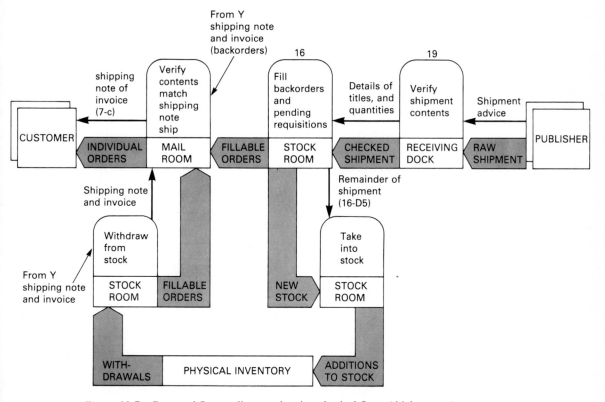

Figure 11.7　Gane and Sarson diagram showing physical flows (thick arrows) as well as data flows (thin arrows).

ology. The MCAUTO version of the complete methodology is called STRADIS; the graphics software for the methodology is STRADIS/DRAW. Figure 11.9 shows a data flow diagram created with STRADIS/DRAW.

MCAUTO lists the following advantages of using its graphics tool:

- Significant cost and time savings
- Reduction in labor needed to redraft graphics during development
- Significant labor reduction for documentation updates during maintenance
- Elimination of proofreading and potential for introduction of errors on diagram updates
- Capability to produce very large data flow diagrams, as in long-range system planning

The EXCELERATOR tool runs on personal computers. It supports various structured diagramming techniques and links them to a data dictionary.

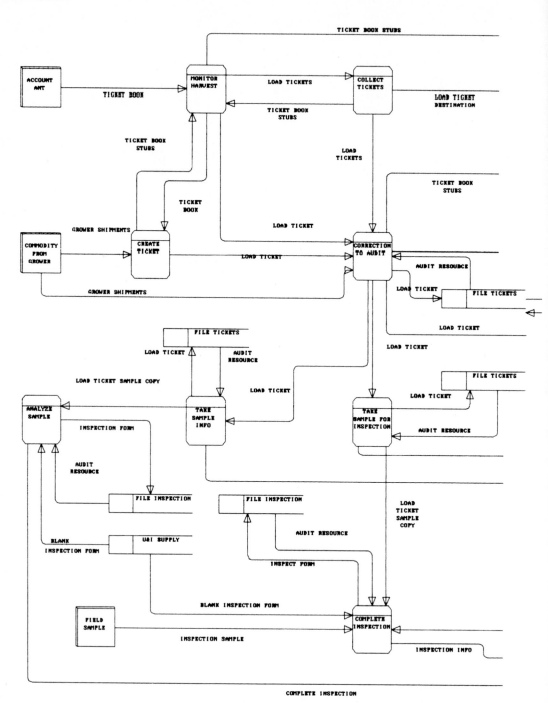

Figure 11.8 Data flow diagram drawn with Gane and Sarson notations [4] and produced on a personal computer with EXCELERATOR, a CASE tool from InTech [6].

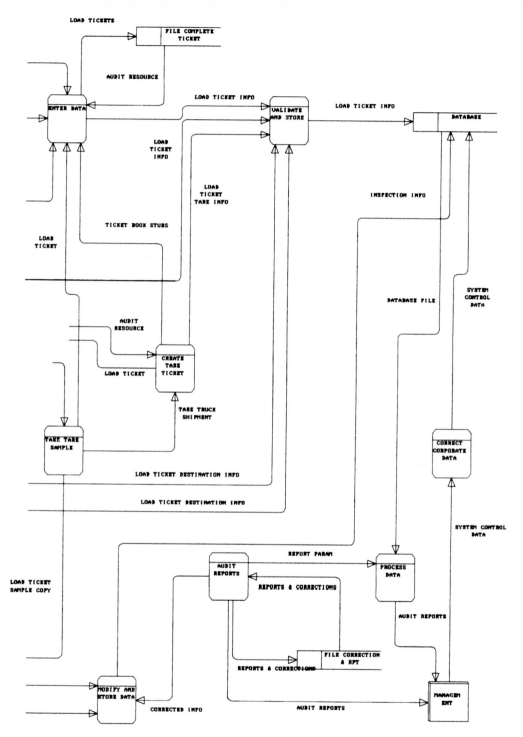

Figure 11.8 (Continued)

161

MCAUTO/IST

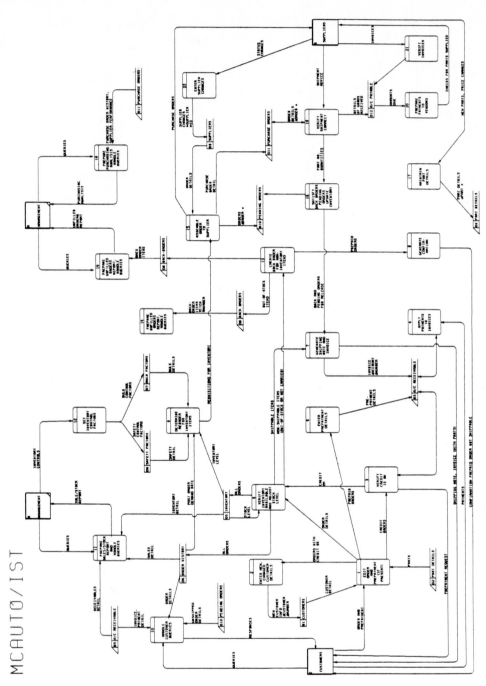

Figure 11.9 Data flow diagram created with STRADIS/DRAW from MCAUTO [5], a CASE tool using Gane-Sarson notation.

COMMENTARY   Data flow diagrams are a very valuable tool for charting the flows of documents and computer data in complex systems. Some organizations extend their use beyond that into the internal structuring of programs. This use can be questionable, as we will discuss later; there are often better techniques.

In many cases we found data flow diagrams to be used badly. Large, complex specifications were created with the help of such diagrams, but the task of cross-checking all of the inputs and outputs of data was not done adequately. The diagrams of this chapter are intended to illustrate this concern.

Figure 11.3 shows the VALIDATE CUSTOMER procedure. This procedure appears in Fig. 11.1. Figure 11.1, however, fails to show CUSTOMER FILE leaving the procedure. The VALIDATE CUSTOMER procedure of Fig. 11.3 creates a new customer record if the order is from a customer who is not yet in the file. This is not reflected in Fig. 11.1.

The incompatibility between Fig. 11.1 and Fig. 11.2 is worse. The ORDER ACCEPTANCE PROCEDURE of Fig. 11.1 has entering it ORDER FILE, CUSTOMER FILE, PRODUCTS FILE, and ORDER RATE FILE, whereas the same procedure in Fig. 11.2 has only CUSTOMER ORDER FILE entering it. The outputs are similarly out of balance.

We did not make up these diagrams. We used diagrams drawn by a highly paid computer professional. When such discrepancies are pointed out, the charts seem surprisingly sloppy. But in practice we found this a common occurrence. Many sets of specifications from which programmers code have data flow diagrams on which the inputs and outputs are inconsistent. After the code has been written, it is expensive to sort out the resulting mess.

We were appalled to find the same types of errors in textbooks and courses. You might like to amuse yourself by checking the data flow diagrams in some of the popular books on structured methodologies.

In some cases the authors of data flow diagrams protest that when they draw the early, high-level diagrams they could not yet know about the detail that will emerge when designing the later diagrams. When an analyst drew Fig. 11.2, for example, he thought merely of an ORDERED ACCEPTANCE PROCEDURE working on a CUSTOMER ORDER FILE and producing a stream of ACCEPTED ORDERS. He had not yet invented the detail shown in Fig. 11.1. It is always true that the early diagrams are sketches, not yet detailed or precise. However, later when the detail is worked out, it ought to be reflected to the higher levels so that the higher levels become correct. In other words, the detail design of Fig. 11.3 should cause us to change Fig. 11.1, and the detail design of Fig. 11.1 should cause us to change Fig. 11.2.

With a computerized tool, this can be done automatically. The detailed inputs and outputs of the lower-level layers can be reflected to the higher-level layers. Amazingly, some computerized tools do not do this. They are merely drawing aids, not linked to the integrity checks that are desirable.

DATA LAYERING   The lower-level charts of a complex system often show, in total, many data items. If all of these data items were individually shown on the top-level charts, the charts would become very cluttered. The top-level charts may therefore show an aggregate data name that encompasses many of the lower-level names. The top-level chart may, for example, show MANUFACTURING DATA BASE as input; the next level shows JOB RECORD, which is part of the MANUFACTURING DATA BASE; the lowest level shows MACHINE-TOOL#, START-TIME, and so on, which are part of the JOB RECORD. This is called *data layering*.

We need drawing conventions to show how the data are layered. Different ways to draw structured data are shown in later chapters.

If detailed data flow diagrams are drawn without thorough understanding and structuring of the data, problems will result. Data analysis and data modeling, discussed later, need to go hand in hand with data flow diagramming. CASE tools should enforce consistent linkages among these different forms of diagrams.

REFERENCES

1. T. De Marco, *Structured Analysis and System Specification*. New York: Yourdon, Inc., 1978, pp. 47–49.

2. E. Yourdon and L. Constantine, *Structured Design*. New York: Yourdon, Inc., 1978, pp. 38–40.

3. M. Page-Jones, *The Practical Guide to Structured Systems Design*. New York: Yourdon, Inc., 1980.

4. C. Gane and T. Sarson, *Structured Systems Analysis: Tools and Techniques*. New York: IST Inc., 1977.

5. STRADIS/DRAW product description, MCAUTO, McDonnell Douglas Automation Company, St. Louis, MO.

6. EXCELERATOR product description, InTech, 5 Cambridge Center, Cambridge, MA 02142.

12 THREE SPECIES OF FUNCTIONAL DECOMPOSITION

Most structured design employs a form of functional decomposition. A high-level function is decomposed into lower-level functions; these are decomposed further; and so on. A tree structure shows the decomposition.

Hierarchical decomposition can be applied to organization structures, system structures, program structures, file structures, and report structures. The term *functional decomposition* applies to functions rather than data. However, similar diagrams are sometimes drawn for the decomposition of both data and functions.

LEVELS OF THOROUGHNESS IN FUNCTIONAL DECOMPOSITION There are three different categories of functional decomposition—three separate *species,* as a botonist would say about trees.

Species I. The most common type of functional decomposition is a tree structure that relates to functions and not to the data that those functions use.

Species II. The second species shows the data types that are input and output to each function. This can be much more thorough, because if it is handled by computer, the machine can check that the data consumed and produced by each functional node are consistent throughout the entire structure.

Species III. The third species is still more thorough. It allows only certain types of decomposition, which have to obey precise rules that are defined by mathematical axioms. The resulting structure can then be completely verified to ensure that it is internally consistent and correct.

We are going to advocate thoroughness, not just because we want to avoid errors in program specifications but also because the thorough techniques have proved in practice to save much time and money. The thorough techniques will lead to a higher level of automation.

SPECIES I FUNCTIONAL DECOMPOSITION: CORPORATE MODEL

The first species of functional decomposition is appropriate for showing the structure of a corporation. At its highest level, functional decomposition is applied to an entire enterprise. A tree-structured chart is used to show the organization as in Fig. 12.1.

Individual divisions or units, such as CATV Bureau in Fig. 12.1, are subdivided to show their *functional areas*. Functional areas refer to the major areas of activity; in a corporation they might be engineering, marketing, production, research, and distribution. Functional areas may be subdivided into *processes*. Processes refer to groups of activities that are necessary in running the enterprise, as shown in Fig. 12.2.

A diagram like Fig. 12.2 is sometimes referred to as a *corporate model* or *enterprise model*. It shows the functions that are necessary in running the enterprise.

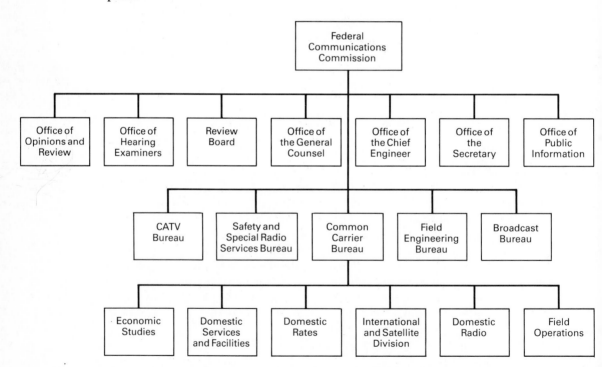

Figure 12.1   A chart decomposing an organization into its component bodies.

ORGANIZATION:	FUNCTIONAL AREAS:	PROCESSES:
CATFOOD DIVISION	BUSINESS PLANNING	Market Analysis Product range review Sales forecasting
	FINANCE	Financial planning Capital acquisition Funds management
	PRODUCT PLANNING	Product design Product pricing Product spec. maint.
	MATERIALS	Ingredient planning Purchasing Receiving Inventory control Quality control
	PRODUCTION PLANNING	Capacity planning Plant scheduling Workflow layout
	PRODUCTION	Ingredients control Mixing and cooking Canning Machine operations
	RESEARCH	Psychological testing Narcotics Package design Catfarm
	SALES	Territory management Selling Sales administration Customer relations
	DISTRIBUTION	Finished stock control Order servicing Packing Shipping
	ACCOUNTING	Creditors and debtors Cash flow Payroll Cost accounting Budget planning Profitability analysis
	PERSONNEL	Personnel planning Recruiting Compensation policy

Figure 12.2 Organization, functions, and processes. The processes may be further subdivided into activities, as shown in Fig. 12.3.

Enterprise models differ in the degree of detail they represent. Some show not only the functional areas and processes but also the detailed activities that are carried out in each process. Some information-planning methodologies refer only to functional areas and processes; some refer to functional areas, processes, and activities. The methods that give the best results are generally the more detailed ones. These need computerization; there is too much detail to manipulate by hand.

Figure 12.2 lists 42 processes. A large, complex corporation might have 30 or so functional areas and 150 to 300 processes. The chart needs to be drawn vertically, rather than horizontally as Fig. 12.1.

The identification of functional areas and processes should be independent of the current organization chart. The organization may change but still have to carry out the same functions and processes. Some corporations reorganize traumatically every two years or so, like the government of Bolivia. The identification of functions and processes should represent fundamental concern for how the corporation operates, independently of its current organization chart (which is often misleading). In some organizations there needs to be basic questioning about whether the functions and processes perceived are sound.

The names given to the processes should be action-oriented nouns such as those in Fig. 12.2. They often end in the suffixes *-ing, -ion,* or *-ment.*

Activities

In each business process, a number of activities take place. For example, one of the processes in Fig. 12.1 is purchasing. In this process, activities such as the following occur:

- Create requisitions for purchase
- Select suppliers
- Create purchase orders
- Follow up the delivery of items on purchase orders
- Process exceptions
- Prepare information for accounts payable
- Record supplier performance data
- Analyze supplier performance

There are typically 5 to 30 activities for each business process. There may be several hundred activities in a small corporation and several thousand in a large, complex one.

This distinction between processes and activities is somewhat artificial. It is better to break the business functional areas into functions and each function

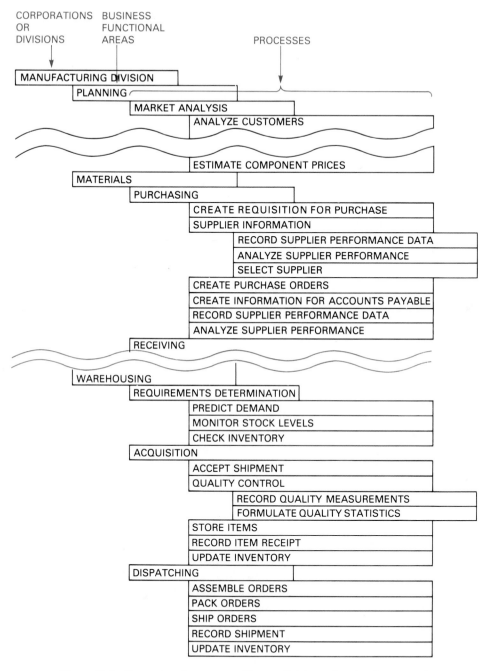

Figure 12.3 Enterprise chart: corporations or divisions, functional areas, and functions. The lowest-level function is sometimes called an activity. Its name should begin with a verb. A procedure (not necessarily computerized) is designed for each activity.

into lower-level functions, continuing until basic activities are arrived at. Figure 12.3 illustrates this hierarchical breakdown of functions. The lowest-level function may be called an *activity,* and its description should begin with a verb, denoting the operation to be performed.

In most corporations the activities have never been charted. When they are listed and related to the data they use, it is usually clear that much duplication exists. Each area of a corporation tends to expand its activities without knowledge of similar activities taking place in other areas. Each department tends to create its own paperwork. This does not matter much if the paperwork is processed manually. However, if it is processed by computer, the proliferation of separately designed paperwork is harmful because it greatly increases the costs of programming and maintenance. A computerized corporation ought to have different procedures from those of a corporation with manual paperwork. Most of the procedures should be on-line with data of controlled redundancy and minimum diversity of application programs. The entry of data in a terminal replaces the need to create carbon copies of forms that flow to various locations. Information becomes instantly available, and procedures should be changed to take advantage of this.

A chart like Fig. 12.3 becomes large. It will be changed and added to many times and so needs to be kept in a computerized form. Small charts can be extracted from the overall computerized chart to show the corporation and its functional areas, an overview of one functional area, or a detailed breakdown of one process.

Functional decomposition can proceed into greater levels of detail until it represents the program modules that are needed for a function, if it is computerized, and the detailed structure of those program modules.

In many cases, top-level planning is not done, and functional decomposition starts at a lower level, sometimes within one department. It is desirable to accomplish top-level planning of data in an organization—the data administration function. The strategic planning of data, discussed in Chapter 40, ought to link to the top-level planning of functions.

End users and user management relate well to charts such as Figs. 12.1, 12.2, and 12.3. They can be encouraged to draw such charts and, where useful, decompose them into the detail necessary for planning computer programs.

Figure 12.4 shows ORDER SERVICING on Fig. 12.2 being broken into further detail to show what happens when an order is serviced and what program modules are needed for this.

SPECIES II FUNCTIONAL DECOMPOSITION

Now let us look at the second species of function decomposition—that in which the functions are related to the data they use.

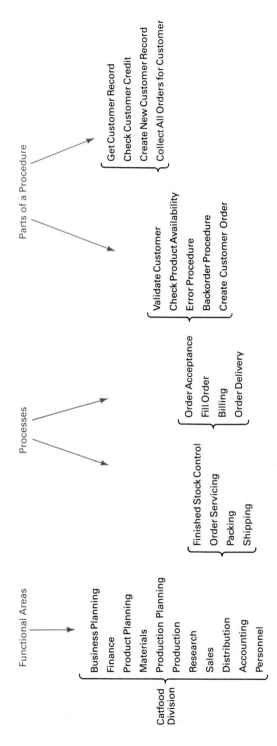

Figure 12.4 Functional decomposition progressing from the highest level to the level of program modules.

A function in computing is an algorithm that takes certain inputs and produces certain outputs. We represent it mathematically as

$$y = F(x)$$

where

F is the function

x is the input(s)

y is the output(s)

Functional decomposition done as in Figs. 12.1 through 12.4 does not take the inputs and outputs into consideration.

We could draw the function $y = F(x)$ as follows:

$$y \;\; \boxed{\;\; F \;\;} \;\; x$$

where x is the input to a block labeled F that produces an output y. This type of diagram is the basis of the HOS notation, which we will discuss later. It relates neatly to mathematical notation but seems unnatural to the uninitiated because the input is on the right rather than on the left. It tends to lead to charts that are wide horizontally and thus difficult to print and manipulate. For most people, it is more natural to use a vertical drawing with the input at the top and the output at the bottom:

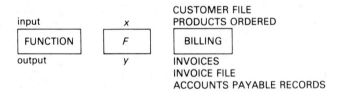

In Chapter 10 we advocated drawing a tree structure with square brackets when designing programs. Figure 12.5 shows the right-hand part of Fig. 12.4 drawn in this way.

We can extend these brackets into a rectangle and show the data they use. This is done in Fig. 12.6. The input data of each function are written at its top right corner, the output at its bottom right corner.

Checking the Use of Data

We can now apply some checks. We can check that the inputs to VALIDATE CUSTOMER are all used by its internal blocks and that its outputs all come

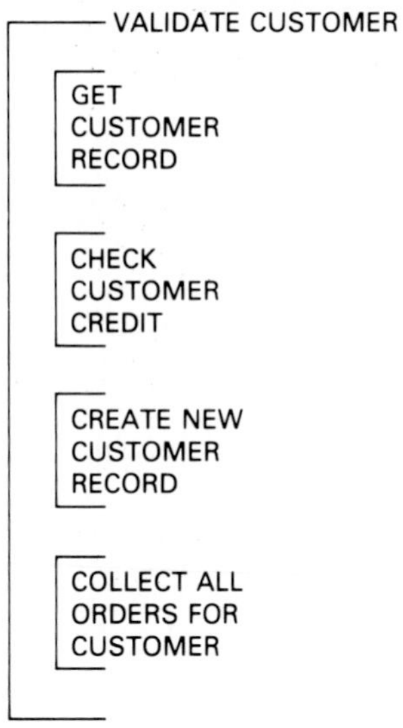

VALIDATE CUSTOMER

GET
CUSTOMER
RECORD

CHECK
CUSTOMER
CREDIT

CREATE NEW
CUSTOMER
RECORD

COLLECT ALL
ORDERS FOR
CUSTOMER

Figure 12.5 Hierarchical decomposition of the function VAL-IDATE CUSTOMER. Figure 12.6 extends this diagram to show the data used.

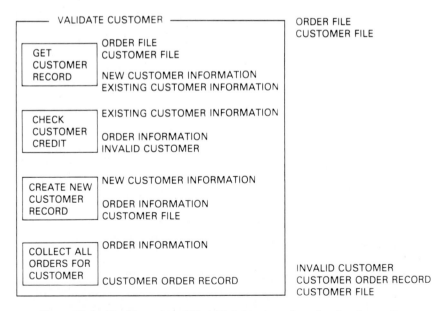

Figure 12.6 The hierarchy of Fig. 12.5 drawn to show the data inputs (top right corners) and outputs (bottom right corners).

from its internal blocks. We can check that no internal block uses data that do not originate somewhere and that no internal block produces data that do not go anywhere. Figure 12.7 uses arrows to show the passage of data among the functions.

Now let us work our way one step further up the tree and show ORDER SERVICING, or at least the part of it represented by the three rightmost brackets of Fig. 12.4. Figure 12.8 shows this.

By checking all the transfers of data, we can be much more thorough than with simple functional decomposition. The chart, however, has become complex, and we have decomposed only one of the four blocks in ORDER SERVICING and within that only one of the five blocks in ORDER ACCEPTANCE. If we decomposed all of the blocks to the same level, the chart would be about twenty times as large and complex. Getting it correct would strain the patience of a monk.

However, failing to get it correct is expensive. It means that our specifications are wrong. It is enormously cheaper to find errors at the specification stage than after the programmers have written code.

Full expansion and checking of the blocks in Fig. 12.8 needs a computer. The analysts should be able to build the diagram a step at a time, usually working from the highest level. They are likely to start with species I functional

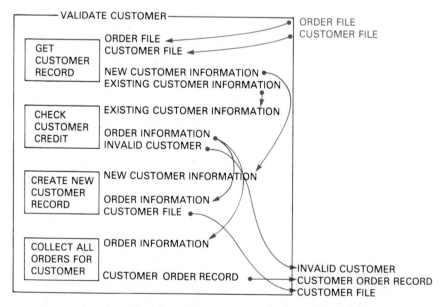

Figure 12.7   The passage of data among the functions in Fig. 12.6. (The left-hand part of this diagram is Fig. 12.5.)

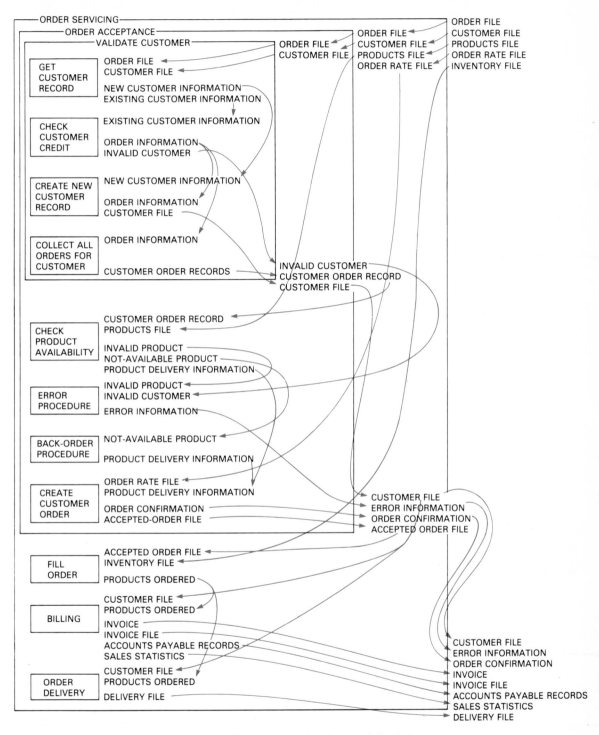

Figure 12.8 An expansion of Fig. 12.7 showing the functions at the three right-hand levels of Fig. 12.4.

decomposition and then add the data. At the lower levels they will discover more details about the data required, and these details need to be reflected upward to the top. The computer can check the consistency and completeness of all the data transfers.

Functional Decomposition and Data Flow Diagrams

Figure 12.8 shows the same information as that in the data flow diagrams of Chapter 11. A functional decomposition chart can be converted into a data flow diagram, and vice versa.

For some situations it is easier to think of system activities in terms of data flow. For others it is easier to think in terms of functions and their decomposition. When carried through to the level needed for program design, both of these become detailed, like Fig. 12.8 with 20 times as many blocks. Both therefore need computerized representation and checking. A computer graphics tool that can relate the two and help the analysts fill in the detail without inconsistencies is needed.

Data flow diagrams tend to be more useful for showing the flow of documents in an organization or the way one business event triggers other events. They give a pictorial representation of the movement of tangible data, which the end users can relate to and be trained to draw and check. As systems analysis moves to the more detailed task of program design, hierarchical structures are more useful. Hierarchical structures will be converted into program code, as we will see later.

SPECIES III FUNCTIONAL DECOMPOSITION

With functional decomposition as normally practiced, we can decompose a function in any way that comes into our head. The third and most rigorous species of functional decomposition allows us to decompose only in certain ways, defined with mathematically precise axioms.

In Fig. 12.7, for example, we have more than one type of decomposition. The first block of VALIDATE CUSTOMER is GET CUSTOMER RECORD. This is always performed. The second and third blocks are CHECK CUSTOMER CREDIT and CREATE NEW CUSTOMER. Only *one* of these two is performed. Which one depends on whether the order is from a new customer or an existing customer.

The originators of the HOS methodology (Chapter 38) concluded that all functional decomposition can be divided into *binary* decompositions. The parent function provides the input data for its binary children and receives the output. Three types of binary decomposition are needed:

Type I. The first function is executed. Its results pass to the second function, which is then executed.

Type II. *Either* the first function *or* the second function is executed.

Type III. Both functions are executed independently.

Using these three binary primitives they discovered that they could keep decomposing until program code could be generated automatically. Each binary decomposition follows rigorous mathematical axioms that enforce correctness so that the entire resulting structure can be proved to be internally correct. We thus have automatic generation of provably correct code [1].

The problem with this is that binary decompositions are so small that the overall design task is tedious. It is like trying to build a complex structure out of small Lego pieces. The solution is to design more powerful forms of decomposition that are themselves built from the primitives and are hence completely checkable. This is rather like building macroinstructions in programming.

Figure 12.9 shows an example of HOS functional decomposition. This is explained in Chapter 38. In Fig. 12.9, the inputs to each block are on its right and the outputs are on its left.

This more precise form of decomposition has several effects. First, it is built in a computer-assisted fashion, step by step, with the computer checking for syntax errors and periodically analyzing the chart to detect any errors in decomposition or use of data. Appropriately skilled analysts can create complex specifications much more quickly than drawing by hand.

Second, the specification that results is free of internal errors, ambiguities, omissions, and inconsistencies.

Third, the decomposition can be continued to a level of detail from which bug-free code is generated automatically.

Fourth, when changes have to be made, they are made on the terminal screen, and all of the consequential changes that should result from any modification are indicated. The program can then be regenerated. In other words, maintenance is easier and faster.

Fifth, the technique seems alien and sometimes difficult to many traditional analysts and programmers. Bright analysts and new graduates often learn it very quickly, but much retraining is needed if a large DP team is to adopt it.

COMMENTARY   When the systems analysis profession has matured beyond its present stage, we expect that most functional decomposition will progress to species II, with data usage being represented and analyzed with computerized tools. Much will progress to species III, with axiomatic control of the decomposition. Species III decomposition will probably progress far beyond that of HOS today, with a powerful library of tools and predesigned control structures. One of the important goals of CASE tools is to check design consistency in every way possible.

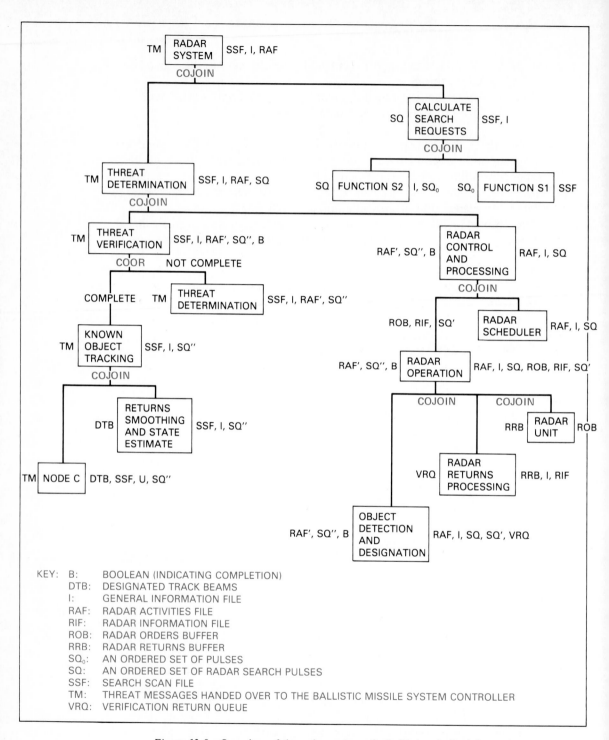

Figure 12.9 Overview of the radar system of a ballistic missile defense system, done with species III functional decomposition, which gives axiomatic checking of the decomposition [2, 3].

REFERENCES

1. J. Martin, *System Design from Provably Correct Constructs*. Englewood Cliffs, NJ: Prentice-Hall, Inc., 1985.

2. W. R. Hackler and A. Samarov, *An AXES Specification of a Radar Scheduler*, Technical Report No. 23. Cambridge, MA: Higher Order Software, Inc., 1979.

3. R. Hackler, "An AXES specification of a Radar Scheduler," *Proceedings, Fourteenth Hawaii International Conference on System Sciences*, Honolulu, vol. 1, 1981.

13 STRUCTURE CHARTS

Structure charts are a form of functional decomposition. Along with data flow diagrams they constitute a commonly used structured design methodology [1].

The basic building block of a program is a module. Structured programs are organized as a hierarchy of modules. The *structure chart* is a tree or hierarchical diagram that defines the overall architecture of a program by showing the program modules and their interrelationships.

Figure 13.1 shows the structure chart for a subscription system. The purpose of the subscription system is to process subscription transactions against a subscription master file. There are three types of transactions: new subscriptions, renewals, and cancellations. Each transaction is first validated and then processed against the master file. For new subscriptions, a customer record is built, and a bill is generated for the balance due. For renewals, the expiration date is updated, and a bill is generated for the balance due. For cancellations, the record is flagged for deletion, and a refund is issued.

The program is represented as a set of hierarchically ordered modules. Modules performing high-level program tasks are placed at the upper levels of the hierarchy, while modules performing low-level, detailed tasks appear at lower levels. Looking down the hierarchy, the modules at each successive level contain tasks that further define tasks performed at the preceding level. For example, the task GET VALID SUB ITEM is composed of two subtasks, READ SUB ITEM and VALIDATE SUB ITEM.

The basic building blocks of structure charts are rectangular boxes and arrows connecting them. Although the smallest possible structure chart contains

181

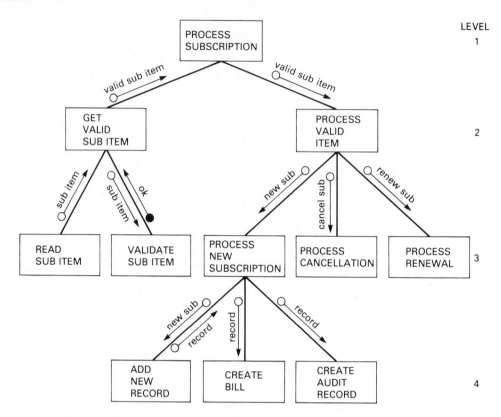

Figure 13.1 The structure chart defines the overall architecture of a program by showing the basic procedural components and their interrelationships. The arrows with an open circle show data passing between the process blocks. The arrow with a filled circle shows control information passing between the process blocks.

only one box, most structure charts contain many boxes and connecting arrows.

Each rectangular box in the structure chart represents a module. Logically, a module is one problem-related task that the program performs, such as ADD NEW RECORD or CREATE BILL. Physically, a module is implemented as a sequence of programming instructions bounded by an entry point and an exit point. The module name is written inside the box:

```
CANCEL
SUBSCRIPTION
```

A descriptive name should be chosen to explain the task the module performs. Other than the module name, the structure chart gives *no* information about the internals of the module.

CONTROL RELATIONSHIPS

Modules are interrelated by a control structure. The structure chart shows the interrelationships by arranging modules in levels and connecting the levels by arrows.

An arrow drawn between two modules at successive levels means that at execution time, program control is passed from one module to the second in the direction of the arrow. We say that the first module *invokes* or *calls* the second module. For example, in Fig. 13.1, the module PROCESS NEW SUBSCRIPTION invokes the module CREATE BILL. After the module CREATE BILL finishes executing, control is returned to PROCESS NEW SUBSCRIPTION. However, we cannot tell by looking at the structure chart whether the module PROCESS NEW SUBSCRIPTION invokes CREATE BILL once or many times or what conditions, if any, are tested to make this invocation decision.

It is possible for one module to invoke several modules (or to have several sons). In the example in the next section, module A has two sons: B and C. Since the structure chart does not show sequence, we do not know in what order a module invokes its sons. A module that has no sons is called a *leaf*.

The rules governing the program control structure are listed in Box 13.1.

COMMON MODULES

It is possible for more than one module to transfer control to the same module. As shown below, module B and module C both invoke module E:

BOX 13.1   Control rules for a structure chart

- There is one and only one module at the top (level 1) of the structure chart. This is where control originates. This module is called the *root*.

- From the root, control is passed down the structure chart level by level to the other modules. Control is always passed back to the invoking module. Therefore, when the program finishes executing, control returns to the root.

- There is at most one control relationship between any two modules in the structure chart. This means that if module A invokes module B, module B *cannot* also invoke module A. A module cannot invoke itself. (The reason for this restriction is that the principle of abstraction as implemented by levels of abstraction does not allow lower-level modules to be aware of the existence of upper-level modules.)

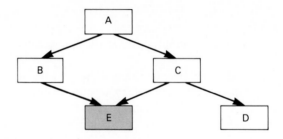

In this case module E is called a *common module*.

This diagram is no longer a tree structure. It is drawn in this way to avoid having to show module E twice.

A common module could itself have a family, as does CALCULATE DE-DUCTIONS in Fig. 13.2.

LIBRARY MODULES   In some cases, the program developer may use pre-defined library modules. This is indicated in the structure chart by a rectangular box with double vertical lines:

Normally, a library module will appear as a leaf on the structure chart.

DATA TRANSFER   When control is transferred between two modules, data are usually transferred as well. Data may be transferred in either direction between the modules. Direction is shown by drawing a small arrow. Data names are written beside the arrow to identify what data are passed.

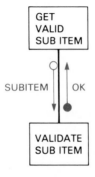

Two basic types of information can be communicated between modules: data and control information [1]. Data are information used in the problem, such as subscription item. This type of information is identified by an arrow with an open circle as its tail, ○—►. It is called a *data couple*. Control information is used by the program to direct execution flow, such as an error flag or end-of-file switch. It is identified by a filled-in circle at its tail, ●—►. It is called a *control couple,* or sometimes a *flag.*

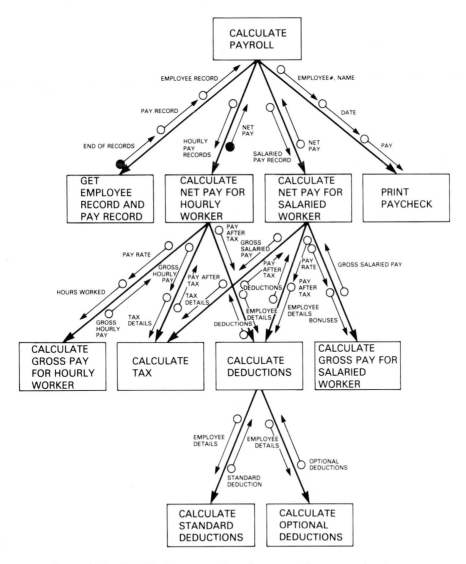

Figure 13.2   Simplified structure chart for a payroll program showing two common modules.

Figures 13.1 and 13.2 show data couples and control couples passing between modules.

Structure charts show small numbers of data types passing. They are not used to show large numbers, as with the outer block of Fig. 12.8. The little arrows attached to vertical links would be inappropriate for this. Even with small numbers, the chart becomes cluttered, as in Fig. 13.2. If there are more than two or three data items passing from one block to another, this usually indicates that the structure chart should be further decomposed.

Although structure charts do show data passing between blocks, we would not class them as species II functional decomposition as described in Chapter 12 because the data inputs and outputs of an integrated hierarchy are not automatically analyzed.

SEQUENCE, SELECTION, AND ITERATION

Three important control structures in program design are sequence, selection, and iteration.

Sequence refers to the order in which blocks are executed. *Selection* refers to the use of conditions to control whether or not a module is executed or which of several blocks are executed. *Iteration* refers to the control of loops.

Structure charts do not show these. They are regarded as detailed internals of the blocks that are shown by a different technique, usually pseudocode (Chapter 18).

It might be thought that the sequence of executing the modules could be shown by the left-to-right sequence of the blocks. Common modules can make this difficult. Yourdon and Constantine stress that the module drawing is independent of sequence of execution [1].

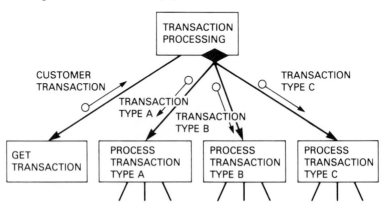

Figure 13.3 The black diamond in the top block is called a *transaction center*. Separate modules are used for processing each type of transaction. The transaction center determines the type of a transaction and transfers control to the appropriate module.

STRADIS/DRAW

MCAUTO/IST

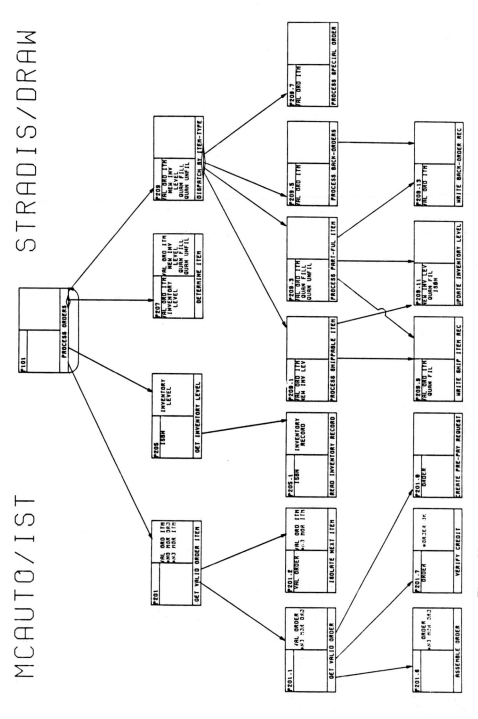

Figure 13.4 Data-structure diagram drawn with MCAUTO's STRADIS/DRAW CASE tool. Data transfers are shown as in Fig. 13.5.

187

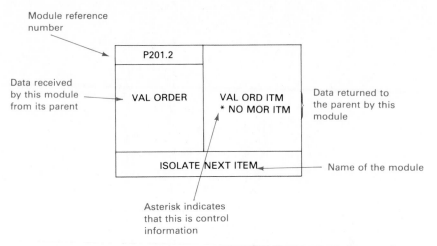

Figure 13.5   With MCAUTO's STRADIS/DRAW (Fig. 13.4), data transfers are placed inside the rectangle instead of being indicated with arrows as in Fig. 13.2.

TRANSACTION
CENTER

Where several types of transactions are processed, a separate program module may be used for each transaction type. The allocation of control to these separate modules may be shown on a structure chart by a black diamond, as shown on Fig. 13.3. This black diamond could have been used in the block labeled DISPATCH in Fig. 13.1 for splitting the control among NEW SUBSCRIPTION, CANCEL SUBSCRIPTION, and RENEW SUBSCRIPTION.

COMPUTER
GRAPHICS

The STRADIS/DRAW software mentioned in Chapter 11 provides an interactive graphics tool for creating, editing, and maintaining structure charts. Figure 13.4 shows a version of a structure chart created with this tool [2].

Because the arrows indicating data transfers become cluttered on structure charts like Fig. 13.2, STRADIS/DRAW puts the data transfers inside the rectangles, as shown in Fig. 13.5. Control flags are marked with an asterisk, as is NO MOR ITM in Fig. 13.5. Even with this approach the data transfers can be cluttered and their names overabbreviated.

EXCELERATOR, from InTech [3], enables structure charts and other types of diagrams to be drawn on the screen of a personal computer and linked to a dictionary. Figure 13.6 shows a structure chart drawn with EXCELERATOR.

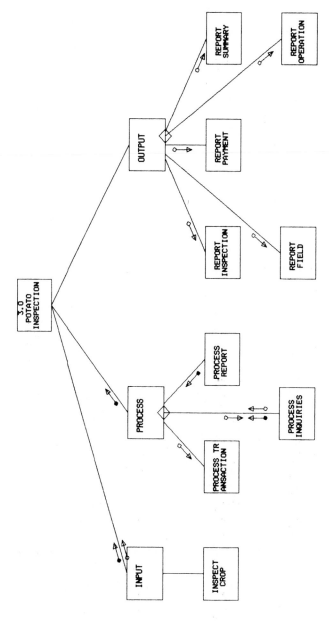

Figure 13.6 A structure chart drawn on the screen of a personal computer with EXCELERA-TOR, a CASE tool from InTech [3]. The items on the diagram are in the EXCELERATOR dictionary. The designer can record and display details of each item.

REFERENCES

1. E. Yourdon and L. Constantine, *Structured Design*. New York: Yourdon Press, 1978, pp. 42–50.

2. *STRADIS/DRAW Reference Manual*. St. Louis: MCAUTO, McDonnell Douglas Automation Company.

3. *EXCELERATOR Reference Manual*. InTech, 5 Cambridge Center, Cambridge, MA 02142.

14 HIPO DIAGRAMS

INTRODUCTION   HIPO stands for *Hierarchical Input, Process Output*.
A *HIPO diagram* is a diagramming technique that uses a set of diagrams to show the input, output, and functions of a system or program. It can give a general or detailed view of a system (or program). HIPO diagrams are inadequate in various ways and have not formed a basis for CASE tools.

Like a structure chart, HIPO shows *what* the system does, rather than *how*. There are three basic kinds of HIPO diagrams:

- Visual table of contents (see Fig. 14.1)
- Overview diagrams (see Fig. 14.2)
- Detail diagrams (see Fig. 14.3)

The *visual table of contents* looks very similar to a structure chart. An example of a visual table of contents for the subscription system is shown in Fig. 14.1. The purpose of this system is to process three types of subscription transactions: new subscriptions, renewals, and cancellations.

Each box in the visual table of contents can represent a system, subsystem, program, or program module. Its purpose is to show the overall functional components and to refer to overview and detail HIPO diagrams. Notice, however, that it does *not* show the data flow between functional components or any control information. It does not show the arrows with open or filled circles that appear on structure charts like that in Fig. 13.1. Also, it does not give any information about the data components of the system (or program).

Overview and *detail* HIPO diagrams give more information on each functional component shown in the visual table of contents. The distinction between them is the amount of detail they show. *Overview diagrams* describe the input, process, and output of the major functional components. According to IBM,

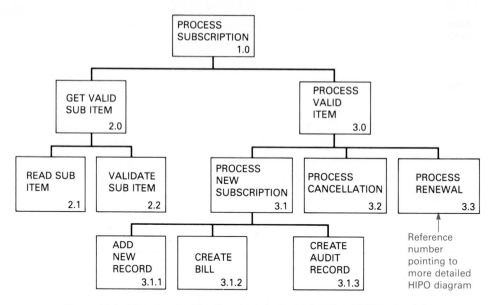

Figure 14.1   The visual table of contents is the highest-level HIPO diagram. It shows the overall functional components of a system or program. It does not give any control information, nor does it describe any data components, as does the equivalent structure chart of Fig. 13.1.

their purpose is to provide "general knowledge of a particular function" [1]. On the other hand, *detail diagrams* provide "all the information necessary to understand the function specified in the next higher [level] diagram" [1]. Overview diagrams are typically used to describe top-level components in the visual table of contents, whereas detail diagrams are used to describe the low-level components. Figure 14.2 is the overview HIPO diagram for the PROCESS SUBSCRIPTION function in the subscription system. Figure 14.3 is the detail diagram for the VALIDATE NEW SUB function in the subscription system.

DIAGRAM COMPONENTS

Overview and detail HIPO diagrams look very much alike. They both consist of three parts: an input box, a process box, and an output box.

In a HIPO diagram, the left-hand box is the *input* portion of the diagram. It shows the input data items, which may be a file, a table, an array, or an individual program variable. Flowchart device symbols are used in overview diagrams to indicate the type of physical device, when it is known. For example, Fig. 14.2 shows that subscription transactions, which are one input to PROCESS SUBSCRIPTION, reside on a tape file and that the subscription master file, which is an output of PROCESS SUBSCRIPTION, is a disk file.

Subscription System
Diagram 1.0 Subscription

Reference number from Table of Contents HIPO diagram

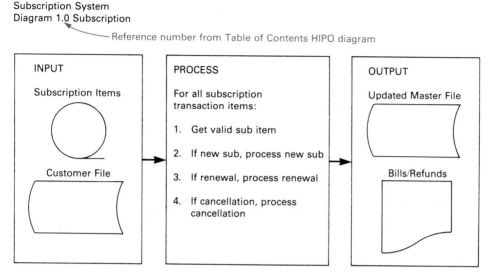

Figure 14.2   An overview HIPO diagram gives general information about the inputs, process steps, and outputs of one particular functional component in a system (or program).

The center box is the *process* portion of the diagram. It contains a list of the process steps to be performed. These steps closely correspond to the subfunctions that were identified in the visual table of contents. For example, in Fig. 14.2, PROCESS SUBSCRIPTION has four process steps, each of which corresponds to the four subfunctions shown in Fig. 14.1. Control information is included to indicate the logic that governs the execution of the process steps. Figure 14.2 shows that all four process steps are performed for each transaction item on the subscription transaction tape.

The right-hand box is the *output* part of the diagram. It shows the output items produced by the process steps. Like an input data item, an output data item may be a file, a table, or a variable.

The three parts of the diagram are connected by arrows to show which input and/or output data items are associated with each process step. For example, in Fig. 14.3, NEW-TERMS and VALID TERMS TABLE are input to process step 3, VALIDATE TERMS. The valid/invalid indicators are the output of process steps 2 and 3.

Whereas the visual table of contents is similar to a structure chart, overview and detail HIPO diagrams are similar to a data flow diagram. Like a data flow diagram, they show the flow of data through processes. However, HIPO diagrams are more difficult to draw than data flow diagrams. HIPO diagrams often require more verbiage and symbols to give the same information as a comparable data flow diagram.

Subscription System
Diagram 2.2.2 Validate New Sub

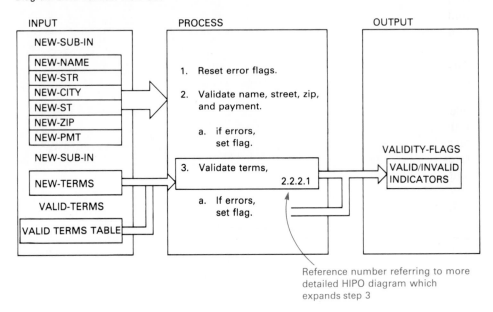

Figure 14.3 A detail HIPO diagram provides the information necessary to understand the inputs, processing steps, and outputs for a functional component. It represents the program design and can be easily transformed into program code.

ANALYSIS AND DESIGN TOOLS

HIPO diagrams are used as both analysis and design tools. At the analysis stage, they are used by the systems analyst to define the system (or program) components in a general way. This general definition then becomes the starting point for system (or program) design. During the design stage, the designer draws more detailed HIPO diagrams to describe each procedural component.

HIPO diagrams are hierarchical and can be used to describe the top-down programming process. During the top-down design process, the process steps in higher-level HIPO diagrams are expanded into a set of lower-level HIPO diagrams. When the design process is finished, there will be one HIPO diagram for each functional component in the program. These HIPO diagrams are then translated into executable code during the implementation step. After implementation, they are retained as system documentation.

COMMENTARY

HIPO diagrams represent another type of procedure design tool. Although HIPO diagrams are a design aid, HIPO diagramming by itself is not a complete design methodology. It does not include any guidelines, strategies, or procedures to guide the analyst in building a functional specification or the designer in building a system or program design.

For smaller programs, HIPO diagrams may be a sufficient tool for program design. However, they quickly become cluttered and difficult to read when there are several process steps or input/output data items to show.

At the general level, a structure chart is usually preferred over a visual table of contents. Although both diagrams provide a hierarchical representation of the basic functional components, only the structure chart shows how the components are interrelated via data. At the detailed level, pseudocode is often preferred over HIPO diagrams because it provides more information in a more compact form, although a HIPO diagram more clearly shows input and output. Showing input and output and how they relate to procedural steps is a strength of HIPO diagrams that some other structured techniques do not have.

HIPO diagrams have no symbols for representing detailed program structures such as conditions, case structures, and loops. Narrative description is used for this.

HIPO diagrams cannot represent data structures or the linkage to data models.

REFERENCE

1. *IBM HIPO: A Design Aid and Documentation Technique* (GC20-185D). White Plains, NY: IBM Corp., 1974.

15 WARNIER-ORR DIAGRAMS

INTRODUCTION   Warnier-Orr diagrams are an alternative to HIPO diagrams or structure charts [1]. They are named after their two principal proponents, Jean-Dominique Warnier and Ken Orr. Like HIPO diagrams and structure charts, they aid the design of well-structured programs. They have certain advantages over these other structured methods. They are easy to learn and to use because they are composed of only four basic diagramming techniques.

A Warnier-Orr diagram represents graphically the hierarchical structure of a program, a system, or a data structure. It draws it horizontally across the page with brackets instead of down the page with blocks, as shown in Fig. 15.1.

Each bracket in the diagram represents a functional breakdown of the item at the head of the bracket. This is similar to a structure chart or a visual-table-of-contents HIPO diagram. In addition to showing hierarchical structure, a Warnier-Orr diagram also shows flow of control through the structure. This is similar to an overview or detail HIPO diagram.

REPRESENTATION   Warnier-Orr diagrams can represent hierarchical data
OF DATA   structures or reports as well as program structures.

Figure 15.2 is an example of a Warnier-Orr diagram of an employee file. The diagram is read from left to right and from top to bottom. The brackets enclose logically related items and separate each hierarchical level. The items are listed vertically. A meaningful name is given to each item. The number of times an item occurs is written in parentheses below its name. For example, in Fig. 15.2, EMPLOYEE FILE occurs once. Within the file body, EMPLOYEE RECORD occurs from 1 to E times as indicated by $(1,E)$.

If an item had the notation $(0,1)$ under it, that would mean that it was

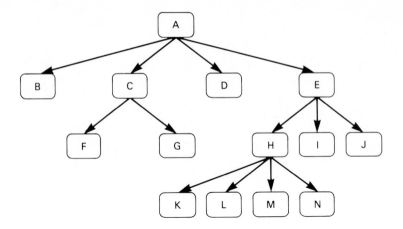

WARNIER–ORR CHART

Figure 15.1 A structure chart or HIPO diagram draws a hierarchical structure down the page with blocks; a Warnier-Orr chart draws it across the page with brackets.

either present or not. Warnier refers to this as an *alternation structure*. The alternation structure can be used with an OR or EXCLUSIVE OR structure. If two vertical items are separated by a +, it means that one or the other or both items are included (i.e., an OR structure). If two items are separated by a ⊕, it means that one or the other but *not* both items are included (i.e., EXCLUSIVE OR). For example, in the employee file shown in Fig. 15.2, an employee is either salaried or hourly but not both.

Figure 15.3 is a sales contract, and Fig. 15.4 is the Warnier-Orr diagram showing the data items included in this contract. Notice that all the contract information is required and that the order information may be repeated. There may be 1 to *N* sets of order information in one sales contract.

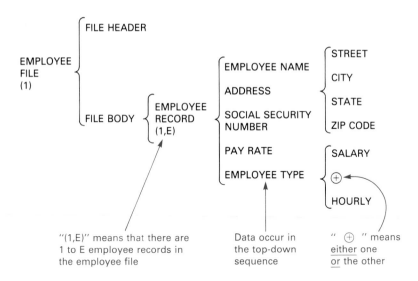

Figure 15.2 A Warnier-Orr representation of an employee file as a hierarchical structure. The parentheses under an item indicate the number of times it is repeated. For example, there is 1 employee file; there are 1 to *E* employee records within the file body. The ⊕ between SALARY and HOURLY means *either* SALARY *or* HOURLY, but not both (mutually exclusive selection). A + would mean either one or the other or both (nonexclusive selection).

REPRESENTATION OF PROGRAM STRUCTURE

Figure 15.5 shows the same type of diagram representing a program structure. It shows the same program structure as the structure chart in Fig. 13.1.

A Warnier-Orr diagram is more powerful than a structure chart because it can show the basic program control constructs: sequence, selection, and repetition.

When representing a program structure, each level in a Warnier-Orr diagram has three parts: BEGIN, process steps, and END. Each level is enclosed in vertical brackets, and the hierarchical structure is read from left to right. To indicate sequence in a Warnier-Orr diagram, the processing steps are included at the same hierarchical level and are written in a vertical column one after another. A structure chart such as Fig. 13.1 does not show sequence.

The number of times a function is executed is indicated by a number or variable enclosed in parentheses below the name of the function. For example, in Fig. 15.5, the function PROCESS SUBSCRIPTION is executed S times where $S \geq 1$. The (1,S) notation indicates a DO UNTIL structure. The termination condition for the structure is defined in the footnote ?1. In Warnier-Orr

THE HOUSE OF MUSIC INC.

A Collins Corporation

Main Office

108 Old Street, White Cliffs, IL 67309

063 259 0003

SALES CONTRACT

Contract No. 7094

SOLD BY	DATE	
Mike	6/10/83	

Name ___ Herbert H. Matlock ___

Address ___ 1901 Keel Road ___

City ___ Ramsbottom, Illinois ___ Zip ___ 64736 ___

Phone ___ 063 259 3730 ___ Customer # ___ 18306 ___

REMARKS:

10 yrs. Parts & Labor on the Piano

1 yr. Parts & Labor on Pianocorder

Delivery Address:

DESCRIPTION	PRICE	DISCOUNT	AMOUNT
New Samick 5'2" Grand Piano model G-1A			
# 820991 with Marantz P-101 # 11359			9500.00
		TOTAL AMOUNT	9500.00
		TRADE IN ALLOWANCE	2300.00
		SALES TAX	
		DEPOSIT	1000.00
		FINAL BALANCE	6200.00

PLEASE NOTE: All sales pending approval by management and verification of trade-in description.

If this contract is breached by the BUYER, the SELLER may take appropriate legal action, or, at its option, retain the deposit as liquidated damages.

Buyer's Signature _____

Figure 15.3   A sales contract.

diagrams, no control logic is included in the body of the diagram; instead, it is included in footnotes below the diagram.

To indicate the selection construct, (0,1) is written below the function name. In Fig. 15.5, the functions PROCESS NEW SUB, PROCESS RE-NEWAL, and PROCESS CANCEL are each selectively performed. The inclusive or exclusive or, + or $\oplus$, is used in conjunction with (0,1) to indicate whether or not at most one alternative can be selected. Note that the $\oplus$ symbols separating PROCESS NEW SUB, PROCESS RENEWAL, and PROCESS CANCEL are used to indicate that a subscription can be of only one type.

However, the diagram body does *not* contain any information about what condition is tested to determine which function is selected. The footnotes ?2, ?3, and ?4 indicate the conditions that are tested to determine which alternative to execute. This is a weakness of the Warnier-Orr diagram. Incorporating the control logic into the body of the diagram would greatly improve its readability.

Box 15.1 summarizes the four basic constructs used to build Warnier-Orr diagrams.

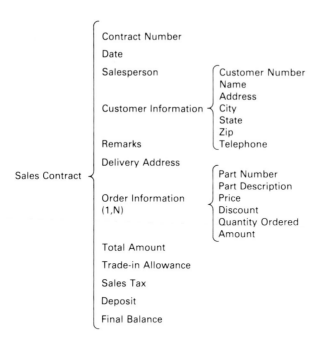

Figure 15.4 The sales contract shown in Fig. 15.3 is represented here by a Warnier-Orr diagram.

CRITIQUE OF WARNIER-ORR DIAGRAMS

Warnier-Orr diagrams have been used extensively to design new systems and to document existing systems. Transferring a Warnier-Orr diagram into structured program code is usually quite simple because of its BEGIN–END block structure format.

Studies have shown that data-structure documentation is more useful to overall program understanding than procedural documentation. Providing good data-structure documentation is a major benefit of Warnier-Orr diagrams.

Warnier-Orr diagrams differ from HIPO diagrams in that they can be used to show the structure of both procedural and data components. They are similar to HIPO diagrams in that they both can be used to describe a system or program at varying degrees of detail during the functional decomposition process. Also, they both offer the advantage of making a program design more visible and understandable as it evolves. At a high level, HIPO diagrams and Warnier-Orr diagrams can give a clear representation of the structure of a system or program. However, when used at a low level, they both can become large and difficult to read.

BOX 15.1 Basic constructs of the Warnier–Orr diagram

Construct	Description	Data Example	Function Example
HIERARCHY name	A bracket is used to enclose the member of a set. Brackets are nested to show hierarchical levels. A bracket is always given a name. Brackets may be nested to show functional decomposition.	Employee file {	Get valid sub item {
SEQUENCE name { item 1 item 2 . . . item n	The sequence construct is used to show the ordering of members in a set by listing them one below another inside a bracket.	Employee { Employee name Employee address Employee number Employee sex Employee salary	Process New Subscription { BEGIN Add new record Create bill Create audit record END Note that BEGIN and END are used to delimit the sequence of steps in a function.
ALTERNATION (also called SEQUENCE or CASE) x (0,1) ⊕ y (0,1) ⊕ z (0,1)	The alternation construct is used to show partitioning into two or more mutually exclusive alternatives. The (0,1) below the name indicates that x occurs once or not at all. The ⊕ is the mutually exclusive or notation separating alternatives. It means that x, y, or z occurs—but only one of the three.	Employee pay type { Hourly (0,1) ⊕ Salaried (0,1)	Process Valid Subscription { Begin Process New Subscription (0,1) + Process Renewal Subscription (0,1) + Process Cancellation (0,1) END

REPETITION

The repetition structure is used to show that something occurs repeatedly. There are three forms:

(1) The first structure shows that the structure named L occurs n times. n may be a variable or a constant value.

(2) The second structure is a DO UNTIL structure that shows that function U occurs 1 to n times.

(3) The third structure is a DO WHILE structure that shows that function W occurs 0 to n times. (Note that Warnier does *not* allow this form in his version of Warnier–Orr diagrams.)

Note: if U and W are data sets, then the notation means that the data set occurs 1 to n or 0 to n times.

L
(n)

U
$(1,n)$

W
$(0,n)$

Employee
$(1,E)$
{
Employee name
Employee address
Employee number
Employee type

Process
Subscription
$(1,S)$

{
BEGIN
Get valid sub item

Process valid item
END
}

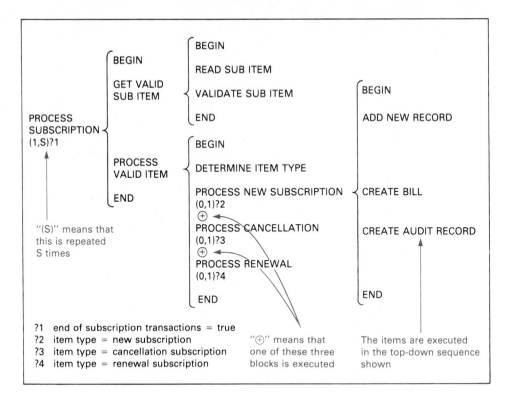

Figure 15.5 A Warnier-Orr diagram for the subscription system shown in the structure chart of Fig. 13.1, the HIPO diagram of Fig. 14.1, and the Michael Jackson diagram of Fig. 16.3.

Warnier-Orr diagrams are preferred over HIPO diagrams. They are a superior diagramming technique, with one exception. Detail HIPO diagrams relate data to processing steps. Warnier-Orr diagrams do not have this valuable capability.

Warnier-Orr diagrams are an alternative to combination approaches such as structure charts and pseudocode or structure charts and Nassi-Shneiderman charts. They offer the advantage of using one technique for both high-level and detail design and for both procedure and data-structure design. The major shortcoming is that Warnier-Orr diagrams do not show conditional logic as well as do other detail-level diagramming techniques. Another major problem is that they are not data-base-oriented. They can only represent hierarchical data structures.

In general, Warnier-Orr diagrams are better suited for designing and documenting small rather than large problems, especially output-oriented problems with simple file structures.

REFERENCE

1. J. D. Warnier, *Logical Construction of Systems*. New York: Van Nostrand Reinhold, 1981, pp. 11–38.

16 MICHAEL JACKSON DIAGRAMS

INTRODUCTION   Warnier-Orr diagrams have the advantage that they represent both data structures and program structures. Michael Jackson techniques [1,2] have the same advantage. In addition, both Warnier-Orr and Jackson emphasize that the program structures should be derived from the data structures. The input data and output data of a program are used to create the program structure.

TREE-STRUCTURE DIAGRAMS   Jackson views program structures and data structures as hierarchical structures. He uses a tree-structure diagram to represent both.

The tree-structure diagram looks very similar to the structure chart presented in Chapter 13 (see Fig. 13.1). Like the structure chart, it is composed of rectangular boxes arranged in levels and connected by lines. When used to show program structure, the tree-structure diagram and the structure chart give the same information, with the following exceptions:

- Only the structure chart shows the data passed between functional components.

- Only the tree-structure diagram shows the control constructs of sequence, selection, and iteration.

A tree-structure diagram is composed of four basic components: sequence, selection, iteration, and elementary.

Sequence

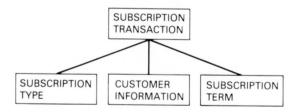

A *sequence component* is made up of a sequence of parts, occurring once each and in a specified order. The order of the parts is shown by reading the diagram from left to right. The example is read: a SUBSCRIPTION TRANS-ACTION is composed of a SUBSCRIPTION TYPE, followed by CUSTOMER INFORMATION, followed by SUBSCRIPTION TERM. Notice that the sequence structure is a two-level structure. The first level names the component; the second level lists its parts.

Selection

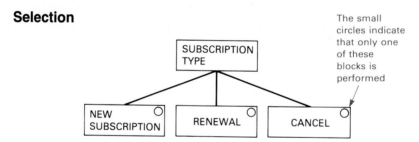

A *selection component* is made up of two or more parts, exactly one of which occurs for each occurrence of the selection component. In the example, a SUBSCRIPTION TYPE is either a NEW SUBSCRIPTION, a RENEWAL, or a CANCEL. The small circle in the upper right-hand corner indicates the parts of the selection component. Like the sequence component, the selection component is a two-level structure. The first level names the component; the second level lists the alternative parts.

Iteration

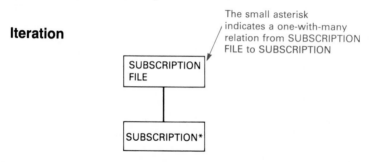

The *iteration component* consists of zero, one, or more occurrences of its parts. In the example, SUBSCRIPTION FILE consists of zero or more SUB-SCRIPTIONS. The asterisk in the upper right-hand corner is used to indicate iteration. Notice again that the iteration structure is a two-level structure.

Elementary

CHARGES

An *elementary* part is drawn in the tree-structure diagram as one rectangular box. It corresponds to the lowest-level data item or program part in the design.

DATA-STRUCTURE DIAGRAMS   Figure 16.1 shows a Jackson representation of data. This is the same employee file that is drawn with the Warnier-Orr technique in Fig. 15.2.

The diagram indicates that an EMPLOYEE FILE is composed of a FILE

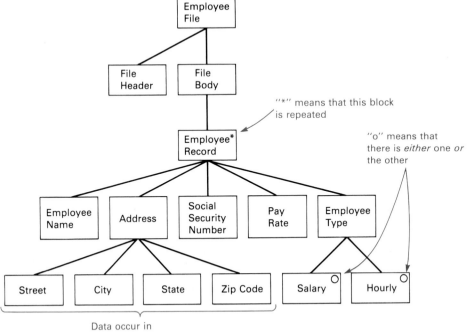

Figure 16.1   Jackson diagramming represents the data stream that enters or leaves a program by means of a hierarchy chart. This diagram uses the same data as the Warnier-Orr diagram of Fig. 15.2.

HEADER, then a FILE BODY. ADDRESS is composed of STREET, CITY, STATE, and ZIP CODE.

The asterisk in EMPLOYEE RECORD indicates that this occurs several times within FILE BODY. This is equivalent to the (1, *E*) indication on the Warnier-Orr chart. Warnier and Orr give somewhat more information than Jackson in that their chart can say *how many times* an item is repeated.

The ○ in the SALARY and HOURLY boxes indicates an either/or situation. EMPLOYEE TYPE in *either* SALARY *or* HOURLY. This is equivalent to the ⊕ in the Warnier-Orr chart of Fig. 15.2.

Like Warnier-Orr, then, a Jackson diagram shows sequence, selection, and iteration.

Figure 16.2 is a tree-structure diagram of the sales contract shown in Fig. 15.3. Figure 15.4 is the equivalent Warnier-Orr diagram.

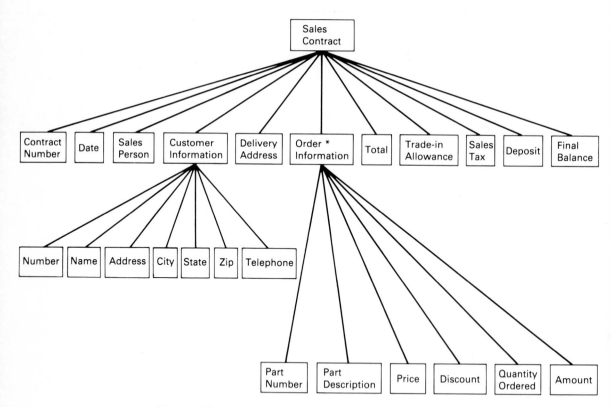

Figure 16.2   Jackson tree-structure diagram representing the sales contract shown in Fig. 15.3. It is equivalent to the Warnier-Orr diagram shown in Fig. 15.4.

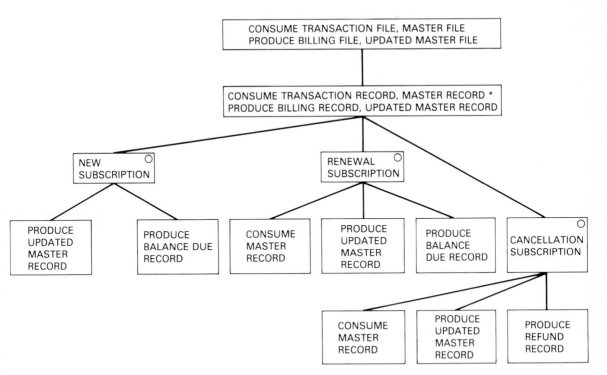

Figure 16.3 The Jackson tree-structure diagram is used to represent a program structure or a data stream. This is the equivalent program structure drawn in the HIPO diagram of Fig. 14.1, the Warnier-Orr chart of Fig. 15.5, and the structure chart of Fig. 13.1.

PROGRAM-STRUCTURE DIAGRAMS

Figure 16.3 shows the same type of diagram for representing the structure of programs.

Again, the ○ in the top right corner of the blocks means selection. Only one of the blocks NEW SUBSCRIPTION, RENEWAL SUBSCRIPTION, and CANCELLATION SUBSCRIPTION is executed. The diagram does not indicate how the choice is made. This is equivalent to the ⊕ in the Warnier-Orr diagrams.

Again, * means repetition. The CONSUME RECORDS PRODUCE RECORDS block is repeated (which means repetition of everything that comprises this block, which is drawn underneath it). The diagram does not indicate what controls the repetition. This is similar to the ''(1, *S*)'' in Warnier-Orr diagrams.

The Jackson representation of data and programs is similar to the Warnier-Orr representation but is drawn vertically instead of horizontally. Compare Figures 16.1 and 16.3 with Figures 15.2 and 15.5.

SYSTEM NETWORK Using Jackson methodology (Jackson System De-
DIAGRAM sign, JSD), one first designs the data structures a program uses, then the input and output data streams,
and finally, from these diagrams, the program structure.

First an overall diagram is drawn showing the data streams that enter and
leave the programs, as illustrated in Fig. 16.3. Rectangles are used for programs, and circles are used for data streams.

This diagram is similar to a data flow diagram, like that in Fig. 11.1,
except that the notation is different and the rules for drawing a system network
diagram are more formal than for a data flow diagram. A data flow diagram
uses circles, not rectangles, for processes and labels the arrows to show the data
streams. Jackson refers to the diagram in Fig. 16.4 as a *system network diagram*.

The rules for drawing a system network diagram are as follows:

- An arrow is used to connect a circle and a rectangle but is not used to connect
  two circles or two rectangles.

- Each circle may have at most one arrow pointing toward it and at most one
  arrow pointing away from it.

A data flow diagram could be used instead.

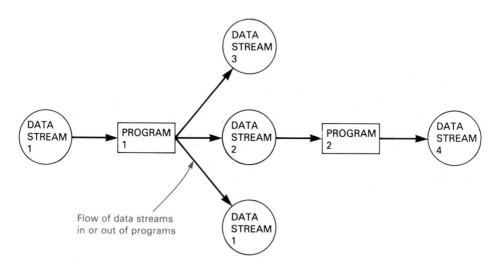

Figure 16.4 A Jackson overview diagram, called a system network diagram.
This gives similar information to that on a data flow diagram. Compare it with
Fig. 11.1.

FROM DATA
TO PROGRAMS

In Jackson's methodology, correct representations of input and output data streams lead to precise structures of programs. We can draw links between the input and output charts to show what data items correspond. Figure 16.5 illustrates this. It shows data structures that are the input and output of a warehouse report program. The connecting arrows show that there is a one-to-one correspondence between SORTED TRANSACTION FILE in the input and REPORT in the output and between ITEM GROUP in the input and REPORT LINE in the output. In other words, one SORTED TRANSACTION FILE produces one REPORT. Similarly, one ITEM GROUP produces one REPORT LINE.

From these data structures is created a corresponding program structure that encompasses all parts of each data structure. This is shown in Fig. 16.6. Where there are one-to-one correspondences between the input and output, the program block says CONSUME: [input] PRODUCE: [output]. This block in the level below may be broken into more detail, showing computational operations

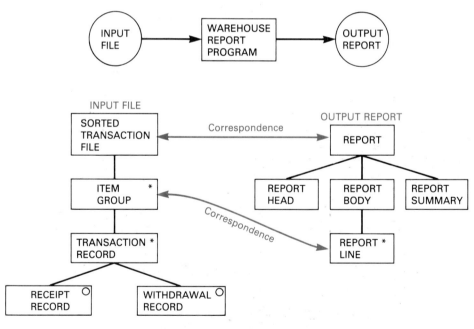

Figure 16.5 On the left is a Jackson drawing of an input file that is input to the Warehouse Report program. On the right is a drawing of the output report that is required from the program. The connecting arrows show one-to-one correspondence between input and output [3].

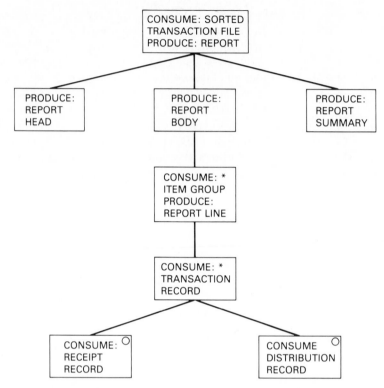

Figure 16.6 A program structure produced from the data structures using Jackson methodology.

or algorithms that link input and output. In Fig. 16.6 there is not a separate block for CONSUME and PRODUCE, as there would be on a structure chart. This is to emphasize that the data items consumed and produced correspond to one another.

Executable program operations can now be allocated to the program structure of Fig. 16.6, as shown in Fig. 16.7. Jackson methodology provides rules for checking both this allocation and the program structure.

Figure 16.8 shows Jackson's formally coded *structure text* derived from the structure of Fig. 16.7. The program operations written on Fig. 16.7 appear in the structure text of Fig. 16.8.

Figure 16.9 shows the structure text converted into a program.

CRITIQUE OF JACKSON DIAGRAMS

Jackson's mapping of input data structures to output data structures is an aid to clear thinking in program design. Major users of the methodology claim that

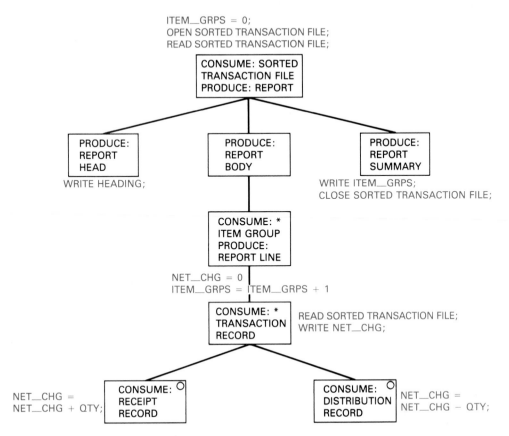

Figure 16.7 Executable program operations allocated to the program structure of Fig. 16.6 [3].

at least for straightforward data processing, it leads to code with fewer problems than other forms of structuring in common use.

It does not help with complex program logic and treats data-base systems as though they were essentially the same as file systems. The structure text of Fig. 16.8 is long-winded and not easy to read. It is longer than the program derived from it in Fig. 16.9 and much longer than the code needed with powerful fourth-generation languages.

Few CASE tools use Michael Jackson diagrams. In general, other techniques have proven more satisfactory as a basis for design automation and code generation. Other techniques are easier to use in joint application design (JAD) sessions with end users.

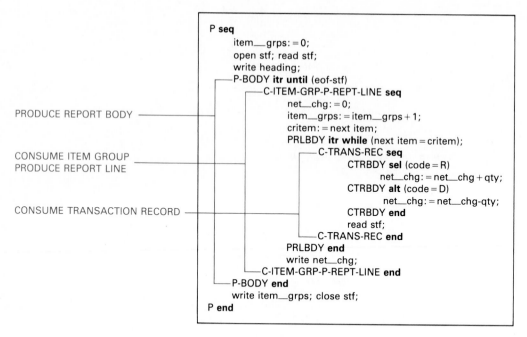

```
P seq
    item_grps: = 0;
    open stf; read stf;
    write heading;
    P-BODY itr until (eof-stf)
        C-ITEM-GRP-P-REPT-LINE seq
            net_chg: = 0;
            item_grps: = item_grps + 1;
            critem: = next item;
            PRLBDY itr while (next item = critem);
                C-TRANS-REC seq
                    CTRBDY sel (code = R)
                        net_chg: = net_chg + qty;
                    CTRBDY alt (code = D)
                        net_chg: = net_chg-qty;
                    CTRBDY end
                    read stf;
                C-TRANS-REC end
            PRLBDY end
            write net_chg;
        C-ITEM-GRP-P-REPT-LINE end
    P-BODY end
    write item_grps; close stf;
P end
```

PRODUCE REPORT BODY

CONSUME ITEM GROUP
PRODUCE REPORT LINE

CONSUME TRANSACTION RECORD

Figure 16.8 Jackson structure text derived from the program structure in Fig. 16.7 [3].

```
PB:        item_grps: = 0;
           open stf;
           read stf;
           write heading;
PBB:       do while (not eof-stf);
               net_chg: = 0;
               item_grps: = item_grps + 1;
               critem: = next item;
PRLBB:         do while (next item = critem);
CTRBB:             if (code = R) then
                       net_chg: = net_chg + qty;
                   else if (code = D) then
CTRBE:                 net_chg: = net_chg-qty;
                   read stf;
PRLBE:         end;
               write net_chg;
PBE:       end;
           write summary;
PE:        close stf;
```

Figure 16.9 Final data-structure design program.

216

REFERENCES

1. M. A. Jackson, *Principles of Program Design*. New York: Academic Press Inc., 1975.

2. M. A. Jackson, *System Development*. Englewood Cliffs, NJ: Prentice-Hall, Inc., 1983.

3. This example is borrowed from one of the wittiest and best articles we have read on structured techniques: G. D. Bergland, "A Guided Tour of Program Design Methodologies," *IEEE Computing* (October 1981), pp. 13–37.

17 FLOWCHARTS

OVERVIEW VERSUS DETAILED STRUCTURE
The diagrams we have used so far do not show the detailed structure of programs; they show the overview structure or architecture. This and the following four chapters discuss techniques for showing program detail.

Techniques for showing overview structure and techniques for showing detail can be subdivided as in the following table. Note that action diagrams and HOS charts cover both the overview structure and the detailed logic.

Techniques for Showing Overview Structure of Programs	Techniques for Showing Logic Detail of Programs (conditions, case structures, loop structures)
Functional decomposition Structure charts Data-flow diagrams Warnier-Orr diagrams Michael Jackson diagrams HIPO diagrams (table of contents) Action diagrams HOS charts	Warnier-Orr diagrams HIPO (Overview and detail) Action diagrams HOS charts Flowcharts Pseudocode or structured English Nassi-Shneiderman diagrams Decision trees Decision tables Finite-state diagrams

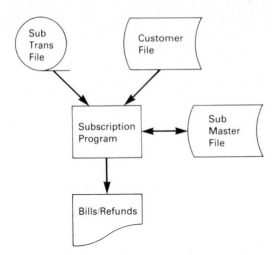

Figure 17.1 The system flowchart is primarily operations documentation used to show the computer operator how to run a system or program.

FLOWCHARTS

Flowcharts were one of the earliest methods used for diagramming. They were used by most analysts and programmers before the era of structured techniques. They are still often encountered today. Flowcharts can be replaced with smaller, cleaner, structured diagrams, and generally we do not recommend their use today. There are two types of flowcharts: system flowcharts and program flowcharts.

System Flowcharts

Figure 17.1 is an example of a system flowchart for the subscription system. It shows the basic input, output, and processing components for a system or program. Usually, input and output are represented as physical files. The processing components represent individual load units or job steps. The same information can be represented in an overview HIPO diagram (see Fig. 14.2).

The system flowchart serves as *operations* documentation, showing the computer operator how to execute the system.

Program Flowcharts

Figure 17.2 is an example of a program flowchart for the module VALIDATE SUBITEM in the subscription system. A program flowchart is primarily a coding tool. It shows in graphic form the sequence in which statements or process blocks will be executed and the control logic that governs their execution. Traditionally, program flowcharts have served two purposes. First, they have been used as a program design tool to plan out detailed and complicated program logic. Second, they have been used as program documentation.

Because program flowcharts provide a sequential rather than a hierarchical representation of a program, they cannot clearly show program structure and the

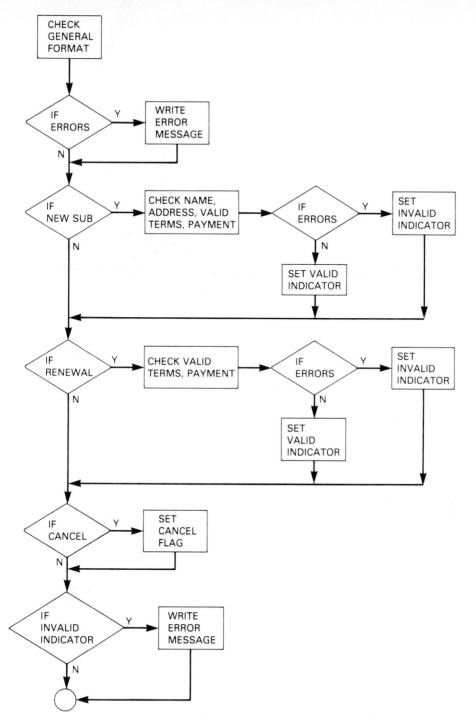

Figure 17.2 Program flowchart for the module VALIDATE SUBITEM in the subscription system. A program flowchart is used to show detailed program logic.

interrelationships between procedural components. The lines with arrows drawn across flowcharts tend to encourage the use of undesirable GO TO statements. Hierarchical diagramming techniques like those in subsequent chapters are preferred over flowcharts to describe program structures and form a basis for computer-aided program design.

Some programmers draw hierarchical diagrams like structure charts or Warnier-Orr diagrams but then draw a flowchart to represent the internal logic of a program module. It is desirable to have *one* diagramming technique that is easy to use both for the overall program structure and for the internal logic.

Some programmers prefer pseudocode to flowcharts. It is a more compact way to describe detailed program logic. A flowchart can easily be three or four times larger than a comparable pseudocode representation. Pseudocode has the disadvantage that it is not graphic.

The pseudocode version of the logic in the flowchart of Fig. 17.2 is shown in Fig. 18.1; a Nassi-Shneiderman version appears in Fig. 19.1, and an action diagram version can be found in Fig. 20.3.

In the case of unstructured programs, flowcharts offer the only graphic technique for describing program form and logic. Experiments have shown that flowcharts showing control flow information made debugging easier than when the source code was used by itself [1].

FLOWCHART SYMBOLS

Figures 17.3 and 17.4 show the flowchart symbols in conventional use.

CRITIQUE OF FLOWCHARTS

Generally, the flowchart is *not* considered a structured diagramming technique. Its utility is limited to small (less than 10,000 line) programs. For larger programs, flowcharts become very cumbersome to use. But even in the case of smaller programs, they normally should not be used as a program design tool. Flowcharts encourage a view of the problem that is likely to lead to a poorly structured program.

At a high level, flowcharts, as commonly drawn, tend to encourage a physical view of the system. The flowcharts for on-line and off-line systems that carry out the same logical functions, for example, are very different. An overall drawing of the functions is needed, leaving a designer free to decide later what should be on-line or off-line. Flowcharts thus tend to encourage a physical view of the system before the overall logical requirements are understood. Gane and Sarson refer to this as being ''prematurely physical'' [2].

Flowcharts can show detailed logic (in an unstructured fashion) but do not give a useful overview of the system functions in the way that data flow diagrams and functional decomposition charts do.

In particular, detailed flowcharts should be avoided as a form of program documentation. Experiments by Shneiderman, for example, could not demon-

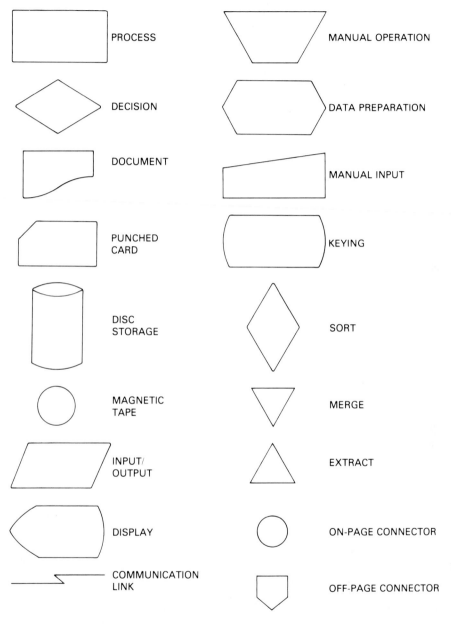

PROCESS	MANUAL OPERATION
DECISION	DATA PREPARATION
DOCUMENT	MANUAL INPUT
PUNCHED CARD	KEYING
DISC STORAGE	SORT
MAGNETIC TAPE	MERGE
INPUT/ OUTPUT	EXTRACT
DISPLAY	ON-PAGE CONNECTOR
COMMUNICATION LINK	OFF-PAGE CONNECTOR

Figure 17.3 Conventional flowchart symbols (from IBM flowcharting template).

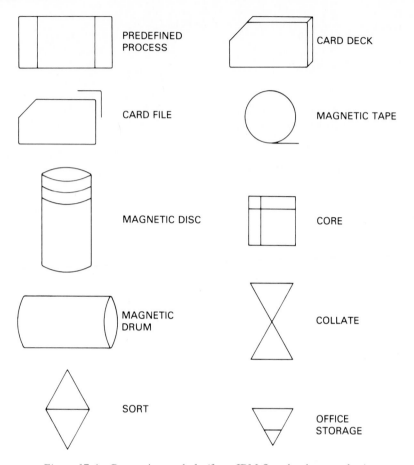

Figure 17.4 Composite symbols (from IBM flowcharting template).

strate that detailed flowcharts aided program understanding, debugging, or modification [3]. When a well-structured program listing is available, pseudocode or graphic documentation (e.g., a Nassi-Shneiderman chart) is more useful. A detailed flowchart is often larger than the program it represents, even though it does not contain declarations or data-structure information.

Useful documentation should be at a higher level than the actual code. Shneiderman comments that to be effective it should probably not be greater than one-tenth of the code length (although this usually does not apply with fourth-generation languages) [4]. Also, it should use problem-related rather than program-related terminology. Flowcharts fail to meet any of these criteria.

REFERENCES

1. J. Brooke and K. Duncan, "An Experimental Study of Flowcharts as an Aid to Identification of Procedural Faults," *Ergonomics,* 23, no. 4 (1980), 387–399.

2. C. Gane and T. Sarson, *Structured Systems Analysis: Tools and Techniques.* New York: IST Databooks, 1977.

3. B. Shneiderman, R. Mayer, D. McKay, and P. Heller, "Experimental Investigations of the Utility of Detailed Flowcharts in Programming," *CACM,* 20, no. 5 (1977), 373–381.

4. B. Shneiderman, "Control Flow and Data Structure Documentation," *CACM,* 25, no. 1 (January 1982), 55–63.

18 STRUCTURED ENGLISH AND PSEUDOCODE

INTRODUCTION   As we stated in Chapter 17, flowcharts do not represent structured design. At a high level they encourage being "prematurely physical." At a detailed level they encourage GO TOs and nonstructured code. They were boycotted by the structured enthusiasts with the comment that they do more harm than good.

At first there was no diagramming technique to replace flowchart representation of program detail. Flowcharts were replaced with structured English and pseudocode. A typical structured methodology draws tree charts like Figs. 13.1, 12.4, 15.3, or 16.2 in which each module is a black box whose contents are not shown on the chart. The contents are represented separately with structured English or pseudocode.

Even at the level of structured English, we believe a picture is worth a thousand words. Analysts and users make mistakes with structured English because it does not reveal the logic structure with the same clarity as a good diagram.

WHY SHOULD ENGLISH BE STRUCTURED?   Typical narrative describing specifications can contain all kinds of ambiguities. The language of lawyers is supposed to be highly professional and precise, but in fact it is common to find ambiguities in contracts. Lawyers achieve what precision they do have at the expense of lengthy language that is often misinterpreted because it is tedious:

> The service fee shall be computed by adding the revenue accruing from sales of tapes on a monthly basis to the monthly rental revenue for tapes and multiplying by twelve percent except in the case where the revenue accruing from the sales of tapes exceeds $US 5000 in any one calendar month in

which case the service fee shall be computed by adding the revenue accruing
from the sales of tapes on a monthly basis multiplied by fifteen percent to
the monthly rental revenue for tapes multiplied by twelve percent; notwith-
standing the above in the circumstance that the revenue accruing from sales
of tapes exceeds $US 8000 in any one calendar month the service fee shall
be computed by adding the revenue accruing from the sales of tapes on a
monthly basis multiplied by eighteen percent to the monthly rental revenue
for tapes multiplied by twelve percent.

In structured English we would say:

```
IF monthly-sales-revenue > 8000
        Fee = monthly-sales-revenue *·18 + monthly-rental-revenue *·12
IF monthly-sales-revenue > 5000
        Fee = monthly-sales-revenue *·15 + monthly-rental-revenue *·12
ELSE
        Fee = monthly-sales-revenue *·12 + monthly-rental-revenue *·12
```

This is easier to read and leads more directly to the program code.

The example just given is simple, and the lawyer's wording is precise.
Many DP situations are much more complex, with multiple nested conditions
and repetitions. There is a greater need for clarity of structure.

AMBIGUITIES

In casual English many ambiguities arise. Consider
the following clause:

All customers who have more than $5000 in their account and who have an
average monthly balance exceeding $500 or who have been customers for
more than five years . . .

There are two possible meanings to this:

1. "All customers (who have more than $5000 in their account AND an average
   monthly balance exceeding $500) OR who have been customers for more than five
   years . . ."
2. "All customers who have more than $5000 in their account AND (an average
   monthly balance exceeding $500 OR have been customers for more than five years)
   . . ."

The parentheses gives the clause more structure and remove the ambiguity.
In general, when a sentence contains both *and* and *or,* there may be ambiguity
that can be clarified with parentheses.

"If A and B and C" should become "If A and (B or C)" or "If (A and
B) or C."

There is another ambiguity in the clause: "average monthly balance." We need to know over how many months the average is taken.

STRUCTURED ENGLISH

Figures 18.1 and 18.2 show typical examples of structured English. They have several important properties:

- They are written in such a way that a user could understand them.
- They are hierarchically structured and use indentation to reveal this structure.
- They have a similar structure to the program code that will be used to implement them.
- Comments that will not be translated into program code are marked with asterisks.

```
VALIDATE SUB ITEM

        * VALIDATE GENERAL FORMAT.
         CHECK GENERAL FORMAT.
         IF ERRORS
                 WRITE ERROR-MESSAGE
         ENDIF.

        * VALIDATE SPECIAL FORMAT.
         IF NEW SUB
                 CHECK NAME AND ADDRESS
                 CHECK FOR NUMERIC ZIP
                 CHECK FOR VALID TERMS
                 CHECK FOR PAYMENT
                 IF ERROR
                         SET INVALID INDICATOR
                 ELSE
                         SET VALID INDICATOR
                 ENDIF
         ENDIF.
         IF RENEWAL
                 CHECK FOR VALID TERMS
                 CHECK FOR PAYMENT
                 IF ERROR
                         SET INVALID INDICATOR
                 ELSE
                         SET VALID INDICATOR
                 ENDIF
         ENDIF.
         IF CANCEL
                 SET CANCEL FLAG
         ENDIF.
         IF INVALID INDICATOR
                 WRITE ERROR MESSAGE
         ENDIF.
```

Figure 18.1 Structured English is a narrative notation used to define procedural logic. This example describes a structured version of the logic shown in the flowchart of Fig. 17.2.

```
ORDER ENTRY:
      OBTAIN CUSTOMER ORDER DETAILS
            IF (CUSTOMER IS VALID)
            THEN SET UP CUSTOMER DETAILS FOR ORDER HEADER RECORD
                  SET UP ORDER DELIVERY ADDRESS FOR ORDER HEADER RECORD
                  WRITE ORDER HEADER RECORD
            ELSE (CUSTOMER IS NOT VALID)
                  ISSUE MESSAGE "INVALID CUSTOMER"
                  EXIT ORDER ENTRY

      REPEAT UNTIL (ORDER IS COMPLETE)
            OBTAIN ORDER LINE ITEM DETAILS
            IF (ORDERED PRODUCT IS VALID)
                  AND IF (QUANTITY ORDERED IS AVAILABLE)
                        THEN SET UP PRODUCT DETAILS FOR LINE ITEM RECORD
                              SET UP QUANTITY ORDERED FOR LINE ITEM RECORD
                              DECREMENT PRODUCT QUANTITY ON HAND BY QUANTITY ORDERED
                              UPDATE PRODUCT RECORD
                              WRITE LINE ITEM RECORD
                        ELSE (QUANTITY ORDERED IS NOT AVAILABLE)
                              SET UP PRODUCT DETAILS FOR BACKORDER RECORD
                              SET UP QUANTITY BACKORDERED FOR BACKORDER RECORD
                              WRITE BACKORDER RECORD
                  ELSE (ORDERED PRODUCT IS NOT VALID)
                        ISSUE MESSAGE "INVALID PRODUCT"
      END REPEAT
      PREPARE PACKING SLIP
      WRITE PACKING SLIP
EXIT
```

Figure 18.2   Structured-English example of typical order-entry logic.

FOUR BASIC STRUCTURE TYPES

Structured English, like any other means of representing program structures, should be designed to show four basic constructs:

1. *Sequence:* Simple, top-to-bottom sequence is used.

2. *Condition:* If a certain condition applies, then a given action will be taken; if not, a different given action may be specified.

3. *Case:* One of several possible cases exists. The structure shows what action is taken for each possible case. A mutually exclusive set of conditions is a *case structure*.

4. *Repetition:* A given set of operations is repeated. The condition that terminates this repetition is shown. Repetition structures are of two types:

   - REPEAT WHILE: The operations are repeated while a specified condition applies. This condition is tested *before* the execution of the operations.

   - REPEAT UNTIL: The operations are repeated until a specified condition exists. This condition is tested *after* the execution of the operations.

Keywords should be used for these structures in structured English. These words should themselves be English so that they are easily understandable by end users. Typical words are as follows:

Sequence

No key word is necessary to show sequence. The sequence may be preceded by a title. The end of the sequence may be indicated with the word EXIT, possibly followed by the sequence title.

Condition

IF and ELSE are commonly used. Sometimes IF . . . THEN . . . is used. THEN is not really necessary; a new line shows what would follow the THEN.
To make clear where an IF clause ends, it is valuable to write ENDIF.

Case

IF . . . ELSEIF . . . ELSEIF . . . ELSE is sometimes used for mutually exclusive conditions. Sometimes the case construct has its own words, different from an IF; for example, SELECT . . . WHEN . . . WHEN . . . WHEN.
To make clear where a case clause ends, it is valuable to write ENDIF, ENDSELECT, and so on.

Repetition

DO WHILE, REPEAT WHILE, and LOOP WHILE are used for repeat-while repetition; DO UNTIL, REPEAT UNTIL, and LOOP UNTIL are used for re-peat-until repetition.
FOR ALL may be used to show that all items in a given set are to be processed; for example, FOR ALL CUSTOMER ORDER RECORDS. FOR EACH may be used to show that *each* item in a given set that meets certain criteria is processed. FOR EACH may be qualified with WHERE; for example, FOR EACH PART WHERE QUANTITY ON HAND > 5000.
To make clear which is the end of the block that is to be repeated, it is necessary to write END, ENDDO, ENDREPEAT, ENDLOOP, or ENDFOR.
In addition to the above keywords, certain keywords may be used to express logic; for example, AND, OR, GT (greater than), LT (less than), GE (greater than or equal to), and LE (less than or equal to).
An installation ought to select a given set of keywords for structured English and make these an installation standard.
In writing structured English, it is useful to capitalize the keywords, names of program blocks, and names of items in the data dictionary. Everything else should be lower-case.

KEYWORDS FROM FOURTH-GENERATION LANGUAGES

Every efficient data processing installation ought to have selected at least one fourth-generation language by now [1]. Many fourth-generation languages contain keywords like those just discussed. If such a language is intended to have major use in an installation, the keywords of the language may be selected as the installation standard for structured English. This has the advantage that the structured English is easier to translate into code, and it may help and encourage the end users to employ the language themselves [2].

BOX 18.1   Rules for writing structured English

- The structures are indented to show the logical hierarchy.
- Sequence, condition, case, and repetition structures are made clear.
- The sequence structure is a list of items in which each item is placed on a separate line. If the item requires more than one line, continuation lines are indented. The end of an item is punctuated with a semicolon (;) (see Fig. 18.3).
- Keywords are used to make the structures clear; for example, IF, THEN, ELSE, ENDIF, REPEAT WHILE, REPEAT UNTIL, ENDREPEAT, EXIT.
- Keywords are used for logic: AND, OR, GT (greater than), LT (less than), GE (greater than or equal to), LE (less than or equal to).
- The choice of keywords should be an installation standard.
- The keyword set may be selected to conform to a fourth-generation language. (They do, however, remain language-independent descriptions.)
- Blocks of instructions are grouped together and given a meaningful name that describes their function.
- Keywords and names that are in the data dictionary are capitalized; names of program blocks are capitalized; other words are not capitalized.
- Comments lines are delimited with a beginning asterisk and a terminating semicolon.
- Parentheses are used to avoid AND/OR and other ambiguities.
- End words such as ENDIF, ENDREPEAT, and EXIT are used to make the end of a structure clear.
- Within these constraints, the wording should be chosen to be as easy to understand by end users as possible.

This concept offends purists who believe that the structured English should be independent of the programming language. In practice, however, tailoring the specifications to a fourth-generation language *does* help, and it is easy for a coder to code them in a different language. All programming languages have condition, case, and repetition constructs that are broadly similar, so select the words of one such language as the set the installation uses.

RULES FOR STRUCTURED ENGLISH

Box 18.1 gives a set of rules to govern the use of structured English. Figure 18.3 presents a version of Fig. 18.2 that follows these rules.

```
ORDER_ENTRY:

    FOR ALL orders
        Obtain CUSTOMER record;
        IF CUSTOMER# is valid
            Set up customer details for ORDER_HEADER record;
            Set up order delivery address for ORDER_HEADER record;
            Write ORDER_HEADER record;
        ELSE
            Issue "invalid customer" message;
            QUIT ORDER_ENTRY;
        ENDIF;
        FOR ALL items ordered
            Obtain PRODUCT record;
            IF PRODUCT# is valid
                IF quantity ordered is available
                    Set up product details for LINE_ITEM record;
                    Set up quantity ordered for LINE_ITEM record;
                    Decrease product quantity on-hand by
                        quantity ordered;
                    Update PRODUCT record;
                    Write LINE_ITEM record;
                ELSE
                    Set up product details for BACKORDER record;
                    Set up quantity backordered for BACKORDER records;
                    Write BACKORDER record;
                ENDIF;
            ELSE
                Issue "invalid product" message;
            ENDIF.
        ENDFOR.
        Prepare package slip;
        Print package slip;
    ENDFOR;
    EXIT ORDER_ENTRY.
```

Figure 18.3   Figure 18.2 rewritten according to the rules in Box 18.1. The keywords used here are those of the fourth-generation language IDEAL.

PSEUDOCODE   We may distinguish between structured English and pseudocode (although sometimes these terms are used interchangeably). Pseudocode uses more formal notation, more oriented to the DP professional, whereas structured English is designed so that end users can read it after minimal training.

In practice, one can observe a spectrum ranging from entirely informal structured English without keywords to a pseudocode notation that is close to the outline of the final program and is difficult for end users to read. Some pseudocode instructions can be translated one for one into similar-looking program code instructions; some are translated into many program instructions.

Figure 18.4 gives an example of pseudocode that most end users would never dare to examine. In this sense, it is very different from Figs. 18.1 to 18.3.

JACKSON'S STRUCTURE TEXT   Figure 18.4 uses Michael Jackson's variant of pseudocode [3]. It shows pseudocode for the program structure shown in Fig. 16.6.

Jackson employs a formal notation for pseudocode, which he calls *structure text*. It accompanies a program-structure chart (or as Jackson defines it, a tree-structure diagram; see Chapter 16) and is used to complete the program design by defining the control logic. Figure 18.5 shows

```
P seq
    item_grps: = 0;
    open stf; read stf;
    write heading;
    P_BODY itr until (eof-stf)
            C_ITEM_GRP_P_REPT_LINE seq
                net_chg: = 0;
                item_grps: = item_grps + 1;
                critem: = next item;
                PRLBDY itr while (next item = critem);
                        C-TRANS-REC seq
                            CTRBDY sel (code = R)
                                net_chg: = net_chg + qty;
                            CTRBDY alt (code = D)
                                net_chg: = net_chg - qty;
                            CTRBDY end
                            read stf;
                        C-TRANS-REC end
                PRLBDY end
                write net_chg;
            C-ITEM-GRP-P-REPT-LINE end
    P-BODY end
    write item_grps; close stf;
P end
```

Figure 18.4   A highly cryptic form of pseudocode, which cannot be read or checked by end users [3].

```
VALIDATE-SUB-ITEM seq
        process CHECK-GENERAL-FORMAT;
        ERROR-CHECK select (ERROR-SW = 'ON')
                write ERROR-MESSAGE
        ERROR-CHECK end;
        VALIDATE-SPECIAL-FORMAT select (SUB-TYPE = 'NEW')
                VALIDATE-NEW-SUB seq
                        check name and address;
                        check numeric zip;
                        process CHECK-TERMS;
                        check payment;
                        ERROR-CHECK select (ERROR-SW = 'ON')
                                set INVALID-INDICATOR
                        ERROR-CHECK alt (ERROR-SW = 'OFF')
                                set VALID-INDICATOR
                        ERROR-CHECK end;
                VALIDATE-NEW-SUB end;
        VALIDATE-SPECIAL-FORMAT alt (SUB-TYPE = 'RENEWAL')
                VALIDATE-RENEWAL-SUB seq
                        process CHECK-TERMS;
                        check payment;
                        ERROR-CHECK select (ERROR-SW = 'ON')
                                set INVALID-INDICATOR
                        ERROR-CHECK alt (ERROR-SW = 'OFF')
                                set VALID-INDICATOR
                        ERROR-CHECK end;
                VALIDATE-RENEWAL-SUB end;
        VALIDATE-SPECIAL-FORMAT alt (SUB-TYPE = 'CANCEL')
                set CANCEL-FLAG
        VALIDATE-SPECIAL-FORMAT end;
        ERROR-CHECK select (INVALID-INDICATOR = 'ON')
                write ERROR-MESSAGES
        ERROR-CHECK end;
VALIDATE-SUB-ITEM end.
```

Figure 18.5 The pseudocode in Fig. 18.1 rewritten using Jackson's structure text notation, which is more formal.

an example of structure text for the module VALIDATE SUB ITEM is the subscription system. Structured English for the same structure is in Fig. 18.1.

Jackson's rules for writing the control constructs of sequence, selection and iteration are as follows:

Sequence

```
N seq
        part-1;
        part-2;
        part-3;
            .
            .
            .
        part-n;
N end.
```

N is the name of the sequence construct. In Fig. 18.5, VALIDATE SUB-ITEM is the name of the first sequence construct listed. The parts are a list of one or more programming-level statements, high-level instructions, or control constructs. The parts are separated by a semicolon (;). The entry point to the sequence construct is **N seq,** and the exit point is **N end.** The indentation shown here is used to clarify the structure. Parts are executed in the order in which they are listed.

Selection

```
N select (condition-1)
      part-1;
N alt (condition-2)
      part-2;
      .

      .

      .

N alt (condition-m)
      part-m;
N end
```

In Fig. 18.5, VALIDATE SPECIAL FORMAT is a selection construct. It has three alternative parts: VALIDATE NEW SUB **seq,** VALIDATE RE-NEWAL SUB **seq,** and set CANCEL FLAG. One of these three alternative parts is executed, depending on the value of SUB TYPE.

The select construct may have two or more parts. Only one part may be executed at one time. The entry point of the select construct is the name **(N)** followed by **select;** the exit point is the name **(N)** followed by **end.** The indentation shown is suggested to clarify the structure.

Iteration

```
N iter while (condition)
         part;
N end
```

The iteration construct is used to represent a loop. Its part is executed repeatedly while the condition is true. The iteration construct has an entry point composed of its name **(N)** followed by **iter** and an exit point composed of its name **(N)** followed by **end.**

Figure 18.4 is similar to Fig. 18.5 but is more condensed by the use of mnemonics.

Three fields are defined, called "RECEIVED," "DISTRIBUTED," and "NETCHANGE," as part of the file called "WAREHOUSE."

```
DEFINE FILE WAREHOUSE
RECEIVED/I9 = IF CODE IS 'R' THEN QUANTITY ELSE 0;
DISTRIBUTED/I9 = IF CODE IS 'D' THEN QUANTITY ELSE 0;
NET_CHANGE/I9 = RECEIVED_DISTRIBUTED;
END
```

The report is then produced as follows:

```
TABLE
FILE WAREHOUSE
SUM RECEIVED AND DISTRIBUTED AND NET_CHANGE
BY PRODUCT
END
```

Figure 18.6   Executable program code written with the fourth-generation language RAMIS II for the problem described with pseudocode in Fig. 18.4 and illustrated in Figs. 16.4 through 16.7. The executable program code is simpler than the pseudocode!

CRITIQUE OF STRUCTURED ENGLISH

Structured English has been a useful tool for describing program logic. We believe that other diagrammatic tools are better, as explained in the next three chapters.

Figure 18.3 represents the form of structured English that we perceive as being generally the most useful.

Figure 18.4 represents a form of pseudocode that we perceive as insufficiently user-friendly. It is difficult to read and even more difficult to write. A nontechnical end user and most ordinary data processing analysts would give up trying to decipher its meaning after the first few lines. If program names are long, the structure text can become a mess and invites mistakes. If program names are not descriptive, it becomes totally unreadable.

It is interesting to reflect that the *executable* program code of some fourth-generation languages is simpler and easier to read than some of the more cryptic breeds of pseudocode. In RAMIS II, for example, the problem pseudocoded in Fig. 18.4 can be executed simply with the code shown in Fig. 18.6.

Use of pseudocode today generally indicates a lack of understanding of today's tools, such as action-diagram editors.

REFERENCES

1. J. Martin, *Fourth-Generation Languages*, Englewood Cliffs, NJ: Prentice-Hall, Inc., 1985.

2. J. Martin, *Application Development Without Programmers*. Englewood Cliffs, NJ: Prentice-Hall, Inc., 1982.

3. G. D. Bergland, "A Guided Tour of Program Design Methodologies," *IEEE Computing* (October 1981), pp. 13–37.

19 NASSI-SHNEIDERMAN CHARTS

INTRODUCTION Flowcharts, as we noted in Chapter 17, are not a good technique for describing structured programs. They give an unstructured view of the world and tend to lead to programs with GO TOs rather than hierarchically structured programs. Nevertheless, psychologists' experiments have confirmed what we might think is intuitively obvious—that clear diagrams do help in creating programs and also in debugging them [1].

I. Nassi and B. Shneiderman set out to replace the traditional flowchart with a chart that offered a structured, hierarchical view of program logic [2]. Nassi-Shneiderman charts are used for detailed program design and documentation. (N. Chapin uses a broadly similar type of diagram that he calls a *Chapin chart* [2].)

Nassi-Shneiderman (N-S) charts represent program structures that have one entry point and one exit point and are composed of the control constructs of sequence, selection, and repetition. Whereas it is difficult to show nesting and recursion with a traditional flowchart, it is easy with an N-S chart. Also, it is easy to convert an N-S chart to structured code.

An N-S chart consists of a rectangular box representing the logic of a program module. It is often used to represent what is in one of the blocks on a structure chart like that of Fig. 13.1. Figure 19.1 shows the logic inside the block VALIDATE SUB ITEM in Fig. 13.1.

The box of the N-S chart is intended to be drawn on one page. It should therefore not have more than about 15 to 20 subdivisions. When an N-S chart becomes too large, subfunctions are separated out and drawn on another N-S chart. It was designed for use with top-down, stepwise refinement methods.

Various structures are nested inside the box of an N-S chart to show the process logic. A branch instruction is *not* permitted.

VALIDATE SUB ITEM:

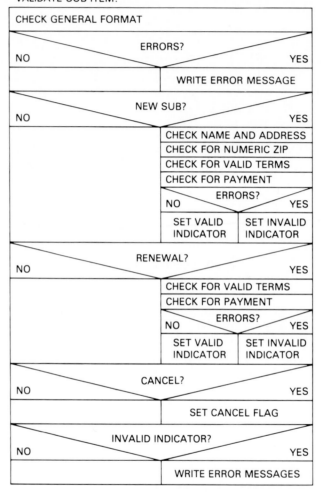

Figure 19.1 A Nassi-Shneiderman chart is used to show the detailed design for a program module. This chart shows the logic inside the VALIDATE SUB ITEM block of Fig. 13.1.

CONTROL CONSTRUCTS

Each basic control construct used in structured programming can be represented by an N-S chart symbol.

Sequence

Sequence is shown by a vertical stack of process boxes:

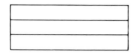

For example, Fig. 19.1 describes the sequence of four processes: CHECK NAME AND ADDRESS, CHECK FOR NUMERIC ZIP, CHECK FOR VALID TERMS, and CHECK FOR PAYMENT.

Selection

Selection (IF-THEN-ELSE) is shown by dividing the process box into five parts. The top half is divided into three triangles. The topmost triangle contains the condition to be tested. The bottom triangles indicate the "true" part and the "false" part of the IF-THEN-ELSE. The bottom half is divided into the "true" process box and the "false" process box, p-1 and p-2, respectively.

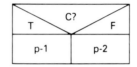

For example, in Fig. 19.1, the last condition test in the chart is to check the INVALID INDICATOR. If the test is true, the process WRITE ERROR MESSAGES is performed. If the test is false, nothing is done, since the false process is null.

Note that the selection structure can be nested. In Fig. 19.1, the condition test for ERRORS is nested within the condition test for RENEWAL.

The condition structure can be extended to the case structure, in which a selection is made from several mutually exclusive choices, as follows:

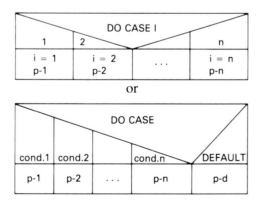

The N-S chart shown in Fig. 19.1 could alternatively have been designed using the case structure shown in Fig. 19.2.

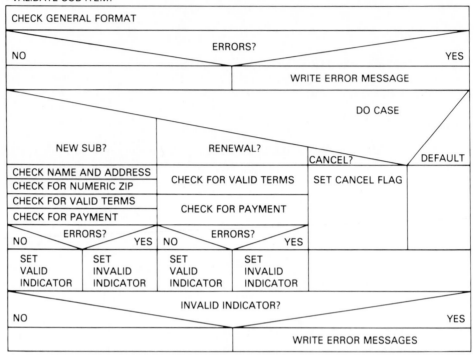

Figure 19.2 The function VALIDATE SUB ITEM from the subscription system can be implemented using the case structure.

Repetition

Repetition is indicated by a DO WHILE or a DO UNTIL structure.

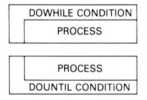

Notice that in the DO WHILE structure the condition is tested first; then, if the condition is true, the process is performed. In the DO UNTIL structure, the process is performed first; then the condition is tested.

In the subscription system, a repetition structure is used to indicate that the subscription process of validating and processing a subscription is performed once for each subscription on the transaction file. This is shown in Fig. 19.3.

Figure 19.3 The function SUBSCRIPTION SYSTEM is repetitively performed until there are no more subscription transactions to process.

CRITIQUE OF THE NASSI-SHNEIDERMAN CHART

The Nassi-Shneiderman chart is a diagramming technique used primarily for detail program design. It is a poor tool for showing the high-level hierarchical control structure for a program. Although it can show the basic procedural components (as in Fig. 19.3), it does not show the interfaces connecting these components.

It is an alternative to traditional program flowcharts, detail HIPO diagrams, and pseudocode. Among these techniques, the N-S chart is the easiest to read and the easiest to convert to program code. However, it is only a procedure design tool and cannot be used to design data structures. And although it is easy to read, it is not always easy to draw. It can take three or four times longer to draw an N-S chart than to write the equivalent pseudocode.

Another major shortcoming of the N-S chart is that it is not data-base-oriented. It does not link to a data model or to a data dictionary.

Action diagrams (next chapter) show all of the information that is on a Nassi-Shneiderman chart and are much easier to use with structured editors. A variety of CASE tools use action diagrams; none that we are aware of use Nassi-Shneiderman diagrams.

REFERENCES

1. J. Brook and K. Duncan, "An Experimental Study of Flowcharts as an Aid to Identification of Procedural Faults," *Ergonomics,* 23, no. 4 (1980), 387–399.

2. N. Chapin, "New Formats for Flowcharts." *Software—Practice and Experience,* no. 4 (1974), 341–357.

3. I. Nassi and B. Shneiderman, "Flowchart Techniques for Structured Programming," *ACM SIGPLAN Notices,* 8, no. 8 (August 1973), 12–26.

20 ACTION DIAGRAMS

**OVERVIEW
VERSUS
DETAILED LOGIC
DIAGRAMMING**

Of the diagramming techniques we have described, some are usable for the *overview* of program structure and some are usable for the *detailed* program logic. Structure charts, HIPO diagrams, and Michael Jackson charts draw overall program structures but not the detailed tests, conditions, and logic. Their advocates usually resort to structured English or pseudocode to represent the detail. Flowcharts and Nassi-Shneiderman charts show the detailed logic of a program but not the structural overview.

There is no reason why the diagramming of the overview should be incompatible with the diagramming of the detail. Indeed, it is highly desirable that these two aspects of program design employ the same type of diagram because complex systems are created by successively filling in detail (top-down design) and linking together blocks of low-level detail (bottom-up design). The design needs to move naturally between the high levels and low levels of design. The low level should be a natural extension of the high level. *Action diagrams* achieve this. They give a natural way to draw program overviews like structure charts, HIPO diagrams, or Warnier-Orr diagrams and detailed logic like flowcharts or Nassi-Shneiderman charts. They were originally designed to be as easy to teach to end users as possible and to assist end users in applying fourth-generation languages.

Glancing ahead, Figs. 20.2 and 20.3 show simple examples of action diagrams. Fig. 20.8 shows an extension of Fig. 20.2.

BRACKETS   A program module is drawn as a bracket:

Brackets are the basic building blocks of action diagrams. The bracket can be of any length, so there is space in it for as much text or detail as is needed.

Inside the bracket is a sequence of operations. A simple control rule applies to the bracket: You enter it at the top, do the things in it in a top-to-bottom sequence, and exit at the bottom.

Inside the bracket there may be other brackets. Many brackets may be nested. The nesting shows the hierarchical structure of a program. Figure 20.1 shows the representation of a hierarchical structure with brackets.

Some brackets are *repetition* brackets. The items in the bracket are executed several times. The repetition bracket has a double line at its top:

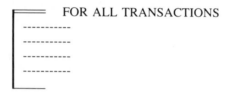

When one of several processes is to be used (mutually exclusive selection), a bracket with several divisions is used:

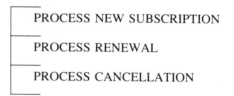

One, and only one, of the divisions in the bracket is executed. This replaces the $\oplus$ of Warnier-Orr diagrams or the $\bigcirc$ of Michael Jackson diagrams, as shown below:

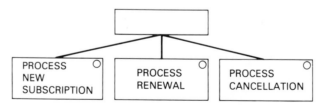

DECOMPOSITION DIAGRAM,
STRUCTURE CHART, HIPO CHART, ETC.

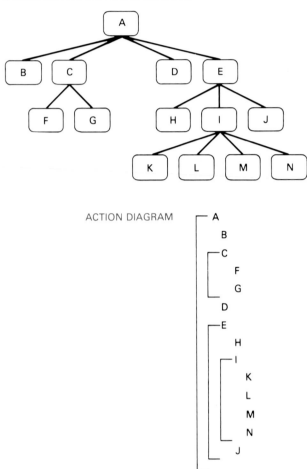

Figure 20.1   Hierarchical block structure and the equivalent action diagram.

**ULTIMATE
DECOMPOSITION**
Figure 20.2 illustrates an action diagram overview of a program structure. Figure 20.2 is equivalent to the Warnier-Orr diagram of Fig. 15.5, the Jackson diagram of Fig. 16.3, the structure chart of Fig. 13.1, and the HIPO diagram of Fig. 14.1. Unlike these charts, however, it can be extended to show conditions, case structures, and loops of different types; it can show detailed program logic.

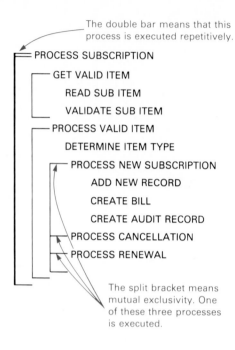

The double bar means that this process is executed repetitively.

PROCESS SUBSCRIPTION

GET VALID ITEM
READ SUB ITEM
VALIDATE SUB ITEM
PROCESS VALID ITEM
DETERMINE ITEM TYPE
PROCESS NEW SUBSCRIPTION
ADD NEW RECORD
CREATE BILL
CREATE AUDIT RECORD
PROCESS CANCELLATION
PROCESS RENEWAL

The split bracket means mutual exclusivity. One of these three processes is executed.

Figure 20.2 High-level action diagram, equivalent to the structure chart in Fig. 13.1, the HIPO diagram in Fig. 14.1, the Jackson diagram in Fig. 16.3, or the Warnier-Orr diagram in Fig. 15.5. This action diagram can now be expanded into a chart showing the detailed program logic. VALIDATE SUB ITEM from this chart is expanded into detailed logic in Fig. 20.3.

Figure 20.3 expands the process in Fig. 20.2 called VALIDATE SUB ITEM. Figures 20.2 and 20.3 could be merged into one chart. Figure 20.3 is equivalent to the flowchart of Fig. 17.2, the structured English of Fig. 18.1, or the Nassi-Shneiderman chart of Fig. 19.1. Glancing ahead, Fig. 20.7 shows *executable* program code written in a fourth-generation language.

This diagramming technique can thus be extended all the way from the highest-level overview to working code in a fourth-generation language. When it is used on a computer screen, the developers can edit and adjust the diagram and successively fill in detail until they have working code that can be tested interpretively. We refer to this as *ultimate decomposition*.

As we will see later, the process of ultimate decomposition can be linked to data-base planning and design.

CONDITIONS

Often a program module or subroutine is executed only if a certain condition applies. In this case the condition is written at the head of a bracket:

IF CUSTOMER# IS VALID

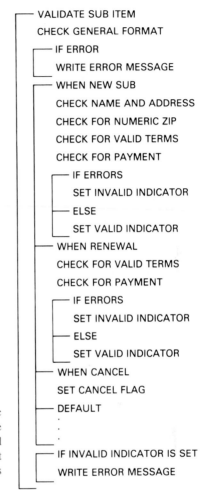

Figure 20.3 Action diagram showing the detailed logic inside the process VALIDATE SUB ITEM. This is the logic shown in the flowchart of Fig. 17.2, the structured English of Fig. 18.1, and the Nassi-Shneiderman chart of Fig. 19.1. This diagram, showing detailed logic, is an extension of the overview diagram of Fig. 20.2.

Conditions are often used to control mutually exclusive choices:

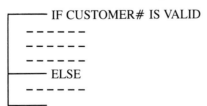

This has only two mutually exclusive conditions, an IF and an ELSE. Sometimes there are many mutually exclusive conditions:

```
┌──── WHEN KEY = "1"
│   ──────
│   ──────
├──── WHEN KEY = "2"
│   ──────
│   ──────
├──── WHEN KEY = "3"
│   ──────
│   ──────
├──── WHEN KEY = "4"
│   ──────
│   ──────
└
```

LOOPS

A loop is represented with a repetition bracket with the double line at its top.

When many people first start to program, they make mistakes with the point at which they test a loop. Sometimes the test should be made *before* the actions of the loop are performed, and sometimes the test should be made *after*. This difference can be made clear on brackets by drawing the test either at the top or at the bottom of the bracket:

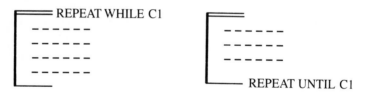

If the test is at the head of the loop, as with a WHILE loop, the actions in the loop may never be executed if the WHILE condition is not satisfied. If the test is at the bottom of the loop, as with an UNTIL loop, the actions in the loop are executed at least once. They will be executed more than once until the condition is fulfilled.

SETS OF DATA

Sometimes a procedure needs to be executed on all the items in a set of items. For example, it might be applied to all transactions or all records in a file:

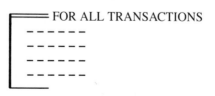

Action diagrams have been used with fourth-generation languages such as NOMAD, MANTIS, FOCUS, RAMIS, and IDEAL. They are a good tool for teaching end users to work with these languages. Some such languages have a FOR construct with a WHERE clause to qualify the FOR; for example,

FOR EACH TRANSACTION WHERE CUSTOMER# > 5000

SUBPROCEDURES   Sometimes a user needs to add to an action diagram an item that is itself a procedure that may contain actions. We call this a subprocedure or subroutine and draw it as a round-cornered box. A subprocedure might be used in several procedures. It will be exploded into detail in another chart that shows the actions it contains.

SUBPROCEDURES NOT YET DESIGNED   Sometimes at the procedure design stage, sections of a procedure may not yet be thought out in detail. The designer can represent this with a box with rounded corners and question marks, ''?'', on the right edge:

COMMON PROCEDURES   Some procedures appear more than once in an action diagram because they are called (invoked) from more than one place in the logic. These procedures are called *common procedures*. They are indicated by drawing a vertical line down the left-hand side of the procedure box:

The use of procedure boxes enables an action diagrammer to concentrate on the parts of a procedure with which he is familiar. Another person, perhaps, may fill in the details in the boxes. This enables an elusive or complex procedure formation problem to be worked out a stage at a time.

The use of these boxes makes action diagrams a powerful tool for designing procedures at many levels of abstraction. As with other structured techniques, top-down design can be done by creating a gross structure with such boxes, while remaining vague about the contents of each box. The gross structure can then be broken down into successive levels of detail. Each explosion of a box adds another degree of detail, which might itself contain actions and boxes.

Similarly, bottom-up design can be done by specifying small procedures as action diagrams whose names appear as boxes in higher-level action diagrams.

TERMINATIONS

Certain conditions may cause a procedure to be terminated. They may cause the termination of the bracket in which the condition occurs, or they may cause the termination of several brackets. Terminations are drawn with an arrow to the left through one or more brackets:

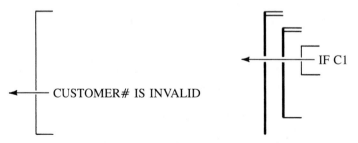

FOURTH-GENERATION LANGUAGES

When fourth-generation languages are used, the wording on the action diagram may be the wording that is used in coding programs with the language, as in the following examples.

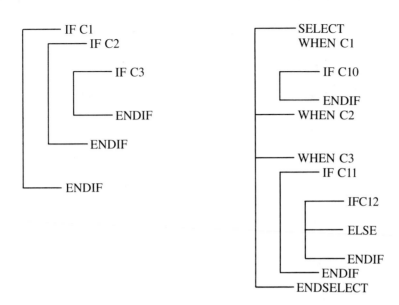

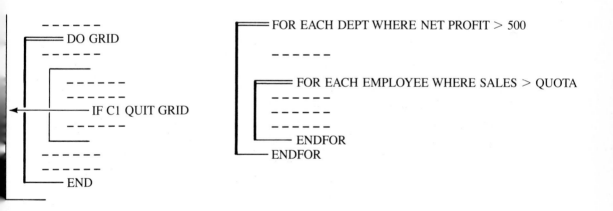

Figure 20.4 shows an action diagram for a procedure using control statements from the language IDEAL, from ADR [1].

DECOMPOSITION TO PROGRAM CODE

Figure 10.21 shows a Jackson diagram of a game program. With action diagrams we can decompose this until we have program code. Figure 20.5 shows

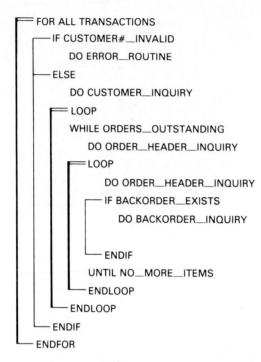

FOR ALL TRANSACTIONS
   IF CUSTOMER#_INVALID
      DO ERROR_ROUTINE
   ELSE
      DO CUSTOMER_INQUIRY
   LOOP
      WHILE ORDERS_OUTSTANDING
        DO ORDER_HEADER_INQUIRY
      LOOP
         DO ORDER_HEADER_INQUIRY
        IF BACKORDER_EXISTS
          DO BACKORDER_INQUIRY

        ENDIF
       UNTIL NO_MORE_ITEMS
      ENDLOOP
     ENDLOOP
   ENDIF
  ENDFOR

Figure 20.4 Action diagrams can be labeled with the control statement of a fourth-generation language and constitute an excellent way to teach such languages. This example uses statements from the language IDEAL, from ADR [1].

an action diagram equivalent to Fig. 10.21. The action diagram gives more room for explanation. Instead of saying PRINT RANDOM WORDS it says PRINT RANDOM WORD FROM EACH OF THE THREE LISTS.

Figure 20.6 decomposes the part of the diagram labeled BUZZWORD GENERATOR. The inner bracket is a repetition bracket that executes 22 times. This is inside a bracket that is terminated by the operator pressing the ESC (escape) key. The last statement in this bracket is WAIT, indicating that the system will wait after executing the remainder of the bracket until the operator presses the ESC key. This gives the operator as much time as he wants to read the printout.

Figure 20.7 decomposes the diagram further into an executable program. This program is written in the fourth-generation language MANTIS, from Cincom Systems, Inc. [2].

TITLES VERSUS CODE STRUCTURE

At the higher levels of the design process, action diagram brackets represent the *names* of processes and subprocesses. As the designer descends into program-level detail, the brackets become *program constructs:* IF brackets, CASE brackets, LOOP brackets, and the like. To show the difference, different colors may be used; for example, the name brackets may be red and the program-construct brackets black. If a black-and-white copier or terminal is used, the name brackets may be dotted or gray and the program-construct brackets black.

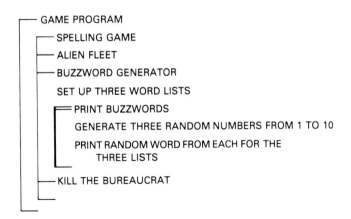

Figure 20.5　An action diagram equivalent to the Jackson diagram of Fig.
10.21.

The program-construct brackets may be labeled with appropriate control
words. These may be the control words of a particular programming language,
or they may be language-independent words.

Figure 20.8 shows the program constructs with language-independent control words. Figure 20.9 shows the same constructs with the words of the fourth-
generation language IDEAL. It is desirable that any fourth-generation language
have a set of clear words equivalent to Fig. 20.8, and it would help if standard
words for this existed in the computer industry.

A simple action diagram editor can be built for personal computers to
speed up the production and modification of programs and help to eliminate

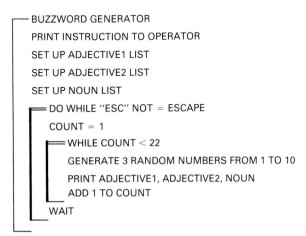

Figure 20.6　Expansion of the BUZZWORD GENERATOR portion of Fig.
20.5.

```
┌─── ENTER BUZZWORD GENERATOR

     CLEAR
     SHOW "I WILL GENERATE A SCREEN FULL OF 'BUZZ PHRASES' EVERY
     TIME YOU HIT 'ENTER'. WHEN YOU WANT TO STOP, HIT 'ESC'."

     TEXT ADJECTIVE1 (10,16), ADJECTIVE (10,16) NOUN (10,16)

     ADJECTIVE1 (1) = "INTEGRATED," "TOTAL," "SYSTEMATIZED," PARALLEL,"
        "'FUNCTIONAL," "RESPONSIVE," "OPTIONAL," "SYNCHRONIZED,"
        "'COMPATIBLE," BALANCED"

     ADJECTIVE2 (1) = "MANAGEMENT," "ORGANIZATIONAL," "MONITORED,"
        "'RECIPROCAL," "DIGITAL," "LOGISTICAL," "TRANSITIONAL,"
        "'INCREMENTAL," "THIRD GENERATION," "POLICY"

     NOUN(1) = "OPTION," "FLEXIBILITY," "CAPABILITY," "MOBILITY,"
        "'PROGRAMMING," "CONCEPT," "TIME PHASE," "PROJECTION,"
        "'HARDWARE," "CONTINGENCY"

     SEED

┌══ WHILE KEY ≠ "ESC"
│   COUNT = 1
│
│  ┌══ WHILE COUNT < 22
│  │   A = INT(RND(10) + 1)
│  │   B = INT(RND(10) + 1)
│  │   C = INT(RND(10) + 1)
│  │
│  │   SHOW ADJECTIVE1(A) + " " + ADJECTIVE2(B) + " " + NOUN(C)
│  │
│  │   COUNT = COUNT + 1
│  └── END
│
│      WAIT
└── END

     CHAIN "GAMES_MENU"
└─ EXIT
```

Figure 20.7 Expansion of the action diagram of Fig. 20.6 into program code. This is an executable program in the fourth-generation language MANTIS [2]. Successive decomposition of a diagram until it becomes executable code is called *ultimate decomposition.*

common types of bugs. A panel for the rapid addition or modification of brackets is shown in Fig. 20.10. A computer can select the control words for any chosen language. The control words are shown in boldfaced type; the other statements are in regular type.

CONCURRENCY   Where brackets may be executed concurrently, they are joined with a semicircular link:

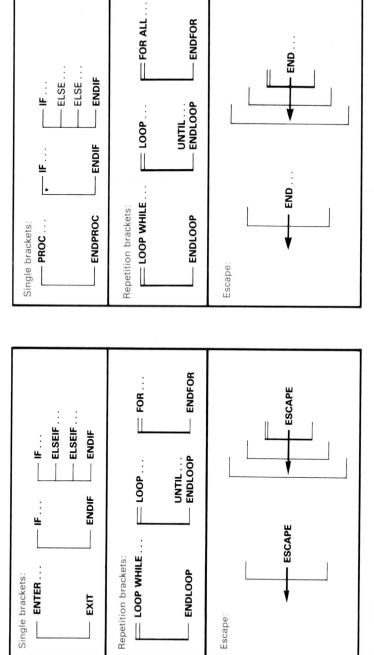

Figure 20.8 Program constructs with language-independent control words.

Figure 20.9 Program constructs with the control words of the fourth-generation language IDEAL.

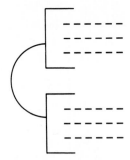

A bracket that relates to a parallel operation on an array processor has the concurrency symbol attached to the bracket:

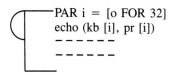

INPUT AND OUTPUT DATA

The brackets of the action diagram are quick and easy to draw. If the user wants to show the data that enter and leave a process, the bracket is expanded into a rectangle, as shown in Fig. 20.11. The data entering the process are written at the top right corner of the block. The data leaving are written at the bottom right corner.

Rectangles can be nested as in Fig. 20.11. We then have species II functional decomposition as described in Chapter 12. This type of functional decomposition is designed for computerized checking to ensure that all the inputs and outputs balance.

The square brackets may be thought of as a shorthand way of drawing rectangles like those in Fig. 20.11.

Single brackets:

    Block:☐   Condition:☐

    Case: 1:☐ 2:☐ 3:☐ 4:☐ More:☐

Repetition brackets:

    For all:☐ Loop while:☐ Loop until:☐

Escape:

    1:☐ 2:☐ 3:☐ 4:☐ 5:☐ More:☐

Figure 20.10 Menu for rapid addition or modification of brackets on an action diagram.

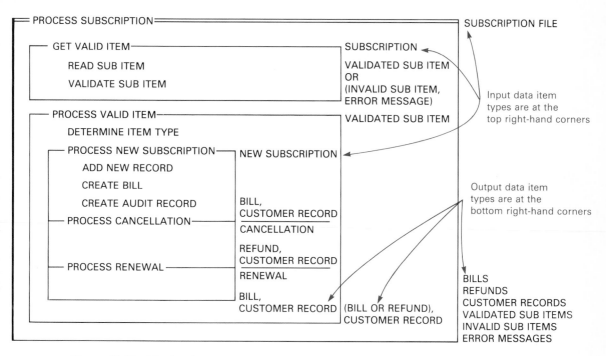

Figure 20.11   The bracket format of Fig. 20.2 is here expanded into the rectangular format used to show the data-item types that are input and output to each process. This is designed for computerized cross-checking.

A diagramming technique, today, should be designed for both quick manual manipulation and computerized manipulation. Users and analysts will want to draw rough sketches on paper or argue at a blackboard using the technique. They will also want to build complex diagrams at a computer screen, using the computer to validate, edit, and maintain the diagrams, possibly linking them to a dictionary, data-base model, or the like. The tool acts rather like a word processor for diagramming, making it easy for users to modify their diagram. Unlike a word processor, it can perform complex validation and cross-checking on the diagram.

The design of simple programs does not need automated correlation in inputs and outputs or diagrams like Fig. 20.11 that show the inputs and outputs. In the design of complex specifications, the automated correlation of inputs and outputs among program modules is essential if mistakes are to be avoided.

In showing input and output data, Fig. 20.11 contains the information on a data-flow diagram. It can be converted into a layered data-flow diagram as in Fig. 20.12. Unlike a data-flow diagram, it can be directly extended to show the program structure, including conditions, case constructs, and loop control.

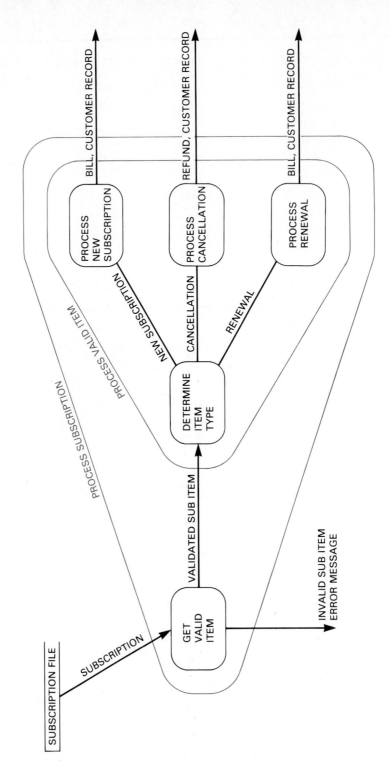

Figure 20.12 Data-flow diagram corresponding to Fig. 20.8.

We think it highly desirable that a programmer sketch the structure of programs with action diagram brackets. These can be drawn on the coding sheet. We have checked many programs written with fourth-generation languages such as FOCUS, RAMIS, IDEAL, and NATURAL, and have discovered that often the coder has made a logic error in the use of loops, END statements, CASE structures, EXITs, and so on. When a coder is taught to draw action diagram brackets and fit the code to them, these structure errors become apparent. The control statements can be fitted to the brackets.

Software, which can run like word processing software on personal computers, can be used for building, editing, and modifying action diagrams and fitting code to them.

ADVANTAGES

Action diagrams were designed to solve some of the concerns with other diagramming techniques. They were designed to have the following properties:

1. They are quick and easy to draw and to change.

2. They are good for manual sketching and for computerized editing.

3. A single technique extends from the highest overview down to coding-level detail (ultimate decomposition).

4. They are easy to teach to end users; they encourage end users to extend their capability into examination or design of detailed process logic. They are thus designed as an information center tool.

5. They can be printed on normal-width paper rather than wall charts, making them appropriate for design with personal computers.

6. They draw the constructs of traditional structured programming and are more graphic than pseudocode.

7. They are designed to link to a data model.

8. They work well with fourth-generation languages and can be tailored to a specific dialect.

9. They are designed for computerized cross-checking of data usage on complex specifications.

Some aspects of this list did not exist when the early structured techniques were designed:

- Computerized editing of an analyst's diagrams
- Computerized cross-checking
- Data models
- Compound relational data-base operations
- Use of personal computers for design

- Fourth-generation languages
- Strong end-user involvement in computing
- Information center management

Chapter 24 extends action diagramming techniques to show data-base operations. Box 20.1 summarizes the diagramming conventions of action diagrams. Box 24.1 adds the symbols used in data-base action diagrams.

Figures 20.13 through 20.18 show examples of action diagrams produced with the action diagramming tool called Action Diagrammer™, from KnowledgeWare [3]. This action diagram editor runs on an IBM PC.

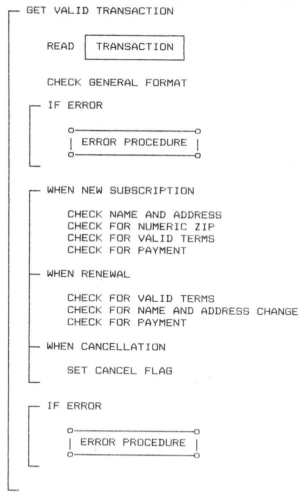

Figure 20.13 An action diagram for the design of the process GET VALID TRANSACTION.

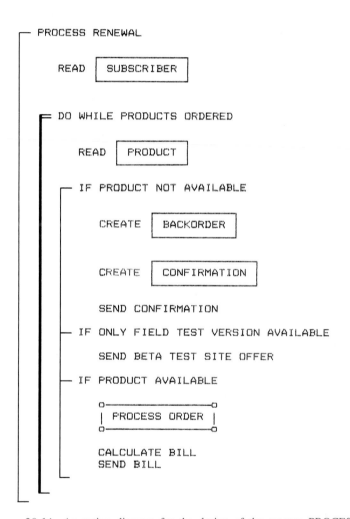

Figure 20.14   An action diagram for the design of the process PROCESS RENEWAL.

```
┌─ <<ORDER_ACCEPTANCE >> PROC
│     EACH CUSTOMER
│
│  ┌─ IF CUSTOMER# VALID
│  │
│  │  ┌─ IF CREDIT_RATING >3
│  │  │
│  │  │     WRITE CUSTOMER ORDER
│  │  │     SET ORDER TOTAL
│  │  │
│  │  │  ┌─ LOOP WHILE EACH PRODUCT
│  │  │  │
│  │  │  │  ┌─ IF PRODUCT# VALID
│  │  │  │  │
│  │  │  │  │  ┌─ IF QUANTITY_ON_HAND > 0
│  │  │  │  │  │
│  │  │  │  │  │     SET LINE_ITEM_PRICE = CATALOG_PRICE
│  │  │  │  │  │     SET LINE_TOTAL = QTY_ORDERED * LINE_ITEM_PRICE
│  │  │  │  │  │     SET ORDER_TOTAL = ORDER_TOTAL + LINE_TOTAL
│  │  │  │  │  │     WRITE ORDER_LINE
│  │  │  │  │  │     EACH ORDER_RATE
│  │  │  │  │  │     SET ACTUAL_USAGE = ACTUAL_USAGE + QTY_ORDERED
│  │  │  │  │  │     WRITE ORDER_RATE
│  │  │  │  │  │
│  │  │  │  │  ├─ ELSE
│  │  │  │  │  │
│  │  │  │  │  │     WRITE BACKORDER
│  │  │  │  │  │     PRINT BACKORDER NOTICE
│  │  │  │  │  │
│  │  │  │  │  └─ ENDIF
│  │  │  │  │
│  │  │  │  ├─ ELSE
│  │  │  │  │
│  │  │  │  │     PRINT ERROR_MESSAGE
│  │  │  │  │
│  │  │  │  └─ ENDIF
│  │  │  │
│  │  │  └─ ENDLOOP
│  │  │
│  │  │     SET ORDER_TOTAL = ORDER_TOTAL * [1 - DISCOUNT / 100]
│  │  │     SET ORDER_STATUS = 0
│  │  │     WRITE CUSTOMER_ORDER
│  │  │
│  │  ├─ ELSE
│  │  │
│  │  │     CALL POOR CREDIT
│  │  │
│  │  └─ ENDIF
│  │
│  ├─ ELSE
│  │
│  │     PRINT REJECT NOTICE
│  │
│  └─ ENDIF
│
└─ ENDPROC
```

Figure 20.15 Executable code for the fourth-generation language IDEAL
[1].
```
```

```
addel ()

*  /* Local Variables */  *****************************************************
   int itab;
   int adlevel;
   int itfrst, itnext, itdel;

*  /* Executable Section */  ***************************************************
   switch (adtab[curline].action)

   case ACT_JUNK:
   case ACT_CASW:
   case ACT_EXIT:
       itfrst = curline;
       itnext = curline + 1;
       break;

   case ACT_BEGL:
   case ACT_BEGB:
       adlevel = 1;
       itfrst = curline;
       for (itnext = curline+1;
            itnext <= numadtab & adlevel > 0; itnext++)
           switch (adtab[itnext].action)  {
           case ACT_BEGL:
           case ACT_BEGB:
               adlevel++;
               break;
           case ACT_END:
               adlevel--;
           }
       }
       if (adlevel > 0)
           aborts ("ad: ? no matching end ??");

       break;

   default:
       itfrst = numadtab;
       itnext = numadtab;
       beep();
   }
   itdel = itnext - itfrst;
   for (itab = itfrst; itab < numadtab; itab++) {
       adtab[itab].action = adtab[itab+itdel].action;
       adtab[itab].count  = adtab[itab+itdel].count;
       adtab[itab].text   = adtab[itab+itdel].text;
   }
   numadtab -= itdel;
   if (curline > numadtab)
       curline = numadtab;

   showbuffer ();
```

Figure 20.16 Code written in the language C, shown with rectangular brackets.

(Continued)

```
* /* Local Variables */ ************************************************
    int itab;
    int adlevel;
    int itfrst, itnext, itdel;

* /* Executable Section */ ********************************************
    switch (adtab[curline].action) {

    case ACT_JUNK:
    case ACT_CASW:
    case ACT_EXIT:
        itfrst = curline;
        itnext = curline + 1;
        break;

    case ACT_BEGL:
    case ACT_BEGB:
        adlevel = 1;
        itfrst = curline;
        for (itnext = curline+1; itnext <= numadtab & adlevel > 0; itnext++
            switch (adtab[itnext].action) {
            case ACT_BEGL:
            case ACT_BEGB:
                adlevel++;
                break;
            case ACT_END:
                adlevel--;
            }
        }
        if (adlevel > 0)
            aborts ("ad: ? no matching end ??");

        break;

    default:
        itfrst = numadtab;
        itnext = numadtab;
        beep();
    }
    itdel = itnext - itfrst;
    for (itab = itfrst; itab < numadtab; itab++) {
        adtab[itab].action = adtab[itab+itdel].action;
        adtab[itab].count  = adtab[itab+itdel].count;
        adtab[itab].text   = adtab[itab+itdel].text;
    }
    numadtab -= itdel
    if (curline > numadtab)
        curline = numadtab

    showbuffer ();
```

Figure 20.16   (Continued)

```
┌── IF ABS(ABS(NUM(col_2)-NUM(col_1))
│       -ABS(lin-2-lin_1))/=1
│       OR ABS(NUM(col_2)NUM(COL_1))
│           +ABS(lin_2-lin_1)=/3
│       OR arriving.status/=free AND
│       arriving.p.color=starting.p.color
│
│       THEN CAUSE illegal;
│         ((king)(*):
│
└── FI;
         (king),(*):
┌── IF ABS(NUM(col_2)-NUM(col_1)) > 1
│       OR ABS(lin_2-lin1) >1
│       OR lin_2=lin_1 AND col_2=col_1
│       OR arriving.status/=free AND
│           arriving.p.color=starting.p.color
│
│       THEN CAUSE illegal;
└──   FI; /*checking king moving to check not implemented*/
    ESAC;
  arriving:=starting;
  RETURN;


┌── ok_rook:
│     PROC (b board,m move)(BOOL)
│ ┌── DO WITH m;
│ │
│ │ ┌── IF NOT (col_2=col_1 OR lin_1=lin_2_ )
│ │ │       OR arriving.status/=free AND
│ │ │       arriving.p.color=starting.p.color
│ │ │
│ │ │       THEN RETURN FALSE;
│ │ └── FI;
│ │ ┌── IF col_1=col_2
│ │ │
│ │ │ ┌── THEN IF lin_1 < lin_2
│ │ │ │
│ │ │ │ ┌── THEN DO FOR 1 :+ lin_1+1 TO lin_2-1;
│ │ │ │ │   ┌── IF board(1)(col_1).status/=free
│ │ │ │ │   │       THEN RETURN FALSE;
│ │ │ │ │   └── FI;
│ │ │ │ └── OD;
│ │ │ │
│ │ │ ┌── ELSE
│ │ │ │
│ │ │ │ ┌── DO FOR 1 := lin_1-1 DOWN TO lin_2 +1
│ │ │ │ │   ┌── IF board(1)(col_1).status/free
│ │ │ │ │   │       THEN RETURN FALSE;
│ │ │ │ │   └── FI;
│ │ │ │ └── OD;
```

Figure 20.17 An action diagram in the CCITT high-level language CHILL
[4], showing a portion of a chess-playing program.   *(Continued)*

```
ELSE

    IF col_2 < col_1

        THEN DO FOR c :+ SUCC(col_1) TO PRED(col_2);

            IF board(lin_1)(c).status/=free
                THEN RETURN FALSE
            FI;

        ELSE
        DO FOR c := SUCC(col_2) DOWN TO PRED(col_1);
            IF boardlin_1)(c).status/=free
                THEN RETURN FALSE;
            FI;
        OD;
    FI;
FI;
RETURN TRUE;
OD;
END OK_ROOK
```

Figure 20.17 *(Continued)*

```
FOR EACH USER INTERACTION
    ACCEPT
    IF ADD..F EQ "*", THEN
        PERFORM APPEND_SHARE_VR    ;*VRWIOS.INC
        IF RECORD LE 0, THEN
            PERFORM DISPLAY_APPEND_ERROR    ;*SCRFINAL.INC
            NEXT FIRST.FIELD

        SCREEN.CHANGE..F="*"

    IF FUNCTION.TYPE:#WT LL "<ACBO>", THEN
        PERFORM WRITE_VR    ;*VRIOS.INC
        IF RECORD LE 0, THEN
            PERFORM DISPLAY_WRITE_ERROR    ;*SCRFINAL.INC
            NEXT FIRST.FIELD

    IF FUNCTION.TYPE:#WT EQ 'r', THEN
        PERFORM DELETE_VR    ;*VRIOS.INC
        IF RECORD GE 0, THEN
        EXIT SCREEN

        PERFORM DISPLAY_DELETE_ERROR    ;*SCRFINAL.INC
        NEXT FIRST.FIELD
```

Figure 20.18 A subroutine written in Application Factory from Cortex [5].

BOX 20.1 Summary of notation used in action diagrams

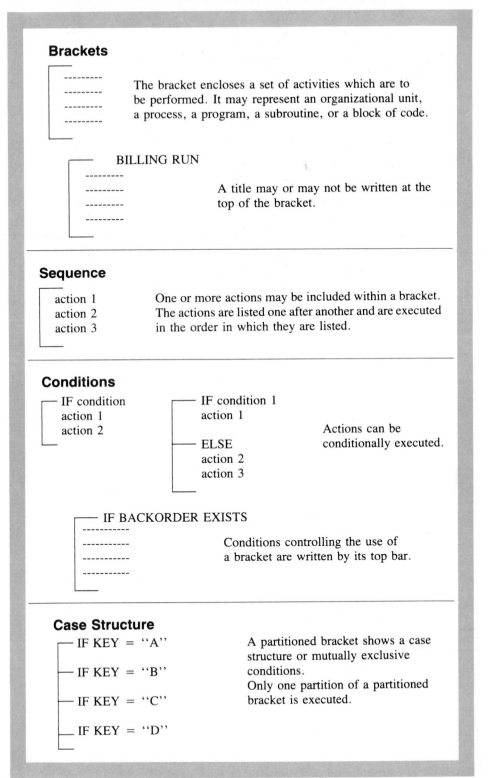

Brackets

The bracket encloses a set of activities which are to be performed. It may represent an organizational unit, a process, a program, a subroutine, or a block of code.

BILLING RUN

A title may or may not be written at the top of the bracket.

Sequence

action 1
action 2
action 3

One or more actions may be included within a bracket. The actions are listed one after another and are executed in the order in which they are listed.

Conditions

IF condition
action 1
action 2

IF condition 1
action 1

ELSE
action 2
action 3

Actions can be conditionally executed.

IF BACKORDER EXISTS

Conditions controlling the use of a bracket are written by its top bar.

Case Structure

IF KEY = "A"

IF KEY = "B"

IF KEY = "C"

IF KEY = "D"

A partitioned bracket shows a case structure or mutually exclusive conditions.
Only one partition of a partitioned bracket is executed.

(Continued)

BOX 20.1 *(Continued)*

Repetition

A double bar at the top of a bracket indicates that the contents of the bracket will be executed multiple times; for example, it is used to draw a program loop.

DO WHILE N > O

Conditions controlling a DO WHILE loop are written at the top of the bracket, showing that the condition is tested before the contents of the bracket are executed.

DO

Conditions controlling a DO UNTIL loop are written at the bottom of the bracket, showing that the condition is tested after the contents of the bracket are executed.

UNTIL NO MORE ITEMS

FOR ALL . . .

FOR EACH . . .
WHERE . . .

Nesting

Brackets are nested to show a hierarchy—a form of tree structure.

BOX 20.1 *(Continued)*

Rectangle Format

The bracket may be expanded into a rectangle. The inputs to the activities in the rectangle are written at its top right-hand corner; the outputs are written at its bottom right-hand corner.

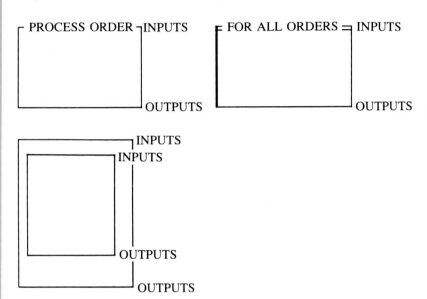

The rectangle format is designed for use with a computer which assists in drawing and cross-checks the inputs and outputs.

Exits

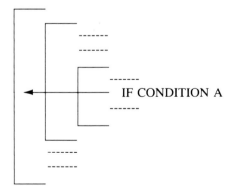

IF CONDITION A

An arrow to the left through one or more brackets indicates that the brackets it passes through are terminated if the condition written by the arrow is satisfied.

(Continued)

BOX 20.1 *(Continued)*

Subprocedures

A round-cornered box within a bracket indicates a procedure diagrammed elsewhere.

A round-cornered box with its right edge made from question marks indicates a procedure not yet thought out in more detail.

Common Procedures

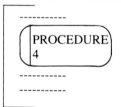

A procedure box with a vertical line drawn through the left side indicates a common procedure— that is, a procedure that appears multiple times in the action diagram.

The following relate to data-base action diagrams which are discussed in Chapters 21 and 22.

Simple Data Action

A rectangle containing the name of a record type or entity type is preceded by a simple data access action: CREATE, READ, UPDATE, or DELETE.

BOX 20.1 *(Continued)*

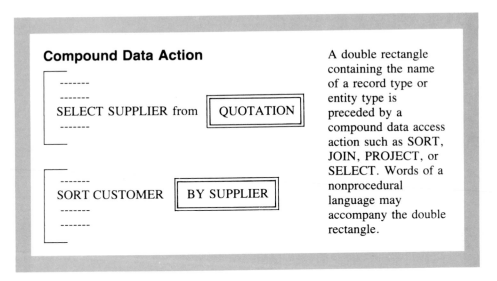

Compound Data Action

SELECT SUPPLIER from | QUOTATION |

SORT CUSTOMER | BY SUPPLIER |

A double rectangle containing the name of a record type or entity type is preceded by a compound data access action such as SORT, JOIN, PROJECT, or SELECT. Words of a nonprocedural language may accompany the double rectangle.

REFERENCES

1. IDEAL manual from Applied Data Research, Inc., Princeton, NJ.

2. *MANTIS User's Guide,* Cincom Systems, Inc., Cincinnati, OH, 1982. The example in Figs. 20.6 and 20.7 are adapted from a program in this manual.

3. Action Diagrammer, from KnowledgeWare, Inc., Atlanta, GA.

4. *CCITT High-Level Language (CHILL),* Recommendation Z.200 (Geneva: CCITT, 1981).

5. Application Factory manuals are available from Cortex Corp., 55 William St., Wellesley, MA 02181.

21 DECISION TREES AND DECISION TABLES

A BROADLY USED DIAGRAMMING TECHNIQUE
Decision trees and decision tables did not originate as computer diagramming techniques. They have much broader applicability. Decision trees and decision tables are used in biology, computer science, information theory, and switching theory. There are four main fields of application [1]:

1. Taxonomy, diagnosis, and pattern recognition
2. Circuit (logic) design and reliability testing
3. Analysis of algorithms
4. Decision-table programming and data bases

DECISION TREE
A *decision tree* is a model of a discrete function in which the value of a variable is determined; based on this value, some action is taken [1]. The action is either to choose another variable to evaluate or to output the value of the function. Thus each action taken depends on the current value of the variable being tested and all previous actions that have been taken. In a formally defined decision tree, a variable is tested only once on any path through the tree. This restriction is to prevent redundant testing.

Decision trees are normally constructed from a problem description. They give a graphic view of the decision making that is needed. They specify what variables are tested, what actions are to be taken, and the order in which decision making is performed. Each time a decision tree is "executed," one path, beginning with the root of the tree and ending with a leaf on the tree, will be followed, depending on the current value of the variable or variables tested.

Consider the description for the subscription system:

In the subscription system, subscription transactions are processed. First, each transaction is validated. Invalid transactions are rejected with an appropriate error message. Valid transactions are processed depending on their type: new subscription, renewal, or cancellation. For new subscriptions, a customer record is built, and a bill is generated for the balance due. For renewals, the expiration date is updated, and a bill is generated for the balance due. For cancellations, the record is flagged for deletion, and a refund is issued.

A decision tree for the subscription system is shown in Fig. 21.1. The root of the tree is the condition test VALID TRANSACTION?, which is answered with YES or NO. If a transaction is valid and it is a new subscription, the path with a YES answer to the VALID TRANSACTION? condition test and NEW SUBSCRIPTION in response to TRANSACTION TYPE will be followed. This path ends with processing a new subscription by building a customer record and generating a bill.

DECISION TABLE

A *decision table* is an alternative model for a function. It shows the function in tabular or matrix form; the upper rows of the table specify the *variables* or *conditions* to be evaluated, and the lower rows specify the *corresponding action* to be taken when an evaluation test is satisfied. A column in the table is called a *rule*. Each rule defines a procedure of the type: If the condition is true, execute the corresponding action.

Figure 21.2 shows a decision table for the subscription system. The rule for processing a new subscription (the second column) tells us that if the transaction is valid, the actions to take are to build a customer record and generate a bill.

A dash in the condition row means "irrelevant." In the first column of Fig. 21.2, the dashes mean that nothing else matters if the transaction is invalid.

The decision table in Fig. 21.2 relates to relatively simple decisions. They

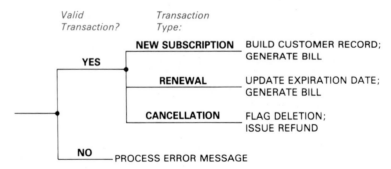

Figure 21.1 A decision tree is a graphic view of the decision logic in a program function.

CONDITIONS				
Valid transaction	NO	YES	YES	YES
New subscription	—	YES	NO	NO
Renewal	—	NO	YES	NO
Cancellation	—	NO	NO	YES
ACTIONS				
Process error message	x			
Build customer record		x		
Generate bill		x	x	
Update expiration date			x	
Flag deletion				x
Issue refund				x

Figure 21.2 A decision table can give a tabular view of the decision logic in a program. This table is equivalent to the decision tree in Fig. 21.1.

A column is referred to as a "rule"

are sufficiently simple that other forms of diagram are probably better and relate more directly to program structure. For example, consider this action diagram:

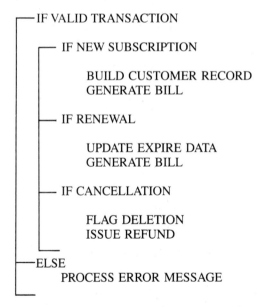

```
┌─IF VALID TRANSACTION

│     ┌─ IF NEW SUBSCRIPTION

│           BUILD CUSTOMER RECORD
│           GENERATE BILL

│     ┌─ IF RENEWAL

│           UPDATE EXPIRE DATA
│           GENERATE BILL

│     ┌─ IF CANCELLATION

│           FLAG DELETION
│           ISSUE REFUND

├─ELSE
│           PROCESS ERROR MESSAGE
└─
```

However, if the decisions relate to complex combinations of conditions, a decision table is a major help in clear thinking. Figure 21.3 shows a decision table where this is the case. Some software exists that can convert decision tables like the one in Fig. 21.3 into program code.

CONDITIONS:	P1						P2						P3						P4						P5						P6						P7					
STATE OF THE INTERFACE / TYPE OF MESSAGE RECEIVED	CALL REQUEST	CALL ACCEPTED	CLEAR REQUEST	CLEAR CONFIRM	DATA	RESET	CALL REQUEST	CALL ACCEPTED	CLEAR REQUEST	CLEAR CONFIRM	DATA	RESET	CALL REQUEST	CALL ACCEPTED	CLEAR REQUEST	CLEAR CONFIRM	DATA	RESET	CALL REQUEST	CALL ACCEPTED	CLEAR REQUEST	CLEAR CONFIRM	DATA	RESET	CALL REQUEST	CALL ACCEPTED	CLEAR REQUEST	CLEAR CONFIRM	DATA	RESET	CALL REQUEST	CALL ACCEPTED	CLEAR REQUEST	CLEAR CONFIRM	DATA	RESET	CALL REQUEST	CALL ACCEPTED	CLEAR REQUEST	CLEAR CONFIRM	DATA	RESET
ACTIONS:																																										
PROCEDURE 1	×																																									
PROCEDURE 2								×																																		
PROCEDURE 3														×																												
PROCEDURE 4																			×	×																						
PROCEDURE 5																									×	×																
ERROR MESSAGE A		×												×																								×				
ERROR MESSAGE B			×						×						×						×											×							×			
ERROR MESSAGE C				×						×						×						×						×						×						×	
ERROR MESSAGE D					×						×						×						×																			
ERROR MESSAGE E						×						×						×						×						×						×						
PRINT INSTRUCTION K															×																×						×					
ERROR PROCEDURE 1	×	×	×			×			×			×			×	×		×			×	×		×			×	×		×			×	×		×			×			
ERROR PROCEDURE 2												×						×						×																		×
LOG OPERATION					×						×						×						×						×						×						×	
SECURITY PROCEDURE																			×																							
SEE DECISION TABLE 13																								×																		
SEE DECISION TABLE 14																							×																			
SEE DECISION TABLE 15																													×						×					×		
SEE DECISION TABLE 16					×						×																														×	

Figure 21.3 Whereas simple decisions like those in Fig. 21.2 can be handled by other methods, complex decisions like those illustrated here require a decision table. Program code can be generated automatically from decision tables.

An attempt to draw the logic of Fig. 21.3 with flowcharts, Nassi-Shneiderman charts, Warnier-Orr diagrams, or other such methods would be clumsy, time-consuming, and prone to errors.

DECISION TREE OR TABLE?

When should you use decision trees and when decision tables? Decision trees are easier to read and understand when the number of conditions is small. Most persons would grasp the meaning of Fig. 21.1 without special training, for example. They might be more bewildered by Fig. 21.2.

If there are a substantial number of conditions and actions, a decision tree becomes too big and clumsy. A decision tree for the situation in Fig. 21.3 would be too large. The patterns in a table like Fig. 21.3 give a clearer idea what is required and encourage visual checking.

A decision table causes the designer to look at every possible combination. Without such a technique, he would probably miss certain combinations. The decision tree does not provide a matrix for every condition and action. It is thus easier to omit important combinations when using a decision tree.

USING DECISION TREES AND DECISION TABLES

Because a decision table or tree maps inputs (conditions) to outputs (actions) without necessarily specifying how the mapping is to be done, it has been used as a system analysis and system design tool. In particular, it has been used to describe the decision-making logic in a functional specification and the program control structure in a program design. For example, De Marco recommends that in structured systems analysis, the process specification can be described by a decision table or tree (see Chapter 36). This is an alternative to using pseudocode, which is not as easy to understand.

Traditionally, flowcharts have been used to represent detailed and complex logic graphically. However, decision tables or trees are preferable because they offer a more compact view of the logic.

Not only can decision tables or trees model program control logic, but they can also model an entire program. Theoretically, they can represent any computable function and therefore replace any program flowchart [2]. The control constructs of sequence, selection, and repetition can be represented by a decision table or tree.

COMMENTARY

Decision tables and decision trees are used as detail design tools for complex program logic. They are seldom used at a high level to show program control structure. In general, they should not be used as a stand-alone design tool. They should be used to supplement other design tools such as structure charts, Warnier-Orr diagrams, and action diagrams.

Decision tables are a valuable tool, especially when used with software that automatically converts them to program code. They have been surprisingly neglected by many DP organizations.

REFERENCES

1. B. Moret, "Decision Trees and Diagrams," *Computing Surveys,* 14, no. 4 (December 1982), 593–623.

2. A. Lew, "On the Emulation of Flowcharts by Decision Tables," *CACM,* 25, no. 12 (December 1982), 895–905.

22 DATA ANALYSIS DIAGRAMS

INTRODUCTION   Many structured techniques represent data as tree structures (hierarchies). This is illustrated for Michael Jackson methodology in Fig. 16.1 and for Warnier methodology in Fig. 15.3.

The data on purchase orders, bank statements, restaurant menus, and most computer printouts can be represented as tree structures. However, some computer input and output data are not hierarchical. Such data can be drawn as tree structures only if certain data items are shown redundantly or if there are no non-tree-structured associations linking the trees. Nonhierarchical data structures are referred to as *plex* or *network* structures.

Plex- or network-structured data are extremely important in the data-base environment. This and the following chapter illustrate the ways in which data-base structures are drawn. This chapter illustrates *bubble charts* and *drawings of record structures;* Chapter 23 illustrates *entity-relationship diagrams* and *data models.*

BUBBLE CHARTS   Bubble charts provide a way of drawing and understanding the associations among data items. This understanding is necessary in order to create records that are clearly structured. Bubble charts form the input to a data modeling process that creates stable data structures. This process is automated.

Bubble charts are a useful way to teach end users and analysts about associations in data. They should employ bubble charts when they start to create logical data-base structures. As these people become more expert, they can avoid drawing charts and represent the same information as input to an automated tool that synthesizes the data structure.

The most elemental piece of data is called a *data item*. It is sometimes also called a *field* or a *data element*. This is the "atom" of data; it cannot be subdivided into smaller data types and retain any meaning to the users of the data. You cannot split the data item called SALARY, for example, into smaller data items that are meaningful by themselves to end users.

In a bubble chart, each *type* of data item is drawn as an ellipse:

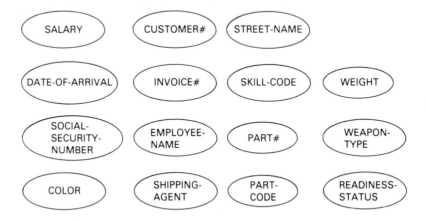

A data base contains hundreds (sometimes thousands) of types of data items. Several thousand types of data items may be used in the running of a big corporation.

To computerize the activities of a corporation, the data items it uses must be defined, cataloged, and organized. This is often difficult and time-consuming because data have been treated rather sloppily in the past. What is essentially the same data-item type has been defined differently in different places, represented differently in computers, and given different names. Data-item types that were casually thought to be the same are found to be not quite the same.

The data administrator has the job of cleaning up this confusion. Definitions of data-item types must be agreed on and documented. Much help from end users is often needed in this process.

ASSOCIATIONS BETWEEN DATA ITEMS

A data item by itself is not of much use. For example, a value of SALARY by itself is uninteresting. It only becomes interesting when it is associated with another data item, such as EMPLOYEE NAME:

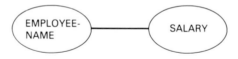

A data base, therefore, consists not only of data items but also of associations between them. There are a large number of different data-item types, and we need a map showing how they are associated. This map is sometimes called a *data model*.

ONE-TO-ONE AND   There are two kinds of links that we shall draw be-
ONE-TO-MANY   tween data items: one-to-one associations and one-to-
ASSOCIATIONS   many associations.

A *one-to-one* association from data-item type A to data-item type B means that at each instant in time, each value of A has *one and only one* value of B associated with it. There is a one-to-one mapping from A to B. If you know the value of A, you can know the value of B.

There is only one value of SALARY associated with a value of EMPLOYEE# at one instant in time; therefore, we can draw a one-to-one link from EMPLOYEE# to SALARY:

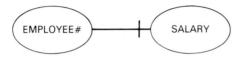

It is said that EMPLOYEE# *identifies* SALARY. If you know the value of EMPLOYEE#, you can know the value of SALARY.

A *one-to-many* link from A to B means that one value of A has *one or many* values of B associated with it. A one-to-many mapping from A to B is drawn with a crow's foot.

Whereas an employee can have only one salary at a given time, he might have one or many girl-friends. We would therefore draw

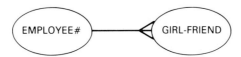

For one value of the data-item type EMPLOYEE# there can be one or many values of the data-item type GIRL-FRIEND.

We can draw both of the above situations on one bubble chart:

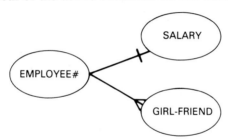

This bubble chart *synthesizes* the two earlier charts into one chart. From this one chart we could derive either of the two previous charts.

The two previous charts might be two different user views, one user being interested in salary and the other in girl-friends. We have created one simple data structure that incorporates these two user views. This is what the data administrator does when building a data base, but the real-life user views are much more complicated than this illustration, and there are many of them. The resulting data model sometimes has hundreds or even thousands of data-item types.

TYPES AND INSTANCES

The terms with which we describe data can refer to *types* of data or to *instances* of those data. EMPLOYEE NAME refers to a type of data item. FRED SMITH is an instance of this data-item type. EMPLOYEE may refer to a type of record. There are many instances of this record type, one for each person employed. The diagrams in this chapter show *types* of data, not instances. A data model shows the associations among *types* of data.

The bubble chart shows data-item types. There are many occurrences of each data-item type. In the foregoing example there are many employees, each with a salary and with zero, one, or many girl-friends. You might imagine a third dimension to the bubble charts showing the many values of each data-item type:

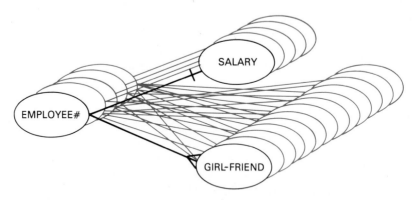

In discussing data we ought to distinguish between types and instances. Sometimes abbreviated wording is used in literature about data. The words *data item* or *record* are used to mean *data-item type* or *record type*.

REVERSE ASSOCIATIONS

Between any two data-item types there can be a mapping in both directions. This gives four possibilities for forward and reverse association. If the data-item types are MAN and WOMAN and the relationship between them represents marriage, the four theoretical possibilities are as follows:

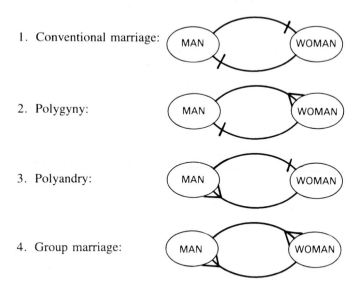

1. Conventional marriage: MAN — WOMAN

2. Polygyny: MAN — WOMAN

3. Polyandry: MAN — WOMAN

4. Group marriage: MAN — WOMAN

The reverse associations are not always of interest. For example, in this following bubble chart

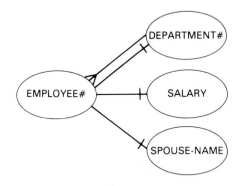

we want the reverse association from DEPARTMENT# to EMPLOYEE# because users want to know what employees work in a given department. However, there is no link from SPOUSE-NAME to EMPLOYEE# because no user wants to ask, "What employee has a spouse named Gertrude?" If a user wanted to ask, "What employees have a salary over $25,000?" we might include a crow's-foot link from SALARY to EMPLOYEE#.

KEYS AND ATTRIBUTES

Given the bubble chart method of representing data, we can state definitions of three important terms: *primary key, secondary key,* and *attribute*.

A *primary key* is a bubble with *one or more one-to-one links* leaving it. Thus in Fig. 22.1, A, C, and F are primary keys. A primary key may uniquely identify many data items.

Data items that are not primary keys are referred to as *nonprime attributes*. All data items, then, are either *primary keys* or *nonprime attributes*.

In Fig. 22.1, B, D, E, G, H, and I are nonprime attributes. Often the word *attribute* is used instead of *nonprime attribute*. Strictly, the primary key data items are attributes also. EMPLOYEE# is an attribute of the employee.

The names of data-item types that are primary keys are underlined in the bubble charts and drawings of records. We can define a nonprime attribute as follows: A *nonprime attribute* is a bubble with *no one-to-one links* leaving it.

Each primary key uniquely identifies one or more data items. Those that are not other primary keys are attributes.

A *secondary key* does not uniquely identify another data item. One value of a secondary key is associated with one or many values of another data item. A crow's-foot link joins it to another data item. Thus a *secondary key* is a nonprime attribute with *one or more one-to-many links* leaving it. In Fig. 22.1, E and H are secondary keys.

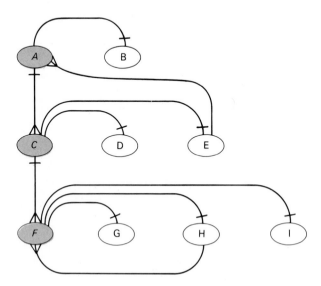

Figure 22.1 A bubble chart showing one-to-one (———+—) and one-to-many (———<) associations among data-item types.

These three fundamental definitions are repeated in the following box for easy reference.

A *primary key* is a bubble with one or more one-to-one links leaving it.

A *nonprime attribute* is a bubble with no one-to-one links leaving it.

A *secondary key* is an attribute with one or more one-to-many links leaving it.

DATA-ITEM GROUPS

When using a data base, we need to extract several views of data from one overall data-base structure. The bubble charts representing these different views of data can be merged into one overall chart. In the bubble chart that results from combining many user views, the bubbles are grouped by primary key. Each primary key is the unique identifier of a group of data-item types. It points with one-to-one links to each nonprime attribute in that group.

The data-item group needs to be structured carefully so that it is as stable as possible. We should not group together an ad hoc collection of data items. There are formal rules for structuring the data-item group; we discuss these in Chapter 40.

RECORDS

The data-item group is commonly called a *record,* sometimes a *logical record* to distinguish it from whatever may be stored physically. A record is often drawn as a bar containing the names of its data items, as in Fig. 22.2.

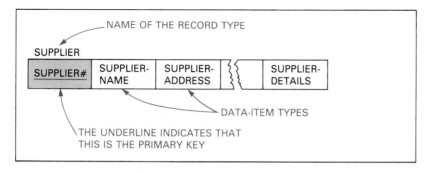

Figure 22.2 Drawing of a logical record.

The record in Fig. 22.2 represents the following bubble chart:

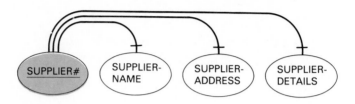

It may be useful to split the SUPPLIER ADDRESS data item into component data items:

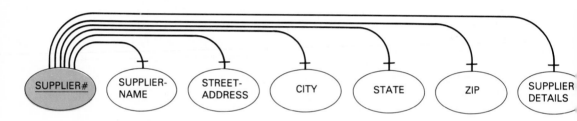

This is useful only if the components may be individually referenced.

Figure 22.3 shows the record redrawn to show that STREET ADDRESS, CITY, STATE, and ZIP are collectively referred to as SUPPLIER ADDRESS but are not by themselves a record with a primary key.

CONCATENATED KEYS   Some data-item types cannot be identified by any single data-item type in a user's view. They need a primary key (unique identifier) that is composed of more than one data-item type in combination. This is called a *concatenated key*.

SUPPLIER#	SUPPLIER-NAME	SUPPLIER-ADDRESS				SUPPLIER-DETAILS
		STREET-ADDRESS	CITY	STATE	ZIP	

Figure 22.3 The record in Fig. 22.2 redrawn to show the decomposition of SUPPLIER-ADDRESS. These components do not by themselves constitute a record or data-item group with a primary key.

Several suppliers may supply a part and each charge a different price for it. The primary key SUPPLIER# is used for identifying information about a supplier. The key PART# is used for identifying information about a part. Neither of these keys is sufficient for identifying the *price*. The price is dependent on both the supplier and the part. We create a new key to identify the price, which consists of SUPPLIER# and PART# joined together (concatenated). We draw this as one bubble:

The two fields from which the concatenated key is created are joined with a + symbol.

The concatenated key has one-to-one links to the keys SUPPLIER# and PART#. The resulting graph is as follows:

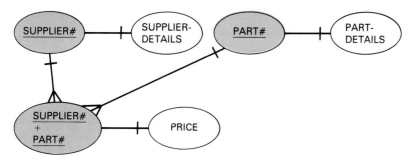

By introducing this form of concatenated key into the logical view of data, we make each data item dependent on one key bubble. Whenever a concatenated key is introduced, the designer should ensure that the items it identifies are dependent on the whole key, not on a portion of it only.

In practice it is sometimes necessary to join together more than two data-item types in a concatenated key. For example, a company supplies a product to domestic and industrial customers. It charges a different price to different *types of customers,* and the price varies from one *state* to another. A *discount* provides different price reductions for different quantities purchased. The *price* is thus identified by a combination of CUSTOMER-TYPE, STATE, DISCOUNT, and PRODUCT:

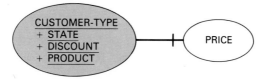

The use of concatenated keys gives each data-item group in the resulting data model a simple structure in which each nonprime attribute is fully dependent on the key bubble and nothing else:

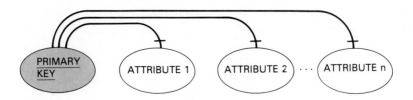

DERIVED DATA

Certain data items are derived by calculation from other data items. For example, TOTAL AMOUNT on an invoice may be derived by adding the AMOUNT data items on individual lines. A derived data-item type may be marked on a bubble chart by shading its "bubble." Dashed or colored lines may be drawn to the derived data-item type from the data-item types from which it is derived, as illustrated in Fig. 22.4. The calculation for deriving the data is written on the diagram.

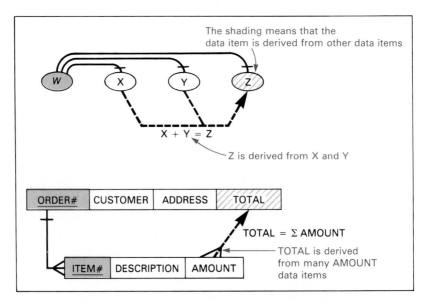

Figure 22.4   Derived data-item types shown on diagrams of data.

Derived data items may or may not be stored with the data. They might be calculated whenever the data are retrieved. To store them requires more storage; to calculate them each time requires more processing. As storage drops in cost, it is increasingly attractive to store them. The diagrams initially drawn are *logical* representations of data that represent derived data without saying whether or not it is stored. This is a later, physical decision.

There has been much debate about whether derived data-item types should be shown on diagrams of data or data models. In our view, they should be shown. Some fourth-generation or nonprocedural languages cause data to be derived automatically once statements like those in Fig. 22.4 are made describing the derivation.

THE HOUSE OF MUSIC INC.
A Collins Corporation
Main Office
108 Old Street, White Cliffs, IL 67309
063 259 0003

SALES CONTRACT

Contract No. 7094

SOLD BY		DATE	
Mike			6/10/83

Name Herbert H. Matlock

Address 1901 Keel Road

City Ramsbottom, Illinois   Zip 64736

Phone 063 259 3730   Customer # 18306

REMARKS:

10 yrs. parts and labor on the Piano
1 yr. parts and labor on pianocorder

Delivery Address:

DESCRIPTION	PRICE	DISCOUNT	AMOUNT
New Samick 5'2" Grand Piano model G-1A			
# 820991 with Marantz P-101 # 11359			9500.00

TOTAL AMOUNT	9500.00
TRADE IN ALLOWANCE	2300.00
SALES TAX	
DEPOSIT	1000.00
FINAL BALANCE	6200.00

PLEASE NOTE: All sales pending approval by management and verification of trade-in description.

If this contract is breached by the BUYER, the SELLER may take appropriate legal action, or, at its option, retain the deposit as liquidated damages.

Buyer's Signature

Figure 22.5   Sales contract. The data-item types on this document are diagrammed in Figs. 22.6 and 22.7.

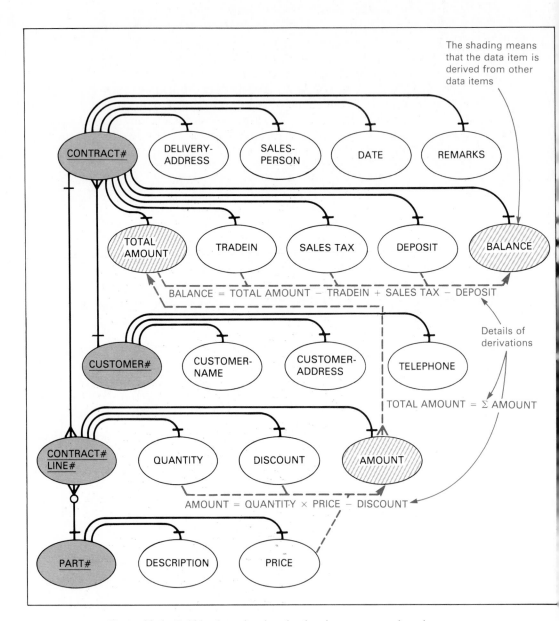

The shading means that the data item is derived from other data items

BALANCE = TOTAL AMOUNT − TRADEIN + SALES TAX − DEPOSIT

Details of derivations

TOTAL AMOUNT = Σ AMOUNT

AMOUNT = QUANTITY × PRICE − DISCOUNT

Figure 22.6 Bubble chart showing the data-item types on the sales contract of Fig. 22.5 and the associations among them. A Warnier-Orr diagram showing the data items in the sales contract appears in Fig. 15.4, and a Jackson tree-structure diagram of the sales contract is shown in Fig. 16.2.

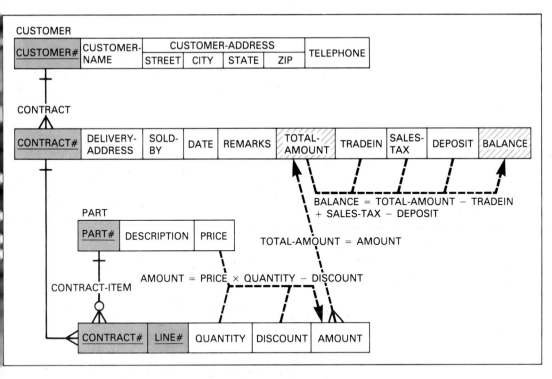

Figure 22.7   Record diagram of the data in Fig. 22.6.

OPTIONAL DATA ITEMS

Sometimes a data-item type is optional. It may or may not exist. For one value of A there may be zero or one value of B. This is indicated by putting an open circle on the link:

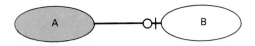

For example,

If the optional bubble is a nonprime attribute (rather than a primary key), it may be treated like any other nonprime attribute when synthesizing the data model.

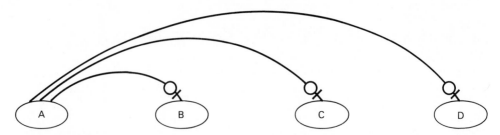

In the mutually exclusive case, one field in a record can be allocated. In the non–mutually exclusive case above, three fields are needed (possibly each with a mechanism for eliminating option fields when not used).

BOX 22.1   Notation used on bubble charts for data analysis. (Compare with Box 23.1.)

A data-item (field) type
is drawn as a named bubble.   (EMPLOYEE)

1:1 Association

- A identifies B.
- B is functionally dependent on A.
- For one occurrence of A there is always one and only one occurrence of B.

1:M Association

For one occurrence of A there are one or multiple occurrences of B.

Optional 1:1 Association

For one occurrence of A there is zero or one occurrence of B.

Optional 1:M Association

For one occurrence of A there are zero, one, or multiple occurrences of B.

BOX 22.1   *(Continued)*

Labeled Associations

A label may be written on an association. This is normally done when two associations with different meanings exist between the same two data-item types.

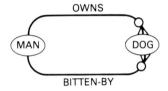

Grouped Data-Item Types

Several data-item types are given a group name but do not constitute a record.

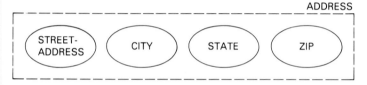

Primary Key

A primary key is a data-item type with a one-to-one link to other data-item types. That is, it *identifies* other data-item types. The name of the primary key data-item is underlined.

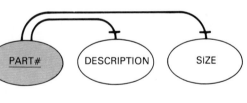

Concatenated Keys

When a primary key consists of multiple data-item types, these are drawn as one bubble. Their names are separated with a " + "

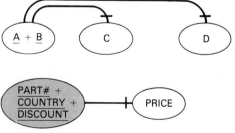

(Continued)

BOX 22.1   *(Continued)*

The components of the
concatenated key are drawn
on the chart.

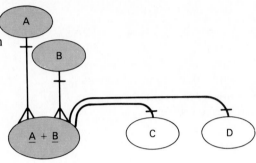

Derived Data

The shading of a bubble means that
this data item is derived
from other data items.

The boldface arrow shows from which
data-item types a derived
data-item type is obtained.

The derivation equation
may be written by the
arrow.

$$X = Y + Z$$

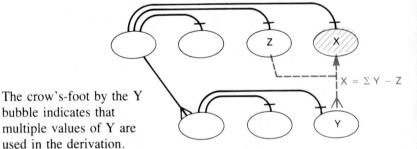

$$X = \Sigma\, Y - Z$$

The crow's-foot by the Y
bubble indicates that
multiple values of Y are
used in the derivation.

23 ENTITY-RELATIONSHIP DIAGRAMS

INTRODUCTION   Chapter 22 contained detailed low-level diagrams of data. This chapter contains high-level overview diagrams of data that are used in strategic or top-down planning [1].

Top-down planning of data identifies the entities involved in running an enterprise and determines the relationships among them. An entity-relationship diagram is developed; this can be decomposed into detailed data models.

To run an enterprise efficiently, certain data are needed. These data are needed regardless of whether computers are used, but computers provide great power in getting the right data to the right people. The data in question need to be planned and described. We need data about these data. Data about data are referred to as *metadata*. A *data model* contains *metadata*.

Data analysts need much help from end users and user executives to enable them to understand an organization's data and to design the data that will be most useful in managing the organization. They need clear ways of diagramming the data. Diagrams like those in this chapter are an essential part of the overall planning of an organization's information resources.

ENTITIES   An *entity* is something, real or abstract, about which we store data. Examples of entity types are CUSTOMER, PART, EMPLOYEE, INVOICE, MACHINE TOOL, SALESPERSON, BRANCH OFFICE, SALES TV AREA, WAREHOUSE, WAREHOUSE BIN, SHOP ORDER, SHIFT REPORT, PRODUCT SPECIFICATION, LEDGER ACCOUNT, JOURNAL POSTING ACCOUNT, PAYMENT, CASH RECEIPT, DEBTOR, CREDITOR, and DEBTOR ANALYSIS RECORD.

The name of each entity type should be a noun, sometimes with a modifier word. An entity type may be thought of as having the properties of a noun. An entity has various *attributes* that we wish to record, such as color, monetary value, percentage utilization, or name.

An *entity type* is a named class of entities that have the same set of *attribute* types: for example, EMPLOYEE is an entity type. An *entity instance* is one specific occurrence of an entity type: for example, B. J. WATKINS is an instance of the entity type EMPLOYEE.

In common usage, the term *entity type* is abbreviated to *entity*. When you see an expression such as ''the CUSTOMER entity,'' be aware that it really refers to an *entity type*.

Using this abbreviation, we describe data in terms of *entities* and *attributes*. The difference between these is that we store information about an entity in multiple data-item types. We do not store information about an attribute in multiple data-item types. If a data-item type that we have been calling an attribute requires information stored about it other than its value, then it is really an entity.

An entity type is represented by a rectangular box. For most entities we store records: CUSTOMER records, PART records, EMPLOYEE records, and the like. The box is sometimes also used to show an entity record type. However, the intent of our data model is to represent the reality of the data without yet thinking about how we will represent it in computers. We may decide to represent it without a conventional record structure.

ENTITY DIAGRAMS   On an *entity-relationship diagram* (often called simply *entity diagram*) the boxes are interconnected by links that represent associations between entity types.

The data in Fig. 22.7 contain four entities: CUSTOMER, PART, CONTRACT, and CONTRACT-ITEM. An entity-relationship diagram can be drawn using the same notation as in Chapter 22:

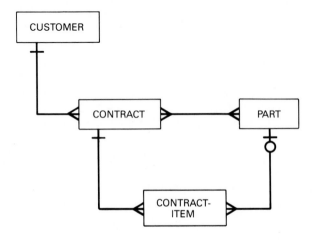

This diagram shows that a customer can have multiple contracts. A contract is for one customer and can be for more than one contract item. There are zero, one, or many contracts for each part. A contract item relates to one contract and one part. Examine Fig. 23.1 to be sure you understand the meaning of the links.

CONCATENATED ENTITY TYPE

Some important information does not relate to one entity alone but to the conjunction of entities. For

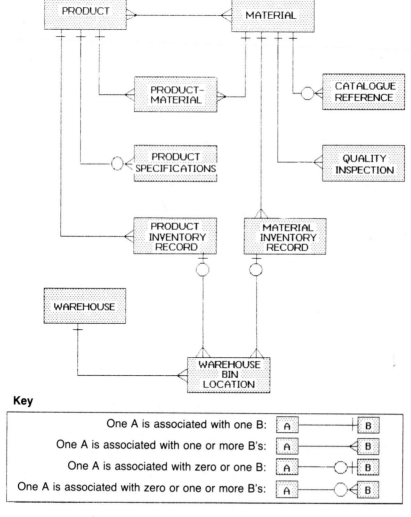

Figure 23.1   An entity-relationship diagram.

example, Fig. 23.1 has a PRODUCT entity and a MATERIAL entity. We want
to record how much of a given material is used on a given product. This requires a concatenated entity, PRODUCT + MATERIAL. It is not information
about the product alone or the material alone. This concatenated entity can be
added to the diagram of Fig. 23.1:

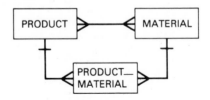

Whenever a link has a crow's foot at both ends, the designer should ask
whether there is any information that would need a concatenation of the two
entities. Usually there is.

Mutually Exclusive Associations

Some associations are mutually exclusive. If A can be associated with either B
or C, but not with both, we draw

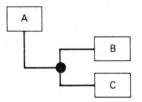

The line branching at the dot indicates that the two links are mutually exclusive.
Suppose, for example, that an aircraft is permitted (say, for regulatory reasons)
to carry cargo or passengers but not both. We can draw the following:

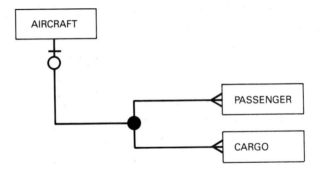

If a driver can be allocated to a truck, car, or motorbike, but only to one of these, we can draw

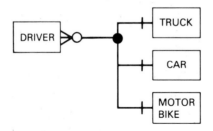

Mutually Inclusive Associations

Some associations are mutually inclusive. In other words, if A is associated with B, it must also be associated with C. We draw this with a line branching (without a dot):

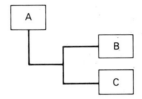

Subset Associations

One association may be a subset of another. In this case the associations are linked by a line with an S around the subset association:

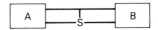

Here the bottom association is a subset of the top one.

Cross-link Associations

Mutual exclusivity, mutual inclusivity, and subset situations are represented by cross-links (links between links). Links may, in principle, be linked with other conditions, though there are few practical applications of cross-links other than those shown.

Looped Associations

Sometimes an occurrence of an entity of a given type is associated with other occurrences of the same type. In this case we draw a loop:

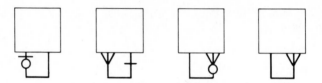

For example, in a zoo data base, we might wish to record which animals are children of other animals and which animal is the mother:

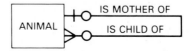

It is normally desirable to label looped associations. Sometimes more than one loop is necessary for the same entity type:

Loops are common in a factory bill of materials. A subassembly is composed of other subassemblies:

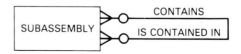

In a personnel data base, some employees manage other employees:

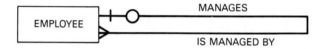

LABELS AND SENTENCES

The link between entities should be thought of as forming a simple sentence. The entity at the start of the link is the *subject* of the sentence, and the entity to which the link goes is the *object*. Here are some links and their corresponding sentences:

AN INVOICE HAS ONE OR MULTIPLE LINE-ITEMS.

PASSENGER SOMETIMES REQUIRES SPECIAL-CATERING.

For entities with two links there are two sentences:

PASSENGER SOMETIMES HAS PURCHASED TICKET(S).
PASSENGER SOMETIMES HAS USED TICKET(S).

Many links have a meaningful link in both directions (which means that they are really two links, one in each direction):

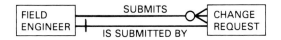

FIELD ENGINEER SUBMITS CHANGE REQUEST.
CHANGE REQUEST IS SUBMITTED BY FIELD ENGINEER.

In this case the two sentences for the same link had effectively the same meaning. That is not always the case, as in this example:

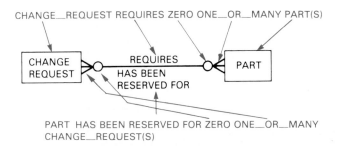

It is desirable that the label on the link compose a sentence, as in the examples just given. This sentence building should be enforced as a discipline of entity analysis. A label that does not form a sentence can be vague:

Some data analysts like to label every link. This takes time, and the additional work is often not worthwhile. The meanings of most links are obvious. Where a link could have alternate meanings, it should be labeled. For example, it may be important to state that a LOADSHEET records *on-board* passengers and baggage, not merely passengers who are booked or who have checked in:

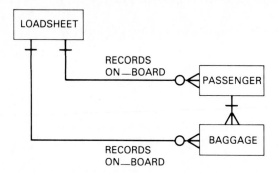

Figure 23.2 shows a telephone-company entity diagram with labeled links.

SUBJECT AND PREDICATE   The information in an information system can be thought of as consisting of statements—factual assertions on topics of concern to the enterprise; for example,

> B. J. Watkins manages the sales department.
> K. L. Jones works for the sales department.
> March had a net after-tax profit of $150,000.
> Order 72193 has a due date of June 17.

Sentences can be passed into a subject-and-predicate form. The predicate can be decomposed into a descriptor and an association that connects the descriptor to the subject:

Subject	Predicate	
	Association	Descriptor
B. J. Watkins	manages	the sales department
K. L. Jones	works for	the sales department
March	had a net after-tax profit of	$150,000
Order 72193	has a due date of	June 17

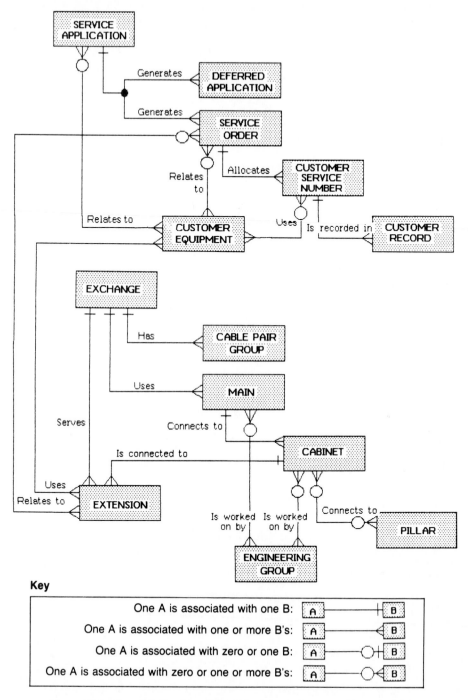

Key

One A is associated with one B:	A ———‖— B
One A is associated with one or more B's:	A ——< B
One A is associated with zero or one B:	A —O‖— B
One A is associated with zero or one or more B's:	A —O< B

Figure 23.2 Part of an entity-relationship diagram for a telephone company, showing labeled associations.

The components of these sentences are entities, links, attributes, or attribute values:

Subject	Predicate	
	Association	Descriptor
B. J. Watkins (ENTITY)	manages (LINK)	the sales department (ENTITY)
K. L. Jones (ENTITY)	works for (LINK)	the sales department (ENTITY)
March (ENTITY)	had a net after-tax profit of (ATTRIBUTE)	$150,000 (VALUE)
Order 72193 (ENTITY)	has a due date of (ATTRIBUTE)	June 17 (VALUE)

All the entities in the table have values. A data model creates a framework into which multiple values can be recorded. The values change; the framework remains the same. The flight-information display at an airport is a framework like a simple data model into which changing values are placed.

For the sentences in our example we can draw a framework that shows the entity types. Attributes can be drawn as ellipses (as in Chapter 22). The frameworks or models for our four sentences are as follows:

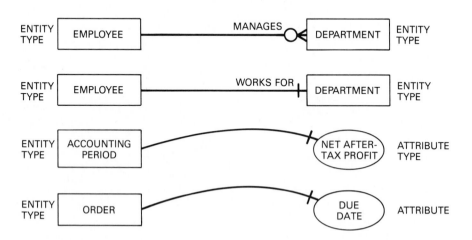

Some research is in progress on advanced forms of data models in which the meaning of the link is encoded so as to be intelligible to computers. This can be used in advanced languages that employ the data base.

BASIC CONSTRUCTS

It will be seen that there are four basic constructs in representing data: entity, attribute, attribute value, and link. Sometimes a more subtle construct is needed, a cross-link. This is a relationship between links; mutual exclusivity, mutual inclusivity, and subset situations are examples. We may also use formulas to show how derived data are obtained.

A simple entity-relationship diagram normally contains *entity types* and *links*. Infrequently, *cross-links* are drawn. As the entity diagram is expanded into a full data model, *attributes* are added, and sometimes formulas for derived attributes. When the model is translated into implementations, the attributes assume *attribute values*.

Integrity checks can be stated on links and attributes. A link can have a maximum and minimum value of cardinality (how many of entity B can be associated with entity A). An attribute may have a maximum and minimum value or a discrete set of values. An entity value may be constrained to be of a stated data type.

Box 23.1 summarizes these constructs.

SEMANTIC INDEPENDENCE

The objective of building entity-relationship diagrams and data models is to create a description of the semantics of data that reflects the actual enterprise and its informational requirements. The task of the data modeler is to capture reality and communicate about it accurately. He tends to be distracted from this task if he has to think about computer hardware or data-base software or if the line between semantics and implementation of data becomes blurred.

A well-structured model keeps one fact in one place (a principle of data normalization discussed in Chapter 40). Each semantic building block is intended to be as independent as possible from the others. This has the following practical payoffs [2]:

- Each construct has but one meaning, and each meaning is captured in just one construct. Exceptions and special cases are minimized. Building, reading, learning, and understanding data models is easier and less error-prone.

- The decisions that a data modeler must make become more distinct and independent, so the analyst can deal with them one at a time. Modeling decisions do not have hidden, unexpected consequences.

- Changes in a logical data model are localized. When some aspect of reality changes, only the constructs that directly represent that aspect need to change. To be stable is the prime virtue for a data model, and in a changing world the best stability is often the ability to change gracefully.

- Well-defined and decoupled primitives are the best building blocks for creating complex structures to represent complex realities, because they can be freely combined into structures whose meaning is clear.

BOX 23.1   Basic constructs used for describing data

ON A DETAILED DATA MODEL

ON AN ENTITY-RELATIONSHIP CHART

- ENTITY TYPE
  An entity is something about which we store data.
  An entity type refers to a class of entities about which the
  same attributes are kept.
- LINK
  An association between two entity types showing how they
  are related.
- LINK CONNECTOR
  A connection between two or more links showing how they
  are related.

- ATTRIBUTE
  A single piece of information about an entity type.
- FORMULA FOR DERIVED ATTRIBUTE
  A means of computing the value of an attribute which is
  derived from other attributes.

- ATTRIBUTE VALUE
  A symbol denoting some quality or quantity which is used
  to describe entities, and which is used as an instance of an
  attribute.

- Modelers and users are free to attend to what they know best—the reality of
  their enterprise and the information they need to know about it.

The clean separation of the semantics of data from other considerations is
referred to as *semantic independence*.

**INVERTED-L
DIAGRAMS**
In a data model designed to be as useful as it can be,
a substantial amount of information needs to be recorded about entities, attributes, and links. Diagrams
like Figs. 23.1 and 23.2 do not have enough space to show all that is needed.

The information can be stored in a data dictionary or "encyclopedia," but it also helps to show it graphically.

An entity can be shown in the form of an inverted L, as shown in Fig. 23.3. This figure shows a subset of a data model with two entities and three links between them. UI indicates which attribute or attributes are unique identifiers of the entity. Names of entity types and attributes are in capitals. Comments or a description may be written against the top part of the L. The vertical part of the L leaves room for listing many attributes and links.

The *cardinality* of a link refers to the number of entities it points to. It may point to zero, one, or many. We may be able to make a cardinality statement more precise than "many": for example, < 30. In a few cases an exact number can be stated. A person has exactly 2 parents. A fiscal year has 12 accounting periods. Cardinality limits are written on the link.

Details about the value of an attribute may be written by its name. Figure

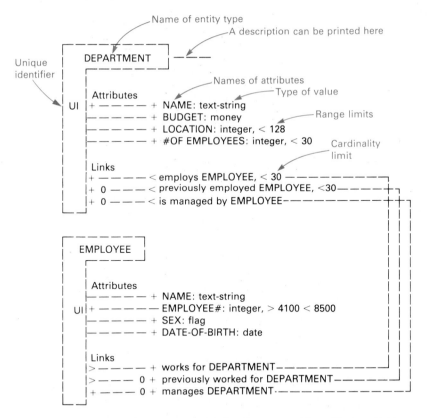

Figure 23.3 A subset of a data model showing two entities with three links between them. Names of entity types and attributes are in capitals. The diagram is designed for printing on a low-cost printer.

23.3 shows the type of value. A PICTURE clause could be written, showing its format. Range limits or other integrity checks may be shown.

Figure 23.3 shows attributes and links against the vertical part of the L. Cross-link associations and complex associations involving multiple attributes or links could also be shown.

ENTITY SUBTYPES   It is sometimes necessary to divide entity types into entity subtypes. In a zoo, for example, the entity type ANIMAL might be subdivided into MAMMAL, REPTILE, FISH, and BIRD. We regard these as entity subtypes *if they have different associations to other entity types*. If, on the other hand, we store essentially the same information about mammals, reptiles, fishes, and birds, we would regard these categories as merely attribute values of the entity type ANIMAL.

We can draw entity subtypes as divisions of the entity type box:

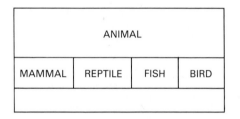

The entity type SATELLITE might be subdivided into LOW-ORBIT and GEOSYNCHRONOUS. LOW-ORBIT SATELLITE has a one-with-many association to the ORBIT DETAIL entity type. GEOSYNCHRONOUS SATELLITE has a one-with-many association with POSITION DETAIL. These two entity types have different attributes.

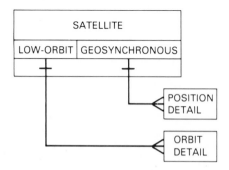

An entity subtype is any subset of entities of a specific entity type about which we wish to record information special to that subtype.

The values of one or more attributes are used to determine the subtype to which a specific entity belongs. These attributes are called the *classifying attributes*.

MULTIPLE SUBTYPE GROUPINGS   The examples we have used show one category of subtyping, drawn as a horizontal band in the entity-type box. There may be more than one independent category of subtyping; if so, we draw a band for each in the entity-type box. The horizontal bands represent independent subtype groupings.

For example, SATELLITE may be subtyped into MILITARY and CIVILIAN, independently of whether it is LOW-ORBIT or GEOSYNCHRONOUS. Again, we store *different* types of information about MILITARY satellite and CIVILIAN satellites.

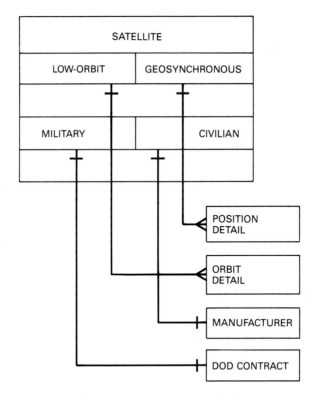

In this illustration each horizontal band contains two *mutually exclusive* entity subtypes. Often the entity subtypes are not mutually exclusive. There may be other entities that do not fit into the subtypes shown. This is indicated by leaving blank space in the horizontal band:

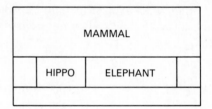

An entity type may contain both mutually exclusive and non–mutually exclusive groupings:

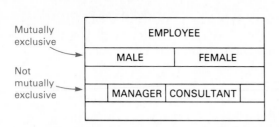

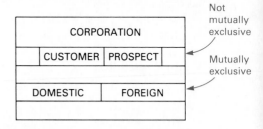

SUBTYPE HIERARCHIES

An entity subtype may itself be subdivided into sub-subtypes:

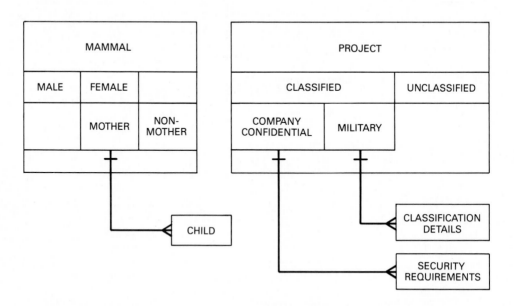

Entity subtypes behave in every way as though they were entity types. They have attributes and associations to other entities.

Ian Palmer stresses that in his experience of data analysis, the newcomer confuses the concepts of entity subtypes and associations among entity types [3]. He emphasizes the importance of recognizing these to be completely different concepts in spite of the fact that most data-base management systems ignore the concept of entity subtypes.

A simple test can help avoid confusion. We ask, "Is A a B?" and "Is B an A?" The permissible answers are *always, sometimes,* and *never.* If both answers are *never,* we are not concerned with subtyping. If both answers are *always,* then A and B are synonyms. If the answers are "Is A a B? Always. Is B an A? Sometimes," then A is a subtype of B.

Let us look at a case that might be confusing. A somewhat bureaucratic organization has people with the following titles: official, adviser, subagent, and representative. Should each of these be a separate entity type, or are they subtypes, or merely attributes?

The cells in the following tables answer the question "Is A a B?"

Is A a B?		B: OFFICIAL	ADVISER	SUBAGENT	REPRESENTATIVE
A:	OFFICIAL		Sometimes	Never	Always
	ADVISER	Never		Never	Never
	SUBAGENT	Never	Never		Always
	REPRESENTATIVE	Sometimes	Never	Sometimes	

The word *always* appears twice. An official and a subagent are *always* a REPRESENTATIVE. These can be subtypes of the entity type REPRESENTATIVE. An official is *never* a subagent, and vice versa, so they are mutually exclusive subtypes. Can there be representatives other than officials and subagents? *No.* Therefore we draw:

REPRESENTATIVE	
OFFICIAL	SUBAGENT

An adviser is *never* any of the others, so that is a separate entity type.

Do we *really* want to regard OFFICIAL and SUBAGENT as entity sub-types, or should they be attributes of REPRESENTATIVE? To answer this we ask, "Do they have associations that are different from those of REPRESEN-TATIVE that we need to include in the data model?" *Yes,* they do. An official supervises a subagent. A subagent is an external employee working for a cor-poration, about which separate records are kept. An association from OFFICIAL to SUBAGENT is needed. This can be drawn inside the entity-type box:

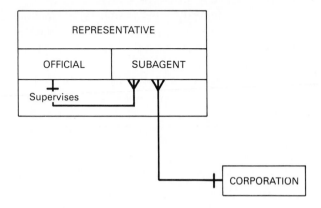

This conveys more information than an attempt at entity analysis without subtyping, which might show the following:

COMPUTER
REPRESENTATION
OF THE DIAGRAM
Entity diagrams can be drawn in a manageable fash-ion for a dozen or so entities. With hundreds of en-tities, the diagram would be difficult to draw and a mess to maintain without computer graphics.

A computerized tool can identify small hierarchies within a more complex structure and assign levels to the structure as illustrated in Figs. 10.17 to 10.20. Figure 23.4 shows a complex entity diagram simplified by drawing the subhierarchies as in Fig. 10.20. The diagram is split into subject areas.

With computer graphics the diagram can be constantly edited, added to, and adjusted in the same way that we adjust text with a word processor. A good computer graphics tool makes change easy; hand-drawn diagrams make change difficult. Hand-drawn diagrams of great complexity discourage modification. Often analysts will do anything to avoid redrawing the diagram. This is a serious concern, because on complex projects the more interaction, discussion, and modification there are at the planning and design stages, the better the results.

A diagram with hundreds of entities, whether computer-drawn or not, is impressive but of little use, except perhaps for the data administrator to hang on his wall in the hope of impressing people. However, with computer graphics, small subset diagrams can be extracted, and these are extremely useful. Subset diagrams relating to specific data subjects are extracted by end users for checking and by analysts for specific projects. On these subset diagrams analysts can create data navigation diagrams and design data-base procedures. Physical database designers employ the subset diagrams for designing data bases. Individual data bases normally employ only a portion of the data represented in a large entity diagram.

Figure 23.5 shows an entity diagram of typical complexity drawn with a computerized tool. In this case the tool enables the diagram to be changed and added to easily. It does not level the diagram, producing subhierarchies as in Fig. 23.4. It does not permit subsets to be extracted automatically for users and analysts. Both of these latter properties are desirable. Figure 23.5 is a computerized COW diagram. Computers should be used to clarify the structure and help in employing its information. We regard Fig. 23.5, then, as an example of how computers should *not* be used.

The complete entity diagram should be kept in computer form, where it can be conveniently updated and manipulated. From it, small subset diagrams should be creatable graphically when the data administrator, end users, or systems analysts need to study them, argue about them, and overdraw access maps on them. The entity diagram should feed the more detailed data modeling process that follows.

NOTATION STYLES   Three notations are used for drawing entity diagrams: arrow notation, crow's-foot notation, and Bachman notation. This chapter has used crow's-foot notation. The table on p. 320 shows the equivalencies among these notations.

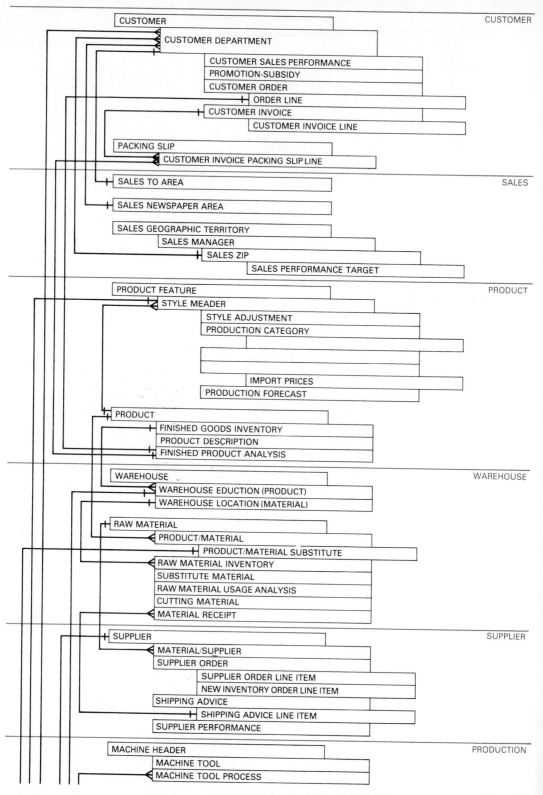

Figure 23.4 An entity chart for a small textile firm.

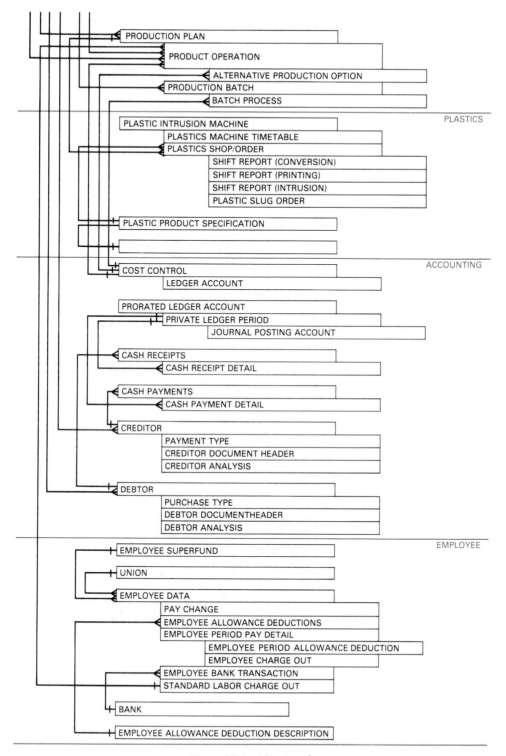

Figure 23.4   (Continued)

Figure 23.5 Portion of an entity diagram of typical complexity drawn with a computerized tool. In this case the tool enables the chart to be changed and added to easily. It does not level the chart, producing subhierarchies as in Fig. 23.4. It does not permit subsets to be extracted auto-

matically for users and analysts. Both of these latter properties are desirable. Consequently, we regard this diagram as an example of how computerized graphics should *not* be used.

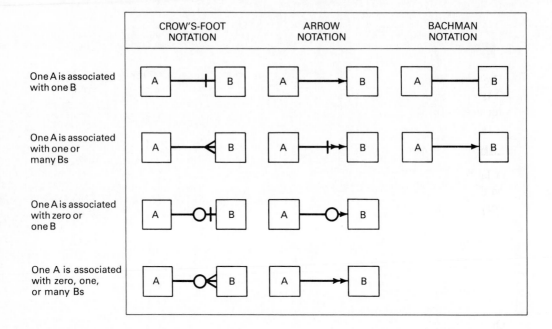

	CROW'S-FOOT NOTATION	ARROW NOTATION	BACHMAN NOTATION

One A is associated with one B

One A is associated with one or many Bs

One A is associated with zero or one B

One A is associated with zero, one, or many Bs

BOX 23.2   Notation used on entity-relationship diagrams

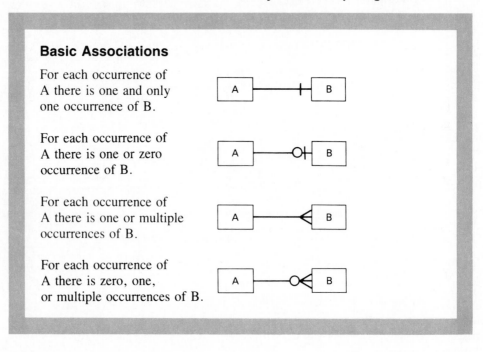

Basic Associations

For each occurrence of A there is one and only one occurrence of B.

For each occurrence of A there is one or zero occurrence of B.

For each occurrence of A there is one or multiple occurrences of B.

For each occurrence of A there is zero, one, or multiple occurrences of B.

BOX 23.2 *(Continued)*

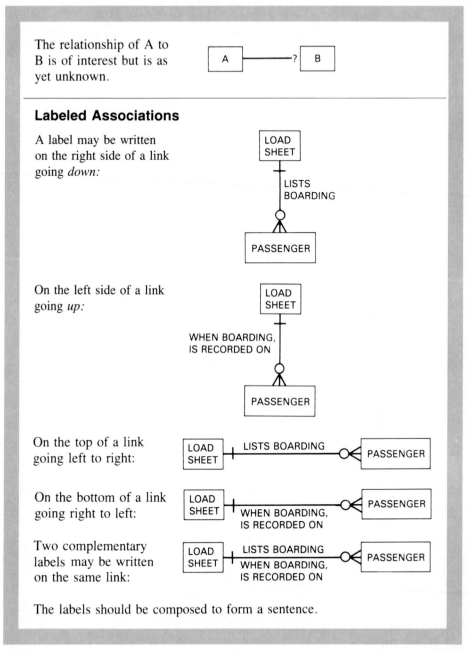

The relationship of A to B is of interest but is as yet unknown.

Labeled Associations

A label may be written on the right side of a link going *down:*

On the left side of a link going *up:*

On the top of a link going left to right:

On the bottom of a link going right to left:

Two complementary labels may be written on the same link:

The labels should be composed to form a sentence.

(Continued)

BOX 23.2 *(Continued)*

Looped Associations

Any of the associations above may be used in a loop. Here an occurrence of an entity is associated with one or more occurrences of entities of the same type.

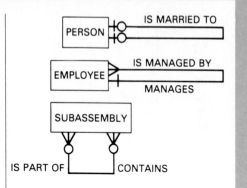

Linked Associations

1. Mutually exclusive associations

   Associations branching from a dot are mutually exclusive. Only one of them can exist for any one occurrence.

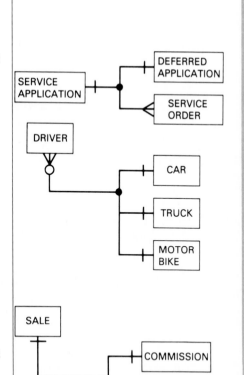

2. Mutually inclusive associations

   Associations connected by a branch are mutually inclusive. All must exist together for any one occurrence.

BOX 23.2   *(Continued)*

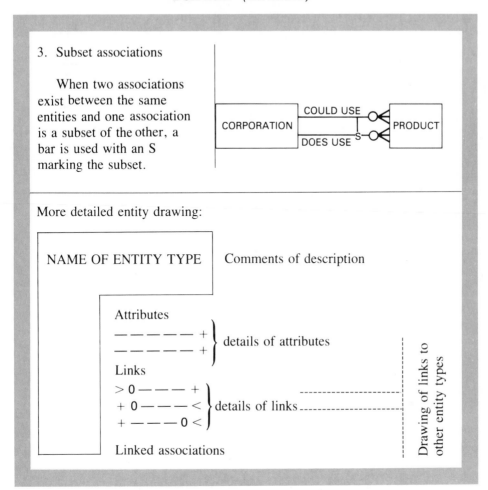

3. Subset associations

   When two associations exist between the same entities and one association is a subset of the other, a bar is used with an S marking the subset.

More detailed entity drawing:

We prefer to use the same notation for bubble charts and entity diagrams so that analysts and users do not have to learn two notations.

Bachman Notation

Bachman notation was an early notation for drawing data-base structures. It deserves a place in the history of systems analysis because it was the first form of data-base diagramming. Bachman notation uses a single-headed arrow for a one-to-many association. It uses an unmarked line for a one-to-one association.

   Bachman notation does not distinguish between the uninteresting association and the one-to-one association. It has no specific way to draw functional dependencies—the single most important input to the detailed data modeling process (see Chapter 41). It cannot draw many of the situations in Box 23.2. We therefore recommend that Bachman notation not be used for entity diagrams, data analysis, or data modeling.

REFERENCES

1. J. Martin, *Strategic Data Planning Methodologies,* Englewood Cliffs, NJ: Prentice-Hall, Inc., 1982.

2. From work done by Ken Winter, Rik Belew, and Bob Walter at Database Design Inc., Ann Arbor, MI.

3. From work done by Ian Palmer at James Martin Associates Ltd., London.

24 DATA NAVIGATION DIAGRAMS

INTRODUCTION   Once a thorough, stable, fully normalized data model exists, the task of the systems analyst and application designer becomes much easier [1]. The designer must determine how he *navigates* through the data base. He needs a clear diagramming technique for this. This chapter discusses the diagramming of data-base navigation; Chapter 25 uses the data-base navigation diagrams for program design.

DIVIDE AND CONQUER   A basic principle of structured design is *divide and conquer*. Complex entangled designs need to be reduced to clean, relatively simple modules. The existence of a thoroughly normalized data model enables complex applications to be reduced to relatively simple projects that *enter and validate* data, *update* data, *perform computations* on data, *handle queries, generate reports and routine documents, conduct audits,* and so on. Sometimes these projects use data in complex ways, with many cross-references among the data.

Many such projects can be performed by one person, especially when fourth-generation languages are used. The main communication among separate developers is via the data model. Most of the human communication problems of large programming projects can be made to disappear. Figure 24.1 illustrates this.

One-person projects are highly appealing. Management can select the person for the job and motivate him highly for speed and excellence. He is in charge of his own success. He is not a cog in a tangled human machine. He will not be slowed down or have to rewrite his code because of other people. When he has finished, management can judge his results and reward him appropriately.

Although one person may be responsible for each of the blocks in Fig.

24.1, a team may sit side by side at terminals so that they can compare notes, see each other's displays, and help each other to understand the meaning of the data.

The divide-and-conquer strategy resulting in one-person projects is made stronger by the use of higher-level data-base languages, and fourth-generation languages in general. With those, one person can often obtain ten times the results in a given time than he could with COBOL. A one-person team can replace a ten-person team. Most fourth-generation languages depend heavily on a data management facility. Nevertheless, with COBOL or PL/I, subdividing projects into small modules is highly desirable, and good data-base management assists this greatly.

SEPARATING DATA FROM PROCEDURES

The information-system needs of some big organizations have grown in complexity as data bases became established. It is possible to use the data in more complex ways. This increase in complexity can be handled only if there is an easy-to-use set of techniques for charting the way through the complexity.

A problem with many structured techniques is that they tangle up the structuring of the data with the structuring of the procedures. This complicates the techniques used. Worse, it results in data that are viewed narrowly and usually not put into a form suitable for other applications that employ the same data.

This chapter and the next assume that the data are designed separately using sound, preferably automated, techniques. The users or analysts who design procedures employ a data model and consider the actions that use that data

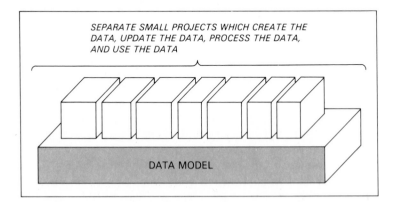

Figure 24.1   A well-designed, stable data model, with appropriate data management facilities, permits application development to be a series of separate, quick-to-implement projects—mostly one-person projects. Communication among the projects is via the data model.

model. Often the data model is designed by a separate data administrator. Sometimes it is designed by the analysts in question.

Data have properties of their own, independent of procedures, that lead to stable structuring. The data navigation diagram is drawn on top of a portion of the data model and links it to the design of the programs that use those data. In this way it forms a simple, easy-to-use bridge between the data model and the procedure design. Any design of a data-base program should begin by sketching the data navigation diagram.

Some fourth-generation languages have enabled data to be used in more complex ways than previously. With some such languages, everything is oriented to the data-base structure. Many users, however, have difficulty learning how to use the full power of the language. They learn to formulate queries and generate reports but not to handle complex data manipulation. One analyst described it as follows: "There is a threshold they cannot get through. It's like flying up through clouds and then all of a sudden the plane breaks out of the clouds and the sun shines." To get through this quickly needs appropriate, ultraclear diagramming techniques, clearly taught.

DATA NAVIGATION DIAGRAMS

The first step in creating procedures that use a data model is to identify the sequence in which the records are accessed. This sequence can be overdrawn on the data model. We will refer to it as a *data navigation diagram*. Information can be created for both the physical data-base designer and the designer of application procedures from the data navigation diagram. The data navigation diagram leads to procedure design with simple *data-base action diagrams* (DAD), which are described in Chapter 25. These in turn lead to structured program code (which is directly applicable to fourth-generation languages).

The complete data model is often too complex for the drawing of access sequences. Only certain entities in the data model are needed. The procedure designer specifies which entities are of concern (see Fig. 24.2).

From the data model, a *neighborhood* may be printed. The neighborhood of one entity is the set of entities that can be reached from it by traversing one link in the data model. Usually this means examining the next-door neighbors in the model. Sometimes the data model may contain extra information saying that additional neighbors should be examined.

The designer examines the neighborhood. He sees the records his procedure will use, plus a few more. He eliminates those he does not want. There may be some he would not have thought about if he had not displayed the neighborhood. There may be some that have *mandatory* links to records he has specified. For example, when a booking record is created, the seat inventory record must be updated.

The designer settles on the group of records his procedure will use. He then has a subset of the overall data model. Usually this is small enough to

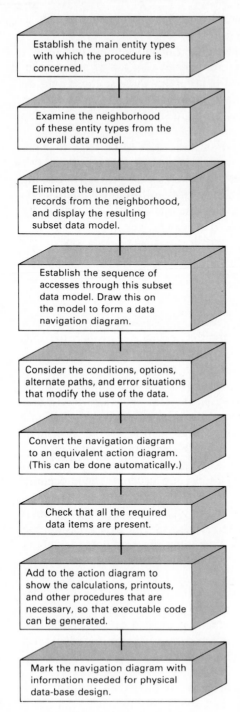

Figure 24.2 Procedure for using data navigation diagrams.

draw on one page. A computerized tool may be available to draw it; if not, it should be drawn by hand.

The designer then makes decisions about the sequence in which his procedure uses the records. He draws this sequence, perhaps with a red pen on the subset data model. He uses a one-to-one link to indicate that one occurrence of a record is accessed and a one-to-many link to indicate that more than one occurrence of a record are accessed.

Data Navigation Diagram for an Order Acceptance System

Consider the design of an order acceptance application for a wholesale distributor. A third-normal-form data model exists, as shown in Fig. 24.3. The designer knows that the application requires CUSTOMER ORDER records and PRODUCT records. The neighborhood of these includes the following records:

> CUSTOMER-ORDER
> CUSTOMER
> ORDER LINE
> BACKORDER
> INVOICE
> PRODUCT
> ORDER-RATE
> QUOTATION
> INVOICE-LINE-ITEM
> PURCHASE-LINE-ITEM

The designer examines the data items in these records. The application does not need any data in the INVOICE, QUOTATION, INVOICE-LINE-ITEM, or PURCHASE-LINE-ITEM records. The ORDER-RATE record should be updated. The designer would have neglected the ORDER-RATE record if he had not printed the neighborhood.

The designer decides, then, that he needs six records and creates a submodel containing these records, as shown in Fig. 24.4.

Figure 24.5 shows his first drawing of the sequence in which the records will be accessed:

1. The CUSTOMER records will be inspected to see whether the customer's credit is good.

2. If the credit is good, a CUSTOMER-ORDER record is created.

3. For each product on the order, the PRODUCT record is inspected to see whether stock is available.

4. If stock is available, an ORDER-LINE record is created, linked to the CUSTOMER-ORDER record, for each product on the order.

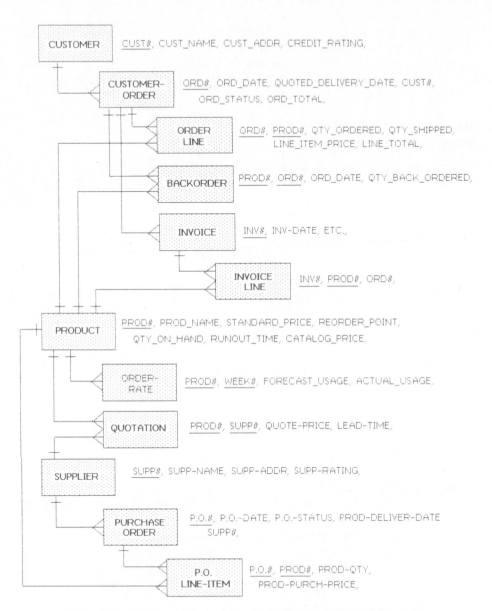

Figure 24.3 Data model for a wholesale distributor. This model is not complete, but because it is correctly normalized it can be grown without pernicious impact to include such things as SALESMAN, WAREHOUSES, ALTERNATE-ADDRESSES, and so on.

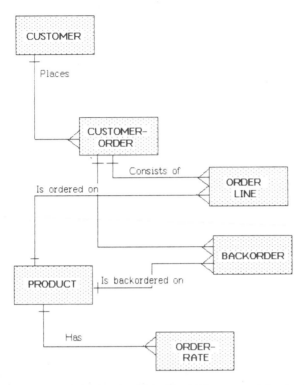

Figure 24.4   Subset of the data model in Fig. 24.3, extracted for the design of the order acceptance procedure.

5. The ORDER-RATE record is updated.

6. If stock is not available, a BACKORDER record is created.

7. When all items are processed, an order confirmation is printed, and the CUSTOMER-ORDER record is updated with ORDER-STATUS, ORDER-TOTAL, and DELIVER-DATE.

Step 2 in Fig. 24.5 is a one-to-many link to indicate that there may be many CUSTOMER-ORDERS for one CUSTOMER.

PROCEDURE DESIGN   The designer now starts to be more precise about what needs to be done with the data.

Initially the *physical* aspects of accessing the data are ignored. Because the data are properly analyzed and structured, the data-base management system (DBMS) can assemble the required data. From the logical point of view, the data navigation diagram is available as though it existed in

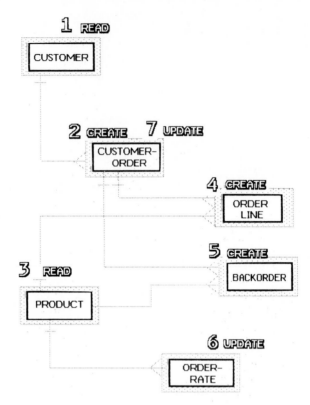

Figure 24.5   Preliminary rough sketch of the data access map, drawn on the
subset data model of Fig. 24.4.

memory just for this designer. Later the data navigation diagram will be annotated with details of numbers of accesses so that it forms valuable input to the
physical data-base designer.

For each step in the data navigation diagram the designer asks three questions:

1. Under what conditions do I want to proceed?
   - Valid or invalid records?
   - Data item >, =, or < certain values?
   - Errors?
   - Results of computations?
   - Matching data items in different records?

2. What do I want to do with, or to, the data?
   - Create, retrieve, update, or delete records?
   - Search, sort, project, or join relations?
   - Computations with the data?

3. What other operations accompany the data-base actions?
   - Print documents?
   - Data-entry screen usage?
   - Security checks?
   - Audit controls?
   - Execution of subroutines?
   - Triggering other transactions?

In Fig. 24.5, the first access is to the CUSTOMER record. The designer asks, "Does a record exist for this customer?" If not, a record must be created. Next, "Is the customer's credit OK?" If it is not, the order is rejected; if it is, the CUSTOMER-ORDER record is created.

The third step in Fig. 24.5 is to the PRODUCT record. The designer asks, "Is this a valid product? Is it discontinued? Is there sufficient product in stock?" If there is insufficient product in stock, a backorder must be placed. If there is sufficient stock, an ORDER-LINE record is created.

The ORDER-RATE record is updated when the ORDER-LINE record is processed.

Finally, the CUSTOMER-ORDER record is updated, with order status, order total, and the estimated delivery date. At that time a confirmation is printed for the customer. Figure 24.6 shows the completed data navigation diagram.

To create the logic and control structures of the program that uses the data base, we recommend *action diagrams*.

The development of the data navigation diagram and the action diagram go hand in hand. Figure 24.7 shows the resulting action diagram, which was automatically created from the data navigation diagram in Fig. 24.6. Figure 24.8 shows the action diagram expanded to show the detailed logic.

PHYSICAL DESIGN   We have said that the data navigation diagram gives information to the physical data-base designer as well as to the application procedure designer. The physical accesses may not be in the same sequence as the logical accesses of the data navigation diagram. In Fig. 24.6, for example, there are two accesses to CUSTOMER-ORDER; in physical practice there would only be one. The first creation of the CUS-TOMER-ORDER record would be in the computer's main memory. This record would not be written on the external storage medium until the second reference to it in the data navigation diagram, after which it is complete.

Again, the ORDER-LINE records in Fig. 24.6 are children of the CUSTOMER-ORDER record, so with most data-base systems it would not be written physically until after the CUSTOMER-ORDER record had been written.

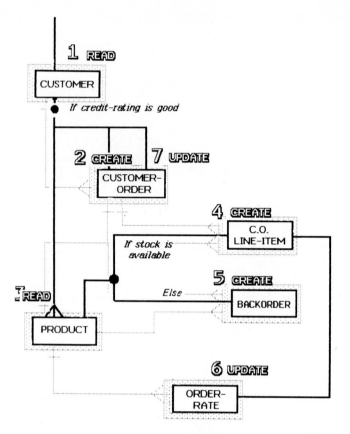

Figure 24.6   The data navigation diagram in Fig. 24.5 drawn, with data-item details, ready for drawing the action diagrams. This diagram could be produced by the customer tool that assists in the data modeling process. Two accesses are shown to CUSTOMER-ORDER. The first reads it; the second updates it. The update of CUSTOMER-LINE-ITEM and ORDER-RATE is done for each PRODUCT access. The update of CUSTOMER-ORDER is not done for each PRODUCT access but for each CUSTOMER-ORDER access. Access 6 is therefore drawn as shown.

It is often the physical-data-base designer who makes such decisions, not the designer of the logical procedure, who draws the data navigation diagram and action diagram.

COMPLEXITY   The subject data model that is used for one application ordinarily does not become very big. It can usually be drawn on one page; so can the associated data navigation diagram.

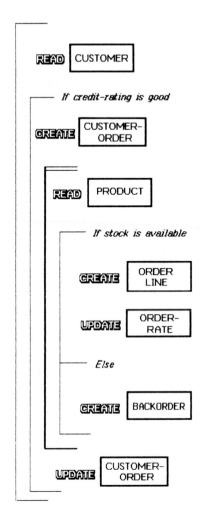

Figure 24.7 The action diagram that was automatically created from the data navigation diagram shown in Fig. 24.6

In some corporations with highly complex data processing, the subset data models never exceed a dozen third-normal-form records. Most do not exceed five.

STANDARD PROCEDURE

It is very simple to teach the use of data navigation diagrams. Together with action diagrams, these should be an installation standard rather than a tool of certain individuals.

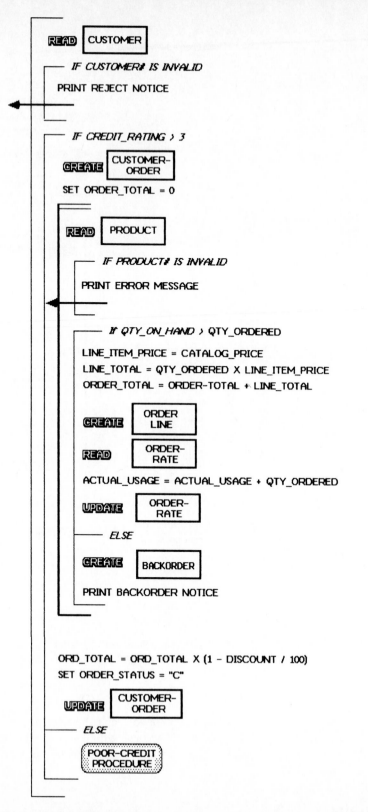

Figure 24.8 The action diagram is expanded to show logical detail of the procedure.

One giant aerospace corporation, where more than a thousand data navigation diagrams were drawn, found that this approach highlighted the transaction-driven nature of good data-base usage. Transaction-driven design had been surprisingly difficult for many analysts to grasp because they had learned techniques that (like many structured techniques) were batch-oriented.

REFERENCE

1. J. Martin, *Managing the Data Base Environment*, Englewood Cliffs, NJ: Prentice-Hall, Inc., 1983.

25 COMPOUND DATA ACCESSES

INTRODUCTION   Traditional data-base navigation, as described in Chapter 24, uses *simple* data-base accesses: CRE-ATE, READ, UPDATE, and DELETE. These carry out an operation on *one* instance of *one* record type.

Some high-level languages permit the use of statements that relate to not one but many instances of records and sometimes more than one record type. We refer to these as *compound data-base accesses*. Examples of such statements are:

    SEARCH

    SORT

    SELECT certain records from a relation or file

    JOIN two or more relations or files

    PROJECT a relation or file to obtain a subset of it

    DUPLICATE

CREATE, READ, UPDATE, and DELETE may also be used to refer to multiple instances of a record type. DELETE, for example, could be used to delete a whole file.

Where a data-base access refers to one instance of record type, we have used a single box containing the name of the record type:

Where a compound access that refers to more than one instance is used, we will use a double box containing the name of the record type or entity type:

Often this double box needs a qualifying statement associated with it to say how it is performed; for example,

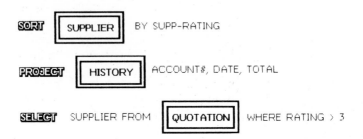

The type of operation is again written in large letters.

RELATIONAL JOINS

A *relational join* merges two relations (logical files or tables) on the basis of a common field [1]. For example, the EMPLOYEE relation and the BRANCH relation might look like this:

BRANCH

BRANCH-ID	LOCATION	BRANCH-STATUS	SALES-YEAR-TO-DATE
007	Paris	17	4789
009	Carnforth	2	816
013	Rio	14	2927

EMPLOYEE

EMPLOYEE#	EMPLOYEE-NAME	SALARY	CODE	MANAGER	CITY
01425	Kleinrock	42000	SE	Epstein	Rio
08301	Ashley	48000	SE	Sauer	Paris
09981	Jenkins	45000	FE	Growler	Rio
12317	Bottle	91000	SE	Minski	Carnforth

These relations are combined in such a way that the CITY field of the EMPLOYEE relation becomes the same as the LOCATION field of the BRANCH relation. We can express this with the statement:

BRANCH.LOCATION = EMPLOYEE.CITY

The result is, in effect, a combined record:

EMPLOYEE#	EMPLOYEE-NAME	SALARY	CODE	MANAGER	CITY	BRANCH-ID	BRANCH-STATUS	SALES-YEAR-TO-DATE
01425	Kleinrock	42000	SE	Epstein	Rio	013	14	2927
08301	Ashley	48000	SE	Sauer	Paris	007	17	4789
09981	Jenkins	45000	FE	Growler	Rio	013	14	2927
12317	Bottle	91000	SE	Minski	Carnforth	009	2	816

This data-base system may not combine them in reality but may join the appropriate data in response to queries or other operations. For example, if we ask for the MANAGER associated with each BRANCH-ID, the system will look up the BRANCH.LOCATION for each BRANCH-ID, search for an EMPLOYEE.CITY data item with the same value, and find the MANAGER data item associated with that.

A join is shown on a navigation chart by linking two or more entity-type access boxes together with a double line:

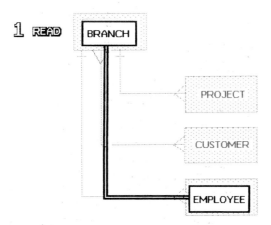

It is shown on an action diagram also by linking the boxes, with an access operation applying the combination:

A statement may be attached to the joined entity types showing how they are joined, like BRANCH.LOCATION = EMPLOYEE.CITY in our example. Often this is not necessary because the joined entity records contain a common attribute that is the basis for the join. For example, the EMPLOYEE record probably contains the attribute BRANCH#, in which case we can simply show

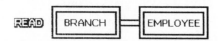

Using this join, we might say SELECT EMPLOYEE-NAME, MANAGER, BRANCH-STATUS, CITY. The result is as follows:

EMPLOYEE-NAME	MANAGER	BRANCH-STATUS	CITY
Kleinrock	Epstein	14	Rio
Ashley	Sauer	17	Paris
Jenkins	Growler	14	Rio
Bottle	Minski	2	Carnforth

We might constrain the join operation by asking for employees whose code is SE and whose salary exceeds $40,000. The result would then be

EMPLOYEE-NAME	MANAGER	BRANCH-STATUS	CITY
Kleinrock	Epstein	14	Rio
Ashley	Sauer	17	Paris
Bottle	Minski	2	Carnforth

With the data-base language SQL (from IBM and others), this operation would be expressed as follows:

```
SELECT EMPLOYEE_NAME, MANAGER, BRANCH_STATUS, CITY
FROM BRANCH, EMPLOYEE
WHERE BRANCH.LOCATION = EMPLOYEE.CITY
AND CODE = SE
AND SALARY > 40000
```

This can be written on an action diagram as follows:

For a simple query such as this, we do not need a diagramming technique. The query language itself is clear enough. For a complex operation, we certainly need to diagram the use of compound data-base actions. Even for queries, if they are complex, diagrams are needed.

AUTOMATIC NAVIGATION

A compound data-base action may require *automatic navigation* by the data-base management system. Relational data bases and a few nonrelational ones have this capability. For a data base without automatic navigation, a compiler of a fourth-generation language may generate the required sequence of data accesses.

With a compound data-base action, search parameters or conditions are often an integral part of the action itself. They are written inside a bracket containing the access box.

SIMPLE VERSUS COMPOUND DATA-BASE ACCESSES

There are many procedures that can be done with either simple data-base accesses or compound accesses. If a traditional DBMS is used, the programmer navigates through the data base with simple accesses. If the DBMS or language compiler has automatic navigation, higher-level statements using compound data-base accesses may be employed.

Suppose, for example, that we want to give a $1000 raise in salary to all employees who are engineers in Carnforth. With IBM's data-base language SQL we would write:

```
UPDATE EMPLOYEE
GET SALARY  =  SALARY  +  1000
WHERE JOB  =  'ENGINEER'
AND OFFICE  =  'CARNFORTH'
```

We can diagram this with a compound action as follows:

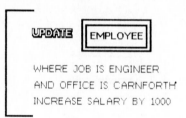

With simple actions (no automatic navigation) we can diagram the same procedure this way:

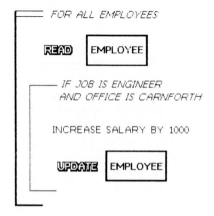

Similarly, a relational join can be represented with either a sequence of single actions or one compound action, as shown in Fig. 25.1. In this example, there are multiple projects of an EMPLOYEE PROJECT record showing how employees were rated for their work on each project they were assigned to. They are given a salary raise if their average rating exceeds 6.

It ought to be an objective of nonprocedural languages to enable their users to achieve as much as possible without *separate* diagramming. The best way to achieve this may be to *incorporate the graphics technique into the language itself.* In other words, executable code is generated from the diagrams.

INTERMIXING SIMPLE AND COMPOUND ACTIONS

Sometimes compound and simple data-base actions are used in the same procedure. Figure 25.2 illustrates this. It uses the data structure shown in Fig. 24.3 and shows the process of reordering stock as it becomes depleted.

As a request for parts is satisfied, the quantity on hand recorded in the PART

THE DATA USED IN THIS EXAMPLE:

EMPLOYEE

EMPLOYEE#	EMPLOYEE-NAME	SALARY	JOB	

EMPLOYEE-PROJECT

EMPLOYEE#	PROJECT#	RATING	

A PROCEDURE FOR GIVING ENGINEERS AN INCREASE IN SALARY, USING SIMPLE DATA-BASE ACTIONS:

```
    FOR ALL EMPLOYEES

  READ    EMPLOYEE

      IF JOB IS ENGINEER

          FOR ALL EMPLOYEE'S PROJECTS

        READ    EMPLOYEE-
                PROJECT

      CALCULATE AVERAGE RATING FOR EMPLOYEE

          IF AVERAGE RATING > 6

      INCREASE SALARY BY 1000

        UPDATE   EMPLOYEE
```

THE SAME PROCEDURE USING A COMPOUND DATA-BASE ACTION

```
  UPDATE   EMPLOYEE    EMPLOYEE
                       PROJECT

  WHERE JOB IS ENGINEER
  AND AVERAGE RATING > 6
  INCREASE SALARY BY 1000
```

Figure 25.1 Illustration of a procedure that may be done with either multiple, simple data-base access commands or one compound access command action.

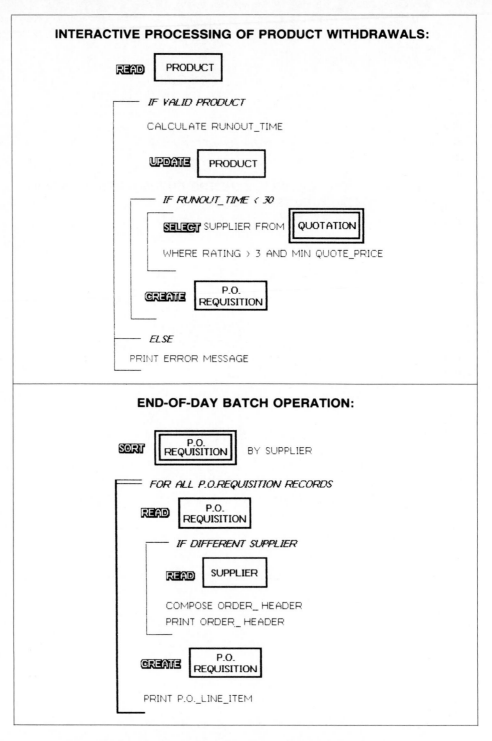

Figure 25.2 Procedures for product withdrawal and reordering using the data structures in Fig. 24.3 and a temporary P.O. REQUISITION file. Two compound accesses are used in these procedures.

record is depleted. Each time this happens the program calculates whether to create an order for more parts from their supplier.

The requests for parts are handled interactively throughout the day. The person designing the procedure decides to create a temporary file of order requisitions, to accumulate such requisitions as they occur, and then to sort them and place the orders at the end of the day. In this way a cumulative order for parts can be sent to a supplier rather than a separate order each time a part reaches its reorder point.

Figure 25.2 shows the results. In the top part of the figure, the selection of suppliers is done with a compound action. This can be represented with one statement in some fourth-generation languages. For example, in SQL it might be

```
SELECT SUPPLIER
FROM QUOTATION
WHERE RATING > 3
AND MIN (QUOTE_PRICE)
```

In the bottom part of Fig. 25.2, the order requisition file is sorted by supplier. This can also be represented by a single fourth-generation language statement:

```
ORDER REQUISITION BY SUPPLIER
```

THREE-WAY JOINS   In some cases three-way joins are useful. Suppose an accountant is concerned that accounts receivable are becoming too high. He wants to phone any branch-office manager who has six-month-old debt outstanding from a customer. The following record structures exist:

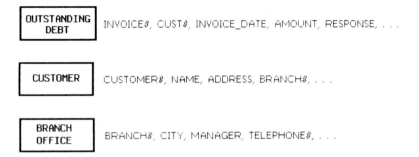

He enters the following query:

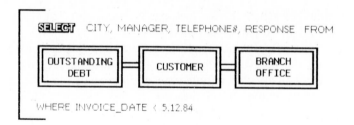

The three-way join is shown in a similar fashion to two-way joins. It could also be drawn on a data model to show a compound access in a navigation chart. Figure 25.3 shows this three-way join expressed with the language SQL.

SEMANTIC
DISINTEGRITY
Unfortunately, compound accesses in high-level database languages sometimes give rise to subtle problems. A user may enter a query with an easy-to-use query language; the query looks correct and the results look correct, but the results are in fact wrong.

The query with a triple join just shown is correct because OUTSTAND-ING_DEBT is associated with *one* CUSTOMER and CUSTOMER is associated with *one* BRANCH. In the data model, these associations are as follows:

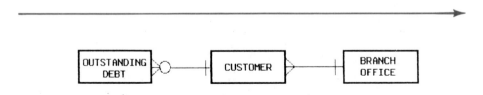

Suppose, however, that one CUSTOMER can be served by more than one BRANCH_OFFICE:

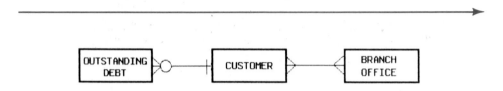

Then the use of the join is incorrect; there is *semantic disintegrity* in the query. The accountant might be phoning a branch manager who is not responsible for a customer's debt.

Again, suppose that two relations were joined as follows:

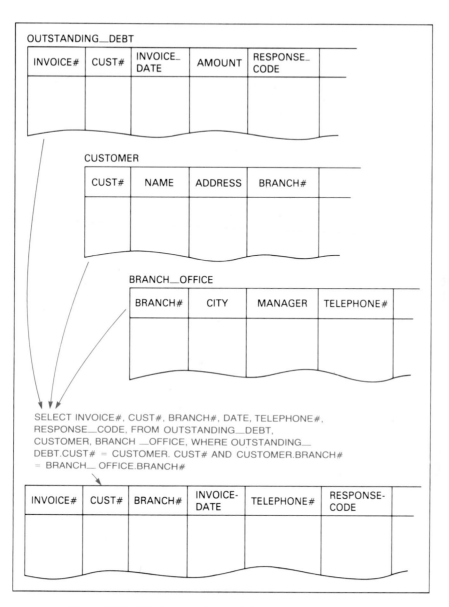

OUTSTANDING__DEBT

INVOICE#	CUST#	INVOICE__DATE	AMOUNT	RESPONSE__CODE	

CUSTOMER

CUST#	NAME	ADDRESS	BRANCH#	

BRANCH__OFFICE

BRANCH#	CITY	MANAGER	TELEPHONE#	

SELECT INVOICE#, CUST#, BRANCH#, DATE, TELEPHONE#,
RESPONSE__CODE, FROM OUTSTANDING__DEBT,
CUSTOMER, BRANCH __OFFICE, WHERE OUTSTANDING__
DEBT.CUST# = CUSTOMER. CUST# AND CUSTOMER.BRANCH#
= BRANCH__ OFFICE.BRANCH#

INVOICE#	CUST#	BRANCH#	INVOICE-DATE	TELEPHONE#	RESPONSE-CODE	

Figure 25.3 Join between three relations expressed with SQL.

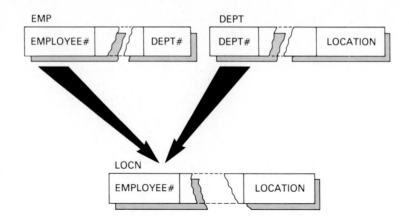

This join is valid if there is a one-to-one association between DEPT# and LO-CATION. It is not valid if there is one-to-many association between DEPT# and LOCATION, because although a department can have more than one location, an employee works in only one location. Drawing data items as ellipses, we have the following associations between data items:

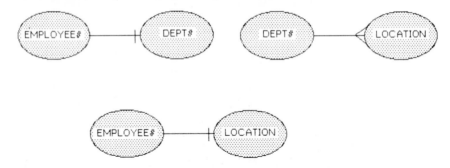

NAVIGATION PATHS

We can understand what a query or relational operation is doing by drawing a navigation path. To perform the join in our example, we start with EMPLOYEE# and find the associated DEPT#. For that DEPT# we find the associated LOCATION. We can draw this navigation path as follows:

Here we have only one-to-one paths, so there is no problem.

If, however, there were a one-to-many path from DEPT# to LOCATION, we would draw

This is invalid because there is *one* LOCATION, not many, for one employee.

We have the possibility of semantic disintegrity if the navigation path has a one-to-many link that is not the first link; for example,

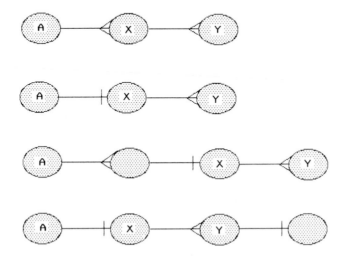

Many values of Y are associated with X, but they might not all be associated with A.

We do not necessarily know whether such a navigation path will be valid or not. Figure 25.4 shows two queries employing a join. Their data and navigation paths are similar in structure. Both use fully normalized data. The one-to-many path makes the bottom one invalid, but not the top one. Because the software cannot tell for sure, it should warn the user that the results might be invalid.

To ensure integrity in relational operations, it is essential that the data be correctly and completely modeled. The designer can understand the effect of compound navigation by drawing appropriate diagrams. Diagrams showing details of the navigation path can warn of the danger of semantic disintegrity. The author has discussed semantic disintegrity more fully elsewhere [2].

FOURTH-GENERATION LANGUAGES

Different fourth-generation languages or high-level data-base languages have different dialects [3]. It would be useful if vendors of such languages would

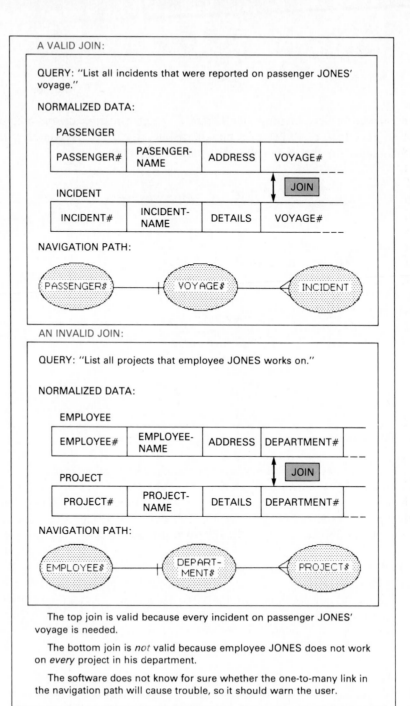

The top join is valid because every incident on passenger JONES' voyage is needed.

The bottom join is *not* valid because employee JONES does not work on *every* project in his department.

The software does not know for sure whether the one-to-many link in the navigation path will cause trouble, so it should warn the user.

Figure 25.4 Two queries with similar data structures using a join.

draw illustrations of the set of control structures and compound data-base accesses their languages employ.

A compound data-base access is rather like a macroinstruction that is decomposed into primitive instructions by a compiler or interpreter before it is executed.

To clarify how a compound data-base access in a language operates, the vendor might draw a diagram decomposing it into simple accesses. This is not always useful because more compound accesses are easy to understand but difficult to draw in a decomposed form (e.g., SORT).

Compound accesses, like simple accesses, need to be converted directly into the code of very high level languages. Often the wording inside the bracket should resemble the resulting code. The dialect of the language is thus incorporated into the diagram. Converting the action diagrams to code can be computer-assisted and ought to form part of an interactive design tool.

The software designer creating a fourth-generation language would do well to start with navigation diagrams and action diagrams, design an easy-to-use technique for charting procedures, and then create an interpreter or compiler with which code can be generated from the diagrams.

The systems analyst needs a computer screen that enables him to edit diagrams rapidly and to add more detail until working code is created.

REFERENCES

1. J. Martin, *Managing the Data Base Environment,* Englewood Cliffs, NJ: Prentice-Hall, Inc., 1983.

2. J. Martin, *System Design from Provably Correct Constructs,* Englewood Cliffs, NJ: Prentice-Hall, Inc., 1985.

3. J. Martin, *Fourth-Generation Languages,* Englewood Cliffs, NJ: Prentice-Hall, Inc., 1985.

26 HOS CHARTS

INTRODUCTION   Functional decomposition is used in most structured methodologies. In Chapter 12 we described three species of functional decomposition, varying in the degree of verification they use. Most functional decomposition in use is species I and employs no verification. Species II employs verification of the use of input and output. In this chapter we describe a much more rigorous form of functional decomposition.

HOS   In conventional practice, functions are decomposed in any way that seems convenient to the designer. In the technique described in this chapter, only rigorously defined forms of decomposition are permitted. These forms of decomposition are precisely defined with mathematical rules at each step; hence the decomposition is provably correct. The decomposition continues until blocks are reached from which executable program code can be generated.

The technique described here is called *higher-order software* (HOS). It was created by Hamilton and Zeldin [1] and is implemented with a CASE tool called USE.IT, available from a company called Higher Order Software [2]. The software automatically generates executable program code. We thus have *ultimate decomposition*. Unlike many code generators, this process can generate code for very complex systems with complex logic.

BINARY TREES   Like other types of functional decomposition, HOS employs tree structures. In its most primitive form it uses binary trees in which each node may be decomposed in one of three ways. From these precisely defined primitives, higher-level control structures that are not necessarily binary are built.

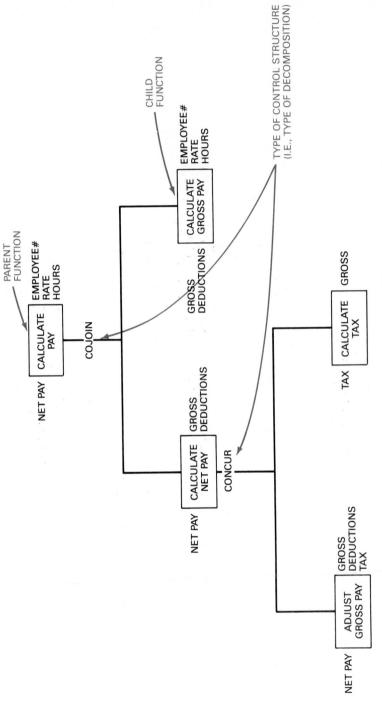

Figure 26.1 Functional decomposition done with HOS. Each decomposition must be of a defined type (COJOIN and CONCUR in this diagram) that obeys precise mathematical rules. The input variables to each function are shown to the right and the output variables to the left.

As in the techniques of Yourdon and Jackson, HOS draws vertical tree structures with the root at the top. Unlike the others, each decomposition is of a specified type called a *control structure*. The type of control structure used is written on the chart as in Fig. 26.1. The decomposition has to obey rules for that control structure that enforce mathematically correct decomposition.

Glancing ahead, Figs. 26.6 and 26.8 show the types of structure that result from HOS design. These charts are called *control maps*.

In HOS diagrams, each subordinate node is drawn below its superior. A branch is described as *entering* a node if it comes from above. It is described as *leaving* a node if it goes to a subordinate node.

If a branch leaves node A and enters node B, node B is referred to as the *offspring* of A. Node A is the *parent* of B.

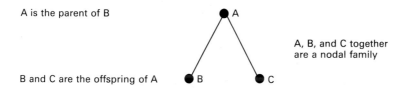

A node of a tree may be regarded as the root of another tree—a tree within a tree. The tree of which an intermediate node is a root is called a *subtree*.

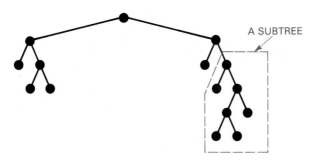

FUNCTIONS   Each node of an HOS binary tree represents a *function*. A function has one or more *objects* as its input and one or more *objects* as its output.

An object might be a data item, a list, a table, a report, a file, or a data base, or it might be a physical entity such as a circuit, a missile, an item undergoing manufacturing scheduling, a train, tracks, or switching points.

In keeping with mathematical notation, the *input* object or objects are written on the right-hand side of the function, and the *output* object or objects are written on the left-hand side of the function.

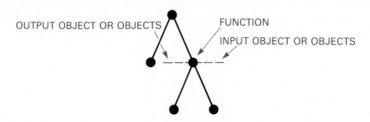

The function may be a mathematical function; for example,

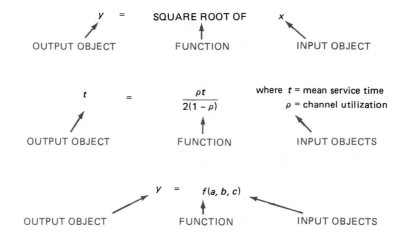

The function may be a programmed algorithm; for example,

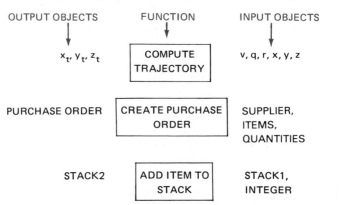

It may be a statement in a nonprocedural language:

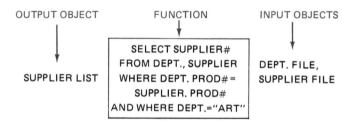

The function may be a program or subroutine specification:

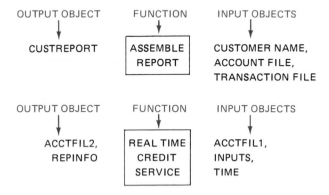

It may be a very broad statement of requirements:

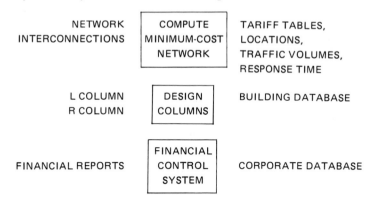

In fact, the notation can express (and decompose) operations that are not necessarily related to computing:

In some cases the object that is the output from a function can be the same item type as the object that is the input. The value of the object is transformed by the function:

TIME2 | INCREASE BY ONE HOUR | TIME1

TIME2 is the same data type as TIME1, but its value has changed.

CAR2 | WRECK | CAR1

CAR2 is the same type of object as CAR1, but it is a different version.

STACK2 | POP | STACK1

When a computer stack is "popped," the top item in the stack is removed so that the next item down becomes the top item. STACK2 is similar to STACK1, but modified.

To add an item to a stack, we use the function PUSH. The following inserts an integer into the stack:

STACK2 | PUSH | STACK1, INTEGER

The top of the stack is represented with the function TOP:

INTEGER | TOP | STACK1

In mathematical notation, we would write

$$STACK2 = PUSH (STACK1, INTEGER)$$
$$INTEGER = TOP (STACK1)$$

If the stack is empty when we do the second of these commands, the output would be a REJECT value.

In mathematical notation, the output of one function is sometimes used as the input to another. Thus, if we do PUSH (STACK, $INTEGER_1$), we obtain a stack with $INTEGER_1$ at the top. Applying the TOP function to this gives us $INTEGER_1$.

We could write these two operations in one statement:

$$INTEGER_1 = TOP (PUSH (STACK, INTEGER_1))$$

Note that we read such mathematics statements from right to left. In $y = f(x)$, we start with x, then we apply function f to it, then we obtain output y.

In the previous example, we start with the inputs STACK and INTEGER$_1$, next apply the function PUSH to these variables, then apply the function TOP to the result, and finally receive INTEGER$_1$ back as output. This notation is used to state some behavior of the relation of the functions TOP, PUSH, and STACK.

FROM REQUIREMENTS STATEMENTS TO DETAILED DESIGN

The HOS tree charts show how broad functions are decomposed into subfunctions. The *root* of the tree is the broadest overview statement. In the tree that results from the final design, the leaves are functions that do not need to be decomposed further. The leaves may be primitive functions, functions already existing and stored in a library, or functions obtainable from an external source.

Design may proceed in a top-down or bottom-up fashion. With top-down design, the broad overview is successively decomposed into functions that contain more detail. With bottom-up design, detailed modules are aggregated to form higher-level modules until the overall goal of the system is reached.

In many methodologies, the requirements statements, the specifications, the high-level design, and the detailed program design are done with different (and usually incompatible) languages. With HOS, one language is used for all of these. An appealing feature of the methodology is that the decomposition tree, formally expressed, goes all the way from broad requirements statements to detailed program design. Automatic checks for errors, omissions, and inconsistencies are applied at each stage. The resulting tree is processed to create the application code automatically.

THREE PRIMITIVE CONTROL STRUCTURES

Unlike most structured methodologies, the HOS decomposition of a function into subfunctions (in other words, the relationship between a node in the tree and its two offspring) is mathematically precise.

A function is decomposed into its offspring using a *control structure*. Three *primitive control structures* are used: JOIN, INCLUDE, and OR. Other control structures can be defined as combinations of these three.

JOIN

Suppose that a high-level function is BUILD-A-STOOL. The stool is to be made from two types of wood, TOPWOOD and LEGWOOD.

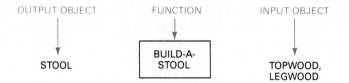

In mathematics we write $y = f(x)$ where y is the result of applying function f to data x. Similarly, to describe our requirement for building a stool we write

STOOL = BUILD-A-STOOL (TOPWOOD, LEGWOOD)

In order to build a stool, two operations are needed. We have to make the legs and the top and then assemble these parts. The BUILD-A-STOOL function can be subdivided into a MAKE-PARTS function and an ASSEMBLE-PARTS function. Two objects are *output* from the MAKE-PARTS function: TOP and LEGS. These objects are *input* to the ASSEMBLE-PARTS function.

STOOL = BUILD-A-STOOL (TOPWOOD, LEGWOOD)

is, then, composed of the following two functions joined together:

TOP, LEGS = MAKE-PARTS (TOPWOOD, LEGWOOD)
STOOL = ASSEMBLE-PARTS (TOP, LEGS)

In the tree notation we represent this as follows:

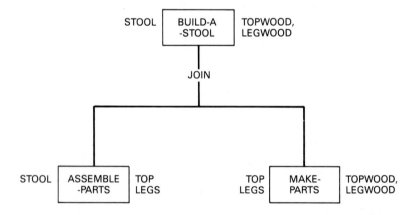

This is an illustration of the use of a JOIN control structure. Here one offspring depends on the other. The output of the right-hand function (TOPS, LEGS) must be the input to the left-hand function.

This input to the right-hand function is the same as the input to the parent. The output from the left-hand function is the same as the output from the parent. The effect of the parent function is thus reproduced.

The diagram must be read from right to left. (TOPWOOD, LEGWOOD) is the input to MAKE-PARTS, which results in TOP, LEGS, which is the input to ASSEMBLE-PARTS, which results in STOOL. Data enter each function from the right and leave it on the left. (Mathematicians sometimes do things differently from ordinary people. The tree is read right to left, not left to right, and it has its root at the top and its leaves at the bottom.)

INCLUDE

The MAKE-PARTS function can be decomposed into two functions, MAKE-TOP and MAKE-LEGS. The top must be made with TOPWOOD, and the legs must be made with LEGWOOD. The two functions composing make parts are thus

$$TOP = MAKE\text{-}TOP \ (TOPWOOD)$$
$$LEGS = MAKE\text{-}LEGS \ (LEGWOOD)$$

These are combined by means of an INCLUDE control structure:

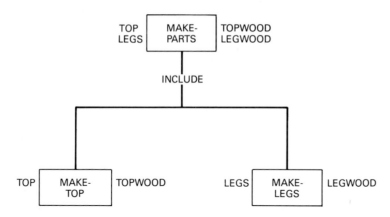

In this control structure the two offspring are independent of each other. They can operate separately and could even be executed on separate machines. Together both offspring use the input data of the parent function, and together they produce the output data of that function.

OR

Let us suppose that the legs can be made in one of two ways, either with a TURN function or with a CARVE function.

We have *either* LEGS = TURN (LEGWOOD) *or* LEGS = CARVE (LEGWOOD). To decide which to do, a Boolean expression is used that can be either true or false. An OR control structure is used as follows:

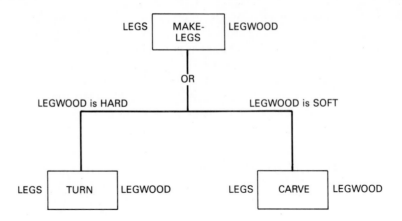

In this control structure, one or other of the offspring achieves the effect of the parent, but not both. The resulting output of each offspring is the same as that of the parent (i.e., LEGS).

Figure 26.2 summarizes the three primitive control structures.

CONTROL MAPS   We can combine the three control structures into one tree as shown in Fig. 26.3. Diagrams like Fig. 26.3 are called *control maps*.

GENERATION OF CODE   By breaking functions down with binary decomposition with the JOIN, INCLUDE, and OR constructs, control structures can be achieved that can be proved correct mathematically [1].

The functional decomposition continues until leaf nodes of the binary tree are reached. These are *primitives* that are known to be correct or *subroutines* that have themselves been created with this method. The design is complete when all parts of the tree reach such leaf nodes. *Program code can then be automatically generated from the resulting structures.*

At each step in the design, its correctness can be automatically checked.

FOUR TYPES OF LEAF NODES   The tree structures have *functions* as their nodes. (A function is also called an *operation*.) Every function is decomposed into lower-level functions showing more detail, except those that are leaf nodes of the tree.

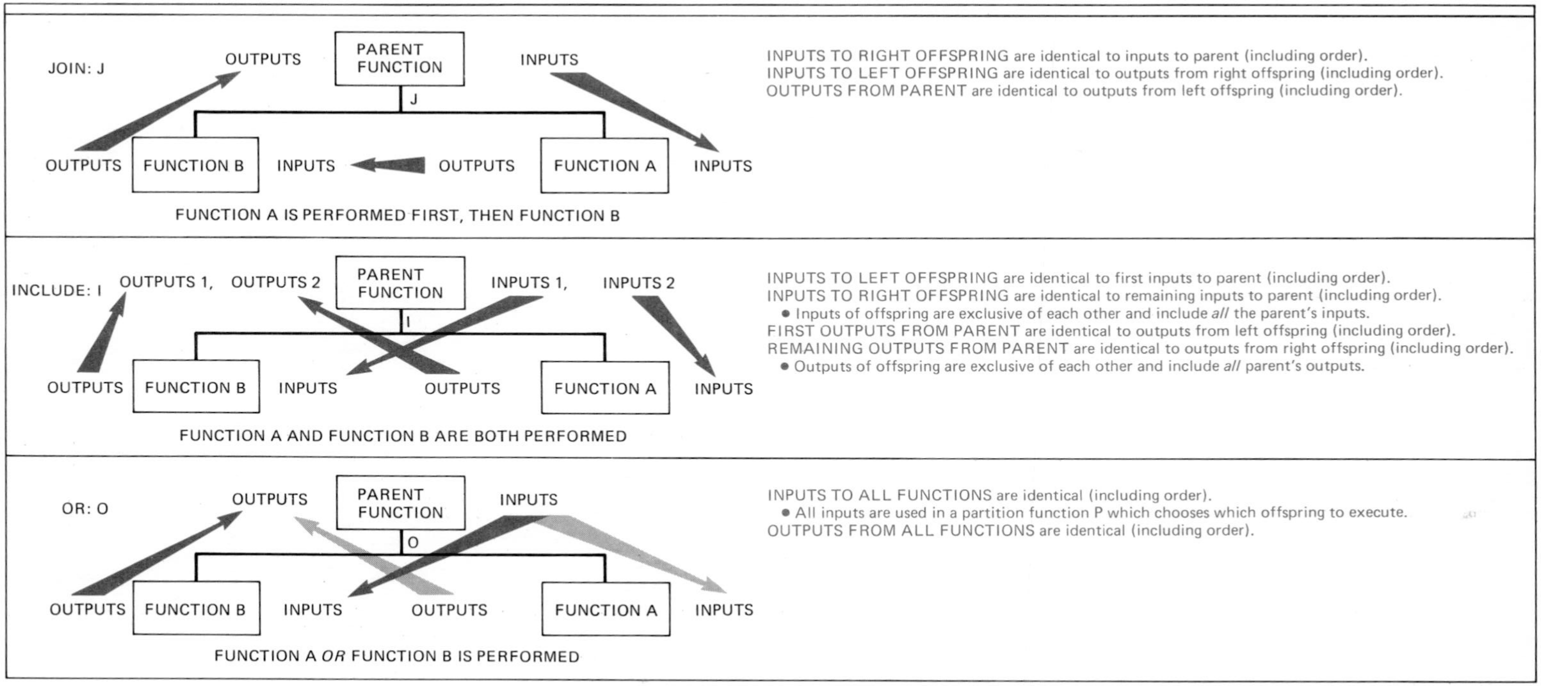
JOIN: J
PARENT FUNCTION
J
OUTPUTS
INPUTS
OUTPUTS
FUNCTION B
INPUTS
OUTPUTS
FUNCTION A
INPUTS
FUNCTION A IS PERFORMED FIRST, THEN FUNCTION B
INPUTS TO RIGHT OFFSPRING are identical to inputs to parent (including order).
INPUTS TO LEFT OFFSPRING are identical to outputs from right offspring (including order).
OUTPUTS FROM PARENT are identical to outputs from left offspring (including order).
INCLUDE: I
OUTPUTS 1, OUTPUTS 2
PARENT FUNCTION
I
INPUTS 1, INPUTS 2
OUTPUTS
FUNCTION B
INPUTS
OUTPUTS
FUNCTION A
INPUTS
FUNCTION A AND FUNCTION B ARE BOTH PERFORMED
INPUTS TO LEFT OFFSPRING are identical to first inputs to parent (including order).
INPUTS TO RIGHT OFFSPRING are identical to remaining inputs to parent (including order).
• Inputs of offspring are exclusive of each other and include *all* the parent's inputs.
FIRST OUTPUTS FROM PARENT are identical to outputs from left offspring (including order).
REMAINING OUTPUTS FROM PARENT are identical to outputs from right offspring (including order).
• Outputs of offspring are exclusive of each other and include *all* parent's outputs.
OR: O
OUTPUTS
PARENT FUNCTION
O
INPUTS
OUTPUTS
FUNCTION B
INPUTS
OUTPUTS
FUNCTION A
INPUTS
FUNCTION A *OR* FUNCTION B IS PERFORMED
INPUTS TO ALL FUNCTIONS are identical (including order).
• All inputs are used in a partition function P which chooses which offspring to execute.
OUTPUTS FROM ALL FUNCTIONS are identical (including order).

Figure 26.2 The three primitive control structures.

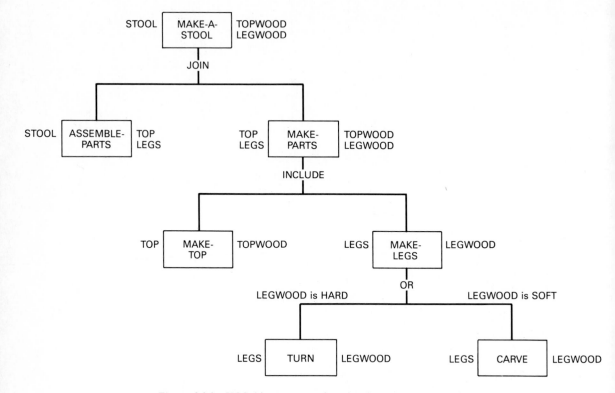

Figure 26.3 HOS binary tree using the three *primitive* control structures: JOIN, INCLUDE, and OR. Other control structures can be defined as combinations of these three. Diagrams like this are called *control maps*.

There are four types of leaf nodes:

1. *Primitive operation* (P). This is an operation that cannot be decomposed into other operations. It is defined rigorously with mathematical axioms.

2. *Operation defined elsewhere* (OP). This function will be further decomposed in another control map, which may be part of the current design or may be in a library.

3. *Recursive operation* (R). This is a special node that allows us to build loops.

4. *External operation* (XO). This function is an external program that is not written with HOS methodology. It may be manufacturer's software or previously existing user programs. Obviously, the HOS software cannot guarantee its correctness.

If there is no non-HOS software (external operations), every operation is ultimately broken down into *primitive operations* that are described mathematically.

The repetitive use of predefined functions is essential. Without this, the binary structures would have too many nodes to be practical for human design. Complex programs require the building of libraries of functions and defined operations (e.g., subroutines). These include completely general functions, such as user-specifiable loop control structures, mathematical operations, elaborate application-independent functions (e.g., data-base operations and report generators), and operations that are specific to given applications (e.g., a backorder subroutine).

STATIC AND DYNAMIC TESTING OF PROGRAMS

We may distinguish between static and dynamic program testing. *Dynamic program testing* is necessary with all programs not built with a rigorous mathematical technique (this includes the vast majority of programs in existence today). Each branch and usable combination of branches must be tested. There are usually so many combinations of branches that it is impossible to be sure that all have been tested. Consequently, saturation testing is done, but in practice not all combinations of paths are exercised and not all possible errors in the code are revealed. Complex software is notorious for containing subtle bugs that can be extremely difficult to track down. Most large programs never become completely bug-free.

Static testing refers to verification that the functions, data types, and control structures have been used in accordance with rules that guarantee correctness. This verification can be performed by a computer with absolute precision. When this static verification is done, there is no need for dynamical testing of *all* the control paths in the control map through the hierarchical structure. A few instances of control paths will be checked to ensure that correct results are being produced.

It is still necessary to check that the specifications are correct and are what the users really need and that nothing has been omitted. For example, does our example represent completely the building of a stool, or is something needed other than legs and a top? The HOS method eliminates most of the effort in saturation testing and tracking down obscure logic errors.

Dynamic testing does not guarantee that code is error-free. You may search for flying saucers, but the fact that you cannot find any does not mean that they do not exist—especially if you do not know what you are really looking for.

EMBELLISHMENTS

We have now described the basic structures of the HOS methodology. Control structures created with this technique are guaranteed bug-free. However, much embellishment is needed in order to make the technique easy to use and powerful.

It has been proved that a computer could execute all arithmetic and logic with only three instructions. However, if you programmed such a computer, you would need tools to make the programming easier—compilers, macroinstructions, libraries of subroutines, report generators, and so on. The same is true with the HOS language. Now that we have the axiomatically verifiable foundation, we can build higher-level control structures out of the three primitives. We can have libraries of defined operations. We can convert data-base models into HOS notation. We can use the HOS language to build report generators, create data-flow diagrams, or translate other problem-definition languages into computable HOS terms. We can specify a computer designed to implement the HOS constructs that can take advantage of future VLSI circuit costs and use multiple parallel processors.

OTHER CONTROL STRUCTURES   Certain other control structures are in common use and are in the HOS manuals. For example, Fig. 26.8 shows two common control structures, COJOIN and CONCUR. In some cases a user builds his own control structures. They are called *defined structures*.

A COJOIN structure, for example, is like a JOIN structure except that the left offspring can have as its input, variables that are input to the parent as well as variables that are output from the right offspring:

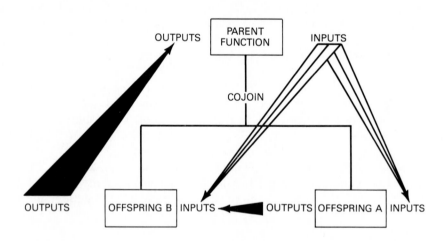

Like other control structures, COJOIN is built from the primitives. Figure 26.4 shows how a COJOIN is composed of a JOIN and an INCLUDE structure.

It is possible to build other control structures out of the primitives. In fact, a long-term question for HOS product developers is, What types of control structures would benefit the users most?

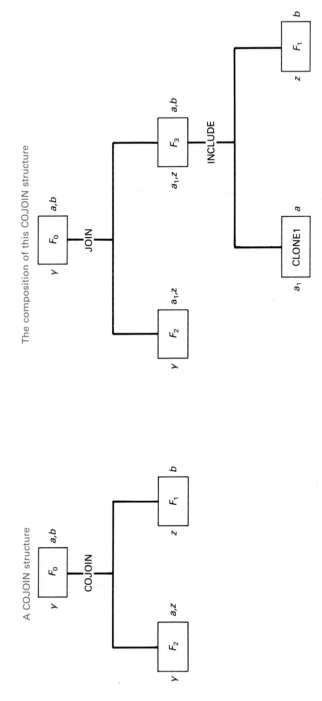

Figure 26.4 A COJOIN structure is built from the primitive structures JOIN and INCLUDE. We can build higher-level defined structures in a similar way.

SIMPLIFICATION   The basic reason for employing defined structures is to simplify control maps. Certain operations appear cumbersome when created with control maps. Because they are designed interactively at a screen, the designer can build and check them quickly. However, it is desirable to replace or simplify repetitively used logic.

An example of this is shown in Figs. 26.5 and 26.6. An operator responds to a menu on a screen with a digit, as on videotex systems, for example. The response triggers one of ten possible actions. Figure 26.5 shows this built with the standard control structures.

The menu response may be a common occurrence. We can create an easy-to-use *defined structure* for handling it. Let us call it MENUSELECT. Its use is shown in Fig. 26.6. The use of MENUSELECT causes the control map of Fig. 26.5 to be generated.

USER FUNCTIONS EMPLOYED IN A DEFINED STRUCTURE   When a defined structure is used, the offspring of a parent are blocks that exist in the original control map from which the defined structure was built. Figure 26.7 shows a control map used repetitively. When it is used, the nodes shown in red may be different. They are OP (operation defined elsewhere) or XO (external operation) blocks and may be defined by the user.

The control map is defined to be a defined structure. It is given a name: DS NAME. When the user employs it, he must provide the three shaded blocks as offspring of the parent whose behavior is described with the defined structure DS NAME. The bottom of Fig. 26.7 illustrates how a user would employ the defined structure.

EXTENDING THE POWER OF HOS   There are two ways of extending the power and usability of the HOS tool. The most common is to build a library of operations, like building a library of subroutines and callable programs. Most HOS control maps contains blocks labeled OP (operation defined elsewhere) or XO (external operation). The user creates OP blocks all the time for operations he has not yet specified in detail or has already specified elsewhere (see Fig. 26.8 for an example). As time goes by, a large library of defined operations grows.

The second way of extending usefulness is to create defined structures. This is rather like creating one's own language or dialect in HOS. Some classes of users already have languages or language constructs that they want to use. They may want to use DO WHILE or REPEAT UNTIL loops, for example. They may want to use menu selection. They may draw data-base action dia-

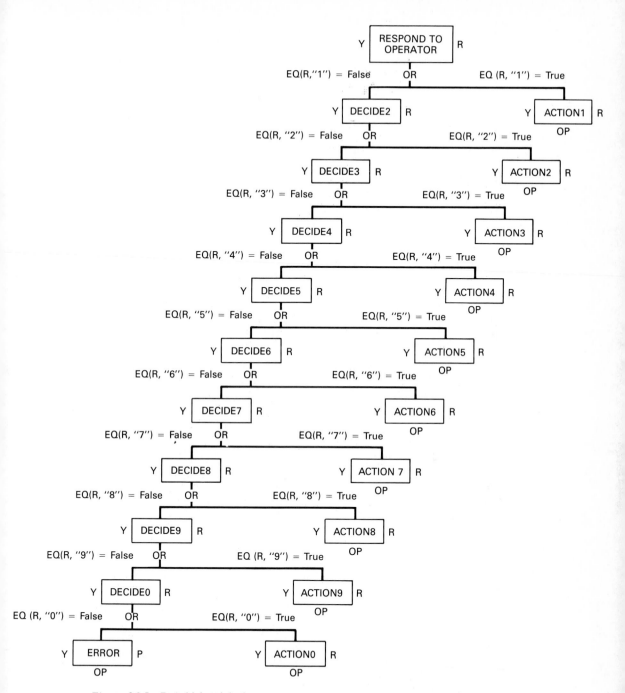

Figure 26.5 R (which might be a user response to a menu) can have any single-digit value. This decides which action is taken. This control map can be replaced with the use of a defined structure as shown in Fig. 26.6.

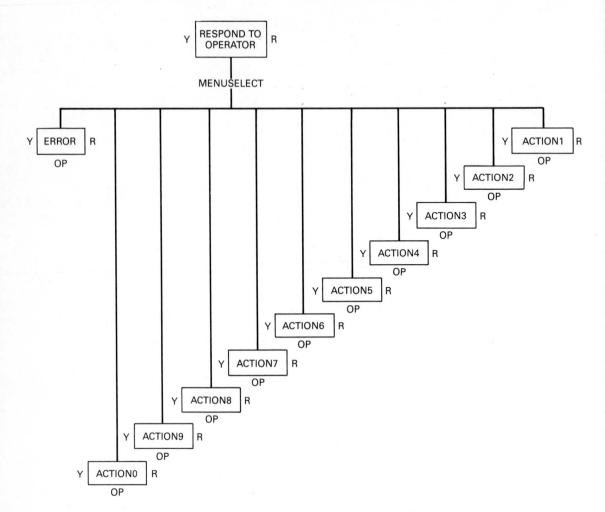

Figure 26.6 Use of the defined structure called MENUSELECT to instantiate the more complex control map of Fig. 26.5.

grams and want to convert them into HOS. There are a variety of such constructs with which different users are familiar, and they would like to employ them to make HOS system development easier.

DISCUSSION   HOS uses much of the philosophy of structured techniques, but it extends the techniques in important

ways:

A control map that we want to use in a defined structure:

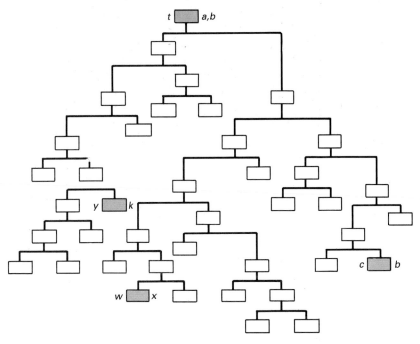

A parent node invoking the defined structure that replaced the above control map:

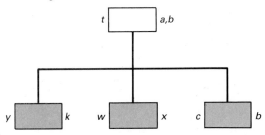

Figure 26.7   A control map that is repetitively used.

1. It is mathematically based so that the control structures are provably correct.

2. It provides computerized graphics with which complex structures can be created rapidly.

3. It automates the generation of executable program code (not merely code skeletons, as with some other tools).

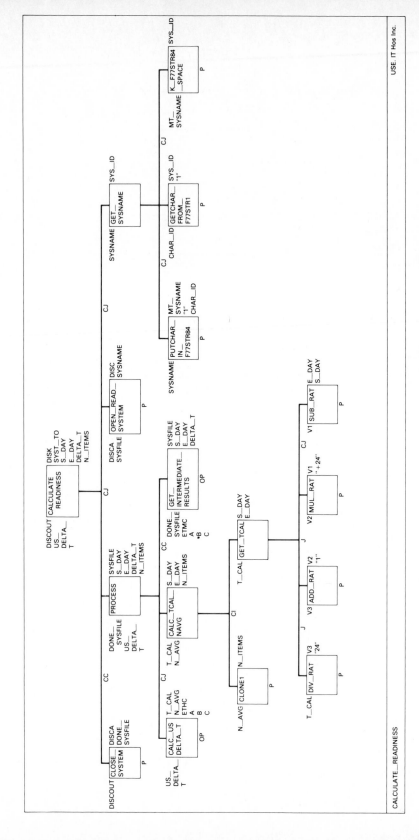

Figure 26.8 Typical HOS chart generated by computer graphics and automatically verified.

4. It eliminates the need for most dynamic program testing.

5. Because of its computerized verification and cross-checking, it is particularly valuable for creating specifications of a level of complexity beyond that which one person can handle. The more complex the system, the greater the benefits.

It is different from the techniques most analysts and programmers are used to, and therefore some find it alien and prefer to use older methods. New graduates, and creative analysts who like to learn new techniques, often make themselves far more powerful with this technique than they could be with conventional structured techniques.

Figure 26.8 shows a typical HOS chart, for the design of packet demultiplexor logic.

HOS methodology is discussed further in Chapter 38.

REFERENCES

1. M. Hamilton and S. Zeldin, *Integrated Software Development System/Higher Order Software Conceptual Description,* TR-3, Cambridge, MA: Higher Order Software, Inc., 1976.

2. *USE.IT Reference Manual,* Cambridge, MA: Higher Order Software, Inc., 1982.

27 A CONSUMER'S GUIDE TO DIAGRAMMING TECHNIQUES

INTRODUCTION   As we have seen, there are many structured diagramming techniques. This chapter gives our views on the ones we recommend. It repeats and summarizes some of the comments made in earlier chapters.

A mature systems analyst ought to be familiar with all the diagramming techniques we have discussed and immediately recognize their equivalences. In any one corporation, a choice must be made to standardize an appropriate group of affiliated techniques.

Box 27.1 shows what each diagramming technique can draw. No technique can draw everything that is needed, so an installation needs a carefully selected combination of techniques.

Figure 27.1 represents the territory for which diagramming is needed. On the left are processes; on the right are data needed for running those processes.

At the top is a broad top-level overview. On the left is the enterprise model showing an organization's functions and processes, like Fig. 10.4. On the right is an overview of the corporate data—the entities and relationships among entities.

One level below is a logical structure representing some level of detail but not yet a program description. The left side refers to the relationship among processes and the data that pass between processes in a given area. The right side refers to the detailed logic modeling of the data for a given area.

The bottom two rows refer to the program structure. First the overall structure and, below, the detailed program logic. The left side refers again to the processes; the right side refers to the data the processes use. The bottom left block is concerned with the details of conditions, case structures, and loops. The bottom right block is concerned with how those procedures use data.

Figure 27.2 shows the candidate diagramming techniques and the areas to which they apply.

BOX 27.1. Summary of the capabilities of diagramming techniques

WHAT CAN BE DRAWN WITH THE TECHNIQUE?	DECOMPOSITION DIAGRAMS	DEPENDENCY DIAGRAMS	DATA FLOW DIAGRAMS	ENTITY-RELATIONSHIP DIAGRAMS	DATA ANALYSIS DIAGRAMS	DATA NAVIGATION DIAGRAMS	HIPO CHARTS	STRUCTURE CHARTS	WARNIER-ORR CHARTS	MICHAEL JACKSON CHARTS	FLOWCHARTS	STRUCTURED ENGLISH	NASSI-SHNEIDERMAN CHARTS	ACTION DIAGRAMS	DATA-BASE ACTION DIAGRAMS	DECISION TREES AND TABLES	STATE-TRANSITION DIAGRAMS	HOS CHARTS
PROCESS STRUCTURES																		
Enterprise model showing corporate functions	YES							YES	YES					YES	YES			
Functional decomposition species I (tree structure only)	YES						YES	YES	YES	YES				YES	YES			YES
Functional decomposition species II (tree structure plus input and output)														YES	YES			YES
Functional decomposition species III (axiomatic control of decomposition)																		YES
Interaction between business events		YES	YES											YES	YES			YES
Flow of data		YES	YES											YES	YES			YES
Nonprocedural (compound) data-base actions															YES			
Control structures — Sequence	YES	YES						YES	YES	YES	YES	YES	YES	YES	YES			YES
Control structures — Conditions	YES	YES								YES	YES	YES	YES	YES	YES	YES	YES	YES
Control structures — Case structure		YES								YES	YES	YES	YES	YES	YES	YES	YES	YES
Control structures — Repetition	YES	YES						YES	YES	YES	YES	YES	YES	YES	YES			YES
Control structures — Loop control										YES	YES	YES	YES	YES	YES			
Good for showing complex logic												YES	YES	YES		YES	YES	
Designed for showing highly complex decisions																YES	YES	
Linkage to data model															YES			YES
Linkage to fourth-generation languages														YES	YES			
DATA STRUCTURES																		
Tree structured data				YES	YES				YES	YES								YES
Plex structured data				YES	YES													YES
Derived data items					YES													
Corporate data models				YES	YES													
Data-base navigation						YES												

CRITERIA FOR CHOICE

The structured revolution first gained momentum in the mid-1970s, and that is when many of the diagramming techniques evolved. A decade later the requirements of diagramming techniques had changed in certain important ways. Just as there was a change from flowcharts (1960s) to structure charts (1970s),

	PROCESSES	DATA
STRATEGIC OVERVIEW	Strategic overview of corporate functions	Strategic overview of corporate data
LOGICAL STRUCTURE	Logical relationship among processes	Detailed logical data model
PROGRAM STRUCTURE	Overall program structure	Program-level view of data
	Detailed program logic	Program usage of data

Figure 27.1   Areas to which the diagramming techniques apply.

so there needs to be a change from third-generation (1970s) to fourth-generation (1980s) techniques. Just as many old flowcharters refused to change or even accept the need for change, so many practitioners of the 1970s techniques also have dug their heels in. Unfortunately, most systems analysts and programmers are still being trained to use older techniques with less computerized assistance, less end-user involvement, less verification before programming, and lower-productivity languages.

The following are important characteristics of today's diagramming methods:

User Friendliness

End users must be more involved in computing. Users should be able to read, check, and critique systems analysts' plans. They should be able to create applications themselves with user-friendly languages or sketch applications they require. User-friendly diagramming techniques are a major aid to spreading computer literacy.

Design for Use with Computerized Tools

Computer-aided systems engineering (CASE), with its combination of computer-aided design and code generation, can greatly speed up the building of systems, improve the quality of results, and make systems easier to test and to change (maintain). The diagramming technique should be signed for ease of

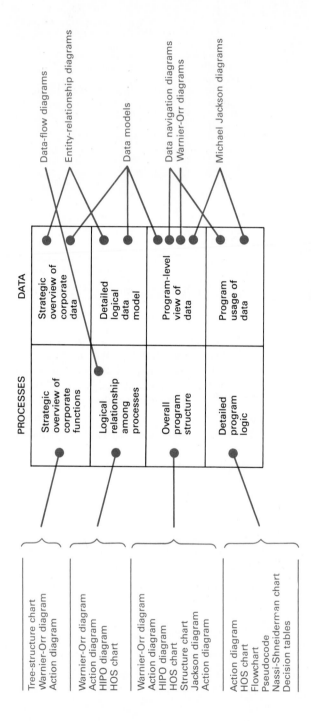

Figure 27.2 Areas in which different diagramming techniques are applicable.

sketching and editing at a computer screen. The computer should fill in many details by using a data dictionary, a data model, drawing techniques, and fourth-generation-language constructs.

Code Generation

Wherever possible, program code should be generated automatically. Some diagramming techniques do not help with this. Some are used to generate code skeletons showing the control structure of programs. Some can generate executable code.

Top-to-Bottom Tool

Some diagramming techniques are appropriate for a high-level overview of systems or programs. Some are appropriate for showing low-level detail with conditions, case structures, and loop structures. It is desirable to have one program representation that can be decomposed steadily from the highest overview to the finest detail. This representation should encourage design refinement one step at a time with computerized editing. Changing representation techniques as the design is decomposed into detail encourages the making of errors.

Rigor

Any possible method should be used to detect and eliminate errors as the system is being specified, designed, and programmed. Some diagramming techniques make possible a high level of automated checking; some do not. This is especially important in the creation of highly complex specifications. Some design techniques, although structured, have resulted in specifications that are full of errors.

Data-Base Orientation

Data-base technology is of great importance and is the foundation of most future data processing. Some structured techniques in common use represent files well, but not the nonhierarchical structures found in data bases. Some do not represent interactive data-base processing well. Good representation of data-base interactions and the use of data models are vital.

Fourth-Generation-Language Orientation

Fourth-generation languages give much faster application development and avoid some of the structuring problems inherent in earlier language. Diagrams of structure designs should be decomposable into fourth-generation-language code, with automated help if possible.

Speed

Productivity of application creation becomes more important as computers out-number programmers by an ever-increasing ratio. Diagramming techniques that are fast to use, both on paper and with computerized tools, are needed.

DATA AND PROCESSES

It is important to have clear diagrams of the structure of data. The design of processes and program structures is easier and more satisfactory if the data design already exists. Some structured techniques have used the same method for drawing data as for drawing processes. This is done in Jackson methodology and Warnier-Orr methodology. It works only for hierarchical data. Hierarchical data structures and hierarchical program structures can be drawn with the same technique. However, many types of data are network-structured, not hierarchically structured, by their very nature. A different technique is needed to represent it.

It is sometimes argued that the data extracted from a data base and used by a programmer are hierarchical; that is, the programmer's logical view of data is hierarchical. However, to impose this constraint tends to prevent the design team from understanding and using data-base navigation and relational concepts.

The data-base world needs correct data modeling. Data models are inevitably drawn differently from program structures. The analyst and programmer need to be thoroughly comfortable with the technique for representing systems and programs as well as that for representing data models. They need to be able to link the data models to their programs. Without this combination, any structured methodology is inadequate today.

DATA FLOW DIAGRAMS

Diagrams that show the passage of data or documents among separate processes are valuable. These enable analysts to draw and understand how complex operations use data. They can draw the flow of work tickets, requisitions, and the like in a factory, or the flow of transactions in a banking system. At a lower level, they can chart the flow of data among computer programs and modules.

Data flow diagrams are easy to understand by both analysts and end users. They have an important role to play.

Data flow diagrams need linking to both the data model that is used and the program structures that result from the diagram. A concern with data flow diagrams is that they are deceptively simple. They can look correct and give the analyst a comfortable feeling when a closer examination of the detail would reveal a different picture. Many specifications for complex systems have been created by analysts drawing large numbers of data flow diagrams leveled (nested) into many layers. When these specifications have been reexamined with more rigorous methods, they have been revealed to be full of inconsistencies, omissions, and ambiguities.

The appropriate role of the data flow diagram needs to be recognized. It is a useful form of overview sketch. It needs to be used in conjunction with thorough data analysis and data modeling (discussed later in the book). It needs to be used in conjunction with techniques for designing the structure of processes.

As commonly drawn, data flow diagrams are not rigorous; they are sketches that are useful aids to understanding. They need to be linked to rigorous techniques for data modeling and functional decomposition. For complex specifications, this *must* be the species II or species III decomposition discussed in Chapter 12, and the checking associated with these forms of decomposition needs to be computerized. The human brain inevitably makes mistakes in specifications that are not computerized, and with complex specifications the quantity of mistakes is horrifying.

THE ESSENTIAL TRILOGY

An analyst, programmer, or end user involved with computing thus needs a trilogy of diagramming techniques. All three are essential. To understand only two of the three is entirely inadequate:

1. Data-flow diagramming
2. Process diagramming, including functional decomposition and the diagramming of detailed logic
3. Data-model diagramming

For the first two of these, the techniques are fairly clear and straightforward. The variants on the diagramming methods are minor. For the third, there is a wide variation because of the potential complexities of programming.

COMPREHENSIVE CAPABILITIES

For the design of processes or programs, it is desirable to select one diagramming technique that can do as much as possible. If it can diagram some aspects of programs and not others, it is going to cause an unnatural break in the design sequence. Worse, it may constrain the thought processes of the designer.

Of the techniques in Box 27.1, action diagrams and HOS charts are the most comprehensive. Each was specifically designed to give top-to-bottom design that could progress from the highest-level sketch of a system down to a level of detail from which code can be generated.

The other techniques have to switch horses in midstream. The most common methodology in North America is the combination of structure charts and pseudocode. In Europe, Michael Jackson diagrams and his "structure text" form of pseudocode are more common than in America. Another combination is Warnier-Orr diagrams and pseudocode. Nassi-Shneiderman charts can replace pseudocode but not higher-level decomposition. Figure 27.3 shows a HIPO chart with a Nassi-Shneiderman chart replacing its central process description.

Action diagrams avoid these clumsy combinations of basically different techniques. As shown in Figs. 20.2 to 20.7, one technique can show the highest-level functional decomposition and can be successively decomposed until executable code is reached. The labeling on the action diagram can be adapted to the dialect of a fourth-generation language.

As shown in Chapter 25, the action diagram can be specifically related to data-base actions, including the compound actions of nonprocedural languages.

With software on a personal computer or terminal, the designer can draw, edit, and change the action diagram quickly. He can link it to a data dictionary, data model, library of previously designed routines, screens, data structures, and so on. He may have the interpreter of a fourth-generation language (or third-generation language such as BASIC or Pascal) running at the same personal computer or terminal.

ULTIMATE DECOMPOSITION

To be fully comprehensive, the diagrams of processes should be extendable all the way from a high-level overview down to executable code in a fourth-generation language as in Fig. 20.7.

DRAWING SPEED

Productivity of analysts and programmers is becoming increasingly important as computers proliferate, and the people who can create software for them remain scarce. We need techniques that are as fast as possible to use.

Diagramming techniques that are excessively time-consuming can be frustrating to programmers under pressure to achieve results quickly. Any diagram of complex procedures is likely to be redrawn many times. It should be quick to redraw. The importance of this is felt particularly when redrawing Nassi-Shneiderman charts, a time-consuming technique. Complex Nassi-Shneiderman diagrams take a long time to change. Warnier-Orr diagrams and action diagrams, on the other hand, are quick and easy to change. Decision tables can represent a complex family of conditions quickly and thoroughly. The same conditional logic would be time-consuming to draw with flowcharts or Nassi-Shneiderman charts.

Diagramming—or more important, successive modification of diagrams— can be speeded up with an appropriate computerized tool. A diagramming method that is susceptible to easy computerized creation and modification on inexpensive personal computers or terminals is needed. The best computer-aided-design software can draw almost any diagram, but it is expensive. A struc-

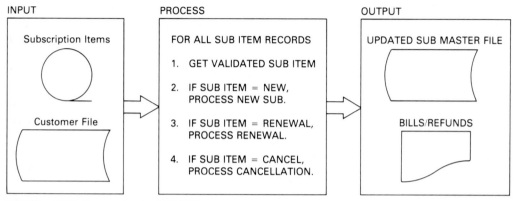

Overview HIPO diagram for the DISPATCH component of the subscription system.

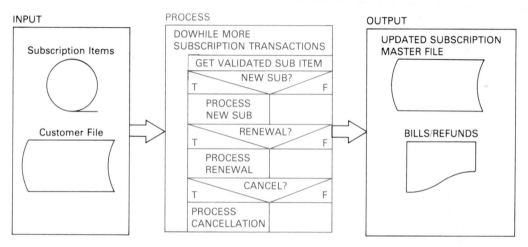

Figure 27.3 A HIPO diagram in which a Nassi-Shneiderman chart replaces the central process description.

tured design technique should itself be designed so that it is not expensive to create good software for it.

Whether or not computerized tools exist, analysts, programmers, and, increasingly, end users argue with sketches on scrap paper and blackboards. Needed is a technique that is good for sketching and can progress to computerized representation. When computer graphics are used, the sketch can be automatically extended and dressed up to make it more respectable-looking and clear to read.

In spite of computer screens, it is necessary to print diagrams that designers and programmers can take home, mail, scribble notes on, and so on. We stressed in Chapter 10 the need to obtain printouts on normal-sized paper rather than wide charts like architects' drawings. The diagrams should be printable on the inexpensive printer of a personal computer. This requires charts that spread out vertically rather than horizontally. It requires techniques that avoid entangled bird's nests of diagrams.

Many of the structure charts, data-flow diagrams, and entity-relationship charts we examined did not meet these criteria. They *could* meet them with different drawing techniques, as shown in Chapter 10. Modularization and multilevel nesting of diagrams can make them printable on small paper but tend to give excessive fragmentation, making them difficult to follow. Action diagrams were designed from the beginning to be printable with inexpensive desk-top printers.

Some analysts, programmers, and their managers love gigantic wall charts with which they can impress their associates. The desire to impress sometimes overrides the more practical concerns of obtaining results in a quick and easy fashion.

INTEGRITY CHECKING

The computer is a wonderful tool for integrity checking. With infinite patience, it can correlate input and output, check data against a dictionary, and apply axioms for verification of correctness. Diagramming methods, and design techniques in general, that facilitate computerized verification to the maximum are needed. The larger and more complex the specification, the greater the need for computerized verification. Where computerized verification has been applied late in the history of complex specifications, it has revealed an appalling mess. The human brain simply cannot accomplish the tedious correlation of detail that is needed, and a large team of human brains with human communication problems is much worse. Errors and inconsistencies tend to multiply as the square of the number of people in the team.

Most structured design uses hierarchical decomposition. We stressed in Chapter 12 that there are three species of hierarchical decomposition. Species I has no rules and is by far the most common. The computer can do little to help check its accuracy. Species II correlates and checks input and output data types throughout the entire design. With this, computerized help is of great value for complex systems. Species III allows only certain types of decomposition; these are rigorously checked to be sure that the entire resulting structure is internally correct.

Species II decomposition is easy to apply. It seems surprising that this level of automated checking is not widespread. Species III is more difficult to apply (though less difficult than the task of programming!). It requires a new level of rigor in thinking about systems; this seems to be the equivalent of culture shock to traditional analysts and programmers. Its payoff, however, is great because it permits a small team, otten one person, to create complex specifications from which correct code is automatically generated. Species III HOS charts are discussed further in Chapter 26.

CODE GENERATION

Computer-aided diagramming and validation are highly desirable but the computer can help in a more powerful way. Wherever possible, it should generate code automatically.

Various methodology vendors claim to have automatic code generation. It is important to distinguish between two types of code generation:

1. Generation of a program skeleton giving the structure of the program but not the detail
2. Generation of executable code

Most methodologies do the former and not the latter. Clearly, the latter is much more valuable. Be aware that many claims of code generation mean the former, not the latter.

Executable code is generated from HOS charts. Tools exist for generating logic modules from decision tables. Action diagrams can be linked to fourth-generation languages for creating executable code.

USER FRIENDLINESS

To achieve increased end-user involvement in computing, the types of diagrams used need to be easy to read and understand. As we discussed in Chapter 10, they should be as self-explanatory as possible. In many cases, end users should be taught to think about systems, using the diagramming technique as a basic aid to clear thinking.

End users learn to read and draw some types of diagrams easily, but not others. Users can quickly understand data flow diagrams. Warnier-Orr diagrams are user-friendly except for their use of symbols such as $+$, $\oplus$, and $(1, N)$. These symbols are quickly learned, but to untrained users they appear as difficult hieroglyphics. Action diagrams, such as those in Figs. 20.2 to 20.4, are very easy to read by end users and can be expanded into successively more detail, encouraging the end user to understand the process of creating detailed applications.

Diagrams that permit the most complete verification are often the least user-friendly. Of the techniques in Table 27.1, the most difficult for users to understand are Michael Jackson methodology and HOS methodology. With computerized tools for diagramming and verification it is possible to build methodologies that are both user-friendly and rigorous. It is highly desirable that computer methodology progress in this way.

COMPUTER GRAPHICS

Systems analysts and business analysts will increasingly use computer graphics to create, edit, change, catalog, and maintain the diagrams they draw. It is important to distinguish between two types of computer graphics:

Manual-substitute graphics. This type of graphics tool merely automates the drawing of diagrams that could be drawn by hand. It speeds up a manual methodology. An example is STRADIS/DRAW, which was illustrated in Figs. 11.9 and 13.4.

Power-tool graphics. This type of graphics performs extensive computations relating to the meaning of what is drawn. It may perform cross-checks, verifications, or design calculations. It may translate one type of diagram into another, for example, a variety of diagram types can automatically be converted into action diagrams [1]. It may translate sketches into more complete designs, asking the designer to make decisions or provide information. Examples are HOS, data-base design tools, and tools for creating specifications from which code can be generated.

Manual-substitute graphics is anchored to design techniques that are commonly performed manually. Power-tool graphics makes possible design techniques that would be far too complex or difficult for most analysts to perform by hand. It facilitates mathematical verification. It makes possible extremely elaborate cross-checking. It can be designed for automatic generation of program code.

HOS, with its axiomatic verification, would be far too difficult to be a good manual technique. It *needs* automation. Its graphics tool is not merely cosmetic but is performing elaborate computation while the designer sits at the screen. The information engineering tools now emerging anchor the designer to centrally maintained data models and encyclopedias, and in some cases perform program generation. Most information-engineering techniques do not work well in practice without automation. They require power-tool graphics.

Once the concept is accepted that systems analysts will employ graphics workstations, new techniques can be devised that are highly powerful but would not work well if done by hand. The challenge in computer methodologies today is to employ such tools to advance the state of the art.

SUMMARY OF PROPERTIES

Box 27.2 lists the same diagramming techniques as Box 27.1 and indicates their properties other than

BOX 27.2   Other properties of diagramming techniques

OTHER PROPERTIES OF DIAGRAMMING TECHHNIQUES	DECOMPOSITION DIAGRAMS	DEPENDENCY DIAGRAMS	DATA FLOW DIAGRAMS	ENTITY-RELATIONSHIP DIAGRAMS	DATA ANALYSIS DIAGRAMS	DATA NAVIGATION DIAGRAMS	HIPO CHARTS	STRUCTURE CHARTS	WARNIER-ORR CHARTS	MICHAEL JACKSON CHARTS	FLOWCHARTS	STRUCTURED ENGLISH	NASSI-SHNEIDERMAN CHARTS	ACTION DIAGRAMS	DATA-BASE ACTION DIAGRAMS	DECISION TREES AND TABLES	STATE-TRANSITION DIAGRAMS	HOS CHARTS
Easy to read	YES	YES	YES	YES	YES	YES	X	YES	YES		o		YES	YES	YES	YES		
Quick to draw and change	YES	YES	YES	YES	YES	YES	X		YES					YES	YES	YES		
User-friendly (easy to teach to end users)	YES	YES	YES	YES	YES	YES	X	Fair	YES				Fair	YES	YES	YES		
Good for stepwise refinement							X	YES	YES					YES	YES			YES
One tool can show high-level structures and detailed logic														YES	YES			YES
Ultimate decomposition (can be decomposed to executable code)														YES	YES			YES
Good for computerized screen editing	YES	YES	YES	YES	YES	YES		YES	YES	YES				YES	YES	YES	YES	YES
Can be printed out on normal-width paper (without excessive division into pieces)			YES	YES	YES				√			YES		YES	YES	YES	YES	YES
Automatically convertible to program skeleton		YES				YES		YES	YES	YES			YES	YES	YES		YES	
Automatically convertible to executable program code														YES (4GL)	YES (4GL)	YES (Code Module)		YES
Problem-related rather than program-related terminology	YES	YES	YES	YES	YES											YES	YES	
Computerized accuracy checking														(can check uses of date)			YES	YES
Rigorous (with computerized checking)																		YES
Good for large, complex specifications which (with computerized assistance) need to be as error free as possible		YES			YES	YES								YES	YES	YES		YES
Oriented to interactive data-base usage and data modeling				YES	YES	YES									YES	YES		

X = High level only   o = Small charts only   √ = Up to a point

those concerned with drawing capabilities. Let us briefly summarize our views on these techniques:

1. Data Flow Diagrams (Fig. 11.1)

- Data flow diagrams are an essential and valuable tool for understanding the flows of documents and data among processes.
- End users can be quickly taught to read, check, and sometimes to draw data flow diagrams.

- Automated tools for drawing and manipulating data flow diagrams exist.
- Although data flow diagrams are an excellent overview tool, they are not good for drawing program architectures. They have been overused and misused in this more detailed area.
- Use of multilayered data flow diagrams for creating complex specifications often results in bad specifications with inconsistencies, omissions, and ambiguities. Data flow diagrams must be linked to other tools.
- Data flow diagrams should be tightly linked to data models; otherwise they can give false representations of data. Often this is not done.
- In some cases, data flow diagrams need improving to show synchronization among separate events.
- Data flow diagrams need improving to show data layering as described in Chapter 11.
- Tools other than data flow diagrams are essential for diagramming the structures of processes, and these should be designed for maximum verification. They could be linked to data flow diagrams.
- They can be drawn so as to be automatically convertible to action diagrams [1].

2. Data Models (Fig. 23.2)

- Data models are an essential tool.
- All systems design should employ data analysis and modeling at an early stage.
- Data models should be used for a top-down strategic view of an enterprise's entities and relationships and for detailed data structures.
- Correct normalization of data is important.
- Bachman notation cannot represent functional dependencies in data and should *not* be used. The notations in Chapter 22 are preferable.
- Automated tools should be used for data modeling, normalization, and presenting analysts or programmers with subsets of data models.

3. Data Navigation Diagrams (Fig. 24.5)

- Data navigation diagrams constitute a simple and essential tool for designing data-base navigation.
- They are adjunct to data modeling.
- They are essential documentation for data-base applications and ought to be an installation standard.
- They need linking to the tool for program design.
- They are automatically convertible to action diagrams.

4. HIPO Diagrams (Fig. 14.2)

- We believe that HIPO diagrams should not be used because other methods are better.

- Data flow diagrams give a much more compact and easy-to-read view of the flows of data.

- High-level HIPO diagrams (visual table of contents) do not give complete control structure information:

  They do not describe the control constructs and control variables governing module invocation.
  They do not describe the input and output data for each procedural component.
  They do not include a link to a data model or data dictionary.

- Detail-level HIPO diagrams (overview and detail HIPO diagrams) are limited to defining procedural components:

  They do not have symbols for representing the basic control constructs of sequence, selection, and repetition.
  They do not include a link to a data model or data dictionary.

5. Structure Charts (Fig. 13.2)

- Structure charts are commonly used for showing program hierarchy in conjunction with data flow diagrams and pseudocode.

- Structure charts do not give complete control structure information:
  They do not describe the control constructs and the control variables governing the invocation of procedural components. (Some structure charts do include some of this information, but it is optional and not necessarily complete.)
  They do not describe the input and output data for each procedural component.
  They do not include a link to a data model, data dictionary, or charts used to define the program data structures.

- Structure charts can become messy when data and control variables are written on them as in Fig. 13.2.

- Structure charts are an early and rather inadequate way of diagramming program structures and ought to be replaced with better techniques.

6. Warnier-Orr Diagrams (Fig. 15.5)

- These are a user-friendly type of diagram for showing functional decomposition and hierarchical data structures.

- Warnier-Orr diagrams are more compact than structure charts, HIPO diagrams, or Michael Jackson diagrams, but they spread out horizontally more than action diagrams.

- They are easy to read, draw, and change but can get cluttered.

- They show sequence, selection, and repetition, which structure charts do not.

- They do not show the conditions or variables that control selection, case structures, or loop structures. (This information is relegated to footnotes.)

- They do not show input and output data for procedural components.

- They do not facilitate any automated checking. They are species I functional decomposition.

- They provide no link to a data model or data dictionary, and there is no link between Warnier-Orr diagrams representing procedural and data components for the same program.

- They are not data-base-oriented. They can represent only hierarchical data structures.

- At a detail level, they degenerate into a form of pseudocode that can be more difficult to read and draw than simple structured English. (Note the BEGIN-END blocks in Fig. 15.5).

- Though we like Warnier-Orr diagrams, we feel that action diagrams have many advantages over them.

7. Michael Jackson Diagrams (Fig. 16.6)

- Michael Jackson methodology, described in Chapters 16 and 33, is claimed to give fewer errors in program structure than Warnier-Orr or Yourdon-Constantine methodologies. In installations we examined, this appeared to be true, but we could find no firm statistics.

- It represents only hierarchical data structures.

- It tends to break down or become very difficult to apply to complex programs.

- It shows sequence, selection, and repetition, which structure charts do not.

- It does not show the conditions or variables that control selection, case structures, or loop structures.

- To show detail design, Jackson diagrams resort to a form of pseudocode (structured text) that is difficult to understand.

- We prefer to use either action diagrams with fourth-generation languages (which is easier) or HOS methodology (which is more rigorous).

8. Flowcharts (Fig. 17.2)

- Flowcharts do not constitute a structured technique.

- They tend to lead to unstructured code, which is difficult to maintain.

- They should be avoided in favor of structured diagramming techniques.

9. Structured English and Pseudocode (Fig. 18.1)

- A picture is worth a thousand words, and pseudocode is not a pictorial technique.
- Code using these techniques is sometimes too lengthy, often longer than fourth-generation-language code.
- Some forms of pseudocode are highly mnemonic and difficult to read.
- Structured English and pseudocode can be helpful to programmers.
- We would replace them with action diagrams, which at a detail level are somewhat similar but have the advantage of being pictorial.

10. Nassi-Shneiderman Charts (Fig. 19.1)

- N-S charts show detailed logic only, not program architecture or functional decomposition.
- They are easy to read and graphically appealing.
- They are easy to teach to end users.
- They are generally an improvement over flowcharts or pseudocode, which they replace.
- They are too time-consuming to draw and change.
- They are not linked to a data dictionary or data model.
- They can show neither high-level program structure nor low-level degeneration into code.
- We prefer action diagrams, which overcome the deficiencies of N-S charts.

11. Action Diagrams (Fig. 20.4)

- Action diagrams represent a later technique designed to overcome many of the deficiencies in earlier techniques.
- They are quick to draw and easy to computerize.
- They are easy to read.
- They are designed to be easy to teach to end users.
- They use a single technique that extends all the way from highest-level functional decomposition to lowest-level logic and coding. They can be decomposed into executable code; all other methods so far require two or three different forms of representation to accomplish this.
- They can have the wording of a chosen fourth-generation language.
- They are designed to spread out vertically, not horizontally, so that an inexpensive desk-top printer can print the charts.

- They provide species II functional decomposition, facilitating cross-checking of inputs and outputs.
- There is a natural progression from a subset of a data model to a data navigation diagram to an action diagram.
- Action diagrams can show nonprocedural data-base operations (compound actions).

12. Decision Trees and Tables (Figs. 21.1 and 21.2)

- These are valuable techniques for representing complex sets of conditions and the actions that result from them.
- Software exists to convert decision tables into program modules.
- Every analyst and programmer should be familiar with them. They are an important tool in a DP professional's tool kit.
- Users can be taught to check decision tables for complex sets of rules or conditions.

13. HOS Charts (Fig. 26.3)

- HOS charts provide species III functional decomposition.
- They are more rigorous than any other structured technique.
- They are mathematically based, creating designs that are provably correct.
- They are automatically convertible to correct program code.
- They are not user-friendly.
- They constitute a tool for a professional analyst.
- Using HOS charts requires a commitment to learn a technique substantially different from traditional techniques.
- HOS charts extend all the way from highest-level functional decomposition to the automatic generation of program code.
- They eliminate most debugging.
- They are extremely valuable for creating highly complex specifications where any other method would give errors, inconsistencies, omissions, and ambiguities.
- Eventually the entire world of structured analysis and programming must move to tools that have this level of rigor and automation.

OUR CHOICE OF TECHNIQUES

Now for the $64,000 question. Which of these various techniques would we select for running a DP operation?

The right-hand side of Fig. 27.2 is fairly clear. The need for data-flow diagrams, data models, and data navigation diagrams is illustrated. The left-hand side offers more choice.

Either HOS methodology or action diagrams offer a single technique that is applicable from top to bottom. HOS is the most rigorous of any structured technique. It gives designs that are guaranteed to be internally consistent and correct, and it automatically generates correct code from them. The designer builds his system with graphics at a computer terminal, and at this terminal the system is easy to modify and maintain.

If the system in question is highly complex, like military systems or the control of complex operations, it is asking for trouble to use methods that do not have the automated verification that HOS has. Experience has shown over and over again what an unholy mess results from the use of traditional structured methods and even worse from nonstructured methods.

The problem with HOS is that it is different from conventional methods. The analysts need training and will take some time to become skilled with it.

In a less complex commercial DP environment, we would employ the most appropriate fourth-generation languages, report generators, and so on, and their associated data management systems. Action diagrams are designed for this environment and work well with traditional languages. They are easy to teach to end users and encourage end users to progress from understanding high-level diagrams of the organization chart and functional decomposition down to diagrams of program detail drawn with the same technique [2].

Decision tables are a valuable tool for handling complex conditions and actions like those in Fig. 21.3. Analysts should understand this tool and use it when appropriate, preferably with automated code generation.

Figure 27.4 shows our preferences. We would want all analysts in a DP organization to be thoroughly trained to use the techniques in Fig. 27.4.

It is desirable to use computerized tools for automating the process of data modeling and third-normal-form design (Chapter 40), automatic extraction of views of data from the models and creating and editing action diagrams, and linking these to the data models. Such computerized tools can provide extensive cross-checking and verification that data are designed and used correctly. Species II functional decomposition is needed with computerized verification that the inputs and outputs are consistent.

CHALLENGE

The challenge of the future is to adapt these drawing techniques and the software that goes with them into a systems engineering tool kit that is easy and fast to use and provides the most rigorous checks possible on the emerging design. This tool kit should generate executable code from the detailed diagrams. The diagrams should be easy to edit and change because complex designs change and evolve constantly during their creation. It should be possible to change the diagrams while enforcing rigor so that maintenance can be performed quickly.

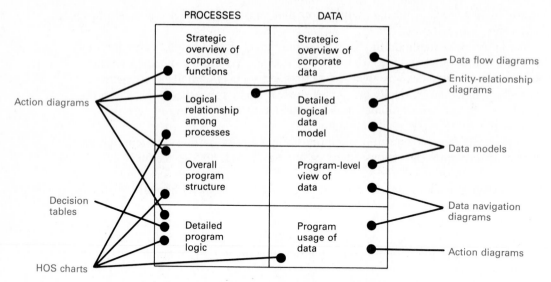

Figure 27.4   Choice of diagramming techniques.

It is possible to have an analyst's workbench that generates provably bug-free programs and specifications that are internally consistent and correct. The challenge today is to adapt this rigor to other techniques that are user-friendly and as powerful as possible.

REFERENCES

1. James Martin: *Recommended Diagramming Standards for Analysts and Programmers,* Prentice-Hall, Inc., Englewood Cliffs, NJ, 1985.

2. James Martin and Carma McClure, *Action Diagrams: Clearly Structured Program Design,* Prentice-Hall, Inc., Englewood Cliffs, NJ, 1985.

28 STRUCTURED ANALYSIS AND DESIGN TECHNIQUES

SOFTWARE ANALYSIS AND DESIGN

Analysis is the process of defining the requirements for a solution to a problem. During analysis the needs of the users are examined, and the properties that the system should possess to meet those needs are defined. Also, system constraints and performance requirements are identified. The functions to be performed are precisely defined, but how these functions work is not addressed. The major output of analysis is the functional specification.

Design follows analysis. It is the process of planning how the system will be built—that is, determining the procedural and data components needed and how these components will be assembled to form the computer solution. Algorithms are developed to describe what each component is to do. The functional specifications, the problem requirements, and constraints defined in the analysis phase are used as input to the design process.

THE DESIRE TO SKIP ANALYSIS

In many software development projects, the analysis phase has been glossed over because it does not lend itself well to structuring with the existing technical tools and methods. It presents a people-oriented rather than a machine-oriented problem. Requirement analysis focuses on the interface between the user and the computer. Traditionally, software developers have preferred to ignore this interface in favor of more easily definable technical issues.

CHANGING REQUIREMENTS

Some requirements are hard; some are optional. Some are likely to change in the future, and some will vary with the needs of a particular user or the capability of a particular computing facility.

Requirements are not static. They change with time, people, and new technologies. In practice, the analysis phase of program development spills over into the rest of the life cycle and must, at least in part, be repeated as the user and the system developer learn more about the problem to be solved.

During analysis, problem requirements are defined, and a problem solution is proposed. First, the problem is studied to determine its parts and their interrelationships. It is of the utmost importance to understand the problem thoroughly *before* defining a solution. If the structure of the solution does not follow from and resemble the structure of the problem, the resulting system will be difficult to change and to maintain. Not anticipating the likelihood of changing requirements has been a major cause of building inflexible, unmaintainable software systems. Only after the problem is well understood can a workable solution be proposed.

SYSTEM SPECIFICATION

The result of the analysis phase is the system specification, which describes how the system will meet the problem requirements. A specification includes definitions for reports, data structures, data bases, external files, internal tables, functional components, and interfaces with other systems—in short, the system components and the interfaces connecting these components. It offers the user and the developer a concrete description of the system components to avoid confusion on the user's part and errors on the developer's part.

The specification should be precise, testable, and formal. For example, "the system will have the capability of processing 100 transactions per second" is a well-defined and testable specification. Also, the specification should be understandable to system analysts, program developers, and end users since it is the principal means of communication between these groups. *Understandable* means that the system components and how the system solves the user problem can be understood at varying levels of detail.

POOR SPECIFICATION AND EXPENSIVE ERRORS

The completeness and correctness of the specification affect the success of the entire software development effort. The specification is used to develop project schedules, manpower assignments, test plans, and user documentation. If the specification is incomplete or incorrect, it can cause schedule delays, poor testing, and incorrect user documentation. A software system built from a poor specification cannot be expected to be reliable or useful.

Developing a sound system specification is the most crucial phase in software development because specification errors can be very expensive if they are not detected and corrected in the early phases. For example, correcting a specification error during the maintenance phase may be 100 times more expensive than if it had been corrected during the analysis phase [1].

IMPORTANCE OF ANALYSIS

Early structured techniques ignored problem-solving methods and user-related issues. The focus was almost entirely on solving technical software problems associated with coding and testing. After realizing that many systems that were technically sound were still software failures because of poorly understood system requirements, structured techniques were developed to bring structured philosophy to bear on requirement analysis problems. All of the basic problem-solving strategies of the structured philosophy—divide and conquer, abstraction, formality, and hierarchical organization—were introduced to the system analysis process. The best-known and most widely used structured technique for requirement analysis and specification is called *structured analysis*.

Structured analysis uses a top-down functional decomposition method to define system requirements. Its objective is to produce a structured specification that provides a concise, easy-to-understand model of the system.

A BUILDING ANALOGY

If we were going to build a one-room mud hut, we would not need to do much planning before construction. Only a few basic materials and tools would be needed. The construction process would involve a few, simple steps, done by one person. If a mistake was made or a change was necessary, the hut would be easy to modify or rebuild.

At the other extreme, if we were going to build a huge skyscraper, we would need a detailed architectural plan. Creating this plan would be our first step, as no professional builder would attempt such a project without a sound plan. Otherwise, how would we determine what building materials were needed, how many workers to hire, or what jobs to assign to them? If the plan were incomplete or incorrect, the cost to change the building or to modify the construction schedule could cause serious financial problems, possible unsafe conditions, and expensive legal consequences.

Building a single-family house falls somewhere in the middle. An experienced builder could probably construct it without a blueprint, but in most cases this would be inefficient and sometimes foolhardy. By skipping the design phase, the builder could begin actual construction sooner. However, the whole project might take longer to complete. Without a sound design, the house could be of poorer quality because its structure and construction materials would be chosen on the basis of availability rather than quality considerations. Also, because the buyer would not have been given an opportunity to review the plan and perhaps modify his requirements before construction began, he might be less satisfied with the outcome.

We can draw a strong analogy between constructing buildings and constructing computer programs. It is as important to plan a program as it is to plan a building.

IMPORTANCE OF DESIGN

In large projects, design errors often exceed coding errors. In a TRW study of errors detected during or after acceptance testing, design errors outweighed coding errors 64 percent to 32 percent (see Fig. 28.1) [2]. Not only did more design errors occur, but they were also more costly to correct than coding errors. Design errors took more time to detect and to correct than coding errors. In a study by Shooman and Bolsky, it was determined that correcting a design error during the coding phase required twice the effort of correcting it during design and ten times the effort if not found and corrected until testing [3]. In other words, design errors often dominated software projects in terms of their number and their cost to fix, especially when not detected early. More care given to design means lower-cost, more reliable systems.

A system design is the blueprint for system implementation. If the blueprint does not exist or if it is incorrect, it should be no surprise when a less-than-acceptable system is produced. Such systems often are poorly organized and poorly documented and become a nightmare to support later.

On the other hand, a good system design can improve software readability and reliability, reduce software complexity and cost, and increase job satisfaction for software developers.

TRW Study	Design Errors	Coding Errors
Total	64%	36%
Found after implementation	45%	9%
Average diagnostic time	3.1 hours	2.2 hours
Average correction time	4.0 hours	0.8 hours

220 Errors

Figure 28.1   In large software projects, design errors often exceed coding errors. Not only do more design errors occur, but they are more costly to correct than coding errors.[2]

In traditional program development, the importance of design is often underestimated. At most, only about 15 percent of the total development effort is spent on the design step. In many software projects, the design step has been skipped. As a result, many serious problems and some long-term consequences have arisen. The development effort becomes a management nightmare because there is no plan for what is to be done. This makes it difficult to assign personnel tasks. System developers become frustrated, unproductive, and eventually unsatisfied with even state-of-the-art projects because there are no mechanisms by which their efforts can be recognized and fairly rewarded. Finally, the system that is produced is often unreliable, inflexible, inefficient, and unmaintainable because it is made up of a conglomeration of discoordinate, poorly tested, and probably undocumented pieces.

A SYSTEMATIC DESIGN APPROACH

The objective of applying structured techniques to the software design process is to combat these problems by offering a systematic approach for system and program design. In essence what this means is that the software developers are first given the opportunity to plan what they are going to do and to evaluate the goodness of that plan before coding and testing begin. The importance of such a plan cannot be overemphasized. The larger the program or system to be built and the more developers involved, the more important this plan becomes. As Freeman explains:

> Design is the primary tool for controlling and dealing with a mass of detail and its attendant complexity. The abstraction processes of design permit us to deal with large masses of detail without becoming bogged down. The regularity and structure of design methods and techniques serve to guide us through complex chains of reasoning where we might otherwise become lost. [4]

TYPES OF SOFTWARE DESIGN

Design is performed between the analysis and implementation steps of the software development process (see Fig. 28.2). The functional specification describing what the program must do is input to the design process. The purpose of design is to devise representations or plans of the software to be built to meet the functional specification. The plans outline the architectural structure for a system or program and provide a detailed blueprint for building the actual program(s).

Design is typically divided into two types:

1. Architectural or system design
2. Detailed design

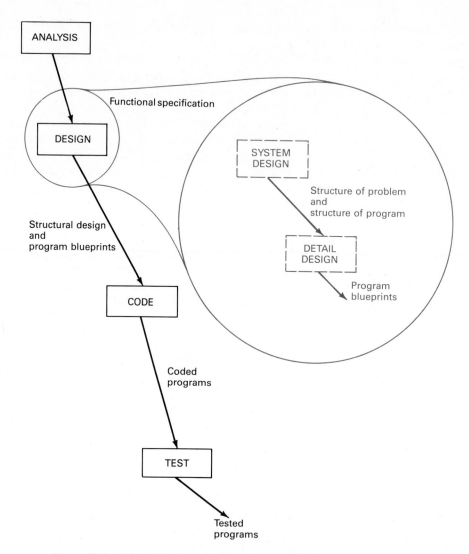

Figure 28.2   Design lies between the systems analysis and program implementation steps in the program development process.

During the first step, *system design,* a high-level design is created in which the basic procedural components and their interrelationships and the major data representations are defined. The program architecture is designed in a manner that follows from and matches the structure of the problem to be solved.

During the second step, *detailed design,* specific algorithmic and data structure choices are made. The system-level design is refined to produce the detail design. Often several levels of refinement are necessary. The refinement process is complete when precise algorithms and data structures covering all major program components have been defined.

STRUCTURED DESIGN METHODOLOGIES

There are several structured design methodologies. All employ functional decomposition as their primary design mechanism. For the most part, they are manual methods supported by few automated aids.

The most widely used structured design methodologies have been top-down design, Yourdon's structured design, Jackson design methodology, and Warnier-Orr design methodology. Now, more rigorous, more automated information engineering techniques are tending to replace the earlier, more casual, hand-drawn techniques.

Top-down design is the most informal structured design methodology. It uses a step-by-step process that begins with the most general functional view of what is to be done, breaks this view down into subfunctions, and then repeats the process for each subfunction until all subfunctions are small enough to be implemented into program code.

Yourdon's structured design is a composite of design strategies, evaluation aids, and graphic documentation techniques. Structured design is a refinement of the top-down design method. It adds design guidelines to systematize the design process further and to measure the quality of a design.

The *Jackson design methodology* is also a refinement of the top-down design method. The major difference between the Jackson design methodology and top-down design or Yourdon's structured design is that it is a data-driven design technique, whereas the others are process-driven. The Jackson design methodology begins with a design of the data structures. The program structure is derived from the data structures. The methodology assumes that the problem has been completely specified prior to design and that the program will be implemented in a second- or third-generation procedural programming language.

The *Warnier-Orr design methodology* is another data-driven design technique. However, its focus on system output differentiates it from other structured design methods. The Warnier-Orr philosophy is that the system output completely and absolutely determines the data structure, and the data structure, in turn, determines the program structure. The Warnier-Orr design process begins with a hierarchical description of the system output. The input structures and program structure are derived from the output structure.

These design methodologies are described and evaluated in the chapters that follow.

REFERENCES

1. V. Haase and G. Koch, ''Developing the Connection Between User and Code,'' *Computer* (May 1982), 10–11.

2. B. Boehm, R. McClearn, and D. Unfrig, "Some Experiences with Automated Aids to the Design of Large-Scale Reliable Software," *IEEE Trans. on Software Engineering,* 1, no. 1 (March 1975).

3. M. Shooman and M. Bolsky, "Types, Distributions and Correction Times for Programming Errors," in *Proceedings of the 1975 International Conference on Reliable Software, ACM SIGPLAN Notices,* 10, no. 6 (August 1975), 347–357.

4. P. Freeman, "The Context of Design," in *Tutorial on Software Design Techniques* (No. EHO 161-0), New York: IEEE Computer Society, 1980, pp. 2–4.

29 STRUCTURED ANALYSIS

A CRITICAL STEP   Analysis is a critical step in developing software systems and programs because it affects all the development steps that follow. It is difficult because of communication problems, changing system requirements, and inadequate estimating techniques.

It is difficult to describe system requirements in a precise, computable form. The language of the user and the language of the developer are so different that effective communication is rare. Although it is seldom realistic, the system developer would like to freeze requirements and then build a system to match. But requirements present a moving target that continues to change throughout system development, and for that matter, throughout the entire life cycle.

Specifications should be a model of the system. They should be easy to build, easy to understand, and easy to change.

A STRUCTURED   Structured analysis proposes to solve these difficul-
DISCIPLINE   ties by providing a systematic, step-by-step approach to performing analysis and by producing a new, improved system specification. To accomplish its aim, structured analysis focuses on clear, concise communication.

There are two similar versions of structured analysis: Gane and Sarson [1] and De Marco and Yourdon [2, 3]. Both represent a structured discipline based on the following structuring concepts:

- Top-down, hierarchical organization
- Divide and conquer
- Graphic communication/documentation tools

Structured analysis uses the top-down, functional decomposition method to define system requirements. The system specification produced by the structured analysis process is a top-down, partitioned model of the system to be built. Because the specification is a graphic model that is concise and easy to understand, the user can become familiar with the system long before it is implemented. This provides an opportunity for system review to discover and correct errors and misconceptions as early as possible during the development process. Because the specification is partitioned into small, manageable pieces, it is easy to modify to reflect any changes in the requirements that occur during the life cycle.

De Marco defines analysis as "the process of transforming a stream of information about current operations and new requirements into some sort of rigorous description of the system to be built" [4]. He explains that the major difference between classical analysis and structured analysis is a new system specification that is much more rigorous and much more user-friendly than the gigantic, impossible-to-read, narrative specification produced by classical analysis methods.

SYSTEM SPECIFICATION

The system specification is the link between analysis and design. It provides a description of the requirements of the system to be built. The primary purpose of analysis is to produce a system specification that defines the structure of the problem to be solved as the user views it. The purpose of design is to define the structure of a solution in a form that is compatible with the structure of the problem and with the user's requirements. Advocates of structured analysis suggest that by using the same construction method (functional decomposition) for both the specification and the design, the two can be brought closer together and are more likely to represent a system that will meet the user's needs and expectations. Structured analysis was designed to be compatible with and to provide the best possible input to structured design. When structured analysis precedes structured design, the specification is in the form needed by structured design, so the design process can begin immediately. (The structured design methodology is discussed in Chapter 31.)

The system specification produced by the structured analysis process is called a *structured specification* and has the following characteristics:

- It is graphic—a graphic model of system processes or procedures
- It is partitioned—able to show system components at varying levels of detail
- It is a top-down hierarchical model—evolved by using functional decomposition
- It is logical—as opposed to a physical model of system processes or procedures

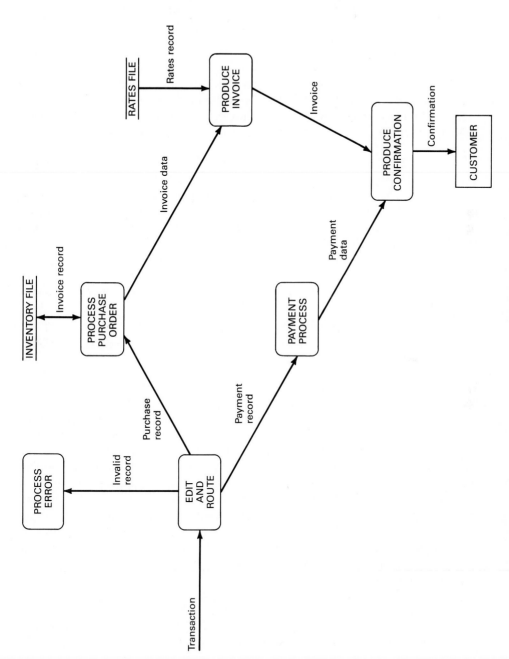

Figure 29.1 A data-flow diagram is a network representation of a system showing the system processes and the data connecting those processes.

The structured specification is composed of data flow diagrams, a data dictionary, and process specifications.

DATA FLOW DIAGRAM

A data flow diagram is a network representation of the processes (functions or procedures) in a system and the data connecting these processes. It shows what a system/procedure does, but not how it is done. It is the central modeling tool of structured analysis and is used to partition the system into a process hierarchy.

Figure 29.1 is an example of a data flow diagram. PRODUCE INVOICE is one of the system processes. Each process is represented by a process box on the diagram. The name of the process is written inside the box. Arrows are used to show the movement of data flows through the processes. The name of the data is written alongside the arrow. INVOICE DATA is the output of PROCESS PURCHASE ORDER and the input to PRODUCE INVOICE. The straight lines—for example, INVENTORY FILE—show data stores—the files and data bases used by the system.

Data flow diagrams can be used in a top-down manner to show system processes in greater and greater detail. At lower levels, the higher-level processes are exploded so we can look inside a process to see what more detailed processes and data flows are involved. (Data flow diagrams are discussed further in Chapter 11.)

DATA DICTIONARY

Data flow diagrams by themselves can provide only an informal description of the system. The data dictionary is used to add rigor to the specification. The *data dictionary* is a set of formal definitions of all data appearing as data flows or data stores on the data flow diagrams. The definition of each data item consists of the data components that make up the data item and the relationships among them. It is a hierarchical definition that defines components and successive subcomponents of each data item. The hierarchy is complete when bottom-level components are defined in terms of data elements that have no logical meaning if subdivided further. Possible data relationships include the following [5]:

AND	Connected data items must be used together.
OR	At least one connected data item must be present.
OPTIONAL	A data item may be present or not.
ITERATIONS	Zero, one, or more connected data items must be present.

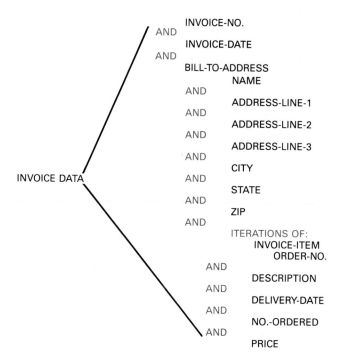

Figure 29.2   A data dictionary is a set of formal definitions of all data appearing as data flows or data stores on the data-flow diagrams for a system.

Figure 29.2 shows an example of the data dictionary entry describing IN-VOICE DATA, which is the data item passed between the processes PROCESS PURCHASE ORDER and PRODUCE INVOICE in the data flow diagram shown in Fig. 29.1.

PROCESS SPECIFICATION

A process specification, or *minispec,* describes what happens inside a process box in a data flow diagram.

A minispec is usually about one page long and explains how the input data are transformed into output data. A minispec is written in structured English (pseudocode), as a decision table or decision trees.

Figure 29.3 shows an example of the process specification for the process EDIT AND ROUTE from the data flow diagram in Fig. 29.1. (Pseudocode is discussed in Chapter 18, and decision tables and decision trees are discussed in Chapter 21.)

```
EDIT AND ROUTE.
    GET A TRANSACTION;
    IF PURCHASE TRANSACTION TYPE
        VALIDATE PURCHASE FIELDS;
        IF ERROR
            SET ERROR INDICATOR;
            PERFORM PROCESS ERROR
        ENDIF;
        PERFORM PROCESS PURCHASE ORDER
    ELSE IF PAYMENT RECORD TYPE
        VALIDATE PAYMENT FIELDS;
        IF ERROR
            SET ERROR INDICATOR;
            PERFORM PROCESS ERROR
        ENDIF;
        PERFORM PAYMENT PROCESS
    ELSE
        SET ERROR INDICATOR;
        PERFORM PROCESS ERROR.
```

Figure 29.3   Structured English (pseudocode) is used to describe the processing steps inside a process box on a data flow diagram.

STEPS OF STRUCTURED ANALYSIS

As shown in Box 29.1, De Marco defines structured analysis as a seven-step process:

Step 1. Document the current way things are done in the present user environment. The output of this step is the current physical data flow diagram. It shows locations, personnel, names, and manual and automated procedures and uses the users' terms.

Step 2. Use the current physical data flow diagram from step 1 to create the logical model of the current system. The logical model, like the physical model, is represented as a data flow diagram. The difference between the two models is that the physical model shows the physical details of how particular users currently do things, while the logical model portrays what is done at an abstract level, separating out any current particulars from the fundamental business procedures.

Step 3. Develop the new logical model for the system to be built. The logical model from step 2 is the starting point. It is modified to incorporate the changes for the new system. It includes both manual and automatable processes and is represented as a set of data flow diagrams describing the system at varying levels of detail. Step 3 involves the major part of the work effort for the structured analysis process.

BOX 29.1 Structured analysis process

De Marco's Seven Steps of Structured Analysis	Gane and Sarson's Five Steps of Structured Analysis
STEP 1: BUILD A CURRENT PHYSICAL MODEL	
STEP 2: BUILD A CURRENT LOGICAL MODEL FROM THE PHYSICAL MODEL STEP 3: BUILD A LOGICAL MODEL OF THE NEW SYSTEM TO BE BUILT • Build a structured specification consisting of data flow diagrams, a data dictionary, and process specifications.	STEP 1: BUILD A CURRENT LOGICAL MODEL STEP 2: BUILD A LOGICAL MODEL OF THE NEW SYSTEM • Build a structured specification consisting of data flow diagrams, a data dictionary, and process specifications. • Build a logical data model by expressing the contents of data stores in third-normal form.
STEP 4: CREATE A FAMILY OF NEW PHYSICAL MODELS STEP 5: PRODUCE COST AND SCHEDULE ESTIMATES FOR EACH MODEL STEP 6: SELECT ONE MODEL STEP 7: PACKAGE THE SPECIFICATION INTO SUBSYSTEMS	STEP 3: DESIGN A PHYSICAL DATA BASE STEP 4: CREATE A NEW PHYSICAL MODEL OF SYSTEM STEP 5: PACKAGE THE SPECIFICATION INTO SUBSYSTEMS

Step 4. Create the new physical model for the system to be built by identifying the human/machine interface. More than one possible data flow diagram is created to represent varying degrees of automation.

Step 5. Produce cost and schedule estimates for each alternative physical model developed in the previous step.

Step 6. Select one of the physical models to be used to specify the functions and requirements of the system to be built. Management, rather than the analyst, will probably make this decision, based on the estimates produced in step 5.

Step 7. Package the structured specification by putting it in final form. It consists of a set of data flow diagrams, a data dictionary, and minispecs.

Gane and Sarson define a similar process for structured analysis (see Box 29.1) [1]. The major difference is that Gane and Sarson include a data modeling step in which the contents of the data stores shown in the data-flow diagrams are carefully defined, possibly in third-normal form. Gane and Sarson include data modeling in step 2 of their version of structured analysis. Then, in step 3, the logical data model is used as input to physical data-base design.

CRITIQUE OF STRUCTURED ANALYSIS

Whereas the most advanced structured techniques are available for the coding phase of software development, probably the least advanced are available for system analysis and specification. Structured analysis is an example of an early, informal analysis methodology. It represents more the beginnings of an analysis method than a full-fledged methodology. As such, it offers some distinct improvements over classical analysis approaches but still falls short of what is needed in a complete analysis methodology.

Perhaps the greatest improvement structured analysis offers is changing the system specification from a large, unreadable tome to a user-friendly, graphic model (i.e., a data flow diagram). A high-level data flow diagram can be drawn quickly and can be changed easily as the user and the analyst learn more about the problem to be solved.

However, the data flow diagram is not a complete or rigorous representation of the system. Although a set of leveled data flow diagrams can show hierarchical organization by exploding process boxes, a data flow diagram shows no logical nesting of data flows and no control information. Also, it is common to find omissions and other mistakes in data flow diagrams since there is no checking mechanism [6]. Although the structured analysis method is based on data flow, its emphasis is on process components, with data analysis receiving only secondary attention.

Another basic improvement that structured analysis offers is the application of the divide-and-conquer principle to both the analysis process and the system specification. Divide and conquer is the only reasonable strategy for handling large problems and specifying their solutions. The analysis process should be divided into steps, and the specification should be divided into easy-to-understand, easy-to-change pieces. De Marco divides the analysis process into seven steps; Gane and Sarson divide it into five similar steps. Both approaches use an informal application of the functional decomposition method to divide a problem into its component parts. But neither methodology offers sufficient guidelines to provide the rigor necessary for defining a precise, computable specification. Not only is the analyst not given adequate guidelines for how to subdivide a problem or how to check for the completeness and correctness of specifications, but he is also not given adequate guidelines for stopping the subdivision process. For example, De Marco states:

> This process of successive partitioning continues down to the primitive level, where nodes cannot be further partitioned, or are judged small enough to specify via minispec. [5]

Advocates of structured analysis recommend the structured specification as the link between analysis and design. The data flow diagram is used as the base on which to build a structured design and ultimately a structured program. However, a big leap of faith is required to supplement the lack of rigor when transforming a data flow diagram into a structure chart representing a structured design.

WHEN TO USE STRUCTURED ANALYSIS

Structured analysis should be used only for small, simple problems. Although it is informal and not computable, data-flow diagramming is the most valuable part of structured analysis. It is easy to use and quite user-friendly. It can be used to discover the basic processing components and data flows in a system. It should be followed by more formal data modeling. (Data modeling is discussed in Chapter 41.)

For larger, more complex systems, data-flow diagramming can be used to sketch a high-level view of the system. But beyond this point, other, more rigorous analysis and specification methods should be used to develop a precise, computable specification. The HOS methodology, discussed in Chapter 38, is one such specification method.

REFERENCES

1. C. Gane and T. Sarson, *Structured Systems Analysis: Tools and Techniques,* New York: IST Databooks, 1977.

2. T. De Marco, *Structured Analysis and System Specification,* New York: Yourdon, Inc., 1978.

3. E. Yourdon, "The Emergence of Structured Analysis," *Computer Decisions,* 8, no. 4 (April 1976).

4. T. De Marco, *Structured Analysis and System Specification* (Guide 47) Chicago: IBM Guide, 1978.

5. T. De Marco, *Specification Modeling,* (Guide 50), Chicago: IBM Guide.

6. N. Chapin, "Some Structured Analysis Techniques," *Data Base* (Winter 1979), 16–23.

30 TOP-DOWN DESIGN

Top-down design is an informal design strategy for breaking problems into smaller problems. It has the following objectives:

- To systematize the design process
- To produce a modular program design
- To provide a framework in which problem solving can more effectively proceed

Top-down design is a step-by-step process that begins with the most general function, breaks it down into subfunctions, and then repeats the process for each subfunction until all subfunctions are small enough and simple enough to be coded in actual programming instructions. The top-down design process is applicable to the design of a module, a program, a system, or a data structure.

DESIGN PROCESS   The top-down design process can be divided into two parts. In the first part (step 1), an initial design is defined. In the second part (steps 2–*n*), the design is systematically expanded:

- *Step 1*. The program design is represented in terms of high-level procedural and data components.
- *Steps 2*–n. In steps, the procedural and data components are defined in more and more detail. This part of the top-down process is an application of the stepwise refinement method discussed in Chapter 6.

The stepwise refinement process can be viewed as two parallel processes (see Fig. 30.1):

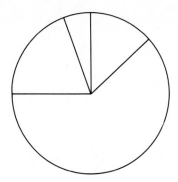

- Divide big problem into easier-to-solve smaller problems.

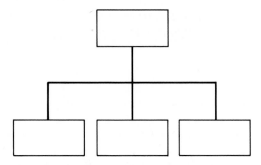

- Produce a hierarchy of program components.
- Start at the top component and proceed down the hierarchy.

Figure 30.1   The refinement process can be viewed as two parallel processes: a decomposition process in which the problem is broken into pieces, and an assembly process in which the program components are defined.

- A decomposition process in which, in steps, the problem is broken into parts
- An assembly process in which, in steps, the program components are defined

DECISION MAKING   The stepwise refinement process is a decision-making process. At each design step, decisions must be made. The designer must use his judgment to determine which of many possible design alternatives is best. No order in which to make design decisions is suggested as part of top-down design, but some general guidelines have been developed:

- Make decisions that will separate the problem into parts whereby the components within each part are logically related.
- When making design decisions, consider alternative designs.
- Attempt to make the easiest decisions first.
- Decide as little as possible at each step.

PRINCIPLES OF TOP-DOWN DESIGN

In addition, there are some basic principles that the designer should follow for successful application of the top-down design approach:

- Input, function, and output should be specified for each module designed at each design step.
- Implementation details should not be addressed until late in the design process.
- At each level of the design, the function of a module should be explained by at most a single page of instructions or a single-page diagram. At the top level, the overall design should be describable in approximately ten or fewer lines of instructions and/or calls to lower-level modules.
- Data should receive as much design attention as processing procedures because the interfaces between modules must be carefully specified.

DOCUMENTATION FOR TOP-DOWN DESIGN

A top-down design is documented in narrative form, graphic form, or a combination of the two. For example, a structure chart like the one shown in Fig. 30.2 may be used to represent the design. Accompanying the structure chart is a pseudocode description of each module in the structure chart (see Fig. 30.3). (Structure charts and pseudocode are discussed in Chapters 13 and 18.)

Alternatively, HIPO diagrams can be used to document the design since they, like structure charts, can show the hierarchical architecture of a system or program. Detailed HIPOs, like pseudocode, can show the processing steps performed by a module. (HIPO diagrams are discussed in Chapter 14.)

TOP-DOWN DESIGN OF DATA

The concept of top-down design applies just as much to the design of data as it does to the design of procedures. Usually, data structures are designed in parallel with the procedural structure, but sometimes the data structures are designed before the program structure. The designer may first

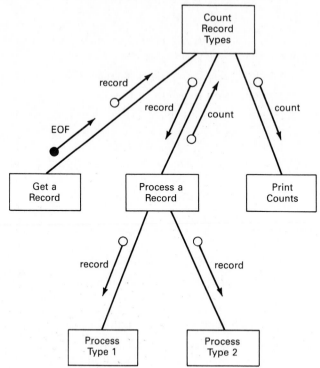

Figure 30.2 A structure chart can be used to represent the design.

identify the files required, then identify the records within files, then provide a specification of each field within a record. The program structure is designed thereafter.

If the top-down design is to proceed successfully, some aspects of data design must be done in detail at a relatively early stage. Otherwise, it will be impossible to describe the data interfaces connecting the modules.

WHEN TO USE TOP-DOWN DESIGN

Top-down design became a popular design approach in the early 1970s. It was a great advancement over the ad hoc design methods used previously because it offered an organized way of attacking larger problems. Unfortunately, it does not provide enough guidelines on how to subdivide a problem, when to stop subdividing, or how to measure the quality of a de-

Pseudocode for COUNT RECORD TYPES Example

COUNT-RECORD TYPES.

    OPEN FILE.
    MOVE 'N' TO NO-MORE RECORDS.
    MOVE 0 TO COUNT-1, COUNT-2.

    PERFORM PROCESS-A-RECORD
        UNTIL NO-MORE-RECORD = 'Y'.
    PERFORM PRINT-COUNTS.
    CLOSE FILE.
    STOP RUN.

PROCESS-A-RECORD.
    READ FILE AT END MOVE 'Y' TO NO-MORE-RECORDS.
    IF FIRST-FIELD = '1'
        PERFORM PROCESS-TYPE-1
    ELSE
        PERFORM PROCESS-TYPE-2.

PROCESS-TYPE-1.

    WRITE SECOND-FIELD.
    MOVE SPACES TO SECOND-FIELD.
    ADD 1 TO COUNT-1.

PROCESS-TYPE-2.

    ADD 1 TO COUNT-2.

PRINT-COUNTS.

    WRITE COUNT-1, COUNT-2.

Figure 30.3 Pseudocode is used to explain the processing steps performed by each module in the structure chart.

sign. It relies greatly on the experience and judgment of the designer. Inexperienced designers often believe that by evolving the design in steps a correct design will automatically result. Of course this is not the case. A poor design can be systematically produced just as easily as a good design.

The top-down design approach is appropriate for the design of small, simple programs. For large programs and systems it is too informal a strategy to be used exclusively to guide the design process.

31 STRUCTURED DESIGN

SYSTEMATIC DESIGN APPROACH

Structured design, as defined by Stevens, Myers, Constantine, and Yourdon [1,2], is a composite of techniques, strategies, and methods for designing software systems and programs. It provides a step-by-step design procedure for system design and detail design.

Some steps involve developing the design; some involve documenting the design; and still others involve evaluating and improving the quality of the design. Each step is supported by a set of design strategies, guidelines, and documentation techniques.

Structured design is a refinement of the top-down design method. All the principles of top-down design remain valid in structured design, but structured design adds many other guidelines to systematize the design process further and to measure the quality of a design. For example, design strategies like transform analysis and transaction analysis guide the designer in ordering design decisions. Design measures like coupling and cohesion provide the designer with techniques for evaluating the quality of a design. The product of structured design is a structure chart showing the program procedural components, their hierarchical arrangement, and the data connecting them (see Fig. 31.2).

Designing programs and systems is a decision-making process that involves many technical decisions. The objective of structured design is to provide a procedure that enables designers to make these decisions in a systematic way. Figure 31.1 shows the four basic steps in the structured design process:

1. Represent the design as a flow of data through a set of processes.
2. Represent the design as a hierarchy of functions (or procedural components).
3. Evaluate and improve the design.
4. Prepare the design for the implementation step.

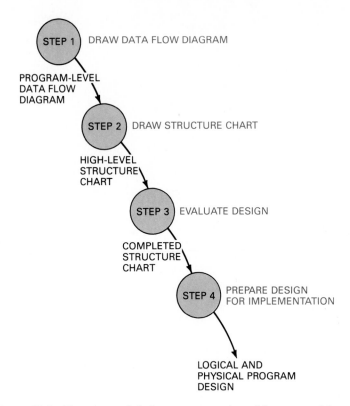

Figure 31.1   The structured design process consists of four sequential steps.

STRUCTURED DESIGN: STEP 1: DRAW DATA-FLOW DIAGRAM

The first step in structured design is to represent the design problem as the flow of data through a system. The system is composed of processes that operate on (or transform) the data. These processes and the data linking them become the basis for defining the program components.

A *data flow diagram* (see Chapter 11) is used to represent this first view of the program design. In Fig. 31.1 we used a data flow diagram to depict the structured design process. Each circle in the diagram represents a process. In Fig. 31.1, there are four processes, corresponding to the four steps in structured design.

STEP 2: DRAW STRUCTURE CHART

The second step in structured design is to represent the program design as a hierarchy of functional components. A structure chart (see Chapter 13) is used to show this view of the design. Figure 31.2 shows an example of a structure chart for the employee skills system. The purpose of this program is to produce a report summarizing employee skills by department.

The structure chart is derived from the data-flow diagram produced in the

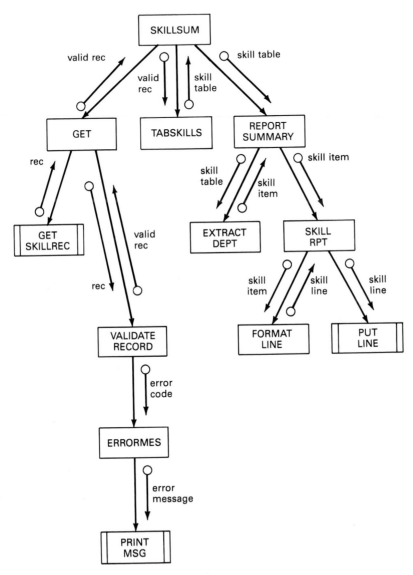

Figure 31.2 The structure chart is a hierarchical diagram that shows the basic procedural components of a system or program and the interrelationships between the components.

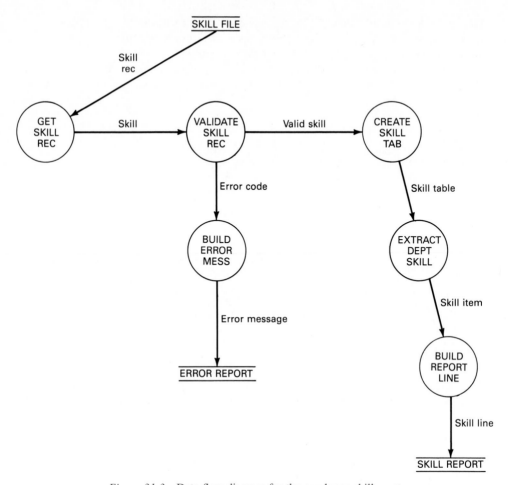

Figure 31.3   Data flow diagram for the employee skills system.

first step. Figure 31.3 shows a data flow diagram for the employee skills system.

Structured design provides two design strategies to guide the transformation of a data flow diagram into a structure chart: transform analysis and transaction analysis. These two strategies provide two structure models that can be used singly or in conjunction to derive a hierarchical design.

Transform Analysis

Transform analysis is an information-flow model used to design a program by identifying the primary functional components and high-level inputs and outputs for these components [3].

The data flow diagram is the primary input to the transform-analysis process. The first step of transform analysis is to divide the data flow diagram into three types of parts: input, logical processing, and output. The input portion of the data-flow diagram includes processes that transform input data from physical (e.g., character from terminal) to logical form (e.g., internal table). It is called the *afferent branch*. In Fig. 31.3, the afferent branch consists of the processes VALIDATE SKILL REC, GET SKILL REC, and BUILD ERROR MESS. There may be more than one afferent branch in a data flow diagram.

The output portion of the data flow diagram transforms output data from logical form (e.g., internal error code) to physical form (e.g., error report print line). It is called the *efferent branch*. There may be more than one efferent branch. In Fig. 31.3, there is one efferent branch consisting of the processes EXTRACT DEPT SKILL and BUILD REPORT LINE.

The logical processing portion contains the essential logical (or internal) processing and is farthest removed from physical input/output considerations. It is called the *central transform*. The central transform for the employee skills system consists of one process, CREATE SKILL TABLE. There may be several central transforms in one data flow diagram.

Figure 31.4 shows the data flow diagram from the employee skills system with each part indicated. The central transform always lies between the afferent and efferent branches on the data flow diagram.

In step 2 of transform analysis, the structure chart is derived by drawing one functional component for each central transform, for each afferent branch, and for each efferent branch. Either the central transform or a new functional component is placed at the top level (root) of the structure chart. The other functional components form the second level.

This is a high-level version of the structure chart; it will be refined in the next step of transform analysis. Figure 31.5 shows the high-level structure chart for the employee skills system. Notice that a new functional component, SKILL SUM, has been created and appears as the root of the structure chart. Also notice that the type of data passed between functional components is indicated on the chart.

Next, in the third step of transform analysis, the structure chart is redefined by adding the subfunctions required by each of the high-level functional components. Many levels may be added. This process of breaking functional components into subfunctions is called *factoring*. Factoring includes adding read and write library modules, error-handling modules, initialization and termination processing, identifying common modules, and the like.

Figure 31.2 shows the fully factored structure chart for the employee skills system. Although it contains more components, the completed structure chart should retain a simple, straightforward relationship to the data flow diagram. The data flow diagram represents the problem components. The structure chart represents the corresponding program components.

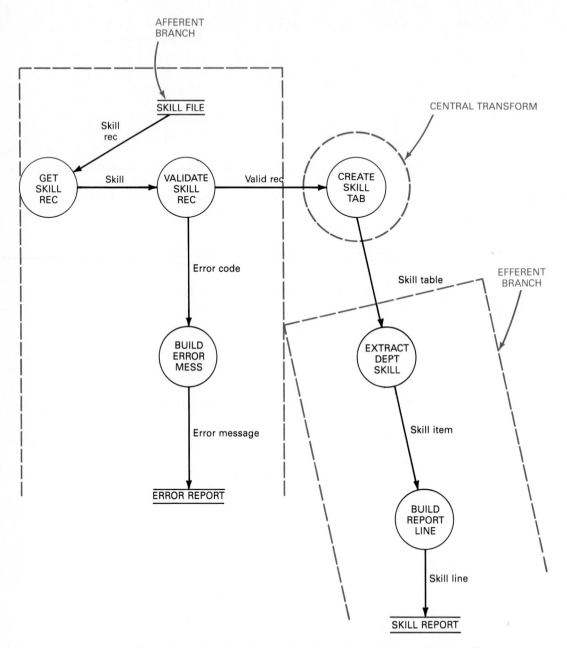

Figure 31.4 Data-flow diagram for the employee skills system with afferent branches (input), efferent branches (output), and central transform (logical processing) indicated.

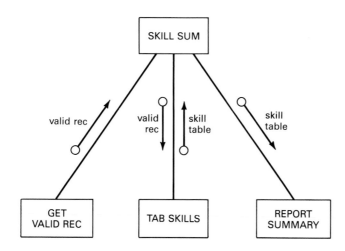

Figure 31.5   High-level structure chart for the employee skills system.

As summarized in Fig. 31.6, transform analysis is a three-step process that begins with a data flow diagram and ends with a fully factored structure chart.

Transaction Analysis

Transaction analysis is an alternative design strategy to transform analysis. It is useful when designing transaction processing programs [4]. A transaction is any element of data that triggers an action.

The general structure chart for a transaction processing program is shown in Fig. 31.7. At the top of the structure chart is one transaction-center module, and below it are several transaction modules. There is one transaction module for each transaction type. Each transaction module, along with its subfunctions, is responsible for processing all the activities for one transaction type. The transaction-center module is responsible for determining the transaction type and then calling the appropriate transaction module to process the transaction.

Every transaction carries a tag identifying its type. Transaction analysis uses this tag to divide the system into transaction modules and a transaction-center module. Figure 31.8 summarizes the basic steps in transaction analysis.

Figure 31.9 is the data flow diagram for a subscription system. The purpose of the system is to process three types of transactions (new subscriptions, renewals, and cancellations) against a subscription master file. The transaction center is the process DISPATCH, where the type of transaction is determined and the transaction is routed to the appropriate process. The transaction modules are PROCESS NEW SUB, PROCESS RENEWAL, and PROCESS CANCEL.

Figure 31.10 shows the high-level structure chart for the subscription sys-

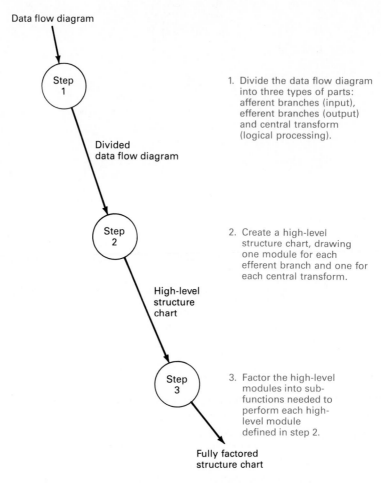

Data flow diagram

Step 1

1. Divide the data flow diagram into three types of parts: afferent branches (input), efferent branches (output) and central transform (logical processing).

Divided data flow diagram

Step 2

2. Create a high-level structure chart, drawing one module for each efferent branch and one for each central transform.

High-level structure chart

Step 3

3. Factor the high-level modules into sub-functions needed to perform each high-level module defined in step 2.

Fully factored structure chart

Figure 31.6 Transform analysis is a three-step process that begins with a data flow diagram and ends with a fully factored structure chart representing the program design.

tem. In the last step of transaction analysis, the structure chart is refined to define all the functional components in the program. Figure 13.1 shows the complete structure chart for the subscription system.

Combination Strategies

In practice, neither transform nor transaction analysis can be used exclusively to design most large programs. Often a combination of the two strategies is needed. For example, when transform analysis alone cannot identify a reasonable central transform, transaction analysis is used to break the system or pro-

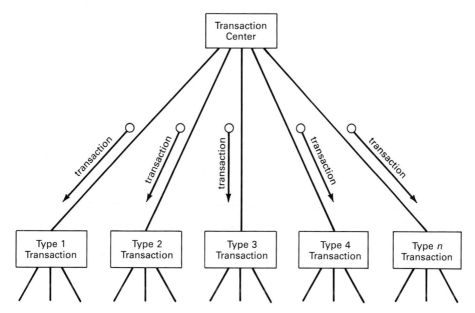

Figure 31.7 The general structure-chart model for a transaction processing program has one transaction-center module at the top and, below it, one transaction module for each transaction type.

gram into subsystems. Then either transform analysis or transaction analysis is used to design each subsystem. If defining the root module as a transaction center makes it too complex, several transaction centers can be identified.

STEP 3:
EVALUATE
THE DESIGN

The third step in structured design is to evaluate the quality of the design created by using transform and/or transaction analysis. Since there are many possible designs for one program, we need a way to measure design quality objectively. Coupling and cohesion are the two major evaluative techniques provided by structured design (see Chapter 5).

Coupling measures the degree of independence between modules. When there is little interaction between two modules, the modules are described as *loosely coupled*. When there is a great deal of interaction between two modules, the modules are described as *tightly coupled*. A high-quality design means that the modules are as loosely coupled as possible.

Five types of coupling are possible between two modules: data, stamp, control, common, and content. Data coupling is the loosest and best type of coupling; content coupling is the tightest and worst type of coupling. Figure 31.11 describes each type of coupling.

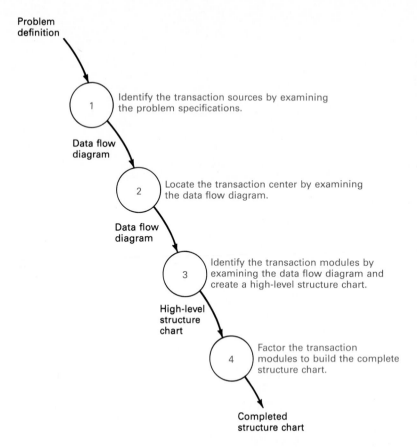

Problem
definition

① Identify the transaction sources by examining the problem specifications.

Data flow
diagram

② Locate the transaction center by examining the data flow diagram.

Data flow
diagram

③ Identify the transaction modules by examining the data flow diagram and create a high-level structure chart.

High-level
structure
chart

④ Factor the transaction modules to build the complete structure chart.

Completed
structure chart

Figure 31.8 Transaction analysis is a four-step process that begins with an examination of the problem definition and ends with a factored structure chart.

Cohesion measures how strongly the elements within a module are related. The stronger the better. Figure 31.12 shows the seven levels of cohesion. Functional cohesion is the strongest, most desirable level; coincidental is the weakest, least desirable level.

To measure the coupling and cohesion for each designed module, the structure chart is examined. The type of coupling is determined by looking at the data passed between modules. For example, in Fig. 31.2, **skill table** is passed between SKILL SUM and REPORT SUMMARY. **Skill table** is a composite data item made up of several individual data items. If all the data items in **skill table** are referenced in REPORT SUMMARY, the two modules are data-coupled. If only a subset of the data items in **skill table** is referenced in

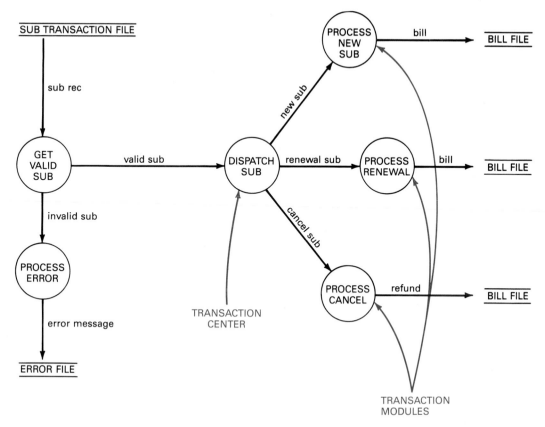

Figure 31.9 Data-flow diagram for the subscription system showing the transaction center and transaction modules.

REPORT SUMMARY, the two modules are stamp-coupled. Either case is considered loose coupling and is acceptable. When several data items are passed between two modules, the two modules are coupled according to the worse type of coupling among the data items passed.

The level of cohesion can be most easily determined by describing the module function in one sentence and then applying the guidelines listed in Box 31.1 [5]. Since it is not possible to draw a sharp line between levels of cohesion, module cohesion is usually described as lying in some range (e.g., sequential or communicational) rather than at one particular level. For example, in Fig. 31.2, we could describe the module TABSKILLS as follows:

> The purpose of the module TABSKILLS is to build a skill table using the information in the SKILLS file.

BOX 31.1   Guidelines for determining the level of module cohesion

- If the module's function can be described fully in a simple sentence, the level of cohesion is probably functional.

- If the only way to describe the module's function is using a compound sentence, its level of cohesion is most likely sequential, communicational, or procedural.

- If the description of the module's function contains time-oriented words like *first, next,* or *after,* the module probably has temporal or procedural cohesion.

- If the module's function is described as performing some operation for a class of items (e.g., all types of transactions), the modules probably has logical cohesion.

- If the module's function can be described as "initialization," "cleanup," or "housekeeping," the module probably has temporal cohesion.

- If the module's function cannot be described, it probably has coincidental cohesion.

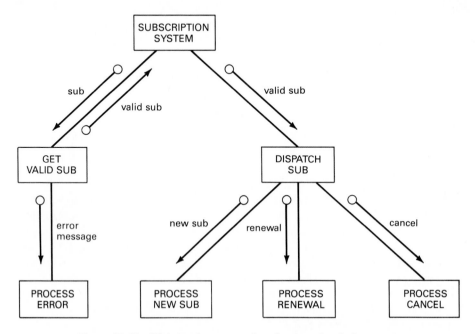

Figure 31.10   High-level structure chart for the subscription system.

(tight)

CONTENT COUPLING: Two modules are content coupled if one module refers to or changes the internals of another module (e.g., a branch or fall through from one module's code into another module).

COMMON COUPLING: Two modules are common coupled if they share the same global data areas (e.g., FORTRAN COMMON,PL I EXTERNAL attribute.)

CONTROL COUPLING: Two modules are control coupled if data from one is used to direct the order of instruction execution in the other (e.g., a flag set in one module and tested in a compare in another module).

STAMP COUPLING: Two modules are stamp coupled if they communicate via a composite data item (e.g., record or COBOL group item). The composite data item may contain pieces of data that are not used by a module even though they are passed to it.

DATA COUPLING: Two modules are data coupled if they communicate via a variable or array (table) that is passed directly as a parameter between the two modules. The data is used in problem-related processing, not for program control purposes.

(loose)

Figure 31.11   The five types of coupling.

Based on this description, the level of cohesion of this module is probably functional because its task can be described by one simple sentence.

STEP 4: PREPARE THE DESIGN FOR IMPLEMENTATION   The last step of structured design is to prepare the design for implementation. This is called *packaging* the design [6]. Packaging is the process of dividing the logical program design into physical implementation units, called *load units*. Each load unit is brought into memory and executed as one unit by the operating system. The purpose of packaging is to define physical system components that can be executed in an actual computer environment. It is *physical design*. Packaging is guided by the logical design and should be performed in a way that preserves a good logical design. Packages should be loosely coupled and have high cohesion. Modules packaged together should be functionally related.

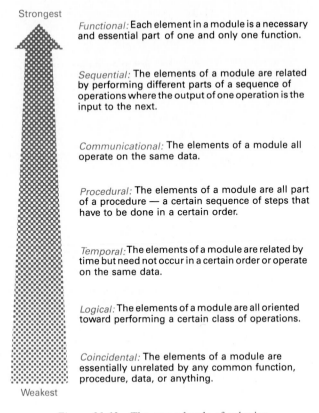

Strongest

Functional: Each element in a module is a necessary and essential part of one and only one function.

Sequential: The elements of a module are related by performing different parts of a sequence of operations where the output of one operation is the input to the next.

Communicational: The elements of a module all operate on the same data.

Procedural: The elements of a module are all part of a procedure — a certain sequence of steps that have to be done in a certain order.

Temporal: The elements of a module are related by time but need not occur in a certain order or operate on the same data.

Logical: The elements of a module are all oriented toward performing a certain class of operations.

Coincidental: The elements of a module are essentially unrelated by any common function, procedure, data, or anything.

Weakest

Figure 31.12   The seven levels of cohesion.

Packaging is performed in steps (see Fig. 31.13). Some steps are performed before the design; others are best performed at the end of the design phase.

Predesign Packaging

At the end of analysis, the system is packaged into jobs and job steps. A *job* is a sequence of one or more job steps. A *job step* is a main program and its subprograms. The data flow diagram is packaged at this point by establishing three boundaries:

1. Hardware boundaries

2. Batch/on-line/real-time boundaries

3. Operating-cycle boundaries

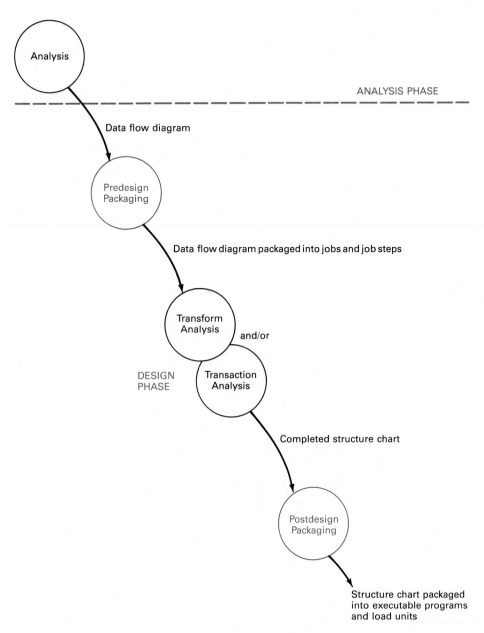

Analysis

ANALYSIS PHASE

Data flow diagram

Predesign
Packaging

Data flow diagram packaged into jobs and job steps

Transform
Analysis

and/or

DESIGN
PHASE

Transaction
Analysis

Completed structure chart

Postdesign
Packaging

Structure chart packaged
into executable programs
and load units

Figure 31.13 Packaging is performed in steps. Some steps (*predesign packaging*) are performed before the design phase; other steps (*postdesign packaging*) are performed at the end of design.

BOX 31.2 Packaging guidelines

ITERATION RULE:	Modules that are iteratively nested within each other should be included in the same load unit.
VOLUME RULE:	Modules that are connected by a high volume call should be included in the same load unit.
TIME-INTERVAL RULE:	Modules that are executed within a short time of each other should be placed in the same load unit.
ADJACENCY RULE:	Modules that execute adjacently in time (one after another) or use the same data should be included in the same load unit.
ISOLATION RULE:	Optionally executed modules should be placed in separate load units.

Postdesign Packaging

Each job step, represented as a data flow diagram, is passed on to the design phase. During design, the job step is defined in terms of a structure chart. At the end of the design, each structure chart is packaged into executable programs and load units. The smallest possible load unit is one module; the largest possible load unit is the entire structure chart.

The primary task of postdesign packaging is to determine how modules will be grouped into load units. The basic packaging rule to follow is to group into one load unit all modules usually executed one after another. Box 31.2 lists some additional packaging rules suggested by Yourdon and Constantine [7].

REFERENCES

1. W. Stevens, G. Myers, and L. Constantine, "Structured Design," *IBM Systems Journal,* 13, no. 2 (1974).

2. E. Yourdon and L. Constantine, *Structured Design,* Englewood Cliffs, NJ: Prentice-Hall, Inc., 1979, pp. 171–201.

3. M. Page-Jones, *The Practical Guide to Structured Systems Design,* New York: Yourdon, Inc., 1980, pp. 39–56.

4. Yourdon and Constantine, pp. 202–222.

5. Page-Jones, pp. 137–178.

6. Yourdon and Constantine, pp. 250–261.

7. Ibid., pp. 276–289.

32   AN EVALUATION OF STRUCTURED DESIGN

STRUCTURED
DESIGN
OF THE CREDIT
VERIFICATION
SYSTEM

The structured design methodology, presented in Chapter 31, can be used to design systems and programs. As an example, consider the design for a credit verification system [1]. The credit verification system receives information about charge purchases from terminals at the point of sale. The incoming charge information is validated for completeness and correctness of the store numbers. For valid charges, the customer credit record is accessed to examine the customer's current balance. Then the amount of the charge, the customer's credit limit, and the current balance are examined to determine whether the charge can be authorized. If so, an authorization number is generated using a special algorithm. In addition, a check digit, which is calculated using the account number from the transaction record and the customer credit record, is verified. Depending on the outcome of the verification checks, an affirmative or negative response or a request for reentry is formatted and sent.

The design for the credit verification system can be developed by using the structured design process with the transform analysis strategy.

The design process begins with a data flow diagram representing the credit verification system. A sample data flow diagram (DFD) is shown in Fig. 32.1. Many other data-flow diagrams could be drawn to represent the credit verification system. For example, more detail could be shown. Process circles representing procedures for check-digit calculation, balance verification, and authorization-number generation could have been added to the DFD.

APPLYING
TRANSFORM
ANALYSIS

Transform analysis is used to convert the data flow diagram into a structure chart representing the functional components of the program. The first step of

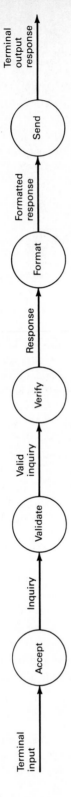

Figure 32.1 A data-flow diagram represents the basic procedural components and the flow of information connecting them for the credit verification system.

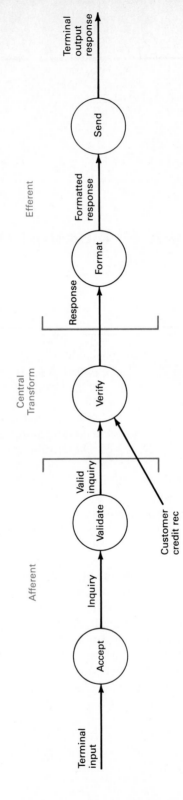

Figure 32.2 The first step of transform analysis is to identify the afferent (input) and efferent (output) data streams and the central transform (logical processing).

transform analysis is to divide the data flow diagram into its input, transform processing, and output parts. Figure 32.2 shows these parts. There is one input (or afferent branch) consisting of the ACCEPT and VALIDATE processes. There is one output (or efferent branch) consisting of the FORMAT and SEND processes. The transform processing (or central transform) is the VERIFY process. When the data flow diagram is as simple as this, there is no question of what to include in each part.

The second step is to create a high-level structure chart (see Fig. 32.3). One module is drawn for each afferent branch (GET VALID INQUIRY), for each efferent branch (PUT RESPONSE), and for each central transform (VERIFY CHARGE). The module VERICHARGE SYSTEM is added as the root of the structure chart, and the module GET CUST REC is added to handle access to the customer credit record. Also, the structure chart shows the data passed between the modules.

Next, the structure chart is factored by breaking the high-level modules into their subcomponents. A completed structure chart is shown in Fig. 32.4.

EVALUATING THE QUALITY OF THE DESIGN

Structured design stresses the importance of checking the quality of the design. The structure chart should be checked against the data flow diagram to make certain that it matches the problem components. Alternative structure charts should also be considered.

There are many possible variations for this design. For example, the CHECK STORE CODE module could have been incorporated into the VALIDATE INQUIRY module along with the other validation checks. Or instead of just one module, FORMAT RESPONSE, which handles all three types of re-

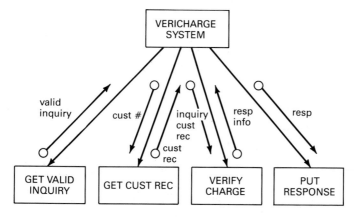

Figure 32.3 The second step of transform analysis is to convert the data-flow diagram into a structure chart showing a high-level view of the design architecture of the program.

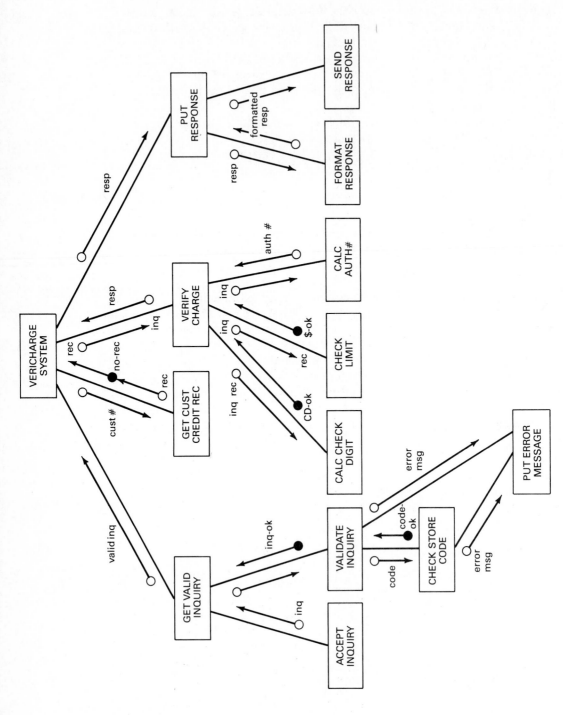

Figure 32.4 At the end of the structured design process, a complete structure chart showing all the procedural components of the system (program) and their interrelationships represents the completed program or system design.

sponses, three separate response modules could have been created. Module coupling and cohesion measures can be used to determine which variation is best (see Chapter 31).

The level of cohesion for the module VALIDATE INQUIRY in Fig. 32.4 may be as high as functional, depending on what operations are performed to validate an inquiry record. If the task of checking the store code were combined with the task of validating the inquiry record, the level of cohesion for VALIDATE INQUIRY would drop to logical. This change weakens the design.

On the other hand, refining FORMAT RESPONSE into three subfunctions improves the design. FORMAT RESPONSE could act as a transaction center calling the appropriate formatting module:

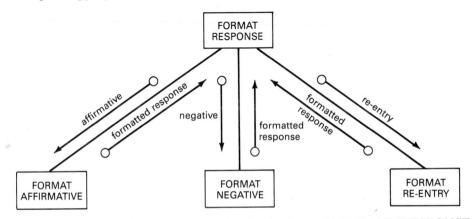

This change improves the level of cohesion of FORMAT RESPONSE from logical or communicational-to-functional, and the level of cohesion for each of its three subfunctions would be functional.

In addition to cohesion considerations, there are also coupling considerations. The goal is to minimize (or loosen) the coupling between modules. As an example, consider the coupling between VERICHARGE SYSTEM and VERIFY CHARGE:

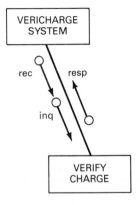

There are three data items passed between these two modules: **rec, inq,** and **resp.** The data items **rec** and **inq** are both composite data items made up of many individual items, only a subset of which are probably needed by VER-IFY CHARGE. This means that VERICHARGE SYSTEM and VERIFY CHARGE are stamp-coupled. To improve the coupling to the data-coupling level, only the data items needed by VERIFY CHARGE should be passed to VERIFY CHARGE, as shown here:

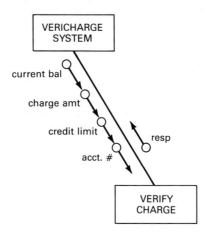

These are a few possible design improvements for the credit verification system. There are others. A complete evaluation of the design involves determining the level of cohesion for each module and the data coupling between each pair of modules in the structure chart.

CRITIQUE OF STRUCTURED DESIGN

The structured design approach views systems as having three basic tasks:

1. Collection and transformation of input data into a form ready for processing.

2. Data processing with the purpose of transforming input data into output results.

3. Transformation and dispersement of the results into final output form.

The structured design process therefore becomes one of identifying these tasks and representing them in a hierarchical form. Transform analysis and transaction analysis are the two primary strategies used to guide this process.

CRITIQUE OF TRANSFORM AND TRANSACTION ANALYSIS

Transform analysis and transaction analysis are nothing more than forms of functional decomposition that use a data flow diagram to identify basic input, process, and output components. The rules that guide these techniques are very vague. For example, the designer is told that there are two methods for finding the processing component called the central transform [2]:

1. Look for it by examining the data flow diagram.
2. Eliminate the input and output branches on the data flow diagram; what is left is the central transform.

When the basic input, processing, and output components have been identified on the data flow diagram, they are hierarchically arranged in a structure chart. This is accomplished by picking up the data flow diagram by its central-transform circles and letting the input and output circles hang down as the leaves on the structure chart (see Fig. 32.5).

Next, the structure chart is refined by using a process called factoring. Like transform and transaction analysis, factoring is a form of functional decomposition. And like transform and transaction analysis, the rules that guide factoring are very vague. For example, there are two guidelines for stopping the factoring process [3]:

1. Stop factoring when there are no more well-defined functions to factor out.
2. Stop factoring when the interface to a module is as complicated as the module itself.

As shown in Fig. 32.6, factoring is simply the successive application of the structured design system model where input data are transformed into output data. There are three substrategies for factoring [4]:

Afferent factoring. Factor out a new module to perform the transform necessary to deliver data upward. Then factor out another afferent module to get new data. Next, factor the new transform module in the same way. Stop factoring when the ultimate physical input (e.g., card) is reached.

Efferent factoring. Factor out a new module to perform the next transform necessary to deliver data downward. Then factor out another efferent module to bring the data closer to their final output form. Stop factoring when the physical output form is reached.

Central-transform factoring. Look for subcomponents that will accomplish the high-level processing task.

The input-transform-output system model of structured design requires that input processing be placed in the afferent branches and output processing in the

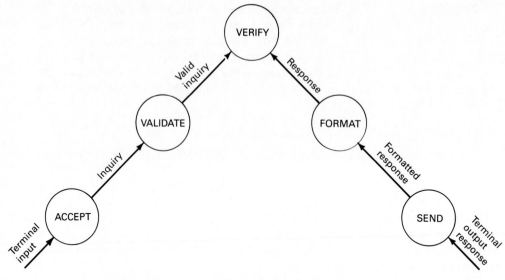

(a) Data-flow diagram hanging by its central transform circle

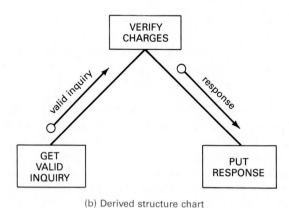

(b) Derived structure chart

Figure 32.5   Design structures for the credit verification system.

efferent branches; whatever is left belongs to the central transform. This is an artificial design restriction that we should question because it can distort the structure of the program. For many problems, requiring this separation of input, output, and logical processing violates the design goal of organizing pro-

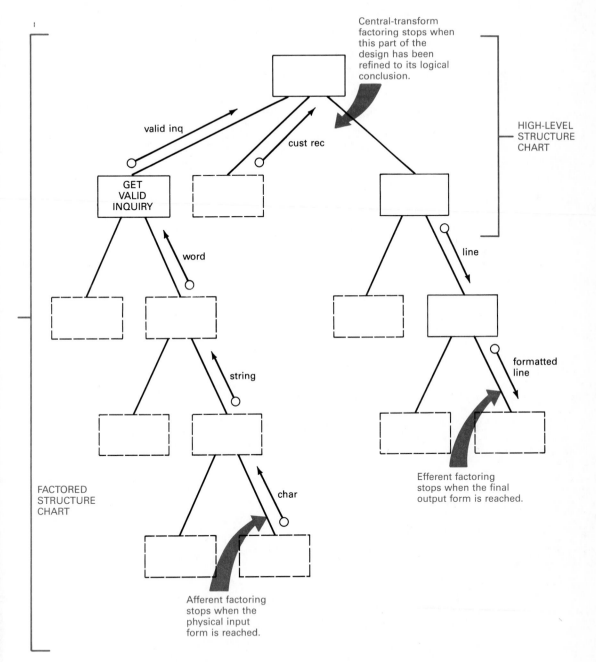

Central-transform factoring stops when this part of the design has been refined to its logical conclusion.

HIGH-LEVEL STRUCTURE CHART

valid inq

cust rec

GET VALID INQUIRY

word

line

string

formatted line

char

FACTORED STRUCTURE CHART

Efferent factoring stops when the final output form is reached.

Afferent factoring stops when the physical input form is reached.

Figure 32.6 Factoring is the process of breaking high-level functional components into more detailed subcomponents in successive steps.

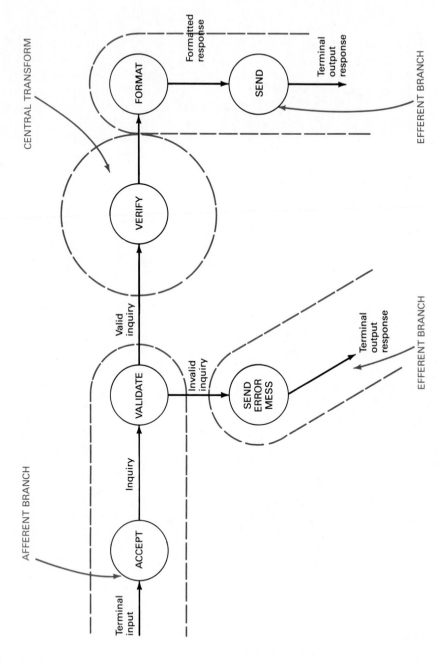

Figure 32.7 Data flow diagram for the credit verification system showing the process for sending error messages identifying invalid inquiries.

gram components to resemble problem components for ease of program understanding and change.

For example, consider another version of the data flow diagram representing the credit verification system discussed earlier in this chapter. This second
version is shown in Fig. 32.7. In this version, a new process, SEND ERROR
MESS, is added to the data flow diagram. Its purpose is to identify invalid
inquiries and send the appropriate error message. Notice that this function is
indicated on the final structure chart for the credit verification system shown in
Fig. 32.4. When SEND ERROR MESS is added to the data flow diagram, we
see it as an efferent (output) branch hanging off an afferent (input) branch. This
violates the structured design rule that requires that afferent and efferent data
branches be separated by a central transform. Structured design forces the designer to insert another central transform, which is an artificial convention not
required by the problem. The other choice is not to show this part of the process
in the data flow diagram. Neither choice leads to a clearer understanding of the
problem components.

COMPARISON WITH TOP-DOWN DESIGN

The strategies of transform analysis, transaction analysis, and factoring offer no real improvement over
the simple functional decomposition method of top-
down design. The introduction of new terminology
such as *afferent streams, efferent streams,* and *cen-
tral transforms* confuses rather than enhances the top-down design process.
Also, the process breaks down when used for the design of large systems with
many input, output, and transform processing streams. The combination strategy
of using transaction analysis to divide the system into more manageable pieces
and then using transform analysis to design each piece can be difficult to apply in practice. No guidelines are offered to accomplish this top-level division.

With the exception of beginning with a data flow diagram to identify high-
level process components and data flow, the designer is well advised to use the
simpler top-down design method and avoid becoming entangled in structured
design terminology and substrategies, for when he finally cuts through the terminology, he will find that what remains is the advice to follow common sense
and experience. As Yourdon and Constantine explain,

> It should be kept in mind that these design strategies . . . will still require
> the judgment, experience, and common sense of the designer. The situation
> is roughly comparable to a cook attempting to use a cookbook in a *haute
> cuisine* restaurant: There is no way to avoid those standard cookbook
> phrases of "season to taste" or "stir gently until ingredients are thoroughly
> mixed." [5]

CRITIQUE OF
COUPLING AND
COHESION

Yourdon suggests coupling and cohesion measures to guide the design process [4]. Modules should be loosely coupled. Modules should have high cohesion.

Intuitively, these seem to be quality characteristics to strive for in a good design. However, the problem is that coupling and cohesion measures are difficult to apply in practice. They are qualitative measures that are tedious to apply manually and impossible to automate. In practice, they are only informally used in the form of rough guidelines such as these:

- Pass as few data as possible between modules.
- Minimize the use of control data (flags, switches, etc.).
- A module should perform one function.

In the Yourdon five-day workshop on structured design, coupling and cohesion measures are never used to evaluate an entire design. There is no class or homework exercise in which the students used coupling and cohesion to evaluate the quality of a program design. The reason is that a structured design (a fully factored structure chart) does not provide all the information needed to apply the measures.

To measure the coupling between two modules, all the data passed between the modules must be defined and included on the structure chart. There are two problems here. First, data design is not part of the structured design process. The designer may not know what the program data structures are, what data items are composite items, and what data items are atomic since these decisions are often made *following* structured design. But without this information, the type of coupling between modules cannot be determined.

Second, not all data passed between modules may be indicated on the structure chart. There is not enough space between modules to make it practical to indicate more than two or three items without creating a traffic jam of data couples flowing between modules. In Fig. 32.4, data couples are crowded and difficult to read. Imagine how cluttered the chart would become with even more data couples. Also, the notation invites mistakes. Control couples are indicated by a filled circle at the end of the arrow (•—→). Data couples are indicated by an open circle at the end of the arrow (○—→). It is far too easy to confuse one for the other. Finally, there is no checking mechanism to determine if all data couples have been indicated or not. With only partial or incorrect data-couple information, it makes no sense to attempt to measure coupling.

To measure cohesion we must look inside at the internal components of a module. However, a structure chart allows only a black-box view of the modules. This means that cohesion measures are reduced to the sort that were suggested by Yourdon and Constantine in Chapter 31: Describe the module function with one sentence. Then evaluate the sentence according to the guidelines presented in Box 31.1.

Advocates of structured design claim that coupling and cohesion represent important advancements toward formalizing the design process. We feel that this position must be questioned in light of their inability to be applied.

LACK OF DATA DESIGN The lack of data design is an extremely serious omission from the structured design methodology. Yourdon skirts the issue by suggesting that some data design is done in the analysis step as part of creating the system specification and some is done during detail design (program design). Structured design does not discuss the role of data bases or data dictionaries in program design. This limits the utility of the structured design methodology to designing simple programs with simple file systems. But for these simple design problems, the top-down design method discussed in Chapter 30 is easier to use and therefore is recommended.

REFERENCES

1. E. Yourdon, *Structured Design,* DELTAK Multimedia Course, Chicago, Illinois, 1983.

2. M. Page-Jones, *The Practical Guide to Structured Systems Design,* New York: Yourdon, Inc., 1980, p. 186.

3. Ibid., p. 138.

4. E. Yourdon and L. Constantine, *Structured Design,* Englewood Cliffs, NJ: Prentice-Hall, Inc., 1979, pp. 187–222.

5. Ibid., p. 246.

33 JACKSON DESIGN METHODOLOGY

JACKSON DESIGN VERSUS STRUCTURED DESIGN

Like structured design (discussed in Chapter 31), the Jackson design methodology is a refinement of the top-down design method. It formalizes the top-down design process by providing the following:

- Well-specified design process steps
- Graphic diagramming techniques
- Methods to evaluate the correctness of the design

Both the Jackson design methodology and structured design separate the implementation phase from the design phase by deferring decisions about implementation and by completing the whole design before the implementation phase is begun. A common aim of both methodologies is to make the structure of the program reflect the structure of the problem in order to create easy-to-understand and easy-to-change programs.

The major difference between the two is that the Jackson design methodology is based on an analysis of data structure, while structured design is based on an analysis of data flow. One is data-oriented, the other process-oriented. The Jackson approach advocates a static view of structures, whereas the Yourdon structured design approach advocates a dynamic view of data flow.

DATA-DRIVEN PROGRAM DESIGN

The Jackson design methodology is a data-driven program design technique. Its approach is to derive the program structure from the data structure(s). It assumes that the problem has been fully specified and that the program will be implemented in a second- or third-generation procedural programming language. Thus systems analysis and program implementation concerns lie outside the design process.

Jackson views a program as a sequential process. It has inputs and outputs that are viewed as sequential streams of records. Jackson suggests that we think of each data stream as a tape file to enforce the idea of decoupling programs and limiting communication to a simple, serial protocol. The design process consists of first defining the structure of the data streams and then ordering the procedural logic (or operations) to fit the data structures. As shown in Box 33.1, the design process consists of four sequential steps [1]:

1. *Data step*. Describe each input and output data stream as a hierarchical structure.

2. *Program step*. Combine all the data structures produced in the first step into one hierarchical program structure.

3. *Operations step*. Make a list of executable operations needed to produce the program output from the input. Then allocate each operation on the list to a component in the program structure.

BOX 33.1 Jackson program design procedure

DATA STEP:

Draw a tree-structure diagram for each input data stream and each output data stream in the program.

PROGRAM STEP:

Take all the data structures defined in the data step and form them into a single program structure.

OPERATIONS STEP:

Make a list of executable operations necessary to produce output from input. Then allocate each operation on the list to a component of the program structure. (Progress from output toward input.)

TEXT STEP:

Transcribe the program structure into structure text, adding the conditional logic that governs the execution of loops and selection structures.

4. *Text step*. Write the ordered operations, with conditional logic included, in the form of structure text, a formal version of pseudocode.

Jackson design methodology uses three diagramming techniques to describe a program design (see Chapter 16):

- *System network diagram:* flow of data streams between programs
- *Tree-structure diagram:* hierarchical representation of program and data structures
- *Structure text:* formal pseudocode

The Jackson design process is illustrated with the design of the employee skills system.

EXAMPLE: EMPLOYEE SKILLS SYSTEM

The purpose of the employee skills system is to produce a summary of employee skills by department. We can assume that the report is a simple list. It has one header and no page numbers. The format is as shown:

DEPT	SKILL	No. of EMPLOYEES
01	DRILL PRESS	6
01	WELDING	3
02	PAINTING	1
03	PAINTING	1
.	.	.
.	.	.
.	.	.

The input for the program is the SKILL FILE. It is a simple sequential file whose records are in skill-number within department-number order. The record format is as follows:

dept	skill	employee-no.

One employee may have several skills.

Figure 33.1 is a system network diagram for the employee skills system. The diagram shows that the employee skills system is composed of one program, EMPLOYEE SKILLS PROGRAM, and two data streams, SKILL FILE and SKILL REPORT. (System network diagrams are discussed in detail in Chapter 16.)

Programs in a system network diagram are not necessarily implemented as

Figure 33.1 The system network diagram for the employee skills system shows that there is one input data stream, SKILL FILE; one output stream, SKILL REPORT; and one program, EMPLOYEE SKILLS PROGRAM. In Jackson terminology, SKILL FILE is *consumed* by the EMPLOYEE SKILLS PROGRAM to *produce* SKILL REPORT.

separate programs. They may be implemented as subroutines or in-line procedures. Likewise, data streams are not necessarily implemented as physical files. They may be implemented as internal tables or direct-access records.

Data Step

The first step in the Jackson design methodology is to represent each data stream as a hierarchical structure. A tree-structure diagram is used. Figure 33.2 shows the tree-structure diagrams for the input and output data streams. (Tree-structure diagrams are discussed in Chapter 16). The purpose of the tree-structure diagram of a data stream is to show the order in which data records are accessed by the program. It is very important that the *complete* data stream be *correctly* represented in the tree-structure diagram. Correct data structures are the key to a correct design since the program structure is derived from the data structures.

Program Step

The second step is to combine the data structures into one program structure. There are two parts to the program step. First, all correspondences between the components of the data structures are identified by studying the data streams and the problem specification. In Fig. 33.2, the red arrows show that SKILL FILE in the input tree corresponds to SKILL REPORT in the output tree. This means that when the Employee Skills program is executed, one instance of the output data stream, SKILL REPORT, is produced from one instance of the input data stream SKILL FILE. There is a one-to-one correspondence between the two data streams. Jackson refers to this one-to-one correspondence as a *consume-produce relationship*.

There is also a one-to-one correspondence between DEPT-SKILL GROUP and SKILL-LINE. One instance of DEPT-SKILL GROUP is consumed to produce one instance of SKILL-LINE.

When a program component corresponds to only an input component, it is of the *consume* form; correspondingly, when a program component corresponds to only an output component, it is of the *produce* form.

To find consume-produce relationships, the designer examines the data

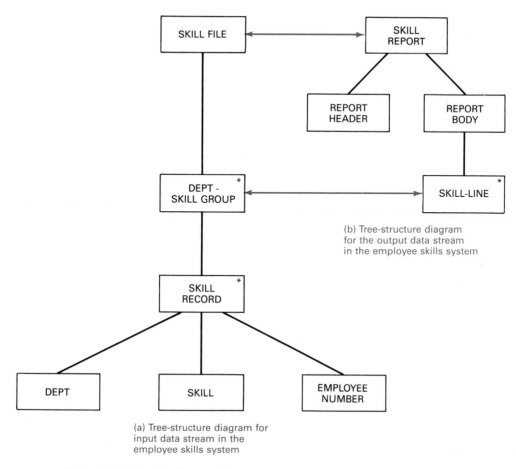

(b) Tree-structure diagram
for the output data stream
in the employee skills system

(a) Tree-structure diagram for
input data stream in the
employee skills system

Figure 33.2 The Employee Skills program has one input data stream and
one output data stream. The tree-structure representation of a data stream
shows how the records are opened.

structures and asks the question, "Does one instance of this, result in one instance of that?"

The program structure is built starting at the top level and using one rectangle to represent each set of corresponding data components. Then the program structure is filled in by adding rectangles to match each noncorresponding
data component. The complete program structure encompasses all data structure
components. The program structure for the Employee Skills program is shown
in Fig. 33.3. It is a tree-structure diagram using the same notation used in the
data structure diagrams. The name of each program component is derived from
the corresponding data component name. The term CONSUME or PRODUCE
is prefixed to each name to indicate whether the program component involves

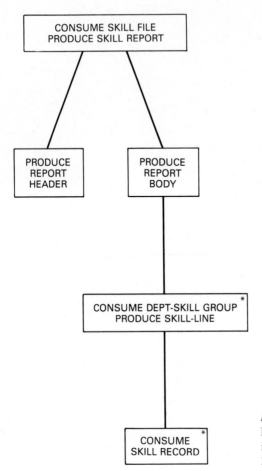

Figure 33.3 The program structure for the Employee Skills program is a composite of its input and output data structure shown in Fig. 33.2.

"consuming" input data or "producing" output data. Sometimes CONSUME and PRODUCE are abbreviated as C and P to shorten program component names. These naming conventions enable the reader easily to identify the input and output data streams in the program structure.

Program-Structure Verification

The second part of the program step is to verify the correctness of the program structure. This is done by reducing the program structure into its component data structures. The procedure showing that the program structure has been derived from data stream A is as follows:

- Eliminate the CONSUME and PRODUCE prefix from the program component names.
- Eliminate the program component names that are not part of data stream A and eliminate any boxes with all names crossed out.
- If the program structure is correct, then what remains is data stream A.

Figure 33.4 shows how the program structure for the Employee Skills program can be reduced into its output data stream, SKILL REPORT.

The procedure is applied to each data stream in turn. If the program structure can be reduced to each of its data structures, it is assumed to be correct.

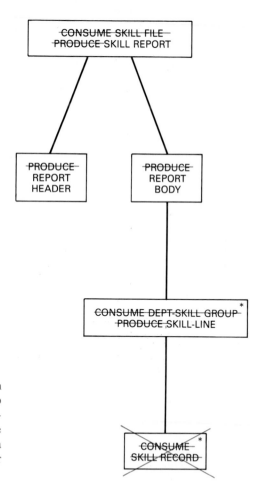

Figure 33.4   The correctness of the program structure is demonstrated by reducing it into its data-structure components. In this example, the program structure for the Employee Skills program is reduced into its output data stream, SKILL REPORT. The data tree for SKILL REPORT is shown in Fig. 33.2.

Operations Step

The operations step has three parts:

1. The executable operations required by the program to convert its input into its output are listed. The list is derived by starting at the output and working back toward the input. Operations are determined by referring to data structures, which are in turn reflected in the program structure.
2. Each operation is allocated to the appropriate place in the program structure.
3. Correctness is verified by checking that all outputs are produced and all inputs are consumed.

Figure 33.5 shows the program structure and the executable operations for the Employee Skills program. Each operation is allocated to a program component, as shown by the numbers.

Text Step

The last step in the Jackson program design process is the text step. In the text step, the program-structure diagram, along with its accompanying operations, is translated into structure text.

Structure text is a formal type of pseudocode (see Chapter 18). It has strict rules for writing the control constructs of sequence, selection, and iteration, but elementary programming-level instructions (e.g., read statement) are written informally.

The structure text for the Employee Skills program is shown in Fig. 33.6. Program component names were shortened for convenience's sake. For example, the full name for SKILL-REPORT is CONSUME-SKILL-FILE-PRODUCE-SKILL-REPORT. The full name acts as a pointer to the part of the program structure and data structures involved in this part of the code.

The control conditions governing the execution of the select and iteration structures are added to the structure text in this step. The condition logic for EMPLOYEE is indicated in parentheses in Fig. 33.6.

At the end of the text step, the program design is ready for implementation into program code. The system network diagram, the data-structure trees, the program-structure tree, and the structure text form the complete design package.

DESIGNING SIMPLE PROGRAMS

The design method illustrated with the Employee Skills program is applicable to a narrow class of sequential file processing programs that Jackson defines as *simple programs*. The properties of a simple program are as follows [2]:

PROGRAM STRUCTURE:

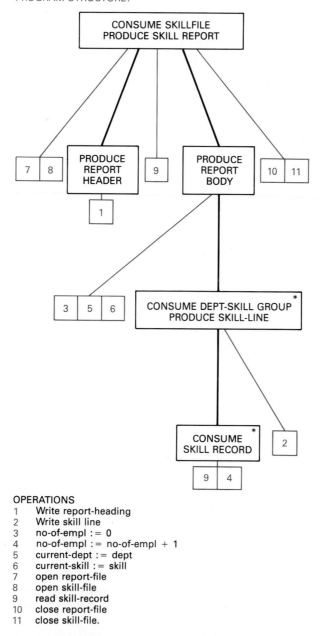

OPERATIONS
1   Write report-heading
2   Write skill line
3   no-of-empl := 0
4   no-of-empl := no-of-empl + 1
5   current-dept := dept
6   current-skill := skill
7   open report-file
8   open skill-file
9   read skill-record
10 close report-file
11 close skill-file.

Figure 33.5   The operations step lists the executable operations required by the program and allocates them to the appropriate program component.

```
SKILL-REPORT seq
  open skillfile;
  open reportfile;
  write report-header;
  read skill-record;
  REPORT-BODY iter while (not end-of-file)
    DEPT-SKILL-GROUP seq
      no-of-empl := 0;
      current-dept := dept;
      current-skill := skill;
      SKILL-RECORD iter while (dept = current-dept
        and skill = current-skill)
        no-of-empl = no-of-empl + 1;
        read skill-record
      SKILL-RECORD end
      move no-of-empl to skill-line;
      write skill-line;
    DEPT-SKILL-GROUP end
  REPORT-BODY end;
  close skillfile;
  close reportfile;
SKILL-REPORT end
```

CONDITION LOGIC

Figure 33.6   The last step in the Jackson design methodology is to translate
the program structure into structure text, a formal version of pseudocode.

- When the program is executed, nothing needs to be remembered from a previous execution.

- The program input and output data streams are sequential files that we can assume function like magnetic-tape files (records are read and written in some order).

- The program structure is formed by merging all the program input and output data structures.

- The data structures must not conflict at any level (e.g., the records must be compatibly ordered).

- Each time the program is executed, one or more complete files are processed.

DESIGNING COMPLEX PROGRAMS

Jackson divides programs into two types, *simple* and *complex*. Most typical data processing programs are complex. The Jackson design process described above is called the *Basic Design Procedure*. It can be used to design simple programs but is not directly applicable to complex programs. A complex program must first be divided into a sequence of simple programs, each of which can then be designed using the Basic Design Procedure.

Most programs fail to meet the criteria for a simple program because their data structures conflict or because they do not process a complete file each time they are executed.

**STRUCTURE
CLASH**

Suppose that in the employee skills system, the SKILL FILE is ordered by employee number within department number. The output, the SKILL RE-PORT, is a summary of skills in department-number order. Then the input and output data structures would conflict (see Fig. 33.7). This situation is called a *structure clash*. If the structure clash is not resolved, the program structure will not match the data structures. Program control variables (e.g., program switches and flags) will have to be introduced to force-fit the structures together. The result will not be a clean, simple program architecture that is easy to understand and easy to implement. An important element in the Jackson design methodology is to recognize and resolve structure clashes, repeating design steps when necessary so that the final design is simple and clean.

To resolve a structure clash, the problem is broken into two or more simple programs by expanding the system network diagram. A structure clash is usually recognized during the program step of the design process when the designer looks for correspondences between data structures. To correct it, the designer must back up and begin the design process again with an expanded system network diagram.

The structure clash in the employee skills system is called an *ordering structure clash* because the data structures are ordered differently. This type of structure clash can be resolved in three ways:

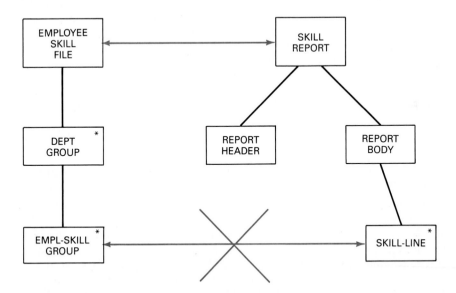

Figure 33.7   The input data structure is in employee-number-within-department-number order. The output data structure is in skill-within-department-number order. The conflict in the order of the structures is called an *ordering structure clash.*

- By dividing the program into two programs
- By defining an intermediate data stream that connects the two programs (the data stream is written by the first program and read by the second program)
- By defining two data structures to represent this one intermediate data stream (each structure corresponds to one of the clashing structures)

Figure 33.8 show the expanded system network diagram for the employee skills system. The two programs are CREATE SKILL GROUPS and CREATE SKILL REPORT. The new intermediate data stream is SKILL GROUP. The two data structures for SKILL GROUP and the new program structure are also shown in Fig. 33.8. Now that the structure clash has been resolved, CREATE SKILL GROUP and CREATE SKILL REPORT can be designed as simple programs.

Jackson defines two other types of structure clashes, *boundary* and *interleaving*. They are both recognized and resolved in the same manner as ordering clashes.

PROGRAM INVERSION

Breaking a complex problem into a set of simple programs offers some significant advantages. As Jackson explains:

> The simple program is a satisfactory high level component. It is a larger object than sequence, iteration or selection; it has a more precise definition than a module; it is subject to restrictions which reveal to us clearly when we are trying to make a single program out of what should be two or more. [3]

In general, viewing a program as a sequence of simple programs connected by serial data streams simplifies the design but can cause serious efficiency problems when the design is implemented. Jackson introduces a technique called *program inversion* to deal with efficiency concerns.

Program inversion combines the best of two worlds: simple design and efficient implementation. It is a coding technique that allows a program to be designed to process a complete file (a property required of a simple program) but to be coded so that it can process one record at a time. It involves coding methods for eliminating physical files and introducing subroutines to read or write one record at a time. The structure text is not affected, nor is the design. In this way, there are many possible implementations for the same design.

Program inversion is used to combine simple programs to achieve efficient implementation. It is important to note that it is *not* used during the design phase. The Jackson design philosophy strongly adheres to a strict separation between the design and implementation of programs.

Expanded system network diagram for employee skills system

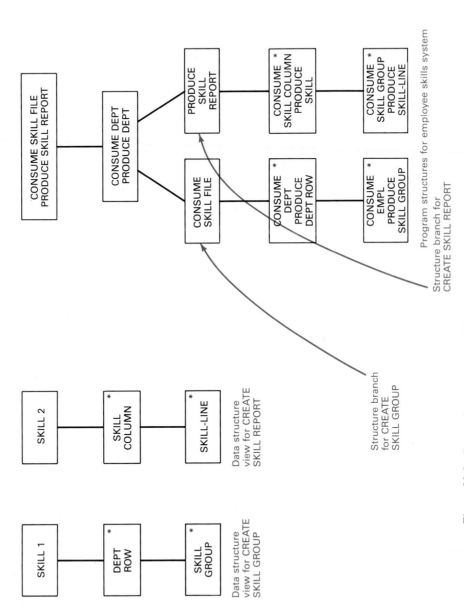

Program structures for employee skills system

Structure branch for
CREATE SKILL REPORT

Structure branch
for CREATE
SKILL GROUP

Data structure
view for CREATE
SKILL REPORT

Data structure
view for CREATE
SKILL GROUP

Figure 33.8 To resolve a structure clash, the system is expanded by decomposing the program into a sequence of simple programs.

REFERENCES

1. M. A. Jackson, *Principles of Program Design,* New York: Academic Press, 1975.

2. M. A. Jackson, "Constructive Methods of Program Design," in *Proceedings, First Conference of the European Conference in Informatics,* 44 (1976).

3. Ibid., p. 341.

34 AN EVALUATION OF JACKSON DESIGN METHODOLOGY

CONSTRUCTIVE DESIGN METHOD

Jackson design methodology is a *constructive design method*. To be constructive a method must be decomposed into steps that can be performed and verified independently. Figure 34.1 is a tree-structure diagram representing the steps in the Jackson design process.

Top-down design (discussed in Chapter 30) and the Yourdon-Constantine structured design methodology (discussed in Chapters 31 and 32) are also constructive design methods. The difference is that only the Jackson method centers around data structure design.

This emphasis on data-structure design is the major strength of the Jackson design methodology. For most data processing application programs, data-structure design is more crucial than procedure design because most data processing systems have relatively simple control flow but complex data structures. This is borne out by the fact that data-structure errors are more common than procedural logic errors [1].

The Jackson design methodology is also concerned with program structures—what the allowable pieces are and how they are arranged. It produces a hierarchical program structure that is derived from hierarchical data structures. Jackson's position is that the key to building a complete and correct program structure is to begin by building data structures. The design of the subscription system is one example that illustrates this position.

DESIGNING THE SUBSCRIPTION SYSTEM

In Chapter 31, the subscription system was designed using the transform-analysis method of structured design. The subscription system processes subscription transactions against a subscription master file. There are three types of transactions: new subscriptions, renewals, and cancellations.

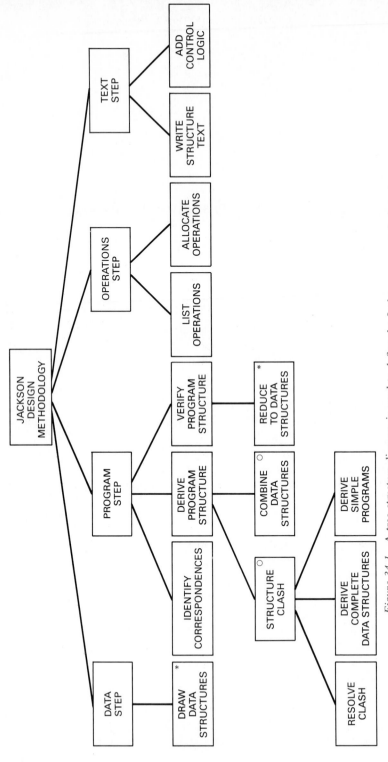

Figure 34.1 A tree-structure diagram is used to define the Jackson program design process.

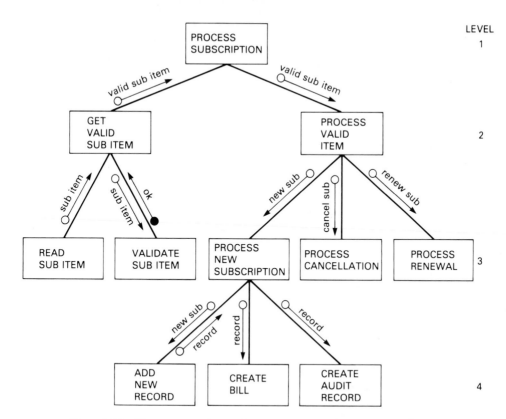

Figure 34.2   The structure chart defines the overall architecture of a program by showing the basic procedural components and their interrelationships. The arrows with an open circle (○——) show data passing between the process blocks. The arrows with a filled circle (●——) show control information passing between the process blocks.

Each transaction is first validated and then processed against the master file. For new subscriptions, a subscriber record is built and a bill is generated for the balance due. For renewals, the expiration date is updated and a bill is generated for the balance due. For cancellations, the record is flagged for deletion.

Figure 34.2 shows the structure chart representing the design of the subscription system. The structure chart was built using the structured design methodology. It was derived by applying functional decomposition to the procedural components. The structured design process does not include a step for defining data structures.

Figure 34.3 is the program-structure diagram for the subscription system. This diagram was built by applying the Jackson design methodology to the sub-

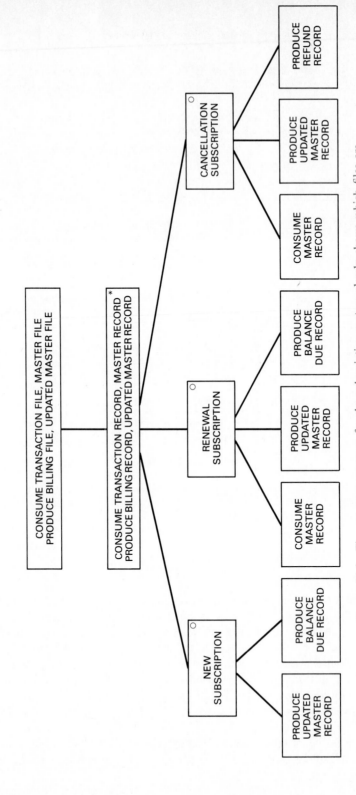

Figure 34.3 The program structure for the subscription system clearly shows which files are consumed and which are produced by the program. The accompanying procedural logic is not part of the program-structure diagram. It is found in the structure text.

scription system problem. The first step was to define the data structures shown in Fig. 34.4. The next step was to derive the program structure by combining all four data structures.

There are differences between the two program designs. The most important difference is that in the Jackson version the need to read, update, and produce a new-subscriber master file is clearly shown. Looking at the Yourdon-Constantine version, we do not see the subscriber master file referenced at all. When the Yourdon-Constantine design is implemented, the programmer must add the logic to read, update, and write the subscriber master file without design

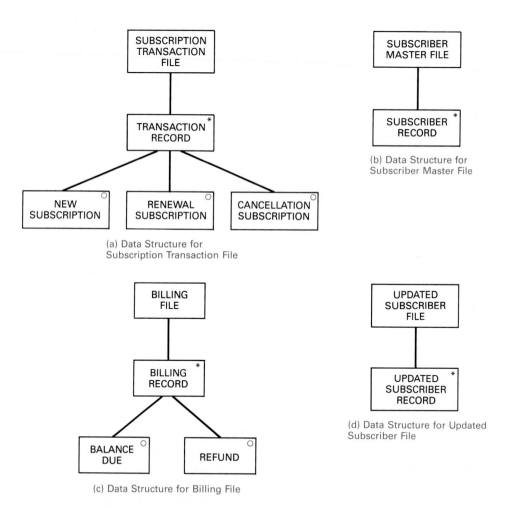

Figure 34.4 There are four data structures for the subscription system. These structures are combined to form the program structure for the subscription system shown in Fig. 34.3.

information to guide him. The Jackson design is therefore preferred over the Yourdon-Constantine design because it provides the more complete design.

Comments on Designing Data First

In the typical data processing application system, data design should be the starting point. It is the basis for building a good, stable program design. In this respect, the Jackson design methodology is superior to the other design methodologies discussed in this section. However, in the areas of control logic design and design verification, the Jackson design methodology is weak.

Comments on Control Logic Design

While we can fault the Yourdon-Constantine structured design methodology for slighting data-structure design, we must fault the Jackson design methodology for slighting control logic design.

Yourdon's position is that data-structure design should be done in a manner that does not interfere with the program control structure. The control structure is designed. Then the data structures are designed to preserve module independence. Data-structure design is not really included in the structured design methodology.

Jackson's position is that the control logic is trivial since it is dictated by the data structures. In the Jackson design methodology, the condition logic that governs the execution of loops and selection structures is added during the last part of the last step in the design process. There are no guidelines for performing this step or checking its correctness.

Both positions are wrong because they deal with only part of the design problem. Designs are full of both data design errors and logic design errors. The design of both data and logic should be more thoroughly guided and verified.

Comments on Design Verification

Verification is an important part of the constructive method. Each step should be performed independently and verified independently. Jackson subscribes to this requirement by including a verification step in each basic design step. But for most steps, verification is only an informal check. Jackson's position is that if something is wrong, it will undoubtedly become apparent in the next step because the pieces will not fit together. For example, if the data structure is incorrect, this will become apparent when the designer attempts to derive the program structure from it.

However, a more formal checking procedure is included only at the end of the program step. The correctness of the program structure is verified by reducing it to each one of the data structures.

Jackson's informal approach to design verification is a result of designing only simple programs. The whole design process becomes obvious and trivial for simple programs. Verification too becomes trivial. The Jackson approach is to use simple programs as building blocks in solving complex problems. The designer decomposes a complex problem into simple programs and never needs to design anything more complex than a simple program.

This line of reasoning, however, breaks down when we consider the interface between the parts. By verifying each simple program, we verify only the parts. But verifying the parts does not mean that we have verified the whole. How the whole is verified is unclear in the Jackson design methodology. This is a serious omission in a design methodology because incomplete verification often leads to design oversights and errors.

LIMITATIONS OF THE JACKSON DESIGN METHODOLOGY

The major weakness of the Jackson design methodology is that is not directly applicable to most real-world problems. First, the design process assumes the existence of a complete, correct specification; this is rarely possible for most data processing applications. Second, the design process is limited to simple programs. Only a very small segment of data processing programs are simple programs. Third, the design process is oriented toward batch-processing systems. It is not an effective design technique for on-line systems or data-base systems.

Too Much and Too Little

The Jackson design methodology offers too much and too little. In the case of simple programs, it is overkill. Following each detailed step probably leads the designer to the same design that he would have arrived at by using a less formal method such as top-down design. The less formal method would require only a fraction of the time. The design of a simple program is often so trivial that a correct design is intuitively obvious by reading the problem description and jotting down some pseudocode. The only benefit that the Jackson design methodology offers in this case is its emphasis on data-structure design. The design process should start with the design of data structures since this is likely to lead to a more complete design.

In the case of complex programs, the Jackson design methodology is inadequate in several areas. The methodology offers few guidelines for designing complex programs. Jackson describes the methodology as "being developed from the bottom up" [2]. How to apply it to small problems is clear, but how to apply it to larger problems is not; and this is, of course, where the designer needs the most help. Also, the methodology forces on-line systems and data-base systems to be designed as though they were batch-processing systems.

Problems with Complex Program Design

To design a complex program using the Jackson design methodology, it must first be decomposed into a network of simple programs. The decomposition technique is to assume that the program is a simple program and follow the basic design procedure. Begin by drawing the system network diagram. Take each data stream in the system network diagram and represent it in a tree-structure diagram. Then look for correspondences among the data components across the diagrams. If the data structures conflict, there is a structure clash, and this cannot be a simple program. The structure clash is resolved, and this resolution results in a decomposition of the program into two programs connected by an intermediate data stream. One complex program may involve many structure clashes; the resolution of each results in a further decomposition of the program.

Structure Clash Problems

Resolution of a structure clash complicates the design by introducing an intermediate data stream. Unlike the other data streams, this intermediate data stream is represented by two different data structures. One data structure is compatible with the simple program that consumes it; the other is compatible with the simple program that produces it. Although one structure must be transformed into the second, this transformation (e.g., sort) is not part of the design.

In Chapter 33, SKILL GROUP was created to resolve an ordering structure clash in the Employee Skills program. Figure 34.5 shows the system network diagram. There are two simple programs, CREATE SKILL GROUP and CREATE SKILL REPORT, connected by the data stream SKILL GROUP. SKILL 1 and SKILL 2 are the two data structures for SKILL GROUP. Figure 34.5 also shows the program structure. Although there are two simple programs, there is only one program structure. From the program structure we can tell only by the component names that the two simple programs are represented. But we cannot tell how one data structure (SKILL 1) is converted into the second data structure (SKILL 2).

How the designer arrives at a program structure that combines all simple programs is not explained in the methodology. The system network diagram, the data structures, and the program structure for a simple program all appear to describe the same design. But for a complex program, these pieces of the design do not obviously fit together. Double data structures, hidden program steps, and combined program structures, a normal part of the design of a complex program, can confuse and frustrate even the most experienced of designers.

Program Inversion Problems

Program inversion is another technique that complicates the design of complex programs. The design of the credit verification system illustrates this problem.

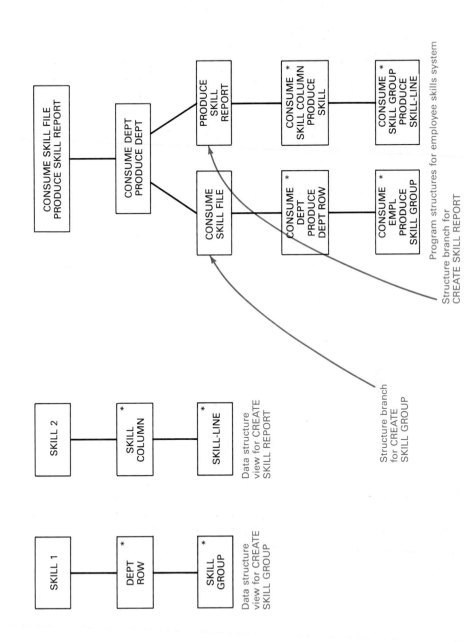

Figure 34.5 To resolve a structure clash, the system is expanded by decomposing the program into a sequence of simple programs.

477

DESIGNING THE CREDIT VERIFICATION SYSTEM

In Chapter 32, we designed the credit verification system using the Yourdon-Constantine structured design methodology. In this chapter, the credit verification system is designed using the Jackson design methodology.

The credit verification system receives information about charge purchases from terminals at the point of sale. The incoming charge information is validated for completeness and correct use of the store numbers. For valid charges, the customer's credit record is accessed to examine the customer's current balance. Then the amount of the charge and the customer's credit limit and the current balance are examined to determine whether the charge can be authorized. If so, an authorization number is generated. In addition, a check digit, which is calculated using the account number from the inquiry record and the customer's credit records, is verified. Depending on the outcome of the verification checks, an affirmative or negative response or a request for reentry is formatted and sent.

Figure 34.6 is the data flow diagram for the credit verification system. Figure 34.7 is the structure chart for the system. Both diagrams are part of the design produced by following the structured design methodology.

System Network Diagram for the Credit Verification System

The Jackson design methodology begins with a system network diagram. The system network diagram for the credit verification system is shown in Fig. 34.8. It looks very similar to the data flow diagram shown in Fig. 34.6. There are, however, some notable differences. The data flow diagram shows the flow of data items through processes. A data item could be a variable, a record, or a whole file. A process could be a program, a module, or a piece of either a program or a module. A system network diagram shows the flow of data streams between simple programs. A data stream is an ordered set of records. The properties of a simple program are listed in Box 34.1. From this comparison, we can see that a system network diagram is more formally defined than a data flow diagram. While the data flow diagram can be used to show a system at varying levels of detail, the system network diagram represents a system only at the simple-program level. Jackson uses the simple program as the principal building block in design. The Yourdon-Constantine methodology, on the other hand, uses the module. The notion of a module can change, depending on the point in the design process, but the notion of a simple program remains constant throughout the design process.

Looking at Fig. 34.8, we see that the credit verification system has two input data streams, CREDIT INQUIRY and CUSTOMER CREDIT RECORD, and one output data stream, RESPONSE.

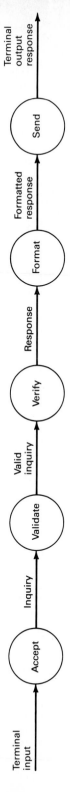

Figure 34.6 Data-flow diagram representing the basic procedural components of the credit ver-ification system and the flow of information connecting them.

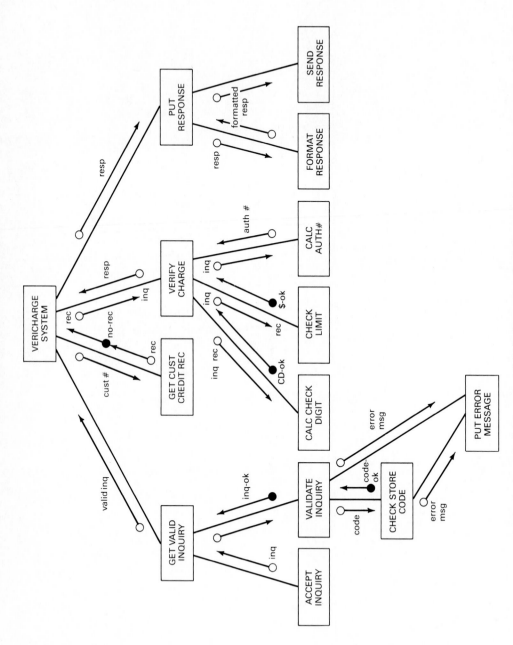

Figure 34.7 At the end of the structured design process, a complete structure chart showing all the procedural components of the system (program) and their interrelationships represents the final program or system design.

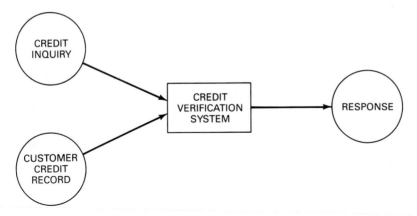

Figure 34.8   The system network diagram for the credit verification system shows that there are two input data streams, CREDIT INQUIRY and CUSTOMER CREDIT RECORD, and one output data stream, RESPONSE.

Record-Level Versus File-Level Design Problems

The first step in the Jackson design methodology is to create a hierarchical tree-structure diagram to represent each data stream. The tree-structure diagrams for the three data streams in the credit verification system are shown in Fig. 34.9. However, a closer look at these diagrams reveals a serious problem. Each data structure must represent the *complete* structure of a data stream. This is key to creating a complete and correct program structure. However, the data structures

BOX 34.1   Properties of a simple program

- When the program is executed, nothing needs to be remembered from a previous execution.
- The program input and output data streams are serial files that function like a tape file.
- The program structure is formed by merging all input and output data structures.
- The data structures must not conflict on any level.
- Each time the program is executed, one or more complete files are processed.

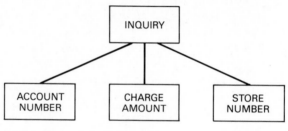

(a) Data Structure for Inquiry

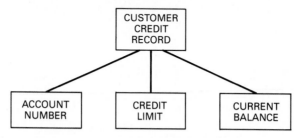

(b) Data Structure for Customer Credit Record

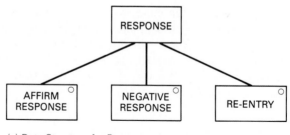

(c) Data Structure for Response

Figure 34.9 There are three data structures representing the three data streams for the credit verification system.

in Fig. 34.9 are incomplete. They represent the data stream at record level and therefore cannot show the relationships between records. What is needed to show all the relationships is a file-level representation for each data stream. The file-level representation shown in Fig. 34.10 leads to a batch-processing view of the design in which whole files are consumed and produced.

But this change introduces another problem. It appears from the problem description that the program needs a record-level design. It takes one inquiry from the terminal and one customer credit record from the CUSTOMER CREDIT FILE and produces one response. It does not consume and produce complete files. This is true for many on-line conversational programs.

To reconcile the file-oriented view required by the Jackson design methodology to represent all data relationships and the record-oriented view required by the problem, Jackson proposes a file-oriented design and a record-oriented implementation. A coding technique called *program inversion* is used to merge these two views.

Program Inversion of the Credit Verification Program

Program inversion involves the creation of an I/O subroutine, which we can call PX, for a program we call P. PX is a file processing procedure that performs one of three possible operations each time it is invoked:

1. Open file X
2. Read (or write) one record of file X
3. Close file X

Jackson calls the creation of program PX the "inversion of P with respect to file X" [3].

The credit verification system requires a triple inversion: one inversion to read a record from the INQUIRY file (program PI), one inversion to read a record from the CUSTOMER CREDIT FILE (program PC), and one inversion to write a response record from the RESPONSE FILE (program PR). Figure 34.11 shows an informal system network diagram depicting these inversions. The CREDIT VERIFICATION PROGRAM is the main program. It has three subroutines, PI, PC, and PR, which are called to perform read and write operations.

These inversions are only apparent when looking at the program code. They are not shown in the formal system network diagram, the program-structure diagram, or the structure text. Figure 34.10 shows the data structure and the program structure for the credit verification system.

Comments on Designing the Credit Verification System

The need to force a batch-processing view on all design problems is a Jackson design methodology kludge that complicates rather than simplifies the design. Having to deal with one view for the design and another view for the implementation makes the program difficult to understand. Also, it violates the fundamental programming principles that the design should be structured to resemble the problem as closely as possible and that the code should be a true representation of the design with nothing added, changed, or deleted.

Jackson's batch-processing view is outdated since it ignores the reality that many modern data processing applications require data-base systems, not simple

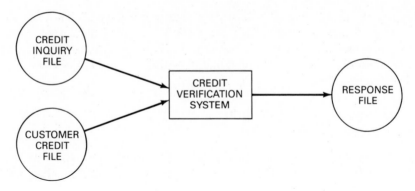

(a) System Network Diagram for the Credit Verification System

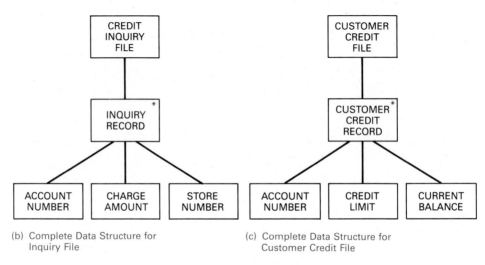

(b) Complete Data Structure for
    Inquiry File

(c) Complete Data Structure for
    Customer Credit File

Figure 34.10   A complete data-structure representation of each data stream
in the credit verification system is a file-level representation.

serial files. Modern data processing does not think in terms of tape files that
must be read in record-order sequence from beginning to end. Rather, it thinks
in terms of flexible data structures that provide the information in a form that is
convenient to and matches the problem requirements.

Also, not all data structures are hierarchical. Since the Jackson design
methodology can deal only with hierarchical data structures, this restriction se-
verely limits the class of problems to which the methodology can be applied.

SUMMARY

In general, the Jackson design methodology is more
difficult to use than other structured design methodol-

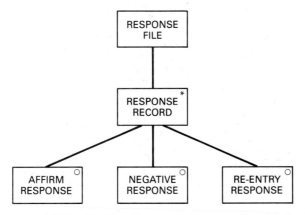

(d) Complete Data Structure for Response File

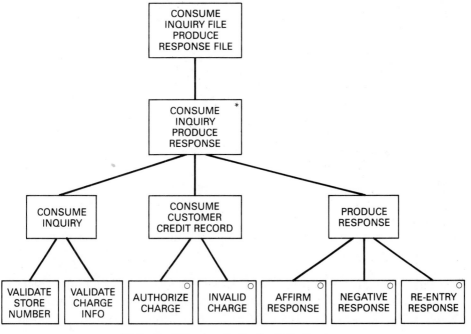

(e) Program Structure for the Credit Verification System.

Figure 34.10   (Continued)

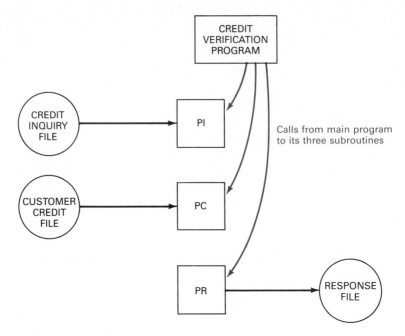

Figure 34.11 An informal system network diagram shows the three program inversions for the Credit Verification program. The inversions are transparent to the design and affect only the actual program code.

ogies. The steps are tedious to apply. For problems with complex data structures, the extra effort may be worthwhile because the resulting program structure is likely to be more complete and correct. Thinking about data structures from the beginning is crucial to a good design. Unfortunately, the methodology will be helpful for only a certain class of problems, serial file systems. It breaks down completely when applied to data-base systems.

For simple problems with simple data structures, the extra effort is probably not worthwhile. The designer is advised to use the simpler top-down design method with the early part of the design effort devoted to data-structure design.

REFERENCES

1. R. Adrion, M. Branstad, and J. Cherniavsky, "Validation, Verification and Testing of Computer Software," *Computing Surveys,* 14, no. 2 (June 1982), 159–191.

2. G. D. Bergland, ''A Guided Tour of Program Design Methodologies,'' *Computer* (October 1981), 13–37.

3. M. A. Jackson, ''Constructive Methods of Program Design,'' in *Proceedings, First Conference of the European Conference in Informatics,* 44 (1976).

35 WARNIER-ORR DESIGN METHODOLOGY

BACKGROUND   The Warnier-Orr design methodology originated with Jean-Dominique Warnier at CII Honeywell-Bull in Paris in the late 1950s. He called the methodology the *logical construction of programs* (LCP). In the mid 1970s, Ken Orr, drawing on the Jackson design methodology, modified Warnier's LCP to create a methodology he called *structured program design* (SPD). The hybrid form of LCP and SPD, called the Warnier-Orr methodology, is the form that we present in here.

SET THEORY   The Warnier-Orr design methodology uses set theory from mathematics to describe program designs. A *set* is an ordered collection of objects that share one or more common characteristics (e.g., the set of integers or the departments in a company). In mathematics, a set is denoted by listing its members and enclosing the list within brackets. For example, the departments in a company form a set indicated by

{accounting, marketing, production, purchasing}

The Warnier-Orr methodology uses a similar notation for sets, except the right-hand bracket is deleted and the members of the set are listed vertically rather than horizontally:

$$\left\{ \begin{array}{l} \text{accounting} \\ \text{marketing} \\ \text{production} \\ \text{purchasing} \end{array} \right.$$

The Warnier-Orr diagram, the central design tool of the Warnier-Orr methodology, is composed of nested set brackets. An example of a Warnier-Orr diagram is shown in Fig. 35.11. Warnier-Orr diagrams are used to show the hierarchical structure and process flow of activities, functions, or data.

TOP-DOWN   The Warnier-Orr methodology is a top-down method
APPROACH   because it uses functional decomposition to derive a
                          program design. Like structured design (discussed in
Chapter 31) and Jackson design (discussed in Chapter 33), it is a refinement of the basic top-down design approach (discussed in Chapter 30) since it provides a step-by-step procedure for deriving the design. Box 35.1 summarizes the six steps in the Warnier-Orr design procedure [1].

In some versions of the methodology, the order of steps 3, 4, and 5 is modified as follows [2]:

3. Design the Logical Process
4. Develop the Physical Data Base
5. Perform Event Analysis

However, regardless of the version, the general design direction remains the same: output, process, input design, with logical design preceding physical design considerations.

BOX 35.1   Steps in the Warnier-Orr design procedure

1. DEFINE THE PROCESS OUTPUTS
   Represent each program output as a hierarchical data structure.

2. DEFINE THE LOGICAL DATA BASE
   Define all the data elements needed to produce the program output(s).

3. PERFORM EVENT ANALYSIS
   Define all the events that can affect (change) the data elements in the logical data base.

4. DEVELOP THE PHYSICAL DATA BASE
   Define the physical files for the input data.

5. DESIGN THE LOGICAL PROCESS
   Design the program processing logic that is needed to produce the desired output from the input.

6. DESIGN THE PHYSICAL PROCESS
   Add the control logic and file-handling procedures to complete the program design.

DATA-DRIVEN APPROACH
The Warnier-Orr methodology is similar to the Jackson methodology in that both are data-driven approaches. They both derive the program structure from the data structure. Also, they both work with only hierarchical data structures, and both stress that logical design should be separate from and precede physical design.

The major difference between the two is that the Jackson design methodology merges all input and output data structures to form a single program structure, whereas the Warnier-Orr methodology derives the program structure and the input data structures from the output data structures. The Warnier-Orr design philosophy is that the program output completely and absolutely determines the data structure, and the data structure, in turn, determines the program structure. For this reason, it is called ''output-oriented analysis'' [3].

DESIGN OF THE EMPLOYEE SKILLS SYSTEM
The Warnier-Orr design methodology is illustrated with the design of the employee skills system. In Chapter 31, this system was designed using the Yourdon-Constantine structured design method, and in Chapter 33, it was designed using the Jackson design method. The purpose of the employee skills system is to produce a summary report of employee skills by department. Each employee may have several skills.

The Warnier-Orr diagram is used to represent the design at varying levels of detail. At the beginning of a design problem, it can be used to sketch the overall problem. Figure 35.1 uses the Warnier-Orr diagram to sketch the employee skills system problem. Even in this first view of the design problem, we can see that the focus is on the system output.

Step 1: Define the Output

The first step in the Warnier-Orr design procedure is to describe the program output as a hierarchical data structure. The Warnier-Orr diagram is used to show

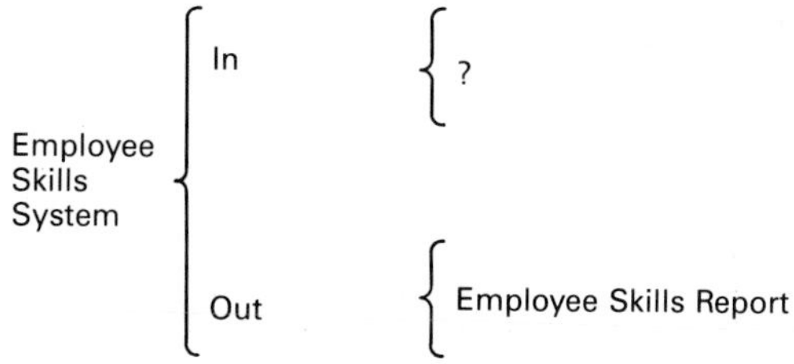

Figure 35.1 The Warnier-Orr diagram is used to represent a design at varying levels of detail. This first view is a rough sketch of the employee skills system design problem.

its hierarchical structure graphically. The designer works from a detailed description of the program output and computational algorithms to define the output data items and arrange them in a hierarchical order. Warnier and Orr provide three guidelines for identifying the hierarchies [4]:

1. Look for repetition of a data item, and create a hierarchical level for each.
2. Look for alternative data items, and create a hierarchical level for each.
3. Look for logical groupings of data items, and group them in a vertical list at one hierarchical level.

Figure 35.2 shows the report for the employee skills system. Figure 35.3 shows the Warnier-Orr diagram representing this report as a hierarchical structure. The diagram indicates that the employee skills report is organized by department and within department by skill. There are one or more departments in the report, and there are one or more skills within each department. For each skill listed in the report, the total number of employees in that department with that skill is given.

This first step is critical since, according to Warnier, the entire design is dependent on the output data structure. It provides the logical framework for the program structure [4].

Step 2: Define the Logical Data Base

In step 2 of the Warnier-Orr design procedure, the logical data base is defined. It consists of all the data needed to produce the program output. The following steps are followed to build the logical data base:

1. List all the data items that appear on the report.
2. Map each data item in the list onto its appropriate place in the output data structure. This is called the *logical output structure*.

DEPT	SKILL	NUMBER OF EMPLOYEES
01	DRILL PRESS	6
01	WELDING	3
02	PAINTING	1
03	PAINTING	7
.	.	.
.	.	.
.	.	.

Figure 35.2 The output for the employee skills system is the employee skills report. It totals the number of employees with a particular skill in a particular department.

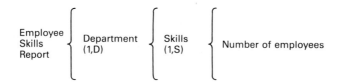

Figure 35.3   The Warnier-Orr diagram is used to show the hierarchical structure of program output. The employee skills report in Fig. 35.2 is represented hierarchically here. This is the output data structure.

3. Remove all constants and derived data items from the logical output structure to create the *logical input structure*.

4. Remove all but the first occurrence of each redundant data item from the logical input structure.

5. Resolve any hidden hierarchies.

Figure 35.4 lists all the data items in the employee skills report. Report titles and constants are included in the list. Figure 35.5 shows the logical output structure for the employee skills report. It indicates where in the data structure each data item of the output will occur.

To convert the logical output structure into the logical data base, the constants and derived data items must be deleted. A derived data item is data that can be computed from other available program data. After deleting constants and derived data, what remains is primary data, or the logical input structure. Figure 35.6 shows the logical input structure for the employee skills report.

Next, any data redundancies are removed by deleting every occurrence but the first occurrence of any primary data item that appears in the logical input structure. In this example, there are no redundant data items.

Finally, the output data structure is examined to reveal any hidden hierarchies. A hidden hierarchy may occur if the output description is not complete. For example, suppose that the employee skills report is to include only production skills and is to exclude other possible skills, such as clerical, sales, or accounting. Another possibility is that the report is to include only male employees. These output qualifications are not apparent by looking at the report layout. Figure 35.7 shows the data structures that represent these variations of

"DEPT"
Department Number
"SKILL"
Skill Description
"NUMBER OF EMPLOYEES"
Employee Skill Count

Figure 35.4   Data items in the employee skills report.

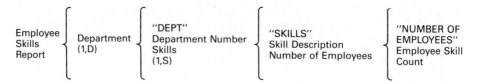

Figure 35.5 The logical output structure shows all the report data items mapped onto the output data structure.

the employee skills report. Note the addition of hierarchical levels to provide for the hidden hierarchies.

The last step in producing the logical data base is to check for hidden hierarchies. If the logical data base is insufficient to produce the complete report output, the cause may be a hidden hierarchy.

The logical data base for the employee skills report is the same as the logical input structure shown in Fig. 35.6, since there are no data redundancies or hidden hierarchies. In this problem the logical data base is a subset of the logical output structure, but this is not always the case. Although they do not appear on the output, some primary data items may be necessary input to the program in order to derive all the output data.

Step 3: Perform Event Analysis

Step 3 of the Warnier-Orr method is to perform event analysis. This involves examining entities and attributes and the events that affect them. Warnier defines an *entity* as a data item that shows the hierarchical relationship among data items. In general, an entity is the name of a hierarchical bracket. An *attribute* is associated with an entity. The attributes are the data items that are not entities (i.e., not names of brackets). The logical data base is used to define the entities and their attributes. Figure 35.8 lists the entities for the logical data base of the employee skills system shown in Fig. 35.6.

For each entity, event analysis is performed by asking the following questions:

Figure 35.6 The logical input structure shows all the primary data items in the report. It is derived from the logical output structure by deleting all constants and derived data.

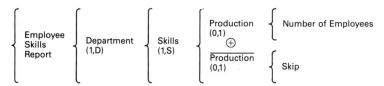

This is the correct data structure for the employee skills report that includes *only* production skills. The horizontal bar over **Production** is the negation operator; it means "not **Production**."

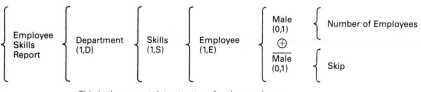

This is the correct data structure for the employee skills report that includes skills only for male employees.

Figure 35.7 Hidden hierarchies can occur if the complete data description is not obvious from examining the report layout.

1. Which attributes may change?

2. What events cause the attributes to change?

The purpose of performing event analysis is to discover any oversights in the data items needed to produce the program output and to determine what logic is required to update data items in the normal course of using the system.

  Event analysis is classified as physical design by Warnier because it con-

ENTITY	ATTRIBUTE
Employee Skills Report Department Skills	------- Department Number Skill Description

Figure 35.8 The entities for the employee skills report are the names of the brackets in the logical data base. The attributes are the remaining data items in the logical data base.

cerns defining real-world events that can affect the attributes associated with an entity [5]. For example, renumbering the departments in a company is one real-world event that would change the attribute **Department Number.** The basic idea behind event analysis is to design the program in a way that handles data changes that may be needed when using the system.

As shown in Fig. 35.8, there are three entities in the employee skills report. Since only the entities **Department** and **Skills** have attributes, event analysis is performed for each of these entities. It is unlikely that either **Department Number** or **Skill Description** will change. What is more likely is the addition of new departments or new skills. For this particular application, these additions are of no concern.

Step 4: Develop the Physical Data Base

Step 4 of the Warnier-Orr design methodology is also concerned with physical design. In this step the input files are designed. They are composed of the primary data items in the logical data base designed in step 2. Multiple records and/or files are defined, depending on where the data are referenced in the logical input structure. For example, data items that are needed only once at the beginning of the report are separated from data items needed to produce each line of a multi-line report.

The primary data items for the employee skills report are **Department Number** and **Skill Description.** These two data items are grouped together to form a record for each employee. If the records are sorted in skill-within-department order, the data are in the correct form and order to produce the program output. We can refer to this physical file as the Skill File:

Department Number	Skill Description	Employee

Step 5: Design the Logical Process

The next step is to define the logical process that transforms the input into the desired output. The framework for the logical process is the data structure that was derived in the first step of this design process. The logical output structure, derived in step 2 of the design process, is used to guide the designer in filling in the logical detail. The logical process is represented by a Warnier-Orr diagram.

Figure 35.9 shows the data structure and logical output structure for the employee skills system. The first step is to add BEGIN and END portions to each hierarchy. They hold the initialization and termination logic for each logical level (e.g., zero out counters, close files). Next, the logical process detail is filled in from the bottom to the top of the data structure. The design direction moves from the highest hierarchical level toward the lowest. At each level the designer asks, "What actions must be performed to produce the output needed at this point in the structure?"

In the employee skills system, the first bracket to fill in is the END logic for the employee skills report. Since the logical output structure indicates that no output is produced at this level, no logic is needed. The next level to examine is the **Department** END bracket. Again the logical output structure indicates that no logic is needed since there is no output at this point in the structure. The same is true at the **Skills** level.

The last level to fill in is **Number of Employees.** Since this is the lowest-level bracket, it does not really need separate BEGIN and END portions. The logic at this level is simple enough to include steps performed one after another. An examination of the logical output structure tells the designer that the following data items are to be printed on one line of the report:

Department Number

Skill Description

Employee Skill Count

Employee Skill Count is the number of employees in a department with a particular skill. To produce the **Employee Skill Count,** the Skill File is read. One employee may have several skills and thus has one record for each skill.

The logic at the **Number of Employees** level is as follows:

$$
\text{Number of Employees} \atop (1,\text{E})
\left\{
\begin{array}{l}
\text{Add 1 to Employee Skill Count} \\
\\
\text{Print Department Number, Skill Description,} \\
\text{Employee Skill Count} \\
\\
\text{Get Next Skill record}
\end{array}
\right.
$$

The designer continues to define the process logic by filling in the BEGIN portion of each bracket. The design direction is from the lowest-level to the highest-level bracket.

The BEGIN portion at the **Skills** level contains logic to set the **Employee Skill Count** to zero. Each time a new skill is encountered in the Skill File, the skill count must be reinitialized. The BEGIN portion at the **Department** level requires no logic.

Finally, the BEGIN portion at the highest level includes printing the report heading line and reading the Skill File for the first time.

Figure 35.10 shows the logic thus far added to the design structure for the employee skills program.

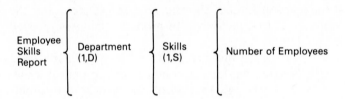

(a) Data Structure for the Employee Skills System

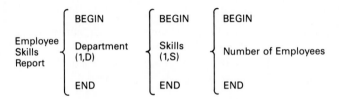

(b) Logical Output Structure for the Employee Skills System

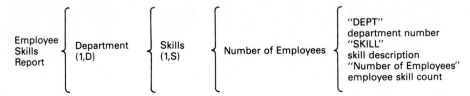

(c) Framework Structure for the Logic Process
Design in the Employee Skills System

Figure 35.9   In the Warnier-Orr methodology, the program structure is derived from the program output structure(s).

Step 6: Design the Physical Process

In the last step of the Warnier-Orr design procedure, the designer adds the control logic and file-handling procedures to the design. Warnier refers to this step
as *physical process design* because these considerations are dependent on the
programming language rather than the problem [6]. To emphasize the separation
between logical and physical design, the control logic is not included in the
Warnier-Orr diagram representing the design. Instead, it is placed in footnotes
(see Fig. 35.11).

Each repetition bracket is interpreted as a DO UNTIL structure. To find

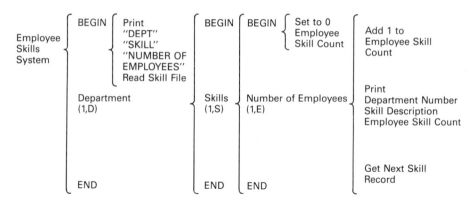

Figure 35.10   To build the program design, the processing logic is added to the data structure.

the termination condition, the reader is referred to the appropriate footnote. For example, in Fig. 35.11, the **Department** bracket,

Department
(1,D)?2

is interpreted as

DO Department Process
UNTIL End of Skill File = true

Figure 35.11 represents the final design for the Employee Skills program. The control logic for the three program loops, **Department, Skills,** and **Number of Employees,** has been added in the form of footnotes, **?1, ?2,** and **?3.** As part of the necessary loop control logic, three new variables are created, **End of Skill File, Current Department,** and **Current Skill.** Each of these variables is initialized at the beginning of the appropriate repetition structure.

Control logic also must be added for **Employee Skill Count.** For each change in skill, a report line is printed, **Current Skill** is updated, and **Employee Skill Count** is reset to zero. For each change in **Department,** a line is printed and **Current Department** is updated. Footnotes **?4** and **?5** indicate the conditions tested for **Skill change** and **Dept change.** Note that the horizontal bar over **Dept change** and **Skill change** in the diagram indicates negation of the condition test (i.e., no change in **Department,** no change in **Skill**).

The final logic added to the diagram concerns file handling. The file open and close instructions are added at the beginning and the end of the employee skills system bracket.

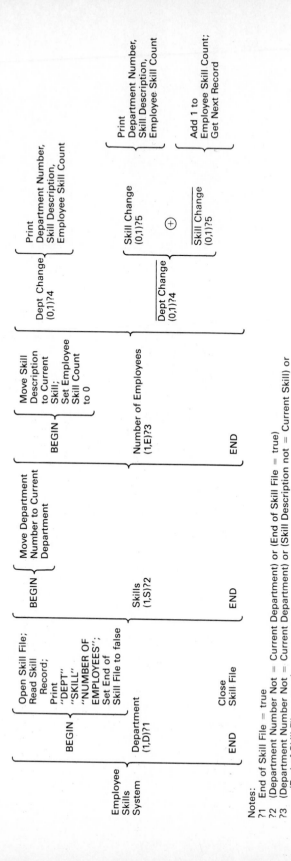

Figure 35.11 The complete program design for the employee skill system represented as a Warnier-Orr diagram.

Notes:
?1   End of Skill File = true
?2   (Department Number Not = Current Department) or (End of Skill File = true)
?3   (Department Number Not = Current Department) or (Skill Description not = Current Skill) or
      (End of Skill File = true)
?4   Department Number Not = Current Department
?5   Skill Description Not = Current Skill

REFERENCES

1. D. Higgins, *Program Design and Construction,* Englewood Cliffs, NJ: Prentice-Hall, Inc., 1979.

2. K. Orr, *Structured Systems Development,* New York: Yourdon Press, Inc., 1977, pp. 81–106.

3. Higgins, p. 38.

4. Ibid., pp. 35–48.

5. Ibid., pp. 73–81.

6. Ibid., pp. 111–122.

36 AN EVALUATION OF THE WARNIER-ORR DESIGN METHODOLOGY

INPUT-PROCESS-OUTPUT MODEL

Like other structured design methodologies, such as the Yourdon-Constantine approach and the Jackson approach, the Warnier-Orr methodology is founded on the basic input-process-output model for a system:

INPUT ⟶ PROCESS ⟶ OUTPUT

Data are entered into a system as input, are operated on (or transformed) by a process, and leave as output.

This is the basic model used for all structured design. However, the order in which the model is built depends on the particular design methodology that is followed.

The Yourdon-Constantine approach views the process part as the fundamental part of the system model, whereas the Jackson approach views the input and output parts as most important. But unlike either of these methodologies, the system output is the focus throughout the entire Warnier-Orr design process. The Warnier-Orr position is that output is the principal purpose of developing a system (program). They define output as the information ultimately used by the end user [1]. For example, a terminal screen of data or a printed report is output. In their view, output is the most important part of the system model.

The basis of the Warnier-Orr philosophy is that system correctness depends on a thorough understanding of the system output. The Warnier-Orr design process begins with a complete description of what output the system is to produce. As Orr explains, this is because what the system is to produce is really its requirements. "Requirements are primarily concerned with outputs and the logical rules for their derivation" [2].

This view leads to a "backward" design approach [1], which, although claimed to be, is not really top-down design. Using the Warnier-Orr methodology, the designer begins by defining the system output and works backwards through the basic system model to define the process and input portions of the design:

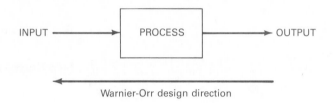

Warnier-Orr design direction

Figure 36.1 is a Warnier-Orr diagram showing the steps in the Warnier-Orr design methodology. As shown in the diagram, the process begins with defining the structure of the system output. The system input structure and the system processing structure are derived from the output data structure. The output of each design step is represented as a Warnier-Orr diagram.

OBJECTIVE OF THE WARNIER-ORR DESIGN METHODOLOGY

The primary objective of the Warnier-Orr methodology is to design reliable systems that can be easily adapted to changing user needs. According to Warnier, one way of achieving this objective is through better communication among analysts, users, and programmers. The Warnier-Orr diagram is the communication vehicle that Warnier recommends because it is easy to understand and because it separates the logical and physical aspects of the design [3].

BENEFITS OF THE WARNIER-ORR DIAGRAM

Perhaps the greatest strength of the Warnier-Orr design methodology is the Warnier-Orr diagram. This one diagramming tool is used to represent all aspects of the design throughout the design process. This serves to link the various design components—the data structures, the logical data base, and the physical and logic processes. For small, output-oriented problems, the entire design can be represented in a single Warnier-Orr diagram. The employee skills system designed in Chapter 35 illustrates this point (see Fig. 35.11).

The diagram encourages the design of a well-structured program since it can represent all the structured constructs: sequence, selection, and repetition. Also, it has no mechanism for representing the GO TO structure to discourage the designer from building programs with GO TOs. A Warnier-Orr diagram

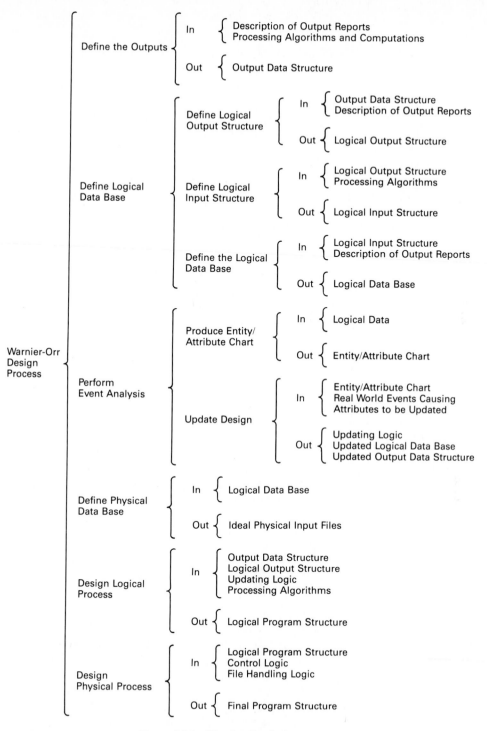

Figure 36.1 Warnier-Orr design process.

represents sequences of actions organized hierarchically, allowing sequence, selection, and repetition as the only means of relating these actions.

PROBLEMS WITH THE WARNIER-ORR DIAGRAM

However, the Warnier-Orr diagram is also the source of many of the deficiencies of the Warnier-Orr design methodology. Orr's position is that data structures can be very complex and therefore must be defined exactly [4]. The Warnier-Orr diagram is used for this purpose. The problem is that the Warnier-Orr diagram limits the design to a strict hierarchical model for data and processes. Network-like data structures cannot be described by the Warnier-Orr diagram; therefore, they are not permitted. Orr ignores the fact that not all data bases are hierarchical [4]. Since many data bases are not hierarchically organized, the Warnier-Orr design methodology is not suitable for designing these types of structures. For that matter, the methodology does not address the design of data-base systems or the role of data dictionaries. This is a serious omission from what is claimed to be a general-purpose design methodology.

Another problem is that the Warnier-Orr diagram includes control logic for loop termination and condition tests only as footnotes, rather than an integral part of the diagram. Warnier claims that because control logic is not really part of the logical design, it should be separated from it [5]. Although this may be true, designing the program control structure is a critical and difficult part of program design. Historically, incorrect program loops and condition tests have been the source of many program errors. The Warnier-Orr design methodology postpones control logic design until the final step of the design process. The methodology provides no guidelines for control logic design. The designer is simply told to insert it at the proper place in the program structure.

Also, the designer must remember that the $(1,m)$ notation under a bracket label implies a DO UNTIL repetition construct, since nowhere in the diagram is this explicitly defined. In this example,

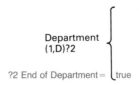

the **Department** loop is a DO UNTIL construct. To find out what condition is tested to terminate the loop, the reader must look at footnote **?2.**

Introduction of control logic often requires the creation of new variables to act as switches, flags, and end-of-file markers (e.g., **End of Department**). In the Warnier-Orr methodology, these control variables are introduced in the last step of the design procedure. Also, the logic needed to set and reset their values is added during this step. The methodology builds the logical data base to list all the input data items required to produce the desired program output much earlier, in step 2 of the methodology. However, it provides no comparable structure to list control variables, nor are the new variables added to the logical data base. Further, it does not include a step to check that each control variable has been correctly initialized and reset. Since a common cause of program errors is incorrectly setting or resetting control variables, this is a serious deficiency of the methodology.

BRACKETED PSEUDOCODE

Looking back at the Warnier-Orr diagram in Fig. 35.11, we see that it is a form of 'bracketed' pseudocode where nesting occurs along the horizontal. This format causes the diagrams to grow across the horizontal. For larger problems with several levels of nesting, the diagram quickly becomes many pages wide. Also, for larger problems involving many pseudocode instructions, the diagram quickly becomes very crowded. The designer is forced to attempt to squeeze the logic into the diagram or redraw the diagram. The temptation is to summarize the logic, consequently leaving out important details. The methodology does not include a step to check that all the steps to produce the output are included in the design. It simply assumes that the designer will have no trouble in correctly listing all the processing logic at the proper place in the structure.

MAJOR CRITICISMS

Our major criticisms of the Warnier-Orr design methodology arise from its extreme output orientation. We seriously question the methodology's basic premise that all data structures and the program architectural structure can and must follow from the output. We find that a design approach built on this premise is appropriate only for small, report-oriented design problems. When applied to larger problems, the methodology breaks down in several areas:

1. Difficulty of handling designs of problems with multiple output structures.
2. Inability to represent nonhierarchical data structures.
3. Inability to design data-base systems.
4. Inadequate input design guidelines.
5. Inadequate logic design guidelines.

DESIGN OF THE SUBSCRIPTION SYSTEM

Each design step for the employee skills system in Chapter 35 was carefully guided by the Warnier-Orr methodology. But the employee skills system is an extremely simple example with one input file, one output report, and a straightforward processing algorithm. Since most design problems are not this simple, we must ask how well the methodology guides the design of more complex problems with multiple input and output files.

Consider, for example, the subscription system design problem. The purpose of the subscription system is to process three types of transactions (new subscriptions, renewals, and cancellations) to update a Subscriber Master File and send out bills and refunds. For new subscriptions, a subscriber record is built and a bill is generated for the balance due. For renewals, the expiration date in the existing subscriber record is updated and a bill is generated for the balance due. For cancellations, the existing subscriber record is flagged for deletion and a refund is issued.

The rough Warnier-Orr diagram of the subscription problem shown in Fig. 36.2 indicates that there are multiple inputs and outputs in this design.

PROBLEMS WITH
MULTIPLE OUTPUT
STRUCTURES

The first step of the Warnier-Orr design process is to represent the system output in hierarchical form. In this case, two Warnier-Orr diagrams are needed— one for bills and one for the updated subscriber file (see Fig. 36.3).

According to Fig. 36.1, the next step is to define the logical data base from the logical output structure and the logical input structure. At this point the methodology becomes vague. The designer is told to take the logical sum of the output data structures to create one logical output structure, but no other guidance is provided. In this problem this is a straightforward task because both bills and master records are in subscriber order. The logical sum of **Bills/Refunds** and **Updated Subscriber Master File** is shown at the top of Fig. 36.4.

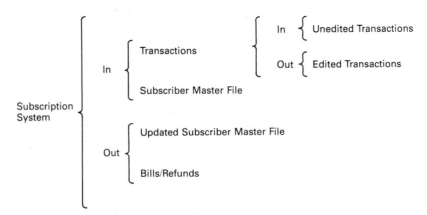

Figure 36.2   A rough Warnier-Orr diagram is used to represent the subscription system at the beginning of the design process.

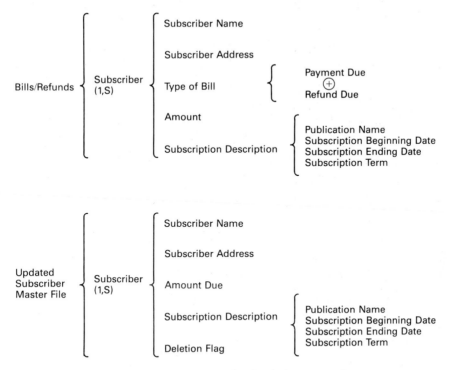

Figure 36.3   The first step in the Warnier-Orr design process is to represent the system output in hierarchical form. The subscription problem has two outputs, **Bills/Refunds** and **Updated Subscriber Master File.**

However, there is one notable difference between the two outputs that alters the structure shown in Fig. 36.4. The updated subscriber file contains all the subscribers, whereas the bills files contain a bill or refund only for the subscribers for whom a transaction was processed. To reflect this difference, the logical output structure must be defined as shown at the bottom of Fig. 36.4.

This requirement is not apparent from examining the system output. Although the methodology suggests that requirements are known from an examination of the output, this is seldom true in practice. By introducing the premise that all follows from the output, the methodology may be misleading the designer.

Orr refers to the problem of overlooked requirements as the "hidden hierarchy" problem [6]. He suggests that this is a common design mistake. When it occurs, the designer must redraw the data structure to include the hidden hierarchy.

For more complex design problems, many requirements may not initially be apparent from an examination of the system output. Since the methodology

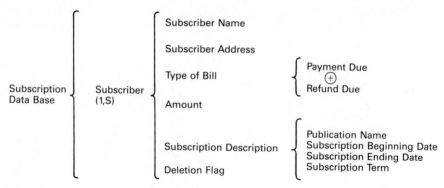

(a) Logical Sum of **Bills/Refund** Data Structure and **Updated Subscriber Master File** in Fig. 36.3

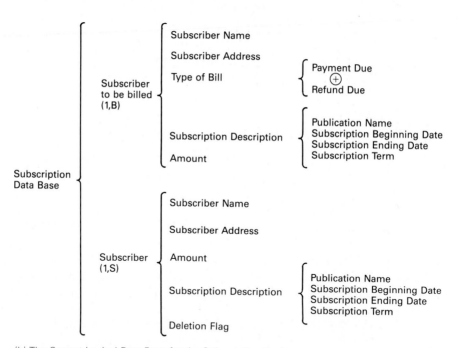

(b) The Correct Logical Data Base for the Subscription System

Figure 36.4   Logical data base for the subscription system.

offers little assistance here other than to keep looking, there is a real danger that the designer may not discover all the hidden hierarchies. This may lead to an incorrect design.

INCOMPATIBLE HIERARCHIES

Suppose we add to the subscription problem the requirement that bills are processed monthly, but the Subscriber Master File is updated weekly. Figure 36.5 shows how this new requirement changes the output structures.

This new requirement introduces another problem. The two output structures are now hierarchically incompatible. Weeks is not a subset of months.

Sometimes this problem can be solved with a technique called "hierarchy inversion" [7]. The incompatible hierarchy is dropped from the structure, its process code is transferred to the next lower hierarchical level, and control logic is added in the lower level to determine when to execute the transferred logic.

Another solution is to create two separate programs, one to produce bills/refunds and one to update the Subscriber Master File. In this problem, the second solution seems better. However, the Warnier-Orr methodology does not advise the designer on how to make this choice.

INADEQUATE INPUT DESIGN GUIDELINES

In the Warnier-Orr methodology, the ideal input structure(s) are derived from the problem output structure. In the subscription problem where the input consists of the old Subscriber Master File and Subscription transactions, it is easy to achieve the ideal input structure(s). In other problems, the ideal input structures may be difficult to achieve because the physical input files already exist and are not compatibly ordered with the ideal input. To solve this incompatibility problem, the Warnier-Orr methodology advises writing another program to convert the existing input into the ideal input. However, the methodology provides no guidelines for input conversion other than to work backwards in steps from ideal to actual input. In some cases this may require only a simple file sort to reorder the data. In other cases several files may have to be merged and the data may have to be completely restructured. Although the Warnier-Orr methodology dismisses input conversion as a simple step, it may be more difficult than producing the output.

OVEREMPHASIS ON OUTPUT

In general, the output orientation of the Warnier-Orr methodology leads to an underestimation of the difficulty of input and process design. The Warnier-Orr methodology suggests that the design of input structures and process logic will fall neatly into place once the output has been correctly structured. According to Orr,

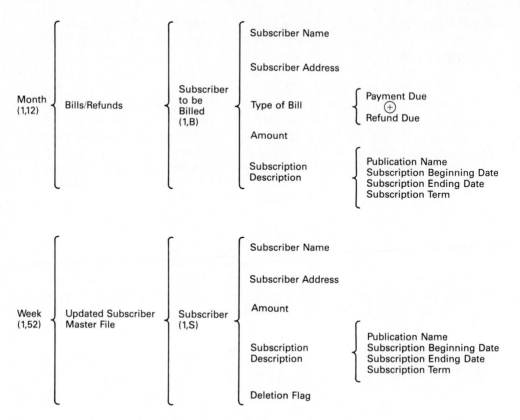

Figure 36.5 Logical output structures for the subscription system that produces monthly bills/refunds and weekly updated Subscription Master Files.

> . . . thinking about outputs is hard work. On the other hand, talking about input is much easier for the hard questions can be left until later. [8]

In his book *Structured Systems Development,* Orr begins the design process with a Warnier-Orr diagram similar to the one shown in Fig. 36.2 for the Subscription system [9]. As he demonstrates the Warnier-Orr design methodology, the output portion of the diagram is developed in great detail. On the other hand, not one design example in the book expands the input part of the design as shown in Fig. 36.2. The reader is left to assume that the methodology is somehow applicable to input design as well as to output design.

    The same criticism applies to process logic design. Somehow the process logic steps are assigned to their appropriate place in the problem structure. But how the designer defines these process steps is not explained. Also, no checking is done to assure that the logic is correct and complete.

RECOMMENDATIONS   The Warnier-Orr methodology is suitable for a small class of design problems: simple, report-oriented systems. For these problems, the methodology provides the designer with an easy-to-follow set of design steps leading to a structured design. Using the Warnier-Orr diagram to represent the design at each step helps clearly to convey and evolve design structures.

For very simple report designs, the methodology becomes too tedious to follow in detail. Instead, most designers will find it sufficient to use an abbreviated version of the methodology that begins with defining the output structure using a Warnier-Orr diagram and then fills in the logic needed to produce the output.

For design problems other than report-oriented systems, the Warnier-Orr methodology is not recommended. It is an inadequate methodology because it recognizes only hierarchical structures, it is not data-base-oriented, and it does not provide checks verifying the completeness and the correctness of a design.

REFERENCES

1. K. Orr, *Structured Systems Development,* New York: Yourdon Press, Inc., 1977, pp. 13–22.

2. Ibid., p. 14.

3. J. D. Warnier, preface in K. Orr, *Structured Systems Development.*

4. Orr, pp. 49–62.

5. D. Higgins, *Program Design and Construction,* Englewood Cliffs, NJ: Prentice-Hall, Inc., 1979, pp. 111–122.

6. Orr, p. 47.

7. Higgins, pp. 139–141.

8. Orr, p. 21.

9. Ibid., p. 59.

PART V MORE AUTOMATED TECHNIQUES

37 A HIGHER LEVEL OF AUTOMATION

Part IV of this book described the structured techniques that evolved in the 1970s. The predominant trend today is the achievement of a higher level of automation of the system creation process.

Automation is needed because it speeds up the creation of systems and can lower their cost, but there is also a more fundamental reason for automation. The human brain is limited in what it can achieve. It makes many errors when handling complex detail. It has difficulty, in most cases, handling mathematical or very precise techniques. Once techniques are automated, we can step up to more rigorous methods.

The analyst using modern tools creates his designs at a workstation in a computer-aided fashion. The workstation will help him to create and edit diagrams. The diagrams will have sufficient precision that they become a language themselves, and from this language executable code will be created. Much greater precision and verification are needed with the CASE tools than with the early structured techniques.

PROBLEMS WITH SPECIFICATIONS

One of the biggest problems in computing today is the creation of specifications for complex systems. Systems analysts create specifications that are full of errors, omissions, and inconsistencies. The methodologies of Yourdon and Constantine, De Marco, Jackson, and Warnier and Orr all attempt to improve the quality of specifications and make some improvement over the state of the art before structured techniques. Their methods, however, are not rigorous, and the specifications that result are still full of problems in most cases. New, computer-aided methods that have greater rigor and can automatically generate code are now coming into use.

The authors recently examined the situation in a large aerospace company relating to the specification of an exceedingly complex system. The original specifications were created with data flow diagrams and English-language descriptions. This took many person-years and resulted in many data flow diagrams layered to many levels. The specifications were redesigned using the HOS methodology described in Chapter 38. This redesign revealed a horrifying quantity of omissions, inconsistencies, and errors. A similar reexamination of most complex-project specifications has taken place with other tools that check consistency. The results have been similar.

Programmers cannot get away with the errors they make because their programs are run on a computer that brutally reveals the errors. Specification writers, however, using traditional methods, can get away with murder. Their specifications cannot be directly tested for accuracy with a computer. The errors, omissions, ambiguities, and inconsistencies are not clearly visible. CASE tools help to avoid this problem.

SPECIFICATION LANGUAGES
Various attempts were made in the 1970s to create computer languages for expressing specifications in order to impose discipline on what was a horrifyingly sloppy process. Most of the early specification languages still did not have the absolute precision of a programming language. To give a specification language that precision, it should be possible to generate executable code from it automatically. If a specification has this precision, we say that it is *computable*.

Specification languages that enforce computability in specifications greatly increase the degree of precision required from the analyst. It is desirable that the analyst use these languages on-line at a workstation so that the workstation helps and guides him and detects errors at the earliest possible moment. The technique should employ graphics as effectively as possible to help visualize and build the design. The graphics editor should not merely aid the building of diagrams but should also incorporate as much automated verification as possible.

Computable specification languages will become the basis of most pre-specified computing (as opposed to ad hoc uses of computers at a workbench screen). The users or analysts create a formal specification that can be steadily refined with spreadsheet tools and nonprocedural languages until code can be generated. Inconsistencies, ambiguities, and omissions that make the specifications noncomputable are flushed out. The analyst, like the programmer before him, is confronted with the ruthless discipline of the machine.

Specification languages that enforce computability in specifications are already in use. At the time of writing, most analysts do not employ them. Some analysts would prefer a more casual existence in which their work is not automatically checked.

COMPUTER-AIDED SPECIFICATION DESIGN

The word *language* might be misleading. The specification may be a drawing or succession of drawings, just as the specification for an engineering mechanism is a succession of drawings. The engineer's drawings are very precise and are drawn with formal rules. They are, in effect, a language with which specifications are stated.

Today's computers have powerful graphics capability. We can create and manipulate drawings on a screen. We do not need to create a work of art or a drawing with the elegance of, say, Victorian architects' drawings of cathedrals. We need clear diagrams of the logic of computer applications that can be refined and automatically checked for accuracy and consistency so that program code can be generated from them.

As users change their minds or the details of the requirements become better understood, the design can be adjusted and the programs regenerated. Ideally, the specification language should be sufficiently easy to understand that users can employ it or at least study the specifications and be involved in valuable discussions about them with the analysts.

A *report generator* is a form of specification language. With an easy-to-use tool, the user specifies the information he wants on the report. This specification is then fed into software that generates the required code. A report specification is very simple. We need to find computable means of specifying more interesting applications.

A good report generator makes extensive use of defaults. It makes its own assumptions about what format of report would be most valuable to the user. Similarly, with more complex specifications the software should make intelligent assumptions wherever it can in an attempt to minimize the work of the analyst and maximize the quality of the result. The analyst should be given a means to override the defaults where desirable.

A report generator is an almost trivial example of creating specifications; at the opposite extreme, CASE tools have been employed for creating specifications for military and aerospace systems of mind-boggling complexity. Here a computer language is needed with the capability to check the accuracy of the interfaces and use of data types. The design tool reveals ambiguities, inconsistencies, and omissions because it has to create computable specifications. The human mind simply cannot spot ambiguities, inconsistencies, and incompleteness in highly complex specifications. And a team of human minds is worse because they create pieces that do not mesh exactly.

The exercise of taking manually created specifications and converting them into a design in which a CASE tool checks for validity and consistency, revealing the sheer horror of the mess we make in manual design of complex systems.

TWO TYPES OF LANGUAGES

In the early days of the computer industry, computer languages were thought of only as programming languages. Initially they were close in syntax to the instruction set of the machine. Human language is very different from machine language, so attempts were made to humanize the programming languages by employing English words.

The standardization of languages like COBOL, FORTRAN, and ADA presented programmers with what in effect were virtual computers hiding the physical details of actual computers, which differed from machine to machine. The programming language, however, remained a statement of how to execute a set of operations in terms of computer resources.

Understanding the requirements of a complex system and writing specifications for it need a very different type of language. In the early days (and often still today), requirements and specifications were expressed in English. Human language, however, is ambiguous and imprecise. Specifications written in English were usually incomplete and almost always open to misinterpretation. The effort to make them more thorough led to documents more voluminous than Victorian novels and far more boring. It became clear that many of the problems with systems were not the programmers' fault but the fault of the specifiers.

Because of this, a variety of techniques grew up for designing and specifying systems. The most commonly used were the structured techniques of the chapters in Part IV. In addition, attempts were made to create specification languages. These languages had little or no resemblance to programming languages. They took a variety of forms. Sometimes a formal programming language was used, sometimes a diagramming technique. There were generalized languages intended to specify any type of program. There are also specialized languages, narrow in scope, most of which are not referred to as "specification" languages. These include report definition languages, data-base query and update languages, languages that could generate certain patterns of commercial DP application, and languages for special functions such as financial analysis, circuit design, and coordinate geometry.

Experience with specification languages indicates that the best form of computable specification is usually a set of diagrams in a CASE tool designed to build up knowledge of the design, in which the diagram is requested to fill in details.

COMPUTABLE SPECIFICATIONS

The computer industry thus acquired two breeds of languages, one for requirements analysis, problem description, and system specification, and one for programming.

It was generally considered desirable that the specification languages be independent of machine resources or programming because the specifications were a fundamental statement about requirements and these requirements could be met with a variety of types of hardware and software. Furthermore, the hardware and software would change while the requirements remained the same.

Programming languages had to be computable. This guaranteed rigor and sufficiency in these languages. Most of the *specification* languages and techniques that grew up were not rigorous and did not enforce logical consistency. They were not computable.

It was generally assumed that the output of the specification language was meant to be used by a programmer, who then coded the programs in a different language. This led to the problems associated with conventional programming. *We believe that this assumption is wrong* for the future of computing. The specification language should be processable so that program code can be *generated automatically,* as with today's report generators and application generators. This means that the specification language requires more rigor than the specification techniques of the 1970s. The specification should contain enough detail and be precise enough to be automatically converted into program code.

Although programming languages have the desirable property of computability, they are not suitable for stating system specifications because of their semantics. What is needed is a specification language that is computable with semantics appropriate for high-level conceptualization of systems. The property of computability will then permit resources to be allocated and programs created automatically (and hence without the errors programmers make).

AUTOMATION OF DESIGN

Many specification techniques were designed to be used by hand. It is only when computers are used that rigorous methods are practical. Humans make too many errors and find rigorous techniques too tedious to use rapidly and thoroughly by hand. Creating design techniques to be run with computerized tools enormously expands the scope of what is practical. Today the hardware for running computerized tools is inexpensive, so future techniques should be designed to employ computers.

Design will never be completely automated. Human inventiveness and creativity are its most important aspect. Humans will always want to argue at a blackboard and draw sketches on paper, so the technique should provide ways to make simple drawings of concepts.

Figure 37.1 shows the essentials of computerized system design. There should be a specification language that is rigorous but has an interactive, user-friendly dialogue. Most people think and design with pictures, so an interactive graphics facility is desirable. The design so created should be capable of being analyzed to check its accuracy and consistency. The design and its analysis should be based on formal rules and axioms. The analyzer should check that the mathematical rules have been obeyed so that the logic structure is guaranteed to be consistent.

Once it has been checked, the software should generate program code. Some tools generate code in conventional programming languages. This provides programs that are *portable* among different machines (insofar as the languages are portable). It is, however, more efficient to generate machine code

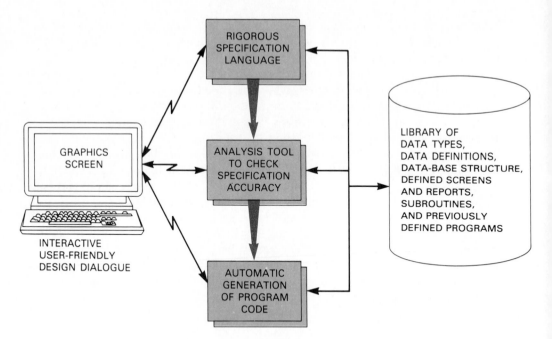

Figure 37.1 CASE tools should employ specification techniques which are user-friendly and rigorous, have tools for on-line accuracy checking, employ a library for the building of complex systems, and be capable of generating code automatically.

and avoid the additional step of compilation, which can degrade code efficiency.

To generate code automatically, a specification must be rigorous. A rigorous specification cannot be created in one shot. It requires much successive refinement. Each step in this refinement needs to be rigorous.

A specification process designed for automation is likely to produce a succession of formal representations of the system that can steadily be broken down into more detail. Different individuals are likely to be involved at different levels of detail. It helps if all use the same type of diagram.

At the highest level, a chart may have a few blocks that represent the broad requirements of the system. At the lowest level, charts have enough detail for automatic generation of program code. Separate portions of the design will be developed separately. The technique must be such that separately developed portions of the design can be linked together without interface problems. When changes are made, as they often are, at a low level in the design, these should be automatically reflected upwards so that the high-level representations of the system can be checked.

INTEGRATION OF DEFINITION LEVELS We commented that with many systems the requirements definition is written in one way, usually in English; the specification is created with a different technique; and the implementation is yet again different—a programming language. When the requirements are translated into the specification there are errors, and when the specification is translated into code there are errors. It is difficult and costly to keep the requirements current once the specification is begun or to reflect program changes in the specifications. When the programs are maintained, the documentation or higher-level systems descriptions are often not changed accordingly. They become out-of-date.

The specification is usually verified on a self-contained basis with only occasional ad hoc checks to the requirements documents. The programs are tested in a self-contained way with only occasional ad hoc checks to the specifications.

The evolution through the development phases is usually not formally traceable.

The solution to this is to have one set of diagrammatic techniques which are formally linked in a CASE tool, with which requirements, specifications, and details can be expressed. The requirements statements are decomposed into greater detail and become the specifications. The specifications are decomposed into greater detail until sufficient detail is reached that code can be generated automatically. When changes are made at a lower level, these are automatically reflected upwards. There is then structural integrity among the requirements, specifications, and detail. In fact, these words cease to have sharp demarcations. A high-level description is decomposed into successively more detailed descriptions.

The documentation does not slip out of date when successive maintenance changes are made because these changes require regeneration of program code from the specification language. The entire structure, top to bottom, reflects the change. Subsequent maintainers will then have a clear and detailed description from which to work.

A COMMON COMMUNICATION VEHICLE A major reason for problems with systems is inadequate communication between users and developers or between requirements definers and programmers. The most successful requirements-definition projects are those where the implementers and users work on and understand the requirements together. The implementers understand better what the users need. The users understand better the constraints of implementation. Each group can trigger creativity in the other, so that the combination produces something better than either group alone. A few exciting projects catch fire when there is excellent understanding between the instigators and implementers.

A good CASE tool should build a bridge of understanding between the users, requirements planners, specifiers, and implementers. Common diagram types should be usable by all of these. The high-level view of the users or requirements planners should be decomposable into the detail needed by the implementers. The high-level planners or specifiers should be able to choose the level of detail they want in specifying the system. Changes made at lower levels should reflect into this higher-level specification to preserve integrity of the levels.

A language that provides this communication bridge accelerates implementers' understanding of the user requirements and enables the user or planner to understand his requirements better. Particularly important, it reveals misunderstanding among the users, planners, and implementers.

A developer may be better able to evaluate cost trade-off possibilities if he and the users employ a common way of looking at system specifications. This may save much money. Early feedback from the developer to the users is always beneficial.

INTEGRATED TOP-DOWN AND BOTTOM-UP DESIGN

The development methodology should facilitate both top-down and bottom-up design and should integrate them. There is a perennial argument about which is best. In practice, almost all complex systems design uses both. Pure top-down design is impractical. Pure bottom-up design would be a mess. Bottom-up design leads to interface problems if uncontrolled. In writing a book, we use a mixture of top-down and bottom-up design. We have to start with a table of contents. But writing the details always causes us to change the table of contents. It is the same in systems design, and a tool is needed that allows the changes and inventions that occur when modules are being worked out in detail to be reflected naturally into the higher-level specifications.

A change made in one lower-level module may affect others, and it is desirable that this ripple effect be immediately traceable. The designer needs to be able to add requirements from the top or the bottom. Detailed work at a lower level frequently causes data-type references to be changed at a higher level. This continual adjustment can occur easily and should be largely automatic.

Often detailed design is done on one part of a system before another. The design tool should permit this to occur naturally and not cause later interface problems. On some systems, one component is developed to completion while specifiers are still debating the concepts of another. Detailed design in one area should not be held up in waiting for complete top-down specification of the layers above (it is normal to write one or more chapters of a book before the table of contents is complete). The top level is not *really* complete until the lower levels are done and the necessary iterations have taken place.

MATHEMATICALLY RIGOROUS LANGUAGES

To achieve the rigor that is necessary, some CASE tools will be mathematically based. With USE.IT, described in the following chapter, everything specified relates to data types, functions, and control structures that are based on mathematical axioms. This permits the building of constructs that are provably correct. As separate modules are interlinked, this is done with provably correct interfaces.

Everything in the system is built from mathematically based primitives. The primitives are interlinked in provably correct fashions. Everything that uses them and obeys the rules is then provably consistent. The mathematically based interfacing rules distinguish this library concept from a conventional subroutine or program library. Increasingly large constructs can be built from what is in the library and then stored in the library with the knowledge that they are correct. As the library builds up, the developers will have less work to do, and there will also be less to verify because it is known that everything in the library is bug-free.

The mathematical rules would be far too tedious and difficult to enforce by hand, so such a method depends on having a fully automated tool.

USER FRIENDLINESS

Particularly important is the user friendliness of the specification language. It may use mathematical techniques to enforce correct logic and interfaces between modules, but the complexity should be completely hidden. The telephone system is exceedingly complex and designed with mathematics, but most of its users know nothing about Erlang equations.

It is likely that different dialects of a specification technique will be needed, as well as different forms of representation. These should be built from the same fundamental set of primitives. If separate systems are defined from the same primitives, technical arguments can be resolved by breaking them down to the primitives to see whether there is real disagreement. With most requirements documents and specifications, there is no means of analyzing them into common primitives.

Once the underlying structure of primitives exists, higher-level constructs should make the specification technique as powerful as possible and as user-friendly as possible.

PROPERTIES NEEDED

Box 37.1 lists the porperties desirable in a specification. Box 37.2 lists the properties desirable in a specification technique.

BOX 37.1 Desirable properties of a specification

A proper specification should:

- Be free from errors.
- Have conceptual clarity.
- Be easy to understand by managers, analysts, and programmers.
- Be presentable in varying degrees of detail.
- Be easy to create.
- Be computable (i.e., have enough precision that program code can be generated automatically).
- Be formal input to a program code generator.
- Be easy to change.
- Be complete.
- Be traceable when changes are introduced.
- Be independent of hardware.
- Employ a data dictionary.
- Employ a data model based on formal data analysis.
- Employ a program module library with automatic verification of interface correctness.
- Employ computerized tools that make it easy to manipulate and change.

SPECTRUM OF SPECIFICATION LANGUAGES

The properties of being user-friendly and being rigorous often seem in conflict. Rigorous languages are not user-friendly; user-friendly languages are generally not rigorous. We could rank specification techniques on a scale with rigorous methods on the right or nonrigorous methods on the left. (See Fig. 37.2)

Traditional English specifications are at the extreme left. They may be (fairly) readable but are entirely nonrigorous. Sometimes software is employed for formatting, editing, and storing specifications. This makes them easier to access, change, and manipulate but does not make them more rigorous. Some text specification formatters have additional capabilities. They detect keywords and format-specification phrases and generate tables of contents and indexes.

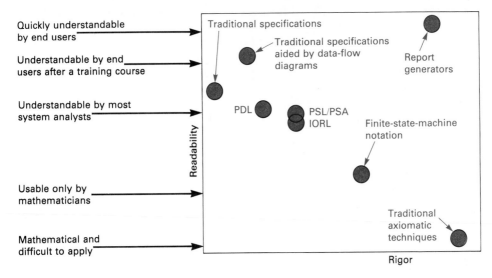

Figure 37.2 Spectrum of specification languages.

The program design language PDL is an example [1]. This improves the specification readability with clauses such as

IF CUSTOMER_CREDIT_CODE < 3
THEN ORDER IS REJECTED

It helps designers to find and cross-reference items in the specifications. It does no consistency or ambiguity checking, so there is little increase in rigor.

Another text approach advocates the use of a limited, well-defined, fairly nonambiguous subset of English [2]. This lessens the scope for misinterpretations and gives slightly more precision to the specifications. Software tools can help search for ambiguities and inconsistencies in such specifications [3].

Clear diagramming techniques in general help analysts to conceptualize systems and clarify complex flows and interrelationships. Diagrams that are too symbolic, however, are not necessarily understood by end users. Most analysts find their diagramming techniques very useful and assume that users find them useful too. In practice, many users are bewildered by the diagrams, thinking that they are more technical than they really are. Users sometimes complain that they understand the written specifications but not the diagrams.

Data flow diagrams represent a step toward formality, and most end users can be taught to read them without difficulty. They are an improvement over unstructured text but are still far from rigorous. They do not possess the desired property that program code be generated from them automatically. Much more detail is needed. Much more is needed to enforce consistency and completeness.

PSL (Problem Statement Language), with its associated PSA (Problem

BOX 37.2   Desirable properties of a specification tool

- It should provide a way to think about systems that improves conceptual clarity.

- It should be easy to learn and use. At its higher levels, it should be usable by non-DP personnel.

- It should be computable, and program code should be generatable from it automatically.

- It should be designed for maximum automation of systems analysis, design, and programming.

- It should be rigorous so that its designs are correct and consistent.

- The axioms or techniques used to enforce rigor should be hidden from the average user.

- It should be versatile enough to remove the need for manual use of programming languages.

- It should extend from the highest-level conceptualization of systems down to the creation of enough detail for program generation. In other words, one tool should suffice for complete system creation. The more detailed versions of a specification should be a natural extension of the more general ones. The high-level specifier should be able to decide into how much detail he wants to go before handing over to the implementer.

- It should be a common communication medium among managers, designers, implementers, verifiers, maintainers, and documenters.

- It should use graphic techniques that are easy to draw and remember.

- It should employ a user-friendly computerized graphics tool for building, changing, and inspecting the design. The graphics should be formal input to automated design.

- It should employ testing tools that assist in verification and permit simulation of missing modules so that partially complete designs can be tested.

- It should employ an integrated top-down or bottom-up design approach. Most complex systems come into existence through a combination of top-down and bottom-up design. The technique should allow certain elements of a system to be specified in detail while others, possibly parents or ancestors in the hierarchy, are not yet defined.

- It should indicate when a specification is complete (so that code can be generated from it).

BOX 37.2 *(Continued)*

- It should employ a hierarchy that descends into steadily increasing levels of detail. It should guarantee that each decomposition is logically valid and each lower level completely replaces the one above it.

- When modifications are made lower in the hierarchy, these should be quickly and perhaps automatically reflectable in the higher levels.

- It should employ an evolving library of subroutines, programs, and all the constructs the language employs. The primitive constructs will be in the library, so everything added to the library will be defined in terms of what is already there. The library becomes, in effect, an extendable requirement-definition language. Everything in such a library employs the common primitives and has been verified by the software.

- It should link automatically to data-base tools, including a dictionary and a directory that stores conceptual data-base models.

- It should guarantee interface consistency when subroutines or callable programs are used or when separate systems intercommunicate. Formal techniques should guarantee logical interface consistency as well as data consistency.

- The specification should be easy to change. It should be able to accommodate the unexpected. It should be easily changeable by persons who did not create it.

- All elements of a system should be traceable. All accesses and changes to data should be traceable throughout the system. This process should ensure that the inputs to each operation could come only from the correct source.

- The language may permit several dialects or several types of nonprocedural representation. These should all translate to a common set of control structures and a common set of rules for verifying correctness.

- A common set of primitives may be used to which the proofs of correctness apply. All nonprimitive structures and semantics should then translate to the primitives.

- Default options may be used where they simplify specification (e.g., with the formatting of screens or reports).

- The language should be independent of hardware or other resources that are likely to change. It should be translatable into different resource environments.

Statement Analyzer), is one of the best-known specification languages [4]. It divides system functions into subfunctions, precisely specifying the inputs and outputs of each. The analyzers perform consistency checking between functions. For example, no function is allowed to use a data item not generated by another function. PSL is further to the right on our scale, but it is still far from completely rigorous or capable of automatic program generation. Another language for functional decomposition and input/output specification is IORL (Input/Output Requirements Language) [5]. Although these do some useful specification checking, they cannot check detailed logic or specify the order and timing constraints needed in real-time systems.

A more rigorous approach is the use of *finite-state machine notation*. This permits complex logic to be described in terms of entities that have discrete *states*. The analyst determines what types of stimulus cause a state to change. The state of an entity is a function of the previous state and the inputs received. The output is a function of the inputs and the state when those inputs are received. State diagrams are drawn to represent the possible states and the stimuli that change them. Associated with the diagrams is a table showing all possible states and stimuli to make sure that all combinations have been thought about.

Finite-state machine notation has been used extensively in defining complex protocols for computer networks [6] and communications switching systems. The CCITT standards committee for international telephony and networking has a language for protocol specification based on this approach, SDL (Specification and Description Language) [7]. Other, more generalized specification languages use this approach, for example, RSL (Requirements Statements Language) [8].

Finite-state machine notation is further to the right. It is a major step in the direction of rigorous logic specification but not sufficiently so for automatic program generation. Some manufacturers' network software designed with finite-state machine notation has exhibited mysterious and infuriating misbehavior. Finite-state machine notation is extremely difficult for most end users to understand. It is not normally used in general data processing or in most scientific computing, and in general it has a limited class of applications. It is possible to build software that translates finite-state machine representation into English-like constructs to aid in user checking [9].

Computable specification languages are found in narrowly focused areas. Probably the most commonly used example is report generators. Broadening the scope somewhat, we have nonprocedural languages for querying, updating, and sometimes manipulating data bases. These are linked to graphics languages and decision-support aids. Very different types of specification or problem-statement languages exist for certain specific applications, for example, coordinate geometry, CAD/CAM, architects' drawings, and the building of telephone switching systems [10].

The CASE tools provide completely general specification tools which are easy to use and yet which do much to enforce rigor in the design. To build software without this computer-enforced rigor will one day seem like building a bridge without stressing calculations.

A major challenge of the computer industry today, then, is to create with graphics tools, specification techniques that are rigorous, powerful, and user-friendly and that automatically generate program code.

REFERENCES

1. S. H. Caine and E. K. Gordon, "PDL: A Tool for Software Design," *AFIPS Conference Proceedings,* 44 (1975).

2. B. E. Casey and B. J. Taylor, "Writing Requirements in English: A Natural Alternative," IEEE Workshop on Software Engineering Standards, San Francisco, August 1981.

3. R. Balzer et al., "Informality in Program Specifications," *IEEE Transactions on Software Engineering,* SE-4(2), 1978.

4. D. Teichroew and E. A. Hershey III, "PSL/PSA: A Computer-Aided Technique for Structured Documentation and Analysis of Information Processing Systems," *IEEE Transactions on Software Engineering,* SE-3(1), 1977.

5. C. R. Everhart, "A Unified Approach to Software System Engineering," *Proc. Compsac 80,* IEEE Computer Society, Los Alamitos, CA, October 1980.

6. J. Martin, *Architectures for Distributed Processing* (Savant Technical Report No. 6), Carnforth, Lancs., England: Savant Institute, 1979.

7. CCITT, "SDL User Guidelines" (Study Group X1, Working Paper 3–1, 3–4).

8. M. W. Alford, "A Requirements Engineering Methodology for Real-Time Processing Requirements," *IEEE Transactions of Software Engineering,* SE-3(1), 1977.

9. A. M. Davies, "Automating the Requirements Phase: Benefits to Later Phases of the Software Life Cycle," *Proc. Compsac 80,* IEEE Computer Society, Los Alamitos, CA, October 1980.

10. The COSS-RL language designed for the definition of central-office switching systems at GTE Laboratories, Waltham, MA.

38 HOS METHODOLOGY

INTRODUCTION

In Chapter 26 we discussed the HOS technique for species III functional decomposition. This chapter extends Chapter 26 to discuss the software and methodology of HOS.

HOS (higher-order software) methodology is the basis of a CASE tool for creating computable software specifications based on a set of mathematical axioms. The axioms, or rules, if obeyed completely, *guarantee that the resulting design is logically complete and consistent* [1]. Executable program code is generated from the design automatically. The technique thus creates bug-free programs. It can create executable programs from complex specifications. It has been used, for example, to create software for missile systems, cryptography, packet switching, and on-line banking systems.

USE.IT

Verification with the HOS axioms would be far too tedious for most analysts to carry out by hand. Its general usability depends on automation with user-friendly software. Software called USE.IT automates the application of the HOS methodology. USE.IT is an integrated family of automated software tools that provide the following:

1. A language for expressing functions and their decomposition into other functions

2. An interactive screen facility for constructing and manipulating the control maps and allowing the user to correct errors interactively

3. A library of data types, primitive functions, and previously defined modules

4. An analyzer routine for automatically checking that all the rules that give provably correct logic have been followed

5. A generator that automatically generates program code.

USE.IT may be regarded as a system specification tool which, unlike other such tools, precisely checks the logic of the specification. It is much more than this because it automatically generates the required code.

It may be regarded as an application generator. Most generators can generate reports, data-entry software, or data-base operations but cannot create *any* type of software. They can usually generate only a specified class of applications. The HOS system can generate *any* application and is particularly useful with highly complex logic.

The HOS software that generates code is separate from the software that allows the logic of the application to be specified and built. The logic of the application remains independent of machines and of programming languages. It can operate on any computer in any language for which a generator module exists. A program written in FORTRAN or PASCAL could thus be recompiled in COBOL or ADA.

USE.IT consists of three major components, AXES, ANALYZER, and RAT, shown in Fig. 38.1.

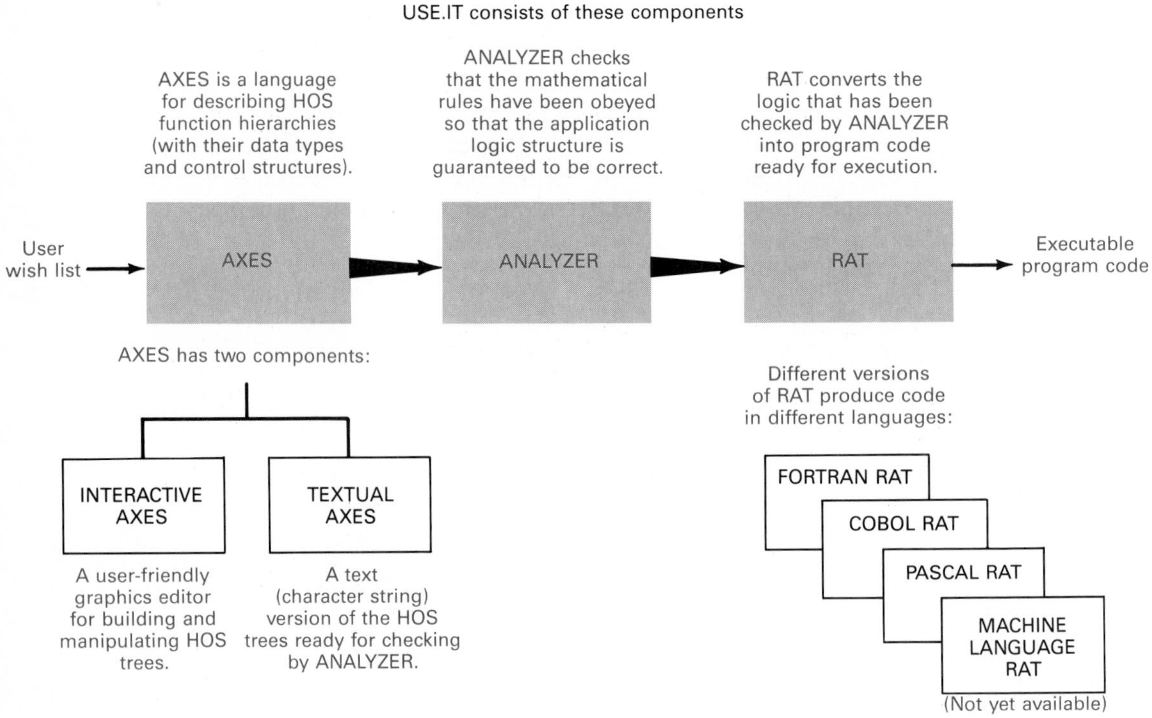

USE.IT consists of these components

AXES is a language for describing HOS function hierarchies (with their data types and control structures).

ANALYZER checks that the mathematical rules have been obeyed so that the application logic structure is guaranteed to be correct.

RAT converts the logic that has been checked by ANALYZER into program code ready for execution.

User wish list → AXES → ANALYZER → RAT → Executable program code

AXES has two components:

INTERACTIVE AXES

TEXTUAL AXES

A user-friendly graphics editor for building and manipulating HOS trees.

A text (character string) version of the HOS trees ready for checking by ANALYZER.

Different versions of RAT produce code in different languages:

FORTRAN RAT

COBOL RAT

PASCAL RAT

MACHINE LANGUAGE RAT

(Not yet available)

Figure 38.1   The components of USE.IT, the software for implementing the HOS methodology.

JOIN, INCLUDE, AND OR   Chapter 26 described the use of the three basic HOS control structures, JOIN, INCLUDE, and OR. HOS's mathematical rules apply to these three structures. Complex structures built with these three primitives can be axiomatically verified.

Figure 38.2 represents the primitive functions in the form of a dynamics graph [2]. This representation makes it clear that JOIN represents a sequence of operations, INCLUDE breaks a function into separate *independent* activities, and OR represents *alternate* operations.

The dynamics graph is a projection of the tree representation and is a useful translation for certain purposes. It may aid an implementer in understanding the timing and storage relationship trade-off from a different viewpoint. A dynamics graph could be annotated with timing information in the physical design.

However, the dynamics graph tends to hide the hierarchical relationships (as do data-flow diagrams). The HOS control maps could be automatically translated into dynamics graphs.

The INCLUDE function could be implemented with two separate processors. A system with multiple INCLUDEs could run on a multiprocessing computer configuration.

With the JOIN, in Fig. 38.2, f_2 cannot complete its processing before f_1 has been processed. The storage for z does not need to be allocated until f_1 has generated its value. The storage for y need not be allocated until its value is generated by f_2. When f_2 has completed its references to z, the storage for z may be released. The storage for f_1's instruction may be released when z is generated. If z is a single object, f_1 must be sequentially processed before f_2. However, if z has a structure $z_1, z_2, \ldots z_n$, the execution of f_2 may begin before f_1 has finished.

Similar implementation considerations apply to the other functions. This affects the techniques used for generating program code from the HOS tree.

GENERATION OF CODE   By breaking functions down with binary decomposition with the JOIN, INCLUDE, and OR constructs, control structures that can be proved correct mathematically can be achieved [3].

The functional decomposition continues until leaf nodes of the binary tree are reached. Leaf nodes are *primitives* that are known to be correct or *subroutines* that have themselves been created with this method. When all parts of the tree reach such leaf nodes, the design is complete. *Program code can then be generated automatically from the resulting structures.*

At each step in the design, its correctness can be automatically checked.

AXES is the language for describing the functions, data types, and control

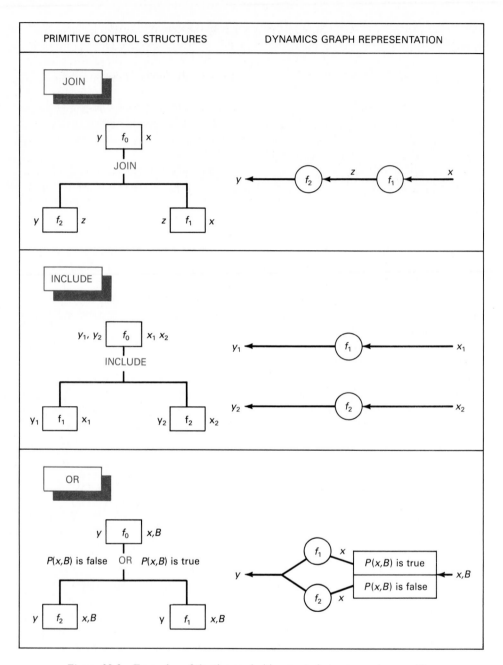

Figure 38.2 Examples of the three primitive control structures shown with a dynamics graph representation. With a JOIN the functions are executed sequentially. With an INCLUDE both are executed independently. With an OR one or other function is executed.

structures. Unlike a programming language, it can express a broad statement of requirements, such as

STOOL = MAKE-STOOL(TOP,LEGS,LATHE,HANDTOOLS)

This statement of requirements is successively decomposed until primitives or predefined modules from which program code can be generated are reached. The target system objects provide a foundation for the user's statement of the problem and need not necessarily be computer-oriented.

There are two major components of AXES: a powerful graphics editor, which allows the HOS trees to be built and manipulated on a graphics screen in a user-friendly fashion, and a textual version of the same information, which makes the control maps ready for checking by ANALYZER.

ANALYZER checks that the mathematical rules have been obeyed. It checks for syntactical errors first, then checks that the data-type transfers are correct and that there are no omissions or inconsistencies in the data types or function descriptions.

RAT (Resource Allocation Tool) uses the output of ANALYZER and automatically generates executable program code. There are several versions of RAT to generate programs in different languages: a FORTRAN RAT, a PASCAL RAT, a COBOL RAT, and so on. A machine-language RAT would avoid the need for a subsequent compilation step.

The term RAT can be used as a verb: We talk about the AXES control charts being ''ratted'' into different languages.

(The term was invented and is much used by the creators of HOS, Margaret Hamilton and Saydean Zeldin, two charming women who would probably stand on a chair if they saw a mouse.)

FOUR TYPES OF LEAF NODES

The tree structures have *functions* as their nodes. (A function is also called an *operation*.) Every function is decomposed into lower-level functions showing more detail, except those that are leaf nodes of the tree.

There are four types of leaf nodes:

1. *Primitive operation* (P). This is an operation that cannot be decomposed into other operations. It is defined rigorously with mathematical axioms.

2. *Operation defined elsewhere* (OP). This function will be further decomposed in another control map, which may be part of the current design or may be in a library.

3. *Recursive operation* (R). This is a special node that allows looping.

4. *External operation* (XO). This function is an external program that is not written with HOS methodology. It may be manufacturer's software or previously existing user programs. The HOS software cannot guarantee its correctness.

If there is no non-HOS software (external operations), every operation is ultimately broken down into *primitive operations* that are described mathematically.

The repetitive use of predefined functions is essential. Without this, the binary structures would have too many nodes to be practical for human design. Complex programs require the building of libraries of functions and defined operations (e.g., subroutines). These include completely general functions such as user-specifiable loop control structures, mathematical operations, elaborate application-independent functions such as data-base operations and report generators, and operations that are specific to given applications (e.g., a backorder subroutine).

CO-CONTROL STRUCTURES

To build complex logic with the JOIN, INCLUDE, and OR control structures would be tedious. HOS provides the user with other control structures that are themselves built out of the JOIN, INCLUDE, and OR and can therefore be automatically verified for correct use.

HOS provides four commonly used nonprimitive HOS structures:

COJOIN

COINCLUDE

COOR

CONCUR

These provide more flexibility in dividing the parent variables among the offspring functions. In addition to these, the user can design his own control structures rather like macroinstructions or can use already existing designed structures from a library.

Suppose, for example, that the input to the MAKE-PARTS function discussed in Chapter 26 includes the tools needed:

TOP,LEGS = MAKE-PARTS (TOPWOOD, LEGWOOD,
LATHE, HANDSAW, HANDTOOLS)

We cannot split these inputs into separate discrete lists, one for MAKE-TOP and one for MAKE-LEGS. To solve this problem a function similar to the INCLUDE function is used, but with more flexibility in handling repeatedly used values. It is called COINCLUDE.

Like INCLUDE, COINCLUDE allows two offspring functions to be combined into one parent function. MAKE-TOP and MAKE-LEGS, for example, can be combined into MAKE-STOOL. The inputs to the offspring functions are taken freely from the inputs to the parent functions. The outputs from the offspring functions (but not necessarily all of them) are combined into the outputs of the parent function.

The decomposition of MAKE-PARTS may, for example, be as follows:

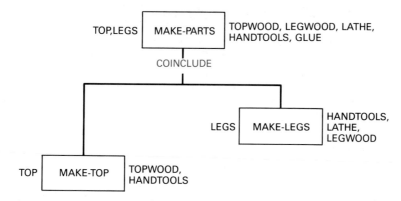

Here there is more freedom than with an INCLUDE structure in *ordering, selecting, omitting,* and *repeating* variables.

The parent's input variables are *reordered* in the input to the right offspring. With the three primitive structures, the ordering of variables is important.

Only certain parent inputs and offspring outputs are *selected* for use. GLUE is *omitted* as an offspring input. HANDTOOLS is *repeated* as an input to both offspring.

As with the primitive control structures, exact rules govern the use of variables in the co-control structures. These structures and their rules are summarized in Fig. 38.3.

To illustrate the co-control structures we will draw dynamics graph projections of them (as we did with the primitive structures in Chapter 37). Like data-flow diagrams, these show functions as circles and the transfer of data types as lines. We draw the flow going from right to left because this is how an HOS chart is read.

COJOIN

The following are examples of uses of the COJOIN structure:

1.

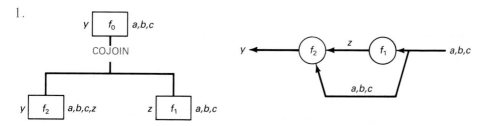

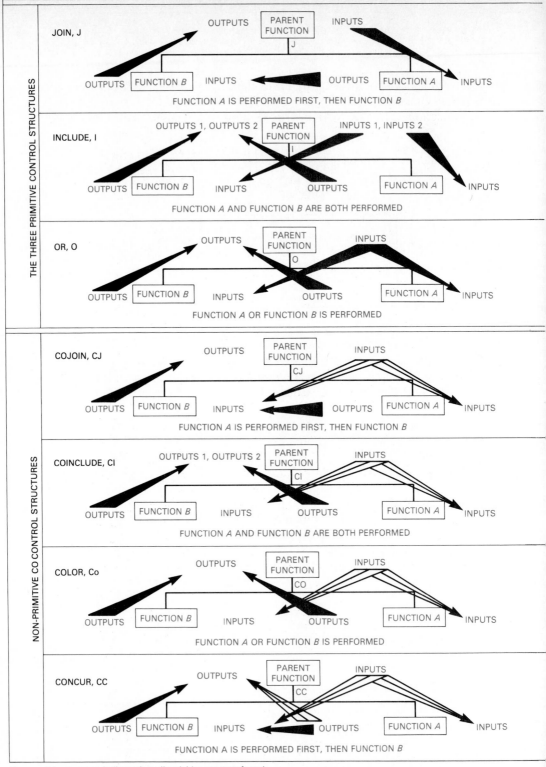

The nonstriped arrows indicate that *all* variables are transferred.
The striped arrows indicate that *some but not necessarily all* variables are transferred.

Figure 38.3 The HOS control structures and movement of variables.

INPUTS TO RIGHT OFFSPRING are identical to inputs to parent (including order).
INPUTS TO LEFT OFFSPRING are identical to outputs from right offspring (including order).
OUTPUTS FROM PARENT are identical to outputs from left offspring (including order).

INPUTS TO LEFT OFFSPRING are identical to first inputs to parent (including order).
INPUTS TO RIGHT OFFSPRING are identical to remaining inputs to parent (including order).
  • Inputs of offspring are exclusive of each other and include *all* the parent's inputs.
FIRST OUTPUTS FROM PARENT are identical to outputs from left offspring (including order).
REMAINING OUTPUTS FROM PARENT are identical to outputs from right offspring (including order).
  • Outputs of offspring are exclusive of each other and include *all* parent's outputs.

INPUTS TO ALL FUNCTIONS are identical (including order).
  All inputs are used in a Partition function P which chooses which offspring to execute.
OUTPUTS FROM ALL FUNCTIONS are identical (including order).

INPUTS TO RIGHT OFFSPRING are a subset of the parent's inputs.
INPUTS TO LEFT OFFSPRING come from either the parent's inputs or the
  outputs of the right offspring.
OUTPUTS FROM PARENT are identical to the outputs from the left offspring.

INPUTS TO RIGHT AND LEFT OFFSPRINGS come from the parent's inputs.
ALL OUTPUTS FROM PARENT come from *either* the outputs of the left offspring
  or the right offspring.
  The first outputs of the parent are identical to those of the left offspring.
  The last outputs of the parent are identical to those of the right offspring.

INPUTS TO BOTH OFFSPRINGS are a subset of the inputs to the parent.
  A partition function P uses some input from the parent to determine which offspring function is used.
OUTPUTS FROM ALL FUNCTIONS are identical.

INPUTS TO RIGHT OFFSPRING are a subset of the inputs to the parent.
INPUTS TO LEFT OFFSPRING come from the outputs of the right offspring and
  from the inputs to the parent; none must necessarily come from the parent.
OUTPUTS FROM THE PARENT come from the outputs of the left and right offspring. Each offspring contributes
  at least one output of the parent.

Figure 38.3   (Continued)

Unlike a primitive JOIN, here the left offspring uses the inputs to the parents.

2.

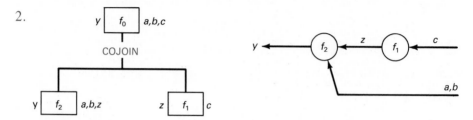

Here the input variables to the parent are split into separate inputs to the two offspring.

3.

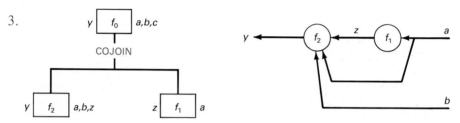

Here c, an input to the parent, is not used by either offspring. The offspring share a, but only the left offspring uses b.

COINCLUDE

The following are examples of uses of the COINCLUDE structure:

1.

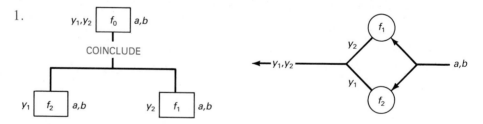

Unlike a primitive INCLUDE, the offspring here share the variables from the parent.

2.

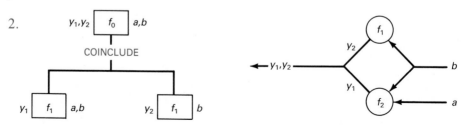

Here both offspring use b but only the left offspring uses a.

3.

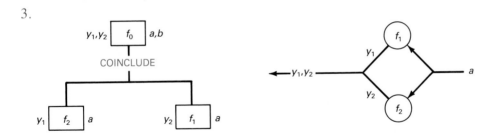

Here one of the inputs to the parent, b, is ignored. Both offspring use the other input, a.

4.

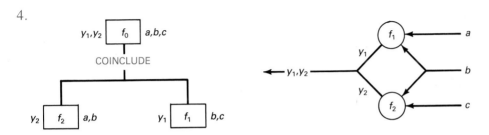

Here different offspring use different parent inputs, and the first output of the parent is from the right, not left, offspring.

COOR

The following are examples of uses of the COOR structure. In each of them a condition, $P(B)$, is tested. One or other of the offspring is used, depending on whether the condition is true or false.

1.

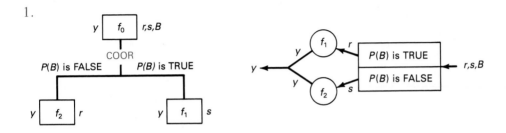

Unlike a primitive OR structure, here the two offspring use different variables from the parent's input.

2.

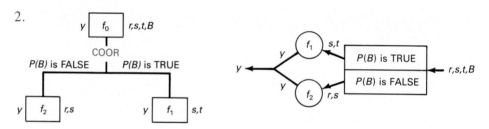

The offspring may share some of the parent's variables and not others.

3.

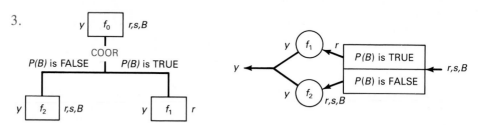

Here one of the offspring employs the Boolean itself.

CONCUR

The following are illustrations of uses of the CONCUR structure:

1.

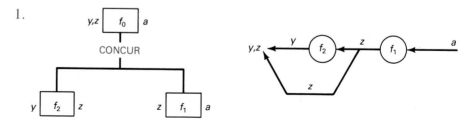

Unlike a JOIN or COJOIN, here the output of the right offspring appears in the output of the parent.

2.

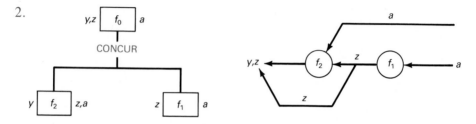

Here the input to the parent is used as input to the left offspring, along with z.

3.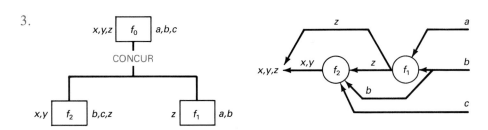

Here the parent inputs are split between the two offspring, with *b* being shared by them.

4.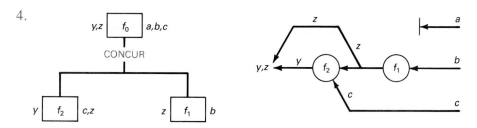

Here one of the inputs to the parent is not used.

   Figure 38.4 shows the four co-control structures applied to the acquisition of stools.

LOCAL VARIABLES   Programs often employ local variables that are not part of their input or output. They are generated and used internally in the program.

   The same is true with HOS control maps. A JOIN or COJOIN produces and uses a local variable. In the following structure, *Z* is a local variable.

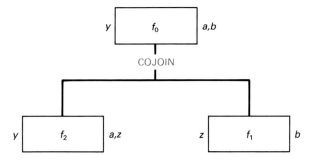

   Local variables are the only ones that are not part of the input or output of the top node of the control structure.

N-WAY BRANCHES   So far we have drawn binary trees. HOS also permits one parent node to have more than two offspring. In this case, the offspring are dealt with a pair at a time from right to left.

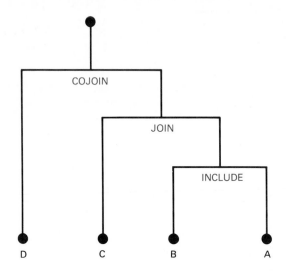

In the diagram, an INCLUDE operation is performed between A and B. The results of that are then used in a JOIN operation with C. The results of that are then used in a COJOIN operation with D.

An *N*-way branch in the tree is thus a shorthand way of drawing multiple binary branches.

INTERACTIVE   The key to making the HOS method easy to use is an
GRAPHICS EDITOR interactive graphics editor. The HOS tree structures can be displayed on a screen, manipulated, and checked in a quick and easy manner.

The designer can work in a top-down fashion, decomposing high-level functions, or in a bottom-up fashion, combining low-level functions. At each stage, the design is checked for correctness. The designer can add comments to any node. Rather like a film editor, he can cut out subtrees and save them, hanging them on a ''hook'' for future use.

A designer working at a low-level node may discover the need for a data type that is not included in the nodes at the top of the tree. He can add this data type and quickly include it in the higher-level nodes.

The graphics editor displays three types of images. These are shown in Figs. 38.5, 38.6, and 38.7.

Figure 38.5 shows the editor in *display-tree mode*. An overview of an HOS tree is shown, giving only the names of the nodes. If the entire tree is too

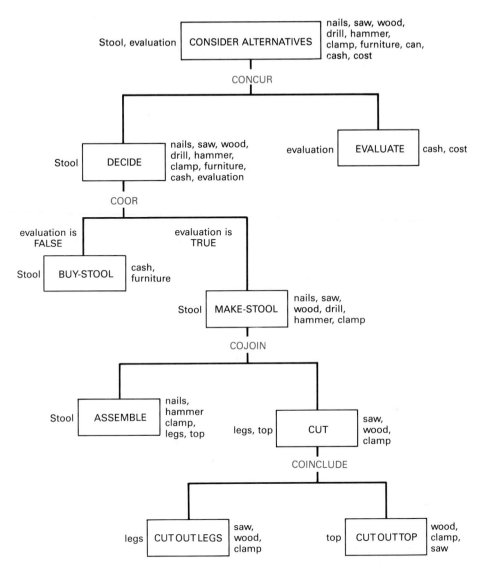

Figure 38.4   The four co-control structures used together to describe the construction of a stool.

big to show on one screen, the user can in effect move the screen "window" around the tree.

With a cursor positioned at some point in the tree, the user may switch to *edit mode*. He then sees details of up to six nodes, as shown in Fig. 38.6. He can move the cursor to any part of this diagram and can make changes to func-

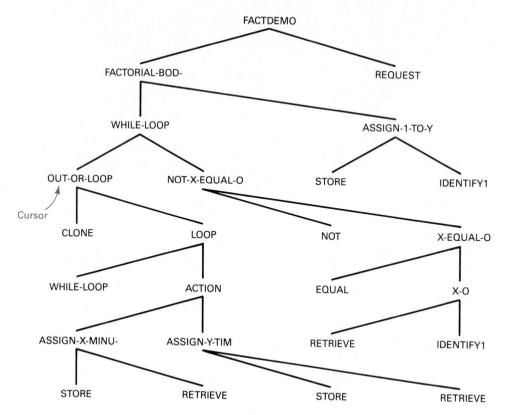

Figure 38.5 The graphics editor in display-tree mode. With the cursor in the position shown, the user may transfer to edit mode and receive the screen shown in Fig. 38.6.

tions, data types, or control structures. If he moves the cursor off the screen, the node to which he moves it becomes the center node.

To see more details of a node, the user can move to *display-documentation mode*. He then obtains a screen like Fig. 38.7 with only one node but with documentation and error details. The other modes also give abbreviated error messages.

In *insert-documentation mode,* the user can enter comments into a screen like Fig. 38.7.

The input and output data are shown at the right and left, respectively, of the boxes in Figs. 38.6 and 38.7. Sometimes a node has too many data types to display. Three dots, as shown in Fig. 38.6, indicate this, and the user can scroll up and down a list of data.

Underneath each box on the screens are details about control structures. The letters J, I, O, CJ, CI, CO, and CC under a box mean JOIN, INCLUDE, OR, COJOIN, COINCLUDE, COOR, and CONCUR, respectively. DS means

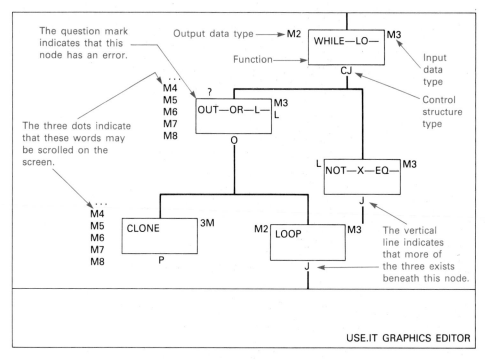

Figure 38.6   The graphics editor in edit mode.

DEFINED STRUCTURE. A function that was decomposed as a defined structure would have the name of the defined structure under the box, for example,
DO WHILE LOOP.

If the box is a leaf node and requires no more functional decomposition,
one of the following appears under the box:

P   Primitive operation

OP   Operation defined elsewhere

XO   External operation

R   Recursion

Figure 38.8 shows a design for a digital clock [4]. On the screen shown is
one primitive operation, CLONE 1, which simply makes an extra copy of its
input variable. There is one OP node. The cursor is placed at the CC indicator
under the TICK function. By pressing the ↓ key, the user can display details
of the CC structure, as shown in Fig. 38.9.

The graphics editor is easy to use. Its syntax is simple but powerful. Most
commands are entered by only one keystroke. A systems analyst can build a

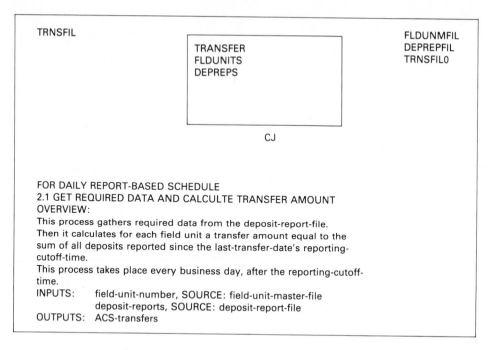

Figure 38.7   The graphics editor in display-documentation mode.

complete function tree quickly if he understands the application well enough, and he can check it for consistency and completeness. He has available to him a library of data types, primitives, previously defined operations, and previously defined control structures.

Pressing the ↑, →, ↓, or ← key moves the cursor from box to box or to boxes that are off the screen. Pressing the space bar moves the cursor around the lettering of a box in a clockwise fashion: first the output, then the function, then the input, then the structure description under the box. The designer may change or insert lettering.

Pressing the ! key deletes a node and all its progeny from the tree. Pressing the * key moves a node to the center of the screen.

Pressing the & key followed by a digit N removes a node and its progeny and stores it in storage location N. The user might think of this as being like hanging this subtree on hook N, as a film editor might, for future use. Pressing the $ key followed by a digit N reattaches the subtree at the cursor position.

To convert the tree structure to text, the nodes must be listed in a given sequence. Top-to-bottom, right-to-left sequencing is used as shown in Fig. 38.10. After each node in the text, the indicator beneath the node in the graphics version is enclosed in square brackets. For a leaf node this indicates the type of

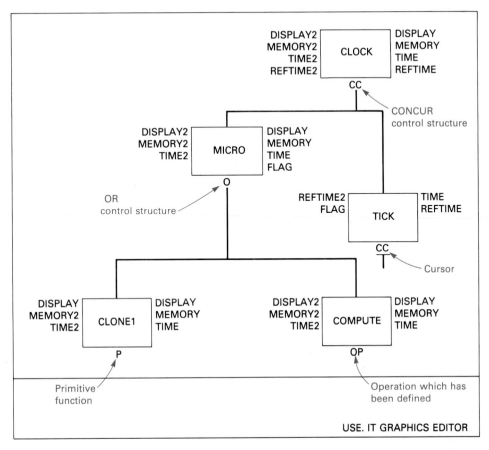

Figure 38.8 A graphics representation of the design of a digital clock. The cursor is on the control structure under TICK. By pressing the ↓ key, the user obtains the chart of TICK shown in Fig. 38.9.

leaf, for example, [P]. For a nonleaf node the square bracket shows the control structure with which it is decomposed, for example, [CI].

SIMULATION

It is sometimes desirable to run the code that has been generated and examine its operation before a system is completely implemented. There may be unimplemented data types and associated unimplemented primitive operations.

When ANALYZER is used in such a case, it will prompt the user for the names of the unimplemented data types:

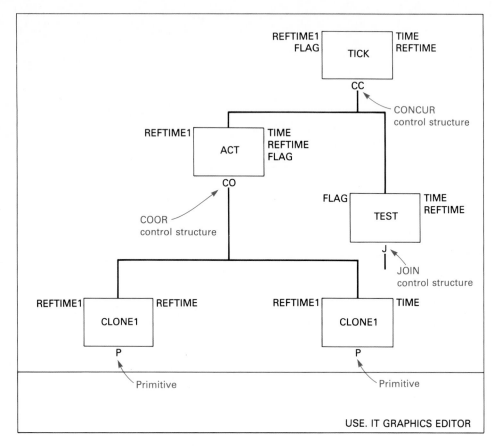

Figure 38.9   An expansion of the control structure for TICK in the design of
the digital clock shown in Fig. 38.8.

ANALYZER types:	ENTER THE NAMES OF UNIMPLE-
	MENTED DATA TYPES
Using person types:	RUNNER

Following this, the RAT may generate program code and insert *prompts*
into each node that references a primitive operation with an unimplemented data
type. When the system is executed, it will operate normally until it reaches one
of these nodes.

Consider a system that will calculate a runner's pace per mile. The AXES
chart is as follows:

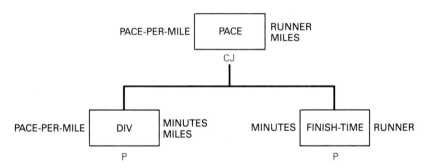

Suppose that in this specification RUNNER is an unimplemented data type associated with an unimplemented primitive operation, FINISH-TIME. FINISH-TIME needs to do a data access to find the value of MINUTES for each value of RUNNER. We can test the incomplete code for this module because USE.IT allows us to simulate the unimplemented node manually. To test the module we type:

RUN PACE

The system responds:

```
$ RUN PACE
C FORTRAN CODE FOR HOS MODEL: PACE
C PRODUCED BY USE.IT F4-RAT 3.02:30-MAR-1983 1
TOP NODE INPUT : RUNNER<INTEGER> =
```

We respond by entering the runner's number: 101. The system then asks for the other top-node input:

TOP NODE INPUT: MILES<RATIONAL>:=

We respond to typing in a rational number: 6.2. The system then attempts to execute the code and reaches the unimplemented primitive FINISH-TIME.

It tells us the line of code at which the pseudonode occurs, tells us its input, and asks us to supply the output:

```
$RUN PACE
C FORTRAN CODE FOR HOS MODEL: PACE
C PRODUCED BY USE.IT F4-RAT 3.02 : 30-MAR-1982 1
TOP NODE INPUT: RUNNER<INTEGER>:= 101 RET
TOP NODE INPUT: MILES<RATIONAL>:= 6.2
PSEUDO-NODE: MINUTES FINISH TIME(RUNNER) AT LINE 9
    INPUT : RUNNER <INTEGER> =          101
    OUTPUT: MINUTES <RATIONAL>:=
```

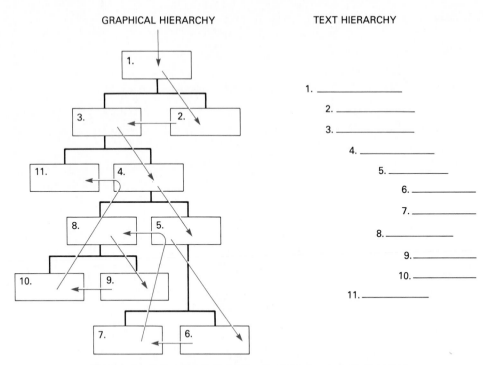

The tree is represented in text using the following sequencing rules:

- Start at the top.
- If a node has offsprings, list the right offspring first.
- When the descendants beneath the right offspring
  are listed, list the left offspring.
- Use indentations equivalent to the depth in the tree.

Figure 38.10   An illustration of the top-to-bottom, right-to-left sequencing of an AXES tree structure in AXES text.

We supply the output, and then the program module completes its operation and prints the value of PACE-PER-MILE.

EXTERNAL MODULES OF CODE

Sometimes previously existing programs need to be incorporated into code generated by USE.IT. USE.IT RATs can generate interfaces to such programs provided that

1. They are callable in the language in question.
2. The non-Rat-generated programs have valid interfaces and work correctly.

1.0   PACKET DEMULTI PLEXOR3:

    Function PACKET_DEMULTI_PLEXOR3 processes data OUTA, OUTB.IN as input producing OUTA_EN,OUTB_EN,IN_EN as output. It is related to its 3 subfunctions via a CJ/CJ structure.

    The present specification presents the architecture for a packet demulti-plexor. This demultiplexor reads messages sent from the host via IN, the input line, determines which of two output lines, OUTA or OUTB, should receive the message, and transmits the message on the appropriate line. If the message is a termination message, then the demultiplexor terminates without further transmission. IN_EN, OUTA_EN, and OUTB_EN represent the final states of the respective input and output lines at the completion of a demultiplexing cycle.

                                                        ── Designer comments
                                                           associated with the
1.1   RECEIVE MESSAGE: HOS blocks.

    Function RECEIVE_MESSAGE processes data IN as input producing IN_RECV,MESSAGE,IF_END as output. Operation RECEIVE_MESSAGE is not a completed module.

    This operation senses the input line, IN, and returns the next message received (MESSAGE), a flag set to TRUE if the message is a transmission termination message (IF_END), and the resulting state of the input line (IN_RECV).

Figure 38.11   Documentation in U.S. Department of Defense standard format, automatically generated by USE.IT.

Of course the RAT cannot ensure the correctness of program code from outside sources.

The module that calls the outside program must have a node in it that represents the interface to that outside program. This is a leaf node in the HOS tree labeled [XO] (external operation).

The input list and output list of the node must contain the arguments and return parameters of the called routine.

GENERATION OF   USE.IT has an automatic documentation generator
DOCUMENTATION   that generates documentation in U.S. Department of
                           Defense format, with standard paragraph numbers,
and so on.

Design and documentation of systems are inextricably linked. Good design ought to produce documentation and be expressed in documentation. Documents are the visible part of the design process.

Ideally, system documentation ought to have two characteristics. First, it ought to be useful to people and should help them understand the system and maintain and improve it. Second, it ought to be machine-readable and computable so that it permits automation of design procedures that are done inefficiently by humans (including verification, design calculations, and program coding).

A major problem with maintenance of software is that when maintainers change the design, they often do not change the documentation. The documentation slips out of phase with the code and becomes useless.

With USE.IT the design *is* the documentation. The designer can put comments in any of the blocks. A high-level system description may be associated with the high-level blocks. The low-level blocks often need no description added to them. A person maintaining the software works by changing the control map, and from this both new program code and new auxiliary documentation are generated.

Figure 38.11 shows documentation generated by USE.IT [5].

REFERENCES

1. *USE.IT Reference Manual,* Cambridge, MA: Higher Order Software, Inc., 1982.

2. W. R. Hackler and A. Samarov, *An AXES Specification of a Radar Scheduler* (Technical Report No. 23), Cambridge, MA: Higher Order Software, Inc., 1979.

3. M. Hamilton and S. Zeldin, *Integrated Software Development System/Higher Order Software Conceptual Description* (TR-3), Cambridge, MA: Higher Order Software, Inc., 1976.

4. *Annotated Model of a Digital Clock* (Educational Series No. 1), Cambridge, MA: Higher Order Software, Inc., 1982.

5. A. Razdow, N. Albertson, Jr., and D. Rose, *Designing Systems by Documenting them with USE.IT,* Cambridge, MA: Higher Order Software, Inc., 1979.

39 THE IMPACT OF DESIGN AUTOMATION

THE REVOLUTION   Techniques like the one in Chapter 38 portend a fundamental revolution in computing. USE-IT was one of the first tools to demonstrate what is possible. Now a variety of tools exist, varying in their rigor and completeness, some of which are easier to use than USE-IT. There are two aspects to the revolution: first, the effect on coding and debugging, and second, and perhaps more important, the effect on the specification of systems.

EFFECT ON   The ad hoc coding process, which is so vulnerable to
PROGRAMMING   the frailties of the human coder, disappears. This is
                       how the computer world must progress. Program coding as we know it today *must* disappear. It is too error-prone and too expensive, and it creates results that are too difficult to modify. In the typical programming department, Murphy's Law has become a Constitutional amendment. Programming is an inhuman use of human beings because it asks them to do something beyond their capabilities—produce perfect, intricate, complex logic that can be easily understood and modified. That is a task for computers, not humans.

Our brain cannot handle complex logic and intricate detail without making mistakes. We need a creative partnership between our brain, which is creative, and an electronic machine that is precise at handling immense detail.

Complex software created with ad hoc methods has an amazingly large number of combinatorial paths that must be tested. In practice, there is no way they could possibly all be tested thoroughly. An attempt is made at saturation testing in which the system is flooded with large numbers of test cases. In saturation testing it may be difficult to notice or track down an error if it occurs, and many errors may lurk in paths that the saturation testing does not happen to reach.

Because of this, most large systems are never fully debugged. They occasionally do mysterious things. A high-level check is placed on them so that they do not lose accounts or have dramatic errors. Most of their minor disasters can be caught when they happen and recovered from. On some software there is a lengthy list of bugs that have been observed but not yet caught. There are probably many others that have not yet been observed.

When this report was being written, *MIS Week* reported that only 30 bugs remained in a certain system [1]. We could ask, "How do you know?" If there are 30 bugs that you cannot find, there are probably many more hiding in the woodwork. In a later issue, the publication said that 600 out of 900 bugs had been fixed on the same system.

When a complex system is developed with HOS, including one with many loops, all possible paths are built from primitives that are mathematically verified. *There are no unknown paths.*

Dynamic program testing is necessary with all programs not built with a rigorous mathematical technique (this includes the vast majority of programs in existence today). Each branch and usable combination of branches ought to be tested, if this were possible. With HOS, most errors are caught with *static* verification, and some with tests of specific instance to ensure that correct results are being created.

EFFECT ON SPECIFICATIONS

An improvement in programming techniques, even a dramatic improvement, is not enough by itself. The biggest problem with most programming is that the specifications are inadequate. The technique of Chapter 38 is a form of specification language. Specifications are created with the aid of a graphics tool that reveals their inconsistencies and errors. Where the statement of specifications is inadequate (as they all are in the beginning), it is adjusted and broken into more detail until provably correct code can be generated from it.

Programmers have an irresistible desire to start coding something, and managers have a comfortable feeling that work is under way if code is being produced. To produce code without rigorous specifications, however, is ultimately very expensive. The code has to be modified, and the cost of modifying it is usually much higher than the cost of creating it in the first place.

A basic principle of structured analysis is that more work is needed at the front in specifications to save time later in expensive code modification and maintenance. The problem with most structured analysis techniques, however, is that they are not rigorous. When using them, it is still true that most of the errors in delivered code are caused by imprecise specifications. The method of Chapter 38 forces the specifications to be rigorous and bug-free.

People need user-friendly nonprocedural techniques with which they can express their desires to a computer. Because most requirement statements are not computable, the computer must help users to refine their requests successively until they *are* computable.

As automation of programming matures, the specification languages that predominate may be different from the one described in chapter 38, but they need to have the property that they *translate broad human thinking about requirements into a computable form and refine it successively until it is possible to allocate the resources needed automatically and generate bug-free machine code*.

WHAT DOES "PROVABLY CORRECT" MEAN?

The expressions "logically guaranteed system design" [2] and "provably correct structures" have been used in describing the HOS methodology. Just what do we mean when we say that programs or specifications are "logically guaranteed" or "provably correct"?

"Provably correct code" does not mean that the program is necessarily without fault. We can still tell the computer to do things that are stupid. If we create a forecasting program based on the phases of the moon and the behavior of groundhogs, no mathematics will help. Provably correct code will not improve a stockbroker's predictions, for example.

However, the majority of bugs in programs today are caused by the mechanics of programming, inconsistent data, sequence errors, and the like. These can be eliminated. We can create a machine in which the gears and levers mesh correctly.

Mathematics does not eliminate errors in the *concept* of what a program should do. The methodology can create provably correct code for a stupid operation. In old fairy tales, a magic device such as the monkey's paw executes its users' wishes but does not check that the effects will really be good for the users. The fairy tales warned us, philosophically, about wishing for the wrong thing.

We can give wrong instructions to the HOS tool, not because of any philosophical problems but because we are careless. This is a new version of garbage in, garbage out. Ill-conceived requirements or misstated requirements lead to provably correct code for executing those wrong requirements. It is perfectly possible to create a correct control map for solving the wrong problem. The software checks that the control map is correct according to its mathematical rules, but the result is wrong because the wrong problem was solved.

SYNTAX AND SEMANTICS

We can distinguish between syntax and semantics in languages. *Syntax* refers to *how* something is being said. *Semantics* refers to *what* is being said.

The Oxford Dictionary defines *syntax* as "sentence construction; the grammatical arrangement of words (in language); set of rules governing this.'' It defines *semantic* as ''relating to meaning in language.''

Most compilers and interpreters check for *syntax errors*—misspelled words, commands without the required variables, missing END statements, and so on. They cannot check the *meaning* of the language. Languages of higher level than programming languages can make some checks on *what* is being said, not just *how*. The HOS software carries out as much verification as it can of *what* is being said. Do the operations and data references obey the basic axioms? There may be garbage in, garbage out, but the internal logic can be checked for what it is doing. This type of internal semantic check is a major step forward in automated design verification.

It is desirable to represent specifications in a technology-independent fashion because machines and software change. A fixed semantics is necessary for this. This semantics may be expressed with different forms of syntax, such as COBOL, FORTRAN, or ADA. In historical methods the opposite is true: The languages have a fixed syntax but uncontrolled semantics. The HOS specification has controlled semantics that can be translated into several syntaxes.

INTERNAL AND EXTERNAL SEMANTICS

We might distinguish between *internal semantics* and *external semantics*. Internal relates to whether what is being said obeys the rules established in the basic axioms. External semantics relates to whether the system is solving the right problem. Techniques for proving program correctness can deal with internal semantics but not external semantics.

We might say to a science-fiction robot, ''Get me a dry blartini with a twist.'' It will tell us there is a *syntax* error and ask whether the word *blartini* should be *martini*.

If we tell it to get a dry martini made with 7-Up, it will tell us we have a *semantics* error. Our instruction violates a basic axiom of martini making.

If we want a vodka martini and only say, ''Get me a dry martini with a twist,'' the robot might bring a gin martini. Now we have an *external semantics* error that the software has not caught.

You might say that the robot should have detected that our specifications were incomplete. It should have known that there are two types of martini and asked, ''Vodka or gin?'' There are other options. It should say, ''With ice or straight up?'' But where does it stop?

It might say, ''Gordons, Juniper, Beefeater, Boodles, Tanqueray, Bombay, Schenley, Skol, London, Mr. Boston, Burnett's, Crystal Palace, Seagram's, Calvert, Booth's, Fleishmann's, S. S. Pierce, Five O'Clock, Gilbey's . . .,'' and we lose patience and say, ''Fetch the damned thing!''

To be computable, specifications have to have much detail or else default options. Default options are common in the simpler forms of nonprocedural languages such as report generators. They are useful elsewhere. We would like the software to use its own intelligence as far as possible in comprehending our requirements and filling in the details so as to save us work and avoid specification debugging.

STANDARDS

A standards committee concerned with the rapidly evolving standards for data networks produced not long ago a document of several hundred pages specifying the draft standard in fine detail. Its objective was to ensure compatibility between equipment made by different manufacturers. To accomplish this it provided specifications which establish common interfaces and protocols. Like all such standards, it was not provably correct or even provably computable. Among other notations, it contained state diagrams that could easily be transformed into the rigorous notation of HOS. Once in that notation, these could be manipulated by the graphics editor and code automatically generated and tested.

Computer standards committees everywhere should be upgrading their notation to provably correct forms.

Now that we know that it is possible, future standards, future network interfaces, future operating systems, future data-base management systems, and so on, all ought to be built with rigorous provably correct design, which helps eliminate redundancies and enforces rigorously correct interfaces between modules.

Software of all types ought to have a certification stamped on it saying whether it was built with a rigorous mathematical foundation.

VERIFICATION AND TESTING

In an HOS environment we can distinguish between *verification* and *testing*. By verification we mean checking that a system's specification is logically complete and consistent and that it obeys the mathematical rules. By testing we mean checking the correctness by demonstrating that the system really works as it was intended to. *Verification* is performed automatically and statically by the HOS software. *Testing* requires that instantiations of the target system's behavior be checked. Test cases are fed to the system to ensure that its algorithms give the results the designers intended.

In conventional systems development, almost all testing has to be done after programming. This is expensive to do, and it is even more expensive to correct the errors found at that late stage. If errors are caught early, they are less costly by one or two orders of magnitude. Using HOS, most of the errors can be caught early. The software analyzes the high-level specifications, and they can be successively reanalyzed as they are broken down into detail. The designer will also do case tests on modules as he proceeds.

To verify automatically, one has to translate a design into a computable form. The HOS representation allows rigorous verification at each step of the design process [3].

BUILDING HIGHER LEVELS OF TRUST Modules that have been verified and tested are stored in the system library. These are then regarded as proven modules that do not need to be verified again. They are verified *one time only*. Their application may be tested when they are used in newly defined systems.

The library of verified modules grows, and these modules may become linked to form larger modules. All new design should use as many of the library modules as possible. This lessens the amount of verification and testing required.

Systems can thus be defined using techniques that eliminate the need for certain types of verification. If techniques that eliminate data and sequence errors are enforced, there is no need to look for these errors. When you use a computer as part of a system, you do not check its internal wiring. You assume that is correct. We should similarly be able to trust as many software modules as possible and link them into larger trustworthy modules.

The growth and maximal use of the library of verified modules is thus a very important part of the overall reduction of testing time and costs.

IMPROVEMENTS IN PRODUCTIVITY The early experiences with the HOS tools show major increases in application development productivity. There are several reasons for this:

1. There is no program coding; the code is generated automatically.

2. Most dynamic testing and error correction, which consumes so much time, is avoided.

3. With the graphics editor, when an error is corrected or a change is made, the effects of this on other parts of the system are *rigorously* detected and quickly modified.

4. The control maps, although they become large and complex, are highly modular and are created and manipulated quickly and easily with the graphics editor.

5. *Defined operations* and *defined structures* are created to form a powerful macrolanguage for specific application areas or system viewpoints.

6. Early feedback helps to make the system specifications consistent and complete.

7. The library facility largely eliminates interface problems among separately created system modules.

8. The library facility encourages the maximum repetitive use of code modules and the minimum redundant code creation.

There are now many nonprocedural languages and code generators in use. It is typical to observe an order of magnitude improvement in productivity with the good ones [4]. USE.IT, the HOS software, seems to give similar improvements. However, most generators generate relatively simple applications, whereas USE.IT can generate exceedingly complex logic and can interlink many separately developed library modules in a provably correct fashion.

COST SAVINGS

Figure 39.1 shows the typical breakdown of costs of a large software project using the classical life cycle [5].

Using the technique of Chapter 38, the programming costs disappear and the costs of testing largely disappear. There is less maintenance because the original system was thoroughly specified. Maintenance is much easier and faster to perform.

Much more care has to go into the specification stage. It might be thought that specification will take longer because it has to be thorough. In early examples of HOS usage, however, specification and design costs have in fact been halved because of the top-to-bottom communication with the tool, the speed of using the graphics editor, and the automatic detection of errors, inconsistencies, and incompleteness. A committee using imprecise methods takes *much* longer than a small group using precise and powerful methods.

PERCENTAGE OF COSTS

	DEVELOPMENT EFFORT	FINDING AND FIXING ERRORS	TOTAL
INITIAL DEVELOPMENT			
Specification and Design	5	5	10
Programming	5		5
Verification and Testing		10	10
TOTAL	10	15	25
MAINTENANCE			
Residual errors		7.5	7.5
Specification and Design	13.5	13.5	27
Programming	13.5		13.5
Verification and Testing		27	27
TOTAL	27	48	75
OVERALL TOTAL	37	63	100

Figure 39.1   Classical life-cycle costs [4].

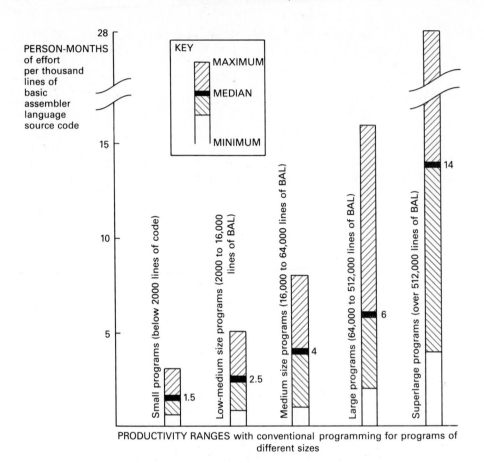

Figure 39.2 Lower programmer productivity is achieved with large programs than small programs [6].

EFFECT OF PROGRAM SIZE

Lower programmer productivity is achieved with large programs than with small programs. Figure 39.2 shows a typical distribution. The productivity achieved with superlarge programs is almost one-tenth that achieved with small programs [6].

There are several reasons why productivity with large programs is worse than with small ones. First, the programming team is larger. This requires more formal interaction between people and gives more scope for miscommunication. Substantial overhead is required to fit together all the pieces of a large program.

Small programs are often created by one person who has all the pieces in his head. With large systems, planning and paperwork are needed to control the development cycle. The various forms of paperwork with large systems sometimes contain an aggregate of over 50 English words for each line of source code in the system [7,8].

In large systems where the programmer works on one project for more than a year, his interest and productivity often decline substantially. On a small program, the programmer can keep working fast to complete the work quickly.

Testing is disproportionately time-consuming with very large programs. The number of combinations that need to be tested tends to increase roughly as the square of the program size. The problems with interfaces between modules become numerous and severe on large programs. Saturation testing becomes lengthy and unsatisfactory in that many bugs are not found. When a bug is corrected, it can have unforeseen consequences in other parts of the program, which in turn are difficult to find.

The HOS technique has a direct effect on all of these problems. It rigorously controls the interfaces among modules. The modules fit together in a provably correct fashion. The generation of code is so much faster than hand coding that a large team of people is not needed. One person can replace ten programmers. Three people can replace a team of 30. This shrinkage greatly reduces the problems of communication among people. The different members of the team all interact with the same graphics representation and library. When any change is made, its consequences are automatically shown on the screen and can be quickly adjusted. The finding of most errors is brought to the front of the development cycle. Saturation testing is largely replaced by static verification. Individual modules, or portions of the system with missing modules, can be tested on-line in a simulated fashion.

In a typical large development project, a programmer sits at his desk and is greeted each morning with a set of memos or documents about changes. He often regards them cynically, feeling that he has neither the time to read them nor the ability to remember to react to them. Somebody, he hopes, is filing them. With HOS, change control is largely automatic. The areas affected by each change are revealed automatically, and the system ensures that all consequential adjustments are made. These adjustments then reside in the on-line graphic representation of the system that every developer uses.

With nonprocedural languages and code generators, many team programming efforts shrink to one-person projects. This can be enhanced by firm high-quality data administration techniques [9].

ERROR STATISTICS

On some large projects, detailed analysis has been done of the errors made. It is interesting to look back and estimate how many errors could have been avoided with the technique described in Chapter 38.

Figure 39.3 shows statistics of the preflight software errors in NASA's moonshot, Project Apollo [10]. These were errors discovered *after* implementation and delivery of code. Far more errors were presumably caught by pro-

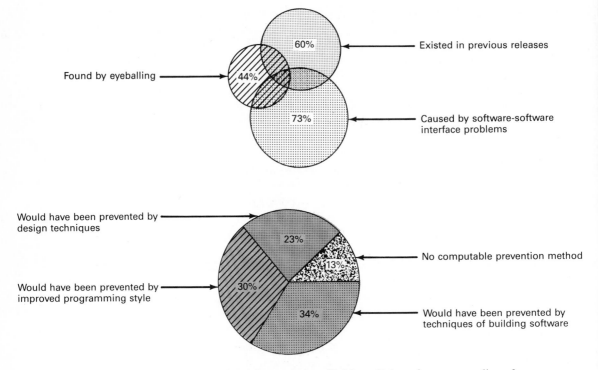

Figure 39.3 A breakdown of the official preflight software anomalies of Project Apollo [10].

grammers during implementation. Fully 73 percent of the problems were software-software interface errors. This is common on large projects. If all software for a project are developed with a methodology like HOS, there should be no interface problems discovered *after* implementation. The interfaces are defined with mathematical precision, and details of all modules and their interface definitions are in the library.

Of the errors, 44 percent were found manually and many by *dynamic* testing runs. With HOS, most would be found in *static* verification.

It was estimated that 30 percent of the errors would have been avoided with better programming style—a good structured programming method. A whopping 87 percent of the errors in the bottom chart of Fig. 39.3 would have been caught by HOS verification methods before code delivery. The remaining 13 percent of the errors were conceptual problems or problems of changing requirements that would not have been caught by mathematical verification. Typically, the specification was incomplete or inconsistent with the original intent of the designer.

Hamilton and Zeldin refer to this residual 13 percent of errors as the ''13 percent problem.'' If code generation and verification are automated and precision is enforced in specification, developers can spend more time at the front of projects checking the high-level HOS charts with the end users and management, trying to flush out any specification faults and omissions.

Both seeing results as quickly as possible and being able to perform simulations at the terminal help developers to catch external semantics errors.

Better front-end methodologies for helping to achieve accurate system conceptualization may reduce the 13 percent. These include thorough data modeling and event diagramming.

HUMAN SYSTEM COMPONENTS

A particularly interesting error occurred on Project Apollo Mission 11. Just prior to landing on the moon, a warning signal informed the astronauts that the capsule should not land. This hair-raising signal was incorrect.

The error was caused by an incorrect entry in the astronaut's checklist of procedures. This caused the astronaut to take an incorrect action with the hardware, which in turn caused the software to think something was true that was not true. Here we have a system error where the system includes interacting hardware, software, and humans.

The HOS technique can be applied to broad systems in which the interaction of the hardware, software, and humans is diagrammed, so that human checklists as well as other system components can be provably correct. This would have prevented some of the problems experienced with nuclear power-station operating procedures, for example.

USE OF OTHER FRONT-END METHODOLOGIES

The HOS software can be made more acceptable and easy to use by linking it to familiar, powerful, or user-friendly front-end methodologies. The extent to which the HOS software encompasses such methodologies is likely to determine its level of success.

Figure 39.4 shows various ways of linking HOS techniques to other front-end techniques. In diagram 1 of Fig. 39.4, the HOS technique is used for creating specifications and the control maps are converted to a familiar representation. Control maps can be converted *automatically* into data-flow diagrams, for example. As shown in diagram 1 of Fig. 39.4, there may be design feedback from the familiar representation to the HOS chart. Software might be created for automatically transforming an HOS control chart into an alternate representation.

Diagram 2 of Fig. 39.4 shows a front-end representation being translated into an HOS representation with the aid of specially designed control structures and defined operations. Chapters 24 and 25, for example, show data access maps and their corresponding data-base action diagrams (DADs). These can be translated into HOS control maps with the aid of control structures designed for this purpose. Chapter 42 shows a data model, possibly created with a tool like Data Designer [11]; this tool could be linked to HOS for *automatic* conversion of the data representation.

Various methodologies are powerful for the overall planning or design of computer systems. It is often desirable to retain these and enhance them. This is easy to do by building special HOS control structures for them and occasionally creating software to convert the output of design tools into HOS notation.

Although powerful front-end methodologies that can enhance the conceptual clarity of systems design or create overview designs for corporate data processing do exist, many of these methodologies are not rigorous. The specifications they create (contrary to the sales claims) are inconsistent, incomplete, redundant, and ambiguous. HOS reveals these deficiencies, so the step of translating their designs into HOS is very valuable. It allows problems to be found at the front end, where they are easily correctable, rather than at the back end, where they are disastrous. Diagram 2 shows design feedback from the HOS representation to the front-end representation.

In one case, a module that was part of a battlefield intelligence system [12] was documented with a mixture of English, equations, and the SREM specification language [13]. Translation of this into HOS revealed and removed many design inconsistencies [12].

The improvement in rigor of the specification methodology may be made more directly than with the off-line feedback of diagram 2. The front-end methodology may itself be analyzed with the HOS technique and consequently enhanced to make it computable or directly convertible into HOS control maps (diagram 3).

IDEF-0 [14] is a specification technique for the design of ICAM systems for computer-aided manufacturing [15]. It uses a type of diagram that represents complex flows and relationships and is easy to use and understand. It is not completely rigorous from a computability point of view. HOS was used to create a computable version of IDEF so that this valuable technique becomes rigorous [16]. Specified was a graphics tool that might be described as an IDEF-0 typewriter [17]. A single keystroke can produce a box, an arrow path, an arrow end, a shift to the next location, and so on. The arrows fall along uniform and predictable paths. This chart becomes part of a computable specification, linked directly to HOS control maps that can be analyzed and from which correct code can be generated.

Tight coupling to powerful front-end methodologies allows the benefits of these methodologies to be retained and allows their users to ''speak their own language.''

INCORPORATION OF NONPROCEDURAL LANGUAGES

Diagram 4 of Fig. 39.4 shows a different type of linkage. The front-end specification is done with the HOS techniques, but certain leaf nodes of the control map refer to the use of other nonprocedural languages. A node might represent an operation done with a report generator, for example, or with a data-base query-update language.

This other nonprocedural language might be used separately from the code generated by the HOS RAT. End users, for example, might employ an end-user language as one facility in the design of a complex system.

Alternatively, the intermediate use of a lower-level nonprocedural language might be translated into the HOS notation. It is then analyzed, together with the rest of the system, and jointly "ratted," as shown in diagram 5 of Fig. 39.4. The control map created by the nonprocedural language becomes a defined operation [OP] in the library.

Combinations of the diagrams in Fig. 39.4 are likely to be used. The linkage to nonprocedural languages in diagrams 4 and 5 may be used in conjunction with the approaches in diagrams 1, 2, or 3.

In particular, we believe that where a tool like HOS is used for commercial DP or complex data-base systems, it needs to be linked to the information engineering tools and methodologies discussed in the following chapters.

SOFTWARE FACTORIES

As computers become increasingly numerous and cheap, it is necessary to create software factories where software can be created in a professional, engineering-like, low-cost fashion.

A methodology like HOS is needed so that standard bug-free building blocks can be created, cataloged, and linked in a manner that avoids interface errors. The building blocks will become larger and more comprehensive as higher levels of trust are developed.

The methodology needs to make certain building blocks modifiable so that they can be adjusted to customers' needs. Some of the building blocks should be highly flexible report generators, document generators, screen handlers, and data-base facilities.

Software factories will often need to produce portable code that runs on all machines. This may be best achieved with an ADA generator, assuming that all manufacturers conform in a single standard specification of the ADA language.

Box 39.1 lists the ways in which a technique like HOS provides solutions to the problems of traditional software development.

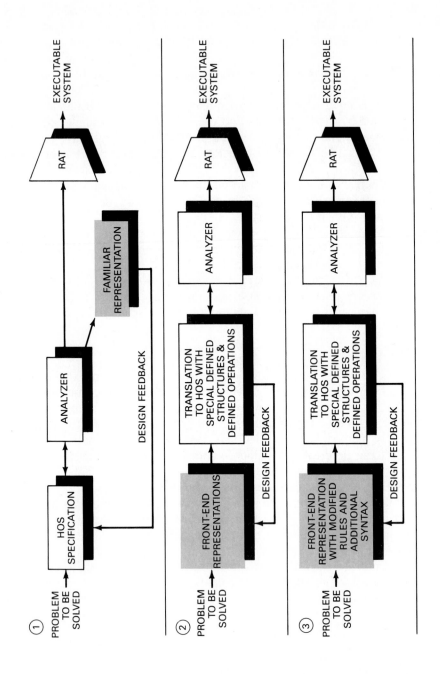

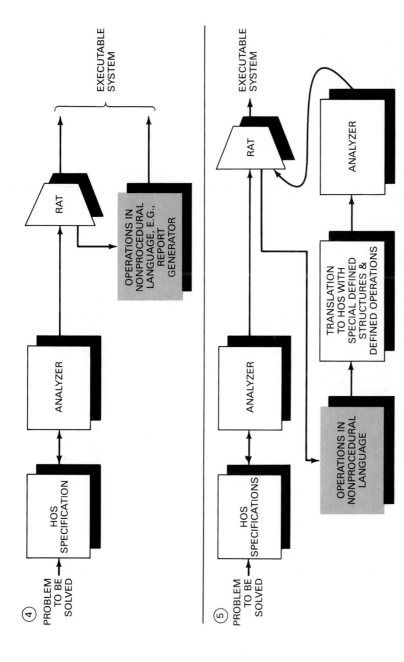

Figure 39.4 Various ways of combining the use of HOS with familiar or easy-to-use specification tools and techniques. In this example, 4 or 5 may be combined with 1, 2, or 3.

571

BOX 39.1 Traditional development versus HOS-like methodology

PROBLEMS WITH TRADITIONAL DEVELOPMENT	EFFECTS OF HOS-LIKE METHODOLOGY
Development takes too long.	Development is much faster.
Development costs are too high.	Major reduction in development costs.
Programming is manual.	Programming is automatic.
Most errors are found *after* coding.	Most errors are found *before* implementation.
Most errors are found manually or by *dynamic* runs.	Most errors are found *automatically* and by *static* analysis.
Some errors are *never* found.	Almost all errors are found.
Mismatch between requirements and specifications. Mismatch between specifications and design. Mismatch between design and coding.	Each level is a precise expansion of the previous level.
Incomplete specifications Inconsistent specifications	Internally complete, consistent specifications are enforced.
Many interface errors and mismatches between subsystems (73 percent of the errors on Project Apollo).	Rigorous, provably correct interfaces between subsystems.
No guarantee of function integrity after implementation.	Guarantee of function integrity after implementation
Large developer teams: severe communication problems.	Small or one-person teams: few communication problems

BOX 39.1   *(Continued)*

Massive paperwork for management control. →	Elimination of most paperwork
Much redundant code development. →	Identification of common modules; use of common modules is made easy.
Separate developers reinventing the wheel. →	Library mechanism with rigorous interfaces encourages the building of reusable constructs.
Maintenance is difficult. →	Maintenance is easy.
Modifications trigger chain reactions of new bugs. →	The effects of all modifications are made explicit and clear.
Successive maintenance degrades the code quality. →	High-quality code is regenerated after each change.
Portability problems. →	A design can be regenerated to different environments.

REFERENCES

1. *MIS WEEK*, February 10, 1982, p. 1.

2. *USE.IT for Logically Guaranteed System Design* (product description folder), Cambridge, MA: Higher Order Software, Inc.

3. M. Hamilton and S. Zeldin, "The Relationship Between Design and Verification," *Journal of Systems and Software,* 1 (Sept. 1979).

4. J. Martin, *Application Development Without Programmers,* Englewood Cliffs, NJ: Prentice-Hall, Inc., 1982.

5. D. K. Lloyd and M. Lipow, *Reliability: Management Methods and Mathematics,* Englewood Cliffs, NJ: Prentice-Hall, Inc., 1972.

6. G. W. Willett et al., *TSO Productivity Study,* American Telephone and Telegraph Long Lines, Kansas City, April 1973.

7. T. C. Jones, *Optimizing Program Quality and Programmer Productivity* (Guide 45), Proceedings, Atlanta, November 1977.

8. T. C. Jones, *A Survey of Programming Design and Specification Techniques,* IEEE Symposium on Specifications of Reliable Software, April 1979.

9. J. Martin, *Managing the Data Base Environment* (Savant Technical Report No. 11), Carnforth, Lancs., England: Savant Institute, 1980.

10. M. Hamilton and S. Zeldin, "Higher Order Software: A Methodology for Defining Software," *IEEE Transactions on Software Engineering* SE-2(1), March 1976.

11. Data Designer, a tool that creates a stable data model from several separately entered representations of data, from Database Design, Inc., Ann Arbor, MI.

12. R. Hackler, *An HOS View of ASAS* (Technique Report No. 32), Cambridge, MA: Higher Order Software, Inc., 1981.

13. M. W. Alford, "A Requirements Engineering Methodology for Real-Time Processing Requirements," *IEEE Transactions on Software Engineering,* SE-3(1), 1977.

14. *Architect's Manual: ICAM Definition Method (Version 0 and Version 1) (IDEF),* Waltham, MA: SofTech, Inc., 1979.

15. *Integrated Computer-Aided Manufacturing (ICAM),* Waltham, MA: Sof-Tech, Inc., 1978.

16. *Computable IDEF* (series of reports prepared for the Air Force Systems Command, Wright-Patterson Air Force Base, OH, Cambridge, MA: Higher Order Software, Inc., 1978–1982.

17. *Computable IDEF: Preliminary Design,* Cambridge, MA: Higher Order Software, Inc., 1982.

40 DATA-BASE PLANNING

INTRODUCTION In the first decades of computing, software has become an unruly mess, far removed from the orderliness one would normally associate with an engineering discipline. The more automated structured methodologies now coming into existence could (in time) gain control of software and eliminate much of the chaos and redundancy.

In data processing there is another mess—the data. The tape and disk libraries have vast numbers of volumes containing redundant, inconsistent collections of data, chaotically organized. What are, in effect, the same data are represented in numerous incompatible ways on different tapes and disks. The grouping of data items into records is such that it leads to all sorts of anomalies and maintenance problems.

The use of specification languages and code generators for computation alone would not eliminate these problems without overall management and control of the *data* in an enterprise. Good CASE tools provide facilities for *data modeling* and link the data models to the design of systems.

One of the important objectives of automated methodologies ought to be to avoid having unpleasant surprises in the later stages of system development. We stressed earlier that discovering problems or changes needed in specifications late in the development life cycle is much more expensive than discovering them early.

In commercial data processing, there can be very expensive surprises late in the development phases, and more often in the maintenance phase, when good *data-base planning* has not been done. The data for commercial data processing can be entangled with many other applications. A large commercial volume library has tens of thousands of tapes and disks, most of them containing different types of data items. One commercial application receives data from, or passes data to, many other applications. If these applications are developed without integrated planning of the data, chaos results. Higher management cannot extract data that need to be drawn from several systems. Expensive conversion is needed, and often important business options are lost because the data are not available in the right form.

The evidence with the use of nonprocedural languages in commercial DP indicates that thorough data-base administration is a vital key to success. These languages make systems development easier than with traditional programming, and it is only too easy for developers serving a particular user group to develop their own data, ignoring the needs of other users. A Tower of Babel grows up in the data if a data administrator does not have firm control.

SEPARATE DEVELOPMENTS WITH INCOMPATIBLE DATA

Traditionally, each functional area in an organization has developed its own files and procedures. There has been much redundancy in data. A medium-sized firm might have many departments, each doing its own purchasing, for example. Before computers, this did not matter; it was probably the best way to operate. After computers, it did matter. There might be a dozen sets of purchasing programs to be maintained instead of one. There might be a dozen sets of incompatible purchasing files. The incompatibility prevented overall management information from being pulled together.

Earlier data processing installations implemented one application at a time. (Many still do.) Integrating the different applications seemed too difficult. Integration grew slowly *within* departments or functional areas. To achieve integration *among* functional areas would have needed new types of management.

Each functional area had its own procedures, which it understood very well. It did not understand the procedures of other areas. Each area kept its own files. The structure of these files were unique to the responsibilities of that area. Unfortunately, data had to pass among the areas, and management data needed to be extracted from several areas. These data were usually incompatible. Worse, individual areas frequently found the need to change their data structures, and often did so without appreciating the chain reaction of problems this would cause. Figure 40.1 shows the environment of this style of data processing.

In this nonintegrated environment, most communication of changes is done by paperwork, which is error-prone, time-consuming, and labor-intensive. Suppose, for example, that the engineering department prepares an engineering change report. It makes several copies, one for production control, one for inventory control, one for accounting, and so on. Production control concludes that the engineering change requires changes to be made to its product file. It requires a new request for materials to be sent to inventory control. Inventory control must determine the effects of the change on its purchasing operations. These affect the costs of raw materials and parts. Inventory control communicates these to accounting. Accounting concludes that a change in sales price is

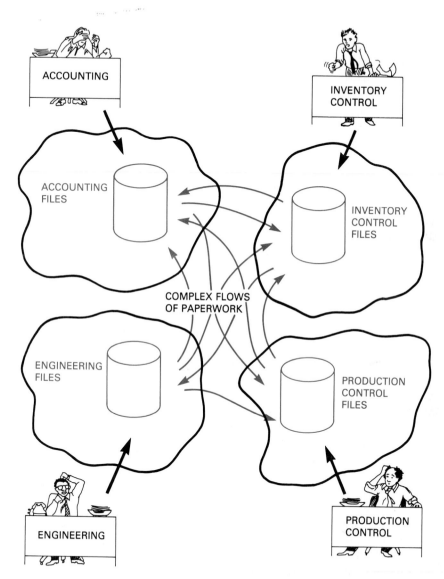

Figure 40.1 Communication of changes in a nonintegrated environment.

necessary to retain profitability. It communicates this to marketing. And so on.

When data for different areas are separately defined and incompatible, this passing of information among the separate systems is complex and inflexible. Manual handling of paperwork is needed. Accuracy is lost. Items slip through the cracks. Changes made to one system can play havoc with others. To prevent harmful effects of change, the management procedures become rigid, and change is made difficult.

In one factory, more than a million dollars' worth of work in progress was unaccounted for on the shop floor due to items' ''slipping through the cracks'' in the paperwork process. This unaccountability was a major motivation for the end-user management to create an on-line system, and that totally changed the administrative procedures of the factory.

The solution to the problems illustrated by Fig. 40.1 is centralized planning of the data. It is the job of a data administrator to create a *model* of the data needed to run an organization. This model spans the functional areas. When it is modularized, it is broken up by data subjects rather than by departmental or organization-chart boundaries. Figure 40.2 illustrates the use of a common data model.

STABLE FOUNDATION

In well-organized commercial DP, the data models become a foundation upon which the procedures are built. A basic reason this has proved to be practical is that the types of data used in an enterprise do not change very much. Although the information requirements of executives change from month to month, the basic entities in an enterprise remain the same unless the enterprise itself changes drastically.

An entity is anything about which data can be stored: a product, a customer, a salesman, a part, and so on. A data model shows the relationships between entities: a *salesman* is an *employee,* a *branch office* has many *salesmen,* and so on.

We store *attributes* that provide data about the entities. For example, a salesman has a given address, territory, quota, and salary, has sold a certain percentage of his quota, and so on. The data model shows what attributes relate to each entity.

The types of entities and attributes that are used in running a corporation usually remain the same, with minor changes. They are the foundation of data processing. Their *values* change constantly. The *information* or types of reports we extract from that collection of data may change substantially. The technology we use for storing or updating the data will change.

When a corporation changes its administrative procedures, the entities and attributes usually remain the same. It may require a small number of new entities or some new attributes for existing entities, so the foundation data model grows somewhat over the years.

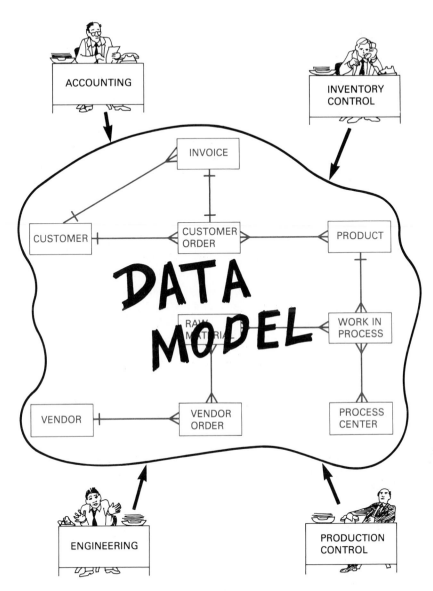

Figure 40.2 When data are consolidated into an integrated data base, data modeling is the key to success. The data structures become more complex, but the data flows are greatly simplified. The data are consistent and accurate. New forms of management information can be extracted quickly with fourth-generation languages. Changes in procedures can be made rapidly with these languages. Paperwork is greatly lessened. The administrative procedures of the organization need to be completely rethought. Fundamentally different analysis and design techniques are needed.

A typical medium-sized corporation has several hundred entities (when redundancies are removed). A large, diversified corporation has more, and a separate data model might be created for each of its subsidiaries. There are often ten or so attributes to each entity, on average.

When computers were first introduced in banks, there were batch processing, many manual procedures, no terminals, and much form-filling. Today, customers use automated teller machines on-line to distant computers, there are large numbers of terminals, and the administrative procedures have changed completely. However, the raw types of data that are stored are the same as 20 years earlier. There has been a huge change in automation, but if a data model had been created 20 years ago, it would still be valid today, with minor changes.

Of course, if the bank decided to diversify into the whiskey distillation business, a fundamentally different data model would have to be created and added onto the existing model.

With some data-base management software, new attributes can be added without causing disruption. New entities can be added. Some types of data system software have more flexibility than others. An appropriate choice is needed.

It might be argued that some enterprises change more than banks in their types of data. That is true, so their data models need to be updated, preferably in an automated fashion.

STABLE DATA BASES

There is a huge difference between data bases that are specifically designed to be *stable* and the files that have been used in traditional data processing. Typical *file* structures tend to change continually because the users' requirements change. No enterprise is static, and management perceptions of what information is needed change rapidly.

Because of the intertwined nature of commercial data illustrated in Fig. 40.1 (and much more complex than Fig. 40.1 in reality), we seek to isolate the programs from the changes in data structures. We use the term *data independence*. *Data independence* means that when the data structure changes, the programs keep running because they are isolated from that change. The programs have a "view of the data that can be preserved even though the actual, physical structure of the data changes.

Data independence is achieved by means of data-base management systems. The most important difference between a data-base management system and a file management system is that data-base management translates between the application program's view of data and the actual structure of the data. It preserves the program's view of data when the actual view changes in either a logical or physical manner. With data-base systems, many application programs can have different views of the same data.

The use of a good data-base management system does not, by itself, give us the protection we need. We also need good logical design of the data structures used.

LOGICAL DESIGN OF DATA BASES

Unless controlled, systems analysts tend to group in records any collection of data items they perceive as being useful. All sorts of anomalies can arise because of inappropriate grouping of data items. Some of these anomalies are subtle and often not perceived.

A data base contains hundreds (sometimes thousands) of types of data items. These data-item types have to be associated into a data-base structure. How do you organize them into a logical structure? What is the best logical structure?

These questions are vitally important because the logical structure is the foundation on which most future data processing will be built. Not only will conventional programs be written to use the data base, but, increasingly, higher-level data-base languages will be used—languages that enable users to extract the information they need from the data base directly, and sometimes to update the data bases. The future corporation will be managed with data-base resources, networks to access the data bases, and end-user software for employing and updating the data.

If the logical structures are designed badly, a large financial penalty will result. A corporation will not be able to employ the data bases as it should, so productivity will suffer. The data bases will have to be modified constantly, but they cannot be modified without much rewriting of application program. The end users will not be served as they need, and because of this, many will try to create their own alternatives to employing the data base.

In the late 1970s it became clear that many data-base installations were not living up to the publicized advantages of data bases. A few rare ones had spectacularly improved the whole data processing function and greatly increased application development speed and productivity. Time and time again the difference lay in the design of the overall logical structure of the data.

One of the arguments for using data-base management systems is that they greatly reduce maintenance. In practice, data-base techniques have often not succeeded in lowering maintenance costs because a need is felt to create new data bases as new applications come along. The reason for this again lies in the logical structuring of the data.

The next chapters describe logical structuring of data. Chapter 41 describes *normalization* of data. Chapter 42 describes *canonical data structures* and the automation of stable data modeling. Chapter 43 describes the automated design of applications that employ data models. Along with these approaches, a good understanding of the nature and definitions of data is needed, and this requires close interaction with end users who are experts on the data.

THE FAILURE OF DATA ADMINISTRATION   Many enterprises have failed disastrously in achieving overall coordination of data. This failure is extremely expensive in the long run—in inflated DP costs, failure to implement needed procedures, and lost business. Box 40.1 lists the reasons for failure of corporate data administration.

It is necessary to make clear to top management the financial importance of successful data administration. It is the job of management to build a computerized corporation, and the foundation of that is the data models used.

BOX 40.1   Reasons for failure of corporate data administration

Many early attempts at corporate data administration failed. The reasons for failure were as follows:

- Organizational politics prevailed, partly because of a lack of strong management with a clear perception of what was to be accomplished.

- The human problems of making different accountants or managers agree on the definitions of data items were too great.

- The magnitude of the task was underestimated, and appropriate computerized tools were not used.

- Methodologies for the design of stable data structures were not understood.

- The necessary data models were too complex to design and administer by hand (and computerized tools were not used).

- There was not an overall architect who could use the design methodology.

- Attempts at data modeling took too long and users could not wait.

- Data-model design was confused with implementation.

Many corporations have achieved successful data administration. Box 40.2 lists the requirements necessary for this to succeed.

BOX 40.2 Essentials for the overall control of data in an enterprise

HUMAN

- Top management must understand the need for building the foundation of correctly modeled data.
- The data administrator must report at a suitably high level and be given full senior management support.
- The span of control of the data administrator needs to be selected with an understanding of what is politically pragmatic.
- The data administrator must be highly competent at using the design methodology, and the methodology must be automated.
- An appropriate budget for data modeling must be set.
- Data modeling should be quite separate from physical data-base design.
- End-user teams should be established to assist in data modeling and to review and refine the data models thoroughly.

TECHNICAL

- Strategic planning of the entities in an enterprise should be done [1]. All entities should be represented in a rough entity model.
- The rough entity model should be expanded into detailed data models in stages, as appropriate.
- The detailed data model should represent all functional dependencies among the data items.
- All logical data groups should be in third normal form (Chapter 41).
- Stability analysis should be applied to the detailed data model [2].
- The entity model and detailed model should be designed with an automated tool [3].
- Defined operations may be associated with the data to ensure integrity, accuracy, and security checks are applied to the data, independent of applications.
- Submodels should be extractable from the overall computerized model when needed for specific projects.
- Ideally, the data modeling tool should provide *automatic* input to the library of the specification language, application generator, or programming language that is used [3].

Box 40.2 lists the essentials for overall control of data in an enterprise. Some corporations have achieved excellent computerized data modeling, and this has both improved their overall usage of computers and made their applications much easier to change and maintain.

REFERENCES

1. J. Martin, *Strategic Data Planning Methodologies,* Englewood Cliffs, NJ: Prentice-Hall, Inc., 1982.

2. J. Martin, *Managing the Data Base Environment,* Englewood Cliffs, NJ: Prentice-Hall, Inc., 1983.

3. Such as Data Designer, from Database Design, Inc., Ann Arbor, MI. The output of Data Designer can be automatically converted to the HOS representation of data.

41 THIRD NORMAL FORM

NORMALIZATION OF DATA

Normalization of data refers to the way data items are grouped into record structures. *Third normal form* is a grouping of data designed to avoid the anomalies and problems that can occur with data. The concept originated with the mathematics of E. F. Codd [1].

With third-normal-form data, each data item in a record refers to a particular key, which uniquely identifies those data. The key itself may be composed of more than one data item. Each data item in the record is identified by the whole key and not just part of the key. No data item in the record is identifiable by any other data item in the record that is not part of the key.

The basic simplicity of third normal form makes the data records easy to understand and easier to change than when data are organized in less rigorous ways. It formally groups the data items associated with each entity type (and also those associated with more than one entity type) and separates the data items that belong to different entity types. Third normal form prevents anomalies that can otherwise occur. It permits rules to be established for controlling semantic disintegrity in query languages.

Data exist in real life as groups of data items. They exist on invoices, bills, tax forms, driving licences, and so on. These groupings are usually not in a normalized form. Not surprisingly, systems analysts have often implemented computer records that are also not normalized. However, data that are not normalized can lead to various subtle problems in the future.

Experience has shown that when computer data are organized in third normal form, the resulting data structures are more stable and able to accommodate change. Each attribute relates to its own entity and is not mixed up with attributes relating to different entities. The actions that create and update data can then be applied with simple structured design to one normalized record at a time.

BOX 41.1 Conversion to third normal form

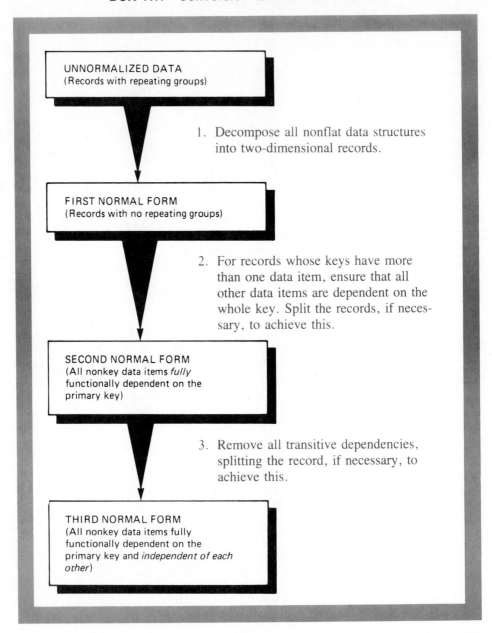

UNNORMALIZED DATA
(Records with repeating groups)

1. Decompose all nonflat data structures into two-dimensional records.

FIRST NORMAL FORM
(Records with no repeating groups)

2. For records whose keys have more than one data item, ensure that all other data items are dependent on the whole key. Split the records, if necessary, to achieve this.

SECOND NORMAL FORM
(All nonkey data items *fully* functionally dependent on the primary key)

3. Remove all transitive dependencies, splitting the record, if necessary, to achieve this.

THIRD NORMAL FORM
(All nonkey data items fully functionally dependent on the primary key and *independent of each other*)

At the time of writing, only a small proportion of existing data bases were in third normal form. Some corporations have several years of experience of operation with third-normal-form data structures. There is no question that they have greatly benefited from this type of design, especially when it is combined with other steps that are part of good data administration [2].

Reacting to the perceived benefits, some corporations have incorporated into their data-base standards manuals the requirement that all data-base structures be in third normal form. Usually this form of·design is better in terms of *machine* requirements as well as in logical structuring, but this is not always the case. Sometimes the physical designer finds it desirable to deviate from third normal form. A compromise is then needed. Which is preferable, somewhat better machine performance or better protection from maintenance costs? Usually the potential maintenance costs are the more expensive.

The data-base standards manual should say that all data will be *designed* in third normal form but that the physical implementation may occasionally deviate from third normal form if the trade-off is fully explored and documented.

To put data into third normal form, three steps may be used. It is put into *first normal form,* then *second normal form,* then *third normal form.* Box 41.1 summarizes this process.

The basic ideas of this normalization of data are simple, but the ramifications are many and subtle, and they vary from one type of data-base usage to another. It is important to note that normalization describes the *logical* not the physical, representation of data. There are many ways of implementing it physically.

Box 41.2 gives the terminology used in discussing data.

FIRST NORMAL FORM

First normal form refers to a collection of data organized into records that have no repeating groups of data items within a record. In other words, they are flat files, two-dimensional matrices of data items. Such a flat file may be thought of as a simple two-dimensional table. It may, however, contain many thousands of records.

Most programming languages give programmers the ability to create and refer to records that are not flat; that is, they contain repeating groups of data items within a record. In COBOL these are called *data tables.* There can be data tables within data tables—repeating groups within repeating groups.

The following COBOL record contains two data groups, called BIRTH and SKILLS.

```
RECORD NAME IS PERSON.
02    EMPLOYEE# PICTURE "9(5)".
02    EMPNAME PICTURE X(20).
```

BOX 41.2   Vocabulary used in discussing data

A clear distinction must be made between the terms *data type* and *data-item type*.

Data type refers to an attribute of the data themselves: data about data. Examples of data types are *integer, rational number, Boolean,* and *alphabetic string*.

Entity type refers to a given class of entities, such as *customer, part, account, employee*.

Attribute refers to a characteristic of an entity type; for example, *color, shape, shipment date, type of account, dollar value*.

Data-item type refers to either an *entity type* or an *attribute*.

Data item refers to a field that expresses an attribute or entity identifier (a special type of attribute) in computable form.

Data-item type refers to a given class of data items. Examples of data-item types are *customer number, account number, address, dollar value, color*.

Entities and data items are *instances* of entity types and data-item types, respectively. For example, DUPONT is an instance of the entity type *customer*. RED is an instance of the attribute *color*. DATA ITEM 4789123 is an instance of the data-item type *employee number*.

In discussing data we sometimes use a shorthand. We say "entity" when we mean "entity type," "data item" when we mean "data-item type," and so on. *Data type* is never abbreviated. That term is especially important in the HOS methodology.

```
O2    SEX PICTURE X.
O2    EMPJCODE PICTURE 9999.
O2    SALARY PICTURE 9(5)V99.
O2    BIRTH.
            O3      MONTH PICTURE 99.
            O3      DAY PICTURE 99.
            O3      YEAR PICTURE 99.
O2    NOSKILLS.
O2    SKILLS OCCURS NOSKILLS TIMES.
            O3      SKILLCODE PICTURE 9999.
            O3      SKILLYEARS PICTURE 99.
```

PERSON

EMPLOYEE#	EMPNAME	SEX	EMPJCODE	SALARY	BIRTH			SKILLS	
					MONTH	DAY	YEAR	SKILLCODE	SKILLYEARS

BIRTH causes no problems because it occurs only once in each record. SKILLS can occur several times in one record, so it is a data table, and the record is not in first normal form. It is not a flat, two-dimensional record. To *normalize* it, the table SKILLS must be removed and put into a separate record:

PERSON

EMPLOYEE#	EMPNAME	SEX	EMPJCODE	SALARY	BIRTH		
					MONTH	DAY	YEAR

SKILLS

EMPLOYEE# + SKILLCODE	SKILLYEARS

The lower record has a concatenated key, EMPLOYEE# + SKILL-CODE. We cannot know SKILLYEARS (the number of years of experience an employee has had with a given skill) unless we know EMPLOYEE# (the employee number to which this refers) and SKILLCODE (the skill in question).

In general, a nonflat record is normalized by converting it into two or more flat records.

If the normalized records in our example were implemented in a CODA-SYL, DL/1, or other nonrelational data-base management system, we would not repeat the field EMPLOYEE# in the lower record. A linkage to the upper record would imply this key:

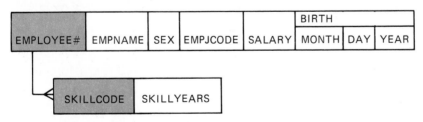

A relational data base *would* employ a separate SKILLS record (relation) with a key EMPLOYEE + SKILLCODE; it thus avoids pointer mechanisms in the logical representation of data.

Here we are concerned not with how the physical implementation is done but with the overall *logical* representation of data. We need to analyze and chart an enterprise's information resources and how they are used. We draw the lower record with its complete concatenated key so that it can stand alone, and the key uniquely identifies the data in the record.

FUNCTIONAL DEPENDENCE

In attempting to lay out the relationships between data items, the designer must be concerned with which data items are *dependent* on which others. Functional dependence is defined as follows:

> Data item B of a record, R, is functionally dependent on data item A of R if, at every instant of time, each value in A has no more than one value in B associated with it in record R. [3]

Saying that B is functionally dependent on A is equivalent to saying that A *identifies* B. In other words, if we know the value of A, we can find the value of B that is associated with it.

For example, in an employee record, the SALARY data item is functionally dependent on EMPLOYEE#. For one EMPLOYEE# there is one SALARY. To find the value of SALARY in a data base, you would normally go via EMPLOYEE#. The latter is a key that identifies the attribute SALARY.

We will draw a functional dependency with a line that has a small crossbar on it:

$$\text{EMPLOYEE\#} \longmapsto \text{SALARY}$$

This indicates that one instance of SALARY is associated with each EMPLOYEE#.

Consider the record for the entity EMPLOYEE:

EMPLOYEE#	EMPLOYEE-NAME	SALARY	PROJECT#	COMPLETION-DATE

The functional dependencies in this record are as follows:

EMPLOYEE#	is dependent on EMPLOYEE-NAME
EMPLOYEE-NAME	is dependent on EMPLOYEE#
SALARY	is dependent on either EMPLOYEE-NAME or EMPLOYEE#
PROJECT#	is dependent on either EMPLOYEE-NAME or EMPLOYEE#
COMPLETION-DATE	is dependent on EMPLOYEE-NAME, EMPLOYEE# or PROJECT#

EMPLOYEE# is not functionally dependent on SALARY because more than one employee could have the same salary. Similarly, EMPLOYEE# is not functionally dependent on PROJECT#, but COMPLETION-DATE is. No other data item in the record is fully dependent on PROJECT#.

We can draw these functional dependencies as follows:

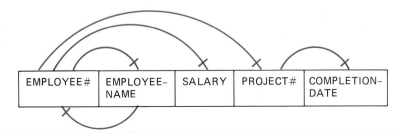

A data item can be functionally dependent on a *group* of data items rather than on a single data item. Consider, for example, the following record, which shows how programmers spent their time:

PROGRAMMER-ACTIVITY

PROGRAMMER#	PACKAGE#	PROGRAMMER-NAME	PACKAGE-NAME	TOTAL-HOURS-WORKED

TOTAL-HOURS-WORKED is functionally dependent on the concatenated key (PROGRAMMER#, PACKAGE#).

The functional dependencies in this record can be drawn as follows:

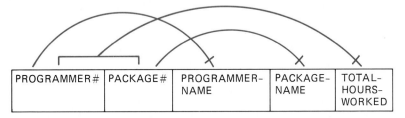

FULL FUNCTIONAL DEPENDENCY   A data item or a collection of data items, B, of a record, R, can be said to be *fully functionally dependent* on another collection of data items, A, of record R if B is functionally dependent on the whole of A but not on any subset of A.

For example, in the record in our example, TOTAL-HOURS-WORKED is fully functionally dependent on the concatenated key (PROGRAMMER#, PACKAGE#) because it refers to how many hours a given programmer has worked on a given package. Neither PROGRAMMER# alone nor PACKAGE# alone identifies TOTAL-HOURS-WORKED.

TOTAL-HOURS-WORKED, however, is the *only* data item that is fully functionally dependent on the concatenated key. PROGRAMMER-NAME is fully functionally dependent on PROGRAMMER# alone, and PACKAGE-NAME is fully functionally dependent on PACKAGE# alone. The lines with bars above make these dependencies clear.

SECOND NORMAL FORM

We are now in a position to define second normal form. First a simple definition:

Each attribute in a record is functionally dependent on the whole key of that record.

Where the key consists of more than one data item, the record may not be in second normal form. The record with the key PROGRAMMER# + PACKAGE# is not in second normal form because TOTAL-HOURS-WORKED depends on the whole key, whereas PROGRAMMER-NAME and PACKAGE-NAME each depend on only one data item in the key. Similarly, the following record is not in second normal form:

PART#	SUPPLIER#	SUPPLIER-NAME	SUPPLIER-DETAILS	PRICE

There are a few problems that can result from this record's not being in second normal form:

1. We cannot enter details about a supplier until that supplier supplies a part. If the supplier does not supply a part, there is no key.

2. If a supplier should temporarily cease to supply any part, the deletion of the last record containing that SUPPLIER# will also delete the details of the supplier. It would normally be desirable that SUPPLIER-DETAILS be preserved.

3. We have problems when we attempt to update the supplier details. We must search for every record that contains that supplier as part of the key. If a supplier supplies many parts, much redundant updating of supplier details will be needed.

These types of irregularities can be removed by splitting the record into two records in second normal form, as shown in Fig. 41.1. Only PRICE is fully functionally dependent on the concatenated key, so all other attributes are removed to the separate record on the left, which has only SUPPLIER-NUMBER as its key.

Splitting to second normal form is the type of splitting that natural database growth tends to force, so it might as well be anticipated when the data base is first set up. In general, every data item in a record should be dependent on the *entire* key; otherwise, it should be removed to a separate record.

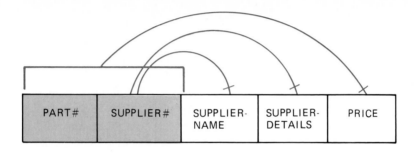

An instance of this record:

PART#	SUPPLIER#	SUPPLIER-NAME	SUPPLIER-DETAILS	PRICE
1	1000	JONES	x	20
1	1500	ABC	x	28
1	2050	XYZ	y	22
1	1900	P–H	z	30
2	3100	ALLEN	z	520
2	1000	JONES	x	500
2	2050	XYZ	y	590
3	2050	XYZ	y	1000
4	1000	JONES	x	80
4	3100	ALLEN	z	90
4	1900	P–H	z	95
5	1500	ABC	x	160
5	1000	JONES	x	140

To convert the records above into second normal form, we split it into two records, thus:

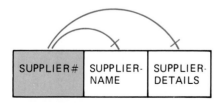
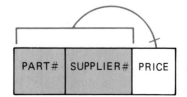

An instance of the above pair of records:

SUPPLIER#	SUPPLIER-NAME	SUPPLIER-DETAILS
1000	JONES	x
1500	ABC	x
2050	XYZ	y
1900	P–H	z
3100	ALLEN	z

PART#	SUPPLIER#	PRICE
1	1000	20
1	1500	28
1	2050	22
1	1900	30
2	3100	520
2	1000	500
2	2050	590
3	2050	1000
4	1000	80
4	3100	90
4	1900	95
5	1500	160
5	1000	140

Figure 41.1   Conversion to second normal form.

CANDIDATE KEYS   The *key* of a normalized record must have the following properties:

1. *Unique identification.* For every record occurrence, the key must uniquely identify the record.
2. *Nonredundancy.* No data item in the key can be discarded without destroying the property of unique identification.

It sometimes happens that more than one data item or set of data items *could* be the key of a record. Such alternative choices are referred to as *candidate keys*.

One candidate key must be designated the *primary key*. We will draw the functional dependencies for candidate keys that are not the primary key *underneath* the record:

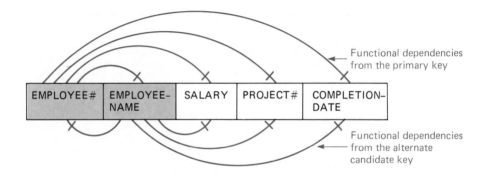

In this illustration, EMPLOYEE-NAME is regarded as a candidate key—an alternative to EMPLOYEE#. This is not generally done in practice because two employees *might* have the same name. Only EMPLOYEE# is truly unique.

The possible existence of candidate keys complicates the definitions of second and third normal form.

A more comprehensive definition of second normal form is:

A record, R, is in second normal form if it is in first normal form and every nonprime data item of R is fully functionally dependent on each candidate key of R. [3]

In the EMPLOYEE record, the candidate keys have only one data item; hence the record is always in second normal form because the nonprime data items *must* be fully dependent on the candidate keys. When the candidate keys consist of more than one data item, a first-normal-form record may not be in second normal form.

THIRD NORMAL FORM

A record that *is* in second normal form can have another type of anomaly. It may have a data item that is not a key but itself identifies other data items. This is referred to as a *transitive dependency*. Transitive dependencies can cause problems. The step of putting data into *third normal form* removes transitive dependencies.

Suppose that A, B, and C are three data items or distinct collections of data items of a record, R. If C is functionally dependent on B and B is functionally dependent on A, C is functionally dependent on A. If the inverse mapping is nonsimple (i.e., if A is not functionally dependent on B *or* B is not functionally dependent on C), C is said to be *transitively dependent* on A.

In a diagram, C is transitively dependent on A if the following relationships exist:

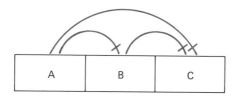

Conversion to third normal form removes this transitive dependency by splitting the record into two:

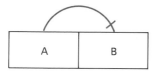 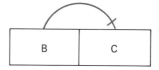

The following record is not in third normal form because COMPLETION-DATE is dependent on PROJECT#.

EMPLOYEE

EMPLOYEE#	EMPLOYEE-NAME	SALARY	PROJECT#	COMPLETION-DATE

A few problems might result from this record's not being in third normal form:

1. Before any employees are recruited for a project, the completion date of the project cannot be recorded because there is no EMPLOYEE record.

2. If all the employees should leave the project so that the project has no employees until others are recruited, all records containing the completion date would be de-

leted. This may be thought an unlikely occurrence, but on other types of files a similar danger of loss of information can be less improbable.

3. If the completion date is changed, it will be necessary to search for all records containing that completion date and update them all.

A simple definition of third normal form is:

A record is in second normal form, and each attribute is functionally dependent on the key and *nothing but the key*.

A more formal definition, which incorporates candidate keys, is as follows:

A record, R, is in third normal form if it is in second normal form and every nonprime data item of R is nontransitively dependent on each candidate key of R.[3]

Figure 41.2 shows the conversion of the EMPLOYEE record to third normal form.

The conversion to third normal form produces a separate record for each entity: a normalized record. For example, Fig. 41.2 produced a separate record for the entity PROJECT. Usually this normalized record would be needed anyway. We need to store data separately for each entity.

STORAGE AND PERFORMANCE

The concept of third normal form applies to all data bases. Experiences has shown that the records of a CODASYL system, the segments of a DL/1 system, or the group of data items in other systems can benefit from being in third normal form.

Objections to third normal form are occasionally heard on the grounds that it requires more storage or more machine time. It is true that a third-normal-form structure usually has more records after all the splitting. Isn't that worse from the hardware point of view?

Not necessarily. In fact, although there are more records, they almost always take less storage. The reason is that non-third-normal-form records usually have much *value* redundancy.

Compare the records in Fig. 41.1. Here records not in second normal form are converted to second normal form by splitting. It will be seen that the lower red part of Fig. 41.1 has fewer *values* of data written down than the red part at the top. There are fewer values of SUPPLIER-NAME and SUPPLIER-DETAILS. This shrinkage does not look very dramatic on such a small illustration. If there had been thousands of suppliers and thousands of parts, and many attributes of both, the shrinkage would have been spectacular.

Again, compare the red parts of Fig. 41.2. Here a record is converted to

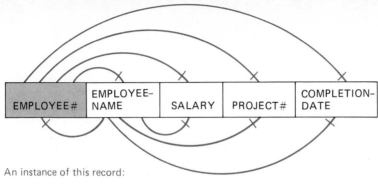

An instance of this record:

EMPLOYEE#	EMPLOYEE-NAME	SALARY	PROJECT#	COMPLETION-DATE
120	JONES	2000	x	17.7.84
121	HARPO	1700	x	17.7.84
270	GARFUNKAL	1800	y	12.1.87
273	SELSI	3600	x	17.7.84
274	ABRAHMS	3000	z	21.3.86
279	HIGGINS	2400	y	12.1.87
301	FLANNEL	1800	z	21.3.86
306	MCGRAW	2100	x	17.7.84
310	ENSON	3000	z	21.3.86
315	GOLDSTEIN	3100	x	17.7.84
317	PUORRO	2700	y	12.1.87
320	MANSINI	1700	y	12.1.87
321	SPOTO	2900	x	17.7.84
340	SCHAFT	3100	x	17.7.84
349	GOLD	1900	z	21.3.86

To convert the above record into third normal form we split it into two records, thus:

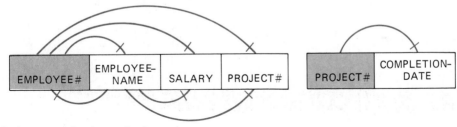

An instance of the above pair of records:

EMPLOYEE#	EMPLOYEE-NAME	SALARY	PROJECT#
120	JONES	2000	x
121	HARPO	1700	x
270	GARFUNKAL	1800	y
273	SELSI	3600	x
274	ABRAHMS	3000	z
279	HIGGINS	2400	y
301	FLANNEL	1800	z
306	MCGRAW	2100	x
310	ENSON	3000	z
315	GOLDSTEIN	3100	x
317	PUORRO	2700	y
320	MANSINI	1700	y
321	SPOTO	2900	x
340	SCHAFT	3100	x

PROJECT#	COMPLETION-DATE
x	17.7.84
y	12.1.87
z	21.3.86

Figure 41.2 Conversion to third normal form.

third normal form by splitting. The number of *values* of data shrinks. There are fewer values of COMPLETION-DATE recorded after the split. Again, if there had been many employees, many projects, and many attributes of those projects, the shrinkage would have been dramatic.

Conversion to third normal form almost always reduces the amount of storage used, often dramatically.

What about machine time and accesses? Often this is less after normalization. Before normalization, many aspects of the data are tangled together and must all be read at once. After normalization, they are separated, so a small record is read.

Also, because there is less value redundancy in third normal form, there is less duplicated updating of the redundant values. Suppose project X slips its completion date (which it does every week!). In the record at the top of Fig. 41.2, the completion date has to be changed seven times; in the third-normal-form version, it has to be changed only once. A similar argument applies to SUPPLIER-NAME and SUPPLIER-DETAILS in Fig. 41.1. The argument would have more force if the examples had hundreds of employees, thousands of suppliers, and many attributes that have to be updated.

There are, however, exceptions to this. On rare occasions, a designer may consciously design non-third-normal-form records for performance reasons.

For our purposes throughout most of this book, third normal form relates to the logical structure of data, not the physical.

SEMANTIC DISINTEGRITY

A further reason for using third normal form is that certain data-base queries can run into problems when data are not cleanly structured. A query, perhaps entered with a data-base query language, can appear to be valid but in fact have subtle illogical aspects sometimes referred to as *semantic disintegrity*. When the data are in third normal form, rules can be devised for preventing semantic disintegrity or warning the user about his query.

CLEAR THINKING ABOUT DATA

Third normal form is an aid to clear thinking about data. It is a formal method of separating the data items that relate to different entities.

A record in third normal form has a clean, simple structure, shown on the top of page 599.

The functional dependency lines all come from the primary key. There are no hidden dependencies not relating to the key. If the key is concatenated, all data items are dependent on the entire key.

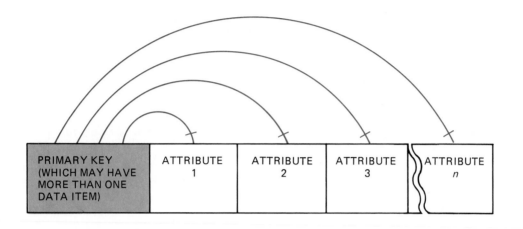

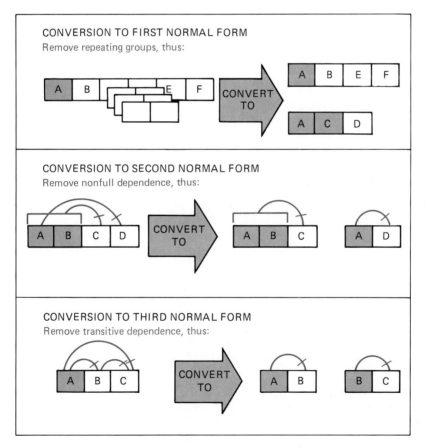

Figure 41.3 A simplified illustration of the three steps in conversion of data to third normal form. Figure 41.4 gives an illustration with real data.

We can give a loose definition of third normal form, which has the advantage of being easy to remember:

> Every data item in a record is dependent on the key, the whole key, and nothing but the key.

If a systems analyst remembers this definition (understanding that it is not rigorous like those earlier in the chapter), he can quickly spot and modify records that are not in third normal form. He should be familiar enough with this that alarm bells go off in his mind whenever he sees records that are not in third normal form.

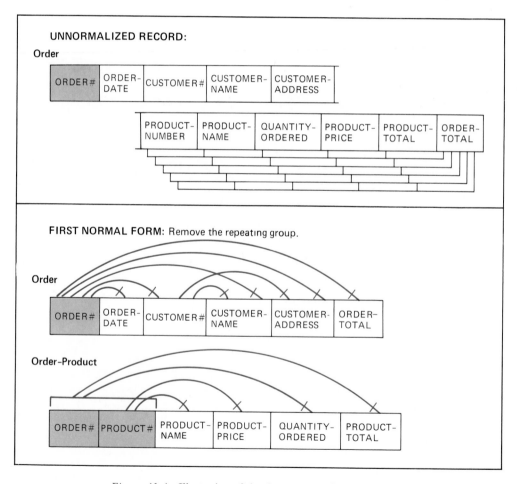

Figure 41.4   Illustration of the three stages of normalization.

SECOND NORMAL FORM: Remove attributes not dependent on the whole of a (concatenated) primary key, as in the ORDER-PRODUCT record above.

Order

ORDER#	ORDER-DATE	CUSTOMER#	CUSTOMER-NAME	CUSTOMER-ADDRESS	ORDER-TOTAL

Order-Product

ORDER#	PRODUCT#	QUANTITY-ORDERED	PRODUCT-TOTAL

Product

PRODUCT#	PRODUCT-NAME	PRODUCT-PRICE

THIRD NORMAL FORM: Remove attributes dependent on data item(s) other than the primary key, as in the ORDER record above.

Order

ORDER NUMBER	ORDER DATE	CUSTOMER NUMBER	ORDER TOTAL

Customer

CUSTOMER NUMBER	CUSTOMER NAME	CUSTOMER ADDRESS

Order-Product

ORDER NUMBER	PRODUCT NUMBER	QUANTITY ORDERED	PRODUCT TOTAL

Product

PRODUCT NUMBER	PRODUCT NAME	PRODUCT PRICE

Figure 41.4   (Continued)

This clean, simple data grouping is easy to implement and to use. There will be complications in store in the future if more complex record structures are used.

For the data-base administrator, third normal form is an aid to precision. A data base in third normal form can grow and evolve naturally. The updating rules are straightforward. A third-normal-form record type can have records added to it or can have records deleted without the problems that could occur with non-third-normal-form record types. Third-normal-form structuring gives a simple view of data to the programmers and users and makes them less likely to perform invalid operations.

Figure 41.3 gives a simplified illustration of the three steps in achieving third-normal-form structures.

A SUGGESTED EXERCISE

Probably the best way for a data processing user to become convinced of the value of normalization is to take a section of his files and write down what third-normal-form records would be used to represent them. A group of systems analysts should then list all the plausible changes that might occur to the files as data processing evolves in the years ahead and see how many of these changes would necessitate restructuring the records in such a way that previously written application programs would have to be changed. Compare this with what reprogramming would be needed if the same changes were applied to the existing records.

In examining existing data bases, it has been our experience that time and time again they are not in third normal form. This spells trouble for the future. Unless it was the conscious policy of management to create third-normal-form structures, the design has been far from these principles.

AN EXAMPLE OF NORMALIZATION

Consider an order record with the following unnormalized structure:

ORDER (*Order number,* order date, customer number, customer name, customer address [product number, product name, quantity ordered, product price, product total] order total.)

The application of the three normalization steps to this example is illustrated in Fig. 41.4.

Application of the **first-normal-form** rule (remove repeating groups) creates two records: ORDER and ORDER-PRODUCT. The primary key is made up of ORDER# and PRODUCT#.

Second normal form removes the product name from the ORDER-

PRODUCT record into a new record: PRODUCT. Product name is wholly dependent on product number; it is only partially dependent on the primary (combined or compound) key of ORDER-PRODUCT: ORDER# + PRODUCT#.

Third normal form removes the customer details from the ORDER record to a separate CUSTOMER record. Customer name and address are wholly dependent on customer number; they are not dependent at all on the primary key of ORDER (i.e., ORDER#). (A customer will not change his name and address with each new order—unless he doesn't intend to pay for it!)

The four resulting records—ORDER, CUSTOMER, ORDER-PRODUCT, and PRODUCT—in Fig. 41.4 are in third normal form.

REFERENCES

1. J. Martin, *System Design from Provably Correct Constructs,* Englewood Cliffs, NJ: Prentice-Hall, Inc., 1985. E. F. Codd mathematics appears in Appendix IV.

2. J. Martin, *Managing the Data Base Environment,* Englewood Cliffs, NJ: Prentice-Hall, Inc., 1983.

3. E. F. Codd, "Further Normalization of the Data Base Relational Model," in *Data Base Systems,* ed. R. Rustin, Englewood Cliffs, NJ: Prentice-Hall, Inc., 1972.

42 AUTOMATED DATA MODELING

INTRODUCTION   Various software tools exist for automating the work
of data modeling. Experience with them has shown
that installations benefit greatly from the use of data models that are generated
and maintained by computer.

It is the task of a *data administrator* to create and be the custodian of the
data model (or models) in an enterprise. We believe that the data model should
be designed and maintained with a computerized tool. The task is too tedious
and error-prone to be done by hand. Organizations without computerized data
models usually have all sorts of inconsistencies and errors in their representation
of data. These become very expensive in maintenance costs, lost application
opportunities, and incorrect information for management.

The technique of canonical synthesis, described in this chapter, would be
too tedious to apply to large installations unless it were automated. Once computerized, it automatically produces fully normalized data models. Like HOS,
it falls into the category of techniques designed for use by computer rather than
use by hand.

Application creators can get into various subtle types of trouble if the data
they use are not correctly modeled. Long and expensive experience has shown
the need for thorough data analysis. The authors have picked apart many examples of specifications, data flow diagrams, and other forms of application
design that are wrong because the designer did not have a correct data model.

A data model shows the functional dependencies and associations among
data items. Functional dependencies in data do not depend on any specific application. They are inherent properties of the data themselves, independent of
how the data are used. The data model, therefore, has a long-term life, whereas
applications often have a short-term life. The logical model of data is a vital
foundation for the building of data processing in an enterprise.

The data in a data model are in third normal form, as described in Chapter

41. However, we need more than simply third-normal-form design of records. The normalized records must be correctly associated into larger structures, and redundancy among data used in different areas must be avoided. Without overall data modeling, different areas could have different normalized data that are highly redundant.

Synthesis of data models is a complex process that has been described in more detail elsewhere [1]. The input to the process is simple in that it can be entered a small step at a time. It needs much human thought about the true nature and definitions of the data. The computerized output of the process can *automatically* become the descriptions of data used in tools for automating application development.

When appropriate automation is used, the difficulties of data administration cease to be *technical* difficulties; they are the human and political difficulties of agreeing about the definitions and uses of data.

THE SYNTHESIS PROCESS

The synthesis process described in this chapter creates a minimal nonredundant data model, designed to be as stable as possible. We refer to it as a *canonical* model. There is one and only one canonical model of a given collection of data items and functional dependencies.

The canonical form of data that we derive in this chapter is independent of whether the data will eventually be represented by means of hierarchical, CODASYL, relational, or other structures. An additional step in deriving a workable schema is to convert the canonical form of the data into a structure that can be supported by whatever software is being used. This is a relatively straightforward step.

The canonical model is sometimes also called a *conceptual model* or *conceptual schema*. This model must be converted into a logical representation that the selected software can handle, and this is then represented physically.

In first deriving the canonical form of the data, we will ignore the question of machine performance. Infrequently used linkages between data will be treated in the same way as linkages of high usage. The resulting minimal data structure will then be reexamined to distinguish between the high-usage and low-usage paths, or paths that are used in real-time operation and batch operation. It will often be necessary to deviate from the minimal structure because of constraints in the software that is used.

The synthesis process can be done largely automatically with a tool that produces third-normal-form structures and good documentation. Such a tool should be used on a companywide basis to design, clarify, unify, and document the corporation's data structures. The tool can be used in conjunction with a data dictionary, as discussed in this chapter.

This chapter introduces the canonical modeling process. It is discussed in more detail, along with practical experience of using it and the role of the data administrator, in James Martin's *Managing the Data Base Environment* [1].

BUBBLE CHARTS

To communicate with the data administrator, end users should be able to draw representations of data structures and understand the diagrams of the data administrator.

Data-base professionals use very complicated words. To involve end users, we must communicate in simple words. Using the bubble charts described in Chapter 22, we could explain the basic ideas of data structures to a child of 10.

Bubble charts provide a way of representing and thinking about data and the associations between data items. They explain the nature of data very simply so that end users can be taught to use them, draw them, and think about their data with them. Bubble charts drawn by end-users can form a vital input to the data-base design process.

SYNTHESIZING USER VIEWS

The data modeling process takes many separate user views of data and *synthesizes* them into a structure that incorporates all of them. The synthesis is done in such a way that redundant data items are eliminated where possible. The same data item does not generally appear twice in the final result. Also, redundant *associations* are eliminated where possible. In other words, a minimal number of lines connect the bubbles in the resulting bubble chart.

The synthesis process is a formal procedure following a formal set of rules. Because it is a formal procedure, it can be done by a computer. This eliminates errors in the process, provides formal documentation that is a basis for end-user discussion, and permits any input view to be changed or new views to be added and immediately reflects the effect of the change in the resulting data model. The computer output can then be *automatically* converted to HOS data representation or representation for other application-generation tools.

ILLUSTRATION OF THE SYNTHESIS PROCESS

As a simple illustration of the synthesis process, consider the four user views of data shown in Fig. 42.1. We want to combine those into a single data model. To start, here is view 1:

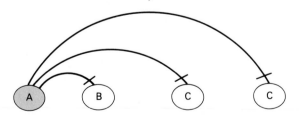

We will combine it with view 2:

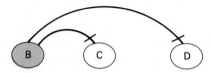

None of the data items appears twice in the result:

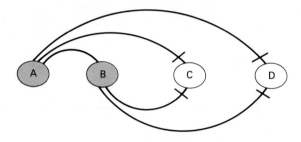

There are, however, some redundant links:

A identifies B.

B identifies C.

Therefore, A *must* identify C.

Therefore, the link A —+ C is redundant.

Similarly, A identifies B and B identifies D; therefore, A *must* identify D. Therefore, the link A —+ D is redundant.

Now the third view is this:

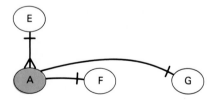

This contains three data items, E, F, and G. When it is merged into the model we get this chart:

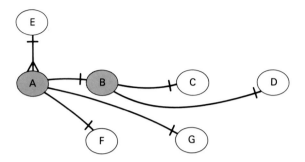

There are no new redundancies, so we will merge in the fourth view:

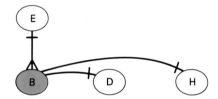

This adds one new data item to the model, H:

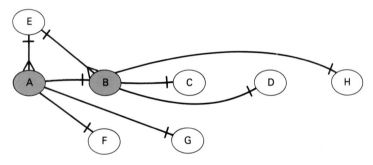

There is now one redundant link: A identifies B; B identifies E; therefore, A *must* identify E. We can remove the one-to-one link from A to E (we cannot change the crow's-foot link from E to A):

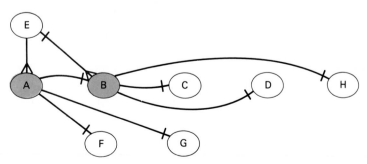

In this resulting structure, there are two primary keys; A and B. (A primary key is a bubble with one or more one-to-one links leaving it.)

We can associate each primary key with the attributes it identifies:

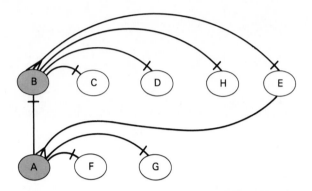

On each linkage between primary keys it is desirable to put the reverse linkage. We should therefore ask, Is the link from B to A a one-to-many link or a one-to-one link?

Suppose that it is a crow's-foot link. The following diagram draws the logical records that result from this design.

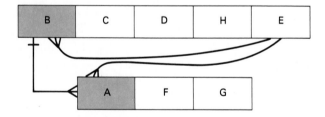

E, here, is a secondary key pointing to both A and B. In old punched-card or batch processing systems, secondary keys, like E, were the *sort* keys. In on-line systems, secondary key paths like those from E to A or B are followed by such means as pointers or indices.

LEVELS OF PRIMARY KEYS

Some of the primary keys themselves identify other primary keys; that is, they have one-to-one links with other primary keys. For clarity, the diagram of the data structure is often drawn with the one-to-one links between primary keys pointing upwards whenever possible. This is normally done in a tree-structure representation of data. The record at the top of the tree is called the root record, and its primary key is a *root key*.

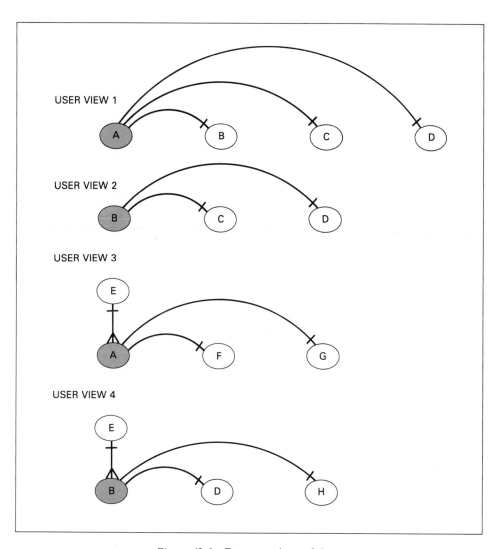

Figure 42.1   Four user views of data.

We can define a root key as follows:

A root key is a primary key with no one-to-one links leaving it to another primary key.

In a tree structure, there is one root key. Structures more complicated than a tree structure (called *plex* or *network structures*) may have more than one root key.

In the last preceding diagram, data item B is the root key.

The definition of *root key* is not fundamental to understanding data, as are the definitions of *primary key* and *secondary key*. It is, however, *useful* to know which are the root keys and root records for planning the physical organization of the data.

The primary keys, or the records they identify, can be arranged into levels. The highest level is the root key, and we will call this depth 1.

A depth 2 primary key has a one-to-one link to a depth 1 primary key.

A depth 3 primary key has a one-to-one link to a depth 2 primary key but no one-to-one links to a depth 1 primary key.

A depth N primary key has a one-to-one link to a depth $N - 1$ primary key but no one-to-one links to a depth M primary key where $M < N - 1$.

The primary keys with the greatest depth in a data structure have no one-to-one links entering them.

Levels can be indicated on a drawing by positioning the data-item groups with different amounts of offset: the depth 1 groups are the leftmost and the deepest groups are the rightmost, as shown in Fig. 42.2.

CANONICAL DATA STRUCTURES

If we have a given collection of data items and we identify their functional dependencies, we can combine them into a nonredundant model. We combine redundant data items and redundant associations so that no redundancy remains.

There is one and only one nonredundant model of a given collection of data. We call this a *canonical model*—a model obtained by following a formal set of rules.

Secondary keys may be added to the model later as the need to search the data is identified. If we consider only primary keys and the grouping of the data items in entity records, the resulting model is *independent of how the data are used*. The structure is inherent in the properties of the data themselves.

Because there is only one nonredundant model and that model is independent of the usage of the data, data designed this way in an enterprise is *stable*. This constitutes a valuable structured technique. *We can structure the data independently of their usage*.

We will define a canonical schema as a model of data that represents the inherent structure of those data in a nonredundant fashion; hence is independent of individual applications of the data and also of the software or hardware mechanisms employed in representing and using the data.

We have stressed that procedures—the way people use data—change rapidly in a typical enterprise. The data themselves have a structure that will not change unless new types of data are added. As new types of data are added, the model can grow in a fashion that does not necessitate the rewriting of existing programs (if the data-base management system has good data independence).

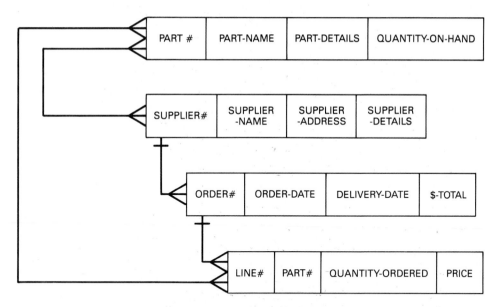

Figure 42.2   Data model with two root keys and three levels of primary key.

Most structured techniques have analyzed procedures first and then decided what file or data-base structures are necessary for these procedures. This has resulted in high maintenance costs because the procedures change. In good information engineering, we analyze the data first and apply various steps to make it stable. Then we look for techniques that enable users to employ those data with as little programming effort as possible—query languages, report generators, and so on. These languages can produce incorrect results if the data are not correctly modeled [2].

CANONICAL SYNTHESIS

The technique we describe takes any number of user views of data and combines them into a minimal set of canonical records with the requisite links between records.

We will represent the user views, or application views of data, by means of bubble charts and will combine them, a step at a time, eliminating redundancies. We will not include every possible link between the data items, only those that end users or application programs employ. The method is tedious to do by hand but is easy to do by computer.

The input to the process must correctly identify the functional dependencies. The output is then automatically in third normal form.

The technique can be applied to the narrow perspective of data bases designed for a specific set of applications or to the broader perspective of building enterprise data models. The entities in a companywide entity chart may be clustered into submodels, which are, in turn, developed in detail using canonical synthesis.

ELIMINATION OF REDUNDANCIES

In the following grouping of data items, the link from X to Z is *probably* redundant:

If we know that X ——+ Y and Y ——+ Z, this implies that X ——+ Z (i.e., there is one value of Z for each value of X). In other words, X identifies Y; Y identifies Z; therefore, X identifies Z.

Why did we say that the link from X to Z is "probably" redundant? Is it not *always* redundant?

Unfortunately, we cannot be absolutely sure unless we know the meaning of the association. As we have illustrated earlier, it is possible to have more than one association between the same two data items:

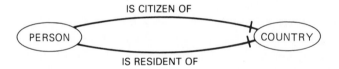

Therefore, before we delete X ——+ Z we must examine the meaning of the associations to be sure that X ——+ Z is *really* implied by X ——+ Y and Y ——+ Z.

In the following case we could not delete it. An employee has a telephone number:

The employee reports to a manager:

The manager also has a telephone number:

Combining these gives the following:

It would not be valid to assume that EMPLOYEE ⟶ TELEPHONE# is redundant and delete it. The employee's telephone number is different from the manager's, and we want both:

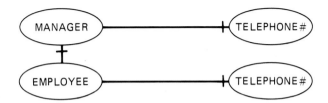

Because TELEPHONE# is an attribute, we can have a separate data item with this name associated with both EMPLOYEE and MANAGER.

The same pattern of associations could have occurred if all the data items in question had been keys:

In this case the links between the three key data items would be left as shown.

Nevertheless, the situation when we have this structure:

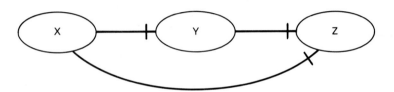

and cannot delete X ⎯⊢ Z is the exception rather than the rule. We have trouble in the case above because of muddled thinking: MANAGER and EM-PLOYEE are really the same type of data item: A manager is an employee. We will use the rule that one-to-one link redundancies can be removed, but each time we use this rule we must look carefully to ensure that we have a genuine redundancy.

Sometimes redundancies can be removed in longer strings of links. Thus in the case

A ⎯⊢ D is a candidate for removal.

It should be noted that one-to-many links cannot be removed. There is nothing necessarily redundant in the following:

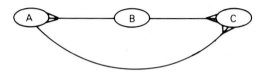

CANDIDATE KEYS

We defined a primary key as a node with one or more one-to-one links leaving it. There is one exception to this definition: the situation in which we have more than one *candidate key;* that is, more than one data item identifies the other data items in a group, as in the following chart:

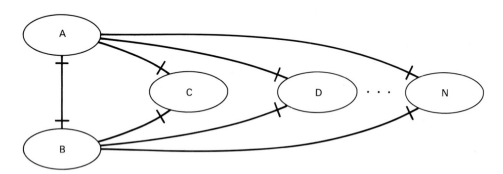

A and B in this case are equivalent. Each identifies the other; hence both identify, C, D, . . . , N. There is redundancy in this diagram. We could remove A ⎯⊢ C, A ⎯⊢ D, . . . , A ⎯⊢ N. Alternatively, we could remove B ⎯⊢ C, B ⎯⊢ D, . . . , B ⎯⊢ N.

The designer might decide that A is the candidate key he wants to employ. A, for example, might be EMPLOYEE# and B, EMPLOYEE-NAME. The designer that deletes the links B ——+ C, B ——+ D, . . . , B ——+ N:

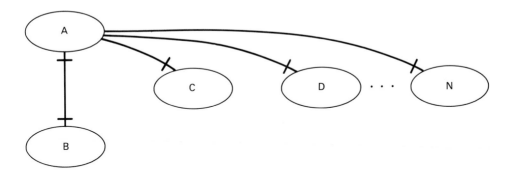

Candidate keys are not too common, as this example or those in Chapter 41 might suggest. EMPLOYEE-NAME would not normally be represented as identifying EMPLOYEE# because two employees could have the same name. EMPLOYEE# is the unique identifier. Occasionally, there is a genuine A ——+ B relationship, which should be left in the graph; for example, EMPLOYEE# ——+ SOCIAL SECURITY#. The designer must make a decision about which redundant links are deleted.

TRANSITIVE DEPENDENCIES

The input views to the synthesis process should contain no *hidden* primary keys. In other words, there should be no *transitive dependencies*.

The following purchase order master record contains a transitive dependency:

ORDER#	SUPPLIER#	SUPPLIER-NAME	SUPPLIER-ADDRESS	DELIVERY-DATE	ORDER-DATE	$-TOTAL

ORDER# is the key. It might be tempting to diagram this record as follows:

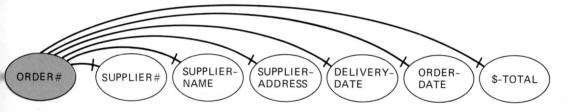

However, SUPPLIER-NAME and SUPPLIER-ADDRESS are identified by SUPPLIER#. The record is therefore better diagrammed as in Box 42.1.

This process of removing transitive dependencies is essentially equivalent to the conversion to third normal form discussed in Chapter 41.

Transitive dependencies should be removed from user views when they are originally diagrammed. This is done before they are fed into the synthesis process.

CONCATENATED KEYS   As discussed earlier, concatenated keys may be necessary. In the earlier example, the price was identi-

BOX 42.1   Avoidance of hidden transitive dependencies in the representation of user views of data

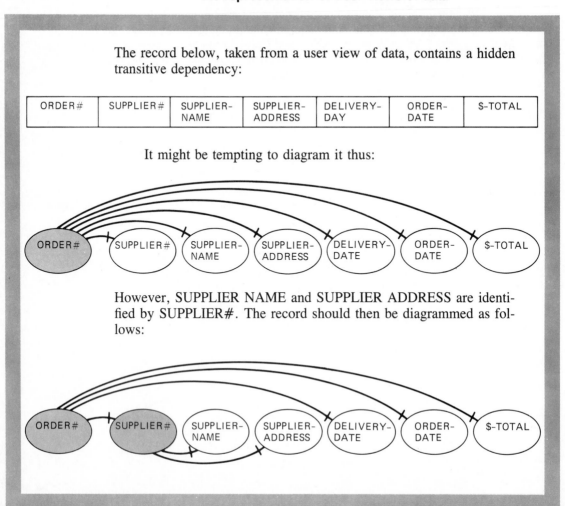

The record below, taken from a user view of data, contains a hidden transitive dependency:

ORDER#	SUPPLIER#	SUPPLIER-NAME	SUPPLIER-ADDRESS	DELIVERY-DAY	ORDER-DATE	$-TOTAL

It might be tempting to diagram it thus:

However, SUPPLIER NAME and SUPPLIER ADDRESS are identified by SUPPLIER#. The record should then be diagrammed as follows:

fied by a combination of CUSTOMER-TYPE, STATE, DISCOUNT, and PRODUCT.

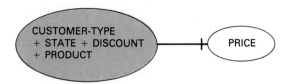

When the modeling process encounters a concatenated key such as this, it automatically makes the component fields of the key into data-item bubbles in their own right in the model. In other words, it explodes the concatenated key like this:

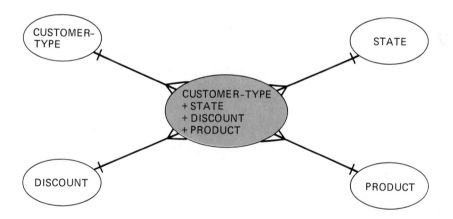

Some of these data items—for example, PRODUCT—might become keys themselves; others may remain attributes.

In the final synthesis, those that still remain merely attributes may be deleted because they already exist in the concatenated key. They are deleted if they are not used as separate data items.

INTERSECTION DATA

In some types of data-base software, data can be related to the *association* between data items. A part, for example, may be supplied by several vendors, each of whom charges a different price for it. The data item PRICE cannot be associated with the PART record alone or with the SUPPLIER record alone. It can only be associated with the combination of the two. Such information is sometimes called *intersection data*—data associated with the association between records.

MANY-TO-MANY ASSOCIATIONS

It is necessary to be cautious with links that have crow's feet pointing in both directions—many-to-many associations. In practice, when a many-to-many association is used, *intersection data* will usually be associated with it sooner or later. If there is no intersection data to start with, they are likely to be added later as the data base evolves. If intersection data are associated with records having keys A and B, those data are identified by a concatenated key A + B. Figure 42.3 shows two examples of intersection data and how they might be handled.

Because of the likelihood of adding intersection data, it is usually best to avoid an A $\rightarrowtail$ —$\leftarrow$ B link in a schema and instead create an extra record having the concatenated key A + B when the data base is first implemented. This avoids later restructuring and consequent rewriting of programs.

MAPPING BETWEEN PRIMARY KEYS

To avoid this problem, when the design procedure gives a mapping *between keys* in one direction, we add the equivalent mapping in the opposite direction. In other words, the line between keys has arrows drawn in both directions. We then have a many-to-many mapping between two keys, A and B:

As the path in either direction might conceivably be traversed, we introduce a third key, A + B, as follows:

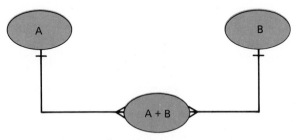

Because we use this procedure, the canonical schema we create will have no many-to-many links between keys unless the association could *never* be used in one direction.

INTERSECTING ATTRIBUTES

A problem that sometimes occurs in the synthesized structure is that an *attribute* may be attached to more

Two examples of intersection data:

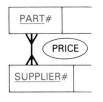

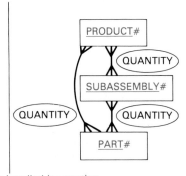

Intersection data could be handled by creating
an exta record (segment) containing the intersection
data and the concatenated key of the records (segments)
associated with it. The keys are shown in red.

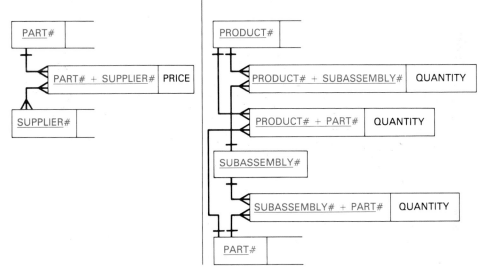

Figure 42.3   Two examples of intersection data.

than one primary key. In other words, it has more than one one-to-one indicator
pointing to it. This is sometimes called an *intersecting attribute*. It cannot remain in such a state in the final synthesis. An attribute in a canonical model can
be owned by only one key.

Box 42.2 illustrates an intersecting attribute and three ways of dealing with it. There should be no intersecting attributes on the final canonical
graph.

BOX 42.2   Reorganizing intersecting attributes

Intersecting attributes must be reorganized. This can be done in one of three ways.

The following graph contains an intersecting attribute:

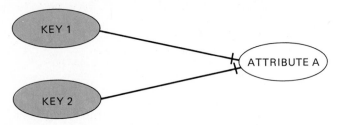

An intersecting attribute can be avoided in one of the following three ways:

1. All but one link to it may be replaced with equivalent links via an existing key:

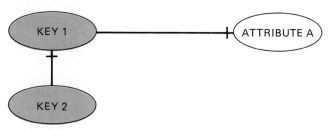

2. Redundant versions of it may be connected to each associated key:

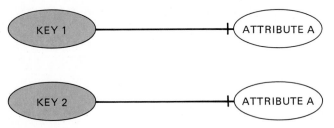

3. It may be made into a key with no attributes:

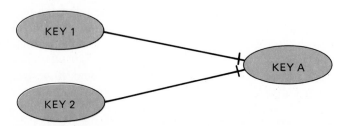

ISOLATED ATTRIBUTES

An *isolated attribute* is an attribute that is not identified by a primary key. It is a bubble with no one-to-one links entering or leaving it, although there will be one-to-many links.

An isolated attribute should be treated in one of the following ways:

1. It may be implemented as a repeating attribute in a variable-length record.
2. It may be treated as a solitary key—a one-data-item record.

An isolated attribute often results from an error in interpretation of the user's data, so the meaning related to it should be checked carefully.

RECORD SEQUENCE

In certain user views, the *sequence* in which the data are presented to the application program or displayed on a terminal is critical. However, the canonical schema does not indicate the sequence in which records are stored. *In general, it is undesirable to state a record sequence in the canonical schema because different applications of the data might require the records in a different sequence.*

In a data base of book titles, for example, one application might want a logical file of book titles in alphabetical order, another might want them ordered by author, another by Library of Congress number. The different sequencing can be indicated by secondary keys, bubbles with a crow's-foot link to BOOK-TITLE.

When the canonical schema is converted to a physical representation, it is necessary to state the record sequencing. This is a statement that should be part of the physical, rather than the logical, description of data. Some *logical* data-description languages require statements about the order of records. This information must then be added when the canonical schema is converted to the software logical schema. Enthusiasts of *relational* data bases stress that the sequencing of the tuples should not be part of the *logical* data description.

AUTOMATING THE PROCEDURE

Canonical modeling done by hand is tedious, but as we have stressed, tools exist for automating it. If these tools are not available, the designer may compromise by identifying the primary keys in all the input views and building a linkage between these by hand. He then adds the attributes these keys identify. The tool saves him time, enforces discipline, helps avoid errors, and provides documents that form the basis of vital communication with end users.

Either way, the designer tackles one input view at a time, checks that it appears correct in its own right, has it merged into the model, and inspects the results. When the program deletes an apparently redundant association, it should ask the designer if he considers it to be genuinely redundant. Each time a programmer or user wants to add new data types or use the data base in a new way, the data-base administrator can enter the new user view and see what effect it has on the existing data base.

The bubble charts showing data, which the systems analyst or end user draws, can be fed into a computerized modeling tool one at a time. The tool synthesizes them into the model structure. It draws the resulting structure and produces various reports.

The output of the modeling process should be studied by concerned users, along with dictionary output, to ensure that the data bases being designed do indeed meet their needs.

Even if the synthesis process is automated, there are several steps that require intelligent human understanding of the meaning of the data. The input must be carefully examined to ensure that the correct keys are used for all data items and that transitive dependencies are removed. When links are removed because they appear to be redundant, the data administrator must check that this reflects the true meaning of the links.

DATA DESIGNER

One tool for data modeling is DDI's Data Designer [3]. User views, portions of user views, or single functional dependencies can be fed to Data Designer one at a time. Data Designer synthesizes them into a nonredundant data model, plots the result, and produces various reports for the data administrator. If the input functional dependencies are correct, the output is in third normal form.

Entries to Data Designer consist of a code character followed by a comma and an input, usually a data item:

```
K, EMPLOYEE#
1, EMPLOYEE-NAME
1, AGE
```

The code character (K and 1 in the example) is called a *modeling command*. Code K is used for indicating the data item *at the start of a one-to-one link*. (K stands for *key*).

The data item at the other end of the link is indicated with a code 1 if it is *one-to-one* association and a code M if it is a *one-to-many* association.

Thus this model

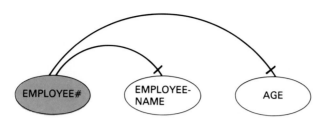

is coded

```
K,  EMPLOYEE#
1,  EMPLOYEE-NAME
1,  AGE
```

and

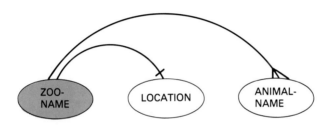

is coded

```
K,  ZOO-NAME
1,  LOCATION
M,  ANIMAL-NAME
```

The reverse association can be coded with a 1 or M *after* the data-item name:

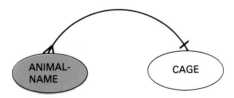

is coded

```
K,  ANIMAL-NAME
1,  CAGE, M
```

The data item labeled K can have a list of data items associated with it without its name being repeated. The list may not contain another K data item. To code two links in a string, two K data items are used:

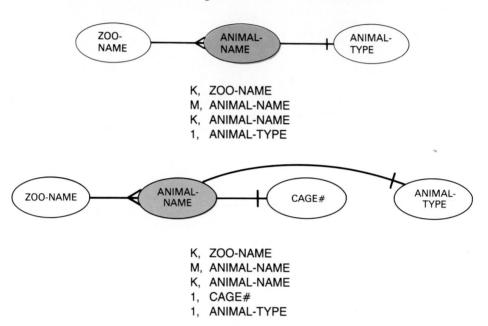

K, ZOO-NAME
M, ANIMAL-NAME
K, ANIMAL-NAME
1, ANIMAL-TYPE

K, ZOO-NAME
M, ANIMAL-NAME
K, ANIMAL-NAME
1, CAGE#
1, ANIMAL-TYPE

To lessen the amount of typing, a name that is the same as in the previous entry need not be repeated:

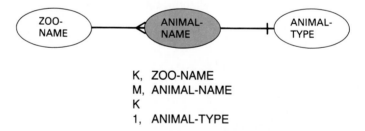

K, ZOO-NAME
M, ANIMAL-NAME
K
1, ANIMAL-TYPE

A concatenated field is represented with one of these data-item *entries,* followed by one or more data items with a C code (C for *concatenated*):

K, ORDER#
C, PART#
1, QUANTITY-ORDERED

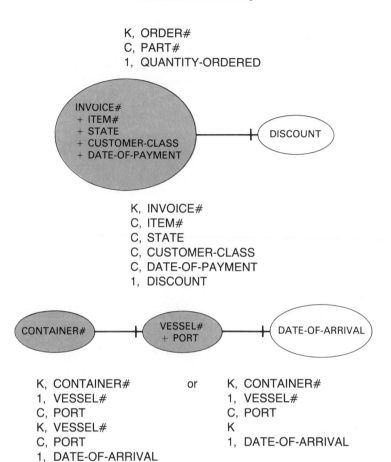

K, INVOICE#
C, ITEM#
C, STATE
C, CUSTOMER-CLASS
C, DATE-OF-PAYMENT
1, DISCOUNT

K, CONTAINER#   or   K, CONTAINER#
1, VESSEL#   1, VESSEL#
C, PORT   C, PORT
K, VESSEL#   K
C, PORT   1, DATE-OF-ARRIVAL
1, DATE-OF-ARRIVAL

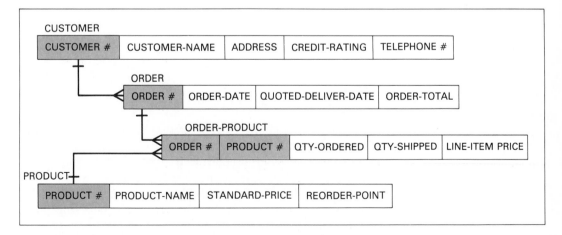

Figure 42.4 A simple data model.

```
● DTYPE:   CUSTOMER
● PRMOP:   CUSTOMER# = CUSTOMER# (CUSTOMER)
● PRMOP:   CUSTOMER_NAME = CUSTOMER_NAME(CUSTOMER)
● PRMOP:   ADDRESS = ADDRESS (CUSTOMER)
● PRMOP:   CREDIT_RATING = CREDIT_RATING(CUSTOMER)
● PRMOP:   TELEPHONE# = TELEPHONE#(CUSTOMER)

● DTYPE:   ORDER
● PRMOP:   ORDER# = ORDER#(ORDER)
● PRMOP:   ORDER_DATE = ORDER_DATE(ORDER)
● PRMOP:   QUOTED_DELIVERY_DATE = QUOTED_DELIVERY_DATE(ORDER)
● PRMOP:   ORDER_TOTAL = ORDER_TOTAL(ORDER)

● DTYPE:   PRODUCT
● PRMOP:   PRODUCT# = PRODUCT# (PRODUCT)
● PRMOP:   PRODUCT_NAME = PRODUCT_NAME (PRODUCT)
● PRMOP:   STANDARD_PRICE = STANDARD_PRICE (PRODUCT)
● PRMOP:   REORDER_POINT = REORDER_POINT (PRODUCT)

● DTYPE:   ORDER_PRODUCT
● PRMOP:   ORDER# = ORDER#_FROM_ORDER_PRODUCT (ORDER_PRODUCT)
● PRMOP:   PRODUCT# = PRODUCT#_FROM_ORDER_PRODUCT (ORDER_PRODUCT)
● PRMOP:   QTY_ORDERED = QTY_ORDERED (ORDER_PRODUCT)
● PRMOP:   QTY_SHIPPED = QTY_SHIPPED (ORDER_PRODUCT)
● PRMOP:   LINE_ITEM_PRICE = LINE_ITEM_PRICE (ORDER_PRODUCT)

● DTYPE:   ORDERS_DATABASE
● PRMOP:   CUSTOMER = CUSTOMER_WITH_ORDER (ORDERS_DATABASE,ORDER)
● PRMOP:   SET_OF_ORDER = SET_OF_ORDERS_FOR_CUSTOMER (ORDERS_DATABASE,CUSTOMER)
● PRMOP:   ORDER = ORDER_OF_ORDER_PRODUCT (ORDERS_DATABASE,ORDER_PRODUCT)
● PRMOP:   SET_OF_ORDER_PRODUCT = SET_OF_ORDER_PRODUCTS_FOR_ORDER (ORDERS_DA-
           TABASE,ORDER)
● PRMOP:   PRODUCT = PRODUCT_OF_ORDER_PRODUCT (ORDERS_DATABASE,ORDER_PRODUCT)
● PRMOP:   SET_OF_ORDER_PRODUCT = SET_OF_ORDER_PRODUCTS_FOR_PRODUCT (ORDERS_
           DATABASE,PRODUCT)
```

Figure 42.5   Representation of the model in Fig. 42.4 in HOS software. The HOS description of the data should be generated automatically from the output of a data modeling tool.

The blank K field on the right picks up the value of the entire concatenated field (the entire bubble), not just part of it.

Using this simple form of coding, one user view after another can be fed to the data modeling tool. It synthesizes them into a structure designed to be stable (a canonical, third-normal-form structure). It prints reports and draws diagrams such as that in Fig. 42.4 describing the resulting model.

Data models produced in this way should be thoroughly checked by users who are experts on the data. The objective of the design and checking is to make the data as stable as possible. A set of steps called *stability analysis* is described in *Managing the Data Base Environment* [1].

CONVERSION TO HOS NOTATION

Figure 42.5 shows HOS code for a data model. This code can be created automatically.

REFERENCES

1. J. Martin, *Managing the Data Base Environment,* Englewood Cliffs, NJ: Prentice-Hall, Inc., 1983.

2. J. Martin, *System Design from Provably Correct Constructs,* Englewood Cliffs, NJ: Prentice-Hall, Inc., 1985.

3. Data Designer and associated tools for data administration are available from Database Design, Inc., 2020 Hogback Road, Ann Arbor, MI 48104.

43 COMPUTER-AIDED DESIGN

INTRODUCTION   The future of computing lies with CASE technology in which the analyst builds applications at a workstation screen and the machine generates executable code. The machine can apply all sorts of cross-checks and validation. It can automate many of the tasks that have been time-consuming in the past. A challenge of computer-aided design is to make the process as user-friendly as possible so that, where appropriate, it can be done by suitably educated end users. End users need to have the ability to solve their own problems with computers where possible. These range from engineers doing complex calculations, to white-collar workers improving their procedures, to business people making complex decisions with the aid of computerized information.

As we make it easier to build applications, it becomes more important that these be anchored into computerized planning of the data. Clean, stable design of data is needed, as described in Chapters 41 and 42. The data can be used with a diversity of tools for application building, including the following:

- Screen design aids, which make it quick and easy to design computer screens at a screen

- Dialogue design aids—an extension of screen design that enables the user to decide interactively which screens to design

- Report generators, which make it quick and easy to design reports and print-outs, sometimes of a complex structure

- An action diagram editor, which enables action diagrams that show intricate logic to be built on a screen with no hanging ENDs, open loops, incorrect case structures, or the like

- A means of converting the action diagrams to code of a specific language, especially a fourth-generation language

- Decision-support aids such as spreadsheet tools for examining and plotting multidimensional data, tools for exploring what-if questions, analyzing trends, and so on

- Graphically oriented specification tools which have the feature of thorough verification of complex specifications

- Other graphically oriented tools for systems analysts, with which the diagrams that analysts build can be converted automatically to action diagrams

- Data-base navigation tools, which aid in navigation through a complex data base and generation of code related to this navigation.

Different types of tools are needed for different types of computer uses.

COMPUTERIZED HELP IN DESIGN

As the analyst goes through the steps of application design, there are certain questions he should ask at each stage. This can be made into a formal procedure. If he is using a computerized tool for carrying out the design steps, the machine should make him address the relevant design questions at each stage. This leads to a better-quality design with well-thought-out controls and should go as far as possible to automatically generating the next stage of the design, until executable code is reached.

In Chapter 24 we discussed the use of data navigation diagrams for building data-base applications. Figure 24.2 gave a set of steps to be used for this.

A formal data model developed with computer assistance (Chapter 42) is the single most important foundation for data processing in which automated techniques are used to make application development fast and relatively easy. It helps to ensure that separately developed systems can interchange data and that systems can be modified without the disruptive effects associated with much maintenance activity today.

Let us assume that a data administrator has built a stable, fully normalized data model and that this is accessible on-line to the application developers. A developer may select the subject area or areas of the data model in which he is interested. We indicated that entity types in a data model are of different levels. Level 1, sometimes called root entity types, has one-to-one associations leaving them going to another entity type. Examples of root entity types are CUSTOMER, PRODUCT, and VENDOR. In diagrams such as Fig. 23.2, the root entity types are the leftmost blocks. The developer may select the root entity types he is interested in. He then examines the lower-level entity types associated with each root and selects those he needs for his application.

When extracting and editing a data submodel to use, the designer may display the *neighborhood* of a given entity type or group of entity types. The neighborhood of an entity type consists of all other entity types that are one link away. The designer may display the attributes associated with each entity type as in Fig. 24.3.

Finally the designer has a submodel, which is the data he will use for his application.

DEVELOPING A DATA-BASE APPLICATION
The figures in this chapter illustrate the building of a data-base application with computer-aided design. At the top of Fig. 43.1 is the data submodel that the analyst extracted from a larger data model. At the bottom is an *instruction panel* with which the computer asks the analyst what actions will be carried out on each entity type. He indicates which entity types the application will create, read, update, or delete. If he indicates "Other," he may receive another panel with relational operations such as SEARCH and JOIN.

When the panel first appears, all of the squares in the "None" column are black. They become white as the analyst indicates data-base actions. This may be used as a means of selecting entity types from a larger submodel.

The computer responds with the screen of Fig. 43.2. The entity types have been marked with the actions that will be carried out on them. The instruction panel now asks the designer to point to each entity type in turn to show the sequence in which the actions will be performed.

Figure 43.3 shows the entity types with sequence numbers on them. The computer now asks the designer about each data-base action in turn. For the first action, Read CUSTOMER, is this done once or many times, always or only sometimes (depending on a condition)? Is the CUSTOMER record accessed by the primary key CUSTOMER# or by some other means?

The designer responds, and the first portion of a navigation diagram appears (Fig. 43.4). On a color screen, the entity-relationship diagram would be a weaker color and the navigation diagram would be superimposed on it in a bolder color, say black.

The instruction panel now asks what happens if the CUSTOMER record cannot be found. All such error conditions need to be dealt with.

The computer now moves on to the second access and questions the designer as shown in the instruction panel of Fig. 43.5. The questions are somewhat different because the second access *creates* a record. The designer indicates, as prompted, that the new record, CUSTOMER-ORDER, is accessed via the CUSTOMER record. He indicates that it is accessed SOMETIMES, so the machine puts an optionality circle on the navigation path from CUSTOMER to CUSTOMER-ORDER, as shown in Fig. 43.6. The instruction panel of Fig. 43.6 asks the designer to state under what conditions a CUSTOMER-ORDER record is created. The designer writes CREDIT-RATING IS GOOD in the

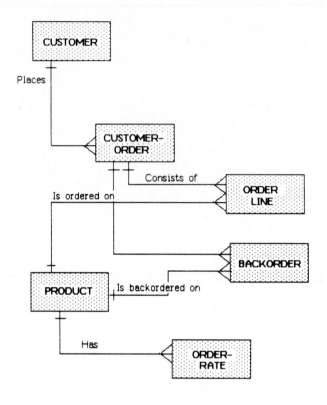

Figure 43.1 In the panel at the bottom, the analyst is asked what actions are to be carried out on each entity type shown in the data submodel at the top.

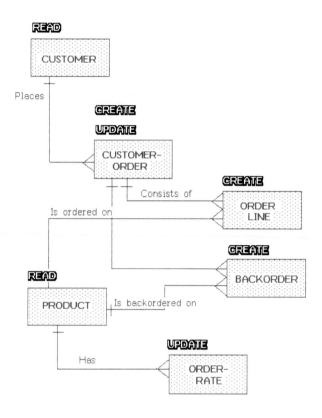

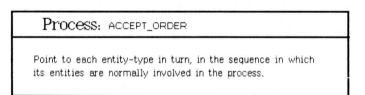

Figure 43.2 The analyst indicates which actions are to be carried out on the entity types.

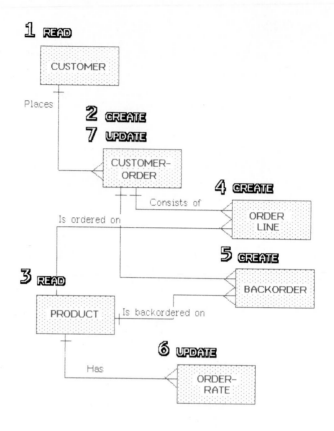

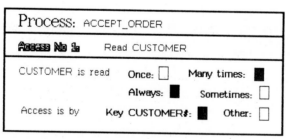

Figure 43.3 The sequence in which the entity types are to be accessed is indicated.

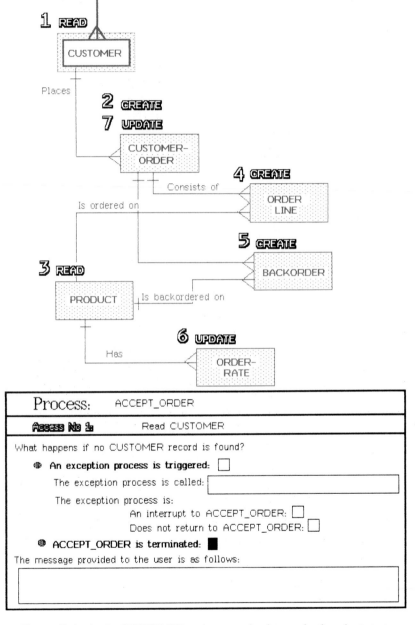

1 READ

CUSTOMER

Places

2 CREATE
7 UPDATE

CUSTOMER-
ORDER

Consists of

4 CREATE

ORDER
LINE

Is ordered on

5 CREATE

BACKORDER

3 READ

PRODUCT

Is backordered on

6 UPDATE

Has

ORDER-
RATE

Process: ACCEPT_ORDER

Access No 1: Read CUSTOMER

What happens if no CUSTOMER record is found?

● **An exception process is triggered:** ☐

   The exception process is called:

   The exception process is:
                  An interrupt to ACCEPT_ORDER: ☐
                  Does not return to ACCEPT_ORDER: ☐

● **ACCEPT_ORDER is terminated:** ■

The message provided to the user is as follows:

Figure 43.4   At the CUSTOMER entity type, the data navigation chart starts to appear.

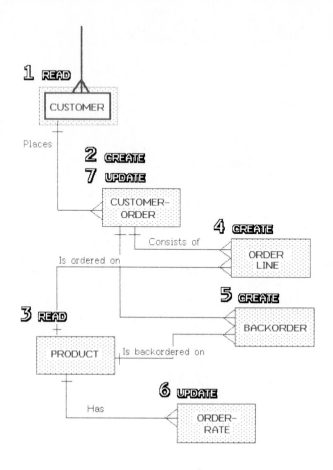

Figure 43.5   The analyst is asked questions about each entity-type access.

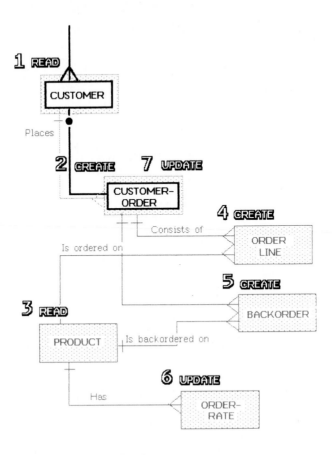

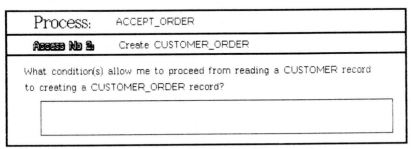

Process: ACCEPT_ORDER

Access No 2: Create CUSTOMER_ORDER

What condition(s) allow me to proceed from reading a CUSTOMER record to creating a CUSTOMER_ORDER record?

Figure 43.6 The analyst is asked for information to define a conditional access.

panel. The machine writes IF CREDIT-RATING IS GOOD against the option-ality circle, as shown in Fig. 43.7.

Figure 43.7 has skipped to a later stage in the dialogue. The navigation diagram has now overlaid much of the entity diagram, and various facts have been recorded about the application design.

The designer has reached access 6, which updates the ORDER-RATE record. The instruction panel shows the data items in the ORDER-RATE record and asks which will be changed. It also asks whether any other data items are needed. For any data item to be changed, it asks the designer, as in Fig. 43.8, to enter the formula or process for computing the new value.

AUTOMATIC
CONVERSION
The navigation diagram of Fig. 43.8 can be automatically converted into the action diagram of Fig. 43.9.

A split screen with appropriate scrolling may be used so that the designer can view both diagrams at once and can modify either one or the other.

The designer may annotate the action diagram with the data items in each entity type, read from the data model. This is shown in Fig. 43.10.

The designer now uses an action diagram editor. He can move a cursor bar up and down the diagram and can make changes with the instruction panel of Fig. 43.11.

Figure 43.12 shows the action diagram with more details added. Such a diagram would show calculations and make references to screen formats, report formats, and so on. These formats can be designed with nonprocedural facilities of many fourth-generation languages, application generators, and COBOL productivity aids.

The action diagram editor may take the application as far as possible before committing to a particular language or generator. It can then be converted automatically to the language in question.

Figure 43.13 shows the action diagram of Fig. 43.12 converted to the language IDEAL, from ADR, Inc. Figure 43.14 shows the same diagram converted to the language Application Factory, from Cortex, Inc. Both Figs. 43.13 and 43.14 are executable code. In a similar way, Fig. 43.12 could be converted to many other fourth-generation languages.

Figure 43.12 is independent of the programming language used. It is, however, designed to be as close as possible to the code representation used in fourth-generation languages and application generators. It can be converted directly into languages such as FOCUS, RAMIS, MANTIS, NOMAD, IDEAL, and CSP. It could also be coded in COBOL, PL/I, ADA, or PASCAL, or it could form the basis for a tool that generates code in these languages.

Fourth-generation languages or application generators of the future ought to assist an analyst or user in creating and manipulating diagrams and then generate efficient executable code directly from the diagram.

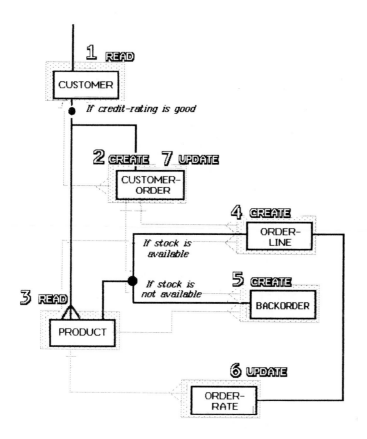

Figure 43.7 The analyst is asked what is entailed in updating a record.

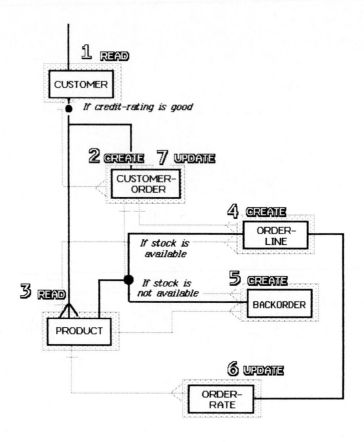

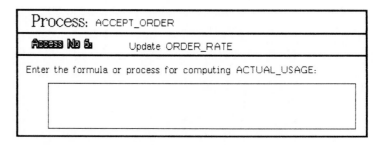

Figure 43.8 The analyst is asked how to change each data item.

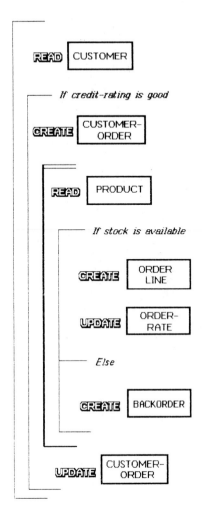

Figure 43.9 An action diagram generated (automatically) from the navigation diagram of Fig. 43.8.

FOUR STAGES

The procedure we have described has four main stages:

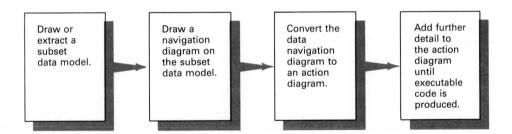

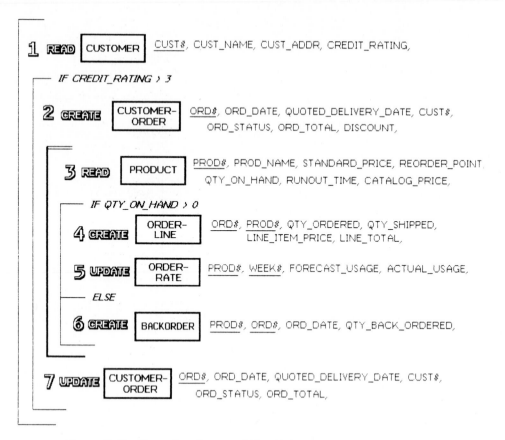

Figure 43.10 The action diagram of Fig. 43.9 annotated with the attributes of each entity type accessed. The condition statements are changed to appropriate attribute names.

These stages are applied both to logical data models and to physical data structures. They are applied to logical data models when *specifying a procedure* and to the more constrained data structures in a data-base management system when *designing a program.* For data-base management systems that directly represent the fully normalized data models, there is no difference between these. Unfortunately, many data-base management systems employ physical data structures that deviate from the conceptual clarity of the entity-relationship model, and with these the navigation diagram may be somewhat different from the navigation diagram drawn on the normalized data model.

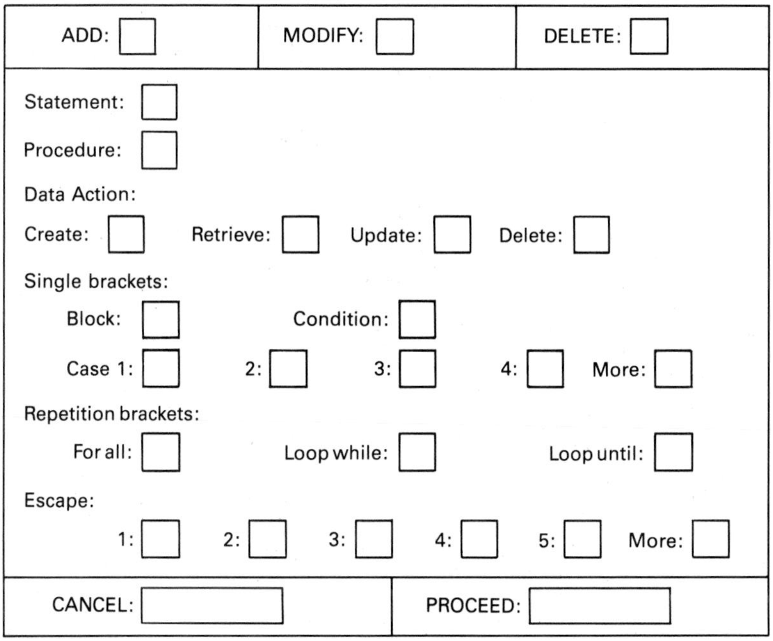

Figure 43.11   An instruction panel for editing action diagrams.

LOGICAL AND PHYSICAL NAVIGATION DIAGRAMS

Navigation diagrams drawn on a logical data model are called *logical navigation diagrams*. Navigation diagrams drawn on a physical data structure are called *physical navigation diagrams*. Sometimes these are also called *logical access maps* and *physical access maps*.

The terms *logical* and *physical* ought to be clear when used about data. *Logical* refers to data as perceived by the analyst or user; this representation of data should be designed for maximum conceptual clarity. *Physical* refers to data as stored in the machine; this representation of data is designed for machine performance. *Logical* is used to describe the fully normalized data model. *Physical* is used to describe the data structured for storage with pointers, chains, rings, tree structures, and the like. Unfortunately, however, there is much confusion about the word *logical* because vendors of data-base management systems such as IBM's IMS have misused the word *logical* to refer to specific data structures that are not necessarily normalized and do not represent the clearly structured data model.

Nevertheless, it is important to understand that the physical data structures

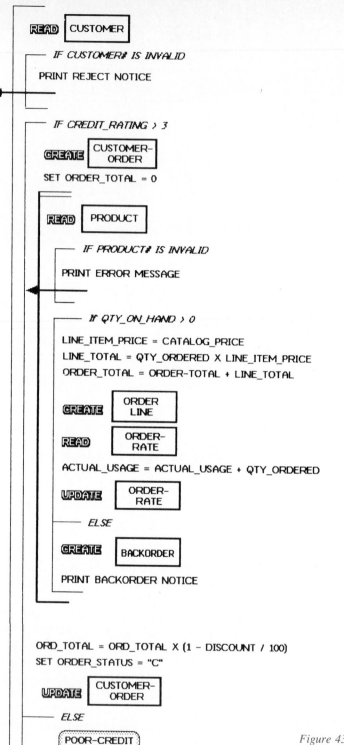

READ CUSTOMER
  ── IF CUSTOMER# IS INVALID
  PRINT REJECT NOTICE

  ── IF CREDIT_RATING > 3
    CREATE CUSTOMER-ORDER
    SET ORDER_TOTAL = 0

      READ PRODUCT
        ── IF PRODUCT# IS INVALID
        PRINT ERROR MESSAGE

        ── IF QTY_ON_HAND > 0
        LINE_ITEM_PRICE = CATALOG_PRICE
        LINE_TOTAL = QTY_ORDERED X LINE_ITEM_PRICE
        ORDER_TOTAL = ORDER-TOTAL + LINE_TOTAL

        CREATE ORDER LINE
        READ ORDER-RATE
        ACTUAL_USAGE = ACTUAL_USAGE + QTY_ORDERED
        UPDATE ORDER-RATE
        ── ELSE
        CREATE BACKORDER
        PRINT BACKORDER NOTICE

    ORD_TOTAL = ORD_TOTAL X (1 - DISCOUNT / 100)
    SET ORDER_STATUS = "C"
    UPDATE CUSTOMER-ORDER
  ── ELSE
    POOR-CREDIT PROCEDURE

Figure 43.12 The action diagram of Fig. 43.10 expanded to show the calculations, printouts, and so on.

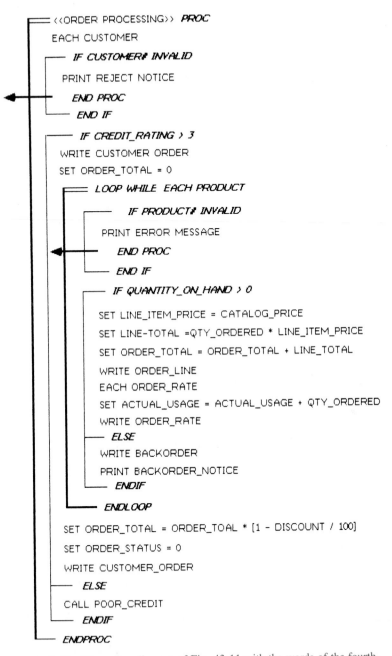

```
<<ORDER PROCESSING>> PROC
EACH CUSTOMER
    IF CUSTOMER# INVALID
    PRINT REJECT NOTICE
        END PROC
        END IF
        IF CREDIT_RATING > 3
    WRITE CUSTOMER ORDER
    SET ORDER_TOTAL = 0
            LOOP WHILE EACH PRODUCT
                IF PRODUCT# INVALID
                PRINT ERROR MESSAGE
                    END PROC
                    END IF
                IF QUANTITY_ON_HAND > 0
                SET LINE_ITEM_PRICE = CATALOG_PRICE
                SET LINE-TOTAL =QTY_ORDERED * LINE_ITEM_PRICE
                SET ORDER_TOTAL = ORDER_TOTAL + LINE_TOTAL
                WRITE ORDER_LINE
                EACH ORDER_RATE
                SET ACTUAL_USAGE = ACTUAL_USAGE + QTY_ORDERED
                WRITE ORDER_RATE
                ELSE
                WRITE BACKORDER
                PRINT BACKORDER_NOTICE
                    ENDIF
            ENDLOOP
    SET ORDER_TOTAL = ORDER_TOAL * [1 - DISCOUNT / 100]
    SET ORDER_STATUS = 0
    WRITE CUSTOMER_ORDER
        ELSE
    CALL POOR_CREDIT
        ENDIF
    ENDPROC
```

Figure 43.13 The action diagram of Fig. 43.11 with the words of the fourth-generation language IDEAL. This is an executable program written in IDEAL.

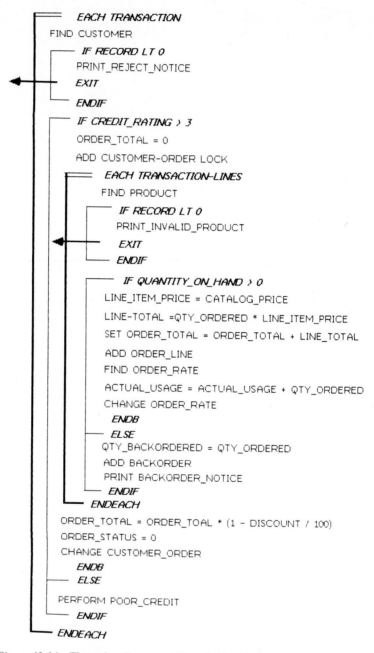

```
         EACH TRANSACTION
FIND CUSTOMER
         IF RECORD LT 0
         PRINT_REJECT_NOTICE
         EXIT
         ENDIF
         IF CREDIT_RATING > 3
         ORDER_TOTAL = 0
         ADD CUSTOMER-ORDER LOCK
                  EACH TRANSACTION-LINES
                  FIND PRODUCT
                           IF RECORD LT 0
                           PRINT_INVALID_PRODUCT
                           EXIT
                           ENDIF
                           IF QUANTITY_ON_HAND > 0
                           LINE_ITEM_PRICE = CATALOG_PRICE
                           LINE-TOTAL =QTY_ORDERED * LINE_ITEM_PRICE
                           SET ORDER_TOTAL = ORDER_TOTAL + LINE_TOTAL
                           ADD ORDER_LINE
                           FIND ORDER_RATE
                           ACTUAL_USAGE = ACTUAL_USAGE + QTY_ORDERED
                           CHANGE ORDER_RATE
                             ENDB
                           ELSE
                           QTY_BACKORDERED = QTY_ORDERED
                           ADD BACKORDER
                           PRINT BACKORDER_NOTICE
                           ENDIF
                  ENDEACH
         ORDER_TOTAL = ORDER_TOAL * (1 - DISCOUNT / 100)
         ORDER_STATUS = 0
         CHANGE CUSTOMER_ORDER
           ENDB
         ELSE
PERFORM POOR_CREDIT
         ENDIF
ENDEACH
```

Figure 43.14   The action diagram of Fig. 43.11 with the words of the fourth-generation language Application Factory. This is an executable program written in Application Factory.

are often different from the fully normalized data model, so physical data navigation may be different from that which is conceived and drawn in the fully normalized data model.

PHYSICAL DESIGN   Initially, the physical aspects of accessing the data are ignored. The navigation diagram is drawn as though the data existed in memory for this application alone. Later, the physical designer adjusts the navigation diagram as appropriate. To help the physical designer, the navigation diagram should be annotated with details of quantities of accesses.

The accesses on the physical navigation diagram may not be in the same sequence as the accesses on the logical navigation diagram. A logical diagram may have two updates of the same record type. Physically, both these updates would be done at the same time. The first update may be done in computer main memory and not written on the external storage medium until the second update can be completed. Similarly, if a parent record has an offspring in a physical data base, the two may be updated together. An offspring record is not created physically until the parent is created, although it could appear first on a logical navigation diagram.

OBJECTIVES OF   The predominant objectives of the design dialogue
THE DESIGN   are the following:
DIALOGUE

1. To speed up the entire development cycle to the maximum, making it possible to create complex applications in days
2. To make the design process as easy to learn as possible, permitting the strongest end-user involvement in the process
3. To automate the documentation (with computer-stored information presented and modifiable diagrammatically) and make the applications easy to change, thus reducing the maintenance burden to a very low level
4. To ensure that all the necessary controls and error conditions are thought about and to build the highest-quality applications
5. To avoid the errors, inconsistencies, ambiguities, and incompleteness of traditional specifications and reduce the need for debugging to a minimal level

The subset data model that is used for one application usually does not become very big. It can usually be drawn on one screen and so can be the associated navigation diagram.

In some corporations with highly complex data processing, the subset data models have never exceeded a dozen third-normal-form records. Most do not exceed six or so.

It is very simple to *teach* the use of data navigation diagrams. These should be an installation standard rather than a tool of certain individuals.

VARIATIONS There can be many variations of the design procedure sketched in this chapter. Various tools provide ways for analysts to conceptualize different aspects of systems and converted them directly into action diagrams and then to executable code.

The designer is likely to use various tools that provide ways to conceptualize different aspects of system design. The separate modules of action diagrams resulting from these tools need to be integrated on the screen with an appropriate library facility.

REFERENCE

1. All are described, and their conversions are illustrated, in J. Martin and C. McClure, *Diagramming Techniques for Analysts and Programmers,* Englewood Cliffs, NJ: Prentice-Hall, Inc., 1985.

44 INFORMATION ENGINEERING

INTRODUCTION   The corporation of the future will be managed to a
                    large extent with the aid of computers. Personal com-
puters will form the nerve endings of a corporate nervous system that connects
them to the mainframe power and data bases they need. Some computing will
be the routine handling of invoices, payroll, inventory, and so on by the large
machines. Much computing will be decision-support operations by individuals
at workstations. Personal, departmental, and central computing will be tightly
interlinked.

In this environment, it is essential to plan for compatibility. The many
machines need to use the same data network. Disks or other media need to
be exchanged among the machines. Software cooperation is needed among the
personal, departmental, and mainframe computers. Particularly important, the
data employed must be compatible, structured for multiple uses, represented in
easily accessible data models, and used with appropriate management controls.

End users in an efficient corporation will be expected to take their own
initiative in using computers. *Information centers* will exist as a part of DP
management to encourage and assist end users, helping them to find and use the
right software tools and to obtain the data they need for processing. Most end
users computing will not involve programming but will employ report generators, spreadsheet tools, decision-support facilities, personal data bases, and a
variety of preprogrammed tools and packages. Some end users do employ programming with the relatively new, easy-to-use end-user languages.

Communication in this environment is extremely important. Users do not
want to key in all the data in the spreadsheets. Those data already exist in other
computers. Accountants want to be able to interchange spreadsheet disks. Decision-support languages need access to centrally collected and maintained data.

Professional computing (by the DP department) needs to use many of the
same data bases. It is desirable for DP to be able to obtain results *quickly* and

to build systems that can be *quickly* changed when necessary. This requires that application generators and fourth-generation languages be used in a cleanly structured fashion, with automatic documentation, where possible, designed for maintenance.

WHAT IS INFORMATION ENGINEERING?

The term *information engineering* refers to an integrated set of methodologies designed to create and operate the environment just described. It relies on fully normalized data models of the data in an enterprise. These models are kept in a computerized form, and workstations use computerized tools to build applications that use the data. These tools are selected or designed to aid and automate systems analysis, develop applications as quickly as possible, and make applications as easy to maintain as possible. A major objective is to avoid the messy problems of conventional development and maintenance.

Whereas most structured techniques are applied to one system, information engineering applies structured techniques to an entire enterprise. It creates data models and process models for the enterprise so that systems designed by separate teams fit together into a designed framework.

The term *information engineering* has been contrasted with the term *software engineering*. The primary focus of software engineering is the *logic* of the computerized processes; it is concerned with structured techniques for specifying, designing, and writing programs. The primary focus of information engineering is the *data* that are stored and maintained by computers and the information that is distilled from these data. Information engineering must also be concerned with structured analysis and code, but it seeks to find tools such as nonprocedural languages, specification languages, application generators, and graphic computer-aided design, which minimize the work of program development.

Data Are Central

The basic premise of information engineering is that data lie at the center of modern data processing. This is illustrated in Fig. 44.1. The data are stored and maintained with the aid of various types of data systems software. The processes on the left in Fig. 44.1 *create* and *modify* the data. The data must be captured and entered with appropriate accuracy controls. The data will be periodically updated. The processes on the right of Fig. 44.1 *use* the data. Routine documents such as invoices, receipts, freight bills, and work tickets are printed. Executives or professionals sometimes search for information. They create summaries or analyses of the data and produce charts and reports. They ask what-if questions and use the data for helping them make decisions. Auditors check the data and attempt to ensure that it is not misused.

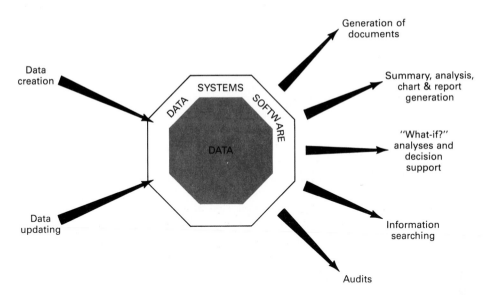

Figure 44.1   Most modern data processing is composed of events that create and modify data, with appropriate accuracy controls, and processes that use, analyze, summarize, and manipulate data or print documents from the data.

The data in Fig. 44.1 may be in several data systems. They may be stored in different ways. They may be distributed. They are often updated and used by means of transmission links and terminals.

A set of *actions* occurs that relates to the data. A simple action applies to one instance of one record. This action may read, modify, create, or delete the record. A compound action applies to an entire logical file or relation or to more than one. It may sort, join, project, read, modify, or delete the relation(s).

These actions are controlled by various *conditions*. Some actions *trigger* other actions. An on-line *procedure* consists of a sequence of actions with associated logic, controlled by certain conditions. We use a diagramming technique to represent these procedures and convert them to highly structured, easily maintainable program code.

Data Are Stable; Procedures Are Not

A second basic premise of information engineering is that the types of data used in an enterprise do not change very much, as we have described. The entity types do not change, except for the occasional (rare) addition of new entity types. The types of *attributes* that we store about these entities also change infrequently. The *values* of data change constantly, like the data in a flight-information board at an airport, but the *structure* of the data does not change much if it was well designed to begin with.

Given a collection of data items, we can represent them in a cleanly structured fashion, as described in Chapters 41 and 42. To do this the data administrator uses automated techniques that build the data models. If well designed, these models change little, and we can usually avoid changes that are disruptive. In information engineering, these models become a foundation on which most computerized procedures are built.

Although the data are relatively stable, the procedures that use the data change fast and frequently. In fact, it is desirable that systems analysts and end users be able to change them frequently. We need maximum flexibility in improving administrative procedures and adapting them to the rapidly changing needs of management. Every business changes dynamically, and the views of management on how to run it change much faster.

The procedures, then, change rapidly (or should), and the computer programs, processes, networks, and hardware change; but the basic types of data are relatively stable. The foundation of data is viable only if the data are correctly identified and structured so that they can be used with the necessary flexibility.

Because the basic data types are stable, whereas procedures tend to change, *data-oriented* techniques succeed if correctly applied where *procedure-oriented* techniques have resulted in systems that are slow to implement and difficult to change. Information engineering seeks to fulfill rapidly management's changing needs for information. We can obtain results quickly, once the necessary data infrastructure is established, by using high-level data-base languages and application generators.

In many organizations, the lack of good data-base design and integration results in hugh maintenance costs and delays. Procedures cannot be changed quickly. New procedures that are urgently needed take years to introduce. Time and time again we hear of board resolutions to implement some new procedures or service and later the idea has to be scrapped or delayed because of the inflexibility of data processing. This directly damages the bottom line.

An objective of information engineering is to create systems that can be modified quickly so that changed procedures can be implemented at once when they are required.

BUILDING BLOCKS OF INFORMATION ENGINEERING
Information engineering provides an interlocking set of methodologies, as shown in Fig. 44.2. In this diagram, each block is dependent on the one beneath it.

The diagram is drawn as a set of building blocks because the blocks are assembled in somewhat different ways by different practitioners.

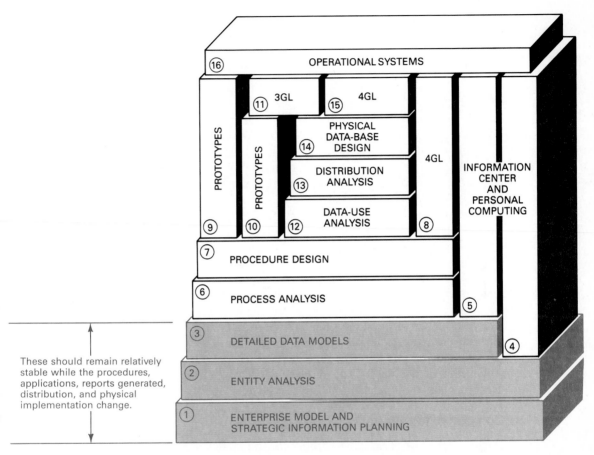

Figure 44.2   The building blocks of information engineering.

Block 1

The block on which all the others rest relates to strategic planning. A hierarchical model of the enterprise is drawn, the objectives of the enterprise and its components are established, and attempts are made to determine what information is needed to enable the enterprise to accomplish its objectives.

Block 2

The next block creates an overview map of the data needed to run the enterprise. This is a top-down analysis of the types of data that must be kept and how they relate to one another. Information analysis is sometimes done across an entire enterprise; sometimes it is done for one division, subsidiary, factory, or portion of an enterprise.

Block 3

The third block is *data modeling*. Information analysis surveys the types of data needed. It creates an information model, which is a broad overview but does not contain all the details needed for data-base implementation. Data modeling creates the detailed logical data-base design and attempts to make it as *stable* as possible before it is implemented. Block 3 is an extension of block 2 that carries it into more detail and applies various checks for stability.

One of the important realizations that led to information engineering is that data in an organization exist and can be described *independently of how those data are used*. Furthermore, the data need to be structured. We must not group any old collection of data items into a record. The data have certain *inherent* properties that lead to correct structuring. These properties are, again, *independent of how the data are used*. If we structure data in a way that violates the inherent properties, it is likely that we will have to restructure them in the future and that restructuring will be expensive because programs using the earlier structure will have to be rewritten. If we structure data in accordance with their inherent properties, the structure will be stable.

The techniques described in Chapters 41 and 42 are used to achieve sound structuring of the data. Data models need to be formally reviewed with end users to make the models as stable as possible [1].

Companywide Planning?

Data modeling is often done without the companywide planning represented by blocks 1 and 2 in Fig. 44.2. Localized data models that relate to a particular business area or particular group of applications are built. Localized models are easier to create and use because they avoid arguments among separate departments or divisions. However, an objective of information engineering is to achieve agreement on data definitions and structures across an organization where those data have to be shared or used in an overall control system.

Blocks 1 and 2 of Fig. 44.2 create an overview of the data needed to run an enterprise. This rough entity model is then divided into clusters, which are sometimes called *subject data bases*, and these are modeled in detail (block 3 of Fig. 44.2). Companywide entity analysis cannot be achieved without top management support, and that is often lacking. To build a fully computerized corporation, it is necessary to harness the perspectives of top management and put the bottom blocks of Fig. 44.2 into place. The techniques of information engineering give top management a plan of action with which to direct the development of information resources.

The bottom three blocks of Fig. 44.2 form a foundation on which most future data processing will be built. Once that foundation, or part of it, exists, it is desirable to employ techniques that can use the data in the data bases and create applications *as quickly as possible*. This requires appropriate application generators, high-level data-base languages, and tools for systems analysts.

Blocks 4 and 5

Many new languages and generators are employable by end users. This direct involvement of end users can bring a vitally needed improvement in the DP process provided that the users do not invent their own data structures. In many cases, users do exactly that, glad of their new-found liberation from the DP programming organization. Where the data are shared data, rather than personal data, the use of end-user languages should be linked into the data models as represented by blocks 4 and 5 in Fig. 44.2.

In some cases, personal computing and information-center computing employ data that are not fully normalized and not represented in the detailed data models. For this reason, block 4 of Fig. 44.2 rests on block 2. On the other hand, where the data needed are in the data administrator's detailed models, the users should employ them. This will save them from having to design their own data, which takes time, and will help to ensure the exchange of data among separately developed systems. Where possible, then, end-user-oriented computing should, like block 5, rest on block 3.

Block 6

Block 6 and those above it relate to the work of professional systems analysts. Block 6 refers to the analysis of a specific business area. The functions of the area are decomposed into *processes,* using decomposition diagrams. De-Dependency diagrams or data flow diagrams may be drawn, showing the interrelations among processes.

In some cases, process analysis is tightly linked to the creation of data models. While the processes are being examined, the entity types needed are considered. The data items needed may be determined and synthesized into a fully normalized data model. If a data model already exists, this will serve to check its accuracy and completeness.

A matrix may be developed that shows which processes use which entity types and how they use them (Fig. 44.3).

Block 7

Block 7 is concerned with the design of procedures. An action diagram of the procedure is created. This may be created from a navigation diagram built on the data model, as illustrated in Chapter 43. Decision trees or tables may be used to design logic where appropriate.

Action diagrams can be generated directly from correctly drawn *decom-*

PROCESS \ ENTITY TYPE	Customer	Order	Vendor	Product	Invoice	Material	Cost	Part	Raw Material Inventory	Finished Goods Inventory	Employee	Sales Territory	Budget	Plan	Work in Process	Facility	Open Requirements	Machine Tool
Customer Order Entry	R	C	R	R			U			U								
Customer Order Control	R	R	R	R		R	R			R					U			
Invoicing	R	R		R	C		R											
Engineering Control				R		R	R	R	R	R					U		R	R
Finished Goods Inventory				R						U								
Bills of Material		R		R			R	R					U				U	
Parts Inventory								R	R	R			U					
Purchase Order Control			R	R		R	R	R	R	R								
Routings															R	R		R
Shop Floor Control		R		R			R	R	R	R								R
Capacity Planning		R							R	R			U		R			R
General Ledger		R			R		R											
Expense												R						
Product Costing		R		R			R	R					U			R	R	
Operating Statements												R		R		R		
Accounts Receivable	R	R										R						
Accounts Payable			R				R	R								R		
Asset Accounting									R	R						R		R
Marketing Analysis	R	R					R						R	U				
Payroll											R							

Figure 44.3 A process/entity-type matrix (C, create; R, read; U, update; D, delete).

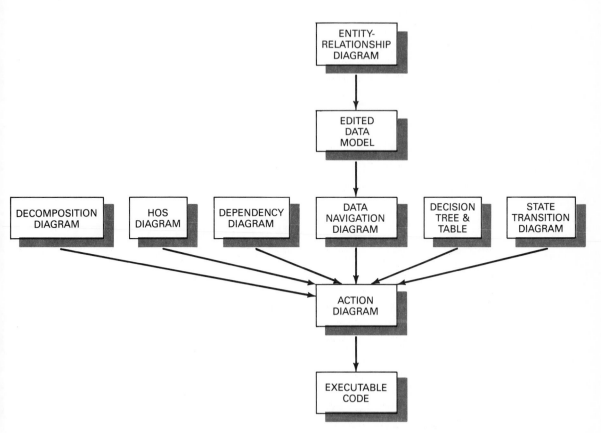

Figure 44.4　Various types of diagrams are automatically convertible to action diagrams and hence to executable code.

position diagrams, dependency diagrams, data navigation diagrams, decision trees, or *state transition diagrams.* Figure 44.4 illustrates this. To speed up the work of the designer, automated graphics tools that enable these types of diagrams to be drawn and changed quickly are desirable. The tools should enforce rigor in the drawing; automatically convert the various representations into action diagrams; facilitate the cutting, pasting, and editing of action diagrams; and convert the action diagrams to code.

　　The use of action diagrams permits the design to be taken as far as possible before committing to a specific language and makes it as easy as possible to switch from one language to another.

　　Figure 44.5 shows the diagramming tools used at the various stages of information engineering.

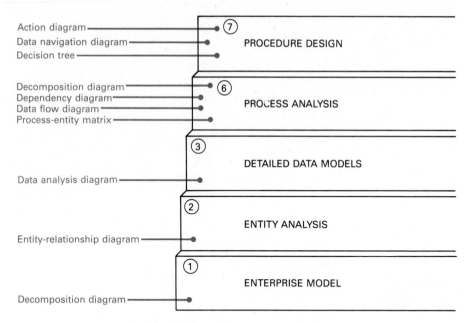

Figure 44.5   Diagramming tools used at different stages of the design.

Blocks 8 and 9

The design in block 7 may be implemented directly in a fourth-generation language such as FOCUS, RAMIS II, IDEAL, Application Factory, NATU-RAL, or MANTIS [2]. Alternatively, such languages or generators may be used to create a *prototype*. The prototype may be successively modified and may eventually become the operational code.

Blocks 10 and 11

In other cases, the prototype may have insufficient machine performance to be the final system. The prototype may be converted to COBOL or some other lower-level language that can be better optimized for performance.

Block 12

Data use analysis (block 12 of Fig. 44.2) provides a formal way of collecting and diagramming the usage information ready for *physical data-base design* (block 14). Data modeling results in a logical design of a data base. A variety of decisions has to be made before that design is implemented physically. The decisions depend on how the data are likely to be used, the usage paths through the data base, and their volumes of use and response time needs. This information is gathered in the stage of block 12.

Block 13

Data models may or may not be split for implementation in separate data bases. This may be done for performance reasons. There are many other possible reasons for distributing data or processing power. Block 13 of Fig. 44.2 is *distribution analysis*.

Block 14

Block 14 relates to the conversion of the data models and procedures into physical data-base design. Some data-base management systems make it advantageous to deviate from cleanly structured third-normal-form data for certain systems where heavy-duty computing makes performance considerations paramount.

The computing environment of Fig. 44.2 differs greatly from the old methods of systems analysis. When performed with automated techniques, it greatly enhances the productivity associated with computer use in corporations. It permits the building of systems that can react rapidly to management's computing and information needs. It can greatly lower the costs of DP maintenance. It represents a major change in the management of DP.

Data-base usage can be further enhanced and application development speeded up by means of another layer added to the conventional data-base models, called *intelligent data base*. An intelligent data model contains logic and rules that are generally executed whenever the data are accessed.

COMPUTERIZATION OF INFORMATION ENGINEERING

Any attempt to do information engineering without computerized tools will become a mess. The data models are too complex to design, draw, and update by hand. Computerized design tools exist to create the models, help check their accuracy, link them to a data dictionary, update them, and make subsets of them available to persons who need to check or use them. These subsets become the basis of individual application building. The application creator can edit the submodel, determine a logical sequence of accesses through it, and use it in an application generator, fourth-generation language, or possible third-generation programming.

ESSENTIAL NEED FOR USER PARTICIPATION

A basic premise of information engineering is that the users of the information must be thoroughly involved. For the first two decades of data processing, systems analysts assumed that they could fully understand the users' data and what the users' information needs were. They were wrong—often catastrophically so. Many of the early management information systems were failures.

Data are full of subtleties and unexpected complexities that are difficult for analysts to discover. Help is needed from the users of the data who *do* understand. In one large bank, a data base that contained an important field called *float* was built. The data administrator thought it was obvious what a banker meant by *float*. However, the data base had to serve both sides of the Atlantic and it was discovered (too late) that a British banker defined *float* differently from his American counterpart. The systems analysts or data administrator could not have been expected to know that, but the bankers said, "Of course they're different; any fool knows that." Data are full of such mismatched definitions and relationships, which can play havoc with data-base systems. To flush them out we need simple techniques for involving the end users—for harnessing the knowledge of the persons who work with the data.

Even more difficult for the analyst is to understand what types of information a user really needs for making decisions. The higher we go in the management tree, the harder it becomes to understand the diversity and complexity of the decision-making processes. Analysts have often guessed what information they think a manager needs or ought to need. Unfortunately, most analysts do not understand the minds of the business people or the subtleties of their decision-making processes. In many cases, members of senior management have never been able to analyze their own decision-making processes and information needs.

The solution to these problems lies in thorough analysis of the data used in running an enterprise and the establishment of these data in systems that permit end users to employ powerful decision-making tools using the data. Once the data are established in appropriate forms of electronic filing, the users must be able to find the data they need quickly and flexibly and to analyze, summarize, and process those data using terminals or personal computers. They should employ their own user-friendly language or work with a specialist who can obtain results for them very quickly—bypassing the lengthy, slow methods of traditional systems analysis and programming in languages like COBOL or PL/I.

The software to make this practical now exists. To employ it effectively, new forms of DP analysis and management are needed. The new techniques need to be integrated into one overall discipline. Information engineering provides a set of linked methodologies that break down the communication barriers between end users, operational management, senior management, and data processing staff.

Some CASE tools specialize in giving the integrated facilities needed for information engineering. They provide a corporate *encyclopedia* in which planning information, data models, and process models are built up. Separate systems are designed using these models. Workbench tools extract data from the central encyclopedia for the building of individual systems. Two such tools are the IEF (Information Engineering Facility) from Texas Instruments [3] and IEW (Information Engineering Workbench) from KnowledgeWare [4].

A HOUSE ON THE SAND

It is enormously tempting to build data systems without the foundation blocks at the bottom of Fig. 44.2. It will become much more tempting as data systems software becomes more powerful and user-seductive.

Most data in an enterprise need to pass from one department to another. Some data need to be gathered from a number of areas to form the information needed for decision making or control. There are not many data with which we can afford uncoordinated, random design by local enthusiasts who wish to be left alone.

Strategic data planning, if done efficiently with a proven methodology, does not cost much when compared to the hidden costs of chaotic data. It is largely a one-time expense, with only a minor cost for keeping it up-to-date. When done, it does not restrict the freedom of local developers. Once they exist, appropriate data systems greatly enhance the freedom to change the corporate procedures.

To build modern data processing without the foundation blocks of Fig. 44.2 is like building a house on the sand. Sooner or later it will be in trouble and have to be rebuilt. Absence of the foundation blocks of data planning is one of the reasons why so much data processing activity steadily bogs down in maintenance. The maintenance caused by absence of planning is enormously more expensive than the planning would have been.

Many corporations have indeed built their MIS house on sand. They have not accomplished the necessary data coordination, either because of lack of understanding of the necessity or methods or because corporate politics has prevented it. It is up to top management to ensure that appropriate foundations are built.

TWO IMAGES

Create in your mind two vividly contrasting images of the use of computers in an enterprise. In the first image, all application creation is done by a hard-pressed DP group using COBOL, with detailed (but nonrigorous) systems analysis and requirements specification. Structured analysis and structured programming are used; these are in fact, the best of the structured software techniques. However, there is an application backlog of years, and an invisible backlog that is even greater. The users seem to be remarkably unsatisfied with the results when they get them. Top management perceives DP as a problem. End users have tried to bypass DP by obtaining their own minicomputers, but this has not been very satisfactory either.

The second image is one in which DP has done entity analysis and data modeling throughout the enterprise and has made the data available on database systems. Users have workstations with which they can access this data. Some use a simple query language designed to be as user-friendly as possible. Others use a language with which they can manipulate the data, extract their own files, perform data entry, and ask what-if questions. Some use spreadsheet and business graphics tools on personal computers. Some use sophisticated decision-support tools. The floor supervisors, expediters, the purchasing, marketing, and personnel departments all create computerized reporting and control procedures with a data-base-oriented application generator. This increases the productivity and efficiency of these departments; decreases the capital tied up in inventory, work in progress, and machine tools; and improves customer service. The financial staff, budget controllers, planners, and engineers create the computing facilities they need with tools like FOCUS, SYSTEM W, NOMAD, and sometimes APL. DP operates an information center designed to give users the maximum help in finding the information they need, processing it or reformatting it to their requirements, and generating procedures and reports. Many DP representatives have become consultants, helpers, and instructors to the end users. Systems analysts work interactively with the end users to create their applications. Almost all data are on-line. Almost all users who need computing have access to terminals. The systems analysts create prototypes of applications interactively, charting complex procedures with CASE tools, which lead to action diagrams, which they can convert directly into code with fourth-generation languages. DP creates the data bases, the networks, and the infrastructure necessary to support this activity. End users of many types throughout the company are inventing how they can use computers to improve their own productivity and are constantly adjusting their own applications.

The second image is what computing *ought* to be like. It needs support facilities created by DP. It needs substantial coordination, which is what information engineering is all about.

Today's software makes it practical for many end users to do their own application generation. Whether they do it themselves or with help from a DP specialist, it needs to be done within a *managed* framework.

REFERENCES

1. J. Martin, *Managing the Data Base Environment,* Englewood Cliffs, NJ: Prentice-Hall, Inc., 1983.

2. J. Martin, *Fourth-Generation Languages,* Englewood Cliffs, NJ: Prentice-Hall, Inc., 1985.

3. Information Engineering Facility (IEF), literature available from Texas Instruments, Dallas, TX.

4. Information Engineering Workbench (IEW), literature available from KnowledgeWare, Atlanta, GA.

PART **VI** VERIFICATION AND TESTING

45 SOFTWARE VERIFICATION, VALIDATION, AND TESTING

THE CASE OF THE $18.5-MILLION HYPHEN

On July 22, 1962, the *Mariner I* space rocket was launched on mankind's first effort to explore the planets, a mission to Venus. The rocket deviated from its course, and ground control gave the order to blow it to pieces. Later, an investigation revealed that the software was at fault. The omission of a single hyphen from one computer program had gone unnoticed and had caused the whole mission to be scrapped. The cost to the American taxpayer was $18.5 million [1].

THE CASE OF THE INFINITE LOOP

Legend has it that in the early days of computing, a certain magazine publisher's computer became stuck in a program loop. It printed the same address on mailing wrappers all afternoon. The wrappers were automatically wrapped around the magazines and automatically franked. The next day some farmer out in the wilds of Nebraska was surprised to see a dozen large trucks rolling up filled with magazines.

DEMONSTRATING SOFTWARE CORRECTNESS

Countless other cases of software errors have proved very embarrassing, costly, and even dangerous. The best protection against such errors is to validate the correctness and overall quality of the software *before* it is used. Therefore, an essential part of software development is to demonstrate the correctness of software programs. This is accomplished through various verification and validation activities. Traditionally, these activities have all been performed near the end of the software development life cycle. And for most

BOX 45.1   Verification techniques used at each software development stage

Representation of Software at a Major Development Phase	Methodologies That Support Verification	Verification Tools and Techniques	
		Manual	Automated
REQUIREMENTS SPECIFICATION	• PSL/PSA (Program Statement Language/Program Statement Analyzer) • ISDOS (Information System Design and Optimization System) • SREP (Software Requirements Engineering Program) • SADT (Structured Analysis and Design Technique) • SAMM (Systematic Activity Modeling Method)	• Inspections • Peer reviews • Walk-throughs • Functional testing	• Data flow analyzer • Assertion generator • Requirements analyzer • Requirements tracer • Functional testing

DESIGN SPECIFICATION	• Top-down design • Structured design • Jackson design methodology • HOS (Higher Order Software) • DECA (Design Expression and Configuration Aid) • SPECIAL	• Inspections • Peer reviews • Walk-throughs • Algorithm analysis • Formal verification • Functional testing	• Formal verification • Data flow analyzer • Analytic modeling of design • Functional testing
PROGRAM CODE	• Structured programming	• Desk checking • Inspections • Peer reviews • Walk-throughs • Formal verification • Structural testing	• Data flow analyzer • Cross-reference map • Control structure analyzer • Interface checker • Code auditor • Debugging compiler • Comparator • Test-data generator • Assertion checker • Performance monitor • Test-coverage analyzer • Report generators • Symbolic evaluators • Structural testing

software, correctness has been demonstrated with only one technique, program testing.

However, several recent software studies have shown that postponing correctness checking until late in the development process makes errors more difficult and more costly to detect and correct [2]. It is on the order of 10 to 100 times more expensive to delay correcting a development error until after the software is operational. Studies have also shown that program testing alone should not be considered an adequate demonstrator of software correctness. Testing can never *guarantee* correctness.

The structured philosophy alters the traditional testing approach by distributing correctness checking throughout the development cycle and by using several techniques and tools to demonstrate software correctness.

Verification

For the final software product to be correct, it must be correct at each stage of its development. The correctness of the requirements specification must be verified; the correctness of the design specification must be verified; and the correctness of the program code must be verified. *Verification* is the demonstration of the consistency, completeness, and correctness of the software as it evolves through each development stage.

As shown in Box 45.1, different verification techniques can be used at each stage of development.

Validation

Whereas verification is concerned with the correctness of software at each stage of development, validation is concerned with the correctness of the final software product. *Validation* is the demonstration that the finished software system correctly meets user needs and requirements. Validation is usually accomplished by verifying the correctness of the requirements specification, design specification, and program code.

Testing

Testing is the technique of demonstrating program correctness by executing the program with a set of sample input data cases.

Testing has been used as the primary verification and validation technique in both traditional and structured software development. The major difference is that testing is usually the only technique used in traditional development, whereas in structured development it is accompanied by other techniques such as design walk-throughs, code inspections, and formal verification. Also, formalized verification procedures to be applied to each development phase and a variety of powerful automated tools have been introduced to the structured development environment. Box 45.1 lists several methodologies and tools that support structured verification activities.

VERIFICATION AND VALICATION TECHNIQUES   Verification and validation techniques range from very informal methods, such as desk checking, to very formal methods, such as proofs of correctness. They include dynamic analysis, in which the program code is actually executed, and static analysis, in which the program algorithms and structure are examined. They also include a variety of manual and automated techniques. Finally, they include methods for studying what functions are performed and how these functions are implemented.

In Box 45.2, verification and validation techniques are divided in four category parts [3]:

1. Dynamic and static techniques

2. Formal and informal techniques

3. Automated and manual techniques

4. Structural and functional testing

Dynamic and Static Techniques

When we think of software verification, we usually think of dynamic techniques, such as program testing, that involve the actual execution of the program. But static techniques are equally important for two reasons. First, dynamic techniques alone are not able to detect all types of software errors. For example, data definition errors, incorrectly initialized variables, and unreferenced variables are often not detected by dynamic techniques. Also, dynamic techniques cannot be used to verify the correctness of a requirements or design specification if they are not written in a formal, computable form.

Static techniques are usually part of dynamic techniques. The use of dynamic techniques normally follows a three-step procedure:

1. Application of static techniques, such as control-flow analysis, data flow analysis, and complexity analysis, to determine what software probes (e.g., path counters and variable tracers) to insert into the program code

2. Execution of the program with probes generating analysis information

3. Analysis of the results of program execution

Static techniques are important in determining appropriate test cases and generating test data needed for dynamic techniques. They are also important in demonstrating software correctness at the early stages of development since they can be used to analyze requirements and design specifications as well as program code.

BOX 45.2 Categories of verification and validation techniques

Category	Description	Examples
STATIC TECHNIQUES	Involves analysis of program specification, design, and code without program execution	• Data flow analyzers • Control structure analyzers • Correctness proofs • Inspections
DYNAMIC TECHNIQUES	Involves actual execution of program code	• Program testing • Data flow analyzers • Assertion checkers
MANUAL TECHNIQUES	Not aided by automated tools	• Desk checking • Inspections • Walk-throughs
AUTOMATED TECHNIQUES	Aided by automated tools	• Structure checkers • Cross-reference mappers • Comparators • Proofs of correctness
INFORMAL TECHNIQUES	Techniques based on heuristic rules	• Desk checking • Informal correctness proofs
FORMAL TECHNIQUES	Techniques based on formal procedures and/or mathematically based rules	• Inspections • Walk-throughs • Formal proofs of correctness
FUNCTIONAL TESTING	Concerned with what program functions are performed but not how they are implemented	• Black-box testing
STRUCTURAL TESTING	Concerned with how program functions are implemented	• White-box testing

Formal and Informal Techniques

Traditional software verification has been treated informally. Methods like desk checking and program testing guided mainly by programmer instinct have been the most frequently used. These informal methods concentrated on program code verification. More formal methods such as formal proofs of correctness, which also concentrate on code verification, have been rarely used in practice.

With the advent of the structured-design revolution, formal methods, in the sense of disciplined procedures, became more widely accepted and applied. These techniques include structured walk-throughs and inspections. Besides being applied to program code, they are also applied to requirements and design specifications. However, formal methods, in the sense of mathematical proofs, were not introduced as part of the structured-design revolution. Mathematically based verification methods are still not widely accepted as practical verification techniques. This is partly because most formal techniques are manual techniques that are tedious to apply to all but the smallest programs.

Automatic and Manual Techniques

Some automated tools are built into the compiler. Others exist as separate pre-processors and postprocessors. They are used to generate test data, to compare expected and actual test results, to generate and check assertions, and to check compliance to standards. Automated tools are most helpful in checking for consistency and correctness. They are not very helpful in checking for completeness (checking that the software performs all intended functions). Completeness errors are often invisible to automated methods because they can only analyze what exists in the specification or the code, not what has been left out. For completeness checking, manual methods are often more successful in detecting errors of omission.

In the 1970s, when testing procedures became more formal and also more complex, the need for automated methods to support software verification grew acute. Without automated tools, any hope of performing a reasonable degree of thorough software verification, especially for large systems, is virtually nonexistent. Still, however, the need for powerful automated verification tools is not fully appreciated even in structured-programming circles. Many programmers must rely too heavily on manual methods and personal instinct because most structured techniques are manual methods.

Functional and Structural Testing

Functional testing, or "black-box testing," is concerned with what functions the software performs but not how the functions are implemented. Functional testing can be applied to a requirements specification, a design specification, or program code. It is used for software validation.

Test cases and test data for functional testing are derived from the external requirements without looking at the design algorithms or the internal program structure.

On the other hand, *structural testing,* or ''white-box testing,'' is concerned with the correctness of program implementation. It is applied to a formal design specification (e.g., Jackson's structured English) or program code. Test cases and test data are derived by analyzing the program algorithms, control structure, data structures, and arithmetic computations.

Both functional testing and structural testing are considered essential components in structured verification methods. Structural testing is more useful in finding consistency and correctness errors, while functional testing is more useful in finding completeness errors.

REFERENCES

1. G. Wallace, D. Wallechinsky, A. Wallace, and S. Wallace, *The Book of Lists #2,* New York: William Morrow and Co., Inc., 1980, p. 486.

2. M. Deutsch, ''Software Project Verification and Validation,'' *Computer* (April 1981), 54–70.

3. R. Adrion, M. Branstad, and J. Cherniavsky, ''Validation, Verification, and Testing of Computer Software,'' *Computing Surveys,* 14, no. 2 (June 1982), 159–191.

46 TESTING

THE TESTING PROCESS

Testing is the process of guaranteeing that a program conforms to specification requirements and works in all cases in which it is supposed to work.

The testing process consists of the following:

- Selecting a set of input data with which to execute the program
- Determining the expected output to be produced
- Executing the program
- Analyzing the results produced from the program execution

A program is *exhaustively* tested if it is executed with every possible set of input data. Exhaustive testing can guarantee the validity of a program, but for most programs it is not practical because an infinite or incredibly large number of possible input data sets exist. Instead, the correctness of a program is usually demonstrated by testing it with a small sample of carefully chosen test cases.

The tester's task is to eliminate unexpected program conditions and failures and to discover any incorrect or deficient implementation of the requirements specification by using a reasonable set of sample test cases. The requirements specification, the design specification, and the program code are used to guide the selection of appropriate test cases.

TESTING HEURISTICS

Although much research has been devoted to developing a test theory, there have been few encouraging results. As of yet, testing still lacks a sound theoret-

BOX 46.1 Where verification and validation techniques are primarily used in testing

Technique	Description	Test Phase			
		Unit	Integration	System	Acceptance
STATIC TECHNIQUES	Involves analysis of program specification, design, and code. Examples: control-structure analysis, correctness proofs, inspections.	✓	✓		
DYNAMIC TECHNIQUES	Involves actual execution of program code. Examples: program testing, data flow analysis, assertion checking.	✓	✓	✓	✓
MANUAL TECHNIQUES	Not aided by automated tools. Examples desk checking, walk-through, inspections.	✓	✓	✓	✓
AUTOMATED TECHNIQUES	Aided by automated tools. Examples structure checkers, test-data generators, cross-reference maps, comparators, proofs of correctness.	✓	✓		

INFORMAL TECHNIQUES	Techniques based on heuristic rules. Examples: informal correctness proofs, desk checking.	✓	✓		✓
FORMAL TECHNIQUES	Techniques based on formal procedures. Examples: inspection, walk-through. Techniques based on mathematical logic. Examples: formal correctness proofs.	✓	✓		
FUNCTIONAL TESTING (Black-box testing)	Concerned with what functions are performed but not how they are implemented.	✓	✓		
STRUCTURAL TESTING (White-box testing)	Concerned with how functions are implemented.	✓			
VERIFICATION	Demonstration of correctness of software as it is developed.	✓	✓	✓	✓
VALIDATION	Demonstration of correctness of final software product.	✓		✓	✓

ical basis. Even in a structured environment, testing is directed by only heuristic rules such as these [1]:

- Test every program statement and every path at least once.
- Test the most important and the most heavily used parts of the program most thoroughly.
- Test modules individually before they are combined. Then test intersections between modules.
- Organize testing so that it proceeds from the simplest to the most complex test cases. This means that tests involving less complicated logic (fewer loops and condition testing) should be executed first. This also means that normal processing with valid input should be tested before exception processing is checked.
- Calculate expected test tests *before* the test is executed.

FOUR-PHASE TESTING PROCEDURE

The structured approach has greatly affected testing as well as the other phases of software development. Testing has been formalized into a four-phase procedure:

1. Unit testing
2. Integration testing
3. System testing
4. Acceptance testing

Ideally, the phases should be performed sequentially. For example, integration testing should be completed before system testing begins. Within each phase, however, testing steps may proceed in parallel. More than one module may be unit-tested at the same time; in the case of integration testing, more than one subsystem of modules may be tested at the same time.

When top-down programming is used, module coding, unit testing, and integration testing are all merged. A module is coded, integrated into the program control structure, and tested. Then another module is coded, integrated into the control structure, and tested. This process begins with the highest-level modules and continues down to the lowest-level modules. System and acceptance testing follow separately after all modules have been added to the control structure.

As shown in Box 46.1, a combination of verification and validation techniques is used to support the four testing phases. Unit and integration testing are primarily verification activities, while system and acceptance testing are primarily validation activities. Also, unit and integrated testing are basically forms of structural testing, while system and acceptance testing are forms of functional testing. Figure 46.1 summarizes the four-phase testing procedure.

UNIT TESTING

Unit testing is structural testing performed at the program module level. Each module, function, or subroutine is usually unit-tested by the programmer as part of the coding step.

The goals of unit testing are to execute each statement in a module, to traverse each logic path in the module, and to test the module with each possible set of input data. This type of testing is sometimes called *coverage-based testing* [2]. Usually, it is impossible to achieve full coverage because the number of tests needed would be staggering. Instead, a smaller set of tests that attempt to

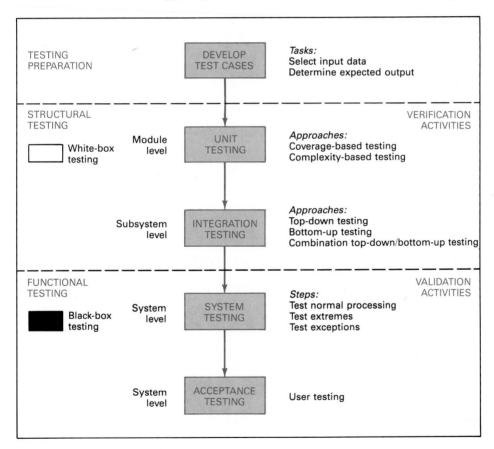

Figure 46.1   The testing process is divided into a four-phase procedure: unit testing, integration testing, system testing, and acceptance testing. As preparation for testing, test cases are selected, the appropriate input data are generated, and anticipated results are calculated.

reveal many of the logic, computation, data-handling, and timing problems in a reasonable amount of time and at a reasonable cost is selected.

Computational testing verifies the quantitative accuracy of arithmetic operations performed in the module. Data-handling testing ensures that valid and invalid data are properly edited, that output data are stored in the proper format and location, that data conversions are correctly performed, that all data are properly initialized, and that all data are referenced.

Coverage-based Testing

The simplest form of test coverage in unit testing is that each statement in the module is executed at least once. Other types of coverage are branch coverage and path coverage. Branch coverage exercises each decision and follows all decision branches. Path coverage exercises all program DD paths (a *DD path* is the sequence of statements starting at the outcome of a decision and leading up to the next decision).

Dynamic Analysis

Unit testing usually concentrates on a dynamic analysis of the program code to reveal errors. The code is executed both manually (e.g., walk-throughs or inspections) and automatically. Execution steps typically include those listed in Box 46.2.

Although dynamic analysis is useful in detecting many types of program errors, it cannot detect all types. For example, dynamic analysis is particularly helpful in checking the program control structure but not very helpful in checking data structures. This is a serious shortcoming because data-structure errors

BOX 46.2   Steps in unit testing

1. A manual code walk-through to determine if the design specifications are correctly implemented by the code

2. Execution of the simplest possible tests to verify the basic structure of the module

3. Execution of tests to examine the module performance on valid input data

4. Execution of tests to examine the module performance on invalid input data

5. Execution of tests to examine the correctness of each loop, especially checking for proper loop termination

are commonly made. For example, studies by Howden and Glass [2] showed that errors in data definition were much more common than errors in procedures.

This suggests that unit testing should concentrate on data analysis much more than has been done traditionally. For example, analysis of data flow can help discover undefined and unreferenced variables.

Static Analysis

Another shortcoming of dynamic analysis is that it is not very effective in checking for program completeness. Since many program errors are a result of omissions (e.g., a partial implementation of the system requirements), techniques other than dynamic analysis should be incorporated into unit testing. These techniques fall into the category of static analysis. They include inspections, data flow analysis, and proofs of correctness linked to the system requirements. They can help discover missing program functions, errors in arithmetic expressions, type declarations, mismatched shared-data areas, module interface errors, and standards violations.

Complexity-based Testing

Complexity analysis is a particularly useful type of static analysis. It formalizes coverage-based testing. Rather than simply executing as many program statements, DD paths, or decision branches as possible, as is the objective in coverage-based testing, the objective of complexity-based testing is to direct the testing effort toward the most complex parts of the code. This is where more errors are likely to have been made.

Complexity analysis can predict where program errors are likely to occur and the types of program errors that are likely to occur. With this information, coverage-based testing can be made more effective by zeroing in on the more error-prone parts of the program. For example, Halstead's metric, n_2, which is a count of the number of distinct operands, can be used to measure the complexity of a program statement, DD path, or module. The statements, DD paths, or modules with large n_2 values have greater complexity and should be concentrated upon during coverage-based testing. Those with lower n_2 values should be executed if time and budget permit.

Other complexity metrics such as McCabe's cyclomatic complexity number and McClure's control variable complexity are discussed in Chapter 5.

INTEGRATION TESTING

Integration testing is a higher form of structural testing. While unit testing is performed at a module level, integration testing is performed at a subsystem level, where a subsystem is a hierarchy of modules. Since modules have been unit-tested prior to integration testing, they can be treated as black boxes, allowing integration testing to concentrate on interfaces between modules. The goals of integration testing are to verify that each module performs correctly within the control structure and that the module interfaces are correct.

Integration testing is performed by combining modules in steps. At each step, one module is added to the program structure, and testing concentrates on exercising this newly added module. Sometimes regression testing is included as a second component of integration testing. In *regression testing,* tests exercise the other modules in the program to determine if they have been adversely affected by the newly added module.

When it has been demonstrated that a module performs properly within the program structure, another module is added, and testing continues. This process is repeated until all modules have been integrated and tested.

There are two basic approaches to integration testing, bottom-up testing and top-down testing.

Bottom-Up Testing

In *bottom-up testing,* the lowest-level modules are integrated and tested first. This means that integration testing proceeds *up* the hierarchical program control structure shown in Fig. 46.2.

The bottom-up approach requires the construction of drivers to simulate

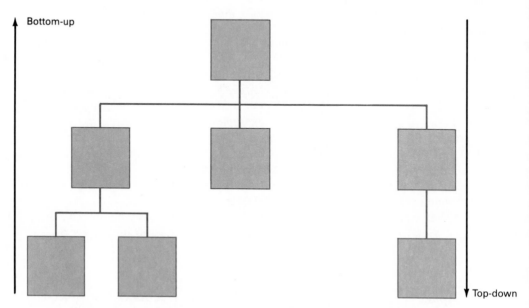

Figure 46.2 In bottom-up testing, the lowest-level modules are integrated and tested first. Integration testing moves *up* the hierarchical program control structure. In top-down testing, high-level modules are integrated and tested first. Integration testing moves *down* the control structure.

the program environment during integration testing. A *driver* is a temporary test program that calls the module that is being tested.

Problems with Bottom-Up Testing

Several problems have been noted with bottom-up testing:

- Driver programs can require a great deal of effort to develop and can be an additional source of errors.
- High-level program functions are tested last and least. (Critical errors often occur at high-level functions, and bottom-up testing may delay their discovery.)
- Interface errors may not appear until late in integration testing. (The later errors are discovered, the more difficult and expensive they are to correct.)

Top-Down Testing

In *top-down testing,* high-level modules are integrated and tested first. This means that integration testing proceeds *down* the hierarchical control structure shown in Fig. 46.2.

Top-down testing requires the creation of dummy modules called *stubs.* When a module is tested, the modules it calls are represented by stubs, which usually just return control to the calling module. As the testing continues down the program structure, each stub is replaced by the actual module code.

Top-down testing offers several important advantages over bottom-up testing:

- The quantity of test data needed grows as integration testing proceeds, allowing the pooling of test data instead of requiring separate test data for each module as it is integrated.
- High-level functions are tested first and most.
- Integration testing can be begun earlier since high-level modules can be coded first and can be tested with stubs.
- Stubs are easier to construct than drivers.

Problems with Top-Down Testing

Although usually preferred over pure bottom-up testing, there can be problems with top-down testing:

- Sometimes stubs can be difficult to construct as the actual module. (This can be time consuming and error prone.)
- Critical low-level functions are not tested until late in the development process. (Problems with critical low-level functions may force a late redesign of several high-level functions.)

Combination Top-Down/Bottom-Up Testing

In small programs, it makes little difference which integration approach is used. In this case, unit testing and integration testing are often merged into one step. But in large projects, more formality and separation of the testing steps is preferred. Also, a combination top-down/bottom up approach, which capitalizes on their advantages and minimizes their problems, is preferred. This combination approach is basically a top-down approach that incorporates a bottom-up approach by deviating from a pure top-down direction to deal with the most critical and/or most complex parts of the program first. Some general guidelines are listed in Box 46.3.

SYSTEM TESTING   System testing is a validation activity used to demonstrate that the entire software program is correct. It is performed following integration testing and is basically functional testing. The objective is to discover any incorrect implementation of the requirements specification.

Typical strategies for system testing include the following:

- Test cases should exercise the most important and most heavily used parts of the program.
- Test cases should represent normal or expected use of the program.
- Test cases should be selected to expose errors under extreme or critical processing conditions.

A thorough system test includes tests to cover each of the listed strategies. Guidelines for system testing are listed in Box 46.4.

BOX 46.3   Guidelines for integration testing

1. Use the top-down approach to test the program control structure and verify the correctness of high-level functions first.
2. Use the bottom-up approach to test modules that interface with the operating system environment in complex or new ways and to test modules that perform the most critical or complex logic in the program.
3. Include regression testing as a component of integration testing.

BOX 46.4   Guidelines for system testing

- The program functional requirements and specifications should be used to build test cases.
- Test cases should be prepared with the expected test results determined *before* the tests are executed.
- Testing should begin with the simplest tests and graduate to the more complex tests, first using constructed and then using live input data.
- System testing should be performed in three steps:

1. *Test normal cases:* Demonstrate that the program will produce correct results for expected input data.
2. *Test extremes:* Test extremes in input volume as well as input values.
3. *Test exceptions:* Use test data that fall out of the acceptable range to demonstrate that the program explicitly rejects all invalid input data.

- When possible, run in parallel with a previous system and compare results.

ACCEPTANCE TESTING

Acceptance testing is another validation activity. It is the purest form of functional testing. The program is treated as a black box; that is, no knowledge of its internal structure is assumed, and testing is based completely on user requirements. Normally, acceptance testing is performed following system testing and involves the user's exercising the software with live data.

TEST DATA

Test data are a crucial element for accomplishing effective and economic testing. Developing test data involves two tasks [2]:

1. Selecting test input data
2. Determining expect output

The theorem of testing states the following:

If there exists a consistent, reliable, valid, and complete criterion for test selection for a program p and if a test set satisfying the criterion is such that all test instances succeed, then the program p is correct. [2]

Unfortunately, it has been shown mathematically that no algorithm exists to find consistent, reliable, and complete program test criteria. This means there is no one best way to generate an optimal set of test data that will exhaustively test a program. Heuristic methods must be used.

If selecting test data is an extremely difficult task, calculating expected results is often even more difficult. In addition to the obvious requirement that test data must show that the program works in the way it was intended, test-data guidelines are listed in Box 46.5.

Types of Test Data

Test data can be divided into three types:

1. *Constructed data:* data that are manually constructed in a selective field-by-field manner or data randomly constructed by an automatic test generator
2. *Modified actual data:* actual data that are modified manually or automatically to produce certain results and to execute certain parts of the program
3. *Actual live data:* used in volume testing and parallel runs

All three types of test data should be used during testing. Constructed data are very useful in the early testing phases since the tester can control data values in each field of an input record. Constructed data are most helpful during unit testing and integration testing when testing for exceptions (e.g., input data that fall out of the acceptable range). To be objective, both manually and randomly constructed data should be used.

Modified actual data are useful when testing normal processing (e.g., the program produces expected results for expected data) during integration and system testing. It can detect errors that might have been overlooked with constructed data. Also, modifying real data will give the tester an opportunity to test error routines.

Actual live data are required for comprehensive testing during system and

BOX 46.5   Guidelines for test data

- Use test data that can obtain as much information as possible with each test so as to make testing complete in a feasible number of test runs.
- Design test data so the results can be calculated before the test is executed.
- Keep test data relatively simple so that the results are simple to check (e.g., keep arithmetic simple).

acceptance testing. Live data are often used in parallel runs with an older system to compare results with the new replacement system.

Selection of Test Data

Test data must be carefully selected to detect as many problems as possible with only a few tests due to time and cost constraints. Three commonly used methods for conducting testing are as follows:

- Testing is done to simulate normal or expected use of the program.
- Testing is done to expose errors under extreme or critical conditions.
- Testing is done to exercise the most complex parts of the program.

A comprehensive-testing approach includes each of these three methods. Test data must be constructed accordingly.

Generation of Test Data

Generating test data requires the ability to distinguish test cases and to describe them relative to the requirements specifications and testing goals. Test cases must be able to produce repeatable results.

Many powerful automated tools have been developed to aid in the generation of test data. They include test-data generators, file comparators, and programming environments. Test tools are discussed in Chapter 48.

Test-data generation for structural testing usually follows a static analysis of the program code to determine what data will provide the fullest test coverage and will support complexity-based testing. Automated tools, such as compilers with cross-reference maps, complexity analysis, and testing probe insertion, can greatly aid static analysis.

Test-data generation for functional testing is usually based on a manual examination of the requirements specification. When the requirements have been formally defined in a requirements specification language such as PSL, automated methods, such as assertion generators and requirements analyzers, can aid test-data generation.

REFERENCES

1. C. McClure, *Managing Software Development and Maintenance,* New York: Van Nostrand Reinhold Co., 1981.

2. R. Adrion, M. Branstad, and J. Cherniavsky, "Validation, Verification, and Testing of Computer Software," *Computing Surveys,* 14, no. 2, (June 1982), 159–191.

3. McClure, pp. 58–65.

47 DEBUGGING

Gloria was one of the best programmers at the British American Insurance Company. But as sometimes happens to even the best programmers, Gloria was having a bad week. She had almost completed her part of the new on-line claims system when an elusive bug brought her progress to a halt. Gloria was determined that no bug would get the best of her, so she searched through listings, test runs, and dumps to find the problem. Although her co-workers offered help, she refused, claiming it would take too long to explain the program and the problem to someone else. By the time another programmer became familiar enough with her problem to be of any real help, she would certainly have it solved.

After a week of searching, Gloria asked Ted, another programmer at BAI, to look at her program. After a few minutes' explanation of the program logic from Gloria and a few more minutes to review the code, Ted pointed out the bug. There was a missing period at the end of a COBOL IF statement. The compiler had not detected the mistake, and the indentation had camouflaged it.

Gloria was both relieved and humiliated. How could she have studied her own program for a whole week without seeing such an obvious mistake?

Gloria's experience is a common one among programmers. Although the error was very minor, it had cost BAI a week of valuable programmer time.

THE DIFFICULTY
OF DEBUGGING
Program testing and debugging usually go hand in hand. *Testing* is the process of executing a program with sample input to demonstrate its correctness. *Debugging* is the process of locating the source of program errors that are discovered by testing.

Some revealing experiments have been performed on the debugging process. Researchers have used both professional programmers and programming students to gain a better understanding of which debugging methods are most useful. The results are both disappointing and surprising. First, the inability of experienced programmers to detect even obvious errors is alarming [1]. Second, computer-based debugging by the original programmer appears to be one of the least efficient debugging methods [2]. Third, no single method used alone is very good [1].

As illustrated in Gloria's story, programmers are not very successful in finding errors. They do not know where to look and consequently often waste a great deal of effort looking in the wrong place. They do not know what errors are most likely to occur. They do not know when they have isolated all aspects of an error and how to track its total effect throughout the program. When they are looking in the wrong place, they find it difficult to look elsewhere because their thinking becomes fixed on one possible cause.

Even in situations where experienced programmers have been given information about the number and the location of program errors, the programmers have been unable to find all the errors. Debugging seems to be very dependent on the individual programmer. In some instances, inexperienced programmers are more successful than experienced programmers at finding errors. Also, when different programmers independently debug the same program, they are likely to find different errors.

DEBUGGING METHODS

There are two basic debugging methods, individual debugging and group debugging. In *individual debugging,* one programmer works alone to find the error(s); in *group debugging,* two or more programmers work together to find the error(s). For each method, there are many variations. For example, an individual may use a computer-based debugging approach that relies mainly on studying the results from program execution tests. Or an individual may use a non-computer-based method in which the program listing is studied (desk debugging). On the other hand, a group of programmers may choose to walk through the program, listing together in an attempt to discover the error.

In his experiments, Myers found that the most cost-effective method for finding errors was to employ two programmers who work independently of one another and later pool their results. This method proved equally cost-effective (in terms of cost per error found) to a single-person method because of little overlap in the errors found by both programmers [3]. Fagan performed experiments with group inspection techniques at IBM. He found that group walk-throughs and inspections were a more effective debugging method (in terms of programmer time and computer time) than when the original programmers debugged their own code individually [3].

Since the ability to detect different types of errors varies with the method used and the individuals involved, a combination approach is probably best.

Based on the results of debugging experiments and studies, the following debugging method is suggested:

1. Two individuals work independently to locate the error using a computer-based testing approach interspersed with individual desk debugging. (These individuals are not the same persons who wrote or changed the code.)
2. The two individuals pool their findings by performing a walk-through review of the program and the error evidence each has gathered.
3. Automatic debugging tools are used to aid the process.

Using more than one debugging method and more than one debugger may seem too extravagant a suggestion when many systems and programming departments are suffering from personnel shortages. But it is a very practical suggestion because this approach will not only enable programmers to find more errors sooner but will also provide an environment in which supportive feedback from peers, programming education, and programmer communication can be enhanced. A better program and better programmers will result.

PROGRAM DEBUGGING TOOLS

Which debugging tools are the most useful? Is the source listing the only essential debugging aid? Are dumps of any use? Does an on-line debugging environment improve programmer effectiveness? Shneiderman suggests the following list of debugging aids [3]:

- Source code listing
- Detailed program specification
- Program flowchart
- Output listing
- Trace of statements executed and variable values
- Access to terminal for program execution
- Clues to type or location of error

He places the source listing at the top of the list, claiming that it is the most important debugging aid. Experiments by Gilb support Shneiderman's claim by showing that simple source code reading is more effective than use of test data in finding errors [4]. Also, Van Tassel believes that desk-checking a source listing can be as effective as studying program dumps [5]. Weinberg suggests that automatically generated flow diagrams can be used to supplement code reading [6].

Box 47.1 lists a set of tools that aid the debugging process. Selection of appropriate debugging tools depends on the problem to be solved and the de-

BOX 47.1 Debugging tools and aids

- Debugging compilers (e.g., University of Waterloo's COBOL WATBOL and FORTRAN WATFIV, Cornell University's PL/I PL/C, IBM's PL/I Checkout Compiler, Stanford University's ALGOL W)
- Cross-reference listers (e.g., TRW's DEPCHT, DPNDCY, FREF for FORTRAN programs)
- Storage map (a common compiler option)
- Source code reformatters (e.g., ADR's MetaCOBOL)
- Automatic flowcharters (e.g., TRW's FLOWGEN for FORTRAN programs)
- Automatic documentors (e.g., General Research's RXVP, Software Rennovation Technology's RE-LEARN)
- Structuring engines (e.g., Catalyst's COBOL Engine; Caines, Farber, and Gordon's FORTRAN Engine)
- Executive monitors and performance monitors (e.g., TRW's PPE)
- Code optimizers (e.g., IBM's PL/I Optimizing Compiler)
- Structure checkers (e.g., TRW's CODE AUDITOR for FORTRAN programs)
- Decision-table processors
- Data dictionaries
- Automated librarians (e.g., NIC's SLICK)
- Data management systems
- Test-data generators (e.g., TRW's ATDG)
- Test-case generators (e.g., General Research's RXVP for FORTRAN programs)
- Compiler-error-checking features (e.g., IBM's COBOL USE command, IBM's PL/I ON SIZE ERROR command, DEC BASIC-PLUS)
- File-compare utilities
- Language debugging packages for dumps, flow trace, variable trace, subroutine trace, subscript checks, and display (e.g., Stanford's ALGOL W, IBM's COBOL and PL/I)
- On-line debuggers providing on-line breakpoints, restarts, and modifications (e.g, DEC BASIC-PLUS)
- Language-conversion packages
- Programmer's workbench (e.g., UNIX)

bugger's personal preference. However, the important point here is that the availability of a powerful set of debugging tools can greatly affect the amount of debugging effort expended. For example, Van Tassel claims that the use of a good debugging compiler (e.g., University of Waterloo's COBOL WATBOL and FORTRAN WATFIV, Cornell University's PL/I, PL/C, and IBM's PL/I Checkout Compiler) can reduce the debugging effort by half [5]. A debugging compiler checks more thoroughly for syntax errors by examining the interaction of instructions as well as the correctness of each single instruction. It also performs checks such as out-of-range subscripts and uninitialized variables during program execution.

LOCATING PROGRAM ERRORS

The last item on Shneiderman's list of debugging aids lists clues to the type or location of the error. Traditionally, programmers have spent too much time looking for errors in the wrong places. Myers found that programmers focused their attention on normal processing at the expense of considering special processing situations and invalid input [1]. Weinberg found that programmers have difficulty finding errors because their conjectures become prematurely fixed, blinding them to other possibilities [6].

Knowing what types of errors are likely to occur and where they are likely to occur in the program can avoid these problems and greatly simplify the debugging process. Two techniques are suggested:

1. Study the program error properties.
2. Measure program complexity.

Program Error Profile

Each program has an error profile identifying which parts (modules) of a program are most error-prone and what types of program errors are most likely to occur. This profile is established during program development because most developers have a favorite subset of programming constructs they use repeatedly and also have certain programming errors that they make repeatedly. Unless a major program rewrite is performed, this profile remains generally unchanged throughout the life of the program.

Error profiles can be determined by studying the program errors found during development testing and the maintenance phase. Boxes 47.2, 47.3, and 47.4 list the error information that should be recorded and studied.

Herndon and Keenan studied the program errors that were discovered during the testing of a real-time communications system [7]. In total, 200 errors were found. The errors were categorized according to the cause of the error:

- *Specification error:* incomplete or incorrect design specification
- *Programming error:* faulty design, logic, or code
- *Testing error:* invalid test procedures
- *External error:* hardware failures or problems in other systems that interface with the system

The majority (58 percent) of the errors found in the communications system were programming errors. Specification errors accounted for 19 percent of the errors found, external errors for 13 percent, and testing errors for the remaining 10 percent. Using this historical error information, we can predict that future problems with this communications system will probably be caused by programming errors.

Schneidewind and Hoffman also performed programming experiments to study program errors [8]. They categorize errors according to the following error types:

- *Design error:* communication error, data design error, etc.
- *Coding error:* syntax error, design misunderstanding, etc.
- *Clerical error:* manual input error, mental error, etc.
- *Debugging error:* inappropriate use of debugging tools, etc.
- *Testing error:* inadequate tests, misinterpretation of results, etc.

BOX 47.2   Error report

ERROR REPORT

ER NO _____

Reported by: _____

Date reported: _____

System name: _____

Severity of error:

_____ High: system does not function

_____ Medium: system functions, but not satisfactorily

_____ Low: system functions, but with minor irregularities

Symptomatic description of error:

_____

_____

_____

_____

BOX 47.3 Error correction data

ERROR CORRECTION DATA

System name(s): _____

Program name(s): _____

Type of error:

_____ Specification error   _____ Debugging error

_____ Design error   _____ Testing error

_____ Coding error   _____ External error

_____ Clerical error   _____ Other _____

Explanation of cause of error:

_____

_____

_____

_____

_____

Life-cycle phase during which error corrected:

Development   Maintenance

_____ Specification   _____ Change/enhancement

_____ Design   _____ Rewrite

_____ Coding   _____ Error correction (of another error)

_____ Testing

Number of modules changes: _____

Number of lines of code added and/or changed: _____

Number of compiles: _____

Number of tests for revalidation: _____

Total number of test runs: _____

Test data available: _____ _____

Modules changed   Number of times previously changed

_____   _____

_____   _____

_____   _____

_____   _____

Times to detect and correct errors: _____ hours

Difficulty of detecting and correcting error:

_____ Low: less than 4 hours

_____ Medium: 4 hours to 16 hours

_____ High: greater than 16 hours

Code style:

_____ Structured

_____ Unstructured

BOX 47.4 Error categories

I. Design Error

  1. Missing cases or steps

  2. Inadequate checking/editing

  3. Initialization error

  4. Loop control error

  5. Misunderstanding of specifications

  6. Incorrect algorithm (math error)

  7. Timing problems

  8. Failure to consider all data types

II. Coding Error

  1. Misunderstanding of design

  2. I/O format error

  3. Control structure error (IF, PERFORM)

  4. Syntax error

  5. Incorrect subroutine usage

  6. Initialization/reinitialization error (e.g., flag)

  7. Indexing/subscripting error

  8. Naming inconsistency

  9. Inadequate checking/editing

  10. Error in parameter passing

  11. Using wrong arithmetic mode

  12. Overflow, underflow, truncation

III. Clerical Error

  1. Slip of the pencil (misspelling)

  2. Keypunch/data entry

IV. Debugging Error

  1. Insufficient or incorrect use of test cases/data
  2. Negligence
  3. Misinterpretation of error source/debugging results

BOX 47.4   *(Continued)*

V. Testing Error

    1. Inadequate test cases/data

    2. Misinterpretation of test results

    3. Misinterpretation of program specifications

    4. Negligence

VI. External Error

    1. Hardware failure

    2. Software reaction to hardware failure

    3. Problems in other systems that interfaced with this one

VII. Specification Error

    1. Incomplete or ambiguous specification
    2. Incorrect problem definition

The error type that occurred most frequently was clerical, followed by coding, design, and finally, testing errors. It is interesting to note that the design errors were caused by the neglect of extreme conditions (i.e., extreme numeric values that cause underflow or overflow or exceed any limits). This agrees with Myers's findings that programmers tend to concentrate on normal processing situations at the expense of off-normal situations. As a general debugging guideline, the programmer should focus the debugging search on examining extreme conditions rather than normal processing. Box 47.5 lists some additional debugging guidelines.

In error discussions, the emphasis is often placed on specification and design errors rather than on clerical and coding errors because these errors are more difficult to detect and correct and because many clerical and coding errors are detectable during compilation. However, clerical and coding errors cannot be entirely ignored by the debugger, for two reasons. First, although they are easier to detect and correct, more coding errors than design errors tend to be made. This was the case in both the Herndon and the Schneidewind studies [7, 8]. The result is that the total amount of effort expended detecting and correcting clerical and coding errors may equal or even be greater than the effort expended detecting and correcting specification and design errors. Second,

BOX 47.5   Debugging guidelines

- Do not use a random approach to debugging. Begin by excluding the unlikely sources of the error. First eliminate the simple cases; then move on to the more difficult cases [5].

- Isolate one error at a time [5].

- Employ defensive programming by making program errors easy to locate with the use of debugging code embedded in the program (e.g., printout of selective variable values, logic traces, end-of-program-logic message). After debugging is completed, leave the debugging code in the program by changing each debugging statement into a nonexecutable comment so the statements are available for future use but do not interfere with normal processing [5].

- Study actual program output carefully, comparing it to samples of expected output. Many errors are observable in the output listings [2].

- Focus attention on data handled by the program rather than solely on program processing logic. Focus on boundary and invalid-input conditions when checking for data-related errors [2]. Check data type, data value ranges, data field sizes, and data value.

- Use the most powerful debugging tools available and a variety of debugging methods (e.g., computer-based and non-computer-based) to avoid becoming locked into considering only one possibility too prematurely.

- Keep a record of errors detected and corrected, noting where the errors occurred in the program and the types of errors that were found; this information can be used to predict where future errors will occur [9].

- Measure program complexity. Programs (modules) with high complexity have a greater propensity for errors and probably will require more time to detect and correct errors. Programs (modules) with high complexity are more likely to contain specification and design errors; programs (modules) with low complexity are more likely to contain clerical and coding errors.

- Use programs with artificially seeded errors to train programmers in debugging techniques; give them immediate feedback on all seeded errors, showing them what they missed [4].

many clerical and coding errors (e.g., uninitialized variable, out-of-range subscript, nontermination of loops) are not detectable by the ordinary compiler.

When searching for a program error, the programmer should not dismiss the possibility that its cause may be a syntax error or a misunderstanding of how the language works. A debugging compiler can greatly aid the programmer in locating these types of errors.

**PREDICTING
ERROR-
PRONENESS**

Program complexity can be used to measure error-proneness by predicting where errors are most likely to occur (in which modules) and the types of errors that are most likely to occur. Knowing the type of errors and where they are likely to occur can be used to select an optimum debugging strategy and tools, leading to the detection and correction of more errors sooner and at a lower cost.

McCabe's cyclomatic number has been found to have a significant relationship with program error occurrence. As defined in Chapter 3, the cyclomatic number is calculated by counting the number of program compares:

$$\text{Cyclomatic number} = \text{number-of-compares} + 1$$

Program errors are more likely to occur in program modules having a high cyclomatic number (>10) than in modules having a low cyclomatic number. In addition, a high cyclomatic number is associated with design errors, whereas a low cyclomatic number is associated with coding errors. The desk-checking debugging method and nonexecution debugging tools such as a debugging compiler are very helpful in finding coding errors. A group walk-through and execution debugging tools such as tracers and on-line debuggers are recommended for finding design errors.

REFERENCES

1. G. Myers, "A Controlled Experiment in Program Testing and Code Walk-through/Inspections," *Communications of the ACM,* 21, no. 9 (September 1978), 760–768.

2. B. Knight "On Software Quality and Productivity," *Technical Directions, IBM FSC* (July 1978), 21–27.

3. B. Shneiderman, *Software Psychology,* Cambridge, MA: Winthrop Publishers, Inc., 1980, pp. 129–130.

4. T. Gilb, *Software Metrics,* Cambridge, MA: Winthrop Publishers, Inc., 1977, pp. 26–49.

5. D. Van Tassel, *Program Style, Design, Efficiency, Debugging, and Testing,* Englewood Cliffs, N.J.: Prentice-Hall, Inc., 1978, pp. 176–237.

6. G. Weinberg, *Psychology of Computer Programming,* New York: Van Nostrand Reinhold Co., 1971, pp. 247–251.

7. M. Herndon and A. Keenan, *Analysis of Error Remediation Expenditures During Validation,* Third International Conference on Software Engineering, May 1978, pp. 202–206.

8. N. Schneidewind and H. Hoffman, "An Experiment in Software Error Data Collection and Analysis," *IEEE Transactions on Software Engineering* SE-5(3), May 1979, 276–286.

9. H. Mills, "Software Development," *IEEE Transactions on Software Engineering,* SE-2(4), December 1976, 265–273.

48 AUTOMATED TEST TOOLS

TEST TOOLS Automated tools are important because their use can greatly improve both program quality and programmer productivity. Automated test tools are no exception. For example, the Hughes Aircraft Company estimates a savings of 4400 person-days in a recent software project due to the use of a formalized test plan supported by automated test tools [1]. The test tools provide a practical means to test the software more exhaustively, resulting in higher error exposure rates at an earlier stage in the software development cycle.

Test tools assist the testing process by creating test cases, generating test data, and analyzing test results. As shown in Box 48.1, there are three categories of test tools [1]:

- Static tools
- Dynamic tools
- Interpretive tools

Box 48.2 lists several examples of test tools currently available. A more complete description of each type of tool is available [2].

GENERAL RESEARCH'S RXVP RXVP is a good example of a multifunctional test tool. It was developed by General Research Corporation as a test and documentation tool for FORTRAN programs. Since RXVP can perform both static and dynamic program analysis, it is considered a combination static/dynamic test tool. It has proved to be a powerful tool for decreasing human effort and human errors in the testing process and for improving the effectiveness of the testing process.

BOX 48.1   Types of test tools

STATIC TOOLS

These tools are used to examine the structure of a program to reveal potential problems in the code, to identify the program control structure and data structures, and to determine test coverage with different input data. They usually analyze the source code and do not involve execution of the program. Examples include data flow analyzers, structure checkers, and cross-reference maps.

DYNAMIC TOOLS

These tools examine the performance of a program as it executes with certain input data. Probes are inserted in the code to follow flow of execution and to keep counts of module invocations, subroutine calls, loop executions, number of statements executed, value ranges of variables, and the like. Examples include variable tracers and path tracers.

INTERPRETIVE TOOLS

These tools use symbolic execution to examine the program. The program is described as a series of symbolic formulas that are executed and verified against a set of predefined assertions. Symbolic execution is still an experimental technique in the automatic theorem-proving research area.

RXVP Experiences

The Karlsruhe Nuclear Research Center has many FORTRAN systems, some as large as 75,000 lines of code, that needed extensive modification and maintenance. Karlsruhe found RXVP to be an immense aid in making program modifications that would otherwise have been impractical [3]. RXVP provided information on the data flow and module invocation structure in their complex programs. This made it possible to investigate thoroughly the impact of modifications on the entire program and to trace possible side effects. In addition, it was helpful in static error detection. Uninitialized variables and variables whose values were set but never referenced were quickly found.

Hughes Aircraft used RXVP to support a formalized testing procedure by providing the following software testing procedures [1]:

- Analysis of the program source code to generate a directed graph of its control structure
- Insertion of probes to interpret and record program flow during execution
- Record of statistics on execution of program statements and variable values during execution
- Report on test coverage based on program execution information

With the help of RXVP, Hughes estimates that they were able to find 400 more errors during testing, a savings of approximately 4400 person-days.

RXVP Analysis Reports

RXVP analyzes FORTRAN source code and produces a data base containing information about the program. Using this data base, the following documentation reports can be generated:

1. Source code listing
2. Module invocation structure
3. Cross-reference report
4. Common block matrix
5. Test-coverage analysis reports

For each program module, a *source listing* is generated. Each statement is numbered and indented according to its nesting depth. Statements are grouped together by DD paths. (A DD path is a sequence of statement executed from the outcome of decision through the next decision.)

In the *module invocation structure report,* all invocations to each module from other modules and all invocations from this module to other modules are listed. The statement number of the invocation is also listed.

A *global cross-reference report* is also provided. For each variable, the modules in which the variable appears, the statement number, and the type of reference are listed.

In addition, the data flow between modules via the COMMON blocks is described in the *common block matrix*. It identifies in which modules the individual COMMON blocks occur and whether or not at least one variable of the COMMON block is referenced in that module.

When the program is executed, a *graphic report* displays the paths executed in each specified module. RXVP offers three trace options: variable trace, DD-path trace, and DD-path summary. The variable trace analysis reports maximum, minimum, first, last, and average values of each variable traced. The

BOX 48.2 Automated test tools

Tool	Description	Examples
CODE AUDITOR	Examines source code to determine if standards have been adhered to.	TRW's CODE AUDITOR for FORTRAN; ADR's MetaCOBOL
COMPARATORS	Compares two versions of data to determine in what ways they differ.	File-compare utilities supplied by computer vendor (e.g., IBM); Software Renovation Technology's RE-LEARN
CONTROL STRUCTURE ANALYZER	Examines source code or design specification to identify control flow for data flow analyzers and test-coverage analysis. Also checks violations of control flow standards.	TRW's FLOWGEN for FORTRAN; RE-LEARN for COBOL; General Research's RXVP for FORTRAN
CROSS-REFERENCE GENERATOR	Shows where each variable is referenced in a program and where each procedure is called.	TRW's DEPCHT, DPNDCY, and FREF for FORTRAN; ADRs MetaCOBOL
DATA FLOW ANALYZER	Checks for data flow errors (e.g., undefined variables, uninitialized variables, illegal sequences of file operations) and traces variable definition and references.	General Research's RXVP; Software Renovation Technology's RE-LEARN
FORMAL VERIFICATION	Applies mathematics to prove the correctness of the program algorithm.	HOS USE.IT
REQUIREMENTS TRACER	Requirements are specified using a formal language. Then reports relationships between inputs, outputs, processes, and data and checks for syntactic specification errors and logic inconsistencies and ambiguities.	U. of Michigan's PSL/PSA

BOX 48.2 *(Continued)*

TEST-DATA GENERATORS	Generates test data needed to execute a program by analyzing program structure or expected input. Also uses random-number generators to derive input.	TRW's ATDG; General Research's RXVP
ASSERTION GENERATOR	Captures functional properties of a program, called *assertions,* for insertion into source code to be used in comparing actual properties with intended properties.	U. of Michigan's PSL
ASSERTION PROCESSOR	Checks program assertions during program execution. Serves as a bridge between formal correctness proofs and heuristic testing methods.	U. of Michigan's PSA
DATA FLOW ANALYZER	Checks for data flow errors (e.g., uninitialized program variables, illegal sequences of file operations) and traces variable definition and references.	General Research's RXVP; Software Renovation Technology's RE-LEARN
PROGRAMMING ENVIRONMENT	Collection of integrated tools to support all aspects of program development.	Bell Labs' UNIX
PERFORMANCE MONITOR	Monitors execution of program to locate possible area of inefficiency.	TRW's PPE
TEST-DATA GENERATOR	Generates test data to execute a program and determine expected input to program.	TRW's ATDG; General Research's RXVP
TEST-COVERAGE ANALYZER	Monitors execution of a program during program testing in order to measure the completeness of test-data sets. Examines statements executed, decision branches executed, and DD paths executed.	General Research's RXVP

DD-path trace analysis reports execution counts by module and by DD path. A summary report lists the number of calls, the number of DD paths executed, and the percentage of DD-path coverage by test cases for each module and for the complete system. Unexecuted DD paths are listed separately, and the variables that control execution of the missed paths are also listed. This greatly aids the tester in creating additional test cases to increase path coverage.

The ultimate testing goal is to execute each statement at least once. The objective of RXVP is to aid this goal by helping to select the minimal number of test cases that can provide 100 percent coverage of all DD paths through the program.

Box 48.3 summarizes the test-support functions provided by RXVP.

SOFTWARE RENOVATION TECHNOLOGY'S RE-LEARN

If all programs were well documented and cleanly structured and if all used third-normal-form data models and data dictionaries for generating the program's data, the testing task would be much easier. Unfortunately, most programs, even well-structured

BOX 48.3 Test-support functions provided by RXVP

PRETEST STATIC ANALYSIS

- Structure analysis to produce a directed graph showing program control structure
- Insertion of software probes into source code to act as tracers during program execution
- Assistance in test-case selection

TEST EXECUTION

- Execution of the program with test probes inserted to record analysis information

POSTTEST STATIC ANALYSIS

- Test-coverage analysis in terms of statement execution and data value ranges programs, fall short of this quality goal. It is often a major detective task to find out how a program works in order to determine how to test it effectively. Several types of structure need to be understood:

- Procedural structure
- Control structure
- Data structure
- Input/output structure

A tool called RE-LEARN, from the Software Renovation Technology, has been developed to perform a very comprehensive static analysis of these four types of program structure [4]. RE-LEARN enables a COBOL program to be analyzed interactively at a terminal screen.

The tool operates in two phases: the LOAD phase and the VIEW phase. The LOAD phase examines the program, conducts research into how it works, and stores information about it that can be interrogated during the VIEW phase. The user can examine the program interactively during the VIEW phase and can produce a variety of views and charts on the screen showing how the program works.

Among these charts are the following:

Structure Chart View

This view gives an overall picture of the program. PERFORMed procedures and CALLed programs are displayed as boxes in a hierarchy chart. The user can traverse the chart, examine data interactions between the boxes, and mark the boxes on the screen for future reference.

Source Code Views

The source code can be viewed in various ways. The user can scroll through the source code, exclude lines, and mark lines. He can ask questions about where variables are used, about control flow, and so on, and see the answers displayed by the appropriate code being highlighted.

Control Trace

The control trace displays the procedural structure of a program. The user can follow the branches, loops, and paths the program follows, can find how switches are used, and can ask questions such as ''How can I get there from here?''

Data Trace

The data trace can answer questions such as ''Where is this variable modified?'' ''Where is this variable used next?'' and ''Where did the value in this variable come from?'' It tells where any variable is used, modified, or referenced. It thus helps the user to determine which control paths are relevant, what data aliases must be examined, and what statements might modify a variable.

Version Comparison

RE-LEARN can display the differences in source code between two versions of a program. This information can be manipulated on the difference display so that interesting differences are more evident.

Subset Facility

Subsets of a program can be displayed; for example,

- Input/output
- Data definitions
- Data manipulation (assignment of values to data items)
- Control
- Procedure calls
- Labels
- Comments

Search Facility

RE-LEARN can search through the program to find variables or answer other questions about the program.

Structure Chart

Figure 48.1 shows a program structure chart created by RE-LEARN's analysis of the program. It shows the *call* relationships among the subprogram units within the program. Here a *call* refers to any method of invoking a unit, including PERFORM and CALL statements and the INPUT and OUTPUT clauses of SORT and MERGE statements.

RE-LEARN draws hierarchical pictures of these relationships. The *called* unit is drawn underneath the *calling* unit. The left-to-right ordering of subordinate boxes is based on the ordering of calling statements in the program. If a unit is called by more than one other unit, it will appear more than once on the chart, in which case it is marked with an asterisk. Unit 14, for example, appears twice in Fig. 48.1.

The structure chart, like other RE-LEARN charts, is usually too big for one terminal screen. RE-LEARN creates a virtual screen that may be longer and wider than the terminal screen. To view the larger virtual screen, the terminal

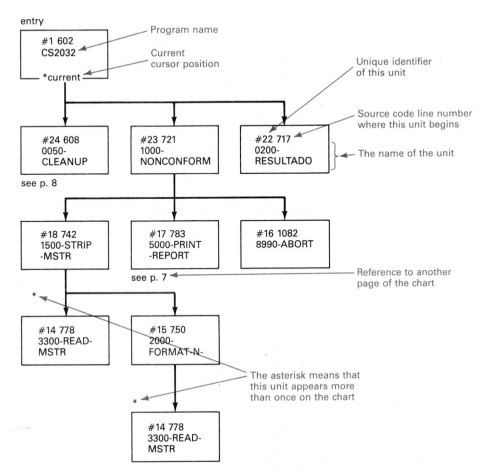

Figure 48.1 Structure chart displayed by Software Renovation Technology's RE-LEARN. The chart may occupy many virtual screens (pages).

screen is scrolled over it like a viewing window. The virtual screen is of such a size that it can be printed. It is also called a page.

The user is given a variety of commands with which he can move around the structure chart and learn various facts from it. There are both graphic commands and a LIST command for displaying tabular information about the units. The user can print either individual screens or the whole chart.

By moving a cursor, RE-LEARN's attention can be on one box on the chart at a time. RE-LEARN writes *** current** at the bottom of this box. Unit #1 is the current box in Fig. 48.1. Various commands for examining or manipulating the chart change the current box. RE-LEARN scrolls the chart so that the current box is within the viewing window. The user can scroll away from this to examine other parts of the chart. Sometimes the subordinates of a box are on a different virtual screen, in which case RE-LEARN writes **see page x** below the box.

The word **entry** is written above a box that is an entry point to the chart, as with unit 1 in Fig. 48.1. The word **exit** is written below a box that exits the program. The word **recursive** is written below a box that calls itself (directly or indirectly).

The commands for manipulating the structure chart enable the user to traverse it along its arrows, to scroll around it, to set up marks on it, to adjust the drawing of the chart, and to carry out various types of searches. The search commands employ the **source** code. The user can tell RE-LEARN to search for source statements of a particular type, for variables, or for patterns of characters.

Figure 48.2 shows the output of the LIST command, which lists all units in a program. Part of the program in Fig. 48.2 is in the structure chart of Fig. 48.1.

Viewing the Source Code

RE-LEARN's *source code view* allows the user to explore the data flow, control flow, and procedure interfaces and generally to review how the program functions. The user can browse, search, compare versions, trace calling sequences, find out where variables are modified, and so on.

The user may examine the whole program or one of the units in Fig. 48.1. He may ZOOM IN to a PERFORMed paragraph in the code. The screen display then excludes all other source code. The user may ZOOM OUT to a high-level view from which the current view was derived.

Whereas in the *structure chart view* the object of current examination is a box (program unit), in the *source code view* it is a line of source code. Many source code view commands operate with the current line of code to produce effects. Many commands move to a different current line.

Particularly useful among the commands that search the source code are the *trace* commands. There are two types of trace, a *data trace* and a *control trace*.

Data Tracing

Data traces enable the users to find out what happens to variables. The variables traced can be simple variables and also files, groups, tables, table elements, or any legal COBOL reference.

A data trace does not display the sequence of the source code, but rather the sequence in which lines of code employ the data item that is being traced. The current line of code may be 350 and the next line 157 because that is where

List of Units in CS2032

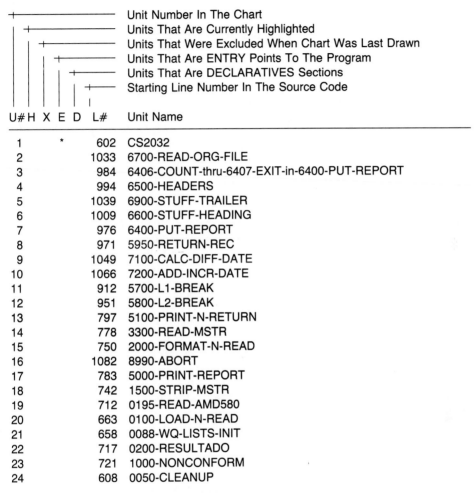

U#	H	X	E	D	L#	Unit Name
1	*				602	CS2032
2					1033	6700-READ-ORG-FILE
3					984	6406-COUNT-thru-6407-EXIT-in-6400-PUT-REPORT
4					994	6500-HEADERS
5					1039	6900-STUFF-TRAILER
6					1009	6600-STUFF-HEADING
7					976	6400-PUT-REPORT
8					971	5950-RETURN-REC
9					1049	7100-CALC-DIFF-DATE
10					1066	7200-ADD-INCR-DATE
11					912	5700-L1-BREAK
12					951	5800-L2-BREAK
13					797	5100-PRINT-N-RETURN
14					778	3300-READ-MSTR
15					750	2000-FORMAT-N-READ
16					1082	8990-ABORT
17					783	5000-PRINT-REPORT
18					742	1500-STRIP-MSTR
19					712	0195-READ-AMD580
20					663	0100-LOAD-N-READ
21					658	0088-WQ-LISTS-INIT
22					717	0200-RESULTADO
23					721	1000-NONCONFORM
24					608	0050-CLEANUP

Figure 48.2 LIST display showing the program's unit. Part of this program is shown in the structure chart of Fig. 48.1.

the data item is used next in the program control sequence. There may be more than one "next use" of the data item.

If the program uses a REDEFINE, giving the data item a different name, this will be traced. Also, if a subroutine returns a different data item derived from the original, this will be indicated.

The user may start the trace at any point by moving the cursor to that position in the source code.

There are three types of data trace:

- *Use:* where the value of a variable is read
- *Modification:* where the value of a variable is set or modified
- *Reference:* both of the above

The trace may proceed in a forward or backward direction. Combined, these give six data trace commands:

	Forward	Backward
Use	NEXTUSE	PREVUSE
Modification	NEXTMOD	PREVMOD
Reference	NEXTREF	PREVREF

The NEXTUSE command, for example, shows all statements reachable from the current statement that could **use** the variable in question. The PREVUSE command shows all statements that could reach the current statement and **use** the variable in question. Similarly, the NEXTMOD and PREVMOD relate to statements that could **modify** the variable, and NEXTREF and PREVREF relate to statements that could **reference** the variable.

The result might be too wide-ranging. The user can limit any RE-LEARN search with various types of "filters." For example, the following command,

! 312–375 | FIND MOVE ALL

would look at source code lines 312 to 375 for all occurrences of the pattern MOVE. If this statement is combined with a trace, it limits the result to statements 312 to 375 that contain the pattern MOVE.

Control Trace

Whereas a data trace shows statements that use or modify variables, a *control trace* shows the control flow statements such as GO TO, PERFORM, IF, ELSE, CALL, and RETURN. It provides a mechanism for simulating conditions and branches and therefore for following a control path.

A *forward* control trace lists all possible paths forward from the current statement. A *backward* control trace lists all possible paths that could have reached the current statement. Destination commands show possible paths from the current statement that could reach a given destination: They tell how you can get *there* from *here*.

The range of such traces can be limited with a variety of filters. The user may pick one of the many paths to or from the current statement and display the source code statements on that path. RE-LEARN will show which program units contain statements in any given control path.

Find

A group of FIND commands will search backward or forward through the text of the source code, looking for given character strings or patterns.

Dead Code

The data trace can be employed to look for unused variables. The control trace can be employed to look for unused program statements.

Version Comparisons

Two versions of source code can be compared by RE-LEARN. A variety of commands can be used for this comparison.

Figures 48.3 and 48.4 are comparison displays, one displaying the old version and one the new version of the source code. The two columns of state-

```
<unit name>                                              <short message>
= = >  _<primary command input>
  OLD     NEW       <long message>-------------------------------------------------------------
*****************************************TOP OF UNIT*********************************************
000001  000001   0050-CLEANUP                                    SECTION
000002  000002      MOVE SPACES TO WQ-AMD580-LISTS-GRP.
000003  000003      PERFORM 0088-WQ-LISTS-INIT VARYING WQ-NDX1
000004  000004         FROM +1 BY +1
000005  000005         UNTIL WQ-NDX1 > WQ-MAX-NUM-OF-JOB-CODES
000006  000006        AFTER
000007  000007         WQ-NDX2 FROM +1 BY +1
000008  000008           UNTIL WQ-NDX2 > WQ-MAX-NUM-OF-GRADES.
        DELETE           . . .                        1 line excluded
000010  000009    OPEN INPUT JOB-AMD580-NULLS-FILE.
        DELETE           . . .                        1 line excluded
000012  000010    IF W2-EOF-JOB-AMD580-NULLS-FILE = '1'
000013  000011       MOVE 'DDNAME CS2032C, FILE EMPTY'
000014  000012                                   TO WX-ABORT-TEXT
000015  000013       PERFORM 8990-ABORT.
        FROM             . . .                        2 lines excluded
  TO    000014    PERFORM 0195-READ-AMD580.
  TO    000015    PERFORM 0196-COMPUTE-AMD580.
  TO    000016    PERFORM 0197-CHECK-AMD580.
  TO    000017    IF IJ-NUMBERS IS ALPHANUMERIC
  ADD   000018       EXHIBIT NAMED IJ-NUMBERS 'DATA NOT NUMERIC'
        DELETE           . . .                        5 lines excluded
000023  000019      PERFORM 0195-READ-AMD580 UNTIL IJ-NUMBERS
```

Figure 48.3   This figure and Fig. 48.4 show comparison displays of two versions of a program. The code of the old version is shown here.

ment numbers on the left show which statements are changed. The programs may be large, so RE-LEARN can display a comparison in which all lines that are the same in the two versions are excluded. Figure 48.5 shows this.

SOFTWARE ENVIRONMENTS

Software environment is the term used for an integrated set of tools supporting each phase of software development, maintenance, and migration to new technologies. Its objective is to improve the software work environment by automatically handling much of the drudgery work of programming, thus freeing programmers for more creative activities.

One type of software environment is a *programming environment*. It aids programmers in the development, integration, and execution of programs. The tools provided by a programming environment typically include an operating system, utility programs, programming language compilers/interpreters, editors, debugging aids, documenters, a file management system, and project management tools.

```
<unit name>                                                     <short message>
= = > _<primary command input>
   OLD      NEW         <long message>------------------------------------------------------------
*********************************************TOP OF UNIT*********************************************
000001   000001    0050-CLEANUP                                      SECTION
000002   000002        MOVE SPACES TO WQ-AMD580-LISTS-GRP.
000003   000003        PERFORM 0088-WQ-LISTS-INIT VARYING WQ-NDX1
000004   000004            FROM +1 BY +1
000005   000005            UNTIL WQ-NDX1 > WQ-MAX-NUM-OF-JOB-CODES
000006   000006          AFTER
000007   000007          WQ-NDX2 FROM +1 BY +1
000008   000008              UNTIL WQ-NDX2 > WQ-MAX-NUM-OF-GRADES.
000009   DELETE     SET WQ-NDX1 WQ-NDX2          TO +1.
000010   000009     OPEN INPUT JOB-AMD580-NULLS-FILE.
000011   DELETE     PERFORM 0195-READ-AMD580.
000012   000010     IF W2-EOF-JOB-AMD580-NULLS-FILE = '1'
000013   000011        MOVE 'DDNAME CS2032C, FILE EMPTY'
000014   000012                                       TO WX-ABORT-TEXT
000015   000013        PERFORM 8990-ABORT.
000016   FROM       PERFORM 0195-PROCESS-AMD580.
000017   FROM       IJ-NUMBERS IS ALPHANUMERIC OR SPACES
   TO                  . . .                          4 lines excluded
   ADD                 . . .                          1 line excluded
000018   DELETE     DISPLAY 'THIS IS FOR DEBUG PURPOSES'
000019   DELETE     DISPLAY 'UP TO THE TEST FOR IJ-NUMBERS'
```

Figure 48.4   Code of the new version of the program shown in Fig. 48.3.

```
     OLD     NEW
     ......  ......              . . .              8 lines excluded
     000109  DELETE  SET WQ-NDX1 WQ-NDX2         TO +1.
     ......  ......              . . .              1 line excluded
     000111  DELETE  PERFORM 0195-READ-AMD580.
     ......  ......              . . .              4 lines excluded
     000116  FROM    PERFORM 0195-PROCESS-AMD580.
     000117  FROM    IF IJ-NUMBERS IS ALPHANUMERIC OR SPACES
        TO   000114  PERFORM 0195-READ-AMD580.
        TO   000115  PERFORM 0196-COMPUTE-AMD580.
        TO   000116  PERFORM 0197-CHECK-AMD580.
        TO   000117  IF IJ-NUMBERS IS ALPHANUMERIC
     ......  ......              . . .              1 line excluded
     000119  DELETE      DISPLAY 'THIS IS FOR DEBUG PURPOSES'
     000120  DELETE      DISPLAY 'UP TO THE TEST FOR IJ-NUMBERS'
     000121  DELETE      DISPLAY 'BEING ALPHANUMERIC IN SECTION'
     000122  DELETE      DISPLAY '0050-CLEANUP'
     000123  DELETE      PERFORM 0190-FIX-IJ-NUMBERS
     ......  ......              . . .              2 lines excluded
       ADD   000121  PERFORM 0199-COMPUTE-ALL-AMD580ES.
       ADD   000122  PERFORM 0200-CHECK-ALL-AMD580ES.
     ......  ......              . . .            950 lines excluded
```

Figure 48.5 Chart comparing two versions of a program, with the lines that are common to both versions excluded.

AT&T's UNIX

UNIX is the most widely available programming environment [5]. UNIX is basically a time-sharing operating system supported by an extensive set of tools. UNIX provides a general environment since it can support different programming languages and different programming methodologies. One particularly powerful feature of UNIX is that it allows the programmer to move more easily from one system to another. For example, while editing a program, the programmer can suspend editing to invoke the mail program. When he has finished answering his mail, he can return to editing his program. Because UNIX is easy to use, it encourage the user to pick and choose from a powerful tool kit as well as to share user-developed procedures and data bases with other users. Underlying the power of UNIX is a consistend design philosophy employing a single, uniform file system.

Programming environments such as UNIX have been designed primarily to support program development efforts. They concentrate on coding and testing aids. In some cases they provide such a powerful tool kit that it is often possible to avoid programming completely.

Programming environments are particularly important to testing because they offer an integrated set of test tools. Most verification and validation tools do not exist as integrated packages. Several different tools (e.g., test-data generators, file comparators, cross-reference mappers, traces) are needed to support testings. This means that the tester must deal with the difficult problem of combining tools that are seldom compatible. This must be done before he faces the difficult task of testing. An integrated set of test tools would greatly simplify the testing task and probably result in more thoroughly tested software.

REFERENCES

1. M. Deutsch, "Software Project Verification and Validation," *Computer* (April 1981), 54–70.

2. P. Powell, ed., *Software Validation, Verification, and Testing Technique and Tool Reference Guide* (NBS Special Publication 500–93), Washington, DC: National Bureau of Standards, 1982.

3. W. Geiger, "Test and Documentation System for FORTRAN Programs," in *Practice in Software Adaptation and Maintenance,* Amsterdam: North-Holland Publishing Co., 1980, pp. 143–156.

4. *RE-LEARN Manual,* San Francisco: Software Renovation Technology.

5. B. Kernigham and J. Mashly, "The UNIX Programming Environment," *Computer* (April 1981), 12–24.

49 AN EVALUATION OF VERIFICATION TECHNIQUES

INTRODUCTION

A critique of validation and verification techniques must center on program testing, since testing is the dominant verification technique. There are many serious problems with testing.

LIMITATIONS OF TESTING

Testing methods are too limited. To detect and correct errors as soon as possible, verification activities must be applied over the entire software life cycle. Requirements specifications, design specifications, and program code must each be verified. But testing methods are usually applied too late in the development process. They are applicable only to program code because requirements and design specifications (even those created with structured techniques) are not representable in a formal, computable form. For this reason, manual verification techniques, such as inspections and walk-throughs, are most commonly used to certify the correctness of requirements and design specifications.

But even in the area of program code verification, testing has limited value. In practice it offers only a limited guarantee of correctness. Most programs cannot be completely tested since complete testing requires the execution of all program paths. Even in a small program, the number of paths can be enormous. For example, in the simple module in the following illustration there are over 206 trillion unique paths. If it were possible to test each of them in a millisecond, the total time taken for the complete test would be over 1600 years.

Structured programming seeks to lessen the number of unique paths that have to be tested—by making modules small, keeping the interface between

717

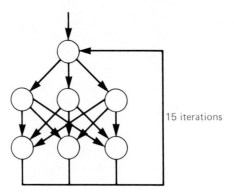

15 iterations

modules simple, and restricting the control structures to ones that are easier to test. However, it is still impossible to test most structured programs exhaustively.

Therefore, we have learned to accept the limitations of testing and to expect software errors in operational systems. Most large systems always contain some errors. For this reason, they occasionally do mysterious things. A high-level check is placed on them so that they do not lose accounts or produce catastrophic errors. Most of the minor disasters can be caught when they happen and recovered from. In some widely used software there is a permanent list of errors observed but not yet repaired.

PROBLEMS WITH TEST TOOLS

Many new, powerful tools have been developed to improve the effectiveness of program testing. Chapter 48 mentioned several automated tools, such as data flow analyzers, control-structure analyzers, test-coverage analyzers, and test-data generators. Unfortunately, two large stumbling blocks hinder their use. First, the high costs associated with their use prevents many organizations from adapting them. Second, there are serious integration problems. Individual tools offer partial benefits. To support testing, especially in the case of large, complex systems, a combination of tools must be used. But grouping tools is often not feasible because of incompatibilities and usage restrictions to certain languages and certain operating systems. Test-support environments that include an integrated package of powerful tools are yet to be developed.

LACK OF THEORY

Without a doubt the most fundamental problem with testing is that there is no solid theoretical foundation for testing. Although much research has been done in this area, little progress has been made. What is worse, more research in this area is likely to lead to a dead end.

TESTING FOURTH-GENERATION-LANGUAGE PROGRAMS

Some testing problems disappear when fourth-generation languages are used. In general, the use of fourth-generation languages simplifies the testing process. How much depends on the particular fourth-generation language and how it is used.

Many fourth-generation languages operate in a data-base environment. They are supported by powerful data dictionaries that can provide data checks as part of the data definition. This eliminates the need to put these checks into the program code and test for them. Since data errors are more common than procedure errors, many possible program errors can be avoided simply by using a powerful fourth-generation language.

Some fourth-generation languages are nonprocedural languages. A nonprocedural language specifies what is accomplished but not in detail how. Some high-level programming languages have nonprocedural capabilities. The language NOMAD is an example. Below is a one-statement NOMAD program:

LIST BY CUSTOMER AVERAGE (INVOICE TOTAL)

The program is complete. It leaves the software to decide how the list should be formatted, when to skip pages and number pages, how to sort into CUSTOMER sequence, and how to complete an average.

A program as simple as this one needs no verification. It is obvious from looking at the output report whether or not the report is correct.

Most fourth-generation language programs are not this simple. They range from a few dozen to a few hundred statements. Several programs can be grouped to form applications. They often do much more than simple report generation. They can be used for any DP application that has been traditionally written in third-generation languages such as COBOL or FORTRAN. These programs do need to be verified. They can contain errors. For example, the wrong algorithm could be programmed. A mistake could be made in an arithmetic expression (such as a plus for a minus). An incorrect default could be assumed. The program could be only a partial solution to the problem.

Testing Nonprocedural Fourth-Generation-Language Programs

Most errors will be functional rather than structural when programming is done at a nonprocedural level. Structural concerns, such as whether a loop is terminated correctly, disappear because the software, not the programmer, constructs loops. But functional concerns, such as whether the program performs the intended function, the entire intended function, and nothing but the intended function, remain as valid as ever.

In this environment, there is no need for structural, or "white-box," testing; but functional or, "black-box," testing, which is used to validate the correctness and completeness of the program, is very essential.

Many of the traditional testing techniques discussed in Chapter 46 are applicable in the fourth-generation-language environment. Also, new automated tools that support functional testing need to be made available in the fourth-generation-language environment. Box 49.1 lists some examples.

BOX 49.1   Test tools that support functional testing

Tool	Description	Examples
COMPARATORS	Compares two versions of data to determine in what ways they differ.	File-compare utilities; Software Renovation Technology's RE-LEARN
REQUIREMENTS TRACERS	Requirements are specified using a formal language. Then reports relationships between inputs, outputs, processes, and data and checks for specification errors, inconsistencies, and ambiguities.	U. of Michigan's PSL/PSA
TEST-DATA GENERATORS	Generates test data needed to execute a program by analysis of program structure or expected input.	TRW's ATDG; General Research's RXVP
ASSERTION GENERATORS	Captures functional properties, called assertions, to be used in comparing actual properties with intended properties.	U. of Michigan's PSL/PSA
PERFORMANCE MONITORS	Monitors execution of program to locate possible areas of inefficiency.	TRW's PPE

Testing Procedural Fourth-Generation-Language Programs

Some fourth-generation languages, such as NOMAD, FOCUS, and NATURAL, have procedural capabilities. Program control constructs such as IF statements and DO WHILE statements are provided. They are similar to those available in third-generation procedural languages; for example,

```
IF (ALL(ITEM-QUANTITY GT 6)) THEN PRINT 'YES';
```

is a NOMAD IF statement. And here is an example of a DO group in NOMAD:

```
IF CODE GT 8 THEN DO;
    PRINT 'INVALID CODE';
    ERRORSCOUNT = ERRORSCOUNT + 1;
END;
```

Using procedural capabilities makes fourth-generation-language programs susceptible to programming errors that are common to third-generation procedural languages. All types of logic errors, such as incorrect loops or incorrect conditional expressions, are possible, but they occur to a lesser degree than in third-generation-language programs because there is much less code to be written. For example, Fig. 49.1 shows a 57-line NATURAL program. The equivalent COBOL program contains over 500 lines.

Notice that the NATURAL program does contain some procedural logic. It has eight IF statements. Each has a potential for containing errors that are not detectable by the system, such as an incorrect operator or misunderstood operator-precedence relations. Consider the IF statement at line 0150:

```
IF *NUMBER (0140) = 0 AND #TRAN = 'D' OR = I or = 'U' DO
```

If the programmer accidentally types $<$ instead of an $=$ sign for the compare *NUMBER (0140) $=$ 0, the statement would still be syntactically correct but semantically wrong. If there were no verification step, this error might go unnoticed, and the program would produce incorrect results.

A form of structural verification is needed to detect logic errors in procedural code. Many of the structural-testing techniques discussed in Chapter 46 are also applicable in this environment. Box 49.2 lists some general guidelines.

Figure 49.2 summarizes the different levels of verification needed for the different types of fourth-generation languages.

```
0010   ************** PROJECT TRACKING SYSTEM **************
0020   SET GLOBALS TR = ON
0030   REPEAT UNTIL #TRAN (A1) = 'E'
0040   INPUT 'PROJECT TRACKING SYSTEM' //
0050       'ENTER A TRANSACTION CODE' //
0060       'A - ADD A NEW RECORD        ' / 'D - DELETE A RECORD      ' /
0070       'I - INQUIRE (LOOK)          ' / 'E - END PROGRAM          ' /
0080       'U - UPDATE A RECORD         ' //
0090   'TRANSACTION:' #TRAN / 'RECORD ID:' #RECORD-ID (A5)
0100   IF #TRAN = 'E' STOP
0110   IF NOT (#TRAN = 'A' OR = 'D' OR = 'I' OR = 'U')
0120       REINPUT WITH 'INVALID TRANSACTION SELECTED, PLEASE REENTER'
0130   ************** SEE IF RECORD EXISTS **************
0140   FIND NUMBER PROJECT WITH RECORD-ID = #RECORD-ID
0150   IF *NUMBER (0140) = 0 AND #TRAN = 'D' OR = 'I' OR = 'U' DO
0160       COMPRESS 'RECORD ID' #RECORD-ID 'DOES NOT EXIST' INTO #MSG (A60)
0170       REINPUT WITH #MSG MARK 2 ALARM DOEND
0180   IF *NUMBER (0140) > 0 AND #TRAN = 'A' DO
0190       COMPRESS 'A RECORD ALREADY EXISTS FOR RECORD ID:' #RECORD-ID INTO #MSG
0200       REINPUT WITH #MSG MARK 2 ALARM DOEND
0210   ********** GET RECORD(S) FOR PROCESSING **********
0220   FIND PROJECT WITH RECORD-ID = #RECORD-ID
0230   IF NO RECORDS FOUND
0240       RESET RECORD-ID DUE-DATE FST-REMIND SEC-REMIND COMP-DATE
0250           PRM-CAT SEC-CAT PER-1 PER-2 PER-3 PER-4
0260   **** DISPLAY RECORD FOR UPDATE OR GET DATA FOR NEW RECORD ****
0270   INPUT 'TRAN:' *OUT #TRAN 19T 'PROJECT TRACKING SYSTEM' //
0280       22T 'RECORD ID:' *OUTIN #RECORD-ID //
0290       10T '-------------------- DATES ------------------------' /
0300       10T '                    DUE DATE:' *OUTIN DUE-DATE    '(MMOOYY)' /
0310       10T '            FIRST REMINDER:' *OUTIN FST-REMIND  '(MMOOYY)' /
0320       10T '           SECOND REMINDER:' *OUTIN SEC-REMIND  '(MMOOYY)' /
0330       10T '          COMPLETION DATE:' *OUTIN COMP-DATE   '(MMOOYY)' //
0340       10T '----------------- SUBJECT CATEGORIES -----------------' /
0350       10T '      PRIMARY CATEGORY:'  OUTIN PRM-CAT /
0360       10T 'SECONDARY CATEGORY:' *OUTIN SEC-CAT //
0370       10T '--------------- RESPONSIBLE PERSON ----------------' /
0380       10T '                 PERSON 1:' *OUTIN PER-1 /
0390       10T '                 PERSON 2:' *OUTIN PER-2 /
0400       10T '                 PERSON 3:' *OUTIN PER-3 /
0410       10T '                 PERSON 4:' *OUTIN PER-4
0420   ************** DELETE THE RECORD **************
0430   IF #TRAN = 'D' DO
0440       DELETE (0220) END OF TRANSACTION WRITE NOTITLE 'RECORD DELETED' DOEND
```

Figure 49.1· This 57-line NATURAL program is equivalent to a 500-line
COBOL program. It does contain some procedural logic, although much less
than the COBOL version.

```
0450   ************** UPDATE THE RECORD **************
0460   IF #TRAN = 'U' DO
0470       UPDATE (0220) DUE-DATE = DUE-DATE FST-REMIND = FST-REMIND
0480       SEC-REMIND = SEC-REMIND COMP-DATE = COMP-DATE PRM-CAT = PRM-CAT
0490       SEC-CAT = SEC-CAT PER-1 = PER-1 PER-2 = PER-2 PER-3 = PER-3
0500       PER-4 = PER-4 END OF TRANSACTION WRITE 'RECORD UPDATED' DOEND
0510   ************** ADD A NEW RECORD **************
0520   IF #TRAN = 'A' DO
0530       STORE PROJECT DUE-DATE = DUE-DATE FST-REMIND = FST-REMIND
0540       SEC-REMIND = SEC-REMIND COMP-DATE = COMP-DATE PRM-CAT = PRM-CAT
0550       SEC-CAT = SEC-CAT PER-1 = PER-1 PER-2 = PER-2 PER-3 = PER-3
0560       PER-4 = PER-4 END OF TRANSACTION WRITE 'RECORD ADDED' DOEND
0570   END
```

Figure 49.1   (Continued)

IMPROVEMENT THROUGH FORMALITY

Improvement of validation and verification techniques is considered a top-priority software issue. Much research is currently being performed in this area. Surprisingly, most is aimed at the improvement of existing testing techniques and support tools in spite of the serious, fundamental flaws in testing. It is doubtful that testing will ever be more than an ad hoc process based on well-thought-out heuristic rules. The structured-design movement has introduced formal procedures to guide the testing process. But we must not mistake this level of formality, that of standards and procedures, for the much higher and much more desirable level provided by mathematical rigor. The low-level formality that testing methods offer cannot solve software reliability problems. What is needed is high-level formality—an entirely different verification technique that is mathematically rigorous.

BOX 49.2   Guidelines for verifying procedural code

1. Conduct a manual walk-through of the code to determine if the specifications are correctly implemented in the code.

2. Execute a simple test to verify the correctness of the control structure.

3. Execute the code with valid input data.

4. Execute the code with invalid input data.

5. Execute the code to ensure proper loop termination.

6. Use a complexity-based testing strategy to concentrate testing on the most error-prone parts of the program.

	Level of Verification Needed	
	Structural Verification	Functional Verification
Simple-Query Facilities		
Complex-Query Facilities		√
Report Generators		some
Graphic Languages		some
Application Generators	some (for algorithmic components)	√
Very High Level Programming Languages	some (for algorithmic components)	√
Parameterized Application Packages		√ (acceptance testing)
Computable Specification Languages		some

Figure 49.2   Different facilities for application creation without conventional programming require different degrees of verification to assure the correctness of the application.

FORMAL PROOF-OF-CORRECTNESS TECHNIQUES

Formal proof-of-correctness techniques should form the base of future verification techniques. They can place software verification on solid theoretical ground. They can be applied to a formal representation of requirements and design as well as to program code. The HOS methodology discussed in Chapters 38 and 39 is a good example.

Proof-of-correctness techniques do not eliminate all possible errors. They cannot guarantee the elimination of errors in *concept* of what the program should do. It is possible to create a correct program that solves the wrong problem or only partially solves the problem. Misstatement of requirements and incomplete requirements lie outside the realm of correctness proofs.

Less Testing

For this reason, any program should be tested. But when a program has been developed using proof-of-correctness techniques such as HOS, the amount of testing needed is dramatically reduced. The need for structural testing virtually disappears. Program verification is accomplished through static proof methods rather than dynamic testing methods. The requirements specification is statically verified, the design specification is statically verified, and the program code is statically verified.

It is important to realize that the need for program validation to check for completeness errors remains. Dynamic program testing is performed to ensure that the program algorithms give the results that the designer intended.

Figure 49.3 compares traditional program verification, which relies mainly on dynamic program testing, and formal program verification, which employs static proof methods and functional testing. The major difference between the two is that formal program verification does not require the structural testing steps. Unit testing and integration testing steps disappear. Correctness proofs allow structural testing to be replaced by formal verification, which is performed earlier in the development process. In effect, structural testing is incorporated into the design phase.

For each step of design, there is a counterstep of verification. At times, the process of design is one and the same as the process of verification. Most data- and procedure-structure errors can be eliminated during design, so there is no need to check for them later in a separate unit testing step. Because interfaces are rigorously defined, most interface errors among different modules of separately developed subsystems are caught during program design. This eliminates the need for a separate integration testing step.

The major similarity between traditional and formal verification is that both perform functional testing for final program validation. The same functional testing methods and tools employed in the traditional process are employed in the formal process. These methods were discussed in Chapter 46.

Fewer Tools

Formal verification simplifies not only the testing process but also the verification tools needed. Tools that support structural testing are for the most part no longer needed. For example, control-structure analyzers, data flow analyzers, cross-reference generators, and test-coverage analyzers are probably not needed. If an automatic code generator is used along with formal correctness proofs, code auditors are not needed. In addition to eliminating many automated tools, some manual verification methods can also be crossed off the list. Inspections, walk-throughs, desk checking, and peer reviews used to examine the correctness of program code can be eliminated.

However, verification tools and methods that support functional testing continue to be very valuable. They are essential for validating program completeness. They aid the generation of test data and the evaluation of test results. Of particular importance are tools and methods that check for completeness by providing a link to system requirements. Box 49.1 lists some tools that support functional testing.

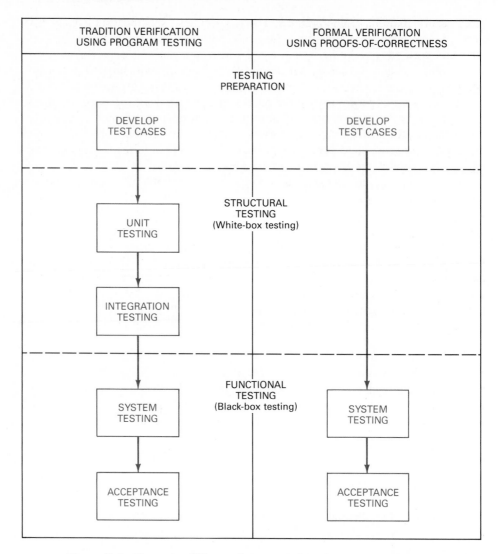

Figure 49.3 The major difference between traditional program verification, which relies mainly on testing methods, and formal program verification, which relies mainly on formal proofs of correctness, is that the need for structural testing disappears. It is incorporated into the design phase.

Benefits of Formal Proofs of Correctness

The net gain from proof-of-correctness techniques is to greatly simplify and improve program verification. Many more errors are found earlier in the development process. This substantially reduces development problems and costs.

Since much of the testing phase can be eliminated, the need for many expensive test tools is lessened.

However, much of the value of formal verification lies in its practical application. Almost no programmers use manual proofs of correctness in practice because they require a high level of mathematical sophistication. Even for simple programs, a level of mathematical maturity is needed far beyond that of ordinary DP analysts and programmers. The mathematical proofs involved are often several times longer than the program itself.

It is only when computers are used that rigorous methods become practical. Humans make too many errors and find rigorous techniques too tedious to use rapidly and thoroughly by hand.

Fortunately, automated proofs of correctness have been developed and successfully used to create larger complex systems. The best example is the HOS methodology, which is completely general and can be applied to the development of any type of system. It is entirely based on mathematical theorems and proofs and so is entirely rigorous. It automatically generates program code that is provably correct.

PART **VII** TOWARD AN ENGINEERING
DISCIPLINE

50 WHERE DO STRUCTURED TECHNIQUES GO FROM HERE?

The first six parts of this book have described the current state of the art of structured techniques. What happens next?

PATTERNS OF EVOLUTION

We can perhaps understand the likely pattern of evolution of software engineering if we examine the patterns of growth in older applied sciences. Figure 50.1 shows the typical growth pattern in the usage of methodologies. A new methodology is born when a few pioneers perceive that an existing methodology is inadequate. They experiment with better techniques. There is a limited early adoption of the new methods as their benefits become demonstrated. We will describe this first phase as *crisis and recognition*.

The early adoption of new methods is often done by pragmatists who initially pay little attention to developing principles. Later there is academic emphasis. Principles are better thought out and the methods are refined. We will use the term *academic emphasis* to characterize this second phase.

Eventually the new methods start to be generally assimilated. Courses are developed, the methods are widely taught, and they become an accepted discipline. The methodology reaches maturity, and there is then little change. Formality and often bureaucracy grow in the practice of the methodology. We will call this phase *assimilation*.

The field of *management science* is a good example of this pattern of evolution. Management science is the application of quantitative techniques (e.g., linear programming, simulation, queuing theory, modeling) to solve management, business, and industrial problems.

There are close parallels between the history of management science and the history of structured techniques. The one major difference is that the rate of growth has been much faster for structured techniques. It took 40 years for

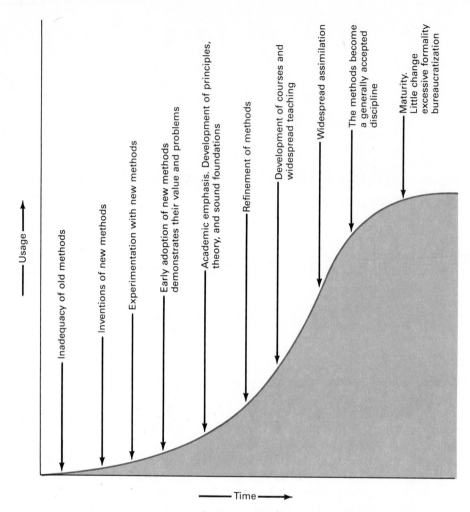

Figure 50.1 The evolution of new methodologies typically follows this growth pattern.

management science to reach a state of maturity. It took structured techniques just over a decade.

PHASES OF GROWTH OF MANAGEMENT SCIENCE

Figure 50.2 shows the three periods of the history of management science [1].

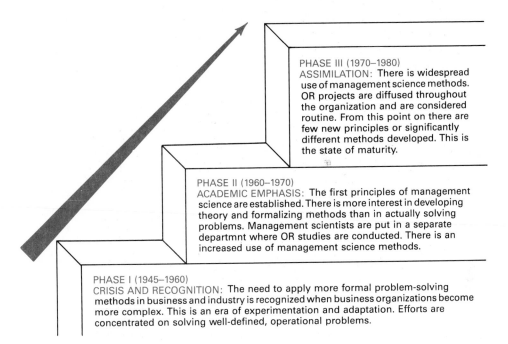

PHASE III (1970–1980)
ASSIMILATION: There is widespread use of management science methods. OR projects are diffused throughout the organization and are considered routine. From this point on there are few new principles or significantly different methods developed. This is the state of maturity.

PHASE II (1960–1970)
ACADEMIC EMPHASIS: The first principles of management science are established. There is more interest in developing theory and formalizing methods than in actually solving problems. Management scientists are put in a separate departmnt where OR studies are conducted. There is an increased use of management science methods.

PHASE I (1945–1960)
CRISIS AND RECOGNITION: The need to apply more formal problem-solving methods in business and industry is recognized when business organizations become more complex. This is an era of experimentation and adaptation. Efforts are concentrated on solving well-defined, operational problems.

Figure 50.2   The field of management science evolved through three phases of growth to reach a state of maturity.

Crisis and Recognition

The first phase began in the mid-1940s when the need to apply more formal problem-solving methods in industry was first recognized. The postwar business boom caused a rapid increase in the size and complexity of business organizations. New growth brought new problems, many of which involved complex interrelated variables and fast-changing situations. Relying solely on intuitive problem-solving methods to deal with complex problems was no longer realistic. A changing business environment demanded more powerful tools and methods. Operations research (OR) methods, which had been used during World War II to improve the utilization of armaments, were adapted to the business environment. When OR methods were combined with decision-making strategies, the practice of OR broadened into the field of management science.

This first phase was an era of experimentation and adaptation. Principles and methodologies from other disciplines were applied for the first time to solve business problems. Mathematicians and engineers migrated from these other disciplines into the management science field. They concentrated their efforts on solving well-defined, operational problems.

Academic Emphasis

The first principles of management science were established during the second phase. There was more interest in developing theory and formalizing methods than in applying management science techniques to solve real business problems.

The limitations of management science and the difficulties of introducing the methods became apparent. Problem areas included disappointing project results, proliferation of highly technical terminology, unsatisfactory experience with outside consultants, inability of management scientists to fit into the business organization, and an inability to demonstrate the cost effectiveness of the methods.

The trend was to create a separate department to perform management science projects and toward increased use of management science. Universities began to offer management science courses.

Assimilation

Widespread use of management science methods occurred in the 1970s. In the 1950s, less than 5 percent of U.S. corporations had special OR or management science groups. In the 1970s, over 65 percent did. OR groups tended to be located organizationally within the MIS department, reporting to top management, and were viewed as part of the strategic planning function.

More attention was paid to developing processes and applying fundamental principles to solve real problems than to the development of theory and abstract techniques. Management science became problem-oriented and solution-oriented. It was concerned not only with problem formulation and solutions but also with implementation viewed as a continuous effort as opposed to a one-time project. The trend changed from performing OR projects primarily by the management scientist to OR projects diffused throughout the organization.

Management science approached the state of maturity. From this point, few new principles or significantly different methodologies were developed.

PHASES OF GROWTH OF STRUCTURED TECHNIQUES

We can use the same three phases of growth to describe structured techniques and to show that this methodology too has probably reached its third stage of growth (see Fig. 50.3) [2].

Recognition and Crisis

During the first phase, the software crisis was recognized as a serious problem demanding immediate solutions. Software development was out of control. Costly and catastrophic software failures were becoming too commonplace. This

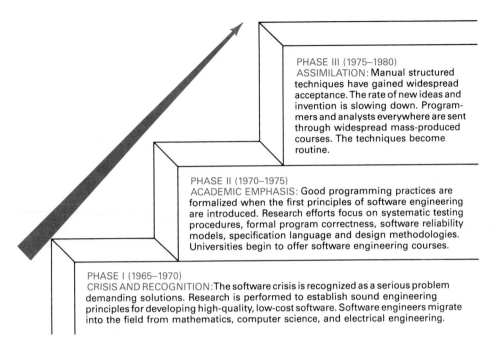

PHASE III (1975–1980)
ASSIMILATION: Manual structured techniques have gained widespread acceptance. The rate of new ideas and invention is slowing down. Programmers and analysts everywhere are sent through widespread mass-produced courses. The techniques become routine.

PHASE II (1970–1975)
ACADEMIC EMPHASIS: Good programming practices are formalized when the first principles of software engineering are introduced. Research efforts focus on systematic testing procedures, formal program correctness, software reliability models, specification language and design methodologies. Universities begin to offer software engineering courses.

PHASE I (1965–1970)
CRISIS AND RECOGNITION: The software crisis is recognized as a serious problem demanding solutions. Research is performed to establish sound engineering principles for developing high-quality, low-cost software. Software engineers migrate into the field from mathematics, computer science, and electrical engineering.

Figure 50.3 Structured techniques evolved through three phases of growth similar to those in Fig. 50.2. (See Fig. 50.4 for what happens next.)

prompted research into sound engineering principles and methodologies for developing high-quality, low-cost software systems.

Academic Emphasis

Good programming practices were formalized when the first principles of software engineering were introduced in the early 1970s. The beginnings of the top-down programming methodologies were established. Early research efforts focused on developing coding methodologies (e.g., structured programming) and a structured programming language (e.g., PASCAL). Later research efforts attempted to formalize programming with the introduction of systematic testing procedures, the notion of formal program correctness, software reliability models, specification languages, and design methodologies. Researchers migrated from other, more established disciplines such as mathematics, computer science, and electrical engineering into the software engineering field. Universities began to offer software engineering courses within the computer science curriculum.

There was more interest in the structure and algorithmic elegance of software systems than in their utility. Software structures were viewed as an end in themselves rather than as a tool for automating processes. The tendency to emphasize the tool over the solution was driven by a fascination with the intricacies of mathematics and logic rather than its application.

Major problems included disregard for human factors and the context in which the system will be used, a tendency to view problems as black or white, and a tendency to take a snapshot view of the system requirements, which does not take into account the impact of changes and leads to rigid, inflexible systems.

Assimilation

By the end of the 1970s, structured techniques reached the third stage of growth. The fundamental principles of software structuring were beginning to be widely accepted and used. Large numbers of programmers and analysts were fed through mass-produced courses on structured techniques. Although the use of structured methods and tools was still increasing, the rate of invention and introduction of new ideas was slowing down. Traditional structured techniques had reached a state of maturity. They approached the plateau of Fig. 50.1.

SHOCK

As traditional structured techniques reached the top of the curve in Fig. 50.1, many measurements were made of the productivity of analysts and programmers using these techniques [3]. It became clear that there were limits to productivity and that these limits were far below what would be needed as computers continued to proliferate, drop in cost, and increase in speed.

The effectiveness of the move to conventional structured techniques is addressed in extensive research done by T. C. Jones [3]. He divides programming productivity improvements into four ranges and discusses what techniques have achieved improvements within these ranges:

1. Methods that may yield up to 25 percent improvement
2. Methods that may yield a 25 to 50 percent improvement
3. Methods that may yield a 50 to 75 percent improvement
4. Methods that may yield more than a 75 percent improvement

Improving Productivity up to 25 Percent

Most of the success stories and firm evidence of productivity improvement using structured techniques with conventional programming languages lie in this range.

Often the baseline for comparison is programs that are unstructured, designed in a bottom-up fashion, with no formal reviews or inspections prior to testing, and no use of interactive methods. If this is the starting point, then almost *any* step toward structured techniques or interactive development will give results. These results are rarely more than a 25 percent improvement (if there are no change in language and no move to programmers of greater talent).

Small programs written by individual programmers benefit from interactive methods [4]. Large programs needing multiple programmers benefit from the better discipline of structured methods [5,6] and from inspections [7].

In one installation we studied, a much heralded move to interactive programming actually *lowered* overall programmer productivity because the programmers made more mistakes. They seemed to be less able to contemplate their code carefully when entering it on a screen than when using off-line coding sheets.

Improving Productivity by 25 to 50 Percent

Achieving more than a 25 percent improvement is more difficult because programming is so labor-intensive. Real people in real life, Jones concludes, cannot move a great deal faster than they already do. To achieve more than a 25 percent improvement requires techniques that replace human effort in some way.

Jones concludes: "It can almost definitely be stated that no *single technique* by itself can improve productivity at the 50% level for programs larger than trivial ones, except for a change in programming language" [3].

Jones states that there are a few stories at the 35 to 40 percent improvement level. Sometimes these related to an unusually backward installation so that the improvement looked better than it perhaps should have.

Improving Productivity by 50 to 75 Percent

Jones concluded that there are only two general ways to achieve programming productivity gains that approach 75 percent:

1. Search out programmers and analysts who have exceptionally high personal achievement. There are a few isolated stories of abnormally high productivity, such as the programming of the New York Times Information System (87,000 instructions in one year by three people: Harlan Mills, Terry Baker, and an assistant who checked the code). This is a productivity four or five times higher than the norm. It is sometimes quoted as a triumph of structured programming, which it is, but it is more a triumph of selecting brilliant individuals and giving them the fullest support. An IBM executive with the project in his area said, "Baker was supported in a way similar to a great surgeon in an operating room" [8].

The best programmers need to be paid more than average ones. The increase in results can far exceed the increase in pay. The salary histogram is not nearly as elongated as the productivity histogram, so it pays to seek out programmers of exceptional productivity and avoid the others.

2. Use program generators, very high level languages, development shared by several systems, or various forms of program *acquisition* in place of program *development*.

Higher Productivity Gains

In stark contrast to the surveys of programmer productivity improvement are the results that have been achieved with data-base user languages, report generators, graphics packages, and application generators. With these, productivity improvements of over 1000 percent are not uncommon [9]. Some of them can only generate certain well-defined classes of applications. Code generators that generate much broader ranges of software are needed.

INADEQUACY   Traditional structured techniques, in short, are insufficient to solve the software crisis. The demands for software are increasing too fast.

Computing hardware has passed through a number of steps that dramatically changed its capability: the coming of magnetic tape in the 1950s, the coming of disks in the 1960s, the coming of terminals and data transmission, the spread of distributed processing, and the arrival of the microcomputer. Computer industry observers have sometimes lamented that there have not been revolutions of equivalent power in software. We are now beginning to see dramatic changes in software, equivalent in their importance to the coming of disks or terminals.

One might reflect with dread on what the computer world might be like in ten years' time if we did *not* have dramatic breakthroughs in software. Computing power is plunging in cost. Big machines are becoming bigger. Small machines are springing up like mushrooms. Numerous machines are being interconnected into computer networks.

IBM has commented that in a few years there will be one computer for every ten employees in the United States. There cannot be one professional programmer for every ten employees. Today there is one programmer for about every 300 employees.

The VHSIC program of the U.S. Department of Defense is creating a microprocessor on a chip with the power of a large mainframe of ten years earlier. Such chips will become mass-produceable, like newsprint. Future computers need to be fundamentally rearchitected so that they can take advantage of such microelectronics. They will have large numbers of microprocessors operating in parallel. Amdahl is creating wafer-scale integration in which one chip 2½ inches square contains the circuitry of 100 conventional chips.

The Japanese have described a fifth generation of computers with which they hope to wrest computer industry dominance away from the United States. They have described a highly parallel mainframe with 10,000 processors capable of executing a combined instruction rate of 10 billion instructions per second and operating with fundamentally different software. Quite separately they are building a parallel supercomputer far faster than any in existence.

Any way we assess the future of the computer industry, computing power will vastly outstrip that of today. But the number of professional programmers will increase only slowly. Somehow or other, one programmer must support a vast increase in processor power.

In the next ten years computers, on average, will increase in speed by a factor of 10 or more. If the most advanced goals of the Japanese and others are realized, the increase could be 1000 or so. This large number is made possible by highly parallel architectures incorporating many processors that are cheaply mass-produced. As computers plunge in cost, many more will be sold. The number of applications in today's data processing centers is growing by 45 percent per year, according to an IBM survey [10]. Ten year's growth at 45 percent multiplies the number of applications by 41. At the same time, the number of installations is growing greatly because of small cheap mainframes, minicomputers, and desk-top machines.

Most estimates of future computing power indicate that the *productivity of application development needs to increase by two orders of magnitude in the next ten years.* Traditional structured techniques improve productivity by 75 percent at best, and usually more like 25 percent.

There is no shadow of doubt that we are going to see a spectacular growth in the quantity and power of computers. We *must* achieve a quantum leap in software creation in order to be able to use the hardware we can mass-produce.

THE AUTOMATION OF AUTOMATION

The quantum leap in software and application building is going to come from automating the tasks that analysts and programmers perform and from using precoded software modules wherever possible. The analyst of the future will have a workstation with a large graphics screen. Like an architect or microchip designer, he will have sophisticated computer-aided-design software. His workstation will often be connectable to a mainframe where a dictionary, directory, design encyclopedia, and software library are centrally maintained to aid and interlink the work of different designers.

Executable code will be generated automatically from the design. In some cases, a high-level design statement with many default options will generate the code, as with today's report generators and nonprocedural languages. In some cases, the designer will decompose his high-level design into lower-level modules until code can be generated. Programmers will be replaced by higher-level designers in most data processing operations.

Does this mean that structured techniques will not be needed? On the contrary, it is *structured* design that makes higher levels of automation possible. The designer will create diagrams like those in Part III of this book at a workstation. The diagramming techniques need to be carefully designed so that their computerization can result in thorough cross-checking and verification and so that executable code can be generated automatically.

Manual programming is one of the most labor-intensive and error-prone tasks that humans perform. The computer industry can achieve its potential only if we can automate the programming task.

RIGOROUS SPECIFICATION

The problem with structured techniques as practiced in most installations is that they are still manual techniques. They are refinements of the manual methods that programmers and analysts have always used. As such, they improve productivity by a small amount only. We can teach a swimmer to swim faster by improving his technique, but the increase in speed is small compared with giving him a motorboat.

Structured techniques have an important part to play in the automation of programming, but to do that, another problem has to be solved. Most structured techniques as currently practiced are not rigorous. Their designs are not computable—in other words, they cannot be converted automatically into executable code. We do now have techniques with which we can create structured specifications that *are* computable and rigorous. When we employ rigorous techniques to examine the data flow diagrams and structure charts that most analysts use, this reveals how sloppy conventional structured design is. Often the diagrams and structure charts are simply wrong. They are clearly not an adequate basis for the automation of programming.

As long as systems analysts and programmers use manual methods, they will be restricted to methodologies with which a humble human can cope. More powerful methodologies will remain academic. They will remain too tedious to be practical unless automated. Now that we know that we can economically automate our methodologies, we are set free to devise powerful techniques— immensely more powerful than those that could be designed by hand.

MEAT MACHINES

Our human brain is good at some tasks and bad at others. The computer is good at certain tasks that the brain does badly. The challenge of computing is to forge a creative partnership using the best of both.

The electronic machine is fast and absolutely precise. It executes it instructions unerringly. Our "meat machine" of a brain is slow, and usually it is not precise. It cannot do long, meticulous logic operations without making mistakes. Fortunately, it has some remarkable properties. It can invent, conceptualize, demand improvements, create visions. Humans can write music, start wars, build cities, create art, fall in love, go to the moon, colonize the solar system, but we cannot write COBOL or ADA code that is guaranteed to be bug-free.

Many of the tasks DP professionals do are tasks that are unsuited to our meat-machine brain. They need the precision of an electronic machine. Humans create program specifications that are full of inconsistencies and vagueness. A computer should be helping the human to create specifications and checking them at each step for consistency. It should not be a human job to write programs from the specifications because humans cannot do that well. A computer should generate the code needed. When humans want to make modifications, as we frequently do, we have real problems if we attempt to change the code. A seemingly innocent change has ramifications that we do not perceive and causes a chain reaction of errors.

If the programs needed are large, we are in even worse trouble because we need many people to work together on them. When humans try to interact at the level of meticulous detail needed, there are all sorts of communication errors. When one human makes a change, it affects the work of the others, but often the subtle interconnection is not perceived. Meat machines do not communicate with precision.

The end user perceives the meat machines in the DP department to be a problem but does not know what to do about it. A major part of the problem is that they are so slow; they often take two years to produce results, and they do not start for a long time because of the backlog. It is rather like communicating with a development team on another solar system where the signals take years to get there and back.

Today there is much that can be automated in the creation of specifications and the generation of programs. We have report generators, application generators, tools for creating data bases, tools for using data bases, computer-aided design of specifications, and software for creating code from specifications. Tools exist for the automation of *all* programming, not just commercial DP systems. The tools differ greatly in their nature.

It is a subtle blow to the dignity of a professional to hear that a major part of what he is paid for can be automated. Subconsciously he wants to disbelieve it and finds all sorts of arguments for opposing the automation. Because of this we find new graduates adopting the new techniques faster than experienced professionals.

THEORETICAL PRINCIPLES

The challenge of software engineering today, then, is the challenge of automating the manual tasks. New methodologies that center around this automation are needed.

The automated tools and nonprocedural languages that exist today were mostly created by craftsman-programmers with no knowledge of computer science theory. There are now hundreds of fourth-generation languages [11], almost all created by pragmatic craftsmen with no interest in the theory of languages. Their products solve very important problems and are changing the perceptions of how DP departments should operate. Most computer scientists (at the time of writing) have taken no interest in the new tools and do not even know their names.

The creators of today's automated tools and fourth-generation languages were reacting to an urgent problem—the software crisis. They have built new tools destined to be the crude forerunners of a software, and later hardware, technology that will change the entire future of computing.

This is similar to previous technological history. Newcomen produced the first steam engine with a piston in 1712. For decades Newcomen's successors in this field were craftsman-mechanics. The scientists of the era took no interest in the principles or theory of steam engines. Forty years after Newcomen's death, an engineer, John Smeaton, did meticulous research in the area, and this resulted in much better steam engines. Later the theoretical principles of thermodynamics and the Carnot cycle enabled engineers to design steam engines of maximum efficiency, and later more powerful steam turbines. Eventually computer scientists will direct their attention to fully automated methodologies, and we will see major improvements.

FUTURE GROWTH OF AUTOMATED METHODS

We thus have the beginnings of another development pattern like those in Figs. 50.2 and 50.3—the evolution of automated software development methodologies. Figure 50.4 shows its likely growth pattern. A question exists about the extent to which academia will be involved. With structured techniques, academia was involved from the start and made a major contribution to the evolution of traditional structured techniques. With some aspects of computing (for example, the early development of personal computers), most computer science departments were conspicuously absent. The initial growth of the set of the methodologies that encompass information engineering, fourth-generation languages, and code generators has come mainly from industry and entrepreneurs. It is desirable that computer science departments increase their activities in these vitally important areas.

Like management science and other established disciplines, software engineering growth has become contained within the boundaries of limiting principles and a fixed mentality. Thus the changes needed are unlikely to emerge from the established experts. Instead, a completely new software discipline, based on radically new principles and technologies, must be built. It is unlikely that *traditional* software engineers who are totally immersed in and often blinded by their current methods will be the instigators of new software directions. The forces of change will often come from outsiders. Most revolutions do not originate within the existing establishment.

It is likely that historians in the future, looking back on the extraordinary evolution of computing, will say that the true computer revolution was the one

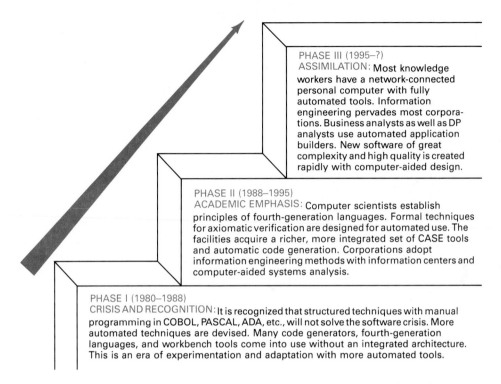

PHASE III (1995–?)
ASSIMILATION: Most knowledge workers have a network-connected personal computer with fully automated tools. Information engineering pervades most corporations. Business analysts as well as DP analysts use automated application builders. New software of great complexity and high quality is created rapidly with computer-aided design.

PHASE II (1988–1995)
ACADEMIC EMPHASIS: Computer scientists establish principles of fourth-generation languages. Formal techniques for axiomatic verification are designed for automated use. The facilities acquire a richer, more integrated set of CASE tools and automatic code generation. Corporations adopt information engineering methods with information centers and computer-aided systems analysis.

PHASE I (1980–1988)
CRISIS AND RECOGNITION: It is recognized that structured techniques with manual programming in COBOL, PASCAL, ADA, etc., will not solve the software crisis. More automated techniques are devised. Many code generators, fourth-generation languages, and workbench tools come into use without an integrated architecture. This is an era of experimentation and adaptation with more automated tools.

Figure 50.4 Automated methodologies evolving through phases of growth similar to the pattern of Figs. 50.2 and 50.3.

that *automated* the processes of design and programming. Manual structured techniques were a necessary preliminary to the automation but were not by themselves the true revolution.

REFERENCES

1. R. Levin and C. Kirkpatrick, *Quantitative Approaches to Management* (4th ed.), New York: McGraw-Hill, 1978, pp. 571–586.

2. A. Wasserman and L. Belady, "Software Engineering: The Turning Point," *Computer,* 11, no. 9 (September 1978), 30–39.

3. T. C. Jones, *The Limits to Programming Productivity,* Guide and Share Application Development Symposium, Proceedings, Share, New York, 1979.

4. G. W. Willett et al., *TSO Productivity Study,* American Telephone and Telegraph Long Lines, Kansas City, April 1973.

5. P. Freeman and A. I. Wasserman, *Tutorial on Software Design Techniques,* IEEE Computer Society, 1977.

6. C. V. Ramamoorthy and H. H. So, "Survey of Principles and Techniques of Software Requirements and Specifications," in *Software Engineering Techniques 2,* Maidenhead, Berkshire, England: Infotech International Ltd., 1977, pp. 265–318.

7. M. E. Fagan, "Design and Code Inspections to Reduce Errors in Program Development," *IBM Systems Journal,* 15, no. 3, (1976).

8. J. Fox, *Software Management,* Englewood Cliffs, NJ: Prentice-Hall, Inc., 1981.

9. J. Martin, *Application Development Without Programmers,* Englewood Cliffs, NJ: Prentice-Hall, Inc., 1982.

10. IBM internal report.

11. J. Martin, *Fourth-Generation Languages,* Englewood Cliffs, NJ: Prentice-Hall, Inc., 1985.

51 THE MOVE TOWARD TRUE ENGINEERING

INTRODUCTION   Since the 1960s there has been a move to change computer programming from a craft-like art to an engineering-like discipline with the objective of introducing a disciplined approach to software development. The field of software engineering emerged to meet this objective. As Bauer explained, *software engineering* is "the establishment and use of sound engineering principles (methods) in order to economically obtain software that is reliable and works on real machines" [1]. The key words in this definition relate to all types of engineering: sound principles and economic, reliable products.

Software engineering, like other engineering disciplines, deals with management and human engineering issues as well as technical ones. It is thus broader than the subject of this book; structured techniques form its core. Unlike other engineering disciplines, its product, software, is nonmaterial. Software development cannot, therefore, be managed and controlled in the same manner as physical products.

SOFTWARE   After the expression "software engineering" had
MISENGINEERING   been in use for almost a decade, C. A. R. Hoare, professor of computing at Oxford, pronounced it a startling contradiction in terms [2]. Engineering as a profession has certain characteristics that were conspicuously absent in the practices of the early "software engineers." Hoare stated:

> The attempt to build a discipline of software engineering on such shoddy foundations must surely be doomed, like trying to base chemical engineering on phlogiston theory, or astronomy on the assumption of a flat earth. [2]

The practices taught in some of the courses on structured techniques were far from rigorous. Programmers trained in such courses produced widely different designs for the same program, and most of these did not work. The inadequate methods became corporate "standards." Maintenance became a nightmare for complex systems.

One of the most vivid descriptions of large programming projects was written by Fred Brooks in *The Mythical Man-Month*.

> No scene from prehistory is quite so vivid as that of the mortal struggles of great beasts in the tar pits. In the mind's eye one sees dinosaurs, mammoths, and saber-toothed tigers struggling against the grip of the tar. The fiercer the struggle, the more entangling the tar, and no beast is so strong or so skillful but that he ultimately sinks.
>
> Large-system programming has over the past decade been such a tar pit, and many great and powerful beasts have thrashed violently in it. Most have emerged with running systems—few have met goals, schedules, and budgets. Large and small, massive or wiry, team after team has become entangled in the tar. No one thing seems to cause the difficulty—any particular paw can be pulled away. But the accumulation of simultaneous and interacting factors brings slower and slower motion. Everyone seems to have been surprised by the stickiness of the problem, and it is hard to discern the nature of it. But we must try to understand it if we are to solve it. [3]

One could not imagine such a description applying to telephone engineering, chemical engineering, or even to a field newer than software, such as microelectronics engineering. Telephone engineering is highly complex. The Bell System is far more complex than even the most elaborate of today's software, but it can be broken down in a mathematically tractable fashion. The problem with software is that we often do not use techniques that decompose the complexity into standard, well-engineered modules.

Brooks comments: "The tar pit of software engineering will be sticky for a long time to come. One can expect the human race to continue attempting systems just within or just beyond their reach" [3].

Since Brooks wrote his classic book, tools and techniques more akin to true engineering practice have come into use. They need improving; we are only part of way down the path to sound engineering of computer applications. One of the biggest problems is that most software creators are not using the tools that exist.

CHARACTERISTICS OF ENGINEERING

Hoare compares the characteristics of engineering as a profession with software engineering as currently practiced [2]. We will extend his comparison:

An engineer has a range of trusted and proven techniques that give a precise result.

A "software engineer" more often concocts his own programs. Hoare comments:

> How many of them are ignorant of, or prefer to ignore, the known techniques used successfully by others, and embark on some spatchcocked implementation of their own defective invention. [2]

The development of an inventory of standardized, verified program components will help improve reliability as well as reduce the tremendous duplication of effort in developing software components common to many programs.

Many programmers do not want to be thought of as engineers. In fact, they regard engineering as a mechanical profession and programming as a higher, more artistic, more creative activity. As for using standardized components—that's what plumbers do!

An engineer is strongly concerned with reliability and predictable performance.

Programmers have become accustomed to accepting software that occasionally does mysterious things. Unpredictability, which would horrify an engineer, is often regarded by computer professionals as part of the nature of the beast.

A fatal attraction to the programmer is the complexity of software, which would

> revolt the instincts of any engineer, but which to the clever programmer masquerades as power and sophistication. The programmer's use of unreliable operating systems, etc., excuses the unreliability of his own code; their inefficiency excuses the inefficiency of his own programs; their complexity protects his work from close scrutiny by his client or manager. [2]

Today we have techniques for achieving high reliability and predictability in software. Elaborate axiomatic verification, like HOS, can be made easy to use and enforce by means of workstations connected to libraries, dictionaries, and encyclopedias. These tools work well on extremely complex projects, yet we find the hair-raising spectacle of the military and the aerospace industry using manual and totally unreliable techniques to build software for missiles. The specifications given to programmers are full of errors, inconsistencies, and omissions because the automated tools for verification have not been used.

An engineer is vigilant in seeking to reduce costs and complexity.

He realizes that these conflicting objectives require a search for the utmost simplicity. Great engineering is simple engineering. Many programmers, by contrast, revel in complexity, finding excitement in projects of a complexity slightly beyond their comprehension. Hoare comments:

> Among manufacturers' software (such as large operating systems) one can find what must be the worst engineered products of the computer age. No wonder it was given away free—and what a very expensive gift it was to the recipient. [2]

Techniques for reducing complexity will be of increasing urgency as we build systems with far more intricate functionality, such as worldwide networks, increasingly elaborate uses of graphics, unmanned weapons systems, uses of artificial intelligence, and intelligent robots.

> An engineer uses designs based on sound mathematical theories.

The theories, principles, and mathematics are represented in manuals, textbooks, and codes of practice. The typical programmer makes up new program designs for each problem, with no mathematical basis. The programmer *could* be better off than the engineer because the directories, help instructions, library of code modules, and soundly based aid could be available at his fingertips at his workstation.

> An engineer recommends designs and techniques to his customers and insists that sound designs and techniques be used.

He often understands the true needs of a client better than the client himself. He encourages the client to sketch and describe what he wants and presents to the client modified designs based on sound engineering. To please the client, the analyst and programmer often concoct ideas that are untried and sometimes unworkable.

> Engineers build prototypes of new designs.

Computer executives often commit to expensive and complex projects without prototyping. Fred Brooks, who managed the building of the first IBM 360 operating system, advises, "Plan to throw one away" [3].

Prototyping is vitally important with end-user systems in which the users are still changing their understanding of how computers might help them. In our view, there is *no* end-user system that should *not* be prototyped or partially prototyped. A cycle of rapidly evolving prototypes is often necessary. Today's software makes it much easier than it used to be to create and modify prototypes rapidly [4].

Engineers employ formal diagramming.

A preeminent textbook on engineering drawing states:

Engineering drawing is the graphic language used in the industrial world by engineers and designers. . . . Thus engineering drawing becomes, with the possible exception of mathematics, the most important single branch of study in a technical school. . . . An engineer without a working knowledge of the engineer's language would be professionally illiterate. [5]

Drawing is similarly a vital language for software engineers, and it can often represent complex constructs in a far more usable fashion than English, pseudo-English, or mathematics.

The engineer today performs computer-aided drawing on a screen, using the computer to perform many checks and calculations. The same should be true of the software engineer.

Many of today's analysts and programmers draw, on paper, sloppy diagrams that are ill-structured, are not automatically checked, and lack an adequate set of defined diagramming symbols.

An engineer respects his tools and demands from them the highest precision, convenience, quality, and reliability.

An engineer develops an ingrained mastery of his tools so that he can use them instinctively, focusing his mental effort and creativity on the client's problem rather than the tool itself.

The tools of the software engineer are becoming elegant and powerful. With computerized graphics workstations networked to central computers, an immensely powerful tool kit becomes practical. Amazingly, many analysts, programmers, and computer scientists do not use the tools that are available. Programmers, like weekend sailors refusing to use motors, often avoid the computerized tools, claiming that their hand methods are more flexible. One of the most famous of the structured programming pioneers wrote about the use of powerful graphics tools: "That is precisely the kind of would-be embellishment the professional software designer is only too happy to ignore" [6].

To build the complex software of the future without powerful computerized graphics for structured design with rigorous verification would be like trying to build a modern jet engine with the tools of a blacksmith.

POWER TOOLS

Perhaps the most important characteristic of future software engineers or information engineers is that they will use power tools. Computers will be used wherever possible to enforce rigor, perform intricate cross-checking, use corporate encyclopedias, and provide analysts with tools and techniques that enable them to tackle complex problems and generate executable code. Structured techniques will use formal graphics charts that the analyst can very quickly create, edit, and modify on his workstation screen. He will be able to scroll, zoom, or page through large charts and library representations of system logic and data. This use of graphics will extend from the top-level strategic planning of the data needed to run an organization (a vitally important subject) down to the representation of intricate logic and the automatic generation of code. Box 51.1 lists ways in which computers can help in the automation of systems analysis, design, and programming.

BOX 51.1   Ways in which computers can help in the automation of systems analysis, design, and programming

- Use of interactive graphics to speed up the creation of diagrams; the editing, expansion, and modification of diagrams; the manipulation of very large diagrams; and the extraction of working subsets from large diagrams
- Automatic generation of code for reports, documents, and graphics charts
- Automatic generation of code for data-base creation, data entry, and updating
- Automatic generation of code for terminal dialogues and screen interaction
- Functional decomposition using interactive graphics
- Species II functional decomposition with cross-checking of inputs and outputs
- Species III functional decomposition with verification of correctness of each decomposition step
- Decomposition on a graphics screen until code can be generated automatically
- Syntax checking of all terminal interaction
- Use of axiomatic verification to perform semantics checking of all constructs used
- Linkage to library routines with complete verification of the correctness of the interface
- Automatic linkage of all routines to a data dictionary and data model
- Extraction of subsets of the overall data model for individual projects
- Interactive creation and editing of a data access map
- Automated canonical synthesis of a data model from user views

BOX 51.1 *(Continued)*

- Automated strategic planning of the data in an enterprise linked to data modeling
- Intelligent data models linked to application generation (the intelligent data model contains details of derived data, validity checks, triggers, and any application-independent logic that can be applied to the data)
- Enterprise modeling that documents the goals, critical success factors, targets for management by objectives, and information resources needed for managing the organization
- Maintenance of an information engineering encyclopedia for the corporation
- Interactive graphics tool for drawing, editing, maintaining, and cross-checking data flow diagrams and linking them to action diagrams and the information engineering encyclopedia
- Intelligent spreadsheet manipulation linked to the data bases and graphics plotters
- Tool for optimizing physical data-base design
- Tool for planning and designing distributed processing and distributed data
- Tools for network design and optimization
- Specification languages, preferably using interactive graphics
- Nonprocedural languages; fourth-generation languages
- Computer-assisted instruction to show how to use the tools, languages, and facilities
- Comprehensive set of decision-support tools
- Tool for creating and editing decision tables and automatically generating program code for this logic
- Tools for aiding maintenance that reveal program structure and show the impact of any modifications
- Project management aids: PERT charts; estimators for people, time, budget; project control
- Word processor and central specification library
- On-line manuals of the methodology, standards, tool operation, and guidelines

Most of the power tools will operate on personal computers. *Not* to use them will become as ridiculous as drilling holes without an electric drill or computing mathematical tables by hand. The personal computer will need connection to mainframes where shared central libraries, dictionaries, models, and encyclopedias are maintained, and sometimes the designer will need mainframe computing power.

Power tools for mechanical functions save time and increase productivity by a large factor. Power tools for systems design and creation also save time and increase productivity by a large factor, but they have another function, which will become even more important. They can *enforce* validity checking, rigorous interfaces between modules, use of a central dictionary and data model, provably correct logic where possible, up-front verification of specifications, and automatic generation of bug-free code.

The challenge of software engineering today is to design these power tools to be as effective as possible.

Structured techniques designed for use with power tools are likely to be different from structured techniques designed for manual use. Computerized techniques can handle vastly more detail and can apply verification and cross-checking techniques that need extensive computation. The choice of permissible constructs with which system logic can be built should be limited to those that can be axiomatically verified. As in HOS, this is likely to result in primitives different from those of classical programming. From the primitives can be built much higher level user-friendly constructs that are decomposable in a rigorous fashion into the primitives.

With automated tools we can build software factories. We can give the software specifiers tools that force them to produce rigorous computable specifications, and we can then automate the generation of program code. We can enable developers to obtain and employ the proven mechanisms of other developers. We can interlink mechanisms to build large, powerful constructs. We can build user-friendly interfaces to complex systems. We have already begun to put in place the bases for grand-scale engineering of software.

INFORMATION ENGINEERING

In commercial data processing and MIS systems, the concepts of information engineering are more important than the concepts of software engineering. A DP professional needs both sets of expertise.

At the 1982 IEEE COMPCON Conference [7], *software engineering* was defined as a composite of the activities in Box 51.2. Many vital aspects of building an enterprise's information resources are missing from this set of activities. Box 51.3 lists the activities that constitute information engineering.

The intent of information engineering is to deliver the right information to the right person at the right time. The extraction and processing of this information can often be done with tools that do not involve professional program-

BOX 51.2   Software engineering curriculum

At the 1982 IEEE COMPCON Conference [7], *software engineering* was defined as a composite of the following activities:

PROGRAMMING METHODOLOGY

Structured programming
Design approaches
Requirements analysis
Specification techniques

PROGRAMMING TECHNOLOGY

Programming environments
Support for methodology
Word processing

MANAGEMENT

Project organization
Life-cycle planning

COMPUTER SCIENCE THEORY

Programming-language design
Programming methods
Analysis of algorithms
System organizations
Hardware/software trade-offs

mers. The design and integration of the information resources are critical and require the use of computerized tools. Excellent tools exist for information engineering; the automated tool kit is a rapidly improving.

RESISTANCE TO
NEW METHODS

The big problem that remains is how to convert a multibillion-dollar industry with vast vested interests

BOX 51.3 Information engineering curriculum

Note: "Automated tools" is not included here as a separate subject because it is assumed to pervade all of the areas listed.

DATA METHODOLOGIES

Data analysis
Data modeling and entity-relationship analysis
Strategic data planning
Information engineering encyclopedia

ENTERPRISE ANALYSIS

Enterprise modeling
Critical-success-factor analysis
Strategic information system planning
Information resource design

SYSTEM DESIGN

Distributed systems
Distributed data base
Networks
Office automation
Information-flow analysis
Structured techniques and their automation
Verification techniques and provably correct design

APPLICATION BUILDING

CASE tools
Specification techniques
Code generators
Fourth-generation (and nonprocedural) languages
Decision-support tools
Maintenance

BOX 51.3   *(Continued)*

END-USER COMPUTING

End-user languages and tools
Personal computers and software
Information center techniques

DP MANAGEMENT

Data administration
Management of end-user computing
Prototyping
Alternate life cycles
Information engineering project management
MIS organization structures

ADVANCED TOPICS

Theory of fourth-generation (and nonprocedural) languages
Theory of specification languages
Knowledge-based-systems
Design of expert systems
Advanced software automation

in earlier techniques. Conventional programming in conventional languages has the momentum of a giant freight train. It will not be deflected from its course quickly.

A major reason for resistance is that DP organizations have struggled to achieve discipline in the DP development process. This process used to be an unruly free-for-all until standards and guidelines were established relatively recently. The standards and methods have assumed the force of law, have been taught to all DP staff in an organization, and are regarded as a vital necessity in the crusade against unmet requirements, unmaintainable code, and nonportable programs. The installation standards, religiously adhered to, have frozen the methodologies of large installations at a time when the technology is plunging into new forms.

One typical corporation with many computer installations in many countries spent much effort in the 1970s perfecting a project management system. This incorporates installation standards, guidelines, and some software for project control. It is referred to as the installation "bible." No DP manager will admit that he does not use it; to do so would be detrimental to his career.

If the bible is followed literally, it prevents DP managers and analysts from using most of the automated methods. It insists that specifications for all applications be created with techniques that are entirely nonrigorous. These are typically an inch or more thick, usually difficult to read, impossible to verify, and full of ambiguities, inconsistencies, errors, and omissions.

One methodology sold and used in many installations consists of 32 two-inch-thick binders that spell out in detail how to create requirements and specifications. They expand the methods *prior to the use of structured techniques* into a bureaucracy that is immensely time-consuming, entirely non-rigorous, and unchangeable, and it prevents automation of code generation.

Many government departments are still issuing application development directives that lock their vast organizations into conventional procedural techniques that prevent productivity, nonprocedural languages, and rigorous methods.

One of the tragedies of the computer industry today is that while true engineering techniques *do exist* for avoiding slow, ad hoc, error-prone programming, most DP executives are sending their staff to courses that teach variants of the messy, nonrigorous manual methods.

REFERENCES

1. F. L. Bauer, *Software Engineering,* Amsterdam: North Holland Publishing Co., 1972, p. 530.

2. C. A. R. Hoare, "The Engineering of Software: A Startling Contradiction," *Computer Bulletin,* December 1975, pp. 34–42.

3. F. P. Brooks, *The Mythical Man-Month,* Reading, MA: Addison-Wesley, 1975, p. 26.

4. J. Martin, *Fourth-Generation Languages,* Englewood Cliffs, NJ: Prentice-Hall, Inc., 1985.

5. T. E. French and C. J. Vierck, *Engineering Drawing,* New York: McGraw-Hill, 1972.

6. Personal communication.

7. R. R. Baldwin, "Reportage on Spring 1982 IEEE COMPCON Conference," *Software Engineering Notes,* 17, no. 2 (April 1982), 13–20.

52 EPILOGUE: THE FUTURE

THE REVOLUTION: ITS CAUSES AND OUTCOME
There is a major revolution happening in software and system design. Yet the users of traditional techniques are as complacent as the Deep South before the Yankee armies swept through.

The revolution is the replacement of manual design and coding with automated design and coding.

Revolutions occur because of dissatisfaction. Users and management are realizing that the immense power of the computer is not being used as it should in most corporations. Data processing is bogged down in problems. Management is not receiving the information it requires from their systems. Many decisions that should be made with the aid of computers are in fact being made with hand methods or inadequate information. Systems are so difficult to change that they often inhibit the implementation of new and important procedures that management requires. Computer users are increasingly hostile to DP but feel powerless to prevent the problems.

Among top managers there is a growing sense of anger that they are spending so much on computing and yet seem unable to change procedures or obtain the information they need. In one corporation with an expensive and elegant worldwide computer network, the chief executive complained to us bitterly that for years he had been asking for daily or even weekly figures on cash balances but seemed no nearer to obtaining these or other information he needed.

For complex systems everywhere, specifications are being created that are full of errors, inconsistencies, and omissions. Data flow diagrams are nested down numerous levels with no verification or cross-checking and often no data modeling. The data throughout large organizations have become an unruly mess. Structure charts are drawn from the data flow diagrams with no rigor. Handwritten code full of bugs is created from specifications full of errors. With these techniques, we often try to build our most complex systems.

In the history of technology, we can observe certain times when a major break with the past methods had to occur. In computing, a set of application development methods has been accepted and slowly refined for more than two decades. We have now reached a point when these are inhibiting the most effective uses of computers. Fundamentally different methods are needed and are coming into use. Unfortunately, many DP organizations are not adopting the new methods rapidly enough.

Steam engines made earlier this century were beautifully intricate machines. They had many polished brass sliding rods, levers, and cams. Engineers had invented elaborate mechanisms for extracting a fraction of a percent of extra performance. They lovingly tuned the mechanisms and held technical symposiums on steam engines long after the electric motor was in use.

In Victorian factories with steam engines, there were overhead shafts 100 feet long with large pulleys and belts going down to each machine tool. With electric power, each machine tool could have its own motor. But the shafts remained in many factories long after their usefulness had ended. New tools often need fundamentally new methodologies. The procedures manuals in DP are often referred to as the "bible" of DP development, and it is heresy to disobey the bible even when new software and techniques render it hopelessly obsolete. The old DP procedures, like the steam-driven shaft and pulleys, can prevent freedom to move flexibly with the new methods.

The automation of automation, as we have stressed, will build on the principles of structured techniques described in Chapter 2. Many early structured techniques use only a fraction of these principles.

The mechanisms that implement the principles or perform verification of correctness can be hidden under the covers. The hard work of verification should be done by machines, not humans, and should be done automatically without anyone having to ask.

Norbert Wiener, the great pioneer of computers, wrote a book whose title will long be remembered: *The Inhuman Use of Human Beings* [1]. His view was that jobs that are inhuman because of drudgery should be done by machines, not people. Among these jobs he did not include that of the programmer! In a sense, the programmer's job is inhuman because we require him to write a large amount of complex code without errors. Error-free coding is not natural for our animal-like brain. We cannot handle the meticulous detail and the vast numbers of combinatorial paths. Furthermore, if we want 1000 lines of code produced per day, the job is even more inhuman. It is a job for machines, not people. Only recently have we understood how to make machines do it.

Once we have the capability to make machines create error-free code, the whole evolution of computers must change. The era of ad hoc hand coding is a temporary aberration in the history of computing.

The automation of automation is the beginning of a chain reaction. We have described how high-level *control structures* can be built out of primitive control structures. Still higher-level ones can be built out of these, and so on. Essential in this is the rigor of the mechanism that enforces correct interfacing among the modules. It is this rigor that allows pyramiding of modules and control structures.

As the pyramids build, we will reach very high level constructs. High-level design languages will allow fast, very complex design. Millions of computers on worldwide data networks will interchange libraries and data bases. Knowledge-based systems will acquire ever more inferences and become self-feeding. Intelligent network directories will allow machines and users to find the resources they need.

As the pyramiding takes us to higher-level semantics, we will have higher-level problems with semantics—external semantics that the internal verification mechanisms will not cover. We will have higher-level forms of garbage in, garbage out, so that higher-level controls will need to be devised for protection. Knowledge-based systems, for example, could be filled by humans with some incorrect knowledge or assertions. Artificial intelligence systems may become very difficult to debug. Self-feeding knowledge bases may constitute a chain reaction that quickly passes beyond our human ability to maintain accuracy controls—a problem for the future.

Once a rigorous basis exists for designing systems and automatically generating code, the objective of software evolution should be to make it as user-friendly and as powerful as possible. The extent to which such software is made easy to use and powerful will determine its acceptance and ultimate value.

The human talent needed to make it user-friendly is quite different from, and even alien to, the human talent needed to make it mathematically rigorous. New and different software houses may succeed by employing rigorous automated techniques as their foundation and by building with it powerful tools that are designed to be user-seductive.

Libraries of constructs need to be built for automating different classes of applications. Here are some examples of application classes that need their own libraries of operations and control structures:

- Commercial procedures
- Financial applications
- Design of operating systems
- Automatic data-base navigation
- Query languages
- Design of circuits with NOR, NAND gates, etc.
- Control of robots
- Cryptanalysis
- Missile control

- Building architecture
- Design graphics
- Network design
- Avionics
- CAD/CAM
- Production control
- Project management
- Decision-support graphics

The list is endless.

A WAY TO THINK ABOUT SYSTEMS

Structured techniques, particularly the more advanced ones that lead to automated verification and use of enterprise data models, are really *a way to think about systems* that leads to higher-precision specification and design. As such, they ought to be taught in business schools and management training courses, as well as computer science schools and systems analysts' courses. At different levels, they can be understood by business people and users and by computer professionals. They can provide a way to bridge the gap.

The concepts of accountants and double-entry bookkeeping can be mapped in structured diagrams. The set of ideas of many disciplines can be represented with functional decomposition. Other types of charts that help human communication are also desirable, but if they are to become the basis of system specifications, enough rigor ought to be imposed upon them for them to be computable so that they can be used for automatic code generation.

THE CHANGING COMPUTER INDUSTRY

Conversion of the computer industry to rigorous design will obviously not happen overnight. The investment tied up in existing hardware, software, and techniques is gigantic. The insularity of the major computer corporations is immense, and so is their resistance to methods that do not originate internally. Techniques like HOS need to have their worth proven on very large projects before they will penetrate much of the computer industry.

The ultimate concern of structured techniques is the control of complexity. This may become more urgent in microchip design than in programming, especially if wafer-scale integration becomes a reality. Computer-aided design with rigorous verification techniques may tend to migrate from microchip design to software design. On the other hand, if software designers forge ahead with new tools as they should, software and chip design will evolve in parallel to conquer the future challenge of immense complexity. Eventually it will be desirable to design the logic of software and microelectronics together to build machines that employ tight cooperation of hardware, software, and firmware.

The challenge of the computer industry today, then, is to master complexity with automated tools. The tools will drastically change both software design and hardware design. Wafers and software need to be designed with an integrated technique that is truly rigorous and produces bug-free design. Vast new libraries of constructs that can be interlinked without interface problems will grow.

The hand programmer and his ad hoc designs will become a romantic part of computer history, like the weavers in their cottages when the industrial revolution began.

REFERENCE

1. N. Wiener, *Inhuman Uses of Human Beings*, Boston: M.I.T. Press, 1975.

INDEX

A

Abstraction, levels of, 41, 67, 83, 84–85, 91, 183
Abstraction, principles of, 15, 16–17, 22, 105, 183
Acceptance testing, 685
Action diagrams, 112, 116, 118, 119, 245–73, 335, 378, 380, 383, 384, 387, 389, 392, 393–94, 395, 396, 643, 646, 647, 648, 657, 659
  brackets in, 246, 258, 259, 269
  case structure, 269
  common procedures, 251, 272
  compound data action, 273
  concurrency in, 256–58
  conditions in, 248–50, 269
  decomposition to program code, 253–54
  exits, 271
  and fourth-generation languages, 252–53
  input data, 258–61
  loops, 250
  nesting, 270
  output data, 258–61
  program constructs, 254–55, 257
  rectangle format, 271
  repetition, 246, 270
  sequence, 269
  sets of data in, 250–51
  simple data action, 272
  subprocedures, 251, 272
  termination in, 252
  ultimate decomposition of, 247–48, 256

ADA, 11, 520, 534, 560
ADR, 253, 254, 640
Afferent branch, 427, 428, 443, 451
Afferent factoring, 447
ALGOL, 72
All-in-one approach, top-down programming, 91
Alternation structure, Warnier-Orr diagrams, 198, 202
Analysis. *See* Structured analysis
ANALYZER, 534, 537, 551
Apollo Project, error statistics, 565, 566, 567
Application Factory, 268, 640, 648
Arrow notation, entity-relationship diagrams, 315, 320
Attributes, data, 286–87, 298, 307, 308, 578, 588
  intersecting, 620–22
  isolated, 623
  Warnier-Orr design methodology, 494, 495
Attribute value, data, 307, 308
Automated data modeling, 605–29
  bubble charts, 607
  candidate keys, 616–17
  canonical data structures, 612–14
  concatenated keys, 618–19
  conversion to HOS notation, 629
  Data Designer, 624–28
  elimination of redundancies, 614–16
  intersecting attributes, 620–22
  intersection data, 619
  isolated attributes, 623

Automated data modeling *(cont.)*
  many-to-many associations, 620
  mapping between primary keys, 620
  primary keys, 610–12
  record sequence, 623
  synthesis process, 606–7
  transitive dependencies, 617–18
Automated test tools. *See* Test tools,
    automated
Automatic navigation, compound data
    accesses, 343
Automation-like design, 557–73
  cost savings, 563
  effect of programming, 557–58
  effect on specifications, 558–59
  error statistics, 565–67
  human system components, 567
  incorporation of nonprocedural
    languages, 569
  productivity improvement, 562–63
  program size, 564–65
  provably correct code, 559
  software factories, 569
  syntax and semantics, 559–61
  use of other front-end methodologies,
    567–68
  verification and testing, 561
Automation, system creation process,
    517–31
  computable specifications, 520–21
  computer-aided specification design, 519
  creating specifications, 517–18
  design, 521–22
  integration of definition levels, 522–23
  mathematically rigorous languages, 524
  specification languages, 518, 525–31
  specification properties, 525, 526
  user friendliness, 525–26, 531
AXES, 534, 535, 537, 552, 554

B

Bachman notation, entity-relationship
    diagrams, 315, 320, 323–24, 390
Baker, F. T., 8, 40

Basic Design Procedure, Jackson design
    methodology, 464
Benson, J., 40
Binary decomposition, 176–77
Binary trees, and HOS charts, 355–57
Bohm, C., 38, 45
Bolsky, M., 402
Bottom-up programming, 17, 41, 91–100,
    104
  and concatenation, 96, 97–98
Bottom-up testing, 682–83
Boundary structure clash, 466
Brackets, action diagrams, 246, 258, 259,
    269
Brooks, F., 40, 746, 748
Brown, P., 40
Bubble charts, 281–87, 292, 294–96, 607

C

Candidate keys, 594, 616–17
Canonical data structures, 581, 605, 606,
    612–14
Cardinality, of a link, 309
Case construct, Structured English, 230,
    231
Case statement, 46, 49
Case structure, action diagrams, 269
CASE tools, 3–14, 28, 29, 62, 64, 105,
    109, 111, 120, 145, 160–61, 162,
    164, 177, 187, 189, 191, 215, 243,
    355, 379, 517, 518, 519, 520, 522,
    523, 524, 530, 533, 631, 662
Central transform, 427, 428, 451
Central-transform factoring, 447
Chapin, N., 239
CHILL, 267
Chunking theory, 80–81
C language, 265–66
COBOL, 11, 13, 28, 59, 60–61, 62–64,
    72, 326, 520, 534, 560, 587, 640
Codd, E. F., 585
Coding. *See* Programming
Cohesion, 75, 78–80, 81, 431, 434, 436,
    445, 452–53

Coincidental cohesion, 79, 80, 436
COINCLUDE control structure, 538, 540–41, 542–43, 547
COJOIN control structure, 368, 369, 538, 539, 540–41, 542–43, 547
Comment block. *See* Module comment block
Common coupling, 76, 77, 78
Common module, 53, 183–84
Common procedures, 251, 272
Communicational cohesion, 79, 80, 436
Complexity-based testing, 681
Complexity metrics, 70–75
Compound data accesses, 339–53
  automatic navigation, 343
  comparison with simple data-base accesses, 343–44
  and fourth-generation languages, 351, 353
  intermixing with simple actions, 344, 347
  navigation paths, 350–51
  relational joins, 340–43, 344
  semantic disintegrity, 348, 350, 351
  three-way joins, 347–48, 349
Compound data action, action diagrams, 273
Computer-aided design (CAD), 12, 631–50
  automatic conversion, 640
  developing a data-base application, 633, 640
  logical and physical navigation diagrams, 645, 649
  objectives of design dialogue, 649–50
  physical design, 649
  variations, 650
Computer-aided diagramming, 120
Computer-aided programming (CAP), 12
Computer-aided specification design, 519
Computer-aided systems analysis (CASA), 12
Computer-aided systems design, principles of, 28, 29, 33
Computer-aided systems engineering. *See* CASE
Computer graphics, 388
  data-flow diagrams, 158–59, 162
  structure charts, 187, 188
  see also Graphics
Concatenated entity type, 299–302

Concatenated keys, 288–90, 295, 618–19
Concatenation, 58
  and bottom-up programming, 96, 97–98
CONCUR control structure, 368, 538, 540–41, 544–45, 547
Concurrency, in action diagrams, 256–58
Condition construct:
  action diagrams, 269
  Structured English, 230, 231
Constantine, L., 12, 19, 75, 78, 186, 423, 438, 451, 452
Consume-produce relationship, Jackson design methodology, 458
Content coupling, 76, 77, 78
Control constructs, 45–50, 58
Control coupling, 76, 77, 78, 185
Control data, 76
Control flow information, 119, 185
Control maps, 357, 364, 366, 370, 371, 373
Control relationships, structure charts, 183
Control structures, 52–53, 186, 357, 361–64, 365, 366, 368–69, 535, 538–45
Control variable complexity metric, 74–75, 681
COOR control structure, 538, 540–41, 543–44, 547
Corporate model, 166
Correctness, proofs of, 26–27, 105, 559, 724–27
Coupling, 75–76, 77, 431, 435, 445, 452–53; *see also* Decoupling
Coverage-based testing, 679, 680
COW (can of worms) charts, 133–34, 315
Cross-link associations, entity-relationship diagrams, 301
Crow's-foot notation, entity-relationship diagrams, 315, 320
Cyclomatic number theory, 73, 681, 699

D

Data:
  attributes, 286, 298, 307, 308, 578, 588

Data: *(cont.)*
  control, 76
  global, 76
  instances of, 284
  shared, 76
  types of, 284
Data administration, 119, 605
Data analysis diagrams, 281–96
  associations between data items,
    282–86, 294–95
  attributes, 286, 287
  bubble charts, 281–87, 292
  concatenated keys, 288–90
  data-item groups, 287, 294
  derived data, 290–91, 296
  keys, 286, 287, 295
  optional data items, 293–94
  records, 287–88
  reverse associations, 284–86
Data-base action diagrams (DAD), 327,
    378, 389
Data-base application, 633, 640
Data-base planning, 575–84
  failure of data administration, 582–84
  logical design of data bases, 581–82
  separate developments with incompatible
    data, 576, 578
  stable data-bases, 580–81
  stable foundation, 578, 580
Data coupling, 76, 77, 78, 185
Data Designer, 624–28
Data dictionary, 119, 154–55, 410–11
Data element. *See* Data items
Data flow diagrams (DFD), 112, 113, 119,
    134, 135, 136, 137, 138, 149–64,
    193, 259, 260, 378, 380, 382–83,
    389–90, 394, 396, 409, 410, 424,
    425, 426, 428, 433, 441, 450
  computer graphics, 158–59, 162
  data dictionary, 154–55
  data flow component of, 149, 150–51
  data layering, 164
  data-store component of, 149, 151
  defining, 149
  functional decomposition, 176
  Gane and Sarson notation, 155–58, 159,
    160–61

  leveling, 152–53
  process component of, 149, 151
  process specification, 154, 411
  symbols used in, 145–47, 156
  terminator component of, 149, 152
Data independence, 23–24, 25, 580
Data information, structure charts, 185
Data-item groups, 287, 295
Data items, 281, 293–94, 588
  associations between, 282–86
Data-item type, 588
Data layering, data flow diagrams, 164
Data-model charts, 138–39
Data modeling, automated, 575, 605–29
  bubble charts, 607
  candidate keys, 616–17
  canonical data structures, 612–14
  concatenated keys, 618–19
  conversion to HOS notation, 629
  Data Designer, 624–28
  elimination of redundancies, 614–16
  intersecting attributes, 620–22
  intersection data, 619
  isolated attributes, 623
  many-to-many associations, 620
  mapping between primary keys, 620
  primary keys, levels of, 610–12
  record sequence, 623
  synthesis process, 606–7
  transitive dependencies, 617–18
Data models, 115, 283, 326, 327, 330,
    380, 382, 390, 395, 396, 579
Data navigation diagrams, 112, 116, 119,
    325–37, 378, 380, 389, 390, 396,
    637, 657, 659
  complexity of, 334–35
  divide and conquer principle, 325–26
  physical design, 333–34
  procedure design, 331–33
  separating data from procedures, 326–27
  standard procedure, 335
Data store, data flow diagram, 149, 151
Data structure diagrams, 112, 378, 389
  and Jackson design methodology,
    209–11, 216
Data structure information, 119
Data type, 588

David, E. E., 4
Debugging, 689–99
    guidelines, 698
    locating errors, 699
    methods of, 690–91
    tools, 691–93
Decision tables, 112, 275–80, 378, 380,
    384, 394, 395, 396
Decision trees, 112, 275–80, 378, 389,
    394, 657
Decomposition:
    binary, 176–77
    diagrams, 378, 389, 657, 658
    top-down programming, 96
    see also Functional decomposition
Decoupling, 76–77, 78
Defined structures, 368, 370, 372
De Marco, T., 12, 155, 156, 279, 407,
    408, 412, 413, 415
Dependency diagrams, 378, 389, 657
Derived data, 290–91, 296
Design automation, principle of, 28
Design techniques, 399–405
    structured design methodologies, 405
    types of, 403–5
Detailed design, 403, 404–5
Detail HIPO diagrams, 191–92, 193, 194,
    197, 391
Diagramming techniques, consumer's guide
    to, 377–96
    code generation, 381, 387
    computer graphics, 388
    computerized tools, 379, 381
    data and processes, 382
    data flow diagrams, 382–83
    data-model diagramming, 383
    fourth-generation languages, 381
    integrity checking, 386–87
    process diagramming, 383
    summary of properties, 388–94
    ultimate decomposition, 384
    user friendliness, 379, 387–88
Diagrams, 109–21
    categories of, 111
    computer-aided, 120
    end-user involvement, 111–12
    functions of structured, 120–21

program documentation tools, 117–18
    utility of documentation, 118–19
    see also Structured diagrams
Dijkstra, E., 11, 18, 38, 39, 40, 83, 84,
    85, 89, 91, 99, 103
Display-documentation mode, graphics
    editor, 548, 550
Display-tree mode, graphics editor, 546
Divide-and-conquer principle, 16, 18–19,
    22, 67, 75, 105, 325–26, 414
Documentation program, 54–59, 117–19
Donaldson, J., 40
DO UNTIL, 46, 48, 50, 242
DO WHILE, 46, 48, 50, 242
Dynamic analysis, of programs, 367,
    680–81, 702

E

Edit mode, graphics editor, 547, 549
Efferent branch, 427, 428, 443, 451
Efferent factoring, 447
Elementary component, tree-structure
    diagrams, 207, 209
Encyclopedia, 11, 13, 662
End-user involvement, 28–30, 32, 33
    and diagramming techniques, 111–12
English. *See* Structured English
Enterprise models, 25, 33, 111, 166, 168,
    169
Entities, 297–98, 307, 578
    Warnier-Orr design methodology, 494,
    495
Entity-relationship diagrams, 112,
    297–324, 378, 380, 389, 396
    basic constructs, 307
    Bachman notation, 315, 320, 323–24,
    390
    computer representation of, 314–15
    concatenated entity type, 299–300
    cross-link associations, 301
    entities, 297–98
    entity subtypes, 310–11
    inverted-L diagrams, 308–10

Entity-relationship diagrams *(cont.)*
  labels, 302–4, 321
  linked associations, 322–23
  looped associations, 301–2, 305, 322
  multiple subtype groupings, 311–12
  mutually exclusive associations, 300–301, 322
  mutually inclusive associations, 301, 322
  notation styles, 315, 320–23
  semantic independence, 307–8
  sentences, 302–4
  subject and predicate, 304, 306
  subset associations, 301, 323
  subtype hierarchies, 312–14
Entity subtypes, 310–11
Entity type, 308, 588
Errors. *See* Debugging
Error statistics, HOS-like design, 565–67
  Project Apollo, 565, 566, 567
Escape, 46, 50, 58
EXCELERATOR, 158, 159, 160, 188, 189
Exits, action diagrams, 271
External documentation, 118–19

F

Factoring, 427, 447, 449
Fan-out, of modules, 80
Field. *See* Data items
Finite-state machine notation, 530
First normal form, 586, 587–90
Flag. *See* Control coupling
Flowcharts, 11, 110, 112, 219–24, 227, 229, 248, 249, 279, 378, 380, 389, 393
  program, 220–22
  symbols, 222, 223–24
  system, 220
FORTRAN, 13, 28, 59, 64, 73, 76, 520, 534, 560
Fourth-generation languages, 28, 29, 381
  and action diagrams, 252–53
  and compound data accesses, 351, 353
  and Structured English, 232
  testing, 719–21

Fraser, A. G., 4
Freeman, P., 403
Fully functional dependency, 591–92
Functional areas, functional decomposition, 166, 167
Functional cohesion, 79, 80, 436
Functional decomposition, 19, 21, 112, 165–78
  and data-flow diagrams, 176
  with HOS, 356
  species I, 165, 166–70, 355, 386
  species II, 165, 170–76, 258, 355, 383, 386, 395
  species III, 165, 176–78, 383, 386, 394
Functional dependence, 590–91

G

Gane, C., 155, 222, 407, 413, 414, 415
Gane and Sarson notation, 155–58, 159, 160–61
General Research Corporation, 701–3
Gilb, T., 691
Global data, 76
GO TO statements, 11, 12, 23, 38–39, 41, 50, 59, 133, 222, 504
Graham, R. M., 3, 37
Graphics, 26, 29, 385
  editor, HOS charts, 546–51
  see also Computer graphics

H

Hamilton, M., 12, 26, 355, 537, 566
Herndon, M., 693, 697
Hierarchical organization, 16, 19–20, 22, 51–52, 67, 105, 133, 139, 140, 165
Hierarchy construct, Warnier-Orr diagrams, 202
HIPO (hierarchical input, process output) diagrams, 112, 114, 118, 191–95, 198, 201, 204, 211, 247, 248, 378, 380, 384, 385, 389, 391

as analysis and design tools, 194
components of, 192–93
detail, 191–92, 193, 194, 197, 391
overview, 191, 192, 193, 197, 391
visual table of contents, 191, 192, 193, 197, 391
Hoare, C. A. R., 4, 18, 26, 38, 746, 747, 748
HOS (higher-order software) charts and methodology, 112, 355–75, 378, 380, 383, 387, 389, 394, 395, 396, 533–56
  binary trees, 355–57
  control maps, 364, 366, 370, 371, 373
  control structures, 361–64, 365, 366, 368–69, 535, 538–45
  defined structures, 368, 370, 372
  dynamic testing of programs, 367
  embellishments, 367–68
  extending power of, 370, 372
  external modules of code, 554–55
  from requirements statements to detailed design, 361
  functional decomposition with, 356
  functions, 357–61
  generation of code, 364, 535, 537
  generation of documentation, 555–56
  graphics editor, 546–51
  leaf nodes, 364–67, 537–38
  local variables, 545
  N-way, branches, 546
  simulation, 551–54
  static testing of programs, 367
  USE.IT, 533–34, 554, 555, 556

I

ICAM systems, 568
IDEAL, 233, 251, 253, 254, 255, 257, 264, 640, 647
IDEF-O, 568
IEF (Information Engineering Facility), 662
IEW (Information Engineering Workbench), 662

IF-THEN-ELSE structure, 47, 49
INCLUDE, control structure, 363, 365, 366, 369, 535, 536, 538, 540–41
Incremental approach, top-down programming, 92
Indentation, 59
Information engineering, 10, 24, 25, 33, 651–64, 752–53
  building blocks of, 654–61
Information hiding, 75
Insert-documentation mode, graphics editor, 548
Integration testing, 681–84
Interleaving structure clash, 466
Internal documentation, 118
Intersecting attributes, 620–22
Intersection data, 619
Inverted-L diagrams, 308–10
Invocation relationship, between modules, 52–53
IORL (Input/Output Requirements Language), 530
Isolated attributes, 623
Iteration construct, 45, 46, 48
  Jackson's structured text, 236
  tree-structure diagrams, 208–9

J

Jackson, M., 12, 357
Jackson design methodology, 112, 115, 145, 204, 207–16, 248, 255, 292, 378, 380, 382, 387, 389, 392, 405, 455–67
  comparison with structured design, 455
  data step, 458
  and data-structure diagrams, 209–10, 216
  designing complex programs, 464
  designing simple programs, 462, 464, 481
  design procedure, 456
  evaluation of, 469–86
  operation step, 462, 463
  program inversion, 466, 476, 483

Jackson design methodology *(cont.)*
 program step, 458
 and program-structure diagrams, 211,
  214
 program-structure verification, 460–61
 structure clash, 465–66, 467, 476, 477
 structure text using, 214, 216, 234–36,
  383, 392, 457, 462, 464
 system network diagram used in, 212,
  457, 478, 481, 486
 and tree-structure diagrams, 207–9, 210,
  211, 457
 using data-driven program design,
  455–57
Jacopini, G., 38, 45
JOIN, control structure, 361–63, 365, 366,
  369, 535, 536, 538, 540–41
Jones, T. C., 736, 737

K

Keenan, A., 693

L

Labeled associations:
 data structure diagrams, 295
 entity relationship diagrams, 302–4, 321
Language Technology, Inc., 62, 64
Layering, of data flow diagrams, 134
Leaf module, 53
Leaf nodes, 364–67, 537–38
Left-to-right trees, 126, 128–31
Leveling, data flow diagrams, 152
Levels of abstraction. *See* Abstraction,
  levels of
Library modules, 184
Lindamood, G., 40
Linked associations, entity-relationship
  diagrams, 322–23
Links, data, 307, 308
Load units, 435

Logical cohesion, 79, 80, 436
Logical construction of programs (LCP),
  489
Logical navigation diagrams, 645
Logical record. *See* Records, data-item
Logic detail of programs, techniques for
  showing, 219, 245
Looped associations, entity-relationship
  diagrams, 301–2, 305, 322
Loops, action diagrams, 250

M

MCAUTO, 158, 159, 162, 187, 188
McCabe, T., 71, 73, 75, 81, 681, 699
McClure, C., 71, 74, 75, 681
Management science, growth of,
  732–34
Managing the Data Base Environment,
  607, 628
MANTIS, 251, 254, 256
Manual-substitute graphics, 388
Many-to-many associations, 620
Martin, J., 607
MENUSELECT, 372
Mesh-structured diagrams, 131–33, 135,
  142, 144
 root nodes in, 141–42
Metrics. *See* Complexity metrics
Michael Jackson diagrams. *See* Jackson
  design methodology
Miller, E., 40
Miller, H., 8, 40, 104
Minispec. *See* Process specification, data
  flow diagrams
Modular programs, 19, 20, 41, 51, 67–81,
  386
 black box model, 68
 complexity metrics and, 70–75
 divide and conquer, 67
 relationships between modules in,
  75–80
 schemes used in, 68–69
 shape of, 80–81
 size of module in, 70

Module comment block, 56, 57, 58
Modules, 181–85
  common, 183–84
  interrelationships of, 183
  library, 184
  properties of, 69
Mutually exclusive associations, entity-
    relationship diagrams, 300–301,
    322
Mutually inclusive associations, entity-
    relationship diagrams, 301, 322
Myers, G., 75, 423, 690, 697
Mythical Man-Month, 746

N

Nassi, I., 239
Nassi-Shneiderman charts, 112, 118, 123,
    204, 222, 224, 239–43, 248, 249,
    279, 378, 380, 384, 385, 389, 393
  control constructs, 240–42
NATO Conference on Software
    Engineering (1968), 37
NATO Conference on Software
    Engineering (1969), 38
Navigation diagrams. *See* Data navigation
    diagrams
Navigation paths, compound data accesses,
    350–51
Nested charts, 134–38
Nested IF, 46, 48–49, 58
Nesting, action diagrams, 270
Network structures. *See* Mesh-structured
    diagrams
Nonprime attributes, data items, 286, 287
Normalization, of data, 581, 585–603
  candidate keys, 594
  first normal form, 587–90
  fully functional dependency, 591–92
  functional dependence, 590–91
  second normal form, 592–93
  semantic disintegrity, 598
  storage and performance, 596, 598
N-way branches, 49, 546

O

One-to-many associations, 139, 283, 294,
    323
One-to-one associations, 138, 283, 294,
    323
OR, control structure, 363–64, 365, 366,
    535, 536, 538, 540–41
Ordering structure clash, 465
Orr, K., 197, 489, 503, 506, 509, 511,
    512
Overview documentation, 54, 55
Overview HIPO diagrams, 191, 192, 193,
    197, 391
Overview structure of programs, techniques
    showing, 219, 245

P

Packaging, structured design, 435–38
Palmer, I., 313
Parnas, D., 75
PASCAL, 11, 28, 534
PDL, 527
Phased approach, top-down programming,
    91
Physical navigation diagrams, 645
Plex structures, 281, 611
PL/I, 11, 13, 28, 59, 326
Power-tool graphics, 388
Primary key, data items, 286, 287, 295,
    610–12, 620
Principle(s):
  of abstraction, 15, 16–17, 22, 105, 183
  of completeness, 21, 22, 23
  of computer-aided systems design, 29,
    33
  of conceptual integrity, 21, 22, 23
  of data independence, 23, 25
  of design automation, 28
  of end-user access, 25
  of end-user involvement, 32, 33
  of enterprise-wide modeling, 25, 33
  of formality, 15, 16, 17–18, 22, 105

Principle(s): *(cont.)*
 of hiding, 21–22
 of information engineering, 33
 of localization, 21, 22, 23
 of logical independence, 22
 of rigorous data analysis, 25
 of software engineering, 33
 of strategic data planning, 25
 of structured techniques, 33
Procedural cohesion, 79, 80, 436
Process, data flow diagrams, 149, 151
Processes, functional decomposition, 166,
   167
Process specification, data flow diagrams,
   154, 411
Productivity, programming, 736–38
Program constructs, action diagrams,
   254–55, 257
Program flowcharts, 220–22
Program instruction comments, 57, 59
Program inversion, Jackson design
   methodology, 466, 467, 483
Programming, by stepwise refinement,
   83–89
 characteristics of, 83–84
Programming, effect on by HOS-like
   design, 557–58
Programming, modular, 67–81
 black box model, 68
 complexity metrics and, 70–75
 divide and conquer, 67
 relationship between modules in, 75–80
 schemes used in, 68–69
 shape of, 80–81
 size of module in, 70
Programming productivity, 736–38
Programming, structured, 29, 37–42
 definitions of, 39, 41–42
 objectives of, 39, 40
Program organization documentation,
   54–57
Program reliability. *See* Proofs of
   correctness
Programs, structured, 45–65
 commentary of methodologies used in,
   103–5
 control constructs, 45–50
 control structure, 52–53

 definitions of, 39, 41–42
 documentation, 54–59
 hierarchical organization, 51–52
 indentation, 59
 modularization, 51
 objectives of, 39, 40
 paths, 53–54
 properties of, 45, 46
 standards, 58–59
 see also Bottom-up programming; Top-
   down programming
Program-structure diagrams, Jackson
   design methodology, 211, 214
Project Apollo, error statistics, 565, 566,
   567
Proofs of correctness, 26–27, 105, 559,
   724–27
PSA (Problem Statement Analyzer), 527
Pseudocode, 112, 117, 118, 204, 222,
   224, 227–37, 279, 380, 383, 393,
   421
PSL (Problem Statement Language), 527

R

RAMIS II, 237
RAT (Resource Allocation Tool), 534,
   537, 552, 554, 555
Recoder, 62, 65
Records, data-item, 287–88, 623
Refinement. *See* Stepwise refinement
Relational joins, compound data accesses,
   340–43, 344
Re-LEARN, 706–14
REPEAT UNTIL, 230
REPEAT WHILE, 230
Repetition control construct:
 action diagrams, 246, 270
 Nassi-Shneiderman charts, 242
 Structured English, 230, 231
 Warnier-Orr diagrams, 199, 202–3
Reverse associations, data structure
   diagrams, 284–85
Root, of tree structure, 133, 610, 611
Root module, 51, 53, 183

Root nodes, mesh-structured diagrams, 141–42
RSL (Requirements Statements Language), 530
RXVP, 701–3, 706

S

Sarson, T., 155, 222, 407, 413, 414, 415
Schneidewind, N., 697
SDL (Specification and Description Language), 530
Secondary key, data item, 286, 287, 612
Second normal form, 586, 592–93
Selection construct, 45, 47, 48, 49, 58
　　Jackson's structured text, 207, 208, 236
　　Nassi-Shneiderman charts, 241
　　tree-structure diagrams, 207, 208
Semantic disintegrity, compound data accesses, 348, 350, 351
Semantic independence, entity-relationship diagrams, 307–8
Semantics, HOS-like design, 559–61
Sentences, entity-relationship diagrams, 302–4
Sequence control construct, 45
　　action diagrams, 269
　　Jackson's structured text, 207, 208, 235–36
　　Nassi-Shneiderman charts, 240–41
　　Structured English, 230, 231
　　Warnier-Orr diagrams, 199, 202–3
Sequential cohesion, 79, 80, 436
Set theory, Warnier-Orr design methodology, 489–90
Shared data, 76
Shneiderman, B., 81, 119, 222, 224, 239, 691
Shooman, M., 402
Simple data action, action diagrams, 272
Simulation, HOS charts, 551–54
Software design, 403–5
Software engineering, 20–23, 33, 745–56
Software factories, 569
Software life cycle, 18

Software Renovation Technology, 706–14
Software science, 71–73
Software verification, validation and testing, 667–74, 676–77
Span of control, of modules, 80
Species I, functional decomposition, 165, 166–70, 355, 386
Species II, functional decomposition, 165, 170–76, 258, 355, 383, 386, 395
Species III, functional decomposition, 165, 176–78, 383, 386, 394
Specifications, 517–31
　　effect of HOS-like design on, 558–59
SQL, 349
Stability analysis, 628
Stamp coupling, 76, 77, 78
State-transition diagrams, 378, 389, 659
Static testing, of programs, 367, 681, 702
Step-by-step approach, top-down programming, 92
Stepwise refinement, 19, 20, 41, 83–89, 91, 104, 417, 418
Stevens, W., 75, 423
STRADIS/DRAW, 158, 159, 162, 187, 188, 388
Structure charts, 56, 112, 113, 119, 181–89, 198, 204, 211, 247–48, 378, 380, 383, 389, 391, 420, 425, 429, 431, 434, 438, 441
　　common modules, 183–84
　　components of, 181–82
　　computer graphics, 188
　　control relationships of, 183
　　control rules for, 183
　　control structures, 186
　　data transfer, 184–86
　　library modules, 184
　　transaction center, 186, 188
Structure clash, 465–66, 467, 476, 477
Structured analysis, 10, 399–405, 407–15
　　data dictionary, 410–11
　　data flow diagram, 410
　　process specification, 411
　　steps of, 412–14
　　system specification, 400, 408
Structured design, 10, 405, 423–38
　　combination strategies, 430–31

Structured design *(cont.)*
  comparison with Jackson design
    methodology, 455
  comparison with top-down design, 451
  evaluation of, 441–53
  postdesign packaging, 437, 438
  predesign packaging, 436, 437
  transaction analysis, 429–30, 432, 433,
    446, 447–51
  transform analysis, 426–29, 430,
    441–43, 446, 447–51, 469
Structured diagramming, 123–48
  COW (can of worms) charts, 133–34,
    315
  data-model charts, 138–39
  left-to-right trees, 126, 128–31
  mesh-structured diagrams, 131–33, 135,
    142, 144
  nested charts, 134–38
  root nodes, 141–42
  sequence of operations, 131–33
  tree structures, 123–25, 126, 127, 128,
    129, 133, 134, 139, 142, 281, 380,
    470, 610, 611
Structured English, 112, 227–37, 248,
    249, 378, 389, 393, 411, 412
  constructs of, 230–31
  and fourth-generation languages, 232–33
  rules for writing, 232–33
Structured programs, 10, 29, 37–42,
    45–65
  commentary on methodologies used in,
    103–105
  control constructs, 45–50
  control structure, 52–53
  definitions of, 39, 41–42
  documentation, 54–59
  hierarchical organization, 51–52
  indentation, 59
  modularization, 51
  objectives of, 39, 40
  paths, 53–54
  properties of, 45, 46
  standards, 58–59
  see also Bottom-up programming; Top-
    down programming
Structured Systems Development, 512

Structured techniques, 3–14
  evolution of, 8–11
  inadequacies of, 738–39
  mathematical rigor of, 11–12
  objectives of, 3–8
  phases of growth of, 734–36
  philosophies of, 15–34
  principles of, 33
  user-friendly, 30, 32
Structure text, Jackson design
    methodology, 214, 216, 234–36, 383,
    392, 457, 462, 464
Subprocedures, action diagrams, 251, 272
Subset associations, entity-relationship
    diagrams, 301, 323
Subtype hierarchies, entity subtypes,
    312–14
Symbols:
  flowchart, 222, 223–24
  structured diagrams, 145–47, 156
Syntax, HOS-like design, 559–61
Synthesis process, data modeling, 606–10
System design, design techniques, 403–4
System design, principles of computer-
    aided, 29
System flowcharts, 220
System network diagram, Jackson design
    methodology, 212, 457, 478, 481,
    486
System specification, 408
System testing, 684, 685

T

Temporal cohesion, 79, 80, 436
Terminations, action diagrams, 252
Terminator, data flow diagram, 149, 152
Testing, HOS-like design, 561
Testing, software, 667–74, 675–87
  acceptance, 685
  bottom-up testing, 682–83
  fourth-generation languages, 719–21
  integration, 681–84
  limitations of, 717–18

system, 684–85
  test data used in, 685–87
  unit testing, 679–81
Test tools, automated, 701–16
  Re-LEARN, 706–14
  RXVP, 701–3, 706
  types of, 702
  UNIX, 715–16
THE Multiprogramming System, 38, 99
Third-normal form, 395, 586, 595–96,
    597, 599
Three-way joins, compound data accesses,
    347–48, 349
Top-down design, 405, 417–21, 423
  comparison with structured design, 451
  of data, 419–20
  documentation for, 419
  principles of, 419
  process of, 417–18
Top-down programming, 17, 41, 91–100,
    104
  Warnier-Orr design methodology, 490
Top-down testing, 683–84
Transaction analysis, 429–30, 432, 433,
    446, 447–51
Transaction center, 186, 188
Transform analysis, 426–29, 430, 441–43,
    446, 447–51, 469
Transitive dependencies, 595, 617–18
Tree-structure diagrams, 123–25, 126,
    127, 128, 129, 133, 134, 139, 142,
    281, 380, 470, 610, 611
  elementary component, 207, 209
  iteration component, 207, 208–9
  and Jackson design methodology,
    207–9, 210, 211, 457
  selection component, 207, 208
  sequence component, 207, 208

U

Ultimate decomposition, 384
  action diagrams, 247–48, 256
  HOS charts, 355

Unit testing, 679–81
UNIX, 715–16
USE.IT, 355, 525, 533–34, 554, 555,
    556, 557, 562
  ANALYZER, 534, 537, 551
  AXES, 534, 535, 537, 552, 554
  RAT, 534, 537, 552, 554, 555
User friendly structured techniques, 30, 32,
    379, 387–88, 525, 531; *see also* End
    user

V

Validation, software, 667–74, 676–77
Van Tassel, D., 691
Verification:
  HOS-like design, 561
  software, 667–74, 676–77
  techniques, evaluation of, 717–27
Visual table of contents, HIPO diagrams,
    191, 192, 193, 197, 391
von Neumann constructs, 11

W

Warnier, J., 12, 197, 489, 506
Warnier-Orr diagrams, 112, 114, 118, 129,
    148, 197–205, 210, 211, 248, 279,
    292, 378, 380, 384, 387, 389,
    391–92, 405, 489–501
  as data-driven approach, 491
  benefits of, 504, 506
  bracketed pseudocode, 507
  design process, 505
  evaluation of, 503–13
  multiple output structures, 508–11
  objective of, 504
  repetition control construct, 199, 203
  representation of data, 197–98
  representation of program structure,
    199–200
  selection construct, 199, 200

Warnier-Orr diagrams *(cont.)*
  sequence control construct, 199, 202
  set theory, 489–90
  steps in, 490
  top-down approach, 490
Weinberg, G., 4, 57, 70, 691
Wirth, N., 18, 37, 38, 40, 83, 91, 104
Woodfield, S., 73

Y, Z

Yourdon, E., 12, 19, 79, 80, 99, 155,
  186, 357, 407, 423, 438, 451, 452,
  453, 455
Yourdon structured design methodology,
  18, 156, 405, 473, 474, 478
Zeldin, S., 12, 26, 355, 537, 566

Information Systems Management and Strategy	Methodologies for Building Systems	Analysis and Design	CASE
AN INFORMATION SYSTEMS MANIFESTO	STRATEGIC INFORMATION PLANNING METHODOLOGIES (second edition)	STRUCTURED TECHNIQUES: THE BASIS FOR CASE (revised edition)	STRUCTURED TECHNIQU THE BASIS FOR CASE (revised edition)
INFORMATION ENGINEERING (Book I: Introduction)	INFORMATION ENGINEERING (Book I: Introduction)	DATABASE ANALYSIS AND DESIGN	INFORMATION ENGINEER (Book I: Introduction)
INFORMATION ENGINEERING (Book II: Planning and Analysis)	INFORMATION ENGINEERING (Book II: Planning and Analysis)	DESIGN OF MAN-COMPUTER DIALOGUES	Languages and Programn
STRATEGIC INFORMATION PLANNING METHODOLOGIES (second edition)	INFORMATION ENGINEERING (Book III: Design and Construction)	DESIGN OF REAL-TIME COMPUTER SYSTEMS	APPLICATION DEVELOPME WITHOUT PROGRAMMER
SOFTWARE MAINTENANCE: THE PROBLEM AND ITS SOLUTIONS	STRUCTURED TECHNIQUES: THE BASIS FOR CASE (revised edition)	DATA COMMUNICATIONS DESIGN TECHNIQUES	FOURTH-GENERATION LANGUAGES (Volume I: Principles)
DESIGN AND STRATEGY FOR DISTRIBUTED DATA PROCESSING	Object-Oriented Programming	DESIGN AND STRATEGY FOR DISTRIBUTED DATA PROCESSING	FOURTH-GENERATION LANGUAGES (Volume II: Representative 4G
Expert Systems	OBJECT-ORIENTED ANALYSIS AND DESIGN	SOFTWARE MAINTENANCE: THE PROBLEM AND ITS SOLUTIONS	FOURTH-GENERATION LANGUAGES (Volume III: 4GLs from IBM
BUILDING EXPERT SYSTEMS: A TUTORIAL	OBJECT-ORIENTED REVOLUTION	SYSTEM DESIGN FROM PROVABLY CORRECT CONSTRUCTS	Diagramming Techniqu
KNOWLEDGE ACQUISITION FOR EXPERT SYSTEMS		INFORMATION ENGINEERING (Book II: Planning and Analysis)	DIAGRAMMING TECHNIQU FOR ANALYSTS AND PROGRAMMERS
		INFORMATION ENGINEERING (Book III: Design and Construction)	RECOMMENDED DIAGRAMM STANDARDS FOR ANALYS AND PROGRAMMERS
			ACTION DIAGRAMS: CLEAF STRUCTURED SPECIFICATIC PROGRAMS, AND PROCEDU (second edition)